T0319091

Institutional economics and economic organisation theory

Institutional economics and economic organisation theory

an integrated approach

Dr. Louis H.G. Slangen

Dr. Laura A. Loucks

Dr. Arjen H.L. Slangen

Wageningen Academic
Publishers

ISBN: 978-90-8686-077-7

First published, 2008

Wageningen Academic Publishers
The Netherlands, 2008

Preface

In the last three decades, there have been several significant changes in the development of economic theory. Although neoclassical economics continues to dominate mainstream thinking at universities, particularly in applied research, there exists a growing interest in the role institutions play in shaping economic behaviour.

Two of the authors who are working at Wageningen University, were uniquely situated to study the role of institutions in the disciplines of agricultural economics and international development. These disciplines not only have historical importance at this university, but they also consider the institutional arrangements that are not well explained by neoclassical economics. For example, the practice of agriculture in the Netherlands, Europe and throughout the world, is often conducted through institutional arrangements such as family farms and agricultural cooperatives for supplying input and processing output. In both cases, the way in which economic transactions are coordinated in order to maximise gains must be understood differently than the standard neoclassical economic analysis would suggest. Land use systems such as tenure contracts and sharecropping agreements are examples of sophisticated institutions that rely on coordination mechanisms other than the price only. Furthermore, the emergence of new modes of organisation such as joint ventures, share the underlying institutional structure of many of agricultural institutions. Similarly, economic organisational theories such as the principal-agent approach have evolved from land use systems to explain how these institutions function, but are nowadays used to understand contractual issues.

This book, entitled *Institutional Economics and Economic Organization Theory: an integrated approach (IE & EOT),* presents one of the first attempts to integrate two emerging bodies of research: institutional economics and organisation theory. The book starts out within the framework of neoclassical economics, but offers answers that have so far remained puzzles in neoclassical economics. One of these puzzles is the existence of the firm as a mode of organisation. If we see the firm as one mode of organisation, an interesting question is why this mode of organisation is sometimes preferred over other modes of organisation, such as contracts, clubs and networks? In this book, we see the firm as a metaphor of a mode of organisation that can be more broadly interpreted.

The integrated approach of IE & EOT also challenges the dominant paradigm in economics of the last 15 years that the market is the best mechanism for carrying out transactions. The market is not the only transaction mechanism; other modes of organisation are also important. Furthermore, certain pre-conditions have to be met for markets to function well. However, this way of thinking does not involve a simple reintroduction of the confrontation between the 'government' and the 'market'. On the contrary, the integrated approach tries to open the 'blackbox' of a diversity of modes of organisation.

This book claims that for a good understanding and adequate explanation of economic behaviour, one needs more than standard neoclassical economics only. It also requires taking into account a broad set of behavioural and institutional factors in a systematic and a coherent way. Otherwise we are making the same mistake as the blind men from the parable (see page 39) of the blind men and the elephant. Single theories are like parts of the elephant in the observation of the blind men. Taken individually, these theories insufficiently explain the variety of behaviour and governance structures that we observe into day's global economy. This book takes an integrated approach and follows the way of diminishing abstraction; it tries to open the 'blackbox' of the role of institutions in daily economic and business life. Through this integrated approach, the book hopes to contribute to a better insight to real world problems. This is, in short, the main purpose of the book.

The book presents the numerous theoretical aspects of New Institutional Economics and Economic Organisation Theory with examples from empirical research. While many of the applications of the concepts are explained with examples from agriculture and natural resources, we consider this a strength of the book. The reason is that many innovative institutional arrangements and important parts of institutional economic theories have emerged from these areas. Moreover, these applications are quite easily understood and often part of our daily life. We also present applications involving firms and the government.

The content of the book

The subject matter presented here has been taught and tested for over six years in a classroom environment. One outcome from this testing period is the first hand experience we have in applying institutional concepts to contemporary real-world situations. Whether it is the collapse of the communistic system in Europe or the recent privatisation of state-owned enterprises worldwide, the analytical framework presented in this book has been successfully used for practical and relevant application. Moreover, we have discovered that students enjoy the learning process when they have the analytical tools to apply their knowledge to real world events. For example, students learn to think critically about how the provision or supply of goods and services should be organised. Spot markets and contestable markets are not always available or suitable. Consequently, new institutional arrangements such as user contracts are replacing earlier forms of governance. What are the effects of these contracts? Do we have enough information to compare costs and benefits? Are there hold-up and lock-in effects? And what can we do about this? Who is able capture the residual income of these contracts, or more generally, of the privatisation and liberalisation processes? Is it the consumer or the producer who benefits?

The book IE & EOT represents the most up-to-date thinking on New Institutional Economics. It not only synthesises a broad and somewhat disperse literature, but it also bridges the gap between institutional economics and Economic Organisation Theory. Moreover, this book applies an adapted version of the original institutional economic framework for analysis proposed by O.E. Williamson, one of the founders of the New Institutional Economics.

Unique features

1. *IE & EOT* is the first textbook to integrate the various theoretical aspects of New Institutional Economics and Economic Organisation Theory into one analytical framework, while maintaining the specific context and meaning of each individual theory. The text is written as a synthesis of academic literature and supported with citations so that the instructor and

students can trace the theory back to the leading academics in the specific field of study. In this way, the discipline of New Institutional Economics can be understood as a collection of parts that comprise the whole. It is like the elephant; the whole is more than the sum of the parts. Moreover, it is the integration of different bodies of knowledge such as the formal rules of the institutional environment, transaction and coordination mechanisms, the role of incentives, and risk-attitude, and property rights that contribute to the unique breadth and depth of institutional economic analysis.

2. The structure of this book is designed to introduce the theoretical aspects of institutional economics and Economic Organisation Theory in a step by step manner according to the order in which these concepts are linked. Chapter 1 gives a short introduction of all the chapters and it also shows links between the topics discussed in the different chapters. Chapters 2 through 11 all begin with a set of key questions, and finish with a Box containing key concepts discussed in each chapter. Each chapter focuses on a specific topic that is integral to institutional or economic organisation analysis. In addition, as the main topic is introduced, the reader is also introduced to the links between the concepts and theories discussed in the different chapters The topics are linked in a spiral-like order so that the interrelationship between theories becomes clear. As the chapters progress, these related theories are developed in more depth. Upon completing the book, the readers have just as much an understanding of the horizontal linkages between theories as they have of each individual theory.

3. The goal of this book is not only to introduce the theory of institutional economics and economic organisation, but also to give examples of how the different theoretical perspectives can be applied. Some chapters contain addition questions on, for example, the calculation of the quasi-rents and the application of the principal-agent theory. This approach is intended to complement the concepts and study material with real-world examples. Many users of the book will be confronted with a lot of new terms or concepts. Therefore the book contains a Glossary that describes the most important terms used through the book.

How to use this book

The organisation of this book is based on the four levels of analysis identified in the institutional economic framework in Chapter 1. This framework serves as a 'roadmap' for understanding what theories are relevant for studying institutional economics and Economic Organisation Theory. While the writing is targeted towards undergraduate students of economics, business and management, the concepts are developed in enough depth for graduate students as well. Furthermore, the text is written in simple language that is understandable for students from a broad range of disciplines.

Such an approach lends itself to a wide range of uses. IE & EOT is an appropriate textbook for teaching both undergraduate and graduate level courses. Furthermore, it can be used as an overview of the literature. Therefore, it is also an interesting road map for academic researchers who wish to familiarise themselves with the fields of New Institutional Economics and Economic Organisation Theory. For courses that focus on specific aspects of institutional economics, but not the entire discipline, a subset of chapters of the book may be used to introduce those theories that are most relevant for a particular course. Similarly, instructors may choose to omit selected chapters and their associated theories, depending on the emphasis of their curriculum. The book is accompanied with a Workbook with questions and exercises. For more information, please visit the publisher's website.

Acknowledgements

A project like this does not take place overnight. It has partly been based on research carried out over the last fifteen years, among which were several EU-projects. Gradually the research products were transformed in lecture materials and, as said, had been taught and tested for over six years in a classroom environment. In 2007 we started a complete revision of the materials, based on more recent research projects and a rigorous investigation of the most recent literature.

Many people have helped us. First and foremost we express our gratitude to prof. Dr. Arie J.Oskam. He offered us the time and resources to write this book. We have benefited from the help of the following colleagues: Dr. Pierre Durpraz, Institut National de la Recherche Agronomique (INRA Rennes), Prof. Dr. Kostas Karantinis, Institute of Food & Resource Economics, University of Copenhagen,Ir. Evy Mettepenningen, University of Ghent and Dr. Nico Polman, Agriculture Research Institute in Den Haag (LEI). Finally, we would like to thank all our Wageningen University colleagues for their support and assistance: Dr. Roel Jongeneel, Dr. Thomas Herzfeld, Dr. Erno Kuiper, Dr. Sudha Loman, Dr. Jos Bijman, student assistant Pieter Heringa, Dineke Wemmenhove, and Karen van der Heide.

Dr. Louis H.G. Slangen

Associate professor, Agricultural Economics and Rural Policy, Wageningen University.
Louis.slangen@wur.nl

Dr. Laura A. Loucks

Senior Researcher and Lecturer, Agricultural Economics and Rural Policy, Wageningen University.
Laura.loucks@wur.nl

Dr. Arjen H.L. Slangen

Assistant professor of International Business-Society Management, Rotterdam School of Management, Erasmus University Rotterdam aslangen@rsm.nl (until August 1, 2008).
Assistant Professor of International Strategy, Amsterdam Business School, University of Amsterdam (as of August 1, 2008).

Wageningen, June 2008

Table of contents

1. Introduction and overview

1.1 Background

From a societal point of view there is a growing interest in the role of institutions[1]. For many people studying agricultural, development, general or business economics this interest in institutions is not unusual anymore, since institutions are important phenomena, both historically and currently, in the Netherlands, the European Union, worldwide, and especially developing countries. For example, agriculture is characterised by special institutions, such as the family farm, cooperatives, and land use systems like tenure with fixed land rents and sharecropping. Some of these institutions, such as sharecropping, formed the underlying institutional structure for new modes of organisation such as joint ventures and franchising, and have formed the basis of theoretical perspectives such as the principal-agent approach.

Developing countries are often characterised by weak or lacking institutions. This absence of high-quality institutions may express itself in low levels of social capital, the absence of laws and property rights, the quality of the government and poor-functioning markets. In many developing countries the necessary conditions for well functioning markets and other governance structures such as contracts are missing.

There have also been several recent developments that have accelerated and increased the relevance and importance of institutions and its underlying field new institutional economics. One important development is the fall of the wall in Germany in 1989. This event marked a new era; the collapse of the communist system. At the time, many people, including famous economists and policy makers, expected rapid economic growth in Central and Eastern European countries. However, this rapid growth did not take off. Rather, it became clear that a sound institutional setting is a pre-condition for well functioning markets. Such a framework for well functioning markets is determined by the level of social embeddedness and its alignment with the formal rules of the institutional environment. It means that not only the governance structure such as the market matters, but also the broader institutional environment.

A second important development is the privatisation of government-owned enterprises. In the last twenty years, thousands of state-owned firms in Africa, Asia, Latin America, and Western and Eastern Europe have gone private (Shleifer and Vishny, 1998: 137). Government-owned firms supplying resources and services such as gas, water, electricity, railways etc. were transformed from public into private firms. At the same time, markets were liberalised. This raises the question of how the provision or supply of goods and services should be organised. Spot markets and contestable markets are not always available or suitable. New institutional arrangements such as contracts with the users of the products are necessary. However, the provision of goods like gas, forces firms and citisens to conclude contracts with large and powerful corporations. What are the effects of these contracts? Can we easily switch from one service provider to another? Do we

---

[1] North (1991: 97) defines institutions as 'the humanly devised constraints that structure policy, economic and social interaction. They consist of both informal constraints (sanctions, taboos, customs, traditions, and codes of conduct), and formal rules (constitutions, laws and property rights)'.

have enough information to compare the costs and benefits? Are there hold-up and lock-in effects forcing us to remain with one company? And what can we do about this? Who is able to capture the residual income of these contracts, or more generally, of the privatisation and liberalisation processes? Is it the consumer or the producer who benefits?

To analyse these types of questions, we need a coherent theory that broadens its focus beyond the conventional governance structures such as the market and government bureaus. New institutional economics provides such a theory, paying more attention to the social embeddedness, the institutional environment, property rights, the mode of organisation, and the ownership structure of firms. Hence, the theory of new institutional economics is very important for analyzing questions such as: (1) what and (2) how to organise activities in our daily lives, in our household, in firms, in organisations (like a government agency) or in some hybrid forms. Which governance structure can and should be used? The market and the government are often seen as the only solution. However, this is often a too simple approach, because not only both can fail, but many transactions (or activities) can also be carried out by other governance structures, often called hybrids, such as clubs and contracts. More attention needs to paid to these other, often-ignored governance structures. Consequently, it is important to know the effects of other governance structures. For example, what are the effects of performance contracts on the behaviour of the police force? How will these contracts influence the behaviour of the individual policeman? Will they result in more fines or more safety? What types of crime will be solved: the easiest ones?

The choice of the governance structure should not only be based on the informal rules of social embeddedness and the formal rules of the institutional environment, but also on the characteristics of goods or services, and the characteristics of human beings. Important characteristics of goods and services are (non)-rivalry and (non)-excludability. In the case of non-rival and non-excludable goods the market will fail, and other governance structures like contracts, clubs, or even in-house production of the government could be a better solution. The choice of governance structure should also take into account the human characteristics of bounded rationality and opportunistic behaviour. In the real world, we have to be aware that individuals have only limited possibilities and abilities to obtain and process information. People are bounded by their inability to obtain information in order to fully comprehend the complexity of a situation. In the words of Simon (1961: xxiv), people are 'intendedly rational, but only limitedly so'. Opportunistic behaviour is often described as an expression of self-interest. These human characteristics can lead to hidden information and hidden actions.

From an economic perspective, institutions also matter. Within economics there is a growing interest in the role of governance structures, social embeddedness and the institutional environment. These developments are partly a reaction to the limitations of standard economic theory which is based on perfect competition and perfectly-functioning markets. Under perfect competition, all the necessary information is included in the prices of a good. A firm is perceived and treated as an economic agent with a single identity. A firm is introduced in traditional neoclassical economic theory as a production function, with clear links between the input and output, and which is in a position to produce a variety of products by using different amounts and combinations of inputs. In its simplest form, the firm is regarded as a 'blackbox' or a production function, without an internal structure but able to produce a large variety of output(s) using different combinations of inputs. Every economic agent has perfect information; that is, all agents know all technically feasible production and consumption plans and all prices in every market. The role of the producer is relatively simple, given the existence of prices for all goods and perfectly functioning markets and complete information (cf. FitzRoy *et al.*, 1998: 6).

However, these assumptions of traditional neoclassical economic theory do not always coincide with reality (cf. Hart and Holmström, 1987: 71). The conditions of perfect competition (numerous buyers and sellers, homogeneous products, complete and symmetric information, etc.) are often not met in practice. Often, the price cannot incorporate all dimensions of a good. Sometimes there is no market price at all. Moreover, not everything is coordinated via the invisible hand of the market. On the contrary, other governance structures such as organisations and contracts are often used instead. Organisations can be very diverse in nature. They can consist of firms, households, government organisations, clubs, etc. Within firms, we see that the price as coordination mechanism is replaced by one or more other coordination mechanisms to ensures the necessary coordination is achieved.

Firms and other organisations do not function as a single unit with a single identity. Viewing a firm as a cooperation of different involved parties (or stakeholders) can reveal the workings of the blackbox. The firm can also be seen as a "nexus of contracts" where each of the concerned parties is driven by self-interests, which can be different and may contradict each other. In the current economic literature, the assumption that a firm can be viewed as a blackbox has generally been relaxed. Many economists now realise that not only differences in external organisation but also differences in internal organisation can have consequences for the functioning and performance of a firm.

The increased interest of economists in the role of organisations and the institutional environment is also a consequence of a number of recent developments in complementary and overlapping areas of economic research. **Firstly**, the (modern) Industrial Organisation theory, New Institutional Economics, Economic Organisation Theory and Evolutionary Theory have all contributed to this. An important conceptual change has been a shift from 'the theory of the firm' where the enterprise was considered as a production function (a technical construction), to one where the firm is viewed as a governance structure (an organisational structure of governance where decision making occurs). **Secondly**, the passive "conduct concept" of firms, where the structure of a sector determines the conduct and performance of firms has been replaced by a more active behavioural view. Firms have the ability to actively change the structure and the constraints under which they operate (Hay and Morris, 1991: 21). **Thirdly**, there has been increased interest in organisations and the institutional environment in which economic activity takes place.

These three developments have together led to: (1) a change in the perception of the behaviour of organisations, such as firms, with respect to their internal organisation as well as the environment in which they operate, and their possibility to react; (2) a focus on the nature and consequences of institutional arrangements – such as contracts or other arrangements – for motivation and coordination; (3) a focus on the role of transaction costs in the economic process; and (4) a focus on the concept of property structure, the effects of property rights, and the effects of distribution of the property rights. Within institutional arrangements such as contracts, a central issue is who has the 'control rights' in this relationship? The answer to this question often determines which party will be able to capture the residual income.

1.2 Overview of the chapters

Before we begin with an overview of the chapters of the book, we have to introduce the central framework of our approach. Figure 1.1 shows the framework and forms the roadmap for the chapters. The figure is partly based on Williamson (2000: 297), but there are some important differences. The far left column gives the period of time needed to realise changes in the different levels of institutions that exist. These four levels of institutions are summarised in the second column.

The main difference between our framework and that of Williamson pertains to the fourth level of institutions. We have placed here the incentive structure while Williamson interprets this level differently (see Box 1.2). These incentives can be based on rewards (carrot), punishment (stick), building-up reputation, credible commitment and career concerns.[2] In Section 4.3 we will extensively discuss the role of incentives, including intrinsic and extrinsic motivation. The

---

[2] In Chapter 4.3 we will extensively discuss the role of incentives, including intrinsic and extrinsic motivation. However, it will also get attention in other chapters such as the principal-agent and contract theory.

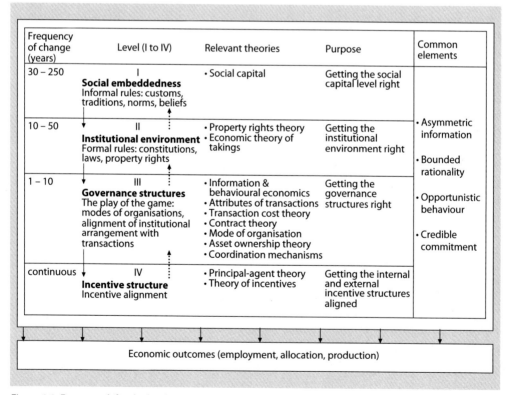

Frequency of change (years)	Level (I to IV)	Relevant theories	Purpose	Common elements
30 – 250	**I** **Social embeddedness** Informal rules: customs, traditions, norms, beliefs	• Social capital	Getting the social capital level right	
10 – 50	**II** **Institutional environment** Formal rules: constitutions, laws, property rights	• Property rights theory • Economic theory of takings	Getting the institutional environment right	• Asymmetric information • Bounded rationality
1 – 10	**III** **Governance structures** The play of the game: modes of organisations, alignment of institutional arrangement with transactions	• Information & behavioural economics • Attributes of transactions • Transaction cost theory • Contract theory • Mode of organisation • Asset ownership theory • Coordination mechanisms	Getting the governance structures right	• Opportunistic behaviour • Credible commitment
continuous	**IV** **Incentive structure** Incentive alignment	• Principal-agent theory • Theory of incentives	Getting the internal and external incentive structures aligned	

Economic outcomes (employment, allocation, production)

Figure 1.1. Framework for the book.

Box 1.1. Different views on the firm.

The **standard neoclassical theory of the firm** is perhaps the oldest and most established view. In its simplest form, the firm is regarded as a blackbox, a production function, without an internal structure but able to produce a large variety of outputs using different combinations of inputs. The theory assumes that every economic agent has perfect information; that is, all agents know all technical feasible production and consumption plans and all prices in every market. Information is distributed symmetrically and every party has access to the same data. The role of the managers, given their (and everyone else's) full information in the neoclassical theory, is simply to maximise the profits or market value of the firm by choosing the optimal production plan. Standard courses in microeconomic go into great detail about the neoclassical theory of the firm (FitzRoy,1998: 6).

Acording to the **transaction costs approach of the firm**, associated with Coase (1937) and Williamson (1975, 1987) the reason *why firms exist* is connected to the 'costs of carrying out a transaction by means of an exchange on an open market' (Coase, 1988: 6). The costs linked to carrying out transactions depend on the nature of the good and the way how the transition is organised; these costs are called transaction costs. The proponents of the transaction cost theory of the firm argue that transaction costs determine structure of the agreements upon which organisations are based, as such, they greatly affect the ultimate form of the mode of organisation itself (cf. FitzRoy,1998: 8).

The **behavioural theory of the firm** postulates the firm as a coalition of (groups of) participants, each with their own objectives (Douma and Schreuder, 2002: 95). By contrast, the standard neoclassical economics assumes that firms are holistic entities that seek to maximise profits. Theories of firm behaviour are based on considering the objectives of individuals and groups within firms. They consider the motives of managers and other groups within the firm. It also argue that lack of information leads firms into choices based on satisfying rather than on maximising behaviour.

The **resource based view (RBV) of the firm** is a way of describing a company's strengths. According to the RBV of the firm, a competitive advantage is based on the possession of certain resources, such as a large-scale plant or experience. The extent to which a competitive advantage is sustainable depends on how difficult or costly it is for other firms to obtain the same resources. In the RBV of the firm, resources are defined quite broadly. These include financial resources, tangible resources (such as plant, equipment, buildings) and intangible resources (such as patents, know-how, brand names, experiences and organisational routines). See also Douma and Schreuder (2002: 192-193).

The **evolutionary theory of the firm** is the newest and least developed of the accepted theories of firm organisation. The unit of analysis under this view is the firm and its productive processes. This theory focuses on three related aspects of organisations: the structure, their strategy, and their *core competency*. A firm is said to have a core competence in a business area if it not only has an advantage in producing a good or service, but also has a similar advantage in the production of innovation and new, related products Firms are able to survive only if they change appropriately in response to changes in demand and technology; in short they must adapt and find new productive scope for their core competencies – the things they do well, in order to succeed (FitzRoy *et al.*, 1998: 8). In the evolutionary theory of the firm the focus is on the development of the organisational form over the time.

> **Box 1.2. Fourth level according to Williamson.**
>
> According to Williamson (2000: 597) the fourth institutional level is the level at which the neoclassical economic analysis works. At this level there is a shift from discrete structural to marginal analysis. This is the level on which standard neoclassical economics and more recently the agency theory or *principal-agent approach* focus. The decision variables in neoclassical economics are prices, input and output. The *principal-agent approach* is concerned with the use of the correct incentives in the case of different risk-attitudes, multi-task factors or multi-principal problems. At this level, marginal analysis and optimisation behaviour dominate. This is also the level of individual decision-makers.

incentives can continuously be changed, and when taken together with other levels, they are very important for the economic outcomes. The third column gives an overview of the theories that are relevant at each institutional level. Most of these theories are related because they all belonging to the fields of New Institutional Economic and Economics Organisation Theory. They will be discussed in separate chapters, but some of them will be presented in the same chapter in an integrated way, so as to show their main similarities and differences.

The fourth column gives the purpose of the four institutional levels. At all levels we have to deal with asymmetric behaviour, bounded rationality, opportunistic behaviour and how to achieve credible commitment. The relevant theories give insight into how we can reduce or avoid the negative effects of these problems. Our framework emphasises that the institutional setting is very important, and the theories, mentioned in the third column, belong to our institutional economic approach.

Some authors (like Ostrom, 1998: 40) also label the theories in the third column as a modern approach to the theory of the firm. If we see the firm as a metaphor for institutional arrangements or governance structures where transactions are carried out, this approach is correct. In the modern theory of the firm, a principal recognises an opportunity to increase the return that can be achieved when individuals are potentially involved in an interdependent relationship. The entrepreneur (we will call him or her the principal) then negotiates a series of contracts with various participants that specify how they are to act in a coordinated, rather than independent, fashion. Each participant voluntarily chooses whether or not to join the firm, but gives up to the principal their discretion over some range of choices. The participants become agents of the principal. After paying each of the agents, the principal retains residual profits (or absorbs losses).

Consequently, the principal is highly motivated to organise the activity as efficiently as possible. The principal attempts to design contracts with his agents that will induce them to act as to increase the return of the principal, and the principal monitors the performances of the agents. Because the agents freely decide whether or not to accept the terms of the principal's contract, the organisation is considered private and voluntary. Furthermore, agents are driven by different types of incentives. When a firm is located in an open market, one can presume that external competition will pressure the principal toward developing efficient internal institutions (Ostrom, 1998: 40).

Opposite to the theory of the firm we have the theory of the state (see Box 1.3). In both the theory of the firm and the theory of the state, the principal or the ruler makes credible commitments to punish anyone who does not follow the rules of the firm or the state. Because they gain the residuals, it is in their interests to punish non-conformance by the agent and subjects. It is also in their interest to monitor the actions of the agents and subjects to be sure that they behave in accordance with the agreement. Both theories thus address how a new institutional arrangement can come about, how credible commitment can be made, and why monitoring must be supplied (Ostrom, 1998: 41). Our approach will be based more on the modern theory of the firm.

As stated earlier, the framework outlined in Figure 1.1 forms the roadmap for the book. All the chapters deal with the theories in the second column of this figure. An exception is Chapter 2, which can largely be seen as an orientation of the New Institutional Economics and Economic Organisation Theory within the different fields of economics.

Box 1.3. The theory of the state.

The theory of the state can be presented in a brief and stylised version. Instead of a principal, we posit a ruler who recognises that substantial benefits can be obtained by organising some activities. If a ruler gains a monopoly through the use of force, the ruler can use coercion as the fundamental mechanism to organise a diversity of human activities that will produce collective benefits. The ruler obtains taxes, labour or other resources from subjects by threatening them with severe sanctions if they do not provide the resources. The 'wise' ruler uses the resources thus obtained to increase the general level of economic well-being of the subjects to a degree sufficient that the ruler can increase tax revenues while being able to reduce the more oppressive uses of coercions. Rulers, like the principals, keep the residuals. Subjects, like agents, may be substantially better off as a result of subjecting themselves to the coercion exercised by the rulers. There is no mechanism, such as a competitive market, that would exert pressure on the ruler to design efficient institutions (Ostrom, 1998: 41).

Chapter 2. Background, origin and position

This chapter deals with the background, origin and position of New Institutional Economics (NIE) and Economic Organisation Theory (EOT). It discusses some common elements and differences with Modern Industrial Organisation (MOI), and Evolutionary theory (ET). Further, it places the NIE in the main stream of economic thinking; the neoclassical economics. The NIE can be considered as an attempt to incorporate a theory of institutions into economics. However, in contrast to the many earlier attempts to overturn or replace the standard neoclassical economy, the NIE builds on, modifies and extends standard neoclassical economy to permit it to come to grips and deal with an entire range of issues that have previously been neglected. What it retains and builds on is the fundamental assumption of scarcity and hence competition – the basis of the choice theoretical approach that underlies microeconomics. What it abandons is instrumental rationality (North, 2003: 17).

The instrumental rationality refers to the assumptions made in neoclassical economics about (1) economic behaviour concerning utility-maximisation by households and profit maximisation by firms; (2) the availability of complete (and/or free or costless) information; (3) completely defined and enforceable private property rights; (4) unlimited market transactions and the market is the only mechanism for carrying out transaction; (5) absence of transaction costs; and (6) completely divisible inputs and outputs. In a world of instrumental rationality institutions are unnecessary (North, 1997: 17).

It is often common to treat both NIE and EOT as equivalents (Hazeu, 2007: 11) and we will largely follow this line. In both theories the fundamental unit of analysis is the transaction. The meaning of the term 'transaction' is synonymous with the economic concept of exchange. Transactions can be carried out by markets, organisations or so-called hybrid forms. According to both NIE and EOT, the market is not the only mechanism for carrying out transactions. Therefore the choice for a transaction mechanism will depend on both its efficiency and effectiveness.

Still, the scope of NIE is somewhat broader than that of EOT. For example, NIE explicitly focuses on: (1) the role and meaning of social embeddedness, including social capital and informal rules in society; and (2) the rules of the game as included in the formal rules of society and the property rights. The area common to NIE and EOT includes, among others, the fundamental question about the reason for the existence and the functioning of different institutional arrangements (like firms, organisations, contracts, clubs, cooperatives). Both, NIE and EOT, make use of information and behavioural economics, principal-agent, transactions costs and contract theory. Our approach is often based on an integration of both.

Concerning the theory of industrial organisation, the term *industrial* refers to *branches of industry* or sectors and not to manufacturing. Until the seventies, the theory of industrial organisation was dominated by the structure-conduct-performance (SCP) approach. The structure includes elements such as the size and number of sellers in the sector, concentration ratio, market power, the degree of product differentiation, the cost structure, the barriers to entry and the degree of vertical integration with suppliers. Conduct refers to the price, research, development, investments, advertising and the like, and conduct results in market performance. Performance is reflected by efficiency, the ratio of prices to marginal costs, product variety, innovation rate, profits and distribution.

In the original SCP approach, the relationships were formulated as mono-causal. New theoretical insights indicate that SCP relationships are fundamentally multi-causal in nature. The structure of a branch of industry or sector is not given exogenously, but is determined by the conduct of the firms. Firms select the degree of product differentiation, their cost structure, degree of vertical integration, etc.

The modern industrial organisation theory (IOT) has slowly usurped the dominant place of the SCP framework. This modern variant is characterised by the theory of the functioning of markets and strategic behaviour of firms which operate in these markets, analysed with models such as game theory models. In this view, it is the agent who makes decisions. Modern IOT provides a link to NIE via the concept of *sunk-costs*, *sunk-investments* and *contestable markets*.

Sunk-costs and *sunk-investments* are related to asset specificity and influence the choice of the best *governance structure*.

In Chapter 2 we will also discuss some common elements of the NIE, EOT, MIO, and ET. Evolutionary economics derives its inspiration of *Darwinisian Evolutionary Theory* and the *criticism of the neoclassical theory*. Concerning the **first source of inspiration**, supporters of evolutionary theory believe that economic phenomena such as **economic change and adaptation** can be adequately described and explained by using Darwinian concepts such as (1) heredity; (2) natural selection (survival of the fittest); and (3) variation, including mutation (= new variation). The analogous economic concepts are routines, selection mechanisms and innovations.

The **second source of inspiration** for evolutionary economists is the fundamental criticism of neoclassical economics. The criticism of evolutionary economics focuses on assumptions about rationality, reversibility, agent homogeneity (the firm as a blackbox), and the static equilibrium concept. In contrast to these assumptions, evolutionary economics supposes and emphasises bounded rationality, irreversibility and path dependency, heterogeneity (variation), change and dynamics instead of static equilibrium. The relationship between New Institutional Economics and Evolutionary Theory expresses itself in the criticism of the neoclassical theory, the use of the same concepts like bounded rationality, path dependency, heterogeneity and both deal with institutions.

Chapter 3. Institutions and levels of institutions

This chapter focuses on the first three levels of the second column of Figure 1.1. It explicitly deals with institutions. They are very important for economic development; good institutions are instrumental to economic development. Institutions is a broad concept. According to North (2003: 23), *institutions are the rules of games of a society, or, more formally, are the humanly devised constraints that structure human interaction. They are composed of both formal rules (statute law, common law, regulations), informal constraints (conventions, norms of behaviour and self-imposed code of conducts), and the enforcement characteristics of both*. In addition to the rules of game we also have the play of the game. Modes of organisation are the players: groups of individuals bound by common purpose to achieve objects. They include firms, clubs, family farms, cooperatives, etc.

We build our approach to institutions largely on the description of North, and extend it towards an improved understanding of the complex world of institutions. For that reason we will distinguish three different types and levels of institutions: social embeddedness, institutional environment and institutional arrangements or governance structures[3]. The social embeddedness is the area of informal rules and the institutional environment generates the formal rules. This approach is expressed in Figure 1.1.

---

[3] Instead of governance structure we can also use the term mode of organisation.

Social embeddedness

Social embeddedness is on the top level. The term 'social embeddedness' refers to the idea that economic behaviour is embedded within social relationships (Granovetter, 1985: 481-482). An important part of the social embeddedness consists of formed norms and values, customs, morals, traditions and codes of conduct, i.e. the informal rules. In most cases, these informal rules change rather slowly.

For analysing the social embeddedness, the concept of social capital is very important. Social capital is largely located at the first level. It is the shared knowledge, norms and values, and expectations about patterns of interaction that groups or individuals bring to repeating activities. The most important component of social capital is trust between people and, to a lesser degree, trust of people in the government. Trust is of great importance between individuals, within a group and organisation, or within a society. A small amount of social capital within a group, organisation or society leads to higher transaction costs. If people trust each other they are prepared to exchange information, cooperate with each other and carry out transactions.

Institutional environment

The formal rules of institutional environment are on the second level; they are also referred to as the formal rules of the game in society. These formal rules include the constitution, laws and other regulations, like those on property rights. At this level the executive, legislative, and bureaucratic functions of the government as well as the distribution of the power across different levels of government are located. The institutional environment differs between countries, and even within countries the basic rules can vary. For example, US legislation differs from Dutch legislation or the legislation of other EU-countries. Also in the US, more values are focused on the individual. An other aspect is that some parts of the institutional environment are more dynamic and change rather quickly, while other parts are less dynamic and change rather slowly. The formal rules like legislation can be changed and implemented more quickly than the above mentioned informal rules.

Governance structures

Governance structures or institutions of governance are on level 3. Another name for governance structures is modes of organisations. Governance structures are the play of the game. The social embeddedness and the institutional environment specifies the rules of the game for the *institutional arrangements* or *governance structure*. We consider *institutional arrangements* and *governance structures* as synonyms. Governance structures consist of a whole spectrum of organisational modes with *markets* at the one end and hierarchies at the other. This spectrum also includes all sorts of hybrid forms such as contracts, clubs, cooperatives, franchising, joint ventures, etc. Such institutional arrangements are organisational modes within which transactions are carried out and implemented. The relevant theories are presented in third column of Figure 1.1.

Finally, the chapter concludes with an application of the theory; the club as a governance structure. This governance structure is an example of a hybrid. Its function can be explained by the club

Box 1.4. Changes in the institutional environment.

The institutional environment in the Western part of the world has developed from a situation where monarchs had the monopoly of violence, with which they protected civilians against theft and robbery, to a situation of a constitutional state and parliamentary democracy. In the past some monarchs used their monopoly of power to rob the people. Slavery, serfdom and toll levy were common. People were hesitant in carrying out productive activities, as they were afraid the monarch would seize any returns. Society has a kind of hold-up problem. In other words, lack of property rights or the erosion of these rights creates a negative incentive for people to undertake productive activities or investments.

Today in a modern constitutional state and parliamentary democracy, the monarch has been replaced by the politician, and the count by a civil servant. Robbery, slavery, serfdom, uncompensated takings and toll collection have been replaced by taxes. In a modern constitutional state and parliamentary democracy, governmental monopoly of violence is restricted by laws and rules. These laws and rules are part of the formal rules of the institutional environment. Together with the informal ones, they form the rules of conduct for governments, firms, households, groups, and individuals.

theory. Its origin can be considered as a reaction on changes in the social embeddedness and the institutional environment.

Chapter 4. Information and behaviour economics, and the role of incentives

In Chapter 4, we address important elements of information and behaviour economics, such as a lack of information, bounded rationality, opportunistic behaviour, self-interest, intrinsic and extrinsic motivation, the use of incentives, risk-attitude, expected utility and loss aversion. These elements underlie the formation of institutions. For example, incomplete information and the limited mental capacity to process information, determines the costs of transacting. The costs of transacting arise because information is costly and asymmetrically held by the parties to the exchange. Institutions are formed to reduce uncertainty in human exchange (North, 2003: 18).

Information economics studies the characteristics and implications of the phenomenon of information. It examines the characteristics, implications of the phenomenon (lack of) information and information-asymmetry. Asymmetric information can give rise to opportunistic behaviour, also sometimes termed as strategic behaviour. Opportunistic behaviour can be described as *a condition of self-interest seeking with guile*. It includes providing of selective and distorted information, making promises which are not intended to be kept, and posing different from what the person actually is. Information-asymmetry affects transaction costs and makes it difficult to achieve an efficient agreement.

The new institutional economics recognises that individuals have only limited possibilities and abilities to obtain and process information; indicated with the term 'bounded rationality'. *Bounded rationality* is said to arise when the cognitive ability of people is insufficient to deal with the complexity of the world. People are not in a position to take all circumstances into account when making a decision. This means that there is an important connection between bounded rationality and the lack or asymmetric information. We will explore the basic concepts of the information economics: asymmetric information, private information, hidden information, hidden actions, its consequences, and what can we do about it.

To reduce the uncertainty in the economy, all sorts of (formal) rules have been implemented over time. Formal rules in society can lead to a better functioning of markets, organisations and hybrid forms for carrying out transactions by defining and protecting property rights, applying monitoring of legal principles, sanctioning violations and creating conflict resolving mechanisms. However, building and preserving social capital can also reduce uncertainty.

Self-interest is often identified with rationality, with the implication that only self-interest individuals are truly rational. However, rationality does not imply self-interest motivations or vice versa. It is argued that there are two kinds of motivations for actions: intrinsic or internal to the individual concerned and extrinsic or external. However, there may be a trade-off between these two kinds of motivation, such that too heavy emphasis on extrinsic motivation can drive out intrinsic motivation. Motivations activated by external factors, such as monetary **incentives** or **direct order** (as in hierarchical governance structure), can crowd out motivations that are internal to the individual, such as more altruistic concerns. However, sometimes extrinsic motivational factors can also reinforce intrinsic motivation if they are seen as supporting self-determination. In that case external motivation is seen as crowding in intrinsic motivation.

Situations, where the driving forces for participants in a transaction is the lack of information, for example, over what others will do, or what others know, or what the next-best alternative is, arise in various forms and involve risks. Moreover the future is uncertain, and the results of projects are often uncertain; it means uncertainties and risks are part of our daily life. Uncertainty motivates people and the creation of institutions or concepts to cope with it. Therefore, in Chapter 4 we will also introduce the concepts of risk, uncertainty, risk-aversity, expected value and expected utility.

These concepts are part of the **theory of expected utility** which is a dominant theory of choice under uncertainty. In the expected utility theory, it is assumed that decision-makers are often risk-averse; i.e. a certain alternative is preferred above uncertain alternative with the same average value. This holds for all games of chance, no matter if it deals about profits or losses. However, according to the prospect theory, the classification whether the outcome is a profit or a loss plays a role in the risk-attitude. An important difference between prospect theory and the expected utility theory

---

Box 1.5. Bounded rationality and observing of contracts.

In situations with bounded rationality it is impossible to make agreements which completely reflect the complex reality in all its facets. The existence of opportunistic behaviour implies that no general trust can be ascribed to an incomplete contract. The question is how can we trust such incomplete contracts? We can rely on incomplete contracts, if the economic actors involved in the contracts are completely trustworthy. Besides trust, incentive mechanisms consisting of rewards (the carrot) and punishments (the stick) can be used for realising credible commitment for observing contracts.

is, therefore, the risk-attitude about gains and losses; people will value gains and losses differently. Most people do not like losses. Loss aversion is a central concept in the prospect theory.

Chapter 5. Attributes of transaction and transaction cost economics

This chapter discusses transaction cost theory, a framework for determining attributes of transactions which are decisive factors for the choice of governance structures and it provides some examples for calculating public and private transaction costs. The transaction cost theory is an important theory within the new institutional economics, because it tries to explain what is the best governance structure, given the characteristics of the transactions and imperfect information.

In the classical article of Coase (1937) 'The nature of the firm', the fundamental question raised is: 'Yet having to regard the fact that if production is regulated by price movements, production could be carried on without any organisation at all, well might we ask, why is there any organisation? Simple put, why do organisations or firms exist? What is their economic function, what determines which transactions take place via the market, and which transaction are completed via a formal organisation in the form of a firm?

For answering the fundamental question raised by Coase we will use the *transaction view*. The most fundamental analysis-unit is the *transaction;* the transfer of goods or services from one individual to another. Transaction is synonymous with the economic concept of exchange. It is a two-sided mechanism: the transfer of goods or services from one individual to another (including the transfer of property rights) and mostly money as a counter performance; i.e. the trade-off between performance and counter performance: *quid pro quo.* Transactions should be organised efficiently as possible. In the *transaction view* the transaction cost theory is at the centre. The size of the transaction costs depends on the nature of the good, the nature of the transaction and the way in which it is organised.

Transaction cost economics frames the problem of economic organisation as the problem of carrying out a transaction. It explains which governance structure has a comparative advantage in carrying out transactions. The empirical object of transaction cost theory is formed by governance structures in which transactions are coordinated and carried out: markets, hierarchies and hybrids lying in-between these two polar cases. According to Williamson (1987: 52-63), the chosen governance structure depends on: (1) the transaction attributes (*asset specificity, uncertainty* and *frequency* of the transaction); and (2) the *human characteristics of the decision-makers (bounded rationality and opportunistic behaviour)*.

In this chapter we will develop a framework for determining attributes of transactions which are decisive factors for the choice of the governance structure. Based on this framework of attributes we can determine which governance structure or organisational mode should be used. The variety of ways of organising transactions found in the real world reflects the fact that transactions differ in basic attributes.

Chapter 6. Principal-agent theory

This chapter addresses the principal-agent theory and its relationship with transaction cost theory. New institutional economics uses this theory to explain how to cope with the uncertainty between a principal and agent. The principal-agent theory offers a comprehensive framework for an analysis of how contracts are to be set up, which incentives should be used given the existence of asymmetric information and the risk-attitude of agent. In most cases, the principal is seen as the 'superior party' in the relationship. The agent can be an employee, but it can also be a more or less independent person who has to carry out a certain task on a contractual basis, like e.g. a civil servant, a farmer, a student, a franchisee, etc. What makes the principal-agent theory particularly relevant and attractive is that in many situations, the interests of the agent do not align with those of the principal.

The principal-agent framework can be used in situations in which a person, the principal, has a certain relationship with another person, the agent. Agents can be seen as (groups of) individuals. An agent performs a certain task, which leads to costs on behalf of the principal. The principal is often not able to observe the actions of the agent directly, but he can observe the output, which is (partly) the result of the actions of the agent. However, in some cases the output can not be measured or it is very difficult to do so. For example, in the public sector the output is not only difficult to measure, but also the relationship between input and output is often unknown. This is elaborated is the final section of this chapter.

Classical issues between different types of people (e.g. on the one hand, owners, managers, ministers and the other hand, workers, civil servants) that can be analysed with this theory are: (1) conflict of interests; (2) information asymmetry and uncertainty; (3) entering into agreements and concluding contracts; (4) questions like how contracts influence the behaviour of the participants? A central problem in principal-agent relationship is how the contract should be designed to motivate the agent to act in a way that serves the interests of the principal. Usually, the agent has better information on his own performance effort as well as his true objectives for complying with the principal's interest.

Chapter 7. Contract theory

Uncertainty often results from the human characteristic of bounded rationality and opportunistic behaviour. A way to cope with this for two parties – who would like to carry out a transition – is writing a contract. They could conclude a contract in which they promise to exchange commodities or service whose prices, quantities or type varied according to specific circumstances (Bates, 1997: 34). The contract is an institutional arrangement for carrying out transactions.

This chapter focuses on contract theory. Important elements are the incompleteness of contracts, the types and properties of contracts, contract compliance and design principles for reducing contractual failure. The chapter concludes with an application of the provision of public goods; the choice between in-house production by the government or contracting out.

Any transaction which is of the type 'You scratch my back, I'll scratch yours' – or as a *quid pro quo* – can be considered as a form of contract. In general, a contract specifies the actions that each party will take (for example the delivery of a good or service by one party and the payment to be made by the other party) and may assign control rights concerning making decisions (cf. FitzRoy *et al.*, 1998: 232).

An important concept in the standard neoclassical economics is a perfectly working market; it is an ideal-type situation. Similarly, we can speak about a complete contract in the same way. It can solve all the problems of motivation and coordination. It is assumed there are no problems concerning property rights. A complete contract specifies what each party is to do in every possible situation, and arranges the distribution of realised costs and benefits for every contingency so that each party individually finds it optimal to abide by the contract's terms. Every contingency is anticipated and all relevant information is available. Such a contract is considered to be complete because, when signed, it can be immediately implemented. All the ordinances in the contract are verifiable, so that one of the parties can call upon a third party, for example a judge, to enforce the contract.

However, as results of three key factors of the new institutional economic – lack of information, bounded rationality and the high transaction costs of obtaining the required information, for monitoring and enforcing of the agreements – contracts are mostly incomplete. It is simply too expensive to take all events into account, specify what should happen in case of each specific circumstance and to control whether the other party or parties adhere to the agreement.

The transaction costs, standard principal-agent and incomplete contract theory are important theories within the NIE and EOT. According to transaction cost theory, asset specificity generates a flow of quasi-rents. This can lead to a dispute as each party to a contractual arrangement attempts to appropriate those rents. The bargaining power and opportunistic behaviour influence the distribution of quasi-rents. Incomplete contract theory states that contracts are incomplete; there will be residual control rights and a residual income. This will lead to a dispute about who has the residual control rights in a contract and who is able to capture the residual income. This is the one who has the 'residual power'. The standard principal-agent approach is usually based on the assumption of a complete contract. Consequently, the standard principal-agent approach assumes there are no quasi-rents, no residual control rights and no residual income. The crux of the principal-agent approach is that the actors have diverse objectives and interests, and the principal has insufficient information over the actions of the agent. Because of asymmetric information, an incentive problem arises. These theories can complement each other quite well, certainly if in the principal-agent approach the assumption of complete contracts is released.

Contracts are governance structures or transaction mechanisms for carrying out transactions. In the case of spot-markets, where the two sides of the transaction take place almost simultaneously, the contractual element is usually downplayed, presumably because it is regarded as trivial. Whenever there is a long-term relation or a long duration between purchase and delivery (*quid* and *quo*), a contract is an essential element of the transaction relation.

Based on five key elements – duration of the contract, the role of the price as coordination mechanism, identities of the parties involved, the special characteristics of the transaction object, the safeguards (e.g. how to deal with unexpected contingencies, the role of written documentation and procedure to be followed in case of conflict of opinion) – we can distinguish a spectrum of contracts. At one end of the spectrum, we have the **classical** contracts, and at the other end, the **relational** contracts and in-between the **neoclassical** contracts. These contracts can be verbal or written and most of them possess the following properties (cf. Milgrom and Roberts (1992: 126-133): (1) voluntary exchange; they contain (2) coordination and (3) motivation mechanisms; (4) they are explicit or implicit; (5) they can be global or detailed. The key elements and properties can be used for analysing contracts.

Because of the incompleteness of contracts we have often to deal with bounded rationality, the chance of opportunistic behaviour, hidden information, hidden actions, lack of credible commitment and lack of trust between contract parties. This causes contractual failures. For reducing contractual failures we have to make use of design principles. These principles discipline people, firms, organisations and the government and control the effects of hidden information, hidden actions and lack of credible commitment or trust. It are essential elements or conditions for realising effective and efficient contracts.

Chapter 8. Coordination mechanisms and governance structures

This chapter deals with coordination mechanisms and governance structures. Firstly, coordination is a central issue in the Economic Organisation Theory. It includes what needs to be coordinated, how coordination is achieved in spot markets, contracts, firms and other governance structures. Secondly, we classify the coordination mechanisms into four groups: (1) the invisible and (2) visible hand, (3) the handbook and (4) the handshake. The combination of these four groups defines a wide variety governance structures along a continuum which extends from pure spot markets via contracts to firms based on vertical integration (= in-house production). We will formulate some propositions that lay the foundation for the relationship between coordination mechanisms and modes of organisation.

Thirdly, we will give an overview and a typology of a continuum of governance structures from spot market to vertical integration based on the key elements: coordination mechanisms, internal or external motivation, the identity of the partners, the duration of the transaction, the enforcement mechanism, financial participation and the level of vertical integration. The chapter concludes with an application to five existing organisational modes, among others, the single owner, partnership and private limited company.

It is important to distinguish between governance structures and coordination mechanisms. Coordination is expressed in the **nature of the coordination mechanism** such as the price, mutual adjustments, contract rules and safeguards or direct supervision. A governance structure or organisational mode often consists of more than just a coordination mechanism. It also includes, for example for a firm, the legal formal rules concerning the legal entity of ownership, the corporate status and tax regimes. However, the relationship between coordination mechanisms and governance structures is also mutually dependent, because the nature of the coordination mechanism also determines for a large part the type governance structure.

Next, there is not always a one-to-one correspondence between governance structures and coordination mechanisms. A given governance structure may, under specific circumstances, use a mix of elements of the four groups of coordination mechanisms. The two extreme governance structures – spot markets and firms as hierarchies (or organisations based on command and control) – use the invisible hand (price driven) and visible hand (direct supervision constraining behaviour) respectively as coordination mechanisms for organising economic activities. The governance structures in-between them will often use a mix of invisible and visible hand, the handbook and the handshake. This means that the application of coordination mechanisms, in practice, often uses a certain mix and is a matter of gradation.

The typology of a continuum of governance structures can be applied to both vertical and horizontal relationships, such as networks, clubs based on self-organisations and more formal clubs. For these modes of organisation, the handshake is an important coordination mechanism. The insight is growing that a variety of hybrid governance structures can been identified. This variety of hybrid governance structures shows that there are different 'ways to organise'. An important number of them consist of different types of contractual relationships. These options also illustrate the shifting boundary of the firm.

Chapter 9. Ownership

This chapter deals with ownership. Important elements are the concepts of ownership, how can we structure the 'organisational mode of ownership' in such a way that it minimises distortions caused by attributes of transactions, who owns a project or a firm, and whose interests should count?

There are two important approaches concerning ownership. One is based on **old** property rights theory and one on the **new** property rights theory. The **old** one deals with ownership as a bundle of property rights, consisting of:
a. the right to use the asset;
b. the right to appropriate the returns from the asset;
c. the right to change the form, substance, and location of the asset;
d. the right to exclude others; and
e. the right of transfer to others through markets or to their inheritances.

In the case of leasing out, a part of this bundle of these rights is transferred to a tenant. For that reason, the income and transfer rights are often especially emphasised as marking the economic meaning of ownership.

The **new** approach has also been labelled as the incomplete contract theory. The **new** property rights approach has been developed over the last fifteen years to explain the optimal allocation of asset property used in firms, organisations or contractual relations (Foss and Foss, 2001: 21). In the **new** property rights theory, having both the residual control rights and the residual income comprises a definition of ownership. This view of ownership is intimately associated with the contractual incompleteness.

In the case of a firm or organisation, where often different stakeholders are involved and different assets are brought in, it is not always simple to indicate who has the residual control rights and who can appropriate the residual income. When there are multiple owners of an asset or firm, they will typically delegate some of the residual control rights to e.g. directors, managers, and board of directors.

Ownership creates strong individual incentives. However, it does not mean that a system of private ownership is always efficient for the society as a whole. Private ownership will be very difficult or create inefficiency in the case of (pure) public goods, providing of certain goods involving a high level of fixed costs, high risky projects, activities leading to monopoly and negative external effects, such as destroying the environment. In spite of these reasons a generally well-accepted rule is that 'getting the property rights right' can improve our welfare. It means a system of clear, enforceable and tradable private property rights will generate socially efficient outcome.

There are two important guidelines for structuring the organisational mode 'ownership' in an efficient way. First, the residual decisions made will tend to be efficient when it is possible for a single identity to have both the residual control rights and to receive the residual income. Second, properly **combining** the two aspects of ownership – **residual control** rights and **residual income** – provides strong incentives for the owner to maintain and increase an asset's value. These guidelines do not only hold for simple assets, but also for more complex ones like a firm.

However, ownership as having residual income is complex. For example, the residual income or payoffs from an asset are often **not one-dimensional;** not all returns are monetary, there may be different **residual elements** associated with each dimension. The result of a project can consist of a variety of rewards (income, royalties, prestige, success, status etc.). A manager who carries out a particular project gains **expertise.** This can have a high value in the future, because he can exploit it. A question will be how these rewards are distributed? Even a simple project can give rise to complications. Most business transactions will be equally complex or even more so. Questions arise such as: are the residuals observable for the different stakeholders within the firm? For whom are the residuals? Or in other words who 'owns' a project or a firm?

'Whose interests should count' is an old discussion. A public limited company means ownership has a collective character; it is from a group of people. The public limited company construction makes it easier to recruit capital. However, it also means the separation of legal ownership and those who managed the firm, and it opens the discussion concerning whose interest should count?

Today investments funds or hedge funds try to take over the strategic parts of the shares of firms. Often they try to strip or split up the firms and selling the best parts of the firm – or make other decisions creating high short-term profits. With the takeover of the strategic part of the shares of a company, investments funds or hedge funds have not the intention of controlling the firm for a long time. The acquisition of strategic part of the shares in a firm is only meant for realising short-term profits. The only interests that count are those of the shareholders of the investment funds. The central question is also here, whose interests should count; the managers, the workers or the shareholders?

Chapter 10. The economics of property rights

This chapter corresponds with Chapter 9. Property rights are an important part of the work of NIE. As explained, ownership can be considered as a bundle of property rights. Based on the same concepts as in Chapter 9, we will elaborate upon two approaches for analysing property rights: the old and the new property rights theory. Next, we will show that both are complements. After that, we will apply the Coase theorem as part of the old property rights theory; meaning the assignments of property rights in a free access situation. It will be worked out in a simple application. However, it is not always easy to allocate property rights to certain assets; for example, it depends on the characteristics of these assets. For non-excludable goods it is very difficult or even impossible to allocate property rights. It would lead to too high transaction costs or it is technically impossible. The chapter concludes with some applications, lessons from the Coase theorem and with the question: is everything we see efficient?

For the economics of property rights theory, both the old and new property rights theories are important. The old property rights theory deals with (1) *property as a bundle of rights* and with (2) *property regimes*. In this view, property is seen as a set of rights. The bundle of property rights refers to what people may and may not do with resources; the extent to which they have them at their disposal, capture their returns, can use, transform and transfer them, and exclude others from their property. The content is important, because if you lease out your land or house, you have to know which of the part of the bundle will be transfer to the tenant. Property regimes refer to property systems for resources or for firms in a nation or in a region. They can consist of government, private, common, or non-property regimes.

The new property rights approach is also named the incomplete contract theory. An important application of the new property rights approach is the property right theory of the firm. A firm is identified as a collection of non-human assets under common ownership, where ownership means holding the residual rights of control. Residual rights are all rights to an asset that are not specifically assigned by a contract or by law to another agent, including the government. In many cases, the holder of residual control rights will, to a large extent, also have the residual income rights. Both are often complementary, that is the reason why residual control rights and residual income often (should) go together. We will address both the old property rights and new property rights approach in Chapter 10, and show that both can be seen as complements.

Property rights as a bundle of rights can be described in terms of the degree of control rights, the division, protection, duration, enforceability, and transferability of the rights. The transferability is strongly related to the well-known Coase theorem. This theorem (1960) states that irrespective of who gets the rights from a free access situation, these rights can be traded to internalise the value of these rights and result in a Pareto-optimal situation The Coase theorem only refers to efficiency, and does not evaluate the fairness in the assignment of the rights. By granting property rights for land, water, fishing and so on to certain groups of people by the government a society can achieve a more equal income distribution. This means, it would be possible, to allocate property rights in such a way as to achieve a more equitable income distribution without adversely affecting allocation efficiency.

However, a number of reasons can prohibit efficient and fair agreements. First, transactions costs can be high as result of bounded rationality and opportunistic behaviour. Second, for some goods – like pure public goods – it is impossible or very difficult to allocate property rights. If we do not have clear and enforceable property rights that can be transferred easily, then efficiency may not be realised. However, if no one clearly owns a valuable asset no one has an incentive to guard its value properly. If property rights are not tradable there is little hope hat assets will end up with those people who can make the best use of them and so value them most.

The third reason prohibiting efficient agreements has to do with weak or inadequate informal rules and formal rules. If property rights are not secure owners will not invest great amounts in assets that they may lose with no compensation, or they may sink valuable resources into protecting their claims. The reason is they have in that case only costs and no benefits. Insecure property rights create hold-up problems. A last reason that hinders bargaining to efficient agreement is a weak and bad government. These reasons are more or less mutual dependent. A weak government, and an inadequate social embeddednesss and institutional environment will lead to high transaction costs. The same holds for unclear and very difficult to transfer property rights. The level of transaction costs can prohibit the transactions.

Answering the question 'Is everything we see efficient?' can not detached from the question: are the property rights 'right'? Given the state of the art of the property rights allocation, if we take into account transaction costs, the current situation is often efficient because the reason why a 'better' outcome was not achieved is that transaction costs of achieving it are too high. For example, the rule *smoking is forbidden* is a cheap solution from the viewpoint of transaction costs.

Chapter 11. Takings

Chapter 10 and 11 are also related, because Chapter 10 deal with the assignment of property rights and Chapter 11 with taking away property rights. The government plays an important role in specifying, protecting and enforcing property rights. Without a government there will be no formal property rights. Takings are the opposite of assigning of property rights by the government; the government takes away the property rights. Lack of property rights or *taking them away* by the government without any compensation influences efficiency and equity in a society.

Assigning of and trade in property rights is connected with the Coase theorem. Takings and land reform have often opposite effects. Therefore, we will also investigate the relationship between the Coase theorem, takings and land reform.

Given the central issue in this chapter, we will address two types of takings: titular and regulatory takings. The titular takings are most far-reaching. Next, we will analyse five arguments for restricting takings and giving compensation, and the incentive effects of takings. The chapter concludes with some applications.

The government needs means of production for preparing, carrying out and regulating her tasks and producing public goods. There are two ways for having the disposal over the required means of production: (1) imposing taxes and use the return of taxes for buying means of production and hiring people for fulfiling the tasks of the government; (2) making use of takings. In the last case the government has directly the disposal over means of production and labour.

However, the power of the government to take away property affects the clarity and certainty over property rights. The social losses associated with the losses of these rights reflect the economic costs of the power of the government to take property. On the one hand, we have the advantages of the delivered public goods. On the basis of these two (losses and profits) elements it is possible to formulate an economic theory of *takings*.

In many countries, the constitution circumscribes the government power to take private property. Mostly the thrust is that the constitution prohibits the government from taking private property for public use, without just compensation. The rule is that taking of private property is only allowed under two conditions: (1) the private property is taken for a public purpose; and (2) the owner is compensated.

Compensated restrictions (takings) and uncompensated restrictions (regulations) result in different incentive effects. If the government does not need to compensate for restrictions, then it will impose too many of them. If there are too many restrictions, resources not being put to their highest-valued use or resources will not be used optimally. Thus uncompensated restrictions result into inefficient use of resources. Firstly, no compensation means no costs for the government and the this creates an incentive to take too much. Secondly, it will lead to less investments by people, in short the hold-problem. Moreover, no compensation also creates the problem of 'who has bad luck'?

1.3 Blind men and the elephant

In standard neoclassical economics, the firm in its simplest form is often seen as a blackbox; it is a production function without an internal structure but able to produce a large variety of outputs using different combinations of inputs. Every economic agent – whether they be a consumer, producer, worker, employee or employer – has perfect information and is able to make the best decision. Consumers strive to achieve utility maximisation and producers strive towards profit maximisation. In short, it is the world of instrumental rationality.

However, by looking carefully at this view, the question can be posed whether it is in reality what it seem to be? The parable of the blind men and elephant makes clear what can happen if we think that we understand what we are observing by only observing individual parts while ignoring how these parts function as a whole. Single theories are like parts of the elephant in the observation of the blind men. Taken individually, these theories insufficiently explain the variety of behaviour and governance structures that we observe into day's global economy. Similarly, by assuming the firm is merely a function of inputs and outputs, we assume we know what it resembles without carefully looking what it is, what is going on and without opening the blackbox of the people involved in the firm. This does not mean that all assumptions of standard neoclassical economics are wrong. But if the analysis of real world problems is partly based on wrong assumptions the conclusions can also be wrong in the end.

This book takes an integrated approach and tries to open the 'blackbox' of the role of institutions in daily economic and business life. Through this integrated approach, the book hopes to contribute to a better insight to real world problems.

The parable of the blind men and the elephant

John Godfrey Saxe

It was six men of Indostan
To learning much inclined,
Who went to see the Elephant
(Though all of them were blind),
That each by observation
Might satisfy his mind.

The *First* approach'd the Elephant,
And happening to fall
Against his broad and sturdy side,
At once began to bawl:
'God bless me! but the Elephant
Is very like a wall!'

The *Second*, feeling of the tusk,
Cried, -'Ho! what have we here
So very round and smooth and sharp?
To me 'tis mighty clear
This wonder of an Elephant
Is very like a spear!'

The *Third* approached the animal,
And happening to take
The squirming trunk within his hands,
Thus boldly up and spake:
'I see,' quoth he, 'the Elephant
Is very like a snake!'

The *Fourth* reached out his eager hand,
And felt about the knee.
'What most this wondrous beast is like
Is mighty plain,' quoth he,
''Tis clear enough the Elephant
Is very like a tree!'

The *Fifth*, who chanced to touch the ear,
Said: 'E'en the blindest man
Can tell what this resembles most;
Deny the fact who can,
This marvel of an Elephant
Is very like a fan!'

The *Sixth* no sooner had begun
About the beast to grope,
Then, seizing on the swinging tail
That fell within his scope,
'I see,' quoth he, 'the Elephant
Is very like a rope!'

And so these men of Indostan
Disputed loud and long,
Each in his own opinion
Exceeding stiff and strong,
Though each was partly in the right,
And all were in the wrong!

MORAL.
So oft in theologic wars,
The disputants, I ween,
Rail on in utter ignorance
Of what each other mean,
And prate about an Elephant
Not one of them has seen!

2. Background, origin and positioning

2.1 Introduction

This chapter deals with the background, origin and position of New Institutional Economics (NIE) relative to neoclassical economics and new emerging economic theories. The purpose of this chapter is threefold: (1) to outline the background, origin and position of NIE; (2) to compare it with Economic Organisation Theory (EOT), modern industrial organisation (MIO), and Evolutionary economics theory (ET); and (3) to analyse its relationship with the standard neoclassical economics.

In Section 2.2 we examine both the linkages and parallels between NIE and EOT. While each theory shares several common elements, there are also differences. In this section, the emphasis will be on the common elements. The differences are also sometimes a matter of taste. NIE and EOT both question the applicability of the standard assumptions of traditional micro-economics. The difference between NIE and EOT becomes most evident in their applications of the theory. EOT focuses mainly on institutional arrangements consisting of organisations such as firms, markets, and hybrid forms among contracts. The scope of NIE is somewhat broader than that of EOT. NIE explicitly focuses on institutions in the form of rules of the game as laid down in the formal and informal rules of society also. Both areas have in common the fundamental question about the reason for the existence and the functioning of firms and organisations; shortly: *why do firms or organisations exist and how do they function*? Both make use of information and behavioural economics, principal-agent, transactions costs and contract theory (See Figure 1.1.). Therefore, these theories are often indicated as the theory of the firm.

The MIO, NIE, EOT, and ET, all share a common achievement in that they have brought about a change in the standard microeconomic view relating to:
1. The theory of firms: a firm is no longer considered as a production function (which is technical construction), but as a governance structure (which is an organisational construction) in which the internal structure has an economic purpose and effects.
2. The passive behavioural view where the structure of a sector specified the conduct and performance of firms is now substituted by a more active behavioural view.
3. The importance of the institutional environment and the institutional arrangements within which economic activity takes place.

Of these various theories, the Evolutionary theory is the newest and least developed. Furubotn and Richter (2005: 40) state that the writings in the field of Evolutionary theory projects lines of thought that complement the research program of New Institutional Economics. However, the two fields are sufficiently distinct in their essential content to warrant separate treatment.

In Section 2.3 we examine the theory of industrial organisation, also known as industrial economics. Until the nineteen seventies, Industrial Organisation Theory was dominated by the structure-conduct-performance (SCP) approach. After this point in time, Modern Industrial Organisation Theory has gradually taken over the dominant position of the structure-conduct-performance framework. This modern variant is characterised by its theoretical focus on the function of markets and the strategic behaviour of firms operating in these markets, using tools such as game theoretic models.

Modern Industrial Organisation Theory (MIO), New Institutional Economics (NIE), and Economic Organisation Theory (EOT) are related and partly overlapping theories. MIO provides a link to NIE via the concepts of *sunk-costs, sunk-investments* and *contestable markets*. *Sunk-costs* and *sunk-investments* are associated with asset specificity and influence the choice of the *governance structure*. This has consequences for the question: what is the most suitable governance structure in the given circumstances? Is it the spot market, a contract or in-house production of the government? This question deals with alternative organisational modes.

The concepts of sunk-investments and non-redeployment can well be explained by the fixed asset and the exit barriers theories. Both theories will be discussed in the Section 2.4. The difference between acquisition costs and salvage value of assets, and the possibility of assets being 'trapped', is explained by the quasi-rent of assets within a certain type of mode of organisation, such as a firm. The concept of being 'trapped' is from the fixed asset theory and connected with the terms asset specificity, 'hold-up' and 'locked in' used in NIE and EOT. Consequently, several important concepts of NIE and EOT have their roots in the fixed asset and exit barrier theories.

Section 2.5 deals with Evolutionary Theory. Evolutionary economics is a relatively young stream which draws its inspiration on the one hand from *Darwinisian Evolutionary Theory* and on the other hand from the *criticism of the neoclassical theory*. Concerning the first source of inspiration, supporters of evolutionary theory believe that economic phenomena such as **economic change and adaptation** can be adequately described and explained by using Darwinian concepts such as (1) heredity; (2) natural selection (survival of the fittest); and (3) variation, including mutation (= new variation). The analogously economic concepts are routines, selection mechanisms and innovations.

The second source of inspiration for evolutionary economics arises from the fundamental criticism of neoclassical economics. The criticism of evolutionary economics focuses on assumptions about rationality, reversibility, agent's homogeneity (the firm as a blackbox), and the static equilibrium concept. In contrast to these assumptions, evolutionary economics supposes and emphasises bounded rationality, irreversibility and path dependency, heterogeneity (variation), and dynamic change rather than static equilibrium.

The close connection between NIE and ET is evident in the criticism of neoclassical economic theory. For example, both use the same concepts such as bounded rationality, path dependency, heterogeneity and both deal with institutions. In addition, they often share common areas of applications. Section 2.6 describes a number of important areas of applications of evolutionary economics.

In Section 2.7 we will discuss the NIE, EOT, MIO, and ET concerning their criticisms of a number of standard neoclassical economics assumptions. These assumptions concern (bounded) rationality, utility and profit maximisation versus satisfying behaviour, asymmetric information and the role of institutions. In contrast, NIE, EOT, MIO and ET emphasise a number of behavioural assumptions regarding the participants of economic processes which are more in line with: (1) what people consider to be important and (2) the type of cognitive capacity that decision-makers possess.

In Section 2.8 we will focus our attention on NIE and standard neoclassical economics, assuming that NIE and EOT are largely overlapping one another. NIE can also be perceived as a complement to the standard neoclassical economics; the *homo economicus* is transformed to a more realistic portrayal of mankind. Some people prefer the term corrections because of their criticism of the assumptions made in the standard neoclassical economics.

Key questions:
- What is the most fundamental unit of analysis in NIE and EOT?
- What are the transaction mechanisms for carrying out transactions?
- What is the way of reasoning behind the Structure, Conduct and Performance approach?
- What is the economic meaning of 'being trapped' and from what theory does it originate?
- Why are sunk-costs, sunk-investments and non-redeployment relevant for NIE and EOT ?
- What economic concepts of the evolutionary theory are based on the Darwinisian evolutionary theory?
- How can we compare and contrast the differences between evolutionary economics and standard neoclassical economics?
- In NIE, what concept replaces the notion of instrumental rationality of standard neoclassical economics?
- What is the relationship between rents, quasi-rents and recoverable costs?

2.2 New institutional economics and Economic Organisation Theory

This book focuses on New Institutional Economy (NIE) and Economic Organisation Theory (EOT). In both theories the fundamental unit of analysis is the transaction. The meaning of the term 'transaction' is synonymous with the economic concept of exchange. It is a two-sided mechanism: the transfer of goods or services from one individual to another or the trade-off between performance and counter performance, *quid pro quo,* and the transfer of property rights. Transactions are organised by governance structures such as markets, organisations or so-called hybrid forms. The governance structure 'market' has a central role in neoclassical economics, however, it is not the only governance structure to organise transactions. To carry out a transaction, you have to collect information, which means there will be costs involved. Therefore, the choice of a governance structure depends on both its efficiency and effectiveness. This theory is also called Economic Organisation Theory, because of choices that have to be made on how well something can be.

The economic analysis of the most fundamental unit, the transaction, focuses on: (1) *coordination* – i.e. what needs to be coordinated, how coordination is achieved in markets, inside organisations and in hybrid forms (such as contracts), which alternatives can be used for achieving coordination between units and how each part of a system fits together; (2) *motivation* and *incentives* – i.e. what and whom needs to be motivated, which incentives are needed, what alternative kinds of incentive systems there are and what needs to be done to make incentive systems effective and efficient; and (3) *demonstrating* that these aspects of organisation matter (Milgrom and Roberts, 1992: 17).

The Economic Organisation Theory is particularly suitable for analysing contractual relationships. Alchian and Demsetz (1972: 794-795) characterise organisations – in forms of firms – in terms of contractual relationships. Jensen and Meckling (1976: 310) view organisations as a nexus of contracting relationships among the individual members of the organisation. These contracts can be internal or external. In the case of an internal contract, there should be a deliverable within the firm, while in the case of an external contract, the provision is delivered by a third party or by the market. The contracting approach in organisation theory emphasises the voluntary nature of people's involvement in (most) organisations: people will only give their allegiance to an organisation that serves their interests. Markets and hierarchies – sometimes regarded as the two major ways of organising economic activity – are actually just two extreme forms of organisational contracting, with voluntary bargaining characterising markets and strict lines of authority characterising hierarchy (Milgrom and Roberts, 1992: 20).

An important question within Economic Organisation Theory is why firms or organisations exist. Many people in the western world work within firms, and most forms of production are realised by firms. In modern economic theory, a firm is an organisation that transforms input into output. Consequently, the efficiency of the whole economic systems depends to a very considerable extent on what happens within these economic units (Coase, 1988: 5-6). In 1937 Coase already stated that markets do not regulate the whole of economic life. If an employee moves from one department to another within the company, he does not do that because of a change in prices. He does it because he is ordered to do so (Coase, 1988: 35). In such cases, the coordination mechanism is not the price mechanism, but a coordination mechanism within the firm itself, such as a direct order.

The term New Institutional Economics (NIE) originated from Williamson (1975). The adjective 'new' was added to distinguish this theory clearly from the work by early Institutionalists. One of the central problems with many of the early Institutionalists was that 'they wanted an economics with institutions, but without theory'. The problem with the work of many (traditional) neoclassical economists is that they practice economics without institutions. NIE tries to provide an economics with both 'theory' and 'institutions' (Langlois, 1986: 5; cf. Nabli and Nugant, 1989: 10; Rutherford, 1994: 9). Nowadays, it can be considered as a complement to traditional neoclassical economics (Hazeu, 2007: 21).

According to Williamson (1998: 23), two recent and complementary fields of economic research have filled in several gaps in (and to a certain extent also as a contrast to) traditional economic theory. The first is NIE and the second is Economic Organisation Theory (EOT). The fields of both NIE and EOT began more or less to gradually take form in the seventies of the last century and thereafter both fields have taken off. According to Williamson (1998: 23), NIE is more inter-disciplinary in nature and is also applicable to neighbouring social sciences. EOT has a better economic-theoretic foundation and is closely linked with MIO. The latter is involved with the functioning of the markets and strategic behaviour of firms which operate in these markets.

Box 2.1. The term New Institutional Economics.

The field of NIE has also been termed as 'theoretical-institutional economics', 'modern institutional economics' and 'neo-institutional economics'. Furubotn and Richter (2005: 10) in their book *Institutions and Economic Theory* suggest that NIE can also be termed as New economics of organisation. Eggertsson (1990: 6) distinguishes between 'neo-institutional economics' based on neoclassical theory and optimisation modelling, and the 'New Institutional Economics' based on ideas about bounded rationality. She uses the adjective *Neo* in place of *New* in order to emphasise the link with neoclassical economics. The prefix 'neo' in neo-institutional economics' refers to the connection between this field and the well-known neoclassical economics. Rutherford (1994: 182) argues that the distinction between 'neo-institutional economics' and 'New Institutional Economics' will be difficult to maintain. The two approaches are quite similar and the name is often simply a matter of taste. We shall be using only the term 'New Institutional Economics' (NIE) from now onwards.

The difference between NIE and EOT is in practise not always easy to identify. There are more or less overlapping areas. How the differences are interpreted by authors and researchers depends on their preferences. Williamson (1987; 1998) bases the naming of *Economic Organisation Theory* on Moe (1984). Moe uses the term *institutions* only as a reference to Coase (1937) and Commons (1934). After which, he gives the impression – without being explicit – that institutions are a form of organisational relationships, and that the behaviour of organisations is determined by these relationships (cf. Moe, 1984: 742-744). EOT is defined by Moe (1984: 739) as a theory which can explain why firms, partnerships, private limited companies, public corporations, and other organisations behave as they do.

Since the nineties of last century and the beginning of this century, there has been growing interest in the economic aspects of organisations. Complete handbooks entitled Economic Organisation Theory started to appear. These included Milgrom and Roberts (1992), Douma and Schreuders (1992; 1998; 2002), FitzRoy *et al.* (1998), Brickley *et al.* (2001), Hendrikse (2003), and books where the most important articles were reprinted (Putterman and Kroszner (eds.), 1996; Groenewegen (ed.), 1996). Furubotn and Richter (1997; 2005:1) called their standard work *Institutions and Economic Theory,* and their central message is that institutions matter for economic performance.

Milgrom and Roberts (1992: 20) consider EOT very appropriate for analysing contracts. They attempt to link the approach of Alchian and Demsetz (1972: 794-795), who model the organisation of types of firms in terms of contractual relationships, with the approach of Jensen and Meckling (1976: 310), who consider organisations to be a nexus of contracts, treaties, and mutual understandings among members of the organisation. The contracting approach to organisations emphasises the voluntary nature of people's involvement in (most) organisations: people will give their loyalty only to an organisation that serves their interests. Furthermore, along with the ability to enter a contract, there are the possibilities for reform, redesign, and abandonment of the organisation by rearranging contractual terms. Markets and hierarchies – sometimes regarded as the major ways of organising economic activities – are actually just two extreme forms of coordination, with voluntary bargaining characterising markets while strict lines of authority characterising hierarchy (Milgrom and Roberts, 1992: 20).

Douma and Schreuder (1998: 14; 2002: 15) describe in their book *Economic Approaches of Organisations*, the integration between studies of organisation and economic theory as the *economic theory of organisation*. They argue that markets and organisations are the two ideal types of coordination of exchange transactions. Markets use the price mechanism as a coordination device, whereas organisations make use of non-price coordination mechanisms, such as authority. Douma and Schreuder emphasise *organisation* as the unit of analysis in their approach, while the *transaction* is the unit in Milgrom and Roberts (1992: 21). Both approaches have the following in common: (1) the fundamental question concerning the reason for the existence of organisations; (2) the functioning of organisations which is also a matter for study EOT, although the emphasis may differ. According to Douma and Schreuder (1998: 14; 2002: 15) '*there is a family of economic approaches of organisations*'. Also in the Dutch work of Moerland (1992) and Noorderhaven (1997) we see an approach similar to the EOT of Douma and Schreuder (1998; 2002). The study subject is once again the organisation.

FitzRoy *et al.* (1998) in their book *Management and Economics of Organization* also focus on this same subject as Milgrom and Roberts (1992). As pointed out by Douma and Schreuder (1998: 14; 2002: 15), the developments within EOT are continuing. FitzRoy *et al.* (1998) discuss not only markets, contracts, and organisations, but also institutions such as property rights (cf. p.172), which until now have only been included in NIE and rarely in EOT (except Milgrom and Roberts, 1992, Chapter 9). The book of Hendrikse (2003) *Economics and Management of Organizations* is strongly oriented on economic organisational questions, but less so on issues such as property rights, social embeddedness, and institutional environment. Hybrids as governance structures – such as contracts and clubs – are largely left out of consideration.

A completely different line of thinking is followed in the standard book of Furubotn and Richter (1997: xiv; 2005: xiv). In their approach, NIE is perceived as a combination of transaction costs theory, property rights analysis, and contract theory (2005: xiv). Their objective is to provide a critical overview of the theoretical contributions of NIE from the nineteen sixties onwards. They devote particular attention to incomplete contract theory. Considering the circumstances which give rise to most contracts, this theory has considerable social relevance.

Without striving for completeness, we can see in reality a certain division of labour exists. Business economists and economists who focus on organisational and management problems have a preference for using the term EOT. General economists prefer to use the term NIE (cf. Hazeu, 2007: 29). We believe that the two terrains overlap to a considerable extent, and that both are perceived as a correction and a complement to standard neoclassical theory. An analysis based on NIE often contains elements of EOT and the marginal principle, optimisation, and striving for effectiveness and efficiency remain important guidelines within NIE.

The literature suggests that the economic theory which is used in EOT is to a considerable extent borrowed from – or overlaps with – NIE. As said, NIE goes somewhat further, and deals with a broader terrain. However, no clearly marked out terrain can be designated. According to Hodgson (1998: 175), even among its supporters there is no unanimous consensus on what exactly should be understood by the term NIE. The terrain is still being developed. As we have already mentioned, the developments in EOT also continue. In addition to markets, contracts, and organisations, there is also an increasing interest in institutions such as property rights.

The scope of NIE is, therefore, somewhat broader than that of EOT. NIE explicitly focuses on institutions in the form of rules of the game as laid down in the formal and informal rules of society. Partly based on Rutherford (1994: 2-3), we will use the following scope for NIE: (1) role and meaning of the social embeddedness, including social capital and the informal rules; (2) the area of formal rules of the game as included in the formal rules of society and property rights. The discussion on property rights dates back to Demsetz (1967) and Alchian and Demsetz (1972), but we will distinguish the old and new property right approach; (3) the area of public choice processes including rent seeking and activities of shifting coalitions, and principal-agent relationships between politicians and government's bureaucrats; and (4) the area common to NIE and EOT, regarding the fundamental question about the reason for the existence and the functioning of institutional arrangements (like firms, organisations, contracts). Both make use of information and behavioural economics, principal-agent theory, transactions costs and contract theory. The principal-agent theory was developed by Stiglitz (1974) and Jensen and Meckling (1976), contract theory by Hart and Holmström (1987), and transaction cost theory originated from Williamson (1987). Finally, a strong distinction between NIE and EOT is not always fruitful. Therefore, we will use a more integrated approach.

2.3 Industrial organisation theory

The theory of industrial organisations, or industrial economics, investigates markets and the results of markets. The term *industrial* refers to the *branch of industry* or a *sector* and not to manufacturing. Until the seventies, the theory of industrial organisation was dominated by the structure-conduct-performance (SCP) approach. The emphasis lay on empirical research on how well the various branches of industry were doing (cf. Van Witteloostuijn, 1994: 770). This approach assumed that the structure of a sector determines conduct and performance. The elements of the structure of a sector include: the size and number of sellers in the sector, market concentration ratio, market power, the degree of product differentiation, the cost structure, the barriers to entry, the degree of vertical integration with suppliers, etc. Conduct refers to the price, research and development, investments, advertising and so forth, and leads to market performance. Performance is reflected by efficiency, the ratio of prices to marginal costs, product variety, innovation rate, profits and distribution (cf. Tirole, 1993: 1).

Following this approach, a number of empirical studies were conducted, initially neglecting the *conduct link* in the SCP-framework. This was based on the argument that the *conduct* of firms can only be analysed in the context of market results. However, representatives of the structuralist school, such as the founder Bain (1968), assume a relatively permanent structure where both conduct and performance are determined. Gradually over time, greater attention has been devoted to the *conduct variables* under the influence of the behaviourists, including Scherer (1980), one of the most important representatives. According to the behaviourist school of thought, the economic performance of a firm is also determined by the inter-relationship between firms and their followed strategy. If oligopolies can coordinate their actions by means of cartels, collusion, or price leadership, then their resulting interdependence can lead to collective profit maximisation.

The main problem with the original SCP approach was that the relationships were formulated as mono-causal. New theoretical insights indicate that SCP relationships are fundamentally multi-causal in nature. The structure of a branch of industry or sector is not given exogenously, but is determined by the conduct of the firms. Firms select the degree of product differentiation, their cost structure, degree of vertical integration, etc. It means there is not only a path from *structure to behaviour/conduct* but also from *behaviour/conduct to structure*. Factors outside the sector are also important such as the demand side and the government. Figure 2.1 give a view of the modern SCP-approach.

After 1970, modern industrial organisation theory (MIO) has slowly usurped the dominant position of the SCP framework. This modern variant is characterised by the importance attached to theory concerning the functioning of markets and the strategic behaviour of firms which operate in these markets, analysed with models such as game theory models (cf. Van Witteloostuijn, 1994: 771). In these models, the economic agents or firms, whether new entrants or established firms, are all considered to be rational. Everyone takes the action of everyone else into account: the so-called strategic interaction. The level of aggregation is not the branch of industry but the

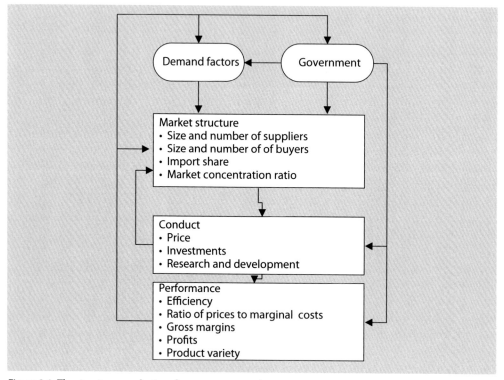

Figure 2.1. The structure conduct performance approach.

agent who makes decisions. In the case of monopoly (a good is sold by only one firm) or perfect competition (all actors are price takers), the nature and magnitude of strategic interaction is too small for a formal use of game theory (Mas-Colell *et al.*, 1995: 217).

Game theory is often applied in economics as it is commonly the case that a number of persons have to make decisions, rather than just one individual. Since the nineteen eighties, game theory has been popular for branches of industry or sectors with few enterprises. If the institutional framework within which decisions are to be made plays an important role, it must be further specified. The sequence of the decisions made and the available information for the various parties must also be indicated (cf. Hendrikse, 1992: 36).

By giving more attention to economic *theory* and the use of a *game-theoretic* approach, the SCP approach has been gradually replaced by an approach where the focus is more on the distinction between *short-* and *long-run* decisions. Long-run decisions are generally taken only once in a while. The construction of a new factory building, cattle barn, or greenhouse is an example of such a decision. Once the decision is made, it is not possible to reverse it easily, and a reversal of the decision entails costs that cannot be recovered. These are known as *sunk-costs*. Short-run decisions are made regularly, and can be reversed or changed without incurring major costs. Long-run decisions are in this view decisive for short-run decisions. Sunk costs create typical problems, such as quasi rents, and have consequences for the best mode of organisation.

Sunk-costs are strongly related to *sunk-investments;* sunk-investments often result in sunk-costs. Both are often used as synonyms. Sunk-investments are investments which generate profits in case of a particular application but have little value in another application. Sunk-investments are related to the concepts of fixed asset and asset specificity. An asset is said to be a fixed asset if the asset is 'trapped' or sunk in a certain use or relationship and an asset is said to be specific, i.e. there is asset specificity, when the investment has a higher value inside a specific relationship than outside it. Asset specificity is a measure of non-redeployability. Such investments are called sunk investments, because part of these costs are sunk into the relationship, i.e. cannot be recovered elsewhere (Hendrikse, 2003: 207). The importance of sunk-investments becomes clear in:
- so-called *contested market* forms;
- fixed asset and exit barriers theory;
- the asset specificity concept, and therefore the sunk aspects of investments, as typified by Williamson.

Box 2.2. Game theory.

Game theory is a method which describes and analyses situations where decisions are taken by a number of persons. It differs from *decision theory,* which is applied in situations in which there is only one decision-maker and so is a special case of game theory. In decision theory situations, all variables are selected by one person, and all other influences are taken to be exogenous parameters. The costs and profits are completely determined by this person. However, this is not the case in game theory situations, where profits and losses are affected by the decision (choice) of others also. Therefore, the *interactions* between decision-makers are crucial in game theory (cf. Hendrikse, 1992: 36).

Box 2.3 Sunk costs and quasi-rents

The difference between sunk costs and opportunity costs can be explained by the quasi-rent concept. A cost is said to be sunk if, once paid, it can never be recouped. An opportunity cost of an activity is the value of the next-best alternative. Sunk costs are taken into account (as full costs) when an investment decision is taken. However, these costs cannot be recovered once they are made, therefore only the salvage value of these costs counts. The salvage value is the value in the next-best alternative. For sunk investments, these values are often low or even zero, for example, the construction costs of a railway. The difference between the value of an investment in its current use and the value of the investment in its next-best alternative use is called the quasi-rent (cf. Hendrikse, 2003: 208). This is numerically worked out in Section 2.4 and more extensively in Appendix 2.1. The quasi-rent is not the same as a rent. A rent is the return from an activity above the minimum required to attract resources to that activity. The quasi-rent is always at least as large as the rent.

When an individual assesses the quasi-rent of some particular activity, he/she ignores any sunk cost (e.g. the value of factual investment in the past) and focuses instead on the payments of what he/she could earn elsewhere (the opportunity cost). Quasi-rents are also created whenever specialised non-salvageable investments are made; for example, when an individual works for an organisation and he is asked to carry out a task that cannot be transferred outside the firm. Having made the investment, the individual will earn a higher wage than he/she can earn in the next-best alternative. If an individual has invested in an activity that cannot be recovered if he/she leaves, this person is now earning a quasi-rent. In the case of a firm operating in the short run, quasi-rents are simply the excess of the total receipts over total variable costs (Furubotn and Richter, 2005: 565). Quasi-rents have the potential to be widely useful for proving incentives, for example concerning the choice of the governance structure (cf. FitzRoy, 1998: 305-307).

The *contested market* received considerable attention in the seventies of last century (cf. Baumol *et al.*, 1982). A perfectly contested market is one in which entry and exit is free and without costs. Sunk costs and sunk investments do not arise in this case. The theory of the contestable markets, and in particular the issue of ultra-free entry into markets, has been very influential in the field of economics and public policy[4]. Contestability theory holds that if a firm can freely enter a market, undercut prices, sells its output while at least covering its costs and then exit the market before the incumbent firm(s) responds, then the incumbent firm(s) will price optimally. According to the theory the threat alone is sufficient to induce competitive prices. Contestability has received serious criticisms on the grounds of both robustness of its predictions and the realism of its assumptions (cf. Baumol *et al.*, 1982). An import assumption is that the contestability theory requires that entrants incur no sunk costs. It also means that there is no asset specificity, or more in general no transaction costs connected with entering and leaving of a market.

A *sustainable* market situation is a necessary condition for a contested market. Such a market exists when demand and supply are in line with each other, with a price high enough to cover

---

[4] The idea in the EU about liberalisation of the energy, telephony, railway and other formerly public sectors supposes the entry of competitive firms. However, in most of these sectors a free entry for firms is almost impossible, because of the costs of the network or infrastructure. Some media like internet offer possibilities for a low cost entry to markets, or a hit-and-run entry.

costs, and low enough to make it impossible for rivals to increase their market-share by lowering prices. A market can be said to be perfectly contested if new firms are confronted with the same cost curves as the existing firms, and it is possible for firms to leave the market without incurring losses. In sum, a perfect contested market requires three conditions. **First**, there are no sunk costs. **Second**, potential new firms should have no disadvantage compared to existing firm concerning entry to production technology and product quality. **Third**, firms which enter the market should be able to apply *hit and run* tactics.

MIO offers a refined definition of the term 'competition' in markets with imperfect competition which begins with exogenous basis conditions for supply and demand (see e.g. Clarkson and Le Roy Miller (1982: 6); Van Cayseele and Schreuder (1990: 309)). It offers a coherent framework for research into how changes in the institutional environment – public law, private legal rules, anti-cartel policy, etc. – affect functioning of a market, firm's behaviour, and market results. Network utilities, relative high investments (including high fixed costs) and relative low maintenance costs, sunk costs, free entry, control of strategic resources, economies of scope are very important issues in MIO.

MIO provides a link to NIE via the concept of *sunk-costs and sunk-investments*. The concepts of sunk-investments and non-redeployment can also be well explained by the fixed asset and the exit barriers theories. Both theories will be discussed in the next section. *Sunk-costs* and *sunk-investments* are related to asset specificity and influence the choice of the best *governance structure*. Or in other words it has consequences for the question: how to organise? What is the best or most suitable governance structure given the circumstances? Is it a spot market, a contract, vertical integration, or in-house production of the government? The question deals with feasible organisational alternatives. For example, the problem of sunk costs can be reduced by the choice of the mode of organisation.

The question of 'which organisational form is the most feasible' is relevant for criticising the conventional economic theory of market failure. According to this theory, markets are beset with market failure whereas 'omniscient, omnipotent, benevolent' governments would reliably administer efficacious remedies. However, do such government bureaus or agencies exist? We have to recognise that all feasible forms of organisation – government included – are flawed (Williamson, 2000: 602). Because we do not live in a first-best world, we have to analyse the best way to organise activities for each transaction, even the organisational form.

The presence of imperfect competition explains why vertical integration (= in-house production) or contracts are attractive as alternative governance structures as a reaction to market imperfection (P > MC) as well as to increased market power. The theory of the firm, including the transaction costs approach, offers a good explanation for alternative modes of governance – e.g. from contract to vertical integration. More generally, there is a need is to identify and explicate the properties of alternative modes of governance – spot markets, classical, neoclassical, and relational long-term contracts, firms, bureaus, etc. – which differ in structural ways (cf. Williamson, 2000: 602). The NIE and EOT open the possibility to look for modes of organisation which are better able to deal with risk and uncertainty; for example, contracts instead of the spot market.

Although MIO, NIE, EOT are related and overlapping theories, a distinction can be made regarding their application. NIE and EOT focus more on internal organisation and MIO on the external organisation in a branch of industry or sector. But this distinction is not very sharp. There is also a development within MIO to incorporate in the theory the internal structure and organisation of firms and how organisations influence behaviour (cf. Clarkson and Miller, 1982: 7-8; Hay and Morris, 1991: 21; Tirole, 1993: 4). According to Tirole (1993: 4) *the intersection between (economic) organisation theory and Industrial organisation theory is one of the most interesting areas for theoretical research in the years to come.*

2.4 The fixed asset and exit barriers theory

It should be emphasised that the concepts of sunk-investments and non-redeployment can be well explained by the fixed asset and the exit barriers theories. The fixed asset theory has been developed by Johnson (1958), formalised by Edwards (1959), and popularised by Hathaway (1963). This theory can be used to explain, for example, why fixed resources were 'trapped' in agriculture; organised mainly in family farms. Important concepts in this theory are acquisition costs and salvage value. The acquisition cost of an asset is the value of the asset at the moment of decision making. If the asset must be purchased on the market, the acquisition cost is equal to the market price.

The salvage value is based on the current opportunity costs. In general, the salvage value for assets, once acquired, are often lower than the acquisition costs. The difference between acquisition costs and salvage value is to be expected for almost all resources and can be directly attributed to resource positioning and transactions costs (Johnson and Pasours, 1981: 3). Furthermore, acquisition costs in the fixed asset theory are often measured at the historical purchase price, whereas the salvage price results from evaluations of salvage opportunities at a point later in time (cf. Johnson, 1958: 77-78).

The neoclassical analysis, however, is almost devoid of explanations as to why assets are fixed in a firm, making it necessary to apply the opportunity costs principle. When it became apparent in the development of economic thought that land and capital goods have many things in common, this difficulty was met, in part with the concept of quasi-rent. Questions involving fixed assets, the length of the period in which capital goods are fixed, and quasi-rents tend to be avoided in the neoclassical analysis by assuming perfect factor markets (i.e. markets in which firms can buy and sell inputs at the same prices). The neoclassical theory does not explain clearly how and why resources move into firms as variable inputs, and become fixed. An asset will be defined, very simply and crudely, as fixed 'if it ain't worth varying'. More elegantly stated, an asset will be defined as fixed so long as its marginal value product, in its present use, neither justifies acquisition of more of it, or its disposition. If the acquisition costs and salvage value of an asset are substantially different, the asset can remain fixed while the price of the product it produce varies (Johnson, 1958: 77-79).

The exit barrier theory of Caves and Porter (1976) is similar to the fixed asset theory developed by Johnson twenty years earlier. Emphasis is placed here on the 'limited salvage value' of durable specific assets. Resources become durable, because once purchased, their value in use exceeds their salvage value. Durable assets include not only traditional, long-lived, specialised equipment but also capital goods and intangible assets. Intangibles, such as trade-marks, have a low salvage value because of the limited markets. Labour with specific skills has a greater in present use than in other uses not requiring the skill. Exit barriers are alleged to result in persistently 'subnormal' profits. Exit barriers arise because resources are durably committed to an activity of the firm (Caves and Porter, 1976: 40)[5].

Both the fixed asset theory and the exit barriers theory focus on resource allocation where resource values in use have fallen below the acquisition prices, but not below salvage values. If the rates of return are evaluated on the basis of current opportunity costs, the implication is that the resources are rationally attracted or retained in their current use rather than being 'trapped' there, and the rates of return are competitive with current alternatives. The appropriate focus of fixed asset theory is therefore on the reasons of divergence between acquisition costs and salvage value of assets.

For explaining the fixed asset theory, we take as an example the factor of production labour in the agricultural sector. At the moment that someone would like to become a farmer, we assume that his acquisition costs are 30,000 euro. This is also shown by P_a in Figure 2.2. At the moment of decision making, he can also earn outside the agricultural sector the same amount of money. When, for example, after 20 years he applies for a job outside the agricultural sector he cannot, or minimally, use his experience in agriculture. Consequently, he will be considered as an unskilled worker. Therefore, we assume that his salvage value is only 20,000 euro (P_s). This value is the market price[6] of his labour outside his farm. The value of his labour within the farm is shown by the VMP-curve (value marginal product).This curve is also the demand curve for his labour within his farm and indicates that the value of his labour within-the farm (P_w) is 25,000 euro. The quasi-rent as explained in Box 2.3 is here 5,000 euro. It should be noticed that quasi-rent may also include non-monetary elements, such as being independent.

The acquisition costs and salvage value concepts have been used by many economists to explain the economic organisation of the agricultural sector in family farms[7]. In the example given in Figure 2.1 the (family) farm is a good organisational mode for creating quasi-rents; the value of the assets in use exceeds their salvage value.

We will give another numerical example in which two parties are involved: a farmer/tenant and a landowner. This example does not refer to labour such as above, but to a capital good as an asset. The farmer/tenant is 55 years old and leases a large plot of land from the landowner. He would like to improve the land with an investment, e.g. a new drainage system. The total investments for this activity are 50,000 euro (TC = 50,000). An amount of 40,000 euro are for the tenant recoverable

---

[5] While some assets of the firm can be easily divested or moved in geographic space in order to increase profits, durable specific assets can be attached to the specific activity of the firm for the duration of the asset's lifetime. This is the meaning of the term "durably committed". Hence, if the inputs associated with durable specific assets command consistently low earnings, the firm carries this loss as a financial liability. Shortfalls of quasi-rents earned by these inputs are shared among the firm's creditors just as any debt, but without the collateral (Caves and Porter, 1976: 40).

[6] This is also the opportunity cost of his labour.

[7] Van den Noort (1969: 63-64; 1984: 71-72).

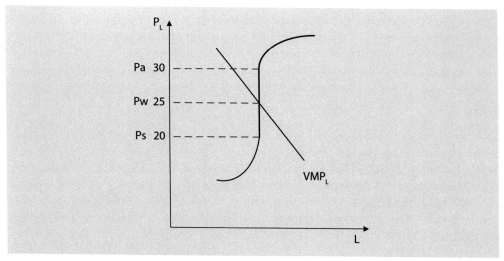

Figure 2.2. Acquisition costs and salvage value for an asset.
Remark: the S-curve is the supply curve of the factor of production. This curve is between P_a and P_s price inelastic. The demand curve for labour is line VMP_L. This curve is represent also the value of the marginal product of the farmer. The difference between the value of his labour within-the farm (P_w) and the salvage value (P_s) is the quasi-rent.

given his age and the expected time period of 10 years that he can use the land, while an amount of 10,000 euro are his sunk costs (SC = 10,000).

The tenant would like to use the land for 10 years. Then, he we would like to stop with farming. This means that the sunk costs (10,000 euro) are not recoverable for the tenant given his age and the expected time period he would like to farm. After 10 years, the sale value of the land is 15,000 euro higher, as a result of the land improvement, than it would be without this investment. However, this is only a gain for the landowner. The remaining amount (50,000 – SC) of 40,000 is recoverable by the tenant with his higher income from farming. The total return of the investment is 40,000 + 15,000 = 55,000 euro. The total costs for the tenant are 50,000 euro, while an amount of 10,000 euro are his sunk costs.

The remaining amount of 15,000 euro is recoverable elsewhere in the relationship between tenant and landlord. The rent of the investment is defined as the part of the revenue higher than the minimum amount necessary to start the activity. In this example the rent equals 55,000 – 50,000 = 5,000 (total return on investment minus the total investment cost). Therefore, the rent is defined from the view point of starting an activity, i.e. the investment. For a more extensively explanation see Appendix 2.1.

The next question is: what is quasi-rent of the investment[8]? The quasi-rent refers to an activity that is still going on, or in our case the investment that has been carried out. The quasi-rent of

---

[8] This is analysed from the viewpoint of the investment as a transaction.

the investment is here the value of the investment minus the value of the next-best alternative of the investment; in this case, it is a sunk investment. At the moment that the investment has been carried out, the value of next-best alternative is equal to the recoverable costs from the investment (= 40,000), under the assumption that the landowner will not sell the land and will not drive away the tenant during the 10 year period. The quasi-rent in this example is 55,000 – 40,000 = 15,000. Quasi-rents emerge when specific investments are made.

An intriguing question is what will happen in the above example. Is the farmer/tenant prepared to make this investment? This is probably not the case since the quasi-rent of the investment will go the landowner. There are three possible alternatives:
1. The investment will not will take place; this is called the hold-up problem. An efficient investment or transaction will not take place, because one party is afraid that the other party will capture the rent.
2. Farmer/tenant and landowner try to conclude a contract including the distribution of the (quasi-) rent; The results of this distribution will depend on the bargaining power of the involved parties and but that process will involve transaction costs; An alternative could be a long-term contract complemented with government regulation for a compensation for the improvement [9]
3. An organisational mode is chosen in which the farmer is also the owner of the land, see Box 2.4. In this way, the problem of distribution of quasi-rent is avoided.

As explained above, sunk-investments are related to the concept of asset specificity. Assets are said to be specific, meaning there is asset specificity when the investment has a higher value inside a specific relationship than outside it. Both examples show that asset specificity can be considered a measure of non-redeployment. We have to deal with sunk investments, because part of these costs are sunk into the relationship, i.e. cannot be recovered elsewhere.

The difference between acquisition costs and salvage value of assets, and the possibility of being 'trapped' of assets are not unique to the agricultural sector, but are also common to other branches

---

[9] In the Netherlands, tenants can get the end of contract period a compensation for the carried out improvements.

Box 2.4. Farmer is the owner of the land.

Suppose the farmer is also the owner of the land and he would like to stop with farming when he is 65 years old. For simplicity, we assume that the amounts of money are the present values, i.e. they are all expressed in the value at this moment. The total cost of this activity are 50,000 euro (TC = 50,000). An amount of 40,000 euro are for the farmer recoverable given his age and the expected time period of 10 years that he can use the land, while an amount of 10,000 euro can not be recovered by his extra yearly income. However, after 10 years the value of his land will increase with 15,000 euro. The rent of his investment is defined as the part of the revenue higher than the minimum amount necessary to start the activity. It can be calculated as follows:

Rent: total return – total costs = (40,000 + 15,000) – 50,000 = 5,000 euro

of industry. The difference between acquisition costs and salvage value of assets can explain the quasi-rent of assets within a certain type of mode of organization or governance structure, such as a firm. It can also be stated the other way around; the firm exists because of the quasi-rent. The concept of being 'trapped' of the fixed asset theory is called in the NIE and EOT 'hold-up' in the *ex-ante* and 'locked in' in the *ex-post* situation. This means that important concepts of NIE and EOT have their roots in the above described theories.

2.5 Evolutionary theory

Evolutionary economics is an emerging research stream which draws its inspiration on the one hand from the Austrian economist Schumpeter and Darwinian evolutionary theory, and on the other hand from a fundamental criticism of neoclassical economics. *An evolutionary theory of economic change* by Nelson and Winter (1982) is recognised to date as a standard work in this field. Another standard work is *Technical change and economic theory* which is a collection of contributions by Dosi, Silverberg, Nelson, Freeman and Soete (1988). A well written study about evolutionary economics is found in Boschma *et al.* (2002). In this book, the building blocks of evolutionary economics are elaborated. The emphasis is not only on the theory, but also on its various applications and policy implications.

To determine the core of this stream of thought, we need to go to its source of inspiration: (a) the *Darwinisian Evolutionary Theory* and (b) the *criticism of neoclassical theory*. Supporters of evolutionary theory believe that economic phenomena such as **economic change and adaptation** can be adequately described and explained by using Darwinian concepts such as (1) heredity; (2) natural selection (survival of the fittest); and (3) variation, including mutation (= new variation). The analogous economic concepts are routines, selection mechanisms and innovations. **First** we discuss the Darwinian concepts routines, selection mechanisms and innovation.

Routines

Economic activities within firms, organisations and consumers can be characterised by specific **routines** and **rules of thumb.** These routines come to be established in the course of time. They are limited in number because it is expensive (in terms of money and time) to develop or discover new routines. Routines refer to all regular and predictable behaviour patterns. Routines explain why people and firms are resistant to change. The behaviour of the firm is generally stable and routinized, because in a world of uncertainty (resulting from incomplete information) we rely on our own existing knowledge and experience as much as possible when making decisions. It means that firms and individuals often fall back on routines for decision making. The term *routines* can be connected with skills. These skills have two features in common. First, they require exercise. It is not enough to read how to bike, it must also be practised; learning by doing is involved. Second, some automatic behaviour or tacit knowledge is often involved; it is knowledge that is difficult to communicate (Boschma *et al.*, 2002: 25).

Routines fulfil two functions in organisations. First, they function as the memory of the organisation. Organisations remember largely by doing. Routines that are not used for some time wither away. Second, routines can be seen as a stabilising force in an organisation. They keep possible conflicts within an organisation under control; in that sense they present a truce in an intraorganisational conflict (Douma and Schreuder, 2002: 231).

Routines have often been incorporated in specific and irreversible investments, which involve high sunk costs and because of that they have often a stable character. Irreversible investments are for example, education and training of workers and development of technology. Changing of routines requires enormous investments (switching costs) and the effect on the competitiveness of the firm is often uncertain. The higher the switching costs the less quickly a firm will change (Boschma *et al.*, 2002: 27). Routines will often create path dependency and lock-in effects (See also Box 2.5 and Box 5.4).

Selection mechanisms

In Evolutionary economics, the forces influencing competition processes are called the selection environment. This selection environment consists of markets, institutions and the spatial environment. They function as a kind of filter, through which adapted firms can survive, and less well adapted firms will disappear. These selection forces form the explanatory framework of Evolutionary economics, because they factor-in a certain level of continuity (besides routines) (Boschma *et al.*, 2002: 27).

The selection-environment specifies ultimately which routines and innovations will survive and which do not. The firms which are able to endure the selection correctly will continue to grow, while the others decline or disappear. Concerning adapting to the selection-environment, there is one important difference from Darwinian biology, which argues that adaptation to the environment occurs in the form of mutations that emerge by coincidence. In contrast, evolutionary economics supposes that adaptation occurs due to the purposeful and intelligent action of entrepreneurs (cf. Hendrikse 1992: 3). They reveal purposeful (enterprising and adaptive) search-behaviour. Firms survive in markets by developing or adapting innovations.

Selection by market forces will favour firms that happen to find better techniques or which happen to use better search rules than others. Their features – the techniques or search rules that make them successful – will spread in the population of firms, partly by expansion and partly by imitation. In that process, however, new mutations of routines will be generated (Douma and Schreuder, 2002: 233). Selection can also take place via the capital market. Banks have limited resources to finance starting firms or firm which would like to expand. Firms have to compete for capital injections. Banks have to balance on basis of the expected return and the risk of the investments.

Institutions are also an important selection mechanism. Rules of law, values and norms, collective agreements between social partners and quality norms reduce the quantity of products which firms can supply and influence the way how they produce these goods. Institutions are often specific for countries or regions, and can have a large influence on the competitiveness of firms in certain areas (Boschma *et al.*, 2002: 28).

This means that evolutionary theory also deals with institutions. The emphasis is less on the individual behaviour that leads to the emergence of institutions, and more on the function performed and the contribution of the institution to the welfare or success of the social unit. In other words, in order to explain an institution, we have to first know its contribution to the survival of society or an organisation (like a firm) in question. The initial birth (development) of an institution does not require to be explained. Institutions may arise due to coincidence, unexpected events, or as a result of the standard process of the *invisible hand*, or even as a result of a conscious objective. An important view here is that the selection process is *'non-man made'* and is the result of the environment.

Selection is viewed as an enormous evolutionary mechanism that investigates the pattern of organisations at every point of time as it were, and tests their ability to fulfil their role (Rutherford, 1994: 85). The evolution of institutions and their performance implications are affected strongly by their path-dependency nature. Path dependency means that history does matter: the direction and scope of institutional change cannot be divorced from its earlier course or past history. Because of their path-dependency characteristics, institutions are the *carriers of history*, reproducing themselves well beyond the time of their usefulness (cf. Saleth and Dinar, 2004: 27).

The spatial structure of an economy can also be an important selection mechanism. It deals, for example, with the presence of natural resources, the availability of labour, and access to the market. Firms in remote areas could have higher cost for certain production factors, because the transportation costs are a function of the distance. The presence of an agglomeration or complex of firms or an integrated chain for service supply, processing, marketing and transportation plays a role in the cost price and the price formation. Spatial structure can function as a learning environment (cf. Boschma *et al.*, 2002: 29).

Innovation

Mutations in evolutionary biology lead to new variations in the population. According to Evolutionary economics, **innovations** are sources of new variations in the economy.

Innovations in firms make it possible for them to survive in the market. An important question is why firms in a world of persistent routines and strong competition are going on with innovations? According to Nelson and Winter (1982), firms turn to innovation when they are threatened in their existing routines: search is failure-induced. Innovations are broadly defined as 'changes in routines'. They concern changes in products, in production technologies, in organisational forms and in markets etc. Changes on population-level arise according to Nelson and Winter (1982) through *search-effects (adaptive learning)* and through *selection-effects*. In the case of *search-effects* firms adapt themselves via search procedures aiming to carry out the existing routines. In the case of *selection-effects*, firms that are making profits tend to expand and increase their market share at the cost of loss-making firms (Boschma *et al.*, 2002: 30).

Consistent with the focus on innovation, evolutionary economics criticises the conventional neoclassical economic concepts of rationality, reversibility, economic agents homogeneity (the firm as blackbox), and static equilibrium concept. In contrast, evolutionary economics concerns concepts such as bounded rationality, irreversibility and path dependency, heterogeneity (variation), and dynamic change instead of static equilibrium (cf. Boschma *et al.*, 2002: 36). Below, we will further discuss bounded rationality, reversibility, technical lock-in, path dependence, heterogeneity, change and dynamics.

Bounded rationality

The concept of *bounded rationality* plays an important role in the discussion on evolutionary selection of routines of firms in Nelson and Winter (1992: 35). Man's rationality is 'bounded': real life decision problems are too complex to comprehend and therefore firms cannot maximise over the set of all conceivable alternatives. Therefore, relatively simple decision rules and procedures are used to guide action. However, because of the bounded rationality problem, these rules and procedures cannot be too complicated and cannot be characterised as 'optimal' in the sense that they reflect the results of global calculation taking into account information and decision costs. Yet, they may be quite satisfactory for the purpose of the firm given the problems the firm faces.

Irreversibility, technical lock-in and path dependence

Characteristic for evolutionary economics is the analysis of irreversible historical processes. This is an important difference with neoclassical economics in which reversibility is at the centre. An example is the different way in which evolutionary economics and neoclassical economics model technological developments. Neoclassical economics describes technologies as a production function. It is like a blackbox: production factors enter and a product comes out. The reactions on changes in the economic system are unequivocal and independent of time and space. Change processes in the neoclassical economics are therefore characterised by reversibility (cf. Boschma *et al.*, 2002: 40).

The evolutionary economics assumes that the change in technology is often local. Consequently, innovation – induced by a price change – concentrates on certain techniques of the production function: *localised technological change*. If there is an opposite price change, firms will not at all costs return to the old technology. Yet in most cases, the new technology has been superior. This is an example of the irreversible process of economic development.

The meaning of localised technological change and irreversibility can be connected with routines, technical lock-in and path dependence. The notion of technical lock-in is similar to the broader concept of path dependence. The term 'path dependence' was brought to economics by way of an analogy from physics and biology, where it denotes the effects of initial conditions on physical subsystems of biological processes (Spulber, 2002: 12). The relation between routines and path dependence can be described for a firm as follows: the economic behaviour of a firm is largely dependent on its specific history, because it relies on knowledge and experience built up in the past in a specific market and using a specific technology (cf. Boschma *et al.*, 2002: 41). Thus technical lock-in, irreversibility and path dependence mean that history does matter.

Firms operate in an environment of uncertainty, complexity, and change. They do not have free and immediate access to available information over commercial and technical possibilities. Similarly, the behaviour of entrepreneurs is also characterised by bounded rationality (cf. Simon, 1961: 81). In order to control – to the extent possible – this uncertainty, entrepreneurs rely on a general routine of behaviour. Routine behaviour is regular and relatively predictable, conservative and risk-averse. Entrepreneurial behaviour can therefore be characterised as path-dependent. It is based on knowledge and experience in a specific terrain (technology and marketing). The situation in the current period is directly related to the situation in the previous period.

An important reason for path-dependence for a firm or an economy is the technology. As a result of technological adaptation, the related sunk implementation and learning costs involved, a firm or an economy is pushed in the direction of a particular situation or equilibrium. In labour market studies, the phenomenon in which current unemployment is dependent on the past (path-dependence) is termed as *hysteresis*. A possible explanation for this is that for the unemployed, a long period of unemployment results in a loss of skills and work-rhythm, and one feels increasingly discouraged to apply for jobs (Van Beers and Theeuwes, 1998: 353).

Heterogeneity

Neoclassical economics assumes that economic agents are homogeneous and have rational behaviour. However, in evolutionary economics heterogeneity (variation) is at the centre. This heterogeneity has to do with bounded rationality (cf. Boschma *et al.*, 2002: 44). For example, firms are not always completely informed about new innovations. Rather, there is mostly information asymmetry and firms can have different expectations about the technological route or innovation, because of bounded rationality. However, if information about new knowledge or innovations becomes directly public for everyone, it would be useless for firms to develop new innovations or knowledge. This is also known as the fundamental paradox of information: the value of information can only be revealed to another party by disclosing that information, while such disclosure destroys the value of the information (Douma and Schreuder, 2002: 54)

Change and dynamics

Because evolutionary theory (ET) explains economic change, and because it explains a situation in terms of how it has arisen, Nelson (1995: 73-74) states that ET is dynamic in character. This explanation of change (new variation) consists of coincidence, inventions and selection elements. It means that evolutionary economics is focussed on the explanation of changes. It makes the criticism that the neoclassical model does not consider technological change as the most important determinant of economic growth. In the footsteps of Schumpeter, the evolutionary theory proposes that the concept of market equilibrium is realistic only in the short-term. However, what is its relevance in reality, where change and dynamics as a result of innovations are the order of the day (cf. Boschma *et al.*, 2002: 50)? The market is not so much a mechanism for realising equilibrium price but more a mechanism evoking disequilibria. A firm can realise monopoly rents if it implements a radical technological innovation first. Technological innovations influence not only monopoly rents and market structures, but have also important spatial consequences. The developments of new (radical) technological innovations also lead to the movement of firms and sectors to other regions. A well-known example is the Silicon Valley (cf. Boschma *et al.*, 2002: 52).

2.6 Important areas of application for evolutionary economics

According to Boschma (2002: 14) the principles of evolutionary economics can be applied in various areas, such as the economics of innovation, economic geography, economic growth of countries and economic policy. Within each area it is possible to distinguish incremental and radical changes. Incremental changes concern the dynamic stability of economic processes in the short-term, in which change has been embedded in existing structures and takes place gradually. This is worked out in concepts like incremental innovation, learning by doing, routines and lock-in. Radical changes refer to structural changes with an emphasis on the long run. Over time, not only technological innovations take place, but also changes in institutions and consumer needs. The selection environment also changes with the innovations. This is called co-evolution. In the long run perspective, concepts such as radical innovation, structural change and the theory of the long gulfs are at the centre of interest.

Technological development, innovation, path-dependence and selection

Firms operate in an environment of uncertainty, complexity, and change. They do not have free and immediate access to available information over commercial and technical possibilities. The behaviour of entrepreneurs is also characterised by bounded rationality (cf. Simon, 1961: 81). In order to control – to the extent possible – this uncertainty, entrepreneurs rely on a general routine behaviour. Routine behaviour is regular and relatively predictable, conservative and risk-averse. Entrepreneurial behaviour can therefore be characterised as path-dependent. It is based on knowledge and experience in a specific terrain (technology and marketing). The situation in the current period is directly related to the situation in the previous period.

Spatial economics

Based on the concepts of bounded rationality, coincidence, competency and selection, the location behaviour of firms can be described and explained. The location decision depends on the competency of firms as processors of information and co-incidence. Because of bounded rationality, firms have to take care for avoiding lock-in of inefficient routines. On the one hand, firms have specific competencies, but on the other hand locations are characterised by technological specialisations. Large firms are often better able to create an advantage by concentrating their R&D on the most suitable location (cf. Boschma *et al.*, 2002: 88-89).

The evolutionary economics is very suitable for analysing the dynamic interaction between the firm and the spatial environment and the evolution of a firm after the actual location choice in a region. Firms producing products that are located at the beginning of the "product life cycle phase" have strong needs for quick and effective information exchange with the local market, local suppliers, etc. This requires a local labour market with technical know-how which can deliver made-to-measure. Furthermore the local production environment must be flexible to new market development and able to switch quickly over to other inputs. If the product has to be further developed, then direct communication between consumer and producers will be necessary. In later phases of the 'product life cycle phase', products and production processes are more standardised. Direct entry to market information and the neighbourhood of technical skills are less important. Production costs increase in importance, because of a more elastic demand (price elasticity of demand will be smaller in absolute terms) and increasing competition. Internal scale advantage can be utilised, and the level of schooling is less important. This means that the importance of access to low labour costs increases. Therefore firms will move their production locations to low-wage countries over time (Boschma *et al.*, 2002: 90-91).

According to evolutionary economics, the choice for a place of business in other regions or even countries does not appear out of the blue. Rather, before a re-allocation takes place, the local circumstances are thoroughly studied beforehand. Local suppliers of input are practically approached, and no asset specific investments are carried out which would pre-determine the choice of the location. All options are kept open, even if it means withdrawing from the region or country. In the following phase of the location processes, based on a learning process and experience, the bonds with the guest region will be tightened. On the basis of the knowledge taken away from the guest region/country, new products are developed which have been adapted to the local preferences. Market relations with local suppliers of input that can be based mutual trust which eventually grows into sustainable networks. This type of trust facilitates communication and enables cooperation and exchange of knowledge, through which new innovations are realised (Boschma *et al.*, 2002: 92).

It means the dynamic relationship between firm and region evolves as a spatial-evolutionary process. The foreign location becomes less dependent on the parent company and more embedded in the region. In the implementation phase, the uncertainty is relatively high. The firm (as a foreign establishment) located in the guest region is still strongly embedded in the network of concern. The establishment takes over the routines of the parent company. In later phases, the establishment undertakes more within the local environment. Dynamic and independent purchase and knowledge relationships arise within the local environment. However, the local firm-environment is not passively assumed, but rather, goes through a transformation as result of creative and strategic behaviour. Through mutual adjustment of firm and region, the establishment becomes more embedded in the guest region. Because of this process, the firm will lose geographical freedom of actions (lock-in through among other sunk costs). At the same moment it comes loose from the parent company, its routines have been changed and new relational assets have arisen from contact with the local environment (Boschma *et al.*, 2002: 93).

By using evolutionary concepts such as routines, competencies, adaptations, innovation and lock-in we can describe the economic development and dynamic of the region. The term region can be identified based on two criteria. First, a region can be interpreted as a homogeneous area with a economic specialisation (e.g. Westland), a cultural identity (Friesland) or political-governmental unit (The Netherlands). Second, a region can be defined based on internal coherence; interactions take place especially within and hardly outside the region. Both criteria offer possibilities for analysing regions from the view point of evolutionary economics. Boschma *et al.* (2002: 97) give two examples; first, the **innovative environment** and second the **adaptation approach**.

Innovative environment-approach appeals to regions which are strongly innovative and flexible (such as Silicon Valley). These regions are characterised by a local network of a large number of small and medium firms which have been specialised in a certain branch or sector. Spatial

---

Box 2.5. Three types of lock-in.

The first type is the *functional lock-in*. In the course of time, the relationships between firms involved with supplying, production, processing and marketing become rigid. For example suppliers do not feel the pressure to develop new activities (e.g. R&D) because they are convinced of their sales. The second type is the *cognitive lock-in*. All external information is filtered and brought in to conformity with the firm's own knowledge and experience. The third type is *political lock-in*. It is the (suffocating) functioning of local consensus pact consisting of the regional policy makers, employers and employees organisations, and other parties which would like to stay in power. Economic renewal is not stimulated or even blocked, because it is not in their interests to change. It is also called institutional sclerosis: the economic surplus is captured and consumed by the established coalitions, in stead of allocated for investments in growth and development (Boschma *et al.*, 2002: 99-101).

---

neighbourhood plays an important role, because it would influence the collective learning process. Innovative environment-regions are characterised by (1) a mobile labour market; (2) intensive relations between actors; and (3) common values and norms. Employees often change jobs (job-hopping), because of the possibilities of economic expansion in the region and because of the quickly spreading-out of the information in small areas with strong social networks. Job-hopping induces learning effects and local-spin-offs of knowledge. Spatial neighbourhoods facilitate intensive and face-to-face contacts, and offer the possibility for building-up personal trust. Informal social networks will arise, but also economic networks between local suppliers and processors emerge which function on trust. The common values and norms function as kind glue between actors. This enables learning processes. Transaction costs are reduced because opportunistic behaviour is constrained under the penalty of exclusion (Boschma *et al.*, 2002: 97-99).

The *adaptation approach* applies to a region specialised in a traditional branch of industry. An important source of the difficulties was the far-reaching specialisation of the production environment, often completely geared to the specific need of a dominant branch of industry. The infrastructure, suppliers and processors, the research institutes, education system, banks, all the activities were connected to one branch of industry or sector (e.g. textile industry in Twente, mine industry in the Roer area and Limburg). This led to regional lock-in. The real problem was often not the level of adaptation, because the involved firms were still innovative, and the leader in their own field. However, the real problem was the lack of adaptability; new technological routes did not get off the ground. Three types of lock-in can explain the lack of economic renewal (see Box 2.5).

Growth theory

The evolutionary growth theory is based on three concepts. The **first** concept refers to the assumptions about how firms make their decisions, the second to the role of innovations in explaining the success of firms and their economic growth process as a whole, and the third focuses on the competition process between firms as an evolutionary selection process (Boschma *et al.*, 2002: 116). As said, the first concept refers to the assumptions about how firms make their decisions. Firms make use of routines or rules of thumb. These rules are in certain view logical and rational, but do no enable firms to make at each moment a profit maximising decision. Making use of routines means that the behaviour of firms can be typified by bounded rationality (Boschma *et al.*, 2002: 116).

The **second** concept of the evolutionary growth theory emphasises the importance of *innovation and imitation*. Each firm uses a part of its profit for searching to new technology by innovation or imitation. For distributing the profit over innovation, imitation and extension of the capacity firms make use of rules of thumb. A firm can also use a rule of thumb for reserving each period a fixed percentage of the profit for R&D. The use of such a rules of thumb can be typified as satisfying behaviour. An important evolutionary aspect of the evolutionary growth model is the role of coincidence (compared with mutation). Do investments in innovation and imitation lead to new technology or is it coincidence? According to Nelson (1995: 70), the higher the investments in innovation, imitation and R&D, the higher the chance to find a new and better technology. Also is often supposed that new technology of firms is an incremental improvement of the existing technology. This assumption is in line with the idea that technological routines are characterised by a series of small changes within an existing technological setting (Boschma *et al.*, 2002: 111-117).

The **third** concept of the evolutionary growth model is the modelling of competition processes between firms as an evolutionary selection process. Firms will spend a part of their profit to innovation and imitation, and a part for increasing of their production capacity. The speed of increasing the production capacity is dependent on the profit of the last period, and the level of the profit is dependent on the efficiency of the technology used by a firm. Therefore, firms with the most efficient technology are able the increase their market share. The competition process requires that more efficient technologies gain ground at the costs of less efficient technologies (Boschma *et al.*, 2002: 117).

Firms use different technologies through which their cost efficiency will be different (variation). Since the profit of a firm is dependent on the efficiency of the used technology, and the growth of the market share of a firm is directly dependent on the profit, the firm with the most efficient technology will win (selection). In this way, more efficient technologies will spread at the cost of less efficient technologies, and technological development will take place (Boschma *et al.*, 2002: 117-118).

The theory of the firm

The evolutionary theory of the firm is the newest and least developed of the theories of the firm. The unit of analysis under this view is the firm and its productive processes. This theory focuses on three related aspects of organisations: the structure, their strategy, and their *core competency*. A firm is said to have a core competence in a business area if it not only has an advantage in producing a good or service, but also has a similar advantage in the production of innovative and new products. Firms are able to survive only if they change appropriately in response to changes in demand and technology; in short, they must adapt and find a new productive scope for their core competencies – the things they do well, in order to succeed (FitzRoy *et al.*, 1998: 8).

With the help of evolutionary theory, concepts such as routines, search-behaviour, variation between firms (concerning technology, productivity, and profit) can be explained by phenomena such as the increase in labour productivity, increased capital intensity, increase in real wages, and relative constant capital yield (Nelson, 1995: 67-71). The argument is as follows. A successful innovation leads to profits, resulting in capital formation and growth of the firm. This growth compensates for the decline in use of labour resulting from increased labour productivity caused by increased capital intensity. Consequently, the demand for labour will increase. At the macro-level, this results in an increase in wages. Therefore for the firm, it becomes more advantageous to adapt labour-saving innovations or to develop new ones. This will further increase capital intensity. The higher profits will stimulate investments, which cause higher wages, which will in turn put pressure on the return of capital.

2.7 Common elements of new theories

Our first observation is that NIE and EOT have overlapping areas (see also Section 2.2). Second, they also show a certain relationship to MIO and ET. The relationship arises from the doubts that all these theories share over the real-world applicability of a number of standard assumptions in traditional neoclassical economics, by North (2003: 17) called instrumental rationality (see Box 2.6).

All these new theories emphasise a number of **behavioural assumptions** regarding the participants of economic processes which are more in line with: (1) what people consider to be important and (2) the type of cognitive capacity that decision-makers possess. The **first** aspect is reflected in the objectives or objective function of a specific decision-maker; the **second** aspect falls under the concept of bounded rationality. Decision-makers – economic agents or players – refer to persons, consumers, producers, employees, employers, firms, organisations, universities and the government. By formulating an objective function for decision-makers according to the standard neoclassical economics, we can specify for individuals a utility function and for firms a profit-function. However, the more behavioural approach – as followed in the NIE and ET – does not suppose utility or profit maximisation, but a satisfying behaviour, e.g. a preference for an easy life, a desire to remain one's own master or preferring safer returns, even if they are on average smaller (see also risk-averse in next section).

Box 2.6 The instrumental rationality of the standard neoclassical economics

The instrumental rationality of the standard neoclassical economics refers to: (1) the behaviour of economic subjects, concerning rationality, utility-maximisation by households and profit maximisation by firms; (2) the availability of complete (and/or free or costless) information; (3) completely defined and enforceable private property rights; (4) unlimited market transactions; (5) absence of transaction costs; and (6) completely divisible inputs and outputs. The NIE builds on, modifies and extends standard neoclassical economics. What it abandons is the instrumental rationality. The place to begin a theory of institution, therefore, is with a modification of the instrumental rationality (North, 2003: 17-18).

In standard neoclassical economics, households and firms are usually perceived as a 'blackbox', within which everything works perfectly and everyone acts how they are supposed to act. Firms are assumed to strive for profit maximisation and to produce at the lowest cost (cf. De Alessi, 1983: 64-65; Eggertsson, 1994: 3-9). However, the theory says nothing about the internal structure of firms, their hierarchical structure, how decisions are delegated, and who has authority for making decisions. Problems arise like: *who has the power of control and who is able to capture the residual income* (Hart, 1995: 63). People in a firm or organisation do not have the same interests. The standard neoclassical theory neglects incentive problems within the firm (cf. Hart, 1995: 17). These incentives can be based on rewards (carrot), punishment (stick), building-up reputation, credible commitment and career concerns (cf. Dixit, 2002: 702-703).

Regarding rationality, it is most often assumed that individuals and firms make rational choices or decisions. Behaviour is considered rational if an individual acts in accordance with his or her preferences; and does so consistently, which is to say that a specific pattern emerges, which is in keeping with a particular objective, such as utility or profit maximisation. Briefly, rational behaviour is defined as behaviour which is consistent with a particular goal. However, in modern decision theory, the maximisation of expected utility is often used. Probability functions play an important role (cf. Sugden, 1991: 757).

Concerning rationality, we distinguish three forms of rationality (Kreps, 1990: 745): *complete rationality, bounded rationality*, and *procedural rationality*. A *completely rational individual* has the ability to foresee and to anticipate everything that might happen and to evaluate, and choose the optimal course from the alternative possible actions, all in the blink of an eye, without costs. This is the standard view in traditional neoclassical economics. In contrast, a *bounded rational individual* attempts to maximise, but he finds it too expensive to do so. He is unable to anticipate all contingencies, yet with an awareness of his inability, he provides *ex-ante* for the (almost inevitable) time *ex-post* when an unforeseen contingency will arise. Bounded rationality does not consider people to be inconsistent, but only that people are rational within the constraints that they face.

Bounded rationality is said to arise when the cognitive ability of people is insufficient to deal with the complexity of the world. People are not in a position to take all circumstances into account when making a decision. As a result, human behaviour is: '... intendedly rational, but only limited so' (Simon, 1961: xxiv). Bounded rationality does not exclude the possibility of maximising utility or profit. Such maximisation may still be attempted but whether it is attained is another matter (cf. Hendrikse, 1992: 3). Williamson (1987: 30) indicates that it is in the context of bounded rationality that the human quality of opportunism (sometimes also referred to as strategic behaviour) appears.

Procedural rationality is said to arise when the complexity of the problem is significantly greater than the cognitive capacity of the decision-maker. In a similar situation, people act in accordance with strict rules or routines. The behaviour of a procedural rational individual follows fixed rules or routines without being directed towards an objective such as maximisation of utility or profit (Hendrikse, 1992: 18-20). According to this view, an evolutionary approach to economic problems is based on an assumption of *procedural rationality* (Hendrikse, 1992: 35). In this approach, economic development is (as we said earlier) comparable with biological processes such as those described by Darwin.

The utility function is replaced by Darwinian aptitude, and selection occurs via an evolutionary process. While it is true that purposeful firms are involved, the behaviour of an enterprise is still characterised by a number of routines and rules of thumb. Qualities and possibilities of organisations develop slowly, as a result of continuous repetition and adaptation. Experience is translated into routines, without complete understanding of why they work. Evolutionary economics places considerable emphasis on the process aspects (conduct) of firms and their learning asset in creating, developing and transforming these processes. Because the current capacity of firms is to a considerable degree determined by specific history, these capacities also vary. It is not simple, and sometimes it is not possible to imitate the workings of other firms. Skills have to be indeed developed again (cf. Hendrikse, 1992: 35-36). The assumption of *procedural rationality* in the evolutionary approach to economic problems is a very strong one, and will be not shared by everyone.

As indicated, the standard neoclassical economic theory supposes *complete rationality*. Rationality is applied by the pursuit of utility or profit maximisation. All available information is taken into consideration in order to achieve this objective. This is perhaps possible with simple problems, but often the situation is so complex that completely rational decision making is simply not possible.

A last element is the role of institutions. This is indeed a basic argument for applying NIE. In the last few decades, there has been increased interest among economists in the role played by institutions and organisations in the working of economic systems. According to North (2003:17), institutions are the rules of the game of a society. More formally, they are the humanly devised constraints that structure human interaction. They consist of both informal constraints (sanctions, taboos, customs, traditions, and codes of conduct), and formal rules (constitutions, laws and property rights). Institutions are formed to reduce uncertainty in human exchange.

2.8 New institutional economics as a complement to standard neoclassical economics

As said, the NIE is an attempt to incorporate a theory of institutions into economics. How does the new institutional economic approach fit in with neoclassical economic theory? It builds on, modifies and extends the standard neoclassical economic approach to permit it to analyse and deal with an entire range of issues that prior to now were neglected. The deductive character of the economy as a 'applied science' is not rejected, neither is the marginal analysis. It retains and builds on the fundamental assumption of scarcity and hence competition. It views economics as a theory of choice subject to constraints; it employs price theory as an essential part of the analysis of institutions, and it sees change in relative prices as a major influence of change in institutions (North, 2003: 19).

The additions and modifications are given below and are based on a multitude of sources of literature (cf. Nabli and Nugent, 1989: 9-12; Eggertsson, 1990: 3-32; Furubotn and Richter, 1991:

4; Joskow, 1995: 254-255; Williamson, 1987: 15-32; 1998: 24-35; Furubotn and Richter, 1997: 2-8; Furubotn and Richter, 2005: 2-8). Some of the corrections and complements are mutually dependent and related with key elements earlier outlined in this chapter. Most of them are also sketched in Figure 1.1.

Methodological individualism

Society, the government, people, firms, parties and other organisations cannot be considered as a collective unit which behaves and trades like an individual. The firm, organisation or the collective is not per se the focus on which everything is oriented; the firm is not a blackbox. In order to study the behaviour of such social units, we should start with the behaviour of the various individual members and explain that in terms of the positions and actions of these members. They have different interests, information, attitudes and behaviour. This view is linked to the criticism evolutionary economics has on neoclassical economics concerning the idea that all economic agents are homogeneous (the firm as a blackbox). In contrast, economic agents are not homogeneous and do not always behave in a rational manner. Heterogeneity (variation) should be taken into account. This heterogeneity has to do with bounded rationality.

Expanding utility maximisation to individuals and satisfying behaviour

Individuals are supposed to pursue their own interest and to maximise utility, given the limitations imposed by the existing organisational structure. In contrast to conventional practise, the dichotomy between the theory of consumer behaviour and the theory of the firm is removed by expanding the utility-maximisation hypothesis to individual choice. This means that an individual, irrespective of whether it is the manager of a government bureau or a capitalist enterprise is considered to make his own choices and pursue his own objectives within the constraints imposed by the system within which he operates.

Satisfying behaviour emphasises the importance of individual preferences. These could include the preference for an easy life, a flexible work week or part-time work. As said, the behavioural approach – applied in NIE – does not suppose utility or profit maximisation, but a satisfying behaviour e.g. by taking into account bounded rationality or the risk-attitude of the decision-maker. This will be further worked out in Chapter 4.

Bounded rationality

Bounded rationality means that there is a limited mental capacity to process information. Human beings, in consequence, impose constraints on human interaction in order to structure exchange (North, 2003: 18). Consequently, in situations with bounded rationality it is impossible to make agreements which completely reflect the complex reality in all its facets. The contracts which are concluded under these conditions are per definition incomplete contracts. The question is how can we trust such agreements? We need certain mechanisms for contract compliance. If the economic actors involved in the contracts are completely trustworthy, we can rely on incomplete contracts. In addition to trust, the reputation mechanism, rewards (the carrot) and punishments (the stick) can be used for realising credible commitment for observing contracts. Bounded rationality will be elaborated in Chapter 4 and in contract theory in Chapter 7.

Opportunistic behaviour

Opportunistic behaviour is described as *a condition of self-interest seeking with guile* (Williamson, 1987: 30). It includes providing selective and distorted information, making promises which are not intended to be kept, and posing differently from what the person actually is. The phenomena of hidden information, hidden actions and strategic behaviour are also included in Williamson's approach. It is sufficient if agents pose differently from what they are and behave differently from what have promised to do, and it is difficult or expensive to determine who they are and how they behave in reality.

The existence of opportunistic behaviour implies that no general trust can be ascribed to an incomplete contract. If it is difficult and/or expensive to specify *ex-ante* whether or not the economic actors are opportunistic, it is possible that no agreement will be made. Opportunistic behaviour will be elaborated upon in Chapter 4.

Lack of information

In the model of perfect competition, perfect information is assumed. But this assumption will rarely be met in practise. Information can be lacking or is limited. It is also possible that information is available but is not equally available to all parties. In that case, asymmetric information is said to exist. One particular economic actor knows something that other actors do not. Asymmetric information can give rise to opportunistic behaviour, also sometimes termed as strategic behaviour. For this reason, in studies relating to asymmetric information, strategic interactions between players are often considered (Varian, 1993: 446). Markets as well as organisations cannot function well if there is a lack of information or asymmetric information. The analysis of this problem has received considerable attention in the so called Information Economics. Institutions and institutional arrangements, such as contracts or vertical integration are used to reduce the costs of information. Incentives arising from the costs of information can lead to the substitution of contractual relationships for spot markets.

Attitude to risk and uncertainty

Due to a lack of information, individuals have to make decisions under uncertainty. Individuals may try to obtain information, but this can be expensive or in fact impossible. It is possible that they have to make a decision based on the available – but deficient -information. In case of uncertainty, probabilities can be attached to a possible event. Probabilities refer to the likelihood that an outcome will occur. It means that uncertainty can be perceived as a possible event/ outcome occurring with a certain probability. Corresponding with the assumption of bounded rationality, the decision-maker can maximise his/her expected utility. The value of the expected utility depends not only on the subjective probability related to a particular outcome, but also on the risk-attitude of the decision-maker. Three types of risk-attitude are distinguished:

1. risk-neutral, where the individual is not sensitive or indifferent to risk;
2. risk-averse, where the individual prefers avoiding risk; and
3. risk-seeking, where the individual is said to be risk-preferring.

It is also known that most people do not equally value gains and losses; they have often have a loss aversion.

In the standard neoclassical model, the entire matter of uncertainty and risk-attitude is neglected since perfect information is assumed. The new institutional economics offers different mechanisms and methods for coping with risks and loss aversion; ranging from the choice of the governance structure (contract versus spot market transactions) to the effects of the different risk-attitudes, such as the approach used in principal-agent theory. Risk-attitudes and loss aversion will be elaborated in Chapter 4.

Property rights

In the standard neoclassical approach, it is assumed that all resources are owned by specific individuals who have the right to use them for various purposes, and may transfer this right to another individual. According to this approach, property rights are perfectly defined, completely private, enforceable, and can be transferred without costs (cf. De Allesie, 1983: 65; Eggertsson, 1990: 84; Gravelle and Rees, 1992: 10). In reality, private property rights are often absent or not specified, protected or enforceable. Furthermore property rights and ownership are not always clear concepts.

Since, the value of a good depends on how property rights are defined, we have to know what do we mean by property rights. It is a concept with different interpretations. As described in Chapter 1 we will distinguish two important approaches to the property rights theory; the **old property rights** and the **new property rights approach**.

In standard neoclassical economics, both property rights approaches are left out of consideration. However, insights on property rights are very important. As said, **property** is on the one hand an institution, but on the other hand an instrument for the government; it can specify and allocate property rights with special objectives. Property rights are important incentives, they also open the firm as a blackbox, and determine the meaning and value of ownership. In Chapter 9 and 10, we further discuss ownership and property rights.

Box 2.7. Key terms of Chapter 2.

Transaction	Non-recoverable costs
Governance structure	Exit barriers theory
Firms as nexus of contracts	Routines
Why do firms exist?	Rules of thumb
Structure Conduct Performance approach	Path dependency
Sunk costs	Lock-in effect
Sunk investments	Switching costs
Non-redeployment	Selection mechanism
Contestable markets	Bounded rationality
Fixed asset theory	Behavioural assumptions
Being trapped	Firm as a blackbox
Acquisitions costs	Methodological individualism
Salvage value	Satisfying behaviour
Quasi-rent	Opportunistic behaviour
Opportunity costs	Asymmetric information
Asset specificity	Risk-attitude
Recoverable costs	Loss aversion

Appendix 2.1 Return, rent and quasi-rent

There are two different types of rents: (1) rents defined as the benefits from an activity going to a certain resource in excess of what is needed to attract that resource to that activity. This rent is pure surplus. To get this surplus no input is needed; (2) quasi-rents as the benefits from an activity going to a resource that are in excess of the minimum required to keep a resource in its current use.

The implication of getting something for nothing in terms of rents as a pure surplus is fairly clear. Some tremendous examples of these type of rents are provided by the earnings of star soccer players such as Cristiano Ronaldo of Manchester United, Ronaldinho and Thierre Henri of Barcelona, David Beckham, and some professional athletes in the United States and elsewhere. When each of these players is interviewed they often dwell on how they play sport out of love for the game. If this claim is in fact true then all of their earnings represent a rent as a pure surplus, since presumably, out of love, they would play the game for free (cf. FitzRoy *et al.*, 1998: 305).

Rents as a pure surplus are relevant for any 'entry' decision regarding some activity. If an individual or a firm is attempting to pick one of several activities to undertake with some limited resources, it will always choose the activity yielding the largest rent. The concept of the quasi-rent is somewhat different; it focuses more on an 'exit' decision.

Assume there is a firm that would like to start a new activity. All the numerical amounts are expressed in present values, for example, in units of 1000 euro. The return (Y) at the beginning of the activity is 100 and the total costs (TC) are 80. Consequently, the minimum required return

(Yr) is also 80. In this case, the firm's profit is equivalent to the rent (R); i.e. 20. This is expressed in column A in Figure 2.3. Column B gives an overview of the costs of the activity in terms of fixed costs (FC) and variable costs (VC). We assume that both fixed and variable costs are 40.

$$R = Y - Yr \tag{2.1}$$
$$TC = FC + VC \tag{2.2}$$
$$Yr = TC \tag{2.3}$$

Next, we assume that after the activity has started all fixed costs cannot be redeployed to alternative uses; thus they are sunk costs (FC = SC). Column C gives immediately after the start situation the maximal quasi-rent (QR). It can be shown that QR is equal to the sum of the sunk costs (SC) and the rent (R). In the start situation the quasi-rent is:

$$QR = Y - VC \tag{2.4}$$
$$QR = 100 - 40 \tag{2.5}$$
$$QR = 60 \tag{2.6}$$

and

$$QR = SC + R \tag{2.7}$$
$$QR = 40 + 20 \tag{2.8}$$
$$QR = 60 \tag{2.9}$$

In transaction cost economics it is common to use the term recoverable costs (RC). These costs are the total costs minus the sunk costs.

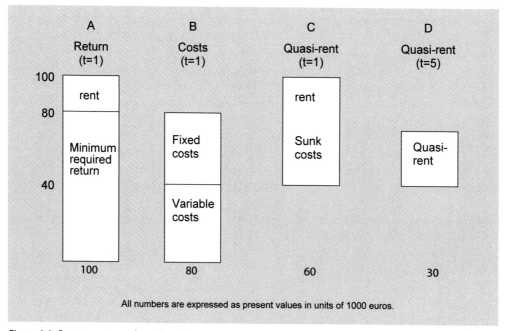

All numbers are expressed as present values in units of 1000 euros.

Figure 2.3. Return, costs and quasi-rent.

$$RC = TC - SC \qquad (2.10)$$
$$RC = 80 - SC \qquad (2.11)$$
$$RC = 80 - 40 \qquad (2.12)$$
$$RC = 40 \qquad (2.13)$$

The quasi-rent equals the total revenue minus the recoverable costs:

$$QR = Y - RC \qquad (2.14)$$
$$QR = 100 - 40 \qquad (2.15)$$
$$QR = 60 \qquad (2.16)$$

In a short-term view the recoverable costs are equal to the variable costs:

$$RC = VC \qquad (2.17)$$
$$RC = 40 \qquad (2.18)$$

After the start of the activity the prices are going to decrease. This has consequences for the return. Suppose, because of a price decrease, the returns fall to 70 in t = 5. What does it mean for the rent and the quasi-rent? There will be no rent anymore (Y < Yr and Y< TC). But what will be the effect of the price decrease on the quasi-rent? In general, the quasi-rent is:

$$QR = Y - RC; \text{ or in our case } QR = 70 - RC \qquad (2.19)$$

In the short-term view the quasi-rent is:

$$QR = Y - VC \qquad (2.20)$$
$$QR = 70 - 40 \qquad (2.21)$$
$$QR = 30 \qquad (2.22)$$

This means the quasi-rent in the short view equals 30.

What can we learn from this numeric example and Figure 2.3? Making use of the quasi-rent is more or less a short-term view. For continuation on the long run of a firm, it is necessary that all the costs are recovered and not only the variable costs. If the price decreases to the level where nothing of fixed costs are recovered anymore, the firm should stop with the production. This point is called the shut-down point. A further decrease in price causes losses larger than the fixed cost and below this point the variable costs can no longer be recovered. This means that if – in a short-term view – the quasi-rent is zero, then the firm should immediately stop the activity. Exit is the only option. In Chapter 5 we use the concept of the quasi-rent extensively. It is a crucial element in transaction cost economics.

Appendix 2.2 Question for review: sunk investments, fixed assets and quasi-rent

Suppose a contractor invests in a specific investment to serve a particular customer. For example, he invests € 100,000 in a machine for removing weeds in streets and parking places. The contractor expects that he can use the machine for 1000 hours a year and for 5 years. In this case, the fixed costs are € 20,000 annually and the variable costs are € 30 per working hour. The only client for the contractor is the local government. In the beginning (t = 0) he concludes a contract with the local government for one year: 1000 hours work and the contract price is € 50 per hour. (For the simplicity we disregard the present value calculation).

a. What type of problem can arise here?

b. What are the returns, the total costs and the amount of rent in first year?

    After one year (t=1) the local government reduces the contract price to € 35 per hour. However, the government is prepared to guarantee the contractor 1000 hours work per year for 4 years.

c. What is the salvage value of the machine after one year (t=1)?

d. Do we have to deal with fixed asset issues and when is exit the only option?

e. What does this offer of the local government mean for the recoverable costs and the quasi-rent of the contractor? Under what conditions are both equal. Please calculate both and if necessary make some assumptions.

3. Embeddedness, institutional environment and governance structures

3.1 Introduction

This chapter is oriented on institutions and their nested levels of analysis. The basis of this chapter is illustrated in Figure 1.1, which is an adapted version of O. E. Williamson's 'Four levels of institutional analysis' (2000). In Section 3.2, we analyse the importance of institutions in economic development and their role in explaining the distribution of wealth. While good institutions and good government are instrumental to economic development, institutions are not always right. Moreover, social interactions are connected across economic scales, from micro to macro and the reverse. However, the effects of institutions and good government are mostly analysed on a macro-level. As we point out in this chapter, they also have important consequences for the micro level; the level of households, firms and organisations. Thus institutional economic analysis is necessarily broad and applied at multiple levels.

For analysing the multiple levels of institutions, we introduce Williamson's classification (2000) in Section 3.3. An important difference between Figure 1.1 and the original scheme of Williamson (see Figure 3.1) is found on the fourth level. According to Williamson, the fourth level is the level at which the neoclassical economic analysis works. However, it is here where we locate the economic incentive structure and relevant theories such as the principal-agent theory. The economic outcome – in terms of income, employment and allocation – is determined by all four levels interacting together. In our approach, the function of neoclassical economy is not exclusive to level four only, but works on all levels and is complemented by institutional economic interactions.

In Section 3.4 we pay special attention to the concept of social embeddedness. Located at the first level, the term social embeddedness refers to the way in which a specific social structure creates norms and values, customs, morals, traditions and codes of conduct. In other words, this is the level from which the informal rules of economic behaviour originate. i.e. the informal rules of the game. The formal rules are found in the second level of analysis which focuses on the institutional environment and is discussed in Section 3.5. The third level of analysis is oriented on institutional arrangements or governance structures and discussed in Section 3.6. While institutional arrangements are considered as the play of the game, they consist of an entire spectrum of possible forms, with *markets* at one end and *hierarchies* at the other. This spectrum also includes all sorts of hybrid forms such as contracts, clubs, cooperatives, environmental cooperatives, etc. Such institutional arrangements are the basis for the organisational modes within which transactions are coordinated and implemented.

In Section 3.7 we look at the hybrid form of governance structure known as the club. The club has several distinct characteristics. These include a voluntary group of individuals who derive mutual benefits from sharing one or more of the following: production costs of activities and services, specific member characteristics or a good characterised by excludable benefits. In this section, we focus our analysis on how the services and benefits of the club are shared and coordinated, for example, in an environmental club.

Using an institutional economic perspective, we can develop a framework – based on theory and literature – for analyzing the institutions necessary for economic and sustainable development. However, both are not the same. Sustainable development encompasses three dimensions: economic, social and environmental. It means more than economic growth only. While institutions are very important for economic growth, they are also fundamental to the triptych dimensions of sustainable development: the economic, environmental and social aspects of an economy, a region, or a sector.

This framework is intended to have practical application. For example, it has been used for developing a questionnaire to investigate the state of institutions and how best to enable them to realise economic and sustainable development. In Appendix 3.1, we will present such a framework. On the one hand, this framework can be used for distinguishing different levels of institutions. On the other hand, this framework serves as an analytical tool by taking into account determinants (or proxy-variables) on different levels of institutions that may account for good performance in the national economy, in sectors of the national economy, government bureaus, firms, organisations and households.

Key questions:
- Why are institutions not always right?
- Why is institutional analysis is important for evaluating whether economic welfare is either created or constrained?
- What is the relationship between the quality of government and the quality of institutions?
- Why is good government an important condition for good institutions?
- Why do we need governance structures? What is their function and purpose?
- Why is the level of social embeddedness important for understanding economic transactions?
- How are new organisational forms related to the interaction between social embeddedness and the institutional environment?
- Why are governance structures comprised of a diversity of coordination mechanisms?
- What new forms of governance are examples of how organisations arise to fill an institutional gap?

3.2 The role of institutions in economic development

Successful development policy requires an understanding of the dynamic way in which economic transactions are conducted and the necessary role institutions play in facilitating change. Succinctly said, institutions are very important for the development of economic activity. However, many studies on economic and also sustainable development consider the institutional structure to be exogenous. The problem then becomes one of 'getting the prices right' so that atomistic agents will behave in a 'correct' (i.e. efficient) manner. *Getting the prices right* follows logically from the prior problem of *getting the institutions right*. In reality, institutions are not always right (cf. Bromley, 1999: 3). Hence it is reasonable to suppose that the same will apply for institutions necessary for economic and sustainable development. In this section we introduce the role of the government as an important institutional actor in the development process.

In recent literature, economists have stressed the idea that good institutions are instrumental to economic development (La Porta *et al.*, 1999: 222). It is also clear that some institutions retard rather than accelerate growth. Regulatory agencies prevent entry, courts resolve disputes arbitrarily and some times dishonestly and politicians use government property to benefit their supporters rather than the population at large (Shleifer and Vishny, 1998: 8). Yet, good government has shown to have contributed to the economic development of European countries over the last millennium and to the economic growth of countries around the world over the last 40 years. Evidently good government is an important condition for good institutions.

From an economic perspective, institutions matter because they affect national welfare, primarily through productivity and employment. For instance, a country's educational institutions may promote human capital formation, which raises labour productivity in the long run. A government's policy on technology may enhance research and development. Labour market regulation, taxation, and social insurance influence labour supply and demand decisions, and search behaviour of unemployment, and thus affect a country's activity rate, the number of working hours per capita (CPB, 1997:3). Comparison of a broad range of countries provides evidence for the importance of institutions and policies on a country's prosperity. In particular, the experiences of those countries with weak institutions showed that the absence of well-developed institutions severely hampered economic growth and cause poverty. Olson (1996: 19) concludes: … 'the large differences in per capita income across countries cannot be explained by differences in access to the world's stock of productive knowledge or to its capital markets, by differences in the ratio of population to land or natural resources, or by differences in the quality of marketable human capital or personal culture. Albeit at a high level of aggregation, this eliminates each of the factors of production as possible explanations of most of the international differences in per capita income. The only remaining plausible explanation is that the great differences in the wealth of nations are mainly due to differences in the quality of their institutions and economic policy.'

The central question in Landes (1998: xx-xxi) *The wealth and poverty of nations* is why poor countries are poor and rich countries are rich. Landes argues that the most important reason for this has to do with institutions or factors related to an institutional context. He refers to: totalitarianism versus democracy; routine, traditionalism and immobility versus tendency to technologically progress; aristocratic, despotic and feudal societies versus societies based on private property rights; differences in norms and values; free markets and the development of new institutional arrangements like associations, cooperations, contracts, and new forms of transaction. These new institutional arrangements make transactions, investments and payments safer and easier, and reduce transaction costs (Landes, 1998: 27-44).

Models of government

In their book, *The grabbing hand*, Shleifer and Vishny (1998) restrict their analysis to the public sector. They distinguish three models of government: the *helping hand model*, the *invisible hand model* and the *grabbing hand model* (p. 2-13). They adopted this perspective to explain the reasons for government intervention and the nature of government decision-making processes.

According to the *helping hand model*, unbridled free markets lead to: monopoly pricing, externalities such as pollution, unemployment, defective credit supply to firms, and to failures of regional development, among other ills. The *helping hand model* focuses particularly on market failure. Solutions ranging from corrective taxes, regulations, and aggregate demand management to price controls, government ownership, and planning are then proposed to cure these sources of market failure (Shleifer and Vishny, 1998: 2).

The traditional alternative to the *helping hand model* is the laissez-faire view of the government- the *invisible hand model*. This model begins with the idea that markets work very well without any government. The government may perform the basic function necessary to support a market economy (such as the provision of law, order, and national defence), but other than delivering these few public goods, the less the government does, the better. The adherents of the *invisible hand models* rarely inquire what the reasons are for massive government intervention in real economies, or focus on the reforms that would constrain the government. Rather, the *invisible hand model* of the government was initially conceived as a prescription for an ideal, limited government. Its irrelevance as a descriptive model is quite obvious, since the government intervenes in economic life much more than any version of the *invisible hand model* would allow (Shleifer and Vishny, 1998: 3).

The third view of government, described by Shleifer and Vishny (1998: 3-4) as the *grabbing hand model*, focuses squarely on politics as the main determinant of government behaviour. The *grabbing hand model* shares with the *invisible hand model* a sceptical view of government, but describes more accurately what it actually does and therefore focuses more on the design of reforms. The *grabbing* and *helping hand model* share their activist interest in reforming government, although as their concepts of government are so different, their ideas of good reforms rarely coincide. The *grabbing hand model* analysis typically looks for ways of limiting government as opposed to expanding its scope.

At the root of the *grabbing hand* analysis are models of political behaviour that argue that politicians do not maximise social welfare, but instead pursue their own selfish objectives. The *grabbing hand model* is helpful for understanding the existing institutions in different countries, the reasons for the ways in which they have been put together, and the benefits and costs of these institutions for economic development and growth. When writing about institutions in a country, such as ownership patterns, regulatory structures, and legal mechanisms, economists used to focus on the benefits of institutional development (e.g. North and Thomas, 1973). Yet more recently, it has also become clear that some institutions retard rather than accelerate growth (e.g. North, 1990; Blanchard and Wolfers, 1999)[10]. Regulatory agencies prevent entry, courts resolve disputes arbitrarily and some times dishonestly, politicians use government property to benefit their supporters rather than the population at large. To understand how such dysfunctional institutions come about and stay around for decades or centuries, we need, according to Shleifer

---

[10] For example, Blanchard and Wolfers (1999: 12-19) have investigated the role of shocks and institutions in the rise of European unemployment. Unemployment in Western Europe got through functioning of social security systems a structural character. The USA has another institution design for unemployment that results in a lower unemployment rate. In USA the institutional arrangement *market* governs the unemployment rate and not the social security system (cf. also Bruinsma (2000:5).

and Vishny (1998: 8), to understand the political objectives and powers of their designers and operators.

Explanations of government failures

Shleifer and Vishny (1998: 239) also discuss a set of explanations for government failures, which, to a large extent, agree with the *grabbing hand model*. They elaborate on recent works by Gambetta *et al.* (1988), Coleman (1988; 1990), Putman (1993), Gellner (1994), and Fukuyama (1995), who have all used concepts such as trust, social capital, and civil society to explain why some countries function better than others. Basing their ideas on these works, Shleifer and Vishny (1998: 239-240) point out that some measures of trust among people in a region – such as participation in non-government associations – are strongly correlated with the quality of government performance in that region.

There are two views on how social capital contributes to better government. In the first, trust promotes cooperation between people, and cooperation leads to better performance of all institutions in the society including the government. In the second view, the essential manifestation of social capital is the presence of non-state institutions in a country that watch, criticise, and restrain the government. Active participation by citisens in such institutions enables them to limit the predatory tendencies of public officials. According to this view, it is countervailing power rather than cooperation among people per se, that improves the performance of the government.

Both views have been tested by a worldwide survey. One question in the survey asked concerning the 'cooperation' view of trust was: *generally speaking, would you say that most people could be trusted, or that you cannot be too careful in dealing with people?* The percentage of people answering 'yes' to this question was one of measures of trust in a country. Next, the survey looked at the relationship between this measure of trust and several proxies for government performance across countries. It examined not only things such as infant mortality and public education expenditure, but also perceived corruption, bureaucratic quality, and judicial efficiency. The result was a positive correlation between trust and government performance across the world, even controlling for per capita income (Shleifer and Vishny, 1998: 240).

The same world wide survey also asked respondents about their participation in a variety of civic activities, including (a) social welfare services, (b) education, art, and cultural activities, (c) local community affairs, (d) activities related to conservation, the environment, and ecology, and (e) work with youth. The percentage of these activities in which an average respondent in a country takes part may measure the intensity of civic participation. This participation variable was related to the proxy variables for government performance. The result was a positive correlation between the intensity of civic participation and government performance across the world, even controlling for per capita income (Shleifer and Vishny, 1998: 240). These results suggest that, in principle at least, low social capital is a valid explanation for the poor performance of Russia's government (Shleifer and Vishny (1998: 240).

Institutional performance and quality of policy

La Porta *et al.* (1999: 222) investigate the determinants of institutional performance and quality of economic policy in a large cross-section of countries. In doing so, the authors present and empirically evaluate a number of theories that focus on economical, political, cultural determinants of government performances. Economic theories of institutions are often oriented on efficiency. They suggest that they are created whenever the social benefits of doing so exceed the cost. The trouble is the absence of institutions and the existence of bad ones (e.g. Demsetz, 1967; North, 1990; Olsen, 1996; Shleifer and Vishny, 1998). In contrast, political theories focus more on redistribution than on efficiency, and hold that policies and institutions are shaped by the desire of those in power to stay in power and to transfer resources to themselves. According to cultural theories, societies hold beliefs that shape collective actions and government (La Porta *et al.*, 1999: 223 -224).

The thrust of economic theory of institutions is that economic development itself creates a demand for good government, and hence the appropriate measure of demand is per capita income. However, good institutions themselves improve economic conditions. For example, we would expect per capita income to be enhanced by better protection of property rights, improved government efficiency, higher quality of private goods, perhaps a big but good government, and perhaps political freedom. Based on data from 152 countries, La Porta *et al.* found a strong association between per capita income and government performance. It appears to be true that richer countries have a better government. However, this performance is also determined to a significant extent by political and cultural factors (La Porta *et al.*, 1999: 224)

Therefore, as well as economic variables, La Porta *et al.* (1999: 223) also look for variables which describe the variation in political and cultural circumstances across countries accounting for the variation in government performance. The political theory of institutions states roughly that institutions and policies are shaped by the desire of those in power to stay in power and to amass resources. Government policies are used to control assets, including people, and to convert this control into wealth. According to La Porta *et al.* (1999: 227), we can analyse the political theories in terms of the control rights of various agents. Modern theories are more nuanced and allow redistributive policy to be shaped by sovereigns, bureaucracies, ethnic groups, religions, and even particular groups.

La Porta *et al.* (1999: 227-228) contrast three types of policy: oriental despotism, European absolutism and limited government. In the case of oriental despotism, the despots had absolute unchecked power through an almost complete control over the military, the aristocracy, religion, and the bureaucracy. These empires were characterised by few property rights, much government intervention, and little government efficiency. They had few laws or civil rights, and relatively small governments (La Porta *et al.*, 1999: 227).

In contrast to oriental despotism, in European absolutism, the power of the monarch was at least partially checked by law, and the Church (Catholic countries) and the aristocracy restricted autocratic control to some extent. As a consequence, these countries had more secure property rights, and greater political rights for the subject, although sovereigns continually tried to restrict these rights to enhance their revenues. Civil law developed in Western Europe as a part of such restrained control by the sovereigns over their subjects. However, government efficiency is not the same as government intervention. Some European countries managed to create relatively efficient bureaucracies, while others such as Italy and France, created 'patrimonial' bureaucracies that used their powers to pursue the personal interests of officials rather than those of the sovereigns (La Porta *et al.*, 1999: 228).

In contrast to the European absolutism, English (later British) government was shaped by the victory of aristocracy over the crown, and resulted in a more limited government, greater political freedom, and a more efficient bureaucracy. Common law was developed, in part, as a mechanism for protecting the subjects from the crown. Perhaps surprisingly, the consent of the governed enabled the British parliament to raise considerably higher tax revenues for military spending than the French kings could ever raise. Though the British government was larger, it was less interventionistic (La Porta *et al.*, 1999: 228).

Cultural theories state that some societies form beliefs and ideas that are conducive to good government, while others do not (see Weber, 1958). To examine these cultural theories, La Porta *et al.* (1999: 224) explored the works of various authors, from Weber (1958) to Landes (1998), all of whom use religion as a proxy for work ethic, tolerance, trust, and other characteristics of a society that may be instrumental in shaping its government. They conclude that trust facilitates collective action and is important for the provision of public goods, whereas cultures of intolerance hinder the performances of government and economic growth (La Porta *et al.*, 1999: 229).

Dimensions of performance of the government

The first step toward understanding what explains the variation in performances of institutions across countries is to describe the dimensions of such performances. Perhaps the most standard view is that a good government protects property rights, and keeps regulation and taxes light. That is, a good government is relatively non-interventionistic. The first dimension of La Porta *et al.* (1999: 225), therefore, focuses on interventionism, especially on the quality of regulation and the security of property rights. One area where the interpretation of interventionism is ambiguous is taxation. Some hold that high taxation is a measurement of high intervention, while others believe high tax rates are imposed with the consent of the government to finance sought-after public goods. Recent interpretations of higher taxes are consistent with the notion that higher tax rates may go hand in hand with better institutions. La Porta *et al.* (1999: 234-235) measure government intervention by an index of property rights protection, an index of the quality of business regulation, and the top marginal tax rate.

A second important dimension can be described as the efficiency of government, or the quality of bureaucracy. When a government intervenes, it can do so reasonably efficiently, or with delays, corruption, and other distortions. When a government taxes, it can do so with relatively high compliance, or with low compliance, which often leads to corruption and arbitrary variation of effective tax rates across similarly situated taxpayers. La Porta *et al.* (1999: 234-235) measured government efficiency using a survey of scores on corruption, bureaucratic delays, and tax compliance. They also include in this category a measure of relative wages of government officials to see if higher wages are associated with more efficient government.

A third dimension of government is the government as a provider of public goods that are essential for economic development, such as infrastructure, schools, health care, police protection, and a court system (cf. La Porta *et al.*, 1999: 226). Government performance of a given country should be assessed in part by evaluating the quality of public good provision such as schooling, infant morality, literacy, and infrastructure. While some of these goods are partly privately provided, governments have come to play a large role in delivering health, education, and infrastructure. A delivery of high quality of these goods, as opposed to just high expenditures, is a sign of a well-functioning government. La Porta *et al.* (1999: 234-235) measure the output of the public sector through infant mortality, school attainment, illiteracy, and an index of infrastructure quality (the lower the degree of infant mortality and illiteracy, the better the performance).

According to La Porta *et al.* (1999: 226), a fourth important indicator of performance is government expenditure on transfers, its own consumption, and public sector employment[11]. High government expenditure in these areas may reflect the citizen's *willingness to pay* taxes because they like what the government is doing, and this reflects good government. Alternatively, high expenditure on transfers and subsidies or on government consumption may reflect high levels of distortionary taxes and redistribution of income, and hence represent a failure to protect the public from government intervention. Examining the determinants of these types of government spending may help us distinguish alternative theories of institutions. La Porta *et al.* (1999: 234-237) measure the size of the public sector by government transfers and subsidies, government consumption, an index of the size of the state enterprise sector, and a measure of the relative size of public sector employment.

A final dimension of good government which La Porta *et al.* (1999: 226) examined is democratic and political rights. Political freedom is a crucial element of good government, and because economic freedom generally goes together with political freedom. The relationship between democracy and economic success over the long span of time indicates that more limited governments have presided over more successful development. La Porta *et al.* (1999: 234-237) made use of indices for democracy and of political rights.

Good government has been shown to contribute to the economic development of European countries over the last millennium, to growth across countries over the last 40 years, and to the successful transition from socialism to capitalism (La Porta *et al.*, 1999: 222). Good government performance is important for realising sustainable development also, and it is from the determinants of good government that we can deduce the determinants of economic and sustainable development.

---

[11] Some measures of the size of the government, such as the size of the state-owned enterprise sector and the relative size of the public sector employment are perhaps more indicative for of the political and redistributive power than oriented on the welfare of the society (cf. Shleifer and Vishny, 1998: 227-253).

However, there is more to economic success than just institutions. Also important is 'the shared knowledge, understandings, norms, rules, and expectations about patterns of interactions that groups of individuals bring to a recurrent activity' (Ostrom 2000: 176); these are often referred to as 'social capital'. Social capital may be correlated with good government, but it can exist outside of good government. It is our contention that social capital is important to sustainable development and also to economic success.

Summarising, we can conclude that institutions and good government are very important for economic growth and welfare. This holds not only for macro but also for micro level. The effects of institutions and good government were analysed more on the macro-level. However, these effects have important consequences on the micro level; the level of households, firms and organisations. In terms of 'theories of the firm' or 'theories of the state' the analytical approach was based more on the theory of firm.

As said, institutions seem to be a broad and also abstract concept, yet when understood, the analysis can be applied on different levels. For analysing the meaning and effects of institutions in society, firms and our daily lives we have to classify them based on a certain number of dimensions. In Appendix 3.1 we will present a framework for classifying institutions. On the one hand this framework can be used for distinguishing different levels of institutions, and on the other hand as an analytical tool for taking into account determinants or proxy-variables on different levels of institutions that may account for good performance in the national economy, in sectors of the national economy, government bureaus, firms, organisation and households.

3.3 Institutional framework: levels of institutions

Over the past several decades, economists have given increasing attention to the role of institutions in the operation of economic systems. The purpose of creating institutions is to provide order and regularity in expected outcomes and to limit the element of uncertainty in transactions. Together with the standard economic constraints, these rules define the choice set, specify the transaction and production costs and thus the feasibility and profitability of economic activities.

One of the first definitions of the term *institution,* originating from Davis and North (1971), argues the importance of distinguishing the difference between institutional environment and institutional arrangements. Davis and North (1971: 6-7) defined the concepts of institutional environment and institutional arrangements as follows. 'The institutional environment is the set of fundamental political, social and legal ground rules that establishes the basis for production, exchange, and distribution. An institutional arrangement is an arrangement between economic units that govern the ways in which these units can cooperate and/or compete'. Consistent with this definition, institutions are usually defined as rules of conduct, or rules of regularity. In the economic sphere, individual transactions are constrained to a considerable extend by the informal and formal rules that structure the exchange. There is no predetermined assumption that the exchange will be efficient. Rather, institutional analysis reveals the reasons why exchanges are often costly and explores the role institutions play in reducing uncertainty in human exchange.

More than thirty years later, North (2003: 17) defines institutions as 'the humanly devised constraints that structure human interaction. They are composed of formal rules (statute law, common law, regulations), informal constraints (conventions, norms of behaviour and self imposed codes of conduct), and the enforcement characteristics of both'. Formulated in this way, institutions are the rules of the game in society. Together they create a behavioural framework within which economic activity occurs. Next, North (2003: 17) distinguishes the difference between institutions and organisations; if institutions are perceived as rules of the game then organisations can be considered as the players. Consequently, the institutional environment does not only delineate the rules of the game within which the institutional arrangements, such as firms and organisations, actually operate, but also prescribes the rules of conduct within which human actions take place. Organisations are trading units through which economic exchanges occur. They include the governments, political parties, firms, labour unions, clubs, etc. The organisations which exist reflect the possibilities provided by the institutional environment. The interaction between institutions and organisations shape the institutional change in an economy (cf. North, 2003:17).

Institutional levels and linkages

Institutional linkages – over time and at a specific time – receive special attention in new institutional economics. Since informal rules play an important role in the incremental way in which institutions evolve, they remain a major source of path dependency. Informal rules change more slowly than formal rules. As a result, there is always tension between altered formal rules and persisting informal rules (Saleth and Dinar, 2004: 27).

Williamson (1998: 26-27) makes – as well as Davis and North (1971: 6-7) and North (1991; 1994) – a distinction between the institutional environment and institutional arrangements (governance structures). However, Williamson (2000: 596-600) goes – based on (1998) – even further. He developed a framework consisting of four levels of institutional economic analysis that are distinguished in Figure 3.1. Each level represents a different process and time period for institutional change. For example, the top level of social embeddedness is considered by Williamson to be the slowest institutional level to evolve. At this level cultural norms, customs, morals, traditions and more informal codes of conduct emerge, forming the underlying social 'fabric' of society. Williamson (1998: 26) suggests that institutional rules at this level take 100-1000 years to be established. However, we have witnessed many types of cultural level shifts in the last one hundred years which suggests that institutional change at this level is not necessarily time dependent.

The second level is referred to as the institutional environment that includes the formal rules of the game in the society. These formal rules include constitutions, laws and property rights. At this level the executive, legislative, and bureaucratic functions of the government are located, as well as the distribution of power across different levels of government. The definition and enforcement of property rights and of contract laws are also important features of this level. The *formal rules of the game* observed here are partly the product of evolutionary processes, and partly the result of political actions. Institutions at this level change in a period of 10 to 100 years. The challenge here is to get the formal rules of the game right.

The third level is where the institutions of governance are located. Governance should be considered as 'an effort to craft order, thereby to mitigate conflict and realise mutual gains' (Williamson, 2000: 599). However, a perfectly functioning legal system for defining contract laws and enforcing contracts hardly exists. Costless court ordering being a fiction, much of the contract management and dispute settlement action is dealt with directly by parties – through private ordering. Analysis at the third level is about the effectiveness and efficiency of different institutional arrangements, or governance structures (e.g. markets, firms, clubs, contracts, in-house production or vertical integration). The challenge here is to get the governance structure right. Possible reorganisation of transactions among governance structures can be done periodically. According to Williamson (2000: 599), the period involved for decisions at this level – i.e. a reorganisation of transactions among governance structures – is between 1 to 10 years.

The fourth level is the level at which the neoclassical economic analysis works. Optimality apparatus, often marginal analysis, is employed. The firm for this purpose is often described as a production function. Adjustment to prices and output occur more or less continuously. Agency theory, which emphasises *ex-ante* incentive alignment and efficient risk bearing, rather than *ex-post* governance, nonetheless makes provisions of which multi-tasking is one (Williamson, 2000: 600).

In the last level that Williamson (2000: 600) distinguishes, there is a shift from discrete structural to marginal analysis. In his view, this is the level on which standard neoclassical economics and more recently the agency theory or *principal-agent approach* focus. The decision variables in neoclassical economics are prices, input and output. The *principal-agent approach* is concerned with the use of the correct incentives in the case of different risk-attitudes, multi-task factors or multi-principal problems. At this level, marginal analysis and optimisation behaviour dominate. This is also the level of individual decision-makers.

Figure 3.1 shows the four levels of institutions of Williamson. In Section 3.4 we will discuss the social embeddedness, in Section 3.5 the institutional environment and in Section 3.6 the governance structures. It should be emphasised that we will not always strictly follow Williamson. Based on the literature and our own research, we will specify our own approach and Figure 1.1 shows our framework. Nevertheless the principles of Williamson's framework are very helpful to structure our analysis. It emphasises that a well-defined definition of institutions depends on the level of analysis.

3.4 Embeddedness and social capital

The first level of institutional analysis (see Figure 3.1) concerns the degree to which economic transactions are embedded in social relations. Granovetter (1985) introduced the term *embeddedness* in his critique of Williamson, arguing that New Institutional Economists presented

Level	Frequency (years)	Core elements	Purpose
Level 1 Social theory	100 to 1000	Embeddedness: informal rules, customs traditions, norms, religion	Often non-calculative; spontaneous
Level 2 Economics of property rights	10 to 100	Institutional environment: formal rules of the game – especially property (polity, judiciary, bureaucracy)	Get the institutional environment right; 1st order economising
Level 3 Transaction costs economics	1 to 10	Governance: play of the game – especially contract (aligning governance with transactions)	Get the governance structures right; 2nd order economising
Level 4 Neo-classical economics / agency theory	continuous	Resource allocation and employment (prices and quantities; incentive alignment)	Get the marginal conditions right; 3rd order economising

Figure 3.1. The four levels of institutions (Williamson, 2000: 597).

an under-socialised view of human behaviour[12]. He disagreed with their claim that institutional arrangements alone could minimise opportunistic behaviour[13]. Conversely, the embeddedness argument holds that (economic) behaviour and institutions are so constrained by ongoing social relations that to construct them as independent is a grievous misunderstanding. Granovetter stressed that economists need to acknowledge 'the role of concrete personal relations and structures (or networks) of such relations in generating trust and discouraging malfeasance' (Granovetter, 1985: 490). Moreover, he emphasised that the value of knowing an individual's reputation was critical information, based on which future economic transactions would either

---

[12] Granovetter argues that Williamson's depiction of human behaviour, characterised by opportunistic behaviour and self-interest, is a narrowly constructed view of what motivates human action. Moreover, he suggests that such a view results in the 'atomisation' of actors by removing them from the social context in which decisions are made. 'Actors do not behave or decide as atoms outside a social context, nor do they adhere slavishly to a script written for them by the particular social categories that they happen to occupy. Their attempts at purposive action are instead embedded in concrete, ongoing systems of social relations' (Granovetter, 1985: 487).

[13] There is some difference in the interpretation of the term social embeddedness between Williamson (1998: 27) and Granovetter (1985: 481-510). This term originates in economic sociology. However, Williamson (1987: 22) adopted the term, but is vague in his description. We will use an interpretation more in line with economic sociology, in which social capital, trust, reciprocity also play an important role. This has consequences for the time period, because social capital and trust can be lost in a short period of time.

Institutional economics and economic organisation theory

be trusted or terminated. In his view, continuing economic relations are closely intertwined with personal relations and trustworthy transactions are knowingly constructed.

However, Granovetter also cautioned against an overly optimistic view of embeddedness. Just as personal relations and networks of relations can generate trust, so they can be used as channels for conducting illegal transactions. For example, diamond trade transactions have been known to be embedded within a densely knit network of actors. Accordingly, they construct rules of conduct easily monitored within the group by the quick spread of information about any misconduct or malfeasance. However, once organised, the temptation is large to use the team for fraudulent transactions, particularly if the probability of an inside informant (cheating) is perceived to be low (Granovetter 1985: 492). As we explain further, social embeddedness is the fundamental level of analysis for understanding the social relationships underlying economic transactions. However, embedded ties alone are not enough for creating orderly economic transactions. Rather, a diversity of social ties is necessary for generating an optimal level of social capital, from which trust is built and credible commitment is created.

The role of social embeddedness was acknowledged by Williamson (1987:22). He adopted the term, but is vague and short in his description. According to Williamson (1998: 27; 2002: 596), the social embeddedness level is where norms, customs, morals, traditions, etc. are located. As examples of people working in this field he referred to Putnam, Leonardi and Nanettie (1993). It was the work of Putnam (1993, 2000) that launched the notion of 'civic life' as a mode of organising and argued that social networks, known as 'Social Capital', are the basis of economic prosperity.

The central thesis of social capital theory is that social interactions in civic life, the day-to-day and face-to face encounters in neighborhoods and communities, are the foundation upon which common values are based and trust is built. In this view, the production of social capital depends on the degree to which social interactions are embedded in a network of social relations. In this sense of the term, social capital is only generated when a network of relations has the capability of creating standards of behaviour and a channel of information flow through which trustworthy transactions are facilitated. In other words, the production of social capital depends somewhat on the level of embeddedness. If social interactions are highly embedded, the likelihood of social capital being produced is greater, to the extent that those relationships extend both horizontally and vertically.

While Putnam popularised the term, the concept of social capital was developed initially by sociologists Pierre Bourdieu (1986) and James Coleman (1988). The focus for Coleman (1988: S. 98) was not so much on the form of social capital, but more on its function. He argued that social capital 'is not a single entity, but a variety of different entities, having two characteristics in common: they all consist of some aspect of a social structure, and they facilitate certain actions of individuals who are within the structure.' (Coleman, 1994: 302). Because norms of reciprocity and shared values are collectively maintained, the benefits gained by conforming are shared by members of the group and amount to a collective good (cf. S.116-118). Consequently, norms and values become social capital to the extent that they are able to solve social dilemmas that would otherwise result in sub-optimal collective outcomes caused by individuals pursuing their private advantage at the cost of collective goods.

Location of social capital

An intriguing question is: where do we locate social capital in the institutional framework[14]? According to Ostrom (2000: 176) social capital is the shared knowledge, understandings, norms and values, rules and expectations about patterns of interaction that groups or individuals bring to repeated activities. In this view, social capital is inextricably linked to the level of social embeddedness within which transactions are conducted. In other words, economic transactions conducted in an institutional context with a low level of social embeddedness are less likely to generate social capital. That said, the economic gains from social embeddedness also come with some cost. The high degree of network density and closed relationships necessary for creating informal exchanges at the micro-scale of inter-community relations, have been found to constrain their network members from making the transition to formal exchanges at the macro-scale of state-society relations (Woolcock, 1998:186). Research on ethnic entrepreneurship has found that the high level of social cohesion required for building trust and connectedness, can also constrain new types of external relations that extend beyond the reach of the embedded network (Portes and Sensenbrenner, 1993: 1321).

The solution Granovetter proposed in his seminal article entitled *The Strength of Weak Ties* involves a social mechanism he refers to as 'coupling and decoupling' such that members of embedded economic groups draw initially upon resources of close network ties, but then bridge into more autonomous ties beyond the micro-level relations, as their need for larger financial transactions expands (Granovetter, 1973 in Woolcock, 1998: 175). Contemporary network analysis and social network theory has built on this initial proposition, noting a common pattern among highly successful organisations (Uzzi *et al.*, 2007: 77). For example, the small-world network consists of a combination of highly clustered internal actor relations which are inter-linked by a relatively short path length of external actor connections (Milgram 1967: 62).[15] In such cases, the degree to which economic transactions are embedded in a pattern of social relations is fundamental for understanding how exchanges are coordinated. Evidently, such patterns comprise the 'base-map' of institutional analysis and are necessarily the structural foundation from which social capital is produced.

Forms of social capital

Social capital takes many different forms, depending on the type of ties that connect people together. For example, the family structure is considered a form of *bonding social capital*, based on close kinship ties in which people share a common set of values, norms of behaviour and social conditions (Putnam, 2000: 22; Woolcock, 2001: 14).Weaker ties among work colleagues or acquaintances may be described as *bridging social capital*, where values are similar and exchanges

---

[14] Or stated in another way: is social capital a coordination mechanism or a component of the underlying level of the social embeddedness? We will argue that it is component of the social embeddedness.

[15] While Granovetter was the first to bring the embeddedness concept to social theory, others have since developed this further into social network theory. In this way, social network theory complements the embeddedness concept by using statistical methods to quantify the density of the social relationships of the involved stakeholders. Using these methods, the structure of relations is more explicitly defined and conceptualised as a form of governance structure.

are mutually beneficial, but particular obligations and demands may be less constraining than with those of closer ties (Woolcock, 2001: 14).

Shared norms are a component of social capital, but specific norms may have different consequences. The norm of reciprocity implies some level of symmetry among those who engage in long-term reciprocal relationships. In this case, the relationship is based on a balance of taking and giving over time. When individuals learn to trust one another so that they are able to make credible commitments and rely on generalised forms of reciprocity rather than on narrow sequences of specific *quid pro quo* relationships, they are able to achieve far more than when these forms of social capital are not present (Ostrom, 2000: 177).

The positive aspects of social capital can lead to more negative aspects as well, if social structures are not dynamically linked across multiple institutional scales (from micro to macro), using a diversity of coordination mechanisms. Studies on entrepreneurship in immigrant communities in the United States propose that social capital is more likely to be present when cultural conditions create an advantage for group members to belong to an embedded intra-community network[16]. While group membership can facilitate access to necessary resources such as strong social support and privileged information with reduced transaction costs, the ability to connect or link with outside groups or networks is often discouraged or constrained (Portes and Sensenbrenner, 1993: 1340).

Hence there exists an embeddedness paradox: the higher the level of embeddedness is, the more likely it is for social capital to be generated. However, at some threshold, the level of embeddedness can potentially constrain the benefits of social capital due to the opportunity cost of not having more autonomous ties linking to outside networks. In this view, social capital can be optimised by a diversity of forms of social ties. While embedded ties are necessary for developing trusting relationships and the associated benefits that can be derived from strong social ties, arm's length ties such as market-based transactions, are also necessary for bridging exchange across institutional boundaries.

Uzzi (1997: 57) expresses this embeddedness paradox in the context of a firm. He argues that the processes by which embeddedness creates a requisite fit with the institutional environment (such that transaction costs are lowered through strong relational ties) are the same processes that can also reduce the organisation's ability to adapt. As a result, successful organisations seem to use a combination of strong and weak social ties to coordinate transactions. In the case of Uzzi's (1997) research in the New York City apparel industry, he found that successful companies frequently used the price mechanism to coordinate routine business between firms. However, critical exchanges in which timing and fine grained information were of importance, were conducted through close personal relationships. The use of embedded networks, coordinated through strong personal ties, had three main components in their use to regulate the expectations and behaviours

---

[16] Portes and Sensenbrenner (1993: 1340) proposed that social capital is high in groups with the following characteristics: (1) distinct cultural characteristics that increases prejudice against them and lowers the probability of entry or exit; (2) engaged in strong confrontation with other groups, often perceived as more powerful; (3) suffering a high degree discrimination and without other alternatives for social honour and economic opportunity; (4) possessing a high degree of internal communication and able to offer rewards to its members.

of exchange partners: (1) trust; (2) fine grained information transfer; and (3) joint-problem solving arrangements (Uzzi, 1997: 42). We discuss these components further below.

While social capital can take many forms, there are underlying similarities among all of the diverse forms. In all forms, individuals who devote time to constructing patterns of relationships among humans are building assets whether consciously or unconsciously. According to Ostrom (2000: 179-180) all forms of social capital share the following attributes:

1. Social capital is formed over time and is embedded in common understanding rather than in physical obvious structures. If used, social capital can be transmitted from one generation to another.
2. Common understanding is hard to articulate precisely in language.
3. Common understanding is easily eroded if large numbers of people are concerned or if a large proportion of the participants changes rapidly – unless substantial efforts are devoted to transmission of the common understandings, monitoring behaviour in conformance with common understandings, and sanctioning behaviour not in conformance with the common understanding.

Components of social capital

Trust is perhaps the most important component of social capital: 'Virtually every commercial transaction has within itself an element of trust, certainly any transaction conducted over a period of time' (Dasgupta, 2000: 329).[17] If one's confidence in an enforcement agency falters, one

---

[17] Dasgupta quotes K. J. Arrow, Gifts and Exchanges, Philosophy and Public Affairs, 1(1972): 357.

Box 3.1. Economic virtues and the social embeddedness.

Butter (2007: 300-302) pleads for more attention for the role of virtues in a democratic society. According to him, there two ways how virtues in an economic welfare analysis could take place: (a) via the individual behaviour, i.e virtuousness for the individual fellow man; (b) via aggregation of individual behaviour to social desired behaviour, i.e. virtuousness in relation to the society by which a person in his individual actions takes into account the costs or disadvantages for others.

Virtuousness in (a) means that you have the intrinsic need to do well for others, without having any benefits for yourself. Doing well for another can be a part of your individual preferences. It should be mentioned that in the long run certain forms of altruism and reciprocity can deal with own interests: "do unto others as you would have them do unto you".

According to Butter (2007: 301), it becomes more important to make use of virtues for realising – via the way of optimising of individual behaviour – a socially desired behaviour. Next, it has to be brought in within the way of economic thinking. One way is to see virtuousness as a part of the social embeddedness and taking into account the relation between virtuousness and values and norms; virtues produce common values and norms. If people have common values and norms, they have – for example – more the tendency to keep the rules (this reduces transaction costs). More in general, democratic virtues contribute to an active participation in the society.

does not trust people to fulfil their agreements and agreements are not entered into (*ibid.* p.332). There is an element of trust in any transaction where one has to decide (make a choice) before being able to observe the action of the other party to the transaction. Further, one has to assume that the other person is not acting with guile, keeping hidden information about himself that can be used to their advantage at the expense of the other party to the transaction. Trust is the catalyst that makes an economy function efficiently.

Yet, the level of trust that is generated from embedded ties is distinctly higher than the level of trust necessary for commercial transactions among actors who are socially detached. Social attachments and affiliations among a network of actors who know each other personally, facilitate norms of exchange and expectations of trust over time (Uzzi and Lancaster, 2004: 321). The economic benefits of such exchanges are not always easily converted to net monetary gains, yet the access to resources that are otherwise unpriced are invaluable to business transactions. For example, economic sociologists researching inter-bank relationships between a syndicate of banks and a client firm, concluded that embedded ties facilitate the exchange of private information flows across a network structure coordinated via relational mechanisms. Thus, social attachments in which an expectation of trust is created, can channel specialised information flows and increase the predictability with which exchange partners share knowledge. Moreover, these exchanges build trust over time such that network members believe that the costs and profits of their knowledge will be shared for mutual benefit over time. In the banking industry, these types of stable self enforcing transaction arrangements are fundamentally important for reducing uncertainty and mitigating shocks in the financial sector (Uzzi and Gillespie, 2002).

Similarly, the level of trust among citizens and their government plays a critical role in economic development. Knack and Keefer (1997) used data from the World Values Survey to show that growth in GDP between 1980 and 1992 was higher in countries where people trusted one another, with the impact greatest in countries that were poorest in 1980. La Porta *et al.* (1997) found trust to be positively correlated with growth in GDP (among other things), but negatively correlated with an index of government corruption. In addition to trust, other elements of social capital include social norms, or behavioural strategies (always do *p* if *q* occurs) subscribed to by all in society, and networks of civic engagement (membership in swim clubs, church organisations, etc.) that enhance cooperation.

Trust is also the expectation of one person about the actions of others that affects the first person's choice, when an action must be taken before the actions of others are known (Dasgupta, 1997: 5). Many economists recognise that trust is an important concept and it plays an important role outside, but also between and within organisations (Douma and Schreuder, 2002: 165-167). Trust lowers the cost of search and monitoring, because trusting people are less secretive and more ready to supply information. Trust reduces the costs of contracting and control because it lowers fears of opportunism and accepts more influence from the partner. In the case of trust, people will deliberate and renegotiate on the basis of give and take ('voice') rather than walk out ('exit') when conflicts arise. According to Nooteboom (1999: 25-28) there are different notions of trust: *trust in people* (behavioural trust, the object is individual people); *trust in the institutional environment* (confidence, the object is the social or natural system) and *trust in organisations* (the object is the intermediate level, the group or community). Organisational trust goes beyond a simple 'aggregate' of behavioural trust. It is a constellation of behavioural trust, with an organisational structure and culture acting as an institutional arrangement that guides the behaviour of both members and staff.

In Nooteboom's approach (1999: 29), the sources of trust are related to North's notion of 'institutional environment' (especially values, norms, codes of conduct) and related to 'institutional arrangements' (especially bonds of friendship or kinship and empathy). Trust can be produced or built up on basis of growing familiarity, existing bonds of kinship, friendship, shared values and norms of conduct, habits and expectations. Nooteboom names this type of trust *process trust*[18]. Some institutions, such as a system of certification, professional standards or rules, can be developed on the basis of a rational design. In the attempt to create conditions for process trust to develop, detailed contracts can be destructive (cf. Nooteboom, 1999: 33).

While trust based on friendship or kinship is often not enough for cooperation, material self-interest and coercion are seldom sufficient either. According to Nooteboom (1999: 30), you 'really' trust someone when you are willing to forego guarantees on the basis of coercion or self-interest. Trust is good and can work (although we try to think why it does), but we have to take into account that trust may not always work (cf. Kreps, 1990: 580). To make sure that it does work we can make use of direct control that one may exercise over conduct by a contract, or by monitoring or threat (coercion). It may also include motives of self-interest that restrain the partner in his opportunistic behaviour; motives such as the preservation of reputation and expectations of future reward from cooperative conduct in the present (Nooteboom, 1999: 29). In short, it means we have to make trust credible[19]. Finally, there is also an important proverb: *trust comes by foot and leaves by horse.*

Trust is more credible when it arises from a foundation of common values and norms of behaviour. If a particular set of beliefs and views of the world are shared, people can more easily communicate with one another and find a common understanding. Moreover, if social interactions are frequent and communication flows are abundant, it is relatively easy to organise people. In this way, common values and norms can serve as a coordination principle for groups, where groups range from a family to a club, from a church to a volunteer group or team of people (a community) working towards a common goal. Common values and norms diminish the incidence of opportunistic behaviour between the members of the group and thereby reduce transaction costs. Effective coordination based on common values and norms coincides with a strong motivation and high commitment of individual members of a group to achieve their common goal (CPB, 1997: 55).

Ostrom (2000) and Dasgupta (2000) provide examples from the development economics literature, demonstrating how common values and norms of reciprocity have guided institutional arrangements for the use of natural resources (land, water, forest, fishing areas, etc.) for centuries. They also show how well-meaning investment projects undertaken by international development agencies can upset such coordination mechanisms, leading to unintended consequences such as

---

[18] Process trust is as much the outcome of a relationship as the basis for it (Nooteboom, 1999: 33).

[19] See also Chapter 7.8.

a reduction rather than an increase in area under irrigation (see for example, Ostrom, 2000). As said, common values and norms are the linkage to social capital.

Reciprocity and social capital

Usually the word *reciprocity* is used to describe *I'll scratch your back if you'll scratch mine*. People provide a service to others, expecting to get something in return. If the service a person provides is not reciprocated to his or her satisfaction, then the service will be withdrawn. Many authors believe that this type of reciprocity[20] (a good deed is always rewarded) is the glue that holds human societies together. It is certainly true that many more ongoing relationships between human beings are buttressed by a understanding of reciprocity than is generally acknowledged (Binmore, 1992: 347-348).

Reciprocity is also an incentive to acquire a reputation for keeping promises and performing actions with short-term costs but long-term benefits. Thus, trustworthy individuals who trust others with a reputation for being trustworthy are willing to engage in mutually productive transactions, so long as they can limit their interaction primarily to those with a reputation for keeping their promises. A reputation for being trustworthy becomes a valuable asset. In evolutionary terms, it increases fitness in an environment in which others use reciprocity norms. Similarly, developing trust in an environment in which others are trustworthy is also an asset. As said, trust is the expectation of one person about the actions of others that affect the first person's choice, when an action must be taken before the actions of others are known. In the context of a transaction, trust affects whether an individual is willing to initiate cooperation in the expectation that it will be reciprocated. Thus, at the core of a behavioural explanation are the links between trust that individuals have in others, the investment others make in trustworthy reputations, and the probability that parties will use reciprocity norms. This mutually reinforcing is affected by past experiences of the parties involved (Ostrom, 1998: 12-13). It means that reciprocity, reputation, and trust can help to overcome the strong temptations of short self-interest.

Reciprocity refers to a family of strategies that can be used in a social dilemma involving (1) an effort to identify who else is involved; (2) an assessment of the likelihood that others are conditional cooperators; (3) a decision to cooperate initially with other if others are trusted to be conditional cooperators; (4) a refusal to cooperate with those who do not reciprocate, and (5) punishment of those who betray trust. All these strategies share the common ingredient that individuals tend to react to positive actions of others with positive responses and the negative actions of others with negative responses (cf. Ostrom, 1998:10). Some of these strategies refer more to simultaneous exchanges of items of roughly equal value, and others to a more continuous relationship of exchange that at any time may be unrequited, but over time is repaid and balanced. Both imply a long-term relationship between people (Pretty, 1999: 82–83).

Summarising, understanding the social embeddedness level of institutional analysis is critical for determining what informal rules are guiding economic transactions. Moreover, the social

---

[20] In their paper *A Theory of Reciprocity* Falk and Fischbacher (1999) present a formal framework of concepts of positive and negative reciprocity, equity and intentions.

Box 3.2 Example of reciprocal behaviour

A well-known example of reciprocal behaviour comes from the game theory. It is the by far the most famous reciprocal strategy, also known as the *tit-for-tat strategy* (cf. Binmore, 1992: 380). An example is the overlapping generations model.

Imagine a world in which there are only two people alive at any stage: a mother and a daughter and we suppose that reproduction is parthenogentic. Each individual lives for precisely two periods. The first of these is a player's *youth* and the second is her *old age*. In her youth, she works, and earns two units of a perishable good. This is wholesome if and only if it is consumed in the same period that is earned. At the end of her youthful stage, each player gives birth to a daughter. The mother then enters her elderly stage during which she is to feeble to work, and so earns nothing.

Everyone would prefer not to consume all their earnings in their youth. All players would prefer to consume one unit in their youth and one unit in their old age. Unfortunately, the consumption cannot be stored, and so the second possibility cannot be achieved unless there are transfers of the good from one player to another.

One equilibrium is for each player to consume everything she earns in her youth. Everyone will then have to endure a miserable old age, but everyone will be optimising given the choices of the others. A more socially desirable outcome would be for each daughter to give her mother one of the two units or the daughter's consumption good. Everyone would then be able to enjoy one unit of consumption in each period of her life. But is such behaviour sustainable as an equilibrium?

Suppose first that each daughter adopts the strategy of giving one unit of her earnings to her mother if and only if her mother behaved similarly in the previous period. This is a Nash equilibrium. No deviant would gain anything if everybody else stuck to their equilibrium strategies. The best a deviant could do is to consume all her own income in her youth, but then her daughter's equilibrium strategy calls for the daughter to punish such selfish behaviour. The punishment consists of the daughter's withholding the gift of one unit of the consumption good that she would otherwise make. The deviant will then be left with nothing in her old age.

Note, however, that a daughter would not want to punish her deviant mother. If she did, she would be punished by her daughter. A *subgame-perfect* equilibrium that sustains the cooperative outcome is easy to find. Each daughter gives one unit of the consumption good to her mother if and only if nobody has ever done anything different in the past. In sum, an individual has to follow a strategy that his opponent followed in the last period (Binmore, 1992: 380-381).

A key point here is that the punishment extends to all descendents of the deviator. Furthermore, societies and cultures institute norms and customs to prevent such intergenerational deviation. Over time, the punishment can be even greater when consequences are imposed by society (collective sanctions such as social shame or outcasting).

context, which underlies economic transactions, is relevant for generating social capital (see Figure 3.2). If transactions are embedded in civic life, or culture, such that values are shared and reputation is built up over time, then people are more likely to be trustworthy. Such embedded ties create the foundation from which a network of trust relations can emerge. This foundation is illustrated as the embedded level of civic life in Figure 3.2. However, the process through which social capital is produced is neither mechanical nor consistent. Rather, this diagram is intended to illustrate that the social context in which economic transactions are embedded, is ongoing, dynamic and continuously constructed and reconstructed. Similarly, these relationships and processes of interaction can be unravelled and destroyed.

The production of social capital is a process of social interaction. In the first level of interaction, coloured grey, we illustrate how culture and every day connections within civic life generate a set of values. Over time, the frequent observation of one another's actions contributes to an understanding of how different individuals will behave. Once an expectation of behaviour is understood, an individual has earned a reputation for how he/she will behave in his/her exchanges, relative to the values shared by a group of individuals. Thus, a trustworthy reputation implies that an individual can be trusted to behave in a consistent manner in honouring these values. Over time, the social interactions that generate a reputation can develop a second level of interaction, known as a network of relations (black in Figure 3.2).

A network of relations can build on social values and the reputation of being trustworthy. Furthermore, if the network builds commitment and trust through relationships in which a balance of give and take is understood, then social capital is produced and information flows will likely be transparent within the group. Once this process is done routinely, we express this with the term ' norms of reciprocity'. Finally, if a network of relationships is comprised of a combination of strong and weak social ties, and extends both horizontally and vertically, then social capital can help to resolve numerous types of social dilemmas across multiple institutional

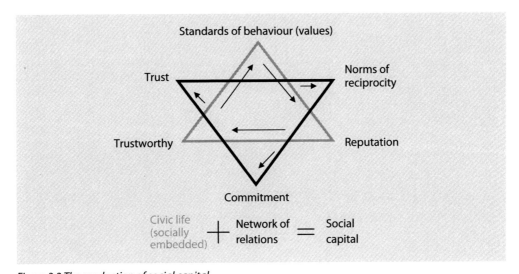

Figure 3.2 The production of social capital

scales. When social capital is high throughout the institutional environment (informal and formal rules), economic welfare (e.g. in GDP per capita) is more likely to be high and governments are more likely to be trusted. The key elements of social capital are as follows:

- trust;
- common norms and values;
- reputation;
- trustworthy;
- norm of reciprocity;
- commitment;
- connectedness or glue that society holds together; and
- active participation in society.

While this list comprises the key elements of social capital, the actual production is organised in a dynamic cycle of interaction between people. Hence, social capital is a product of relationships that contain these key elements and through the process of connecting, trust is built and reinforced over time.

The measurement of social capital

Putnam *et al.* (1993: 88) studied specifically the degree of civic community membership as a measure of social capital. Their method of analysis was based on the assumption that citizens accept their role in collective action (organised group behaviour) as a means of producing collective goods. In so doing, Putnam *et al.* proposed that forms of collective action with high voluntary participation result in higher levels of trust, lower transaction costs and higher economic productivity. Below an example is given of questions used in a similar study for measuring social capital based on trust and passive and active participation in society (cf. Beugelsdijk 2003: 60)[21]. The trust questions are in the first block and the questions about passive and active participation in society are in the second one. The results show that such questions work quite well (see Jongeneel *et al.*, 2008).

---

[21] Both sets of questions have been used for a survey among farmers and in a more general survey.

Trust part. *Survey question: what is your level of trust in the aspects/institutions mentioned below? (1 = very much trust, 2 = much trust, 3 = moderate trust, 4 = little trust, 5 = no trust, 0 = no opinion); (Circle a number).*

		Very much	Much	Moderate	Little	no	No opinion
1.	Society	1	2	3	4	5	0
2.	Your own pressure group	1	2	3	4	5	0
3.	Local government	1	2	3	4	5	0
4.	National government	1	2	3	4	5	0
5.	EU-government	1	2	3	4	5	0
6.	The economy	1	2	3	4	5	0
7.	Future of my holding	1	2	3	4	5	0
8.	The future of farmers in the Netherlands	1	2	3	4	5	0

Passive and active participation in the society part. *Survey question: could you indicate whether you are a member of the following organisations, and if so whether you are also a member of the board of the organisation and to what extent you are involved in the activities of the organisation?*

Organisation	Member		Member of the board		Active participation in the activities of the organisation		
	Yes	No	Yes	No	Always	Sometimes	Never
General Farmers' organisation	☐	☐	☐	☐	☐	☐	☐
Specialised farmers' organisation	☐	☐	☐	☐	☐	☐	☐
Local working parties aiming to improve the agricultural sector	☐	☐	☐	☐	☐	☐	☐
Agricultural organisations directed at nature and landscape management	☐	☐	☐	☐	☐	☐	☐
Church	☐	☐	☐	☐	☐	☐	☐
Sport club	☐	☐	☐	☐	☐	☐	☐
(local) Political party	☐	☐	☐	☐	☐	☐	☐
Other club, namely:	☐	☐	☐	☐	☐	☐	☐
Other club, namely:	☐	☐	☐	☐	☐	☐	☐

3.5 Institutional environment

According to Figure 3.1. the second level of analysis concerns the institutional environment – the rules of the game and the third level focuses on institutions of governance – the play of the game. A first striking difference between the institutional environment and the institutions of governance is that the former mainly defines (or acts as a constraint on) the environment of the latter (Williamson, 1996: 5). A governance structure is a way of implementing and operationalising the 'rules of the game' as defined by the institutional environment.

A second difference is that the institutional environment operates at a higher level of generalisation than institutions of governance such as markets and organisation. In this view, the institutional environment delineates the rules of the game within which such 'governance structures' actually operate. For example, the legal system, which most economists would agree on calling an institution, is a framework which defines the ways in which property rights can be implemented and enforced (Ménard, 1995: 164). Thus the level of analysis is different. This is showed in Figure 3.1. The institutions of governance operate at the level of individual transactions, whereas the institutional environment is more concerned with the composed levels of activity. A third difference is that the institutional environment facilitates and supports the functions of the institutions of governance.

The institutional environment is not a constant, rather, it changes over the years. For example, in the past the monarchs used their monopoly of power to rob the people; slavery, serfdom and toll collection were the order of the day. People were hesitant to carry out productive activities, as they were afraid that the monarch would seize any returns. In these cases, the society has a kind of hold-up problem (cf. Bovenberg and Teulings, 1999: 364-367). In a modern constitutional state and a parliamentary democracy, the monarch has been replaced by the politician, and the count by a civil servant. Robbery, slavery, serfdom, uncompensated takings and toll collection have been replaced by taxes. The governmental monopoly of violence is restricted by laws and rules, and the government protects and enforces the property rights, takes care of the institutional environment (rules of the game) and stimulates the development of efficient governance structures (markets, organisation and third way solutions). This is what we see in the western world and also in many other countries. However, it is not an accepted or normal situation in all the countries of the world.

The institutional environment also differs between countries, and even within countries the basic rules can vary. For example, USA legislation differs from Dutch legislation or the legislation of other EU-countries. Also in the USA, more values are focused on the individual and there are differences between the levels of institutions. Similarly, the rate at which social processes evolve may differ between countries. The social embedding of informal institutions, like values and beliefs, norms, traditions, codes of conduct and religion changes slowly in some nations, while formal rules like legislation can be changed and implemented more quickly in other nations. In other words, some parts of the institutional environment are more dynamic and change rather quickly, while other parts are less dynamic and change rather slowly. For example, ordinary laws can be adapted within one year, while a change in the constitution can take years.

The informal rules of social embeddedness and formal rules of the institutional environment are the rules of the game within the society in which the institutional arrangements operate. Within these rules property rights are defined, implemented, regulated and enforced. Property rights are an important part of the institutional environment. The control rights over the property rights determine who has the power of control within an institutional arrangement, like a firm or a contract, and consequently who has the right over the residual income. The establishment, protection and enforcement of property rights are a very important part of the formal rules of the game. It is for that reason also an important part of the work of the New Institutional Economy (NIE). The origin of this work goes back to Coase (1960), Alchian (1965), Alchian (1967), Demsetz (1967), and Alchian and Demsetz (1972). We discuss property rights in some depth in Chapter 9 and 10.

3.6 Governance structures

On the third level of Figure 3.1, the institutions of governance are located. They refer to the concept 'governance structures'. We consider the terms 'institutional arrangements' and 'governance structures' to have the same meaning. Similarly, the term 'mode of organisation' is often used. However, in the discipline of institutional economics, the term 'governance structure' is more common. While there are several different definitions, the most widely use of 'governance structure' refers to the way in which the 'rules of the game' are implemented and operationalised as defined by the institutional environment. In other words, governance structures are the play of the game. According to institutional economics, instigated by Williamson, individuals and organisations choose a 'contractual format' for carrying out transactions, termed governance structures, from a wide variety of possibilities. In this view, (cf. Hendrikse, 2003: 243) a governance structure can be described as an institutional arrangement consisting of the rules by which an exchange is carried out and administered. It can also be considered as a contractual format chosen to manage a transaction, ranging from a simple spot market transaction, to a long-term relational contract, to a transaction entirely within an organisation or firm (FitzRoy, 1998: 258).

Box 3.3. Governance structures and its linkages.

Transactions are carried out and administered within governance structures; such as markets, (hierarchical) organisations and other institutional arrangements. The results of these transactions are strongly influenced by the level of social embeddedness and the institutional environment. In the western world, the institutional environment has developed from a situation in which monarchs had the monopoly of violence to one with a constitution, a parliamentary democracy and formal rules of law. Concerning the latter, a distinction can be made between regulations under public and private law. The government role in public laws results in direct regulation, such as interdictions, obligations and licences. These prescriptions are direct in character. They have a direct and compulsory influence on the behaviour of people and they often impose considerable limitations on property rights. In private law regulations, the role of government is limited to legislation and to the role of facilitator for a private activities.

The spectrum of institutional arrangements

Williamson's transaction cost economics is also called the markets and hierarchies paradigm. In his view, markets are replaced by hierarchies when price coordination breaks down. His argument is consistent with Coase (1937)[22] who also argued that organisations are primarily characterised by *authority* and *fiat*, the capacity to give orders to agents. One of the earliest extensions of the markets and hierarchies framework was provided by Ouchi (1980). He suggested that a more appropriate framework would encompass markets, bureaucracies and clans. In this extension, hierarchies were substituted by bureaucracies, and clans were added as a third way of transacting. However, most economists would define 'bureaucracies' as a type of organisation (Ménard, 1995: 175). The substitutions of hierarchies by bureaucracies, is in accordance with organisation theorists (Ouchi, 1980: 130-132). According to Ménard (1995: 172), organisations cannot operate exclusively through command; they require also cooperation from their members, which involves their commitment to specific goals, their willingness to endorse or to transform exciting routines and their responsiveness to incentives deliberately designed to maintain or improve their participation.

Williamson (1987: 16) views markets and hierarchies (centrally planned organisations) as the two extremes of the spectrum of the *institutional arrangements*. Coordination is based on prices in the case of *markets* and is based on authority in the case of *hierarchies*. Authority involves the capacity to supervise and to control: it includes the right to make decisions (cf. Ménard, 1994: 237). Many economists subscribe to Williamson's distinction between markets and 'something else' as governance structure. However, they do not support his bipolar distinction between markets and 'something else' as hierarchies. Rather, they prefer the term 'organisations' (Ménard 1995: 170; Douma and Schreuder, 1998: 140; 2002: 163) or bureaucracies (Ouchi, 1980: 133-134), instead of hierarchies for the 'something else'. Moreover, they argue that Williamson has taken an extremely narrow view of non-market coordination. As said above, organisations cannot operate exclusively through authority and direct supervision. They also require the cooperation and commitment of their members. Within organisations there are also other coordination mechanisms, such as mutual adjustment and standardisation of norms (cf. Douma and Schreuders, 2002: 163). We discuss this in more depth in Chapter 8.

---

[22] See Putterman and Kroszner (1996: 89-104).

Box 3.4. A variety in organisations.

Most people work in an organisation of some kind; a firm, or perhaps a public sector organisation such as a hospital, a university or a government department. Almost everyone grows up in an organisation, called family. People are members of clubs. They are very common and important for carrying out activities. For example, we have clubs for sport, culture activities, but also for wildlife and landscape preservation. This means, there is a great variety in the groups in which people for a variety of reasons participate. Therefore, market and hierarchies are a too simple view on the real world given the wide variety of modes of organisation.

Williamson's original formulation of his markets and hierarchies paradigm has been criticised as being too narrow of an approach to modern organisations (see Milgrom and Roberts, 1992: 291; Hart, 1995: 29-30; Douma and Schreuder, 1998: 140; 2002: 163-164). The criticism pertains to two related points:

- It is too simple to see markets and hierarchies as the only two *governance structures* for transactions: there is a third way of transacting.
- Markets and hierarchies should not be viewed seen as two mutually exclusive *governance structures,* hybrid forms also exist.

Douma and Schreuder (1998: 140; 2002: 11, 163) argue that *markets* and *organisations* are the two different types of governance structures. However, they define the phenomenon *organisation* quite broadly. They make a bipolar distinction between markets and organisations, where the latter also includes various hybrid or mixed forms. This approach is closer to reality. Most people work in a certain organisational mode; there is a great variety of reasons why people participate in such organisations. The most important characteristic of such an organisation is that the members cooperate under some form of agreement. This agreement may be based on a formal contract, informal contract, mutual expectation, or just on bonds of kinship. Cooperation or interaction inside an organisation is often more important than a market exchange, although an organisation (like a firm) also has to interact with markets, as when inputs are purchased and outputs are sold (FitzRoy *et al.*, 1998: 1). In many cases, such an organisation does not actually stand completely independent of the market. Organisations such as firms often deal with the market in acquiring input and selling output.

These criticisms on Williamson's bipolar approach led to an extending and refining of his spectrum by introducing hybrid forms as part of the apparatus out of which transaction cost economics works (Williamson, 1991: 269). A hybrid form involves agreements or contractual relations characterised by specific combinations of market incentives and modalities of coordination involving some rules and directives. According to Ménard (1995: 175), hybrid forms often arise when the transactions are *asset specific,* but not specific enough to justify vertical integration, and or when the frequency of the transactions is rather low, and the transactions involve developing personal relationship among the actors. We explain asset specificity further in Chapter 5.

Based on the discussion above, it is good to ask oneself what the most important differences between the governance structures markets, hybrids and hierarchies are. In Table 3.1 we present the four most important attributes in the left column. For each of the three governance structures, we indicate the role of these attributes, denoting strong by (+++), semi-strong by (++), and weak by (+). It should be noticed that this is a stylised approach. In practice, it is possible that governance structures deviate from this more general approach.

The **first** attribute is the incentive intensity. Prices are regarded as highly powered incentives (Williamson, 1991: 275). The role of prices as an incentive mechanism is strong in a market, semi-strong in a hybrid and weak in a hierarchy. The **second** attribute is the administrative control. This is strong in a hierarchy. It refers, for example, to monitoring, and career rewards and penalties. The cooperation within a firm and unwanted (side) effects are checked and controlled by added

Table 3.1. Distinguishing attributes of market, hybrid and hierarchy governance structures (adapted from Williamson, 1991: 281).

	Governance structures		
	Market	Hybrid	Hierarchy
Attributes			
Incentive intensity	+++	++	+
Administrative control	+	++	+++
Adaptation by price coordination	+++	+(+)	+
Adaptation by non-price coordination	+	++	+++

internal controls (Williamson, 1991: 275). Such a control is weak in the market and semi-strong in a hybrid governance structure.

The problem of adaptation

According to Williamson (1991: 278), adaptation is seen as a central problem of economic organisation. Williamson orients his focus more on the adaptive abilities of the market and the internal organisation. The adaptive ability of the price function as a coordination mechanism is well-known in situations where changes in the demand or supply of goods are reflected in price changes, in response to which 'individuals participants .... [are] able to take the right action' (Hayek, 1945: 527 cited by Williamson (1991: 278). The adaptation to which Hayek refers are those for which prices serve as sufficient statistics such that 'changes in the demand or supply of a good are reflected in price changes, in which response individuals participants....'. Williamson (1993: 47-48) refers to this kind of adaptation as *autonomous adaptation*. Whereas the adaptation carried out by non-price coordination refers more to internal coordinating mechanisms. Finally, according to Williamson, the adaptation power in a hybrid is typically less strong than in a hierarchy, because of the lack of power of control.

However, the bipolar approach of Williamson – markets versus hierarchies – does not acknowledge the large variety of organisational modes that comprise a range of governance structures. To understand this variety we to take into account the mix of the applied coordination mechanisms. This will be more extensively discussed in Chapter 8.

As explained above, one fundamental criticism on Williamson is that his approach does not acknowledge the richness of coordination mechanisms; in particular, the forms of non-price coordination are more diverse and complex than authority. While Williamson's argument is consistent with Coase, who argued that organisations are characterised primary by authority, we argue that more attention should be given to coordination mechanisms used within organisations. For example, within organisations there are also other coordination mechanisms, such as mutual adjustment and standardisation of norms. This means we need a more adequate elaboration of the non-price coordination. In our real world a variety of non-price coordination exists.

For that reason, we will distinguish **four** groups of coordination mechanisms. This classification of the coordination mechanisms in these four groups is based on the current state of the NIE theory and is supported by literature (cf. Hennart, 1993: 351; Borgen and Hegrenes, 2005:12-13).

1. **'invisible hand'**;
   The 'invisible hand' refers to the price as coordination mechanism; the (autonomous) adaptation by the price as coordination mechanism is the invisible hand. As shown in Table 3.1, the role of the price as coordination mechanism is strong in markets, semi-strong in hybrids, but sometimes weak in certain hybrids, e.g. a voluntary club, and weak in hierarchies.

2. **'handshake'**;
   The coordination mechanism can often consist of elements such as mutual adjustment and common values and norms of people working together in certain organisations. This group of coordination mechanism is called the handshake group.

3. **'handbook'**;
   The coordination mechanism the 'handbook' consists of rules, directives and safeguards. This coordination mechanism is important for contracts, which belong to the hybrids.

4. **'visible hand'**.
   In a hierarchy the coordination mechanism consists of authority, fiat and direct supervision. We denote this coordination mechanism the visible hand.

As expressed in Table 3.1, the adaptation power in a hybrid is typically less strong than in hierarchy, because of the lack power of control. In the view of Williamson, the strongest adaptation power is derived from authority. However, hybrids often make use of a combination of coordination mechanisms such as the handshake and handbook. In the market as governance structure, the adaptation carried out by non-prices coordination is typically weak. This does not mean that such adaptation is completely absent, because the market is embedded to some degree in social relationships (incl. social capital, values and norms) and the formal rules of institutional environment.

Of course, this embedding holds for all the governance structures. Concerning the formal rules, a distinction can be made between regulations under public and private law. The government role in public law results in direct regulation. They have a direct and compulsory influence on the behaviour of producers and consumers and considerable limitations on property rights. In private law regulations, the role of government is limited to legislation and facilitating private activities (see Box 3.3).

Based on the discussion above, it is clear that we must distinguish between governance structures and coordination mechanisms. Governance structures are more than a single coordination mechanism. For example, they also consist of a supporting structure for carrying out transactions or a certain structure for administrating the transactions. However, the type of governance structures – even if they make use of a mix of them – is strongly characterised by the coordination mechanisms. This is also expressed in Table 3.1. Even the market needs some elements of other coordination mechanisms, such as the handshake.

Box 3.5. The relationship between governances structure and coordination mechanisms.

In Chapter 8 we present a scheme to demonstrate the function of the four groups coordination mechanisms, grouped as the 'invisible hand', the 'handshake', the 'handbook' and 'visible hand'. We also go into more detail about the relationship between governance structures and coordination mechanisms. There are several reasons why the relationship between governance structures and coordination mechanisms deserves special attention. Firstly, there is no one-to-one correspondence between the two, because certain governance structures can combine different coordination mechanisms or make use of a mix of them. Secondly, the distinction between governance structures and coordination mechanisms is the key to understanding the different governance structures and the possibility of combining coordination mechanisms into governance structures. Thirdly, coordination is a central issue in a governance structure. It includes what needs to be coordinated and how coordination is achieved in governance structures such as spot markets, firms and contracts.

The function and purpose of governance structures

Governance structures often emerge in response to various transactional considerations; optimising individuals choose the most efficient institutional arrangement or governance structure for carrying out transactions in a specific environment. This is revealed in the value created by governance structures, including the *quasi-rents* resulting from the use of specific assets. *Quasi-rents* are the return of an asset in excess of the minimum needed to keep the asset in its current use (FitzRoy *et al.*, 1998: 305). This has been explained in Section 2.3 and 2.4. It is assumed that people prefer a governance structure that enables them to keep or to capture the quasi-rents.

It is very difficult to give a fully univocal definition of governance structures. A better way is to look at the common elements as given in the beginning of the this section. **First** of all, a **governance structure** can be described as an *institutional arrangement*. They are embedded in the informal rules of the social embeddedness and formal rules of the institutional environment, as the play of the game.

Secondly, a governance structure in its most simple form is a *transaction mechanism* for carrying out exchange (such as a market). Often, a governance structure includes more; it consists of the rules by which an exchange is carried out, a certain structure for administrating the transactions. It functions as a supporting structure to foster efficiency in transacting (cf. Hendrikse, 2003: 243), and it has often a legal entity, such as a firm. Most governance structures include not only a coordination mechanism but also a motivation mechanism. This motivation mechanism can based on extrinsic or intrinsic motivation or a mixture of both[23].

All these given definitions have in common the idea that – even in its most simple form, such as a market – governance structures are supporting structures or mechanisms for carrying out transactions. They often contain a certain structure for administrating the transactions and

---

[23] See for the explanation Section 4.3.

Box 3.6. The market as governance structure.

The most well-known arrangement or *governance structure* is the market. Ménard (1995: 170) defines the **market** as: *a market is a specific institutional arrangement consisting of rules and conventions that make possible a large number of voluntary transfers of property rights on a regular basis, these reversible transfers being implemented and enforced through a specific mechanism of coordination and motivation, the competitive price system.* In this definition the governance structure as transaction mechanism is at the centre.

are situated within a certain level of social embeddedness and the institutional environment (cf. Ménard, 1995: 175). We find these elements back in a market, firms or organisations, and contracts.

Applied to a firm, a governance structure is concerned with how decisions are made, i.e. the exercise of control rights (by authority and guidance) and income rights. Examples of topics relevant for governance structures include the allocation of property rights, the capital structure, the reward system, the board of directors, the pressure of large investors, the competition in the product and labour markets, the organisational structure, the (management) accounting system and so on. The **control rights** also include who may decide over the use of the asset or the organisation or firm. The **income rights** determine who receives income from the use of the assets. In a governance structure such as the firm, special attention is given to the rules and constraints structuring the ex-post bargaining process over the residual income. That is the amount of return that is left over after everyone has been paid. This could include the total quasi-rent or a large part of it. When taken together, these rules and constraints determine or leave open important questions such as who has the residual control rights and who is able to capture the residual income.

In addition to the firm, a governance structure can also be considered as a contractual format chosen to manage a transaction, ranging from a simple spot market transaction, to a long-term relation contract, to a transaction entirely within an organisation (FitzRoy, 1998: 258). Contracts outside a firm, as a contractual relationship between two parties, are also governance structures. They can be used – just like a market – for the transfer of property rights. For example, a land

Box 3.7. Firms as governance structures.

Firms and, more generally, organisations, have structural properties that strongly influence how agents behave, and what type of decisions they make. The term *firm* can easily be broadened to an organisation. Many decisions to create or allocate resources are made by organisations or at least within organisations. Ménard (1995: 172) defines an **organisation** as: *an organisation is an institutional arrangement designed to make possible the conscious and deliberate coordination of activities within identifiable boundaries, in which members associate on a regular basis through a set of explicit or implicit agreements, commit themselves to collective actions for the purpose of creating and allocating resources and capabilities by a combination of command and cooperation.*

lease contract or rent contract for a house or a office means that property rights (e.g. the use rights) are transferred from the owner to the tenant; contracts are transaction mechanisms for these property rights.

Within each of these three concepts of a governance structure – markets, contracts and firms, there is a certain commonality and internal consistency. They differ in the manner of coordination and the reason for their existence. The manner of coordination indicates which particular means are used for the implementation of activities within each basic concept. The reason for existence shows the specific functions of these devices, whether implicit or explicit.

In reality, there is a broad variety of governance structures, with differences in the reasons for existence and working. The most important reasons are (1) creation of value; (2) distribution of the quasi-rent; (3) changes in the social embeddedness and gaps in institutional environment.

Governance structure and the creation of value

The most important reason why we have governance structures is to create value. Otherwise they would not exist. This value is often more than only a monetary one. The type of governance structure also has implications for the creation of value, because it determines *the efficiency of the* ex-post *bargaining process* concerning the quasi-rents. It is sometimes said that there is no role for a governance structure in the environment described by the Coase theorem, because bargaining is assumed to be efficient and costless. However, in reality there are often inefficiencies in the bargaining process, like transaction costs, lack of power, and lack of information. A governance structure has an impact on the nature and size of these inefficiencies because it has consequences for:
- The information asymmetries between the parties.
- The co-ordination and motivation costs.
- The extent of financial restrictions on the parties.
- The degree of alignment between the parties.

Governance structure and the distribution of the quasi-rents

The type of the governance structure also has consequences for the bargaining over and distribution of quasi-rents. The outcome of the bargaining process is determined by:
- Bargaining power of the involved parties.
- **Specific** contractual agreements concerning control rights (based on observable and verifiable variables) and the allocation of property rights about assets;

In general, control rights are the rights to make any decisions concerning an asset that are not explicitly controlled by law (cf. Milgrom and Roberts, 1992: 289). **Specific control rights** are those rights specified by contracts or rules of law. These rights (and the accompanying obligations) can be observed and verified, for instance by a court of law.
- The **residual control rights** (or residual decision rights) are the rights to make decisions concerning the use, returns, transfer of an asset that are not explicitly controlled by law or assigned by another contract; the question here is: who has the residual control rights and

who is able to capture the residual income? If the distribution of a quasi-rent is not specified *ex-ante* by contract or by rules it can be considered as a kind of residual income[24].

- Availability of alternatives (i.e. the level of sunk costs, sunk investments and lock-in effects).
- Quality of the institutional environment (efficiency and effectiveness of the juridical system, enforcement mechanisms for complying with contracts, conflict resolving mechanisms, professional norms, transparency of the quality of the producer of potential customers, and so on).

These elements directly affect the interests of the involved parties. If the involved parties in a governance structure – e.g. a firm or organisation – have different interests because of:

- different shares in cost and benefits;
- different tax regimes;
- different liabilities (see Box 3.8).

This will influence the relationship between generating and distributing the residual income. In other words, the way in which the quasi-rent is distributed (*ex-post*) has major consequences for the investment behaviour *ex-ante*.

Residual control rights and residual income are not only important in firms but also within each governance structure, especially contractual relationships. There are different types of contracts and different ways for classifying contracts (see Chapter 7). One striking difference exists between complete and incomplete contracts. Complete contracts incorporate all relevant information and specify a course of action for every possible contingency which may occur in the future. If complete contracts can be designed without costs, then all decisions are taken *ex-ante* and the complete quasi-rent is distributed *ex-ante*. According to Hendrikse (2003: 243), in such cases a governance structure adds no value i.e. the choice of governance structure does not matter. If

---

[24] Quasi-rents and residual incomes have a different background; the quasi-rent results from fixed assets and asset specificity, and the residual income from incomplete contracts. This will be discussed in Chapter 5 and 7. However, both explain the distribution issues in a governance structure.

Box 3.8. Difference of interests: debt and equity.

Many firms are financed by a combination of debt and equity. The debt holders – banks, the purchasers of the firm's bonds, input suppliers who offer credit – are lenders. They provide cash in return for a promise to be repaid a fixed amount (perhaps with interest) at a later date. The equity holders get to keep whatever profits are left after paying the dept obligation (remark: there is a difference interest). The equity holder will favour risky investment. They will win big amounts if the investments work out. The debt holders just get their promised fixed payments. If the investment loses money, some of the losses may fall on the creditors who are not fully repaid. It means there is a conflict of interest between the equity and debt holder. If the investment fails the losses are carried by the debt holders. For that reason, debt holders will be more reserved in their approval of risky investments. An ultimate measure for them will be to force the firm into bankruptcy.

---

costless complete contracts are possible, then all possible conflicts could be resolved *ex-ante*. This means a simple governance structure is sufficient; there would be no quasi-surplus and therefore there is no need for *ex-post* bargaining. However, as will be discussed in Chapter 7, designing and concluding complete contracts is rarely possible.

The incompleteness of contracts creates a difference between ex-ante decisions (regarding starting a relationship and interest in specific assets) and ex-post ones (when the residual income is divided). The importance and meaning of a governance structure is crucial if incompleteness of contracts is involved. If an incomplete contract is part of a governance structure, the governance structure can allocate control rights in circumstances for which the contract has made no provisions. This means there is a role for a governance structure *ex-post* if it is costly or impossible to design contracts based on observable future variables. This is the case if certain aspects are not specified. Then there will be an *ex-post* quasi-rent which has to be divided. *Ex-post* investment decisions will determine the size of the quasi-rent (which could have the characteristic of a residual income)[25].

If – in a situation with a market as a governances structure and perfect competition – no residual income is generated, then the competitive nature of the market ensures that the price is equal to the marginal costs and to the marginal return. In this case, there is no use for a governance structure to structure the bargaining process, because the quasi-rent to be bargained about is equal to zero (Hendrikse, 2003: 245). Also if the quasi-rent would have been allocated completely *ex-ante*, then there is nothing to bargain about. This assumes perfect competition and complete contacts. However more typically, we have **incomplete** contracts; consequently you don't know *ex-ante*, if there will be a residual income *ex-post*.

A governance structure also has – besides the creation of value and the distribution of quasi-rents – an impact on the value of the total surplus, because it determines *the level and the distribution of risk*. One aspect in the evaluation of the efficiency of a governance structure is the way it allocates risk to the most risk-tolerant party. The above implies that the purpose of a governance structure is to:

- Provide the most efficient institutional arrangement or governance structures for carrying out transactions. This includes maximising the size of the quasi-rents of assets, while resolving the hold-up problem.
- Maximise the incentives to generate value-enhancing investments, while incentives for developing inefficient influence activities have to be minimised.
- Define the relative position of parties within in particular governance structure. This position depends on bargaining power and having the residual control rights over the bundle of the property rights of the used assets and the ability to capture the residual income. This includes taking care for a fair distribution of the quasi-rent and the residual income.
- Minimise risk, and to allocate the residual risk to the least risk-averse party.

---

[25] A quasi-surplus and residual income are not always restricted to only money.

The origin of governance structures: changes in social embeddedness and gaps in institutional environment

Our real world shows a large variety of forms of governance involved in activities that are neither pure markets nor pure hierarchies. This variety means that we not only should focus on the 'pure categories' but also on the continuum of hybrid governance structures between these forms. Above it is said that governance structures emerge in response to various transactional considerations. However, we also see governance structures come into being as a result of a change in the social embeddedness or a gap in the institutional environment.

A change in social embeddedness can arise as a result of the public good dilemma – in short, a decreased supply and an increased demand for public goods, such as environmental goods. For example, people can become aware of the increasing importance of preserving wildlife, landscape and rural amenities. This can lead to a change in people's values or preferences, followed by a change in society's reference level. The *reference-level* can be the *status quo situation*, or a standard or expectation of the provision-level of environmental goods (cf. Hannemann, 1999: 75). In other words, it depends on what people find 'normal' or as what it should be. One reaction could be that a group of people start to take care for nature and landscape in their surroundings by self-organisation; by founding a club oriented on preserving nature and landscape. The club is in this case the governance structure. The self-organisation in the club reflects the shift in the emphasis of people's concerns about environmental goods.

Another reason for an emerging governance structure could be a change in the institutional environment such as a policy change that leaves an institutional gap. For example, a new government regulation may be introduced that has negative consequences for a certain group of people. The institutional gap thesis states that new associations or organisations emerge in response to institutional shortcomings in existing governance structures (Bergeman, 1996: 43). In such cases, new organisations are created to fill in the institutional gap and resolve transaction cost problems that arise as a result of a change or gap in the institutional environment. The club is an example of a governance structure that can be a useful alternative for carrying out and coordinating certain activities that are consistent with the regulation, yet with fewer negative externalities. In Section 3.7 we present the theoretical background of the club and its application for preserving nature and landscape.

Summarising, getting the institutions right does not only mean getting the social embeddedness and institutional environment right, but also getting the governance structure right. Markets and firms, in the form of a hierarchy, can be seen as the two polar cases of the spectrum of governance structures. The market makes use of market incentives (= prices). Within a hierarchy the coordination can, in the most extreme case, take place through 'planning, command and control'; the decision-making is hierarchical and based on authority, fiat or direct supervision. In-between these two governance structures we see hybrid forms. These hybrid forms often work with a mix of coordination mechanisms, such as prices, mutual adjustment, common values and norms, and other modalities of coordination such as rules. Examples of hybrid governance structures are contracts, cooperatives, and clubs. Markets, organisations and hybrid forms are media (i.e. institutional arrangements) or supporting structures for carrying out transactions. Literature on transaction costs has elaborated the choice between these institutional arrangements. We discuss this further in Chapter 5.

For the new institutional economists, the description and explanation of the institutional levels of analysis: social embeddedness, institutional environment, governance structures, and the analysis of their effects are important areas of study. When taken together, the linkages between these levels formulate the informal and formal rules as the *rules of the game* and different types of governance structures as the *play of the game* (including the market, different types of contracts and firms, the connected the corporate governance discussion). In this way, new institutionalists are getting involved in neoclassical explanatory variables: optimising individuals choose in a specific environment the most efficient institutional arrangement or governance structures for carrying out transactions. This is the link with the transaction cost theory. This theory predicts that the choice of the governance structure depends on the amount and the distribution of the quasi-rents. This is the subject of the Chapter 5.

3.7 Applications of the theory: the 'club' as governance structure and environmental cooperatives

Some important characteristics of clubs

Clubs are very common and are also an important mode of organisation for carrying out activities. We have clubs for sport, culture activities, but also for wildlife and landscape preservation. As explained above, clubs can also arise as a result of a change in the social embeddedness or a gap in the institutional environment; the club as self-organisation or as an alternative for government intervention. The club has some important characteristics as a governance structure. If production costs are shared and the good is purely private, the appropriate structure of a private club is being analysed. The focus of our analysis is the sharing of partly excludable and partly rivalry public goods. A number of aspects of such a club deserve attention[26].

First, members choose to join voluntarily, because they anticipate a net benefit from membership. The utility or expected income jointly derived from membership and from the use of other goods must exceed the utility associated with non-membership status. Furthermore, the net gain in utility or expected income from membership exceeds or equals membership fees or toll payments (Cornes and Sandler, 1996: 347).

Second, clubs involve sharing in the use of an impure public good, the use of the service of the club such as an environmental club, and sharing in the benefits. Sharing often leads to a partial rivalry of benefits as a larger membership crowd one another, detracting from the quality of the service received (Cornes and Sandler, 1996: 348). Crowding and congestion imply that one user's utilisation of the club good, decreases the benefits or quality of the services still available to the remaining users. As such, crowding or congestion depends on the measure of utilisation, which

---

[26] The types of the goods in terms of excludability and rivalry also influence the choice of the governance structure. In case of non-excludable and non-rival goods the market as governances structure will fail. Thus not each governance structure is suitable for these types of goods.

Box 3.9. What is a club?

The club theory has been applied to a wide range of problems including recreation facilities, national parks, wilderness areas, national infrastructure and international organisations. According to Cornes and Sandler (1996: 347) a club is a voluntary group of individuals who derive mutual benefits from sharing one or more of the following: (1) production costs of activities and services; (2) the members' characteristics (e.g. they like playing soccer or golf, the members have land, are farmers, etc.), or (3) a good characterised by (excludable) benefits. These benefits can be internal, which means only for the members and other people are excluded from these benefits (e.g. a card club). However, it also possible that benefits of the club are external. This means that also non-members can enjoy of the benefits (e.g. a club that preserves environmental goods).

could include the number of the members, the total number of the members who use the club's facilities, or the number of visitors to the areas or provisions of the club (cf. Cornes and Sandler, 1996: 348). A club can ration use effectively by means of internal rules as long as the club is small, and the people meet sufficiently frequently and can therefore exercise mutual internal controls over property use.

Internal rules evolve from human experience and incorporate solutions that have tended to serve people best in the past. Examples are customs, good manners, common norms and values. Violations of internal rules are normally sanctioned informally (Kasper and Streit, 1998: 31). The internal rules are more important for cooperatives that are relatively young and small. When clubs grow, there are increasing problems of internal information and informal control. Organisation costs rise as more formal rules have to be implemented (Kasper and Streit, 1998: 182). The coordination mechanism consists of mix of the handshake and (for more formal clubs) the handbook, such as rules, the motivation is often largely based on intrinsic motivation, and for a small part on extrinsic ones.

Club congestion may assume diverse forms: long files, long waits, slower and less services, and a lower quality of the services. As membership size expands, both costs and benefits arise: costs involve increased congestion, while benefits result from cost reduction owing to the sharing of the provision expense associated with the club good. By adding a cost offset to the benefits derived from expanding the membership size, crowding leads to finite membership. This is a second characteristic serving to distinguish club goods from pure public good. For the latter, crowding costs are zero (Cornes and Sandler (1996: 348).

A third distinguishing characteristic of club goods is the existence of non-members. For pure public goods, all individuals can be members without crowding taking place, so that non members do not exist. For club goods, non-members to a given club have two options: they can join another club providing the same good, or they may not join any club offering the club good. If all individuals in the entire population are allocated among a set of clubs with no overlapping or non-assigned individuals, the population is partitioned into a set of clubs. The number of clubs then becomes an important choice variable. When, however, some individuals do not belong to any club supplying the club good, then the population is not partitioned (Cornes and Sandler, 1996: 349).

A fourth distinguishing feature of club goods is the presence of an *exclusion mechanism,* whereby non-members and non-payers can be barred. Without such a mechanism, there would be no incentive for members to join and to pay dues and other fees. The associated cost of operation and provision of an exclusion mechanism must be less than the benefits gained from allocating the shared good within a club arrangement. An analysis of the costs for erection, operation and provision of an exclusion mechanism is important. If, for example, exclusion is not perfect owing to cost considerations, then free riders may utilise the club good. The design of the exclusion mechanism, in terms of penalties and fees, needs to account for providing the proper incentive to both members and free riders. An important question would be if – based on exclusion cost arguments – an exclusion mechanism should include monitoring. The institutional form of a club may be tied to exclusion cost consideration (Cornes and Sandler, 1996: 350).

A fifth distinguishing attribute of club goods concerns a dual decision. Since exclusion is practised, members with user privileges must be distinguished from non-members. Moreover, the provision quantity of the shared good must be determined. Insofar as the membership decision affects the provision choice, and vice versa, neither can be determined independently. For pure public goods, however, only the provision decision needs to be considered – the membership is the entire population (Cornes and Sandler, 1996: 350). So we have to distinguish between the membership decision and the provision decision.

A final feature that differentiates club goods from pure public goods concerns optimality. Voluntary provision of pure public goods is typically associated with a Nash equilibrium that is sub-optimal; thus government provision may be required. In the case of club goods, members or firms can form clubs that collect tolls through an exclusion mechanism. Under a wide variety of circumstances, these clubs can achieve Pareto-optimal results without resorting to government provision (Cornes and Sandler, 1996: 350). When the club decisions are represented as a cooperative action, the resulting outcome will be a Pareto optimum for the members. As noted earlier, members belong to a club because they perceive a net benefit from membership.

Yet the net benefit from membership is not only derived from the Pareto optimality of the endogenous costs and benefits of environmental cooperatives. Rather, the threat of exogenous competing interests and their potential cost effects on the asset value of agriculture land may also fuel the perception that the marginal costs of club membership are lower than the costs of

---

Box 3.10. Institutional form of clubs.

In this literature several possibilities are mentioned for the institutional form of 'clubs', ranging from associations, foundations to cooperatives. The chosen form has consequences for the control rights. For example, an association has members and they have voting rights, and by that some control rights. However, a foundation has no members; this has consequence for the involvement and the control rights of the people. Membership for a cooperative requires a deposit or a bond in addition to a membership fee.

the external threat. Thus, as long as asset values are high and an external threat exists that may reduce the value of farming assets, farmers will likely be motivated to organise in order to reduce the threat of competing interests.

An application of the club theory: environmental cooperatives

In addition to marketable goods such as food, raw materials and ornamental plants, the agricultural sector also produces 'non-marketable' goods like wildlife and landscape. These are called external effects. They are the result of a specific way of using agricultural land. Agricultural landscapes such as 'small-scale landscapes' – characterised by small fields surrounded by hedges or wooded bank, or peatland areas with narrow plots and wide ditches – were a by-product (or joint production) of farming when land use was relatively capital-poor, small-scale and labour-intensive.

Within the last few decades – as a result of a high level of mechanisation, intensification of land use and specialisation at farm and at regional level in agriculture – there was a deterioration of wildlife and landscape and the quality of soil, water and air. While agriculture experienced these developments, higher incomes increased the demand for wildlife and landscape, and for leisure and outdoor recreation. Thus, during the time when the supply of wildlife and landscape decreased, the demand for these amenities actually increased.

The changes on the demand side are a result of changes in the social embeddedness level and the institutional environment. The changes in the social embeddedness meant a change in the values and preferences of people; famers should now pay more attention to nature and landscape, and change in the institutional environment has revealed itself in more government regulation. This implies that the rules of the game for the agricultural sector have changed. The agricultural sector has had to develop new institutional arrangements to meet these changes in the both the social embeddedness level and the institutional environment. One way of achieving this was the environmental cooperative for farmers as a supporting structure to implement and operationalise the changes of the demand side. The environmental cooperative for farmers can be seen as application of the 'club theory'. The 'club theory' gives a theoretical basis for the study of allocation efficiency of quasi -public goods such as nature and landscape. For more background information see Slangen and Polman (2002: 69-90) and Polman and Slangen (2002: 91-111).

In the Netherlands, the first environmental cooperatives arose in the early nineties of the last century. In 2006 there were already approximately 130 environmental cooperatives. For two

> **Box 3.11. Rules of the games.**
>
> The demand for preserving nature and landscape implies that the rules of the game for the agricultural sector are changing. These consist of formal and informal rules. Consequently, the agricultural sector has had to develop new institutional arrangements (e.g. environmental cooperatives) to meet changes in the social embeddednes level and the institutional environment. The governance structure 'environmental cooperative' as a 'club' is a way of reacting to a change in the rules of the game.

reasons it is at the moment more common to speak about 'agricultural nature associations'. First of all, most of them have the legal status of an association, and second the activities of the farmer-members are more oriented on nature and landscape preservation. Nevertheless, we prefer the term *environmental cooperatives* as a kind of brand name. Approximately 70% of the environmental cooperatives is an association, about 20% a foundation and about 9% a cooperative. In total, the environmental cooperatives have 18,000 members of which about 80% are farmers and the rest is non-farmers. About 20% of all land-tied farmers are a member of an environment cooperative.

One application of the 'club' theory is to let farmers take care of the preservation of nature and landscape at the local level. This objective can be pursued through organised cooperation between independent firms. The organised cooperation can be a cooperative association called an 'environmental cooperative'. This approach can be applied as a correction of market failure or an alternative to government intervention. Its advantages include the greater acceptability by farmers, a more effective and efficient approach than those of some alternatives, and lower transaction costs.

An environmental cooperative acting as cooperative association is a governance structure that acts within the existing economic system to correct for market failure. This economic entity is empowered to make decisions solely with reference to its coordination tasks. The resulting risks are borne by the economic subjects. Furthermore an environmental cooperative can be seen as a provision for social regulation with a view to promoting and institutionalising processes of persuasion in society.

The cooperation could address itself to the limitation of environmental pollution by emissions, mineral losses and harmful effects on nature and landscape, or more generally to the preservation and improvement of environmental goods. To keep the environmental cooperative going the cooperation agreement must be attractive for the participating firms. This means that coordinated actions must lead to a better result than uncoordinated action. In addition, environmental cooperatives must not lead to loss of welfare, which means that the benefits to the public must be greater than the costs.

From this and also from an analytical point of view (to realise coordination and motivation of activities) an institutional arrangement like an environmental cooperative should consist of an organised system of goals and instruments that shape the choice-set of farmers. Three main objectives, based on club theory, can be determined for an environmental cooperative:
1. The preservation of nature and landscape and the quality of soil, water and air, summarised as 'preservation of the environmental goods'.
2. The activities of the environmental cooperative must lead to economic benefits for the members. In other words, the economic results must be better than without environmental cooperative.
3. The environmental cooperative must be economically efficient, e.g. lead to a rise in welfare.

The second and third objective can also be seen as prerequisites.

Box 3.12. Coordination in environmental cooperatives.

Activities within organisations are often coordinated without the use of the market. This applies to production of goods and services within firms and government, for consumption within family households or other forms of households, for activities in the fields of recreation and religion. In all these cases there is a form of organisation in which certain activities have to be coordinated. But how does the coordination take place? As well as hierarchical organisations, based on authority, flat and therefore horizontal organisations exist.

In a club the coordination can be based on mutual adjustment, common values and norms, commitment, trust and reputation. These forms of coordination are found in organisations which can be characterised as a network in which people interact in a non-hierarchical way such as in *environmental cooperatives for farmers* (cf. Slangen and Polman, 2002: 81).

An interesting question is: how can we typify the institutional arrangement or governance structure *environmental cooperative for farmers*? On the one hand, an environmental cooperative is an organisation. On the other, it has a relationship with its members who maintain their private property rights and who remain mainly independent farmers. A number of questions arise regarding these contractual relationships. What are the characteristics of the contracts between members and the organisation? How are the property rights of the 'organisation' and the 'members' specified? Who has the residual control rights and who is able to capture the residual income?

Reasons for environmental cooperatives

The first reason why we need a new institutional arrangement such as an environmental cooperative is due to the problems of non-rivalry and non-excludability. Both are reasons for market failure. Typically, wildlife and landscape are characterised by non-rivalry (in consumption and in production, the latter because of the joint production), and to some extent non-excludability because of incomplete property rights. An environmental cooperative for farmers is an institutional arrangement to reduce the cost of delineating the property rights and to extract some income from the asset. Market failure creates an incentive for producers to react collectively. They need an institutional arrangement as a supporting structure for coordination and motivation. The increase in the income potential of an asset has another effect or incentive on the behaviour of its owners. It increases the aggregate gains from cooperation among them, which in return is expected to lead to better delineation of the asset (Barzel 1997: 95). Hence an environmental cooperative for farmers is not only an important institutional arrangement but it is also an important incentive for better delineation of property rights, to generate income, and visa versa.

A second reason that justifies an environmental cooperative (as an institutional arrangement) is that individual farmers need an institutional mechanism to countervail opportunistic behaviour and hold-up problems. The core of the hold-up problem consists of asset specificity together with incomplete contracting. The problem arises in a situation in which each contracting party worries about being forced to accept disadvantageous terms later, after it has made an investment, or worries that its investment may be devalued by the actions of others. The party that is forced to accept a worsening of the effective terms of the relationship once it has made an investment has been 'held up' (Milgrom and Roberts, 1992: 136).

A third reason that justifies environmental cooperatives is that such an institutional arrangement could be used to develop countervailing power of control, building up oligopolistic or spatial monopolistic market power. If farmers pay more attention to wildlife and landscape they will sacrifice gains, on the one hand, from specialising in more regular or prevailing agriculture. On the other hand, the attribute wildlife and landscape is an impure public good or common good. It lies, according to Barzel (1997: 5), in the public domain. The (opportunity) cost for the farmer to produce wildlife and landscape is a private cost and the benefits of the attribute wildlife and landscape are an impure public good. This means that the property rights are different and vaguely defined, which leads to conflicts over the residual control rights and the residual incomes.

The fourth reason is transaction costs. The environmental cooperative for farmers is an institutional arrangement to reduce the transaction cost of delineating property rights and to extract some income from the asset wildlife and landscape. According to transaction cost theory, the **characteristics of human decision-makers** and the **environmental characteristics of the transaction** determine the comparative advantages of a governance structure, i.e. the environmental cooperative. Given the characteristics of the involved goods 'nature and landscape' the environmental cooperative, as a club, is an efficient governance structure for carrying out the connected transactions.

The last reason that justifies environmental cooperatives is also connected with market failure. Traditionally, market failure forms an argument for government intervention. Even if there is a justification for government intervention, an analysis of this interference is necessary. Such analysis casts light on the functioning of the government itself; after all the government can also fail. The reason for government failure can be lack of information, the character of the political decision making process, the bureaucratic way of production, or disincentives arising from taxes, regulation, levies and subsidies (Schram *et al.*, 2000: 32). For impure public goods, an environmental cooperative as a *club* could be an alternative to government provision.

Governance structure and coordination mechanism of an environmental cooperative

As said, the governance structure of an environmental cooperative is a club. The characteristics have been discussed above. The legal status is typically defined as an association. According to Box 3.12 the environmental cooperatives can also be characterised as a network organisation in which people interact in a non-hierarchical way. Moreover, they are mostly self-organised groups. The governance structure *environmental cooperative for farmers* is on the one hand an organisation. But, on the other, it has a relationship with its members who maintain their private property rights and who remain mainly as independent farmers. Often there are management contracts between the environment cooperative and its members. A number of questions arise regarding these relationships: what are the characteristics of the contracts between members and the organisation? How are the property rights of the 'organisation' and the 'members' specified? The answers to these questions depend on the functioning of the environmental cooperatives in practise.

Most environmental cooperatives are flat and horizontal organisations. The coordination within the environmental cooperative is based on common values and norms, and mutual adjustment. It means that the applied coordination mechanism within this governance structure is the 'handshake'. The coordination mechanism for contracts between the environmental cooperative and farmer-members for preserving nature and landscape is based on a combination of the 'handshake' and the 'handbook'. Motivation is for keeping the rules often largely based on a mix of intrinsic and extrinsic motivation[27].

Box 3.13. Key concepts of Chapter 3.

Invisible hand government	Non-price coordination
Grabbing hand government	Handshake
Dimensions of good government	Handbook
Social embeddedness	Control rights
Social capital	Specific control rights
Trust	Residual control rights
Reciprocity	Quasi-rent
Institutional environment	Residual income
Governance structures	Distribution of risk
Market	Club as governance structure
Hierarchies	Characteristics of a club
Hybrids	Exclusion mechanism
Contracts	Club congestion
Coordination mechanisms	
Visible hand	

Appendix 3.1. Framework for analysing institutions and designing better institutions

Institutions are very important for the economic, environmental and social dimensions of sustainable rural development (SRD). In this part we present a conceptual framework developed for analysing the state of institutions and for designing new or better institutions for realising sustainable development of the rural areas. This approach has been used in the project Sustainable Agriculture and Rural areas in Central and Eastern Europe[28] (CEESA). A distinction is made between the social capital, formal and informal rules of institutional environment and institutional arrangements. The framework takes determinants or proxy-variables into account on five different levels that may account for good performance in realising SRD.

The **first level** looks at social capital. Important indicators include the size of social capital, level of reciprocity, intensity of civic participation, the informal rules, reputation, commitment and trust,

---

[27] For more background information see Slangen and Polman (2002: 69-90) and Polman and Slangen (2002: 91-111).

[28] For background information, see Slangen *et al.* (2001 and 2004).

and time consistency of the government and of people. The **second level** looks at the government performance. Indicators or proxy-variables are largely based on macro economic variables. Important indicators on this level include GNP per capita, inflation rate, budget deficit of the government, and public dept in % of GNP. The **third level** looks at the agricultural sector and rural areas. Indicators are based more on sector and regional level variables. Important variables include government expenditure and investment in SD, share of agricultural sector and rural activities in % of GNP, share of population and employment of rural activities of total population and employment. The **fourth level** focuses on the formal rules of the institutional environment for SA. Important indicators include the number and quality of environmental laws protecting valuable areas, property rights and land (and water) use, monitoring, sanctions and conflict resolving mechanisms (e.g. special courts for land and water use dispute), and a social security system for people who have lost their job in the agricultural sector or other rural activities. The **final level** focuses on institutional arrangements, asking what kind of institutional arrangements are used and whether they are sufficient to realise SRD.

The level of social capital has been investigated by survey questions concerning: trust in people, government, processes, participating in the society by passive and active membership in different types or organisations. Related to this it is very useful to look at site of the World Bank (www.worldbank.org). The informal rules of the institutional environment have their bond with people and are often part of social capital. Norms and values become social capital when they are able to solve social dilemmas, such as realising SRD.

The formal rules of the institutional environment important for realising SRD, consist of private and public law, government policy and regulation for protecting the environment, and property rights. It is important to know what types of formal rules there are, and how they perform. Recent literature emphasises the role of the government or government performance in institutions. Good government has been shown to contribute to the economic development of European countries over the last millennium, to growth across countries over the last 40 years, and to the successful transition from socialism to capitalism. So government performance is also important for realising SRD. Determinants of good government on a macro level can used to deduce the determinants for good government regarding SRD.

Figure 3.3 combines the social capital, institutional environment, and the institutional arrangements into one framework. Their performances determine the opportunities for realising Sustainable Development consisting of economic, social or socio-economic and environmental dimensions. Moreover, the framework in Figure 3.3 looks at different levels of determinants that may account for a good performance in realising SRD.

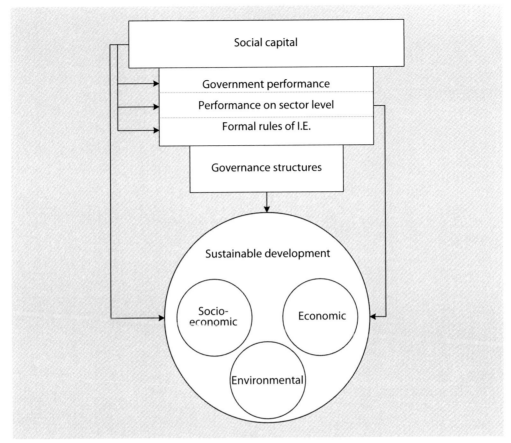

Figure 3.3. Framework of analysing institutional setting for sustainable development.

4. Information and behavioural economics, and the role of incentives

4.1 Introduction

In the neoclassical economic model of perfect competition, perfect information is assumed; that is to say all necessary information is included in the prices. In practise, the conditions of the perfect competition model are not always met. Firstly, the price cannot always represent all dimensions of a good. Sometimes no market price exists. Secondly, there can be uncertainty regarding the quality of the good. Information about it can be lacking or is limited. Thirdly, it is also possible that information is available (for example about the quality) but it is not distributed equally among the participants or parties. This is known as information-asymmetry: information is available but it is not equally available to all parties. In this case, one particular economic actor knows something that other actors do not. Markets as well as organisations cannot function well if there is a lack of information and asymmetric information.

A recent development in economic thinking considers the characteristics of the phenomena of information, the implications of the lack of information and information-asymmetry as a focus of study. For example, the phenomenon of information has led to the origin of information economics (cf. Kreps, 1990: 577-719; Varian, 1992: 440-472; Varian, 2003: 623-641). Information economics is relatively young and belongs to one of the most rapidly growing areas of economic theory in the recent decades (Varian, 1992: 440). The theory examines the characteristics and implications of the missing information and information-asymmetry. Information economics includes situations where the driving force for particular (market) participants is the lack of information, for example, over what others will do, or what others know, or what the next-best alternative is (Kreps, 1990: 578). These situations can arise in various forms.

In this view, we must be aware of the fact that individuals have only limited possibilities and abilities to obtain and process information. Simon (1961: xxiv) uses the term 'bounded rationality' to indicate that decision-makers, who are assumed to be rational, are not *hyper rational*. *Bounded rationality* is said to arise when the cognitive ability of people is insufficient to deal with the complexity of the world. Hence, people are not in a position to take all circumstances into account when making a decision. This means that there is an important connection between bounded rationality, and the lack of information or asymmetric information. In Section 4.2 we will explore the basic concepts of information economics: asymmetric information, private information, hidden information, and hidden actions. We further discuss the consequences of missing information and what we can do about it.

Asymmetric information can give rise to opportunistic behaviour, also sometimes termed as strategic behaviour. For this reason, in studies relating to asymmetric information, strategic interactions between players are often considered (Varian, 1992: 440). Williamson (1987: 30) describes opportunistic behaviour as *a condition of self-interest seeking with guile*. Opportunistic behaviour includes providing selective and distorted information, making promises which are not intended to be kept, and posing differently from what the person actually is. For the phenomena of hidden information, hidden actions and strategic behaviour, agents pose differently from what they are and behave differently from what have promised to do, and it is difficult or expensive to determine who they are and how they behave in reality. In this way information-asymmetry affects transaction costs and makes it difficult to achieve an efficient agreement.

In the psychological literature it is argued that there are two kinds of motivations for action: one intrinsic or internal to the individual concerned and one extrinsic or external. It is also argued that there may be a trade-off between the two kinds of motivation, such that too heavy emphasis on extrinsic motivation can drive out intrinsic motivation. So motivations activated by external factors, such as monetary incentives or direct order (as in hierarchical governance structure), can crowd out motivations that are internal to the individual, such as more altruistic concerns. However, sometimes extrinsic motivational factors can also reinforce intrinsic motivation if they are seen as supporting self-determination. In that case, external motivation is seen as crowding-in intrinsic motivation (Le Grand, 2003: 53). Section 4.3 addresses bounded rationality, opportunistic behaviour, self-interest (and knaves), altruism (and knights), intrinsic and extrinsic motivation, and the use of incentives.

In situations with bounded rationality, it is impossible to make agreements which completely reflect the complexity of reality in all its facets. The existence of opportunistic behaviour implies that no general trust can be ascribed to an incomplete contract. If it is difficult and/or expensive to specify *ex-ante* whether or not the economic actors are opportunistic, then it is likely that no agreement will be made. The contracts which are concluded under these conditions are per definition incomplete contracts. The question is: how can we trust such agreements? We can rely on incomplete contracts, if the economic actors involved in the contracts are completely trustworthy. Besides trust, rewards based on the reputation mechanism (the carrot) and punishments (the stick) can be used for realising credible commitment for observing contracts. Section 4.4 addresses the role of commitment and reputation for observing agreements.

As said, information economics includes situations where the driving force for participants in a transaction is the lack of information, for example over what others will do, or what others know, or what the next-best alternative is. These situations arise in various forms and involve risks. Moreover the future is uncertain, and the results of projects are uncertain; it means uncertainties and risks are part of our daily life. In Section 4.5 we will introduce the concepts of risk, uncertainty, risk-aversion, expected value, and expected utility. These concepts are part of the **theory of expected utility** which is the dominant theory of choices under uncertainty.

However, in the field of risk behaviour a debate is going on between the adherents of the expected utility theory and those of the prospect theory (Kahneman and Tversky, 1979: 263-291). An important difference between prospect theory and the expected utility theory is the risk-attitude about profits and losses; loss aversion is a central concept in the prospect theory. The findings that people commonly value losses more than commensurate gains have been widely reported in the literature for several decades. Because of the consequence of loss aversion we will discuss the prospect theory in Section 4.6.

Key questions:
- What are the characteristics of information and what does lack of information mean?

- What are information revealing mechanisms?
- What are the efficiency problems of moral hazard?
- How can moral hazard be controlled?
- What is the relationship between bounded rationality, opportunistic behaviour and self-interest?
- What is extrinsic and intrinsic motivation and what does the trade-off between both mean?
- What is the relationship between risk (and uncertainty) and the expected value, and what does expected value mean?
- What is the relationship between risk-aversity and expected utility?
- What is an important difference between the expected value and the expected utility?
- What are important differences between the expected utility theory and the prospect theory?
- What problem arise concerning the valuation of gains and losses?
- What does loss aversion mean and what are its consequences?

4.2 Asymmetric information, private information, hidden information and hidden actions

4.2.1 Characteristics of information

The assumption of perfect information is not often met in practise. Information can be lacking or is limited. It is also possible that information is available but is not distributed equally among the participants or parties. This is known as information-asymmetry: information is available but is not equally available to all parties. It occurs when one particular economic actor knows something that other actors do not. Markets as well as organisations cannot function well if there is a lack of information. Market and organisational failure can be a consequence of various aspects connected with the phenomenon of *information*.

The **first** aspect is the developing and spreading of information. Information often has the character of a pure public good, with non-rivalry in use, and non-excludability. Non-rivalry means it can be used several times by different users at the same time. The characteristic of non-rivalry involves the indivisibility of the good 'information', that is, it will be very difficult to divide the good ''information'' into marketable units. This has also as the consequence that it will be very difficult to exclude other people from the use of information if it becomes available. If it becomes available, everyone can make use of it. Non-excludability is a characteristic that arises from a lack of property rights. However, these are often the attributes of the good that make it too costly to secure property rights

The characteristic of non-excludability of information (if it comes available, everyone can make use of it) is also known as the fundamental paradox of information: the value of information can only be revealed to another party by disclosing that information, while such disclosure destroys the value of the information (Douma and Schreuder, 2002: 54). Because everyone has this information and can make use of it. This lack of excludability leads to high transaction costs if we want to exclude people from the use, because of (high) costs linked to exclusion (costs to prevent illegal use, juridical costs, etc.).

A **second** aspect of the information phenomenon has to do with making of the right decision. In order to make the right decision, the person who decides does not only require general information about the properties of the concerned good, but also needs information about the effectiveness and efficiency of the good in the circumstances (of the concerned individual) in which it will be used. In many cases, a decision has to be taken under conditions of uncertainty. For example, I would like to go to my office by bike, shall I take my rain clothes or not? Box 4.1 gives a simple arithmetic example of conditions of uncertainty.

Hirshleifer and Riley (1994: 2) distinguish between *'economics of information'* and *'economics of uncertainty'*. The *economic analysis of information* assumes that individuals, before they take the final decision, try to overcome their ignorance by undertaking actions to generate and collect new information. For example, before a lady decides to take an umbrella with her, she will take the weather forecast into consideration. The *economics of uncertainty* is based on the idea that every individual adapts her (him)-self to the amount of limited information he or she possesses. Given the available information, an individual attempts to choose the best possible action. The decision not to take the umbrella is based on his or her *estimation of the probability* of rain. Box 4.1 gives an example of probability and an exercise on how to calculate the expected value.

Related to this, we sometimes see a difference in the literature between risk and uncertainty. According to Frank H. Knight (1921: 20, 226) cited in Hirshleifer and Riley (1994: 9), a distinction can be made between risk and uncertainty. Risk refers to the situation where an individual is in a position to estimate the probability on the basis of an objective classification. Uncertainty arises in a situation when no objective classification is possible. Hirshleifer and Riley (1994: 10) do not find this distinction useful. They believe that assigning probabilities on the basis of subjective 'degree of belief' is a better approach – as has been used in Box 4.1. We will follow the approach of Hirshleifer and Riley. In Section 4.5 we return to the issues of risk and risk-attitudes in more detail.

4.2.2 Lack of information and asymmetric information

As shown in Figure 4.1, the lack of information can be split up into two categories: asymmetric information and no information at all. Asymmetric information means that information is available, but it is not distributed equally among the participants or parties, or it is not equally available to all partners in a contractual relationship. One particular economic actor knows something that other actors do not. This is known as information-asymmetry: information is available but is not equally available to all parties.

For example, a worker may know better than his employer how much he can produce, but does not reveal it. Similarly, a producer has more insight into the quality of the goods that he produces than the potential consumer. If this type of information is relevant for a potential transaction or for determining efficient allocations and is only known to one of the parties involved, then this information is also called private information. It is private and unobservable or hidden for the other party. Therefore, private information is asymmetric information. It is the inability to observe private information that constitutes the essence of the information problem and introduces risk for the other party. This type of information asymmetry can prevent any agreement from being reached even when an agreement would be efficient under complete information.

Box 4.1. Expected value.

A real estate agent – named Jansen – works for FORTIS, a large investment company in the Netherlands. He receives a sales commission from his employer. For simplicity, suppose that Jansen has three possible incomes for the year. In a good year, he sells many real estates and earns € 300,000, whereas in a bad year he earns nothing. In other years, he receives € 150,000. Probability refers to the likelihood that an outcome will occur. In this example, each outcome is equally likely, and thus has a probability of 1/3 of occurring. The expected value of uncertain payoff is defined as the weighted average of all possible outcomes, where the probability of each outcome is used as weights. The expected value is the central tendency – the payoff that will occur on average. In our example the expected value (EV) is:

$$EV = (1/3 \times 0) + (1/3 \times 150{,}000) + (1/3 \times 300{,}000) = 150{,}000 \text{ euro}$$

Jansen can expect an average earning of 150,000 euro. However, his income is uncertain. The variance is a measure of the variability of the payoff. It is defined as the expected value of the squared difference between each possible payoff and the **expected value.** In this example, the variance (V) is:

$$V = 1/3(0 - 150{,}000)^2 + 1/3 (150{,}000 - 150{,}000)^2 + 1/3 (300{,}000 - 150{,}000)^2$$
$$= 1/3(-150{,}000)^2 + 1/3 (0)^2 + 1/3 (150{,}000)^2$$
$$= 1.5^{10}$$

The standard deviation (SD) is the square root of the variance:

$$SD = 122{,}474$$

Variance and **standard deviation** are used as measures for risk. Higher standard deviations reflect more risk. An event with a definite outcome has a standard deviation of zero. If Jansen is risk-averse – like most people – he prefers a lower standard deviation.

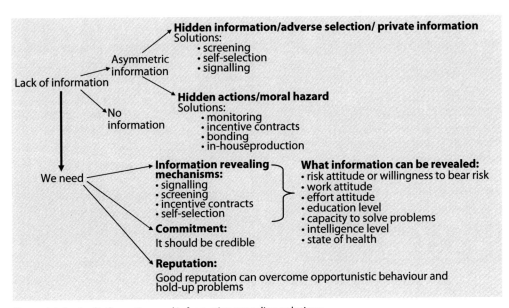

Figure 4.1. Lack of information and information revealing solutions.

As indicated in Figure 4.1, two types of asymmetric information can be distinguished: hidden information and hidden actions. In Section 4.2.3 we will discuss hidden information, adverse selection and private information, all of which can be considered as synonyms. After this, we focus in Section 4.2.4 on ways to solve the problems of hidden information by making use of signalling, screening, and self-selection. In Section 4.2.5 and 4.2.6 we will discuss hidden actions and moral hazard, and ways to control this type of lack of information

A more general approach of for dealing with lack of information is: what can we do in situations with a lack of information (including no information)? Firstly, we can look for information revealing mechanisms. Figure 4.1 gives some examples of them. These mechanisms are used to reveal information about the risk-, work- and effort-attitude, education level etc. Some of these mechanisms are discussed in Section 4.2.4. Secondly, we can look for mechanisms that make it possible to carry out transactions in situations with a lack of information such as credible commitment and a good reputation. Both will be worked out in Section 4.4.

4.2.3 Hidden information or adverse selection

Hidden information is a form of information-asymmetry which also characterises the principal-agent approach (see Chapter 6). It arises when, in a transaction involving a good or service, one party is better informed about one or several variables of the good or service (e.g. quality, cost price, etc.) than the other party (Kreps, 1990: 577). The one party has the disposal of more information than the other. This party has no incentive to disclose information if it is to his or her disadvantage. Instead of *hidden information*, the term *adverse selection* is also used. It is an information problem that exists before the transaction is conducted or the contract is made. Hidden information also includes private information which is relevant for the potential transaction and to which one party is privy to, is not observable, and introduces risks for the other party (cf. Douma and Schreuder, 2002: 57).

Hidden information is, in the language of information economics, an *ex-ante* information problem. It means that an information problem already exists before the transaction is carried out or the agreement is concluded. In insurance economics, the problem of hidden actions is called **adverse selection**. Adverse selection originates from pre-contractual opportunistic behaviour. It arises because of the private information the insurance consumers have before they have purchased the insurance contract, when they are balancing whether the purchase is beneficial. Adverse selection is incompatible with the standard neoclassical economics of markets which assumes all information is instantly available without cost.

However, when the problem of adverse selection is especially severe, there will be no price **at all** at which the quantity of a good supplied by sellers is equal to the quantity demand by buyers. The problem is that the price must be the same to all buyers, no matter what the costs are of serving them, because these costs are not observable by the seller (in the case of adverse selection). Examples are insurance policies for your bike, car, house, travelling, harvest, and for your medical care. The only buyers who – for sure – will pay any given price are those whose private information leads them to believe that the price – e.g. for an insurance policy – is advantageous for them. If the transaction costs for disclosing this private information have to be included in selling the product, then the price will have to rise:

$$P = f(TC, Z)$$ (4.1)

Where TC = transaction costs
Z = all the other costs

The price increase could be so high for the seller to break even that even those who value the good the most will find it not worth while. If the costs are higher than the price (see Equation 4.2) the market can completely collapse.

$$TC + Z > P$$ (4.2)

The standard neoclassical economics is based on the premise that the prices adjust until supply is equal to demand. When there is adverse selection however, changing the prices affects not only the revenues of the selling firm, but also its costs of supplying the product. We use an insurance firm as a **first** example. The average claims made against an insurance firm may be an increasing function of the price (= premium) charged. For the firm, claims are the costs of the product 'insurance':

$$P = f(claims)$$ (4.3)

It means the higher the price, the higher the claims. However, higher claims also mean a higher price, otherwise the firm would go bankrupt.

$$Claims = f(P)$$ (4.4)

The **second** example concerns a bank. The interest rates that a bank charges can affect the selection of the customers who apply for a loan. It is possible that only customers with risky investments may be willing to pay high interest rates. Because of the extra cost connected to these risky investments the cost of a loan will increase. In this case, the saying also holds: bad money drives out good money.

The **third** example regards firms balancing between termination and wage cuts. Firms often prefer terminations rather than wage cuts when they find their wage expenses are too high. Wage cuts are likely to lead to the departure of the most able workers. It means in the case of wage cuts, the best worker will leave the firm first. In most cases, these workers have the best outside job opportunities. This will have consequences for the returns of the firm.

Box 4.2. Incentives for revealing information in adverse selection case.

In adverse selection situations, the agent generally benefits by misrepresenting his information in one way or another. Thus, the principal wants to design a mechanism to elicit the true information. The theory of this is governed by the revelation principle. Suppose the government wants to procure a good or service – a bridge or developing a nature area near a city. The government does not know the unit costs of production; it could be either low (C_l) or high (C_h). Therefore the producer (e.g. an real estate developer) will be tempted to pretend to have high costs so as to receive a high payment, and take the surplus in the form of a profit (if the producer is a private firm) or perks (if it is a non-profit or a public agency). To the extent that competition among rival producers or auditing cannot solve this problem, the government must resort to an incentive scheme suitably designed to reveal the truth. The government should offer a menu of two contracts, specifying the quantity Q the producer will supply and the amount R the government will pay him.

One contract, (Q_l, R_l) is intended for the low-cost case; the other, (Q_h, R_h) is intended for the high-cost case. A high-cost producer has no temptation to cheat. Therefore the payment in that case needs only to cover the full cost: $R_h = C_h Q_h$. But a low-cost producer must be allowed just enough profit to offset what he would have made by pretending to be high-cost, namely the difference in unit costs $(C_h - C_l)$ times the quantity Q_h that he would have sold under this pretence; thus

$$R_l = C_l Q_l + (C_h - Q_l)Q_h$$

(4.5)

Then each cost-type of producer will pick from the menu the contract that is intended for that type. By doing this, the government has to share some surplus or rent with the low-cost type producer. To keep this down, the quantity Q_h will be reduced below the level that would equate social marginal benefits and marginal costs under full information; the amount of the reduction will depend on the probability of the producer being a low-type. If there are more than two types, then the menu will consist of a set of contracts of which one is intended to be chosen by each type of producer, and the payments for each contract are calculated in a way similar to above, so as to secure a truthful self-selection by all types (Dixit, 2002: 700-701).

4.2.4 Signalling, screening and self-selection

In order to eliminate or limit incomplete information, it is possible that an employer carefully observes the behaviour of his personnel to evaluate their productivity. Similarly, a consumer can evaluate the quality of the product of a firm. Employers can be categorised as good or bad depending on how they pay their workers. Producers of good-quality products will generally become known as such, while producers of low-quality products would like to have the *reputation* of good-quality producers. To get this information or to have the image of a good reputation, has associated costs. Incomplete information is a source of transaction costs. For that reason, information economics is also intended for the analysis of transaction costs, including efficiency-loss, caused by asymmetric information. With a view to obtaining as efficient use of the factors of production as possible in society, it is necessary to limit transaction costs as much as possible.

So with this in mind, we have to look for solutions in situations of incomplete information or asymmetric information.

In situations marked by pre-contractual private information, some of the privately informed people would gain if they made their information known (i.e. signalling). Moreover, the uninformed party would gain from getting this information. This means there is often a mutual gain to be had if the desired types of the privately informed agents can make their information known. This creates incentives to find credible ways to reveal the information. One way is for the uninformed party to try to derive the private information from observable actions (or verifiable statements) of the informed party. This leads to different, but closely related, classes of strategies: **signalling, screening and self-selection**. The difference between signalling and screening depends on whether the informed or uninformed party takes the lead (Milgrom and Roberts, 1992: 154).

Signalling

One way to solve the problem of hidden information is by giving signals. Signals can be defined as activities in which the informed party invests so as to make it easier for the other party to find out the private information about hidden characteristics. Good guarantee conditions or extensive and expensive advertisements can be a signal for good quality. In a situation with asymmetric information, a person with good information should often invest more in signals than he/she actually wants. In such a situation, a certain amount of inefficiency is usually unavoidable.

Signalling occurs when the better-informed party makes certain verifiable facts known, which if properly interpreted, may indicated the presence of other unobservable but desirable characteristics. In signalling, the privately informed party takes the lead in adopting behaviour that, properly interpreted, reveals their information. For signalling to be effective, the receiver must believe that the signal is credible. That is, the observable characteristic must clearly point to the unobservable, desirable characteristic (FitzRoy *et al.*, 1998: 247). A signal for the qualification of a worker could be his level of education. For a potential member of an environmental cooperative for farmers, it could also be whether he has followed a course in wildlife and habitats management. Certification schemes and the use of specific labels signal to consumers that a product meets certain quality standards. The purpose of certification is to make a defined level of performance explicitly known. In this way, the label signals credible information about the product that would otherwise be hidden from the consumer.

The best known example of signalling comes from the labour market (cf. Milgrom and Roberts, 1992: 155). Education is perceived as a signal of labour productivity. More educated persons are perceived as highly-productive workers and are being paid accordingly, less-educated persons have low productivity and so receive lower compensation for labour. Whether this is correct depends on two conditions.

First, the level of education which is chosen as the signal of high productivity should be such that the low-educated workers are not prepared or able to reach that level. The level of education should be so high that even by increasing the level of education, the workers could mislead the employers into thinking that their own productivity is high and so should receive a greater compensation. If these self-selection criteria are not met, then the low-productivity workers would obtain the same level of education as the high-productivity workers. The education signal would then provide no information.

The **second** condition is that not having a specific level of education is a suitable signal that the person is not very productive; appearing as a low-educated person should not be the preferred choice of a highly-productive worker. These two conditions are the so-called **self-selection conditions**. The self-selection conditions assure that the signals are credible (cf. Milgrom and Roberts, 1992: 155).

How can we make sure that the signals are credible? The seller of a good, who has complete information at his disposal, can do something to inform the consumers about the quality of the product. The key for such signals is that the sellers of high-quality products (or in the case of an insurance policy, the buyers) know how to distinguish themselves from sellers of low-quality products by being prepared to take actions which sellers of low-quality products **do not** find worthwhile. This is obviously related to costs. Signalling leads to effective revelation of private information. However, it does not come for free. There are costs connected with it. It means that making signals credible involves costs and effort.

The concept of **signalling** can be used to explain a wide variety of phenomena. In our daily world there are a lot of examples of signalling mechanisms which often function as an incentive mechanism also:
- Setting low 'limited' prices as a signal of low cost to demoralise entry by potential competitors.
- Offering of product warranties and money-back guaranties as a signal of product quality.
- Paying dividends by corporations to signal financial strength.
- Farmers who would like to switch to nature and landscape management should signal that they are ready and prepared to preserve nature and landscape in an efficient manner. A signal could be being a (voluntary) member of an environmental cooperative or wildlife and landscape association.

Screening

Signalling occurs from the better informed party. It is also possible that the less-informed party attempts to induce the other party to voluntarily disclose information. This is known as screening. The most important difference between **signalling** and **screening** is which party takes the initiative: the informed or the uninformed. To ensure that the other party voluntarily discloses information, we need to have an information-revealing mechanism. The conditions required for this are termed as the self-selection conditions. In situations in which contracts are used, it involves that the participation-conditions and the incentives-conditions of contracts are made in such a way that agents select the contracts intended for them. Screening leads thus to self-selection. We will come back on the concept of self-selection at the end of this section.

More in general, **screening** refers to activities undertaken by the party without private information (mostly the principal) in order to separate different types (agents) of the informed party (= group

Box 4.3. Scholarship.

Suppose the Ministry of Education has developed two systems for scholarships. Both systems are based on the idea that an average student is able to pass with 60 ECTS a year. The two systems are:

a. A system in which the student will get 400 euro per month, i.e. 4800 euro per year. The money will be transferred at the beginning of each month.

b. A system in which the student will get 150 euro per passed credit. The money will be given at the end of the study year.

Question: what kind of information revealing mechanism is used in system (b) and what will be revealed?

Answer: the used information revealing mechanisms are screening and self-selection. Information about the capacity, effort level, work-attitude and risk-attitude of the student will be revealed in (b).

of agents) along some dimensions. It is the uninformed party who undertakes activities in order to make groups of the informed parties or sort them into separate types. Screening also means that one of the contracting partners demands certain elements in the set of observed characteristics that are correlated with unobserved but desirable elements. According to FitzRoy *et al.* (1998: 248), screening is a strategy sometimes available to an uninformed party that, if successful, will encourage the better-informed party to reveal information. To realise that the informed party reveals voluntarily his private information, we need an information revealing mechanism.

Screening is often done by offering a variety of alternatives, each intended for one of the various types of informed parties, whose choices then effectively reveal their private information. However, the self-selection constraints are crucial in achieving screening: people will choose the alternative intended for them only if it is the best for them in the set of alternatives offered, given what they know. An application is the positive relationship between earnings and age or experiences.

It is empirically well established that wages tend to increase with age and experience. Many factors no doubt contribute to this. Some economic factors are: increasing skills and ability (human capital) with greater responsibility being given to more senior employees who have demonstrated their abilities. However, there is evidence that even after accounting for these effects for them statistically, a positively – sloped age/ wage profile remains: given two workers with the same job assignment, the same responsibility and the same productivity, the older worker will tend to be paid more (Milgrom and Roberts, 1992: 157). Why should this be so?
- One possible answer is a general social preference or norm for paying older workers more and younger ones less.
- A more economic explanation is based on screening designed to reduce employee turnover or walk away. Having employees resign is costly for all firms, but it may be especially costly when, for example, the firm invests significant amounts in training workers. In such cases, firms have an interest in attracting workers who are less inclined to change jobs.

> **Box 4.4. The screening theory.**
>
> The explanation for the relationship between education and performance, productivity and labour participation is often called the screening theory. This theory states that a higher education is a signal for a potentially higher productivity. However, there is also a relationship between signalling and screening. The higher education also shows that the person in question has the potency to obtain more and other knowledge. For that reason, employers will rather have the tendency to hire people with a higher education level. Next to this, it should be mentioned that higher educated people have sometime besides the higher education level other differences with lower educated people also. We can think about intelligence, drive, motivation, better health, etc. These factors also determine which education level is possible.

The screening solution is to design the employment contract in such a way that only the desired types of workers are attracted. The answer to the question *'Why does the older worker tend to be paid more'* is that, it is a screening mechanism. The older ones (1) have more experience; (2) they have – when they are young – an incentive to stay because of the higher pay in the future, and; (3) in the past they have not caused problems such as hidden information or hidden actions, because otherwise they would have been fired.

Another application of the **screening mechanism** is a *performance-based pay system*. Workers or managers who are likely to be most productive in a particular firm tend also to be those with the best outside job opportunities. Offering a performance-based pay system is equal to offering a menu of different contracts, because it allows employees to determine their compensation by how hard they choose to work. It is assumed that paying a wage that is based on measured performance tends to attract and retain the most productive job applicants and to discourage the least productive ones. A pay based on measured output can not only function as a **screening** mechanism but it can also resolve post-contractual moral hazard problems within the firm or organisation (Milgrom and Roberts, 1992: 158).

This can be done by providing incentives for the workers to perform well, even when it is impossible to monitor how hard they are working. The monitoring problems make it often very difficult to contract directly on the workers' providing a high level of effort. If their pay does not depend on their output then they have little direct incentive to exert more than the minimal amounts of effort. Tying pay to productivity provides incentives to raise output. This effect reinforces the screening effect of attracting people who are more productive (Milgrom and Roberts, 1992: 158).

A more general **screening mechanism** is simply making known to the relevant individuals or group what the organisation or club offers and what it expects. This can induce some *self-selection* among potential candidate-members. This kind of actions can be a by-product of other policies. Some examples are:
- Suppose you like to attend your work well-dressed. Do you think it will induce some self-selection concerning the type of organisation where you would like to work?
- Farmer Smit does not like wildlife and landscape conservation. What would be his attitude towards a membership of an environmental cooperative of farmers?

- A contract with little health or pension benefits may be a screening mechanism for young employees (young pilots) who are motivated to work because they need the job experience (hours worked).
- A contract for a professional position in a NGO may emphasise the values of the organisation rather than job benefits. This may act as a screening mechanism for dedicated individuals rather than those seeking high professional rank or income.

The idea of offering menus of contracts is also widely applied in our economy. For example firms can set prices for a whole line of related products such as office copiers, printers and computers. Another example is offering a menu of contracts to salespeople, in which their compensations consist of a fixed part and a flexible part depending on their effort. However, we must be aware that wages are not only costs for the employer, but also a signal. A high wage also means the employer expects a high level of effort from the employee. Another related issue is the effect of salary on the level of innovation. Is wage stabilisation or the freezing of salaries good for the innovation of a firm or an economy?

Self-selection, truth-telling condition and the strategy of being honest

Self-selection has been mentioned briefly in connection with signalling and screening. It is a type of behaviour usually in response to some screening activities, but sometimes to signalling activities also. Self-selection is usually a type of behaviour in response to some screening activities that cause workers to choose from a menu of options and take the one they like best (cf. Kreps, 1990: 638). It means that people use their private information about likely usage to select the best rate plan, type of product, type of contract, type of insurance policy, type of salary (fixed of depending on effort) etc. for themselves. For example, by carefully constructing a menu of options firms make more profits than if they would simple offered the product at one price to all potential customers (cf. Brickley *et al.*, 2001:166).

The logic of **self-selection** is helpful for analysing strategies of firms, workers and consumers also. Well-known examples are: price discrimination, including creaming off the consumers surplus, a price depending on purchased quantity, offering a menu of options to consumers, who must choose among the various versions of a product on the basis of features and prices. The prices and features for each version must be chosen recognising that they will affect the demand for other versions of that product (like a TV, a computer, soft ware, a car, etc.).

> **Box 4.5. Offering a menu of versions.**
>
> If you would like to buy a car, you may choose a standard version or a deluxe version with six airbags, cruise control, navigation system, DVD player, etc. The deluxe version of the car (software) contains additional features that are likely to appeal to more sophisticated car drivers. The same argument holds for computer software. The marginal costs of producing and distributing the standard version and deluxe version are virtually equal. However, the firms mark up the deluxe version more because the typical customer choosing this version is likely to be less price-sensitive than the typical customer choosing the standard version (cf. Brickley, 2001: 166). This characteristic creates the possibility of offering a menu of versions.

Another application is in offering a menu of contracts to salespeople, where the amount of salary and percentage commission on sales vary from a fixed salary to a salary completely depending on commissions on sales. The idea is that salespeople who know that sales in their territories will be especially responsive to their effort will select a high-commission, low fixed salary contracts and be motivated to exert extra effort. Those whose private information indicates that increasing sales will be difficult, will make the opposite choice.

Similar considerations hold for the design of insurance contracts. Different policies are designed for risk classes of buyers. **Self-selection** is achieved by varying the extent of coverage offered and the amount of own or personal risk. This may result in low-risk customers receiving less than full insurance coverage, whereas high-risk individuals purchase full coverage. However, the latter pay a higher amount per unit insurance. The lack of full insurance – e.g. because of their own risk part – for low-risk individuals is a cost of the informational asymmetry. In general, achieving **self-selection via screening** will help overcome the information asymmetry, but it is may be costly (Milgrom and Roberts, 1992: 159).

Self-selection is also important within the contract theory. It refers in this case to a type of behaviour in response to some screening activity that causes potential contract takers to choose from a menu of contracts and sign the one they like best (cf. Kreps, 1990: 638). Suppose the government would like to conclude contracts with farmers for preserving nature, landscape and rural amenities. In the Netherlands, but also in other EU states, this is an important part of the rural policy. In order to realise optimal contracts, we must have a mechanism that ensures that: (1) the participation conditions are met; and (2) a performance incentive exists such that all participants honestly report their optimal strategy.

Such a mechanism is based on the **revelation-principle**. Kreps (1990: 685) and Hirshleifer and Riley (1994: 322) term this mechanism as the direct revelation-mechanism. The word *direct* indicates that everyone voluntarily chooses to be honest. The incentive that we have to give parties to find out who they really are or what their costs really are is also termed the *truth-telling condition* or the *strategy of being honest*. To assure that potential contract-candidates choose

---

Box 4.6. Reducing the of greenhouse gases.

Self-selection can also be applied in the policy for adopting new technology for saving energy or for reducing the emissions of greenhouse gases. Suppose the government would like to make use of levies (taxes) or subsidies. In the case of levies, if agents are not going to purchase the new technology they have to pay more taxes. The problem with subsidies is that they could be paid out to all households (= agents) including those who would have purchased the new technology even without the subsidy. This is called the subsidy-free-rider (Van Soest, 2007: 407). In such cases, the government has too little information to determine whether or not the agent actually needed a subsidy in order to switch to purchase of the new technology. An important question is which instrument can the government use to take care of those agents who actually need the subsidy? A solution would be to offer a menu of tax-subsidies combinations from which agents could choose. The agents (firms or households) are then able to determine the most profitable outcome; either making use of subsidies or avoiding taxes.

---

the contracts intended, we need a particular form of the incentive compatibility condition (= performance incentive), called **self-selection conditions** (Slangen, 1997: 519-520). Building-in of self-selection conditions in contracts reduces the problems of hidden information.

4.2.5 Hidden actions and moral hazard

Similarities exist between hidden information and hidden actions. Both have a common trait in that they are the consequences of the problem of unobservability. The information is unevenly distributed (= information asymmetry). One party has private information that is unobservable for the other party. That information is valuable. It can effect the terms of trade in any transaction. The owner of the private information can decide to disclose it or not. Both hidden information and hidden actions may occur in markets, contracts and in an organisational setting. An important difference is that hidden information is an *ex-ante* problem and hidden actions occur *ex-post*.

Hidden action is a form of information-asymmetry which is characteristic of many *principal-agent* situations (see Chapter 6). *Hidden action* is when one party undertakes specific actions which affect the value of the transaction for the other party, and which the other party cannot fully control or prevent. In general, *hidden action* refers to a situation in which one market-party cannot observe the actions of the other party. Instead of *hidden action*, this is also termed as *moral hazard* (Kreps, 1990: 578, Varian, 1992: 444). Situations of moral hazard provoke unintended use. Hidden action is an *ex-post* phenomenon. It refers to actions in which parties, involved in a transaction or agreement, can undertake after they have made a transaction or an agreement. If these actions cannot be observed by the other party, and the interest of the other party is adversely affected, these hidden actions can hinder the successful carrying out of a transaction or contract. Such hidden actions may even nullify a transaction, contract or a market (Douma and Schreuder, 2002: 56-57).

The moral hazard problem originated in the insurance industry, where it referred to the behaviour of people with insurance who changed their behaviour in a way that lead to larger claims against the insurance firms. It also contains certain types of misbehaviour outside the insurance sector. Several kinds of moral hazard arise frequently in daily life. It includes forms of post-contractual opportunism that arise because actions that have efficiency consequences are not freely observable and so the person taking them may choose to pursue his or her own personal interest at others' expense. For the most part, it is not possible to observe or to verify the relevant behaviour, and

---

Box 4.7. The Dutch cheat insurance (Volkskrant 23 September 2005).

In 2005 the journals reported that the Dutch cheated their insurance firms. A published report of the Union of Insurance firms in 2005 showed that the insurance firms paid almost one 1000 million euro to fraudulent customers. Insurance claims from private persons totalled about 650 million euro of fraudulent claims, and firms had a total of about 300 million euro of fraudulent claims. Travel insurance claims were found to be especially fraude-sensitive. Swindling created extra costs for the insurance firms, but also for the client. Because of the increasing of costs for the insurance firms people have to pay a higher premium.

---

thus it is not possible to write enforceable contracts that specify the behaviour to be adopted (Milgrom and Roberts, 1992: 167).

Moral hazard creates an efficiency problem. For example, an insurance company may not suffer from losses if it would set the insurance premium high enough to cover the extra costs. Still moral hazard will cause an efficiency problem because the extra benefits enjoyed by the insured on account of his or her claim will often not be worth the cost (B < C). This happens because the insured decision-maker does not look at all the costs and benefits associated to his or her decisions (i.e. distribution of the (marginal) B and C over the parties). Moreover the inherent nature of insurance makes it inevitable.

The incentives to alter behaviour will not be a problem if it is easy to determine when behaviour is appropriate and to prevent excessive use. The difficulty or costs of monitoring and difficulty of enforcing appropriate behaviour creates the moral hazard problem. These two difficulties mean that contracting is incomplete because there is no point to writing a contract specifying particular behaviour when the desired actions cannot be observed and consequently the contract cannot be effectively enforced (Milgrom and Roberts, 1992: 167).

Moral hazard may arise in any situation in which someone is tempted to take an inefficient action or to provide distorted information (leading others to take inefficient actions). The reason is that an individual's interests are not in line with group interest and because the report cannot be easily checked or the action accurately monitored. These problems arise in markets, contracts and in other forms of organisations. For example, concerning the market, some firms may find it most profitable to make shoddy or unsafe products when quality is not easily observed, like sport shoes, bicycles etc. of low quality. This can lead to bad buys, but is a form of moral hazard.

Moral hazard is a very common phenomenon that affects a wide array of transactions. As said, it was first identified in the insurance context. However, it has a much broader range of occurrence. For example, moral hazard arises in many institutional arrangements. The mode of organisation – including the **make or buy** approach – is often a response to moral hazard (Milgrom and Roberts, 1992: 179). We will discuss 10 examples of moral hazard. In general, it arises in situations with inefficient actions and distorted information.

Renting

Rented apartments may be less maintained than owner-occupied ones because the renters do not get the full benefits of their efforts at maintenance. How are you driving in a rented car? You are likely to be much more careful in driving a rented car if you are financially responsible for the damage to the car. If you are fully insured, then being careful brings you no extra benefits (Milgrom and Roberts, 1992: 168).

Within organisations

An office employee may spend time during the day studying for a register account exam, or chatting on the telephone and computer with friends when there is work waiting to be done.

Factory workers may call in sick during the hunting or fishing season. On the job, they may exert the least care and effort they can get away with. Senior executives may pursue their own goals of status, high salaries, expensive 'perks', and job security rather than the stockholder' interests, and so they may push sales growth over profits. These examples do not involve insurance explicitly, but they have the crucial feature of insurance: all do not bear the full impact of their decisions. The employees get paid whether they work hard or not, or at least they do not suffer a decrease in pay equal to the full lost value of what they could have produced (Milgrom and Roberts, 1992: 170).

In a principal-agent setting

Each of the above examples can be described in terms of a principal-agent relationship. It refers to a situation in which one individual (the agent) acts on behalf of another (the principal) and is supposed to advance the principal's goals. The moral hazard problems arise when the agent and principal have different objectives and the principal can not easily determine whether the agent's reports and actions are being taken in pursuit of the principal's goals or are self-interested misbehaviour (Milgrom and Roberts, 1992: 170). The principal-agent setting will be explained in Chapter 6.

Private or public insurance

Moral hazard problems arise in both government and private sector insurance programs. However, the problems do seem to be less in the private sector. In part, this is because private corporations:
- cannot sustain huge losses for a long time without going bankrupt; and
- can often not rely on the taxpayers to pay for their financial mistakes.

More in general, private firms have to adapt themselves earlier. Moreover, they have fewer troubles than the government in deciding to terminate the program if the losses being suffered are large. However, the more limited difficulties with moral hazard in private insurance, are also a result of the private sector's unwillingness to undertake a socially desirable insurance program in which the costs associated with moral hazard are high (Milgrom and Roberts, 1992: 178). A good example is the 'rain insurance' for farmers in the Netherlands. Private firms and Farmers organisations also were not prepared to come up with such insurance. After a discussion of years and in the end, with help of the Ministry of Agriculture, Nature and Food Safety, they succeeded in developing such an insurance program.

Moral hazard and employee shirking

In most circumstances, the firm is not paying directly for what the employees are supplying but instead it uses a *proxy* for it. What is actually being supplied are such things as the employees' intellectual and physical efforts. They are paid for the results of these inputs, e.g. sales, written reports etc. The amount and quality of the employees' efforts are difficult to monitor directly. The results of their efforts may be more easily observed. The preferred solution would be to pay them for the difficult observable or unobservable efforts directly. But that is very difficult or even impossible. Thus, firms attempt to motivate employees to choose to work harder or better by rewarding outcomes that are more likely when they behave in the desired way (Milgrom and Roberts, 1992: 179).

Managerial misbehaviour

Corporate executives of corporations are charged with advancing the interests of the shareholders. They are supposed to be overseen in this duty by a board of directors, who are elected by the shareholders. Both corporate executives and board members are considered to be agent of the shareholders. However, the complaint is that corporate executives:
- pursue other goals rather than maximising the long-term value of the firm;
- invest firms' earnings in low-value projects to expand their empires (e.g. by takeovers), instead of paying more dividend to the shareholders. An explanation is that their salary often depends on the empire and on the profit;
- serve the interests of the managers themselves, but not the interests of the shareholders or the workers of the firm.

Hostile takeovers and managerial misbehaviour

A hostile takeover is the acquisition of enough of the shares in a public limited company to give controlling ownership interest in the firm. Successful hostile takeover attempts often result in the replacement of the target firm's senior management and the naming of a new board of directors. Hostile takeovers can often be interpreted as a corrective response to managerial moral hazard: the takeovers displace managers who were pursuing their own interests at the expense of the shareholders (Milgrom and Roberts, 1992: 181-182).

Moral hazard in financial contracts

A moral hazard problem also arises when different stakeholders have different claims on the financial returns from an investment. Financing via debt and equity makes a difference, and this becomes manifest in the case of bankruptcy.

Debt, equity and bankruptcy

Many firms are financed by a combination **debt** and **equity**. The debt holders – banks, the purchasers of the firm's bonds, input suppliers who offer credit – are lenders. They provide cash in return for a promise to be repaid a fixed amount (perhaps with interest) at a later date. The equity holders get to keep whatever profits are left after paying the debt obligations. In a corporation, the equity is lodged with the shareholders, who elect the board of directors to represent their interest in setting policy and in a hiring manager to run the firm. In a partnership, the partners are the equity claimants and with a sole proprietorship (or single owner) the owner is the equity claimant. Absent of serious managerial moral hazard, we should expect that the firm will run in the interest of the equity holders. However, this is not necessarily consistent with the interests of the firm's creditors (Milgrom and Roberts, 1992: 183).

Equity holders will favour riskier investments than the firm's creditors want. The equity holders win big if the investments work out. The debt holders just get their promised fixed payment. If the investment loses money, some of the loss may fall on the creditors who are not fully repaid. It means there is a conflict of interest between equity and debt holders:
- equity holders win big if the investments work out;
- debt holders just get their promised fixed payment;
- but, if it goes wrong the losses are for the debt holders.

Lenders can take measures to protect themselves against a potential moral hazard problem that arises if the firm is organised to maximise the value of its stock. They can do credit checks, monitor performance and they may structure the loans. Sometimes the loan cannot be repaid, or at least a scheduled payment is missing. In these circumstances, the lenders can force the firm into bankruptcy.

Bankruptcy can be seen as an institutional arrangement to protect the value of assets. However, forcing a firm into bankruptcy is an ultimate measure. Once a firm is forced into involuntary bankruptcy, the creditors gain many of the *control rights* that normally belong to equity holders or the managers. Being able to get these rights makes debt holders more willing to lend money than they otherwise would be and encourage the efficient allocation of financial capital. Moreover, the threat of bankruptcy may serve as a check on managerial moral hazard versus shareholder's interest. In the case of bankruptcy, managers may lose their jobs, their perks, and their pensions (Milgrom and Roberts, 1992: 183-184).

Hybrid institutional arrangements

Activities are often organised by hybrid institutional arrangements; a mix of different parties and different modes of organisation. The involved parties have often:
- different responsibilities;
- different shares in costs and benefits;
- different tax regimes; and
- different liabilities levels.

This creates differences in interests between the parties which can cause moral hazard problems. Such a hybrid institutional arrangement can be the basis of a consortium consisting of partners that are single owners, partnerships, limited partnerships, private limited, and public limited companies[29]. In such a consortium the ownership, corporate status, liability and fiscal regimes are different.

A well-known type of a hybrid institutional arrangement is a Public Private Partnership (PPP)[30]. In such projects, the government works together with private parties and often plays different roles: (1) it has often large interests in the realisation of a project; (2) it has to control the quality of

---

[29] For an overview of these differences see Chapter 8.4.

[30] For an overview of possibilities and difficulties of public-private partnership projects see Germis and Vermeylen (2002: 860-863).

the project, the legal procedures and contractual agreements; (3) it has to take care for maintaining the public support. A central question for private investors is whether the government is able to create a stable policy framework for PPP-projects, which are of large-scale and have a long duration. Time-consistency of the government plays an important role here; see Section 4.3. The organisational modes and the interests of the involved partners are different. This can create hidden action problems. Well-known examples of PPP in the Netherlands are: exploitation of the Betuwe Railway, the High Speed Railway, and airports. International examples are the problems of companies such as Shell with projects, among others, in Russia and Iran. As we know from newspapers and other media, this is not without problems. Conflict can arise from the difference in interests of the involved parties.

Ratchet effects

In a principal-agent relationship, the principal tries to apply incentives to stimulate the agent to better performance and he tries to get information about the costs structure of the agent. The activities of the agents often reveal information about his costs structure. After this information is known, the principal has a tendency to adapt the performance reward for creaming off the surplus profits. If the agent becomes aware of this or he/she sees what the principal is up to, he/she will not react on the incentive performance. This phenomenon is known as the 'ratchet effect': the agent sees that good performances today will be punished by stronger norms in the future. Incentive performance will therefore only work if the principal establishes credible commitment to earlier promises to maintain the norms (Teulings *et al.*, 2004: 28).

The ratchet effects played a strong role in the former communist countries. Incentive performances did not work because the state was not able to bind itself in a credible way to earlier promises (Teulings *et al.* 2004: 28). However, today ratchet effects still play a role in firms and government bureaus. The principal often formulates a higher future target or allocates a lower budget future budget if the current goals have been met or even exceed. The dilemma facing the agent is that a better performance today can results in a higher current reward, but is often punished tomorrow by a higher target or tighter budget. For example, by exceeding the current quota, the manager can expect to be 'rewarded' by a higher quota in every subsequent period because output expectations are ratcheted up or raised to a higher level. This would be a perverse dynamic incentive scheme, where good behaviour today is punished tomorrow, so the agent has no incentive to exceed the target or to be careful with spending the entire budget (Hendrikse, 2003: 146).

Government bureaus and departments on local and national levels, and research institutions financed by the government, are making use of the same ratchet incentives. At end of the year, they have to spend the entire budget. If this is not achieved, they will lose the money that is left over and next year they will get a smaller budget. This way of allocating budgets creates an incentive for inefficiency and misbehaviour.

4.2.6 Controlling moral hazard

In order for a *hidden action* problem to arise, three conditions must hold, according to Milgrom and Roberts (1992: 185). **First,** there must be some potential divergence of interests between people. **Second**, there must be some basis for gainful exchange or other cooperation between the individuals – some reason to agree and transact – that activates the divergent interests. **Third**, there must be difficulties in determining whether in fact the terms of the agreement have been followed and in enforcing the contract terms. These three conditions suggest ways to deal with moral hazard problems. The remedies for or ways to limit the hidden actions problems can be grouped into: *monitoring, incentive contracts, bonding* and *'doing it oneself'* (Milgrom and Roberts, 1992: 186-191).

Monitoring

The first remedy is suggested by the third condition: increase the resources devoted to monitoring and verification. The results of monitoring can be the basis for rewards and penalties. For examples, workers are often required to punch a time clock, and their pay is reduced or other punishments are imposed if they arrive too late or quit early. Monitoring may also be used to support a system of rewards for good behaviour.

Difficulties often arise because monitoring actions or verifying reported information is costly or impossible. In some cases, the actions of the agents are not or not completely observable. It means, monitoring actual behaviour, checking, and the verification of reports can be very expensive. Sometimes the costs are prohibitive. Another difficulty is who will monitor the monitor.

Monitoring requires developing sources of information about the agent's truthfulness and performance. However it does not always require direct expenditures of resources. One possibility is to rely on competition among different parties with conflicting interests to develop the required information. Competing sellers will often happily compare the relative merits of their own activities against competing activities of other sellers, i.e. competition between salespeople. The

---

Box 4.8. Who is the monitor?

Suppose that it is difficult for people working together in a group or team to detect shirking of one or more of the team members. However, it would not be that difficult for someone whose only task is to detect shirking. Let us call this person a **monitor**. A team with a monitor would then perform more or better than a team without a monitor. If the value of the additional output from having a monitor is sufficiently high it would be in the interest of all team members to have a monitor. How should the monitor be rewarded for his effort? Suppose the monitor just shares in the proceeds on an equal basis with the other team members. In that case, the monitor has an incentive to shirk himself. So the question becomes, who monitors the monitor. One solution is: give the monitor title to the residual after the other team members have been paid a fixed wage. If the monitor receives the residual, he will not have an incentive to shirk as monitor (Douma and Schreuder, 2002: 121-122). Note that the residuals often consist of the residual income.

In the classical capitalistic firm, the monitor is the owner of the firm, he receives the residual income, has the right to sell the firm, has the rights to hire and fire the workers, and to adjust their wages individually. The monitor is the entrepreneur, and the employees can be seen as 'team members'. However, many firms are no longer organised according to the classical capitalistic firms.

> **Box 4.9. Third party or fire alarm.**
>
> An example in the international policy is the United Nation Security Council (UNSC). It can function as a third party for conflicts in countries or between countries for the public. Concerning the use of force the UNSC retains basically similar preferences as the public, willing to support the use of force in response to genuine threats, reflecting the doctrine of self-defence. This organisation has no incentive to support uses of force inconsistent with these objectives. It means that its approval is a credible signal to the public and a proposed use of force is 'pretty prudent' and therefore consistent with public preferences (Chapman and Reiter, 2004: 890).

danger with relying on competing information providers is that they can have some common interests that are in opposition to the decision-maker's (Milgrom and Roberts, 1992: 186). This can lead to collusion.

Managerial moral hazard is frequently reduced by monitoring provided for free by markets. Managers who do a poor job of generating profits, or having led a firm into bankruptcy will face a greater probability of failure. The fear of unemployment and a reputation for having led a firm into bankruptcy may provide them incentives to do their job quite well. Similarly the 'market for corporate control' provides incentives by threatening bad corporate managers with loss of their jobs following a takeover (Milgrom and Roberts, 1992: 186-187).

A very useful form of monitoring could be **making use of third parties** for monitoring. In this case a third party is used for monitoring the agent and it sends credible signals to the principal. The signals could refer to the actions of the agent (shirking, slack, etc) or the presented information (is it misinformation or not?). To be useful and reliable, the third party has to be **independent, an authority and an expert**. The reported information is sometimes called 'fire alarm'. The advantage of using third party fire alarms is that the principal does not need to expend resources and the reported information is reliable. However, sometimes the value of information depends on the preferences of the principal also.

Incentive contracts

In some situations, monitoring actual behaviour or the veracity of reporting may be simply too expensive to be worthwhile. However, it may be possible to observe **outcomes** and to provide incentives for good behaviour through rewarding the outcomes. If it is possible to observe the results, incentive contracts can be used where good (= desired) outcomes – as a result of good behaviour – can be rewarded. Unfortunately, perfect connections between *unobservable* actions and observed resulting outputs are rare. More often people's behaviour partially determines outcomes, and it is impossible to isolate the effectiveness of their behaviour precisely. For example, a firm's total sales depend not only on the efforts of the sales force but also on a host of other factors. Therefore, rewarding on the basis of results makes the salespeople's incomes dependent on random and uncontrollable factors (Milgrom and Roberts, 1992: 187).

Incentive contracts mean a variable payment depending on the efforts or performances. The incomes become subject to random factors. Most people dislike having their income dependent on random factors. They are risk-averse and would rather have a smaller but certain income, than an uncertain income which is, on average, the same but subject to considerable fluctuation (due to unpredictable and uncontrollable variability). The risk created by incentive contracts is costly to these people. They are not as well off with a risky income as they would be receiving the same expected level of pay for certain, and they thus have to be paid more on average to convince them to accept these risks. From the employer's (= principal's) perspective, this extra income is the cost of using incentive pay (cf. Milgrom and Roberts, 1992: 187).

Moreover, this cost can be a real one to society, one that can reduce overall efficiency. The employer is often more tolerant of risk and better able to bear it than the employees. The employer (or owner) cares little about risk and the employee (or worker) may strongly dislike risk. More in general, it means that in a principal-agent relationship, we suppose the principal has a lower risk-aversity level than the agent. Examples of such relationships are:

- an employer-employee relationship; the employer has a lower risk-aversity level than the employees;
- a franchisor-franchisee relationship; the franchisor has a lower risk-aversity level than the franchisee;
- a university-student relationship; the university has a lower risk-aversity level than the student;
- a soccer club-soccer player relationship; the soccer club has a lower risk-aversity level than the soccer player;
- a landowner-tenant relationship; the landowner has mostly a lower risk-aversity level than the tenant;
- a agricultural cooperative-farmer relationship; the cooperative has a lower risk-aversity level than the farmer.

Tying worker's pay to their job performance means that a source of the variability of the earnings is transferred from principals to agents. However, given the risk-aversity level, transferring risk from the principal to the agents means that the total cost of the given amount of risk in the system will increase. Because the principal cares little about risk and benefits little from its reduction, and the agent strongly dislikes bearing risk. As said, risk compensations are a real cost for the society. The risk compensation depends on the risk-aversity level. It means the agent, who strongly dislikes baring risk is only prepared to bear the risk if he or she will be compensated for it. However, this can be – given the risk-aversity level of the agent – very expensive for the principal. An important question is therefore: how can we reduce the total amount of cost for bearing risk? The solution will be to place the risk as much as possible to the least risk-averse party. It means a redistribution of risk between the involved parties.

The ability to adapt to incentive contracts depends on the contracting parties. Designing efficient incentive contracts involves balancing the costs of risk bearing against the benefits of improved incentives. On the one hand, the benefits of incentives are often higher efforts, better performance and higher output, and on the other hand incentives bring about costs. Resources are needed, e.g. money, and in the case of a high risk-aversity level, the compensation can be very high. Striving for efficient contracts means that it is **inefficient** to use contracts that make risk-averse employees bear avoidable risk unless the contracts also provide useful incentives. The basic idea behind incentive contracts is that of achieving 'goal-congruence'. An appropriately designed reward system causes self-interested behaviour to approximate the behaviour the designer wants. Both parties have a common interest (cf. Milgrom and Roberts, 1992: 188).

Bonding

A third way to link parties to each other and to limit hidden action problems is the posting of bonds (bonding) to guarantee performance. This can be achieved by a guarantee deposit, or the purchase of letters-of-debt (obligations) or by posting of bonds. The bond is a sum of money that is forfeited in the event that inappropriate behaviour is detected, i.e. the deposited amount can be confiscated if undesired behaviour (*shirking* or *cheating*) is discovered. Posting bonds can be a very effective way to provide incentives. However, the problem is that people often will lack the financial resources to post a sufficiently large bond. This is especially the case when gains from cheating are large and the probability of getting caught is small. In this case, for an adequate incentive, the bond would have to be large (Milgrom and Roberts, 1992: 189).

A special type of bonding is **age/wage patterns** or **senior provisions,** combined with a **mandatory retirement**. As mentioned before, pay tends to increase with age and experience. We offered an explanation based on inducing self-selection to reduce employer turnover. Bonding can also be used for preventing hidden actions such as shirking employees. If workers were to post bonds of sufficiently greater values than the benefits of shirking, and if being caught cheating resulted in losing the bond, then they would not cheat. Their value to the firm would be increased by the bond that they have to pay. A bond is efficient when it is efficient for the workers not to cheat and shirk. If the gains from cheating are substantial or the likelihood of getting caught is small, workers may be not prepared to post a big enough bond, and the potential efficiency gain would be lost. An alternative for such a bond is paying people more if they stay longer (Milgrom and Roberts, 1992: 189).

A firm can make a credible commitment to workers, such that, late in their careers, it will pay them **more** than the value of what they produce and thus of what they can earn elsewhere. If the firm pays workers **less** than their marginal product (MP) early in their careers, then the value of the lifetime earnings and the firm's total outlay need not to be affected by this scheme. As the years of the high pay come nearer, however, the high promised wages serve as a bond: workers would give up the dishonest behaviour of shirking. The wage patterns duplicate the effect of a bond. It means that the observed pattern of wages can be explained by a need to make workers value their jobs in order to ensure honest, hardworking behaviour (Milgrom and Roberts, 1992: 190).

Paying people more if they stay longer in a firm or organisation can also be seen as a response on to adverse selection and moral hazard. If workers have had in the past a wrong work attitude or were cheating or shirking frequently, they would have been fired. Paying people more the longer they are in a firm is a signal for good workers. Both views (bond and a response on adverse selection and moral hazard) make clear that mandatory retirement is necessary for efficiency. With wages late in their life exceeding the marginal productivity, some people will want to continue working too long because their pay exceeds the social value of their output. They will not retire voluntarily at the appropriate date. Thus, mandatory retirement is necessary for efficiency; it is the foundation for this mechanism.

'Doing it oneself'

A fourth way to prevent some forms of moral hazard is for the principal to do the work *by himself ('doing it oneself')*. Moral hazard in principal-agent settings can sometimes be overcome by eliminating the agents and having the principals act on their own behalf. However, this is often not possible. For example, you cannot very well be your own surgeon, and it often sacrifices the gains of specialisation (Milgrom and Roberts, 1992: 190).

If it is possible, the contractual relationship will end. One solution is carrying out the transaction by making use of the institutional arrangement, the market, (the buying alternative in the **make or buy** decision). Another solution is vertical integration, i.e., the creation of one organisation that has control over the coordination of all the transactions. It is also called *in-house production* and it is in the **make versus buy** decision the *making by yourself solution. Unified ownership* or the *do-it-yourself* option involves bringing two separate organisations under unified direction (Milgrom and Roberts (1992: 92).

Changing the ownership pattern to bring transactions within a single organisation (unified ownership) can help overcome some moral hazard problems and be a response to inefficiencies arising from bounded rationality and private information (cf. Milgrom and Roberts, 1992: 190). However, bringing two separate organisations within a single organisation involves high transaction costs. They are the transactions costs of internal, non-market organisation. Moreover, a unified organisation is not completely free of the moral hazard problems. Such an organisation has to deal with influence costs, which are a form of moral hazard. Influence costs are the costs of activities that arise in organisations when organisational decisions affect the distribution of wealth or other benefits among members of constituent groups of the organisations and, in pursuit of their selfish interests, the affected individuals or groups attempt to influence the decision to their benefits (Milgrom and Roberts, 1992: 192).

These costs arise when employees divert effort to influence organisational decisions. Influence costs are one of the most important costs of centralised coordination. High costs can be an important reason for considering the boundary of the firm; i.e. are other governance structures more efficient than *in-house production*? These costs can be high if there is a decision-maker with authority who is influenced by employees, often looking out for their own interests (Milgrom and Roberts, 1992: 192).

4.3 Bounded rationality, opportunistic behaviour, self-interest, altruism and the use of incentives

Bounded rationality

Real people are not omniscient nor perfectly far-sighted. They cannot solve arbitrarily complex problems exactly, costlessly and instantaneously, and they can not communicate with one another freely and perfectly. Instead, they are boundedly rational, and they know it. They recognise that they cannot possible foresee all the things that might matter for them. They understand that communication is costly and imperfect and that understandings are often flawed and they know that they are not likely to find the mathematically best solution to difficult problems. They then act in an intentionally rational manner, trying to do the best they can given the limitations under which they work, and they learn (Milgrom and Roberts, 1992: 192).

People have only limited possibilities and abilities to obtain and process information, and the capacity of human beings to formulate and solve complex problems is limited. The concept of *bounded rationality* originates from Simon (1961: xxiii) who describes it as follows: 'The capacity of the human mind for formulating and solving complex problems is very small compared with the size of the problems whose solution is required for objective rational behaviour in the real world'. Human behaviour is: 'intendedly rational, but only limitedly so'. Simon (1961: xxiv) uses the term 'bounded rationality' to indicate that decision-makers, who are assumed to be rational, are not *hyper rational*. (see also Section 2.7).

Bounded rationality has a practical significance in a complex and uncertain environment. It may be too costly or impossible to consider all the consequences of a decision and let the transaction or activity take place in the market. The transaction costs of an internal organisational relation (i.e. the 'make by in-house production' decision) can be lower than that of a market relation (i.e. buy decision). *Bounded rationality* is an important characteristic of the human decision-makers in the transaction cost theory of Williamson (1987:11, 30-31; 1998:303-31). It also plays an important role in Evolutionary theory (see Section 2.5 and 2.6).

Bounded rationality is said to arise when the cognitive ability of people is insufficient to deal with the complexity of the world. People are not in a position to take all circumstances into account when making a decision. This means that in addition to bounded rationality, we also have to deal with the lack of information or asymmetric information.

As said, asymmetric information can give rise to opportunistic behaviour, also sometimes termed as strategic behaviour. Williamson (1987: 30) describes opportunistic behaviour as *a condition of self-interest seeking with guile*. **Opportunistic behaviour** includes providing selective and distorted information, making promises which are not intended to be kept, and posing differently from what the person actually is. For the phenomena of hidden information, hidden actions and strategic behaviour, it is sufficient if agents pose differently from what they are and behave differently from what have promised to do, and it is difficult or expensive to determine who they are and how they behave in reality. These issues affect transaction costs and make it difficult to achieve an efficient agreement. In the previous sections we discussed mechanisms that can be used to limit the effects of hidden information and hidden actions.

Time-inconsistency

A special form of opportunistic behaviour is **time-inconsistency** (= *rules of the game are changed by the party deciding the policy or rules)*. The concept of *time-consistency* is identified and developed by Kydland and Prescott (1977: 475). An important aspect in this concept is *credibility* of a pronouncement, or intended policy, etc. The phenomenon of time-consistency is also related to the theory of rational expectations and shows some similarity with the concept of reputation. In many situations, inefficient outcomes result because promises are not (completely) credible or the intended policy is not realised. In the case of policy, when doubts about credibility or the non-realisation of the intended policy arise, we call this *time-inconsistency*. The changes in the rules of the game of the institutional environment are also a form of *time-inconsistency*.

According to Kydland and Prescott (1977: 474-475) *time-inconsistency* occurs when a policy which originally seems optimal but after a time, or when the time comes to put it into practice, it is no longer considered optimal by the policy makers. This has consequences for the credibility. Without a binding agreement, which keeps the government to the original plan, the government has the decision making competence to change to a new policy which appears better under present circumstances. The problem, if people realise this, is that people will anticipate a change in policy and will act in a manner which results in politicians being unable to reach their original goals. Time-inconsistency is a phenomenon which all decision-makers who attempt to affect the behaviour of others have to deal with. In practice, there are several examples. One example concerns the management agreements for nature and landscape preservation between farmers and the government.[31] The farmers may expect that the government, once the agreement is closed, will lower the compensations. Farmers can be anticipated to be extremely reluctant, then, when it comes to conclude a management agreement (see Box 6.5). This is also consistent with the principal-agent approach. See Chapter 6.

Delegation

One way to enhance the commitment or credibility of government policy is to make use of delegation. Delegation occurs when a principal conditionally grants authority to an agent to act on his or her behalf. The relations between a principal and agent are always governed as contracts, even if this contract is implicit (never formally acknowledged or informal; based on unwritten agreement). Hawkins *et al.* (2003: 2-3) state[32] that the principal retains authority not delegated to the agent in the contract, including all rights to make decisions in contingencies relevant to principal control not defined in the contract. This means that the principal retains the rights of *residual control*. The actors – the principal and the agent – are defined only by their relationship.

---

[31] In a democratic system, it is possible that after the elections there will be new government that could involve a new policy or new rules.

[32] It is questionable whether this statement is right, because the contracts are incomplete. This means we have always to deal with residual control rights and residual income. It is *ex-ante* not clear who will able to capture these residuals.

Delegation occurs between different types of principals and agents. The government can delegate tasks and authority to international organisations. For example, The Netherlands is member of the EU. It means that the Dutch government has delegated different tasks and authority to European Commission, the European Central Bank, etc. According Hawkins *et al.* (2003: 14-15) one of the reasons why government delegates tasks and authority to an international organisation is to enhance the credibility of its policy commitment. To increase credibility through delegation, two conditions must be met. **First**, the preferences of the agent must be stronger than those of the (national) government itself, so that left to its own discretion the agent will adopt a policy that moves the outcome in the direction the national government knows it 'should' go but cannot implement itself. **Second**, there must be some costs to withdraw authority from the agent (Hawkins *et al.*, 2003: 14-15). Consequently, in some cases delegation can be seen as a solution for opportunistic behaviour or **time-inconsistency** of the (national) government.

Not only the government, but also firms can delegate tasks. Inherent in all delegation is the principle of the division of labour. An advantage of delegation could be that tasks are delegated to a more or less specialised agent with the expertise, time, (superior local) information and resources to perform the tasks more efficiently. Without such gains from specialisation, there is little reason to delegate anything to anybody. Delegation has as disadvantage the loss of control rights. As said above, the relations between a principal and an agent are always governed by contracts. However, these contracts are mostly incomplete. This means that there are residual control rights and a residual income. The principal can often not avoid the possibility that the agents will receive some of these residual control rights or even a large part of them, and that the agents are able to capture the residual income. Therefore, determining the optimal degree of delegation involves a trade-off between the advantages of making use of specialised agents with the expertise, time, (superior local) information and resources to perform the tasks more efficiently and the loss of residual control rights and residual income. We will on come back to these issues in Chapter 6.

Self-interest, altruism and use of incentives

As said, opportunistic behaviour can be described as self-interested behaviour. Opposite to the behaviour of self-interest we have altruism. Self-interest is often identified with rationality, with the implication that only self-interest individuals are truly rational. However, rationality does not imply self-interest motivations or vice versa. Le Grand (2003: 27) typifies individuals who are motivated to help others for no private rewards as '*knights*' and self-interested individuals who are motivated to help others only if by so doing they will serve their private interests as '*knaves*'. Both types of people could be bounded rational or rational. It should be emphasised that **altruism** may not be confused with **trust**. For example, I might know you to be a knave, but nonetheless trust you to pursue my self-interest in a particular situation simply because it is a situation in which both our self-interests coincide (for instance, bailing out a leaky life boat)[33]. In that case we can trust each other, even though we both are acting as knaves. Of course, it may be easier on occasion to trust someone to pursue your interests if you think they genuinely have your welfare

---

[33] Please, compare this case with the example of reciprocal behaviour in Box 3.2.

at heart; but feelings of altruism between two individuals are not essential to a relationship of trust existing between them or vice versa (Le Grand, 2003: 29-30).

In the psychological literature it is argued that there are two kinds of motivations for action: intrinsic or internal to the individual concerned and one extrinsic or external. It is also argued that there may be a trade-off between the two kinds of motivation, such that too heavy emphasis on extrinsic motivation can drive out intrinsic motivation. So motivations activated by external factors, such as monetary incentives or direct order (as in hierarchical governance structure), can crowd out motivations that are internal to the individual, such as more **altruistic concerns**. However, sometimes extrinsic motivational factors can also reinforce intrinsic motivation if they are seen as supporting self-determination. In that case external motivation is seen as crowding in intrinsic motivation (Le Grand, 2003: 53).

In the economic evaluation literature, there is little attention given to the role of **altruism**. According to Le Grand (2003: 30) the evidence of the existence of apparently altruistic behaviour comes from a wide variety of sources, including interviews with those who have engaged in an altruistic behaviour laboratory experiment, and empirical tests using observed behaviour. The range of such studies is vast. But the conclusions drawn from them are unequivocal. As Matthew Rabin (1997: 13), an economist reviewing both the psychological and economic literature, says: *it has been experimentally verified that people contribute to public goods more than can be explained by pure self-interest, that those free to allocate money as they choose do not universally grab all the money and that people sacrifice money to retaliate against unfair treatment.*

Based on the interviews of Tismuss among 3,800 people who had given blood to the British National Blood Transfusion Service, it can be concluded that altruistic motivations exist (Le Grand, 2003: 31) (see Box 4.10). Empirical support for Titmuss's arguments came from a study in which a sample of the (American) public was interviewed to discover their attitudes toward blood donation (Lepper and Green, 1978 in Le Grand, 2003: 42). A part of the sample was offered a cash inducement to participate in a blood donation programme and a part not. Of those who indicated they were interested in donating blood, those in the group offered cash compensation were less likely actually to supply it than those in the group that was not. For those who were not interested, the offer of cash compensation made little difference (Le Grand, 2003: 41). Titmuss's position is supported by Frey (1997).

The effects of prices as incentives

The findings of Tismuss and Frey clarify the role of incentives. Intrinsic incentives were replaced by extrinsic incentives. Based on findings of Tismuss and Frey we can argue that changes in the supply of any activity in response to changes in the financial rewards associated with that activity will be the result of the interaction of two effects: crowding-out effects and relative price effects. The crowding-out effect occurs when an extrinsic reward is introduced for an activity (such as the introduction of financial payments) and thereby undermines the intrinsic motivation to perform the activity (which may or may not include altruistic motivations). The relative price effect increases the 'price' of not undertaking the activity relative to that of undertaking it (that is, it increases the money forgone through not doing it) and hence encourages a greater supply of

> ## Box 4.10. Two examples of altruism and the role of prices as incentives.
>
> A well-know example of altruism is that of blood donation (Titmuss, 1973). In his study Titmuss (1973) explored the supply of blood in Britain and the USA. Two economists had argued that the solution to acute problem of Britain's chronic shortage of blood for transfusion purposes was to follow the lead of certain parts of the USA and to begin paying blood donors. Titmuss argued that the introduction of cash payments into a system for supplying blood that previously relied upon voluntary donation would lead to diminution of altruistic motivation and in consequence to a reduction in both the quantity and quality of blood supplied. One of basic arguments concerning altruism of Titmuss was (see Le Grand, 2003: 41) that a market in blood was ultimately degrading for society as a whole. It drove out altruistic motivations for blood donation, replacing then with the cruder calculus of self-interest (Titmuss, 1973: 310-311).
>
> Frey (1997) studied the use of monetary compensation to persuade residents of certain communities in Switzerland to accept a nuclear waste depository located in their community. A survey of more than 300 residents found that more than half (51 percent) supported the siting of the facility in their community, despite a widespread knowledge of the risks involved. The question was then repeated with additional information that the government had decided to compensate all residents of the host community. Varying amounts of compensation were offered to different groups of respondents, some quite substantial (equivalent to 12 percent of Swiss median income in the relevant year). Despite its magnitude, the offer of monetary compensation actually reduced the level of public support for the facility by more than half to 25%. This was not due to any change in the perception of risks involved as a result of the offer of compensation: the researchers checked respondents' perception of risk before and after the compensation was offered and found little difference.

the activity. Which effect is dominant at any time will determine the level of supply of the activity concerned (Le Grand, 2003: 53-54).

The result of this reasoning is that the introduction of financial payments for altruistic activities can lead to a crowding-out effect because it reduces individual' perception of the sacrifices they are making to engage in that activity. According to Le Grand (2003: 54) that impact is not continuous, but begins to dominate only as the value of the payment gets close to fully compensating the individuals concerned for their sacrifices. Below that level it is more likely that crowding-in dominates, with the financial payment indicating social approval of the activity and hence encouraging them to supply more of it. If, on the other hand, the value of the compensation is larger than the monetary value of the opportunities forgone by undertaking the activity (the cost), the relative price begins to dominate and again more of the activity will be supplied.

This can be worked out in diagrammatic presentation. Consider an altruistic activity that, if an individual undertakes it, he or she benefits others. An example could be blood donation, but it could also be the supply of any public service that has that property. We distinguish two situations: one for the **knaves** and one for the **knights** (Le Grand, 2003: 67). **First,** suppose that all individuals undertaking the activity are **knaves**: that they derive no benefit from the fact that the activity is of use to others. In that case, they will require some payment to undertake the activity, with the amount increasing as the amount of the activity increases. An aggregate supply curve for an activity might look as (a) in Figure 4.2. It is a conventional supply curve, with increasing activity as payment for the activity increases.

Second, suppose the individuals are all **knights**. That is they derive some rewards from the fact that others benefits from the activity (in contrast to the knaves). Suppose, too, that the reward they derive is related to the sacrifices that they themselves make to undertake the activity. In that case, the supply curve might look something like that in (b) in Figure 4.2. That figure suggests that individuals are prepared to undertake some sacrifice and to supply a certain amount of the activity, Q, without payment (Le Grand, 2003: 68).

If they are then offered a small payment, they might regard this as a recognition or acknowledgement of their sacrifice and become even more favourably disposed towards the activity; hence supply is 'crowded in', and increases, to say, Q*. However, as the payment increases further, the sacrifice they are making in undertaking the activity lessens, and they begin to derive less intrinsic reward from undertaking it. Hence supply is reduced, with a 'crowding-out effect' dominating. This may, as in the diagram, reduce supply to a point where it is less than the original amount, Q, that people were prepared to supply without compensation. As payment continues to increase, however, the relative price effect begins to dominate, and supply increases again. The two points of the curve are the cost thresholds mentioned in the text (Le Grand, 2003: 68).

According to Le Grand (2003: 55) the theory is also consistent with the social psychologists' argument that crowding-in reflects a reinforcement of intrinsic motivations, and crowding-out a controlling of those motivations. External factors can reinforce intrinsic motivation if they are seen as supporting self-determination or self-esteem. In that case external motivation is seen as crowding-in intrinsic motivation. In the cases where individuals value payment, it is plausible to suppose that this is because they feel reinforced in their actions because, through the provision of payment, the outside world is recognising – and appreciating – the sacrifices that they are voluntarily making. In the cases where individuals appear to regard payment as devaluing their

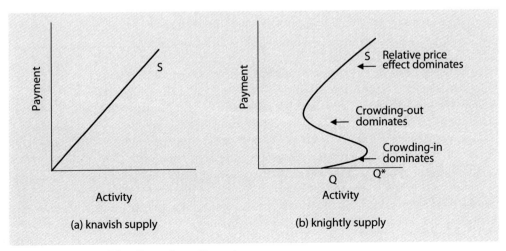

Figure 4.2. Supply and the effects of use of incentives.

altruistic motivation, they may be viewing the payments as controlling – as reducing their sphere of self-determination and self-esteem – and hence they will be demotivating. The individual is no longer making a sacrifice, and has thereby lost a measure of autonomy in what he or she is doing (Le Grand, 2003: 55).

People are motivated to perform altruistic activities because they wish to help others and because they derive some personal benefits from the activities that help others. According the Le Grand (2003:51) the benefits that a person derives from performing an altruistic activity itself is likely to be related to a number of factors. These would include the extent of the help they can offer, the extent to which that help benefits the persons concerned, and probably the degree of approval that the activity concerned attracts form the outside world. However, the motivation to undertake an altruistic activity also seems to depend positively upon the degree of personal sacrifice associated with the activity. Le Grand (2003: 51) terms this the opportunity cost of the activity: that is, the cost to the individual concerned of other opportunities for personal benefits that have to be forgone because he or she has chosen to undertake that activity.

If the cost is too little, the benefits from making sacrifice will also be relatively little and the individual's motivation to perform the activity will correspondingly reduced. For the activity to feel really worthwhile, people need to feel that they have made some effort to perform or to have incurred some significant cost. Too great a cost, on the other hand, will also demotivate them; they will feel that there is a limit to the amount of sacrifice of their interests that are prepare to make for the sake of others. They will therefore feel less inclined to undertake the activity. In other words, there are cost thresholds such that, if the cost falls below the lower threshold or rises above the higher one, people are less likely to perform the activity than if the cost falls in between.

According Le Grand (2003: 52) this 'threshold' account contains some simplistic psychological assumptions and is obviously quite stylised as a description of human behaviour. However, it offers some insights into to apparent contradictions concerning the use of prices as incentives. The blood donation and public reaction to the siting of the nuclear waste disposal facilities indicated that the introduction of prices as incentives devalued that activity. This contrasted with evidence concerning voluntary care giver's activities which suggested that some form of compensation and regarded it as revaluing, not devaluating, their activities (Le Grand, 2003: 52).

'Now the carers who welcome compensation and who do not reduce their activities when offered it (or even do more) may be in the situation where there is still some significant cost of the activity to them: that is, the payment does not fully compensate then for the opportunity cost they incur. Hence some sacrifice is still involved and in consequence they continue to 'value' the activity. The compensation may have actually increased, through indicating a measure of social approval for the activity, the benefit they derive from it, and they may supply more of it. The paid blood donors and those offered a compensation for the nuclear waste disposal facility, on the other hand, may be in the situation where the compensation is adequate or more than adequate to compensate then for their perceived sacrifice. Hence there is no net sacrifice, no altruistic satisfaction from the activity concerned, and the supply is thereby reduced'(Le Grand, 2003: 52).

The above analysis suggests that 'price incentives' can be employed to good effect but that they need to be employed with care. If they are small, then they need not have any crowding-out effect on altruistic motivation; they even complement it. If, on the other hand, they are too great, they may well erode people's sense of sacrifice and thereby reduce their intrinsic motivation to perform the activities concerned. In that case supply will fall. If price incentives increase further, they will increase extrinsic motivation: that is to say, they will appeal to individuals' self-interest, and hence induce further supply of that activity that way (Le Grand, 2003:55).

The amount paid actually paid in any given situation will depend on the level of demand and on the positions of the thresholds for the individuals concerned. If these are known, then the payment issue is relatively simple. If the demand for the activity is relatively low, then the level of altruistic supply, coupled perhaps with a little extra supply crowded-in by some small extrinsic reward, may be sufficient to meet demand. If, on the other hand, demand is relatively high, then the amount paid will have to be sufficient to induce a level of supply through price driven motivations that are more than sufficient to compensate for any fall due to crowding-out of altruistic supply (Le Grand, 2003:55).

In a situation of ignorance concerning the motivational structure, it would be safe to adopt public policy based on the assumption that everyone is price-driven, i.e. motivated by performance-related pay. Of course it can work. However, in practice there are two problems. First, it assumes that the introduction of performance-related pay will have no impact on altruistic behaviour, and it will not crowd out the intrinsic motivation. Second, a system of performance-related pay would require reliable and accurate procedure for measuring and monitoring performance. Such procedures are often difficult to construct and to maintain, especially where quality can be difficult to measure. If quality cannot be properly assessed by the demander the supplier will have an incentive to lower the quality (Le Grand, 2003: 55).

4.4 Commitment and reputation

Commitment

An important element in coordinating and motivating people is commitment. We often have to deal with the problem of imperfect commitment. Imperfect commitment refers to the inability of parties to bind themselves to follow through on threats and promises that they would like to make, but which, having been made, they would later like to renounce. This problem affects both market and non-market organisations, although their nature and impact may differ between organisational forms (Milgrom and Roberts, 1992: 30). Achieving commitment in an organisation or a group is very important because it affects expectations of the members and thereby the behaviour they adopt. Furthermore long-term relationships require commitment.

There are different forms of commitment. Traditional forms include trust, friendship, kinship, ethnicity, religion, etc. These forms of commitment can facilitate economic cooperation without intervention or protection by the government. Consequently, traditional forms of commitment flourish in communities or in areas with little or no government protection. Similarly, traditional forms of commitment often dominate economic life in communities that face a conflict of interest

> **Box 4.11. Credible commitment.**
>
> Another form of commitment is used in the language of game theory. In game theory, a commitment forecloses an opportunity. To illustrate, Julius Caesar sometimes burned the bridges behind him as his army advanced on the enemy. Burning the bridge committed his army to attack by foreclosing the opportunity to retreat. This commitment is achieved by foreclosing the opportunity to run away (Cooter and Ulen, 1997: 170). However, it is also a signal that you are willing to fight. Commitment alone is often not enough, it must also be credible. Burning the bridges behind you is a signal of credible commitment. It is a signal that you are willing to fight.

with the government or that face hostility of the government (cf. Cooter and Ulen, 1997: 196). Common values and norms support commitment to keep agreements, reduce transaction costs and stabilise the underlying relationships.

In situations that generate strong temptations to break mutual commitment, or where there is a lack of common values and norms, sustaining cooperation cannot rely entirely on communication. More robust and long-lasting regimes or organisational modes (e.g. for common pool resources) involve clear mechanisms for monitoring rule conformance and graduated sanctions for enforcing compliance. Monitors – who may be the participants themselves – do not use strong sanctions for individuals who rarely break the rules. Modest sanctions indicate to rule breakers that their lack of conformance has been observed by others. By paying a modest fine, they rejoin the cooperation in good standing and learn that rules infractions are observed and sanctioned. Repeated rule breakers are severely sanctioned and eventually excluded from the group. Rules meeting these design principles reinforce contingent commitment and enhance the trust participants have that others are also keeping their commitments (Ostrom, 1998: 10).

This means commitment alone is not enough, it should also be *credible*. External coercion is also a frequently cited theoretical solution to the problem of commitment. However, this solution does not address what motivates the external enforcer to monitor behaviour and impose sanctions (cf. Ostrom; 1998: 44). A self-organised group (such as a club[34]) must solve the commitment problem without an external enforcer. The members have to motivate themselves to monitor and be willing to impose graduated sanctions to keep conformance high. They have to be self-motivated to observe agreements without making use of an external enforcer.

This means that the crux for bringing about credible commitment (e.g. in **clubs**, such as an environmental club or in **contracts** for nature and landscape preservation by farmers) are monitoring, graduated sanctions and conflict-resolution mechanisms. However, these activities should be carried out on a low cost level. The role of monitoring and credible commitment should be emphasised: without mutual monitoring there can be no credible commitment; without credible commitment there is no reason to propose new rules. Monitoring and graduated sanctions should be undertaken not by external authorities, but by the participants themselves. Mutual monitoring or monitoring by volunteers reduces costs. Farmers who violate the rules are likely to be subjected

---

[34] See Chapter 3.7.

Box 4.12. How to ensure credible commitment for self-organised groups?

According to Ostrom (1998: 94-100), a self-organised group can monitor itself, administer penalties (graduated sanctions), and provide a conflict-solving mechanism to ensure credible commitment. One condition is that it should be possible to do this at low cost. Ostrom (1998: 45) emphasises **first**, the importance of monitoring in such a group: *without mutual monitoring, there can be no credible commitment*. Monitoring and graduated sanctions should preferably be done not by an external authority but by the participants themselves. Monitoring by subordinates or volunteers keeps costs low. **Second**, the persons who break the rules must be confronted with penalties according to the seriousness (= graduated sanctions) and the context of the offence. **Third**, if individuals must follow rules over a long period of time, there must be a mechanism for discussing and resolving differences of opinion. The presence of a conflict-resolving mechanism provides no guarantee that the individuals will keep to the agreement. According to Ostrom (1998: 94-100), it is difficult to imagine how a complex system of rules can be maintained without a conflict-resolution mechanism. Such mechanisms can sometimes be quite informal. Those selected as leaders can also be the basic problem-solvers in case of conflict (Ostrom, 1998: 94-100).

to graduated sanctions, depending on the seriousness and the context of the offence. If individuals are going to follow rules over a long period of time, there must be some mechanism for discussion and for resolving what constitutes a conflict or a difference of opinion.

The presence of a conflict-resolution mechanism does not guarantee that members of a self-organised group, or farmers with an agreement with the government will be able to maintain the rules of agreements. However, it is difficult to imagine how any complex system of rules could be maintained over time without such a mechanism, even quite an informal one. Those who are selected as the leaders could also be the basic mediators or resolvers of the conflict (cf. Ostrom, 1998: 94 -101). To make promises trustworthy, credible commitments need to be established. This is not a problem if the courts can make agreements binding, but in many relational contracts, such court-assured solutions are difficult to attain (Furubotn and Richter, 1997: 276).

Reputation

Reputation is the view formed of an individual or organisation by another based on past experience, and used especially as a basis for forecasting future behaviour. In some cases, it is possible that an individual is able to make favourable information known about him self (e.g. information that he is a desirable contract partner, concerning quality, performance, etc). This impression is made credible by actions in the early period of a long run relationship. That is, over time an individual is able to develop a reputation (Hirschleifer and Riley, 1995: 431). In an environment of imperfect information in which people fear opportunistic or bad-behaviour, reputation is very important. A good reputation can overcome all the problems of opportunistic behaviour, while a bad reputation increases the chance of opportunistic behaviour and hold-up problems (cf. Hart, 1995: 66-67).

Building a **reputation** is one way of showing commitment. However, according to Ostrom (1998: 93-94) it is clear from case studies that even in repeated settings where reputation is important and where individuals share the norm of keeping agreements, reputation and shared values and norms are insufficient in themselves to produce stable cooperative behaviour over the long run. Other ways to realise credible commitment are incentive contracts (with bonuses and penalties) and posting repayable bonds to guarantee performance (see also controlling moral hazard, Section 4.2.4).

If we look at the sources of commitment and trust, there is some overlap (see Section 4.4). Trust is closely related to social norms of behaviour, which are also important elements in commitment. However, commitment can also be realised through more formal rules, or through foreclosing alternatives. Both can have the same effect: reducing hidden actions.

One might say that in each transaction, the decision-maker honours trust in order to encourage future trading partners to offer trust or, in other words, to maintain his of her reputation for honesty. A *reputation* for honesty can be valuable because it can attract (trading) partners. In addition, if it is possible but costly to write detailed contracts, a good reputation can often allow the decision-maker to avoid not only that expense but also the use of costly and error-prone legal contract enforcement mechanisms (Milgrom and Roberts, 1992: 263). One of the ways people enhance the effectiveness of a system of reputations is by narrowing the range of people with whom they do business. Frequent transactions, if they are all of similar magnitude, allow trust to flourish (Milgrom and Roberts, 1992: 266-267).

According to Milgrom and Roberts (1992: 267), the legal system has many disadvantages for contract enforcement. It relies on general rules that may be poorly tailored for particular cases in which disputes arise. Legal procedures are often cumbersome, time consuming and expensive. Judges and juries may often lack enough expertise to evaluate disputes based on technical issues and to apply legal rules appropriately. For this, private practices and common rules have frequently been more important than legal ones for establishing standards of behaviour, discovering facts, ensuring contract compliance and resolving disputes. Often, private rules work by buttressing the *reputation* system itself.

If relationships cover a sufficiently long period of time in which similar agreements have to be repeatedly made, reputation may become important as a coordination mechanism, and common values and norms may develop (Dasgupta, 1991: 79). Common values and norms support a commitment to keep to *ex-ante* agreements. For instance, if a processing firm reneges on an initial agreement with a farmer, the farmer will no longer invest in future relationship-specific assets[35]. Reneging by the processing firm is also a signal to other farmers not to engage in future cooperative arrangements with that firm. Hence, the *reputation* of the user is harmed and it foregoes the benefits of a dedicated supplier relationship.

Nevertheless, a long-term relationship based purely on common values, norms and *reputation* is highly vulnerable to opportunistic behaviour. Consequently, such relationships quickly become

---

[35] Given the non-contractability of relationship-specific investments, incomplete contracts lead to hold-up problems. Changes in asset ownership can affect the severity of the hold-up problem (cf. Hart 1995: 87). However, asymmetric information plays a very limited role in the analysis of hold-up problems.

Box 4.13. One-shot games versus repeated game.

Game theorists speak of *one-shot* games when they wish to emphasise that the recommendation they are offering applies only when the game is to be played once and once only. Rational players have to forgo the full fruits of cooperation in one-shot games like the *Prisoners' Dilemma,* unless some external means of enforcing their pre-play agreements is available. But people seldom play a game just once in real life. Games usually get played over and over again. Repeated games are therefore of much practical importance. If player I breaks his word in a repeated game, then player II has the opportunity to punish him later for his bad behaviour. Sometimes it is enough if player II simply plans to withdraw from their previous understanding. In such circumstances, player I will choose not to shirk on their deal, because the prospective future benefits from continuing his relationship with player II outweigh the momentary advantage to be obtained from revoking (Binmore, 1992: 347).

---

unstable, particularly when economic agents operate in a competitive environment that is changing frequently. In such an environment, bargaining is part of the mutual interaction and common value and norms can not be the sole coordination mechanism (CPB, 1997: 68).

Often the concern with one's reputation may be an effective check on *ex-post* opportunistic behaviour, thus overcoming the temptations to renege or renegotiate. Such concern may even achieve the same results as actual commitment. In contrast, bargaining with terrorists or not punishing naughty children establishes without a doubt, that there is no commitment and invites further challenges. Renegotiating executive pay contracts makes less credible any claims that bad future performance will not be rewarded. Not paying bills or not fulfiling obligations also results in a reputation for being untrustworthy. In a world of costly and incomplete contracts, trust is crucial to realising many transactions. It removes the incentives for opportunistic behaviour by creating a cost offsetting the short-term gains of opportunistic behaviour (Milgrom and Roberts, 1992: 139).

The value of a reputation – and thus the costs incurred in building and maintaining a good one – depends on how often it will prove to be useful. This in turn is related to the frequency of similar transactions, the time horizon over which similar transactions are expected to occur, and the profitability of the transactions. The incentives to build and maintain a *reputation* are larger the more frequent the transaction, the longer the time horizon, and the more profitable the transaction (Milgrom and Roberts, 1992: 139). An important question is which party has the most to lose from a damaged reputation? This is likely to be the one with the longer time horizon, the more visibility, the greater size, the greater frequency of transaction. This outcome also indicates which party in relational contracting should have the discretion to direct activities in unforeseen events. It should be the one with the most to lose from a damaged reputation (Milgrom and Roberts, 1992: 139).

4.5 Risk, uncertainty and risk-aversity

In Section 5.2 we introduced the concepts of risk and uncertainty. As we already said, we will make no distinction between risk and uncertainty, but we can say uncertainties involve risks. The future is uncertain, the results of projects are uncertain; it means uncertainties and risks are part of our daily life. In this section we will further work out the concepts of risk, uncertainty, risk-aversity, expected value, and expected utility. These concepts are part of the theory of expected utility which is the dominant theory of choice under uncertainty (cf. Zerbe and Dively, 1994: 301).

The concept of risk is used in different ways. Risk commonly refers to a positive probability of a bad outcome. We speak of the risk of diving, swimming, skiing or nuclear plants, where the concern is with injury or death. Any time there is a probability, one possibility is worse than the other, so there is risk. Risk of this sort is always present. We are, in this section, largely concerned with income, or financial risks of projects. In a project, the bad outcome refers to a type of variability in benefits or costs streams.

A project whose outcome is uncertain is often called a prospect. When uncertainty exists we can say that there exist *different states of the world*. A prospect then involves more than one state of the world. Two states of the world might be rain tomorrow and no rain tomorrow. As an organiser of an outdoor event, your income may be different according to which state of the world exists, 'rain' or 'no rain'. If it does not rain, your income will be higher than if it does rain.

Expected value

One approach to valuing prospects is to calculate the expected value (EV) of prospects. The EV is a measure of the uncertain outcomes. It is the sum of the values of each alternative outcome times the probability of the outcome. The formula for the expected value is:

$$EV = P_1 X_1 + P_2 X_2 + \dots\dots + P_n X_n \tag{4.5}$$

where P_1 is the probability of receiving the outcome X_1. This can be expressed more concisely as:

$$EV = \sum_{i=1}^{n} P_i X_i \tag{4.6}$$

Each outcome (X_i) is weighted by the probability that it will occur. The **expected value** is the **weighted average of total outcome**. It can be used for choices under uncertainty for consumers and producers. Suppose we have a person who would like to participate in a local lottery – for financing a club house for the soccer club in a small village – with a probability of 10 percent of winning € 100 and 90 percent of paying € 20. Equation 4.7 can be used for calculating the expected value in euro of the person.

$$EV = 0.10 \times 100 - 0.90 \times 20 = -8 \tag{4.7}$$

The expected value approach is also useful in considering ranking alternative projects or prospects. Suppose we have two alternative projects A and B. The costs and payoffs in euro if successful and probabilities of success are given in Table 4.1. We suppose that the costs are independent of probability of success.

Table 4.1. Outcomes of two projects.

	A	B
Probability of success (P)	0.20	0.40
Payoff if successful in euro	4 mln	2 mln
Costs in euro	500,000	400,000

The expected value criterion requires us to choose the project with the highest expected value. For projects A and B the expected values are as follow:

Project A: EV = 0.20 × 4 mln – 500,000 = 300,000
Project B: EV = 0.40 × 2 mln – 400,000 = 400,000

The expected value of B is greater than that of A. If only one project can be undertaken because of budget limitations, space or other physical constraints, then the project with the highest expected value should be chosen if one is using expected values to make the decision (cf. Zerbe and Dively, 1994: 303).

Variability and risk-attitude

The expected value is a very useful and widely used measure. Expected value, however, may not be the best measure of the economic value of a prospect. It considers the probabilities, but does not give full consideration of the variability of outcomes. Consider two alternative projects C and D. Project C has an outcome of € 0 with 50 percent probability and an outcome of € 1 million with 50 percent probability. Project D has an outcome of € 400,000 with 50 percent probability, and an outcome of € 600,000 with 50 percent probability. Table 4.2 summaries the results.

Table 4.2. Results of projects C and D.

	Possible outcome for probability 1	Possible outcome for probability 2	Expected value in Euro
Project C	0.50 x € 0	0.50 x €1 million	500,000
Project D	0.50 x € 400,000	0.50 x € 600,000	500,000

Both projects have equal expected values of € 500,000. But one values them differently, because, there is a great difference in variability of the projects. Project C shows more variability in its outcome and is more risky than project D. Which project do you prefer?

One alternative could be that we define a utility of expected values, which will be the utility associated with the sum that represents the expected values. This can be expressed as U(EV). It represents the utility of the amount of the expected value. However, the U(EV) does not take into account the disutility associated with the variability. If you are more risk-averse you do not like variability. We need a measure that takes into account the risk-attitudes of people and how they perceive more risky results. The question is: which type of project do they prefer if they have a more risk-averse attitude?

As said in Chapter 2, three types of risk-attitudes are distinguished:
1. risk-neutral, where the individual is not sensitive or indifferent to risk;
2. risk-averse, where the individual prefers avoiding risk; and
3. risk-preference, where the individual is said to be risk-preferring.

A risk-neutral individual ranks alternatives according to the value of expected income. Risk-neutral means that an individual is indifferent to risk and he will ask no compensation to induce him to consider a more risky alternative. A risk-averse individual is an individual who with a choice between (1) an alternative with a fixed income (say y_1) to (2) an alternative with uncertain income of which the expected value is identical to y_1, gives preference to the alternative with the fixed income (= y_1). In other words, a fixed amount is valued higher than an uncertain amount which on average would lead to the same yield. In this case, the individual requires to be compensated if he has to bear risk. A risk-preferring person is prepared to accept a lower expected yield under the condition that the distribution in the yield is higher. In the standard neoclassical model, the entire matter of uncertainty and risk-attitude is neglected since perfect information is assumed. However, research has shown that generally individuals are risk-averse. Below we will work out the basic ideas behind the risk-attitudes.

The three attitudes to risk are defined with respect to the relation between the marginal utility of income and the level of income. A decision-maker will be risk-averse, risk-preferring or risk-neutral, according his or her marginal utility of income is diminishing, increasing or constant (Gravelle and Rees, 1992: 562). Figure 4.3 illustrates the graphs of utility functions that respectively represent risk-averse, risk-neutral and risk-preferences.

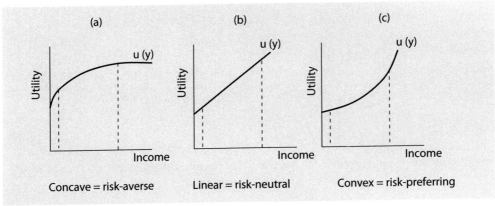

Figure 4.3. How the shape of utility function determines attitudes to risk.

The section between the dotted vertical lines drawn to the curve of the utility function indicates the relevant section of graph for our purpose. For a risk-averse person (a) the utility function $u(y)$ is *concave*, because its derivate $u'(y)$ is decreasing. Thus a risk-averse person has a decreasing marginal utility for money as income (Binmore, 1992: 111).

For a risk-preferring person (c) the utility curve $u(y)$ is *convex*, because its derivate $u'(y)$ is increasing. It means that a risk-preferring person has a increasing marginal utility for money as income. The person with a linear utility function (b) is risk-neutral. A function with straight-line graph is said to be affine. An affine function is therefore simultaneously convex and concave, but not strictly convex and concave (Binmore, 1992: 111).

Expected utility and expected utility function

In spite of the fact that the expected value (see expression (4.5) is a very useful and widely used measure, it has limitations. The reason is that an important factor for determining the value of the expected utility is not only the subjective probability related to a particular outcome, but it also depends on the risk-attitude of the decision-maker. For that reason a better measure is the expected utility (EU). This measure weights the expected euro benefits not only by their probability but also by the marginal utility of income. The expected utility function is often seen as a solution for choice problems in the face of uncertainty.

Utility functions can be written and graphically expressed as depending on the income (or wealth) and utility. Suppose that we are considering two mutually exclusive states such as rain and sunshine, loss or profit, or whatever. Let y_1 and y_2 represent income in state 1 and 2, and let p_1 and p_2 be the probability that state 1 or 2 actually occurs. If the two states are mutually exclusive, so that only one of them can happen, then $p_2 = 1 - p_1$. Given this notation, we can write the utility function as (Varian 2003: 220-221):

$$u = u\,(y_1, y_2, p_1, p_2) \tag{4.8}$$

The utility function of the form:

$$u(y_1, y_2, p_1, p_2) = p_1 y_1 + p_1 y_2 \qquad (4.9)$$

is the expression known as expected value. The expression is the same as Equation 4.5. One particularly convenient form that the utility can take is the following

$$u(y_1, y_2, p_1, p_2) = p_1 v(y_1) + p_2 v(y_2) \qquad (4.10)$$

This says that utility can be written as a weighted sum of some functions of income in each state, $v(y_1)$ and $v(y_2)$, where the weights are given by the probabilities p_1 and p_2.

Von Neumann-Morgenstern utility function as expected utility function

Thus the expression

$$p_1 v(y_1) + p_2 v(y_2) \qquad (4.11)$$

represents the average utility or the expected utility. For this reason, we refer to a utility function with the particular form here as an **expected utility function**. This function is also called a Von Neumann-Morgenstern (N-M) utility function (Varian 2003: 221-222).

What does this mean? When we say that the preferences of a consumer or producer can be presented by an expected utility function, or that the preferences of consumers or producers have the expected utility property, we mean that we can choose a utility function that has the additive form described above. Furthermore, an important property of the N-M expected utility function is that sub-utility indices, which are weighted and added to measure expected utility, are cardinally measurable. It means that not only the amount of the outcome of the expected utility function represents a ranking, but the differences in utility indices have also a meaning of ordering (Boadway and Bruce, 1989: 52).

The **expected utility function** or the N-M expected utility function satisfies the property that it is unique to a **positive affine transformation**. We say that a function is a positive affine transformation if it can be written in the form:

$$v(u) = au + b \text{ where } a > 0 \qquad (4.12)$$

A positive affine transformation simply means multiplying by a positive number and adding a constant. It turns out that if you subject an expected function to a positive affine transformation, it not only represents the same preferences (this is obvious since an affine transformation is just a special kind monotonic transformation) but it also still has the expected utility property (Varian, 2003: 222).

Economists say that an expected utility function is 'unique up to an affine transformation'. This just means that you can apply an affine transformation to it and get another expected utility function that represents the same preferences. But any other kind of transformation will destroy the expected utility property (Varian, 2003: 222).

We claimed above that the expected utility function had some very convenient properties for analyzing choice under uncertainty. Let us apply the expected utility framework to a simple choice problem. Suppose that a student has an income of € 100 per week and is contemplating a gamble that gives him a 50 percent probability of winning € 50 and a 50 percent probability of losing € 50. His income will therefore be random: he has 50 percent probability of ending up with € 50 and 50 percent probability of ending up with € 150. The expected value of his income is € 100 and the expected utility is:

$$½ \, u \, (€ \, 150) + ½ \, u \, (€ \, 50) \quad \text{or} \quad 0.5u \, (€ \, 150) + 0.5u \, (€ \, 50) \tag{4.13}$$

This is depicted in Figure 4.4. The **expected utility** of wealth is the average of the two numbers u (€ 150) and u(€ 50), labelled $0.5u$ (150) + $0.5u$(50) in the graph. We have also depicted the utility of the **expected value** of income, which is labelled u(€ 100). Note that in the diagram of Figure 4.4 the **expected value** of income is less than the **utility** of the expected income. That is:

$$u \, (0.5 \times 150 + 0.5 \times 50) = u \, (100) > 0.5 \, u \, (150) + 0.5 \, u \, (50) \tag{4.14}$$

In this case we say that the student is **risk-averse** since he prefers to have the expected value of his income rather than face the gamble. It means that for risk-averse student the utility of the expected value of income, u (100), is greater than the expected utility of income; $0.5u$ (€ 150) + $0.5u$ (€ 50).

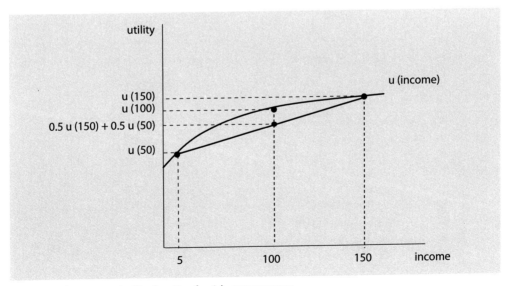

Figure 4.4. The expected utility function for risk-averse person.

It could happen that the preference of the student was such that he prefers a random distribution of income to its expected value, in which we say that the student is **risk-lover.** He prefers risk. This is worked out in Figure 4.5. For a risk-preferring student the expected utility of income, $0.5u$ (€ 150) + $0.5u$ (€ 50), is greater than the utility of the expected value of income, u (100).

Note the difference between Figure 4.4 and Figure 4.5. The risk-averse student has a *concave* utility function – its slope gets flatter as income is increased. The risk-preferring student has a *convex* utility function – its slope gets steeper as wealth increases. Thus the curvature of the utility function measures the attitude of the student towards risk. In general, the more concave the utility function, the more risk-averse the student will be, and the more convex the utility function, the more risk-preferring the student will be. The intermediate case is that of a linear utility function. Here the student is **risk-neutral**: the expected utility of its wealth is the utility of its expected value. In this case the student does not care about the riskiness of his income at all: only about its expected value (Varian, 2003: 225).

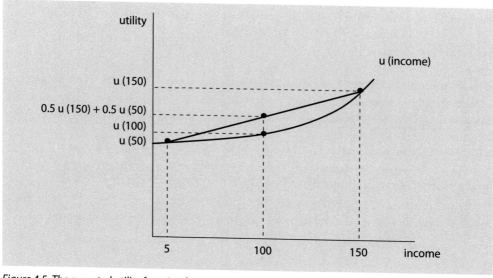

Figure 4.5. The expected utility function for risk-preferring person.

Box 4.15. An example of a risk-neutral and a risk-averse decision-maker.

We are going to make use of the data in Table 4.1. Next we suppose two decision-makers; one is risk-neutral and other is risk-avers. We have learned from above that for the **risk-neutral** decision-maker the expected utility is equal to the expected value. It means for the **risk-neutral** decision-maker the expected utility (EU) is:

For project A: EU = EV = 0.20 × 4 mln – 500,000 = 300,000
For project B: EU = EV = 0.40 × 2 mln – 400,000 = 400,000

For the **risk-averse** decision-maker we suppose that his preferences can be represented by a square root utility function as given in Equation 4.15:

$$EU = p\sqrt{Y} - C \tag{4.15}$$

Where EU = expected utility
Y = payoff if successful
C = costs
p = probability of success

For project A: EU = 0.2 × $4^{1/2}$ mln – 500,000 = 0.2 × 2,000 – 500,000 = -496,600
For project B: EU = 0.4 × $2^{1/2}$ mln – 400,000 = 0.4 × 1414 – 400,000 = -399,434.40

Based on these results, the risk-averse decision-maker would not carry out the projects. It is clear that the results are strongly determined by the expected utility function of the risk-averse decision-maker. If we do not take the square root of Y but we suppose a less risk-averse person, e.g. $Y^{0.8}$, the EU for both projects will be positive (100,000 and 296,000 respectively).

4.6 Prospect theory

In the field of risk behaviour a debate is going on between the adherents of the expected utility theory and the those of the prospect theory (Kahneman and Tversky, 1979: 263-291), a theory for which in 2002 the Nobel price was awarded. The essence of this theory was already given by Adam Smith in 1790: '*We may suffer more when we fall from a better to a worse situation than we ever enjoy when we rise from a worse to a better*'. The 'prospect theory', stems from behavioural economics.

An important difference between prospect theory and the expected utility theory is the risk-attitude about profits and losses; loss aversion is a central concept in the prospect theory. In the expected utility theory decision-makers are often risk-averse; i.e. a certain alternative (e.g. € 1000) is preferred above uncertain alternative with the same average value (e.g. 50% chance on € 2000 and 50% on € 0). This holds for all games of chance, no matter if it deals about profits or losses. However, according to the prospect theory, the (subjective) classification whether the outcome is a profit or a loss plays a role in the risk-attitude.

People feel the pain of a loss (e.g. decreasing share prices) stronger than the joy over profits if the share prices increase. Decision-makers prefer in a loss situation an uncertain loss (e.g. 50% chance on a loss of € 2000 and 50% on a loss € 0) above a certain loss of € 1000 (Van den Assem and Post, 2005: 538). Kahneman and Tversky (1979: 268) show that in the positive domain (see right side of Figure 4.6), the certainty effect contributes to a risk-averse preference for a sure gain over a larger gain that is merely probable. In the negative domain (see left side of Figure 4.6), the same effect leads to a risk-seeking preference for a loss that is merely probable over a smaller loss that is certain. This means that the same psychological principle – i.e. overweighting of certainty – favours risk aversion in the domain of gains and risk-seeking in the domain of losses. It appears that certainty increases the aversiveness of losses as well as the desirability of gains.

Another difference between prospect theory and the expected utility theory is that in the expected utility theory, profits and losses are simply changes in the income levels. However, according to the prospect theory, a decision taker sees profits and losses as a deviation of a subjective reference point or level which does not need to coincide with the income levels. This reference point, for example, can be influenced by personal aspiration and feelings. According Kahneman and Tversky (1979: 277) the carriers of value are changes in wealth or welfare rather, than the final states. The emphasis on the changes as the carriers of value does not mean that the value of particular change is independent of initial position. Value can be treated as a function of two arguments: the asset position that serves as a reference point, and the magnitude of the change (positive or negative) from that reference point.

Many sensory and perceptual dimensions share the property that the psychological response is a concave function[36] of the magnitude of physical change. For example, it is easier to discriminate between a change of 3 °C and a change of 6 °C in room temperature, than it is to discriminate between a change of 13 °C and a change of 16 °C. Kahneman and Tversky (1979: 278) suppose that this principle applies in particular to the evaluation of monetary changes. Thus, the difference

---

[36] See Figure 4.3; a *concave* utility function means its slope gets flatter as income is increased.

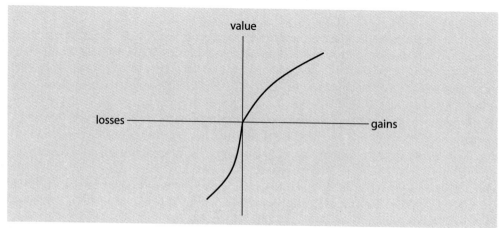

Figure 4.6. A value function (Kahneman and Tversky, 1979: 279).

in value between a gain of 100 and a gain of 200 appears to be greater than the difference between a loss of 1,100 and a loss 1,200, unless the larger loss is intolerable.

Kahneman and Tversky (1979: 279) state that value function is (a) defined on the deviations form the reference level; (b) generally concave gains and commonly convex for losses; (c) steeper for losses than for gains. Thus, a salient characteristic of attitudes to change in welfare is that losses loom larger than gains. A value function which satisfies these properties is displayed in Figure 4.6. The proposed S-shaped value function is steepest at the reference point.

Figure 4.6 shows that individuals relate the improvements or deteriorations in their situation to a point of **reference**, for example their original situation, or the situation that it should be. The 'prospect theory' further states that people give more weight to the deviations from this point of **reference** that they experience as negative than to those that they consider positive. In other words: an improvement is weighed less heavily than a deterioration. The way in which changes are realised and the allocation of property rights play an important role here. People give more (and a negative) weight to a deterioration of a situation that is forced upon them, than they do (positively) to an equally great improvement that they have voluntarily safeguarded. Also people attach more value to the loss of something that they already have than to the attainment of something that is still to come.

The findings that people instead commonly value losses more than commensurate gains have been widely reported in the professional literature for more than three decades. They come from a wide array of survey studies, real exchange experiments, and recordings of the choices made by individuals in their daily lives. One of the earliest reports of these endowment effect disparities were based on survey studies and appeared in the early 1970s. For example, duck hunters said they would be willing to pay, on average, $ 247 to preserve a marsh area important to propagation of birdlife but would demand $ 1044 to agree to its demise (Knetsch, 1999: 4).

Box 4.16. Reference-level.

The public good dilemma of decreased supply and increased demand of environmental goods has gained increasing importance as an item of policy in the EU. This is reflected in the shift in the emphasis of consumer concerns from that of securing adequate food supply towards taking a greater interest in nature, landscape, rural amenities and food safety. Governments have introduced policies not only to persuade farmers, as the custodians of rural resources, to contribute positively to the preservation of nature and landscape but also to avert further degradation.

The shift in the emphasis more to the consumers is connected with the *reference-level*. Hanley *et al.* (1998: 103) defines the *reference-level,* as the level of quality of the environment that the society feels should be present. The *reference-level* can also be the *status quo situation*, or a standard or expectation of the provision-level of environmental goods (cf. Hannemann, 1999: 75). In other words, it all depends on what people find 'normal' or as what it should be.

Box 4.17. Evidence of a disparity.

In an early study involving real exchanges, as opposed to hypothetical ones, participants demanded a minimum to four times as much money to give up a lottery ticket than the maximum sum they were willing to pay to acquire a ticket. A group of individuals in another real exchange experiment were willing to pay, on average, $ 5.60 for a 50 percentage chance to win $ 20, but these same individuals demanded an average of $ 10.87 to give up the identical entitlement. In another example, participants were willing to pay $ 0.96 to acquire a widely available lottery ticket selling for $ 1.00, but these same individual demanded an average of $ 2.42 to give up exactly the same entitlement (Knetsch, 1999: 5).

In sum, there is often not a single value of an entitlement, but different values depending on the whether the entitlement is being gained or lost. The negative value to a community of losing a park will be greater than the value of gaining the same amenity; losing jobs will be more aversive than the benefits of gaining like similar numbers of jobs. In the case of environmental valuations, the valuation disparity has important implications. Given the near universal use of the willingness to pay (WTP) measure to assess losses and reductions in losses, it is important to emphasis that the reported differences of willingness to accept (WTA) is from about 4 to 5 times more than the WTP measures (Knetsch, 1999: 9-12).

The current practice of using the WTP measure, rather than the more appropriate WTA measure, for losses and for reduction of losses for environmental goods will in most cases give rise to systematic understatements of the their values. This will lead to under valuing of activities with negative impacts, such as pollution, risk to health and food safety, as such losses will be underweighed. Similarly, damage fines and compensation for damage or takings of property rights will be too small to provide proper deterrence and restitutions respectively.

Box 4.18. The loss or a shift in property rights.

Through shifting of citizens' preferences, the *reference-level* also changes and hereby also the opinion and attitude over the allocation of property rights between farmers and the government change. If the *reference-level* of a society for the quality of environmental goods rises (the measuring rod is at a higher level), the property rights of these goods will be situated more in the public domain (cf. Barzel, 1997: 5). The result is that people feel that environmental goods, such as nature and landscape, belong more to the society, even though they are located on the land of the farmers. Through such a shift in preferences the allocation of property rights is not fixed. Through changes in allocation of the property rights, the relative decision-power of farmers on the use of their land diminishes. Farmers will say: this *is my land; I have the full property rights*. Through the characteristics – non-rivalry and (to a certain extent) non-excludability – environmental goods such as nature and landscape are not private goods however. Citizens will for this reason, and also because of the shifting of property rights, say: it *is our wildlife and landscape*. The shift in property rights is for the citizens a gain and for the farmers a loss. However the valuation of both is not the same.

These findings have also consequences for the application of the Coase theorem. The usual Coase theorem prediction of finale entitlements resulting from costless exchanges being independent of initial allocations, is often used in the analysis and design of policy reform, including those related to environmental goods. However, this prediction is critically based on the assumption of gains and losses being valued the same. As it now appears this assumption is generally not right. This reduces the validity the Coase theorem and increases the disadvantages of takings, not only for public goods but also for land reform programs. We will come on these issues in Chapter 10 and 11. According to Knetsch (1999: 12), the results will often be quite opposite – final allocations will usually depend on initial distributions.

4.7 Application: bargaining over a sale

The possibility of failing to reach an agreement can arise in a simple problem with private information about values. Consider two people, a **buyer** and a **seller**. The seller owns a unit of some good in which the buyer is interested (e.g. a painting). Each is **privately informed** about the value that he or she places on having the good. However this information is hidden for the other party. Both parties have only an estimation of the value for the other party. The buyer believes that the seller values the good either at 20 Euro or 10 Euro. The seller believes that the buyer values the good at either 5 or 30 Euro. The buyer assigns a probability of 0.2 to the seller's valuing the good at 20 Euro and correspondingly, a probability of 0.8 that it is worth 10 Euro to her. The seller assesses a probability of 0.2 that the buyer's valuation is 5 Euro and a probability of 0.8 that it is 30 Euro. Table 4.3 gives an overview of the probabilities and valuations. Of course, the seller knows what the good is actually worth to her, and the buyer knows what it is worth to him.

If the actual valuations (or reservation prices) are 5 Euro for the buyer and 20 for the seller, it is efficient for the good to remain with the seller – this maximises the total value. It means there will be no trade. This occurs with probability $0.2 \times 0.2 = 0.04$. If the valuations (or reservation prices) are 5 Euro for the buyer and 10 Euro for the seller, again it is efficient for the good to remain with the seller. Again there will be no trade. Because the price offered by the buyer is below the reservation price of the seller. This occurs with a probability of $0.2 \times 0.8 = 0.16$.

Table 4.3. Efficient outcomes with different possible valuations.

Buyer's value	Seller's value	
	10 Euro Probability = 0.8	20 Euro Probability = 0.2
5 Euro Probability = 0.2	Probability = 0.2x0.8=0.16 No trade	Probability = 0.2x0.4=0.04 No trade
30 Euro Probability = 0.8	Probability = 0.8x0.8=0.64 Trade	Probability = 0.8x0.2=0.16 Trade

If the valuations of the buyer is 30 Euro and for the seller 10 or 20 Euro, efficiency demands that a sale occurs and the good will be transferred. This occurs with a probability of 0.64 resp. 0.16. Remark: the valuations of the buyer are in both cases higher than the reservation price of the seller; it means there will be trade. This can be noticed in the last row of Table 4.3.

Based on the information in Table 4.2 we can also calculate the expected values as a guideline for starting bargaining.

Buyer He believes that the seller values the good either 10 or 20 Euro. The expected value is:
EV = 0.8 × 10 + 0.2 × 20 = 12 €

Seller She believes that the buyer values the good either 5 or 30 Euro. The expected value is:
EV = 0.2 × 5 + 0.8 × 30 = 25 €

If the valuations were known, there would not be much difficulty. Both parties would know what the good was worth to the other, and if there is a value gain from transferring the good, they ought to be able to settle on some payment from the buyer to the seller that makes both parties better off. However that is usually not the case.

Figure 4.7 shows the graphical presentation. The expected values are 12 and 25 respectively. Figure 4.7 also shows the bargaining area. It is the area where the values of the buyer and seller overlap each other. Outside this area there will be no trade. According to the belief of the buyer, the seller is – on the one hand – not prepared to sell the good below a price of 10 euro. On the other hand, according to the belief of the buyer, the value of good for the seller is not more than 20 euro. Because of the lack of information about the true willingness to sell (of the seller) and the true willingness to pay (of the buyer) we have to make use of this kind of strategy.

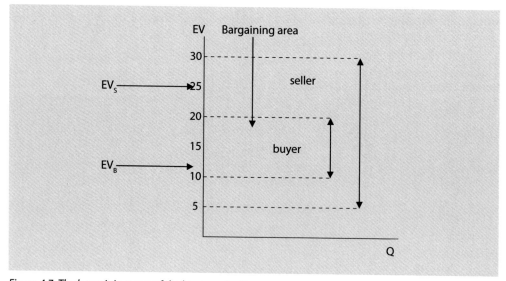

Figure 4.7. The bargaining area of the buyer and seller.

In the standard neoclassical economic approach, we suppose that there is no private information about the valuation of goods. Thus we assume that we know the willingness to sell (of the seller) and the willingness to pay (of the buyer). The way of reasoning is as follows: we have a number of the same goods (see Q), and for the simplicity we suppose only **one buyer** and **one seller**. At a price of 10 euro buyer A would like to buy 30 units of the goods, and at a price of 30 euro 5 units of the goods. At a price of 15 euro the seller is prepared to sell 10 units and at a price of 20 euro 25 units of the goods. The graphic presentation is given in Figure 4.8. The willingness to pay is the area under the demand curve and the willingness to sell is the area above the supply curve. The overlapping area of both is the bargaining area. In Figure 4.8, it is the area ABC.

The area ABC is also the surplus area, consisting of the consumer and producer surplus. The area above the price line P_e is the consumer surplus. It is the difference between what the consumer is willing to pay for a good (indicated by the area under the demand curve) and what he/she has to pay. What he/she has to pay is in Figure 4.8 the price P_e. This price is also called the reservation price; it is the price that a buyer would be willing to pay for an item, given preferences, income and price of other goods. The producer surplus is the area above the supply curve and below the price line P_e representing the difference between the minimum amount the seller will accept for any unit sold (willingness to sell) and its actual price. We also need these concepts for the distribution of the surplus or rents arising as result of the use of relation-specific investments. This will be applied in Chapter 5.3.

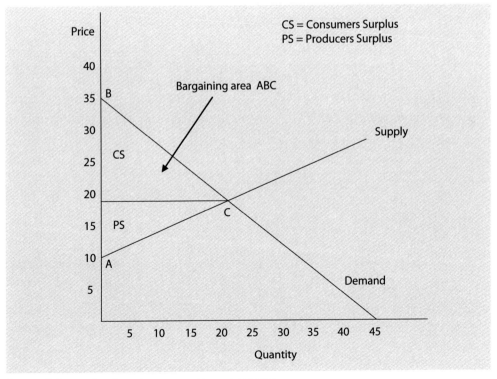

Figure 4.8. Demand and supply curves and bargaining area.

Box 4.19. Key terms of Chapter 4.

Characteristics of information goods	Monitoring
Non-rivalry and non-excludability	Incentive contacts
Lack of information	Bonding
Uncertainty	Doing it oneself
Risk	Opportunistic behaviour
Variance	Time-inconsistency
Standard deviation	Delegation as remedy for time-inconsistency
Information – asymmetry	Self-interest
Hidden information	Altruism
Private information	Internal incentive
Adverse selection	External incentive
Hidden actions	Crowding out effects
Moral hazard	Commitment
Bad money drives out good money	Reputation
Signalling	Expected value
Screening	Risk-attitudes
Self-section	Expected utility
Information revealing mechanisms	Loss aversion

5. Attributes of transactions and transaction cost economics

5.1 Introduction

As we said in Chapter 1, transaction cost theory is an important field in new institutional economics. Williamson (1987; 1998; 2000) has delivered important contributions to transaction cost economics. He considers transaction cost economics to be the product of two recent and complementary terrains of economic research. The first is New Institutional Economics; the second is the New Economics of Organisation. A key conceptual move for both areas of research was to push beyond the 'theory of the firm' in which the enterprise was considered merely as a production function (a matter of technical construction), into a 'theory of the firm as a governance structure' (which is an organisational construction). Work in both of these areas began to take shape in the nineteen seventies and has grown exponentially since (cf. Williamson, 1998: 23).

The attributes of transactions and transaction cost theory are at the centre in this chapter. In the previous chapters we paid attention to sunk investments, asset specificity, governance structures, opportunistic behaviour, bounded rationality and uncertainty. These are all important basic elements in transaction cost economics. This theory tries to explain which type of organisation. or governance structure has a comparative advantage in carry out transactions. According to this theory, the characteristics of human decision-makers and the environmental characteristics of the transaction are especially important in determining the comparative advantages of a transaction mechanism. Concerning characteristics of human decision-makers, transaction cost economics is based on bounded rationality and opportunistic behaviour. Section 5.2 addresses the most important ideas of the founding fathers of transaction cost theory. Williamson in particular has delivered an important contribution to this theory.

In Section 5.3 we apply the basic elements of Williamson's transaction cost theory. The central approach of transaction cost economics (TCE) is to focus on the transaction as the unit of analysis used to explain which organisational mode or governance structure has a comparative advantage in carrying out transactions. While the transaction is the unit of analysis, the governance structures are chosen depending on: (1) the transaction attributes (*asset specificity*, *uncertainty* and *frequency* of the transaction); and (2) the human characteristics of the decision-makers (*bounded rationality and opportunistic behaviour*). We will denote (1) and (2) as the characteristics of the transaction, i.e. the exogenous variables, while the endogenous variable is the choice of the governance structure. We will make use of a number of numerical examples throughout the chapter.

An important study object of TCE are also the governance structures in which transactions are carried out. The results of these transactions are not only strongly influenced by the institutional environment, but also by the social embeddedness of the transaction. Given both, it is important to investigate which transaction attributes are decisive for determining the transaction costs and subsequently for the most suitable governance structure. In Section 5.4 we develop a framework for analysing this question. This framework contains more attributes of the transaction than the initial approach of Williamson.

The chapter concludes with Section 5.5. Here we present two methods for determining transaction costs. In both approaches, the government is one of the contract partners, in this case the contract giver. The other transaction parties are private landowners and farmers. It is common to make a distinction between private and public transaction costs. The private transaction costs are the costs born by private parties and the public transaction costs are the transaction costs for the government. In the last example, based on an EU research project, we make use of the positive approach by investigating step by step what people understand as transaction costs.

Key questions:
- Why do firms and organisations exist?
- What does the transaction view mean and does this view explain the initial organisational mode or governance structure?
- Which factors determine the choice of the governance structure according to Williamson?
- In which situations are long-term contracts and vertical integration efficient governance structures?
- Which factors are important and which steps have to be undertaken to calculate the effects of the so-called fundamental transformation?
- What are the main points of criticism on Williamson?
- How can Williamson's version of transaction cost economics be extended?
- What are the differences between private and public transaction costs and how can they be determined?
- How do transition costs differ from transaction costs?

5.2 Transaction cost theory

In the classical article of Coase (1937) 'The nature of the firm', the fundamental question raised is: 'Yet having regard to the fact that if production is regulated by price movements, production could be carried on without any organisation at all, well might we ask, why is there any organisation? (cf. Putterman and Kroszner, 1996: 91). In simple words, why do organisations or firms exist? What is their economic function, what determines which transactions take place via the market, and which occurs via a formal organisation in the form of a firm. Coase's answer was that there are costs linked to carrying out transactions, and that the size of these transaction costs depends on the nature of the good, the nature of the transaction and the way in which it is organised (cf. Milgrom and Roberts, 1992: 28).

The costs linked to the use of the market mechanism consist of: (1) finding the relevant prices; and (2) the costs of negotiating and the specification of the good to be transferred; and (3) the institutional arrangement to be used to specify and transfer the property rights of the good. It may be difficult or impossible to arrive at a completely specified activity or good which can be used for a *market* transaction. It may be more efficient and effective to enter into an organisational relation, e.g. a long-term labour contract, instead of hiring labour every day via a market. In other words, a firm as an organisational unit can exist only if it can carry out its coordination function at lower costs than by undertaking market transactions each time.

Coase (1992: 715) already came up with this answer in 1932. The use of the price mechanism involves costs. What the price is, has to be determined. Negotiations have to be made, contracts have to be signed, inspections carried out and agreements have to be made to sort out differences in opinions. When taken together, these costs are known as transaction costs. The presence of these costs implies that organisation modes other than the *market* are still preferable; making use of the market would be linked to high costs or would be imperfect in various ways. Reducing the costs of carrying out transactions via the *market* explains, according to Coase, the existence of firms. Thus, the allocation of the factors of production arises via management decisions. In his 1937 article, Coase stated that in a competing coordination system, there is an optimum for planning. A firm as a planning unit can only exist if on the one hand its coordination function can be carried out at lower costs than that by *market* transactions (cf. Coase, 1996: 92).

It has taken a long time for the ideas of Coase to be analysed and understood. One reason for this is that transaction costs are difficult to define. Another argument came from Alchian and Demsetz (1972). They had a conceptual problem with Coase's approach. Alchian and Demsetz (1972: 777) argued that it was not possible to make a distinction between contracts via the *market* and *contracts* between employer and employee. They (1972: 794) considered a firm to be like a *contractual structure*. The acquisition of the resources, the production and the delivery of the end-product are organised via contractual relations. However, the mistake that Alchian and Demsetz (1977) made is that they assumed **complete contracts**. The specification of *contracts*, for all possible future situations which can arise, is not only difficult but would also involve enormous costs.

Jensen and Meckling (1976: 310-311) adopted the Alchian and Demesetz view of firms as a broadly defined contractual structure and stated that organisations such as firms, non-profit organisations and government agencies consist of a *nexus of contracts*. These contracts can be internal or external. With an internal contract, the firm decides to provide the requirements from within the organisation, and with an external contract, the provisions are delivered by a third party. This refers to the classic **make versus buy** decision which has long been a subject of research. The background of the **make or buy** decision is the choice that a firm must make about whether it should make an intermediate good in-house or secure it in some market or via contracts. The **make or buy** decision[37] also refers to the fundamental question regarding the reason for the existence of organisations and how they function.

For answering the fundamental question raised by Coase we will use the *transaction view*. The most fundamental unit of analysis is the *transaction;* the transfer of goods or services from one individual to another. Transaction is synonymous with the economic concept of exchange. It is a two-sided mechanism: the transfer of goods or services from one individual to another (including the transfer of property rights) or the trade-off between performance and counter performance, *quid pro quo*. Transactions should be organised as efficiently as possible. In the *transaction view*, the transaction cost theory is at the centre.

---

[37] The make-or buy decision mostly refers to the backward integration into input production. Most of the literature about manufacturer's decision to make or buy its derives his predictions from transaction cost economics (Lafontaine and Slade, 2007: 648).

Transaction cost economics frames the problem of economic organisation as the problem of carrying out a transaction. The *quid pro quo* refers to concluding an agreement (by sale and purchase) or a contract. In either case, a special assignment must be carried out. This can be done in various ways. Each transaction of a good or service involves costs. There are various views of the concept transaction costs. Arrow (1969: 48), cited in Williamson (1987: 18), has defined transaction costs as 'the costs of running an economic system'. Williamson (1987: 19), views transaction costs as the economic equivalent of frictions in the physical system.

The transaction costs approach is also closely related to the contractual perspective on organisations. According to Williamson (1987: 20-22), transaction cost economics poses the problem of economic organisation as a problem of **contracting**. He (1987; 1991; 1996; 1998; 2000) is primarily responsible for the main contribution in extending transaction cost theory. His work, based on Coase, gives primary importance to transactions. He attempts to explain why institutional arrangements offer comparative advantages in the carrying out of different types of transactions. A particular task is to be accomplished and it can be organised in any number of ways. According to Williamson, the main modes of organisation are *markets* and *hierarchies*. The spectrum of institutional arrangements, within which transactions can be conducted, runs from markets on the one end to centrally planned hierarchical organisations on the other end (Williamson, 1987: 16).

With the transaction costs approach, the firm is perceived as an institutional solution to avoid the costs of the price mechanism (i.e. making use of the market as governance structure. The firm is also considered a mode of organising for certain contracts which are not easy to deal with in a market relationship. The answer to the question of which institutional arrangement (market, organisation or hybrid forms such as a contract) is most suitable in a particular situation depends, according to Williamson (1987: 11, 30-31, 52; 1998: 30-31), on the *human characteristics of the decision-makers (bounded rationality and opportunistic behaviour)* and the *characteristics of the environment (asset specificity, uncertainty and frequency of the transaction)*, in short, the transaction attributes. These aspects which are connected to a transaction determine the size and nature of transaction costs.

This also means that the *characteristics of human decision-makers* and *transaction attributes* of the transaction determine the comparative advantages of the transaction mechanisms *market* and *organisation* (Williamson, 1987: 11, 30-31; 1998: 30-31). The human characteristics on which transaction cost economics is based – *bounded rationality* and *opportunistic* (strategic) *behaviour* – have been described in Chapter 4. The human characteristic *bounded rationality* has a practical significance in a complex and uncertain environment. It may be too costly or impossible to consider all the consequences of a decision and to use the market for carrying out the transaction. The transaction costs of an internal organisational relation (i.e. **make** by in-house production or vertical integration) can be lower than that of a market relation (i.e. **buy**).

Opportunistic behaviour is also a human characteristic consisting of the provision of selective and distorted information, making promises which are not intended to be kept, and pretending to be different from what the person actually is. This means that the phenomena of *hidden information* and *hidden actions* are also included in Williamson's approach. In this view, it is expected or assumed that some of the agents will behave differently from what they appear to be doing and it is difficult or expensive to determine who they are and how they behave in reality.

As said, transaction cost economics tries to explain which institutional arrangement or mode of organisation has a comparative advantage in carrying out transactions. While Williamson (1987: 18) used the term governance structure, we consider all three of these terms, institutional arrangement, mode of organisation, and governance structure, to have a similar meaning. According to TCE, the comparative advantages of these transaction mechanisms are determined by important transaction attributes. They consist of:

- **Asset specificity**
  Within the attribute of *asset specificity* (also called relation-specific investments*)*, a distinction can be made between: *site specificity, physical asset specificity, human asset specificity, dedicated assets* and '*brand name capital*' (cf. Williamson (1987: 55; 1996: 55-56). The *site specificity* refers to the (special) location of the asset, and the place-restriction (e.g. tied to a particular area), reflecting the distance and accessibility in terms of time and money. These characteristics of a good refer to the specific use of an asset as a result of its position. Place-restricted investment can reflect *ex-ante* decisions to reduce supply and transport costs. Such investments are difficult or impossible to change once they have been made. *Physical asset specificity* involves investment in a machine or building which has a narrowly defined use. *Human asset specificity* exists whenever people obtain training or develop their skills which can then only be applied in specialised areas.
  Dedicated assets specificity refers to an investment in a general purpose asset made at the request of a particular transaction partner. The specificity here refers to committing funds to a specified transaction that might have been used elsewhere. In most cases, the manner in which the financial means are obtained is a one-time only event. There is no possibility of developing a structural relation. Finally, the fifth type called *brand name capital specificity*, refers to becoming affiliated with a well-known *brand name* and thus becoming less free to pursue other opportunities. Perhaps the most colourful example of brand name specificity occurs with actors on popular television shows. For example, the personage of actors in a popular television soap can in effect become brands, and this identification in the public's eyes prevent these actors from being taken seriously in other programmes. In such cases, the person is associated with a specific character in a comparable manner as with a well-known brand-name and thus has fewer possibilities for other alternatives (FitzRoy *et al.* (1998: 212).
  According to Williamson (1987: 30), the asset specificity is the most critical dimension for describing transactions. The basic reason is that the more committed one becomes to a transaction, the more one stands to lose from unforeseen events and the possibility that contracting partners may find it in their interests to renegotiate more favourable terms from you given that you have committed (or sunk) assets. The various forms of *asset specificity* make transacting parties fearful of making a commitment that later prove to be *one way,* or its turn out to be non-reversible FitzRoy *et al.* (1998: 212-213).

> **Box 5.1. Asset specificity and sunk-investments.**
>
> An investment is said to be specific, when the asset in which the investment has been incorporated has a higher value inside the specific relationship than outside it. Asset specificity is a measure of non-redeployability. Such investments are called sunk investments, because part of costs are sunk into the relationship, i.e. cannot be recovered elsewhere (for sunk-investments see also Chapter 2). Asset specificity, and therefore the sunk aspect of investments, occurs in so many ways that five types of specific investments are distinguished (cf. Hendrikse, 2003: 207).

- **Uncertainty**

  In addition to asset specificity, Williamson (1987: 52) also distinguishes of the aspects *uncertainty* and *frequency* of a transaction which affects the size and nature of the transaction costs. *Uncertainty* includes possibilities or events which can be anticipated at high cost, as well as events which cannot be anticipated or are difficult to anticipate. In addition, it also includes the sort of uncertainty where one party has information which the other lacks; this is as explained in Section 4.2 asymmetric information. Uncertainty will extensively be worked out in Section 5.3 and 5.4.

- **Frequency**

  The aspect '*frequency*' indicates the intensity with which transactions are handled. With a low frequency, the costs per transaction will be relatively high. If transactions are regularly made, then a special provision can be arranged. The creation of a special structure (governance structure) is only appropriate if transactions are frequent. Such provisions involve, on the one hand, costs which have to be evaluated against the benefits (Williamson, 1987: 60). On the other hand, an increase in the intensity of the transactions can result in scale-effects; with an increase in the number of transactions, the costs per transaction will decline.

Summarising, the human characteristics of *bounded rationality* and *opportunistic behaviour* (including strategic behaviour) together with the environmental characteristics *asset specificity, uncertainty and frequency*, can result in transactions taking place within a specific organisational relationship or structure. In the next section, we will apply these basic elements and demonstrate how transaction costs economic analysis is constructed.

5.3 Transaction cost economics: applying the basic elements

Transaction cost economics (TCE) tries to explain which organisational mode or governance structure (we consider both as synonyms) has a comparative advantage in carrying out transactions. The transaction is the unit of analysis, while governance structures are chosen depending on:

1. the *characteristics of the environment* (*asset specificity, uncertainty* and *frequency* of the transaction); and
2. the *human characteristics of the decision-makers* (*bounded rationality* and *opportunistic behaviour*).

Box 5.2. *Ex-ante* and *ex-post* transaction costs.

Ex-ante costs arise **before** the transaction occurs. In this situation, search-costs by suppliers and consumers arise. This includes the costs of obtaining information about the product, price, quality, amount, time and place. These costs arise in the first phase of the transaction process, i.e. the contact-phase. According to Williamson (1987: 20) the *ex-ante* transaction costs consist of the cost of *drafting, negotiating, and safeguarding an agreement.*

Ex-ante costs also include costs associated with the second phase of the transaction process: the contract-phase, i.e. closure of the agreement. In this phase, costs can appear as a result of *ex-ante* attempts to evaluate problems, uncertainty and risks and to manage them. *Ex-post* costs arise **after** the agreement is closed. These costs include the costs which occur in the third phase of the exchange process; carrying out and controlling observance (the control phase). These costs involve the costs of monitoring, renegotiating and adapting, and may be arbitraged through a third party.

According to Williamson (1987: 21), the *ex-post* costs of contracting take several forms; (1) maladaption costs are incurred when transactions drift out of alignment, including the opportunity costs of maintaining the contract under changed circumstances; (2) the haggling cost is incurred if bilateral efforts are made to correct *ex-post* misalignments, including the adaptation costs in case of changes in the contract; (3) the set-up and running cost associated with the governance structure to which disputes are referred; and (4) the bonding cost of effective secure commitments. A complicating factor is that the *ex-ante* and *ex-post* costs of a contract can be mutually dependent (Williamson (1987: 21).

We will denote (1) and (2) as the characteristics of the transaction, i.e. the exogenous variables, while the endogenous variable is the choice of the governance structure. As explained in Section 3.6, a broad spectrum of governances structures can be distinguished.

The choice of governance structure should take into account the *transaction* and *the organisational mode view*.[38] The transaction view is often used as a starting point for the analysis of the choice of the governance structure, assuming that a governance structure is chosen which minimises total costs, i.e. the joint transaction costs and the production costs. Transaction cost economics simplifies this analysis by assuming that transaction and production costs, e.g. the presence of or absence of economies of scale, are determined separately and can be added together in order to determine the total costs of a certain way of organising. It implies that production costs can be ignored in determining the most efficient governance structure, i.e. the choice of the governance structure is driven by minimising transaction costs (Hendrikse, 2003: 211).

However, the pure transaction view does not explain the initial organisational mode or governance structure, but only that they are different because of the transaction costs for carrying transactions. In transaction cost economics this problem is solved by assuming that an efficient

---

[38] The organisational mode view includes, among others, the legal entity, the used coordination and motivation mechanisms. See also Chapter 8.

governance structure is adopted and that very inefficient ones are not likely to survive[39]. This assumption is connected with the evolutionary theory. Thus, according to the pure transaction view this means that we have the market as a governance structure, because the market is an efficient governance structure.

A more appropriate view is that the initial reason – as explained in Sections 2.4 and 3.6 – for why we have a governance structure is that a governance structure such as the market, adds value by carrying out transactions. Some governance structures are better able to capture the quasi-rents of specific assets than others. This means, we should partially include the organisational mode view. However, the organisational mode view extends further. It also focuses on the ways of coordination and motivation, the corporate status and the legal entity. This will be discussed more extensively in Chapter 8. In transaction cost economics, the emphasis is on the transaction view, but this should also include the value-creation expressed in (quasi-)rents and the distribution of the (quasi-)rents. The distribution of the (quasi-)rents can also be considered as the appropriation of the quasi-rents (Williamson, 1987: 65).

Transaction-specific investments, investments with a low level of redeployment and investments with a high level of asset specificity (which all can be considered as synonyms) are crucial elements in transaction cost theory. As explained in Section 2.4, they create quasi-rents. However, according to transaction cost theory, it is not desirable to start or to have a market relationship when significant transaction-specific investments are involved. This can be illustrated by the numeral example in Section 2.4. The farmer/tenant would disregard the investment in land improvement in the case of a market relationship or a short-term one year contract. However, suppose the farmer/tenant has a land tenure contract of 6[40] years. If the investment is made, then the possibility may arise for *ex-post* opportunistic behaviour of the landowner.

Because of the higher return of the land, the landowner can threaten the tenant that he has to pay a higher land rent, otherwise the landowner is not prepared to continue the land tenure contract after the termination of the contract period (e.g. for a renewal of the contract for a duration longer than 6 years). The bargaining power of the tenant is lowered because of his asset specific (site specificity) investment in land improvement. Hence, he is locked-in. If he does not agree with a higher lease price, he will loss the value of his investment in land improvement. When considering the best governance structure, in this case, a long-term contract between the tenant and farmer, or a farmer/owner structure in which the farmer is also the owner of the land, are both preferable options in which transaction costs are reduced.

The next example is partly based on Hendrikse (2003: 206-209). Consider two parties in the production column 'flowers'; an upstream and a downstream party. The flower auction is the upstream party and the flower growers are the downstream party. Between both parties there exists a certain transaction relationship; the auction sells the flowers of the flower growers. The upstream party (= the flower auction) has spent time and effort on developing a new computer

---

[39] However, this does not guarantee that only efficient governance will emerge.

[40] Given his age, the farmer/tenant will not carry out the investment. But suppose he has a son who would like to continue the farm. In that case farmer could decide to do the investment.

system for processing the flowers delivered by downstream party (the flower growers). The computer system is used by the flower growers on a contractual basis. The total costs for the inventor are 20 million euro where an amount SC of these costs is sunk, i.e. these costs are not recoverable elsewhere. It is a transaction-specific investment. The remaining amount (20 million euro minus SC) is recoverable elsewhere, i.e. a certain part of the computer system can be used for other purposes. We assume the value for the downstream party is 25 million euro. Table 5.1 summarises these figures. The focus of the transaction cost economics is on the quasi-rent. Table 5.1 also shows the relationship between the rent and the quasi-rent. The quasi-rent is always at least as large as the rent.

If we discard the unit of currency, the quasi-rent is the total value minus the recoverable costs or

$$25 - (20 - CS) = 5 + SC \tag{5.1}$$

The party that did the transaction-specific investment is (*ex-post*) tied to the relationship (Compare example in Section 2.4 and Appendix 2.1), because the value is the highest within the relationship. Doing this type of investment is called by Williamson (1996: 61) the fundamental transformation (associated with the concept of 'being trapped'). The quasi-rent of this cooperation is allocated partly according to the contractual agreement made. However, this contract did not cover all possible situations *ex-ante*, so that the allocation of the quasi-rent also depends, to a certain extent, on the *ex-post* bargaining position.

Assume that both parties agree, before the relational-specific investment has been carried out, that the (quasi)-rent will be equally shared. This means that the bargaining power is such that half of the quasi-rent goes to each party, i.e. equal bargaining power. Next, we assume no opportunistic behaviour. With these assumptions, the compensation (= contract price) for the transactions between both parties can be determined before, as well as after, the fundamental transformation. The total rent associated with the transaction is 25 – 20 = 5. Each party receives half of the rent, which means *ex-ante* a contract price of 22.5. The profit for the upstream investor (= producer surplus) amounts to 22.5 – 20 = 2.5 and the profit for the downstream party (= consumer surplus) comes to 25 – 22.5 = 2.5.

Table 5.1. Overview of the costs and benefits.

	Amount in million euro
Value for downstream party (TV)	25
Total costs (TC)	20
Sunk costs (SC)	SC
Recoverable costs (RC)	20 – SC
Rent (R)	25 – 20 = 5
Quasi-rent (QR)	R + SC

However, sunk costs are involved after the specific investment in the computer system is made. Some of the costs invested by the upstream investor are specific to the project and therefore cannot be recovered elsewhere. Next, we assume opportunistic behaviour. The opportunistic downstream party is aware of sunk costs and may claim that there are unforeseen circumstances which make a lower price for using the computer system desirable, i.e. the downstream party may try to appropriate a part of the quasi-rent by insisting on a price reduction. One of the reasons could be a strong increase in gas prices. The upstream inventor cannot defend himself against this appropriation threat, because a portion of his costs are sunk (Hendrikse, 2003: 209).

Suppose the sunk costs are 8 (SC = 8) which means that the recoverable costs are 12. The upstream inventor can refuse to deal further with the downstream party when the price drops below 12 once the investment is done; 12 is the reservation price for the upstream party. This fundamental transformation in the bargaining position, as a result of a specific investment, is summarised in Table 5.2 (cf. Hendrikse, 2003: 209).

Various reasons can be used by the downstream party for lowering the contract price of 22.5. Contracts are mostly incomplete, the future is uncertain and it is impossible to take all the contingencies into account. Moreover, incomplete contracts create the possibilities of opportunistic behaviour; for example, bargaining *ex-post* about the quasi-rent, i.e. 5 + SC, instead of the total rent of 5. In case of a SC of 8 the quasi-rent is 5 + 8 = 13. The assumption of equal bargaining power or strength entails that each party receives 50% of the quasi-rent or 6.5. If the quasi-rent for the downstream party will be deducted from the contract price, ex-ant, the contract price becomes *ex-post* 18.5. This means that downstream party is able to appropriate the quasi-rent. Table 5.3 shows the effects of the fundamental transformation on the contract price.

Based on these results, we can conclude that the party which has made the relation-specific investments finds itself in a disadvantageous position (we shortly call this party A). The other party (named B) has various possibilities of reducing the net revenues of the contractual relationship. Consequently, the contract is incomplete and incomplete contracts are vulnerable for *ex-post* opportunistic behaviour, like renegotiating contracts or even violating the contracts. The

Table 5.2. The reservation prices (in million euro) before and after the fundamental transformation.

	Ex-ante	Ex-post
Upstream inventor	20	12
Downstream party	25	25

Table 5.3. Adapted contract price before and after the fundamental transformation.

	Ex-ante	Ex-post
Contract price	22.5	18.5

landowner of our example in Section 2.4 can increase the land lease price, but can also threaten to break up the relationship to stipulate better contract conditions than those agreed upon first. In the above example, party B may threaten to lower the contract price. The reasons are:

1. the asset specificity or the sunk character of the investments, *ex-post* there are hardly alternatives available;
2. the human characteristics of opportunistic behaviour and bounded rationality; and
3. contracts are incomplete, as a result of bounded rationality, people are not omniscient, and transaction costs; writing complete contracts would involve huge transaction costs. (This will be discussed more extensively in Chapter 7.)

Unspecified contingencies are gaps in a relationship and can be used by one party to improve its position at the cost of the other party. Williamson (1987: 20 – 22) uses the term *ex-post haggling* for describing such activities, where the haggling is about the quasi-rent. *Ex-post* haggling is expressed in various bargaining problems.

These three factors create two related problems: the hold-up and lock-in. Hold-up is more an *ex-ante* problem and lock-in an *ex-post* one. The prospect of hold-up often results in no investment at all. Our farmer/tenant in Section 2.4 can wisely anticipate the possibility that the landowner will increase the land rent as soon as the land improvement project has been realised, or cancel the contract for a new term. The idea that the quasi-rent of the tenant's land improvement will go to the landowner will likely hold the farmer/tenant back from making this investment. If he does the investment without an *ex-ante* agreement with the landowner about the future contract duration and contract price, he will be locked-in by the land-owner.

Similarly, for the upstream inventor we can analyse the options and the numerical results. As shown in Table 5.4 there are three options for the upstream inventor (in Table 5.4 named party A): (1) no investment; (2) investment with equal distribution of the quasi-rent, *ex-ante* agreed in a contract; (3) investment, but distribution of the quasi-rent is determined *ex-post*. For the downstream party (named party B) the option (3) is the best one. Given the opportunistic behavioural assumption of transaction cost economics, party B will choose this option. Party A anticipates this behaviour. He expects that the situation as described in option (3) can arise, which will result in a loss for party A of 1.5 million euro. The investor, i.e. party A will not invest. This is called the hold-op problem; an efficient investment or a surplus-generating investment will not take place. It is a dramatic example of transaction cost.

Table 5.4. The numerical results and the hold-up problem.

Actions by party A	Distribution of quasi-rent	Amount of quasi-rent for party B
(1) No investment	Nothing to distribute	0
(2) Investment	Equal distribution between both parties, determined *ex-ante*	2.5
(3) Investment	Distribution determined *ex-post* and claimed by opportunistic behaviour of party B	6.5

As said, transaction cost economics tries to explain which organisational mode or governance structure will be chosen for transactions. Given relational-specific investments and opportunistic behaviour (in terms of *ex-post* haggling, hold-up and lock-in) we to look at the ability of governance structures to create circumstances such that valuable investments and transactions are carried out. Many organisational modes or contractual relationships can be distinguished. Each organisational mode has its own advantages and disadvantages. According to Williamson, the dimensions of the transaction consisting of the level of asset specificity, degree of uncertainty and frequency, complemented with the human characteristics determine which particular governance structure is most efficient. This expressed in Figure 5.1.

Transactions with a low level of asset specificity are carried out by the governance structure known as the 'market'. In this governance structure, there are often sufficient competitive alternatives available to punish bad behaviour without inducing high costs. Standard products like grain and milk are offered by many suppliers at the same level of quality, and there are may buyers. For standard commodity products, the level of asset specificity and the degree of uncertainty are both low, and transactions regularly occur. Consequently, the market will ensure an efficient allocation (cf. Hendrikse, 2003: 212).

However, transactions with a high level of asset specificity are not well suited for the governance structure of either the 'market' or short-term contacts. In cases of committed assets, the fear will be that the other party will claim the entire surplus. Consequently, a governance structure like vertical integration, in Section 4.2.6 referred to as *in-house production*, offers safeguards against this type of claim, which arises, according to transaction cost theory, from opportunistic behaviour. With the above given payments, it is clear that there will be no investment in a market relationship or a short-term contract, because the fear of being held-up precludes the investment. Vertical integration removes the fear of hold-up, and results therefore in a valuable investment. In our example, the transaction between flower growers and the flower auction could be coordinated by a long-term contract, because vertical integration is not a realistic alternative.

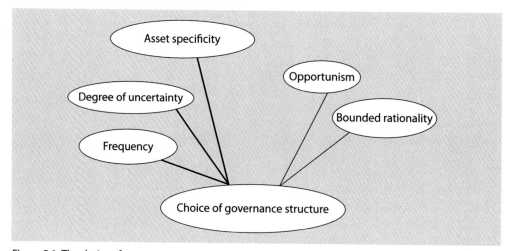

Figure 5.1. The choice of governance structures according to the transaction cost theory.

Consider a relationship between an auto component manufacturer and an automobile company. If the component manufacturer has to invest in specialised equipment for making components that can be sold to one automobile company only, the asset specificity is high for the component manufacturer. As a result, the component manufacturer would be vulnerable to opportunistic behaviour by the automobile company. In this case, vertical integration can be the preferred solution (Douma and Schreuder, 2002: 205).

This means that in a situation with a high level of asset specificity, long-term contracts and vertical integration remain as possible efficient forms of governance structures. The uncertainty which surrounds a transaction is also an exogenous variable determining which governance structure is efficient. The degree of uncertainty is a result of the incompleteness of contracts and the possibilities of *ex-post* renegotiation in order to claim *ex-post* a larger part of the surplus. A high degree of uncertainty provides more possibilities for *ex-post* renegotiation, because the causes for a specific outcome are harder to discover and harder to prove. By bringing those transactions, which involve a high level of asset specificity, inside the organisation (i.e. vertical integration) the *ex-post* bargaining possibility changes or is removed. It aligns previously conflicting interest and eliminates a number of choices. Vertical integration is a way to prevent the hold-up problem, because the conflict of interests between parties is removed (Hendrikse, 2003: 213).

Figure 5.2 summarises the predictions of the transaction cost economics when only the exogenous variables of asset specificity and the degree of uncertainty are taken into account. When the asset specificity is low, transaction cost economics predicts that the market will be an efficient governance structure, even when there is a lot of uncertainty. The reason for the choice between market and hierarchy is explained by Williamson's bipolar spectrum; market versus hierarchy. Markets and hierarchies are the two main governance structures. In his view, markets are replaced by hierarchies when price coordination breaks down. This has been discussed in Section 3.6. A hierarchy is a governance structure able to solve certain problems in situations with high level of asset specificity. However, it also introduces a number of internal organisational problems, which do not outweigh the benefits of vertical integration when there is lot of uncertainty (Hendrikse, 2003: 213). The idea is that uncertainty, as result of bad behaviour, will be punished. In the future, other parties will be not inclined to do business with parties with a bad reputation.

As explained in Section 4.4, the value of a reputation – and thus the costs incurred in building and maintaining a good one – depends on how often it will prove to be useful. A reputation is more

		Degree of uncertainty	
		Low	High
Asset specificity	Low	Market	Market
	High	Long-term contract	Hierarchy

Figure 5.2. Governance structure choice as a function of asset specificity and the degree of uncertainty (Hendrikse, 2003: 214).

valuable when transactions occur more often, the relationship lasts longer, and the transactions are profitable. The reputation mechanism can be used to realise credible commitment for contract compliance. Thus, the market as an appropriate governance structure in cases of high level of uncertainty (Figure 5.2) is disputed[41], yet this is the view of Williamson. Other governance structures which make use of common values and norms, reputation mechanisms and the build-up of trust are also possible, e.g. short or medium terms contacts. When the level of asset specificity is high, then an efficient choice of governance structures is the long-term contract or the hierarchy, depending on the level of uncertainty. In the case of low level uncertainty, a long-term contract is a suitable governance structure, and when the degree of uncertainty is high, the hierarchy is a better choice. The given outcomes given in Figure 5.2 are strongly influenced by the transaction cost economics view of Williamson.

The predictions of the transaction cost economics can also be formulated in terms of the level of assets specificity and frequency with which the transactions occur. This is presented in Figure 5.3. An example of a unilateral governance structure is the vertical integration of in-house production, such that one party has the power. Many buyer-seller relationships have a bilateral character. An example is a long-term contract in which both parties are independent and have comparable power. In the terms of Williamson, this is known as a bilateral governance structure (Hendrikse, 2003: 214).

Transactions between two parties can also be specific and occur infrequently or not very often. In such cases, the exchange is often carried out with the help of an external intermediator. This is indicated by a trilateral governance structure in Figure 5.3.

In spite of the criticism on Williamson, it is fair to say that most of the empirical literature has been supportive of the basic ideas of transaction cost theory, especially concerning asset specificity, uncertainty and frequency. However, it is not easy to feel completely satisfied with the somewhat vague character of some of the concepts in the theory. For example, uncertainty and frequency are broad categories and it is often difficult to find good proxies for them. In addition, it is not always clear what the observability and verifiability status of these variables are. The same holds, but to a lesser degree, for the concept of quasi-rent; it is not easy to measure.

---

[41] Because other alternatives are possible.

		Asset specificity		
		Low	Medium	High
Frequency	Low	Market	Trilateral governance structure	Unilateral
	High		Bilateral governance structure	

Figure 5.3. Governance structure choice as a function of asset specificity and frequency (Williamson, 1987: 79).

Box 5.3. Criticism of Williamson.

In the transaction costs literature, there is some discussion about which transactions should be carried out in the market and which subsumed within hierarchically organised firms (Granovetter, 1985: 483). According to Williamson, transactions that are uncertain in outcome, recur frequently, and require substantial transaction-specific investments are more likely to take place within a hierarchically organised firm. Those that are straightforward and require no transaction-specific investment will more likely take place between firms, that is to say, across a market interface. In this account, the former set of transactions is internalised within hierarchies for two reasons.

The first is 'bounded rationality', the inability of economic actors to anticipate properly the complex chains of contingencies that may be relevant to long-term contracts. When transactions are internalised, it is unnecessary to anticipate all such contingencies; they can be handled within the firm's governance structure instead of leading to complex negotiations. The second reason is 'opportunistic behaviour', the rational pursuit by economic actors of their own advantage, with all means at their commands, including guile and deceit. Opportunism is more mitigated and constrained by authority relations and by the greater identification with transaction partners one allegedly has if both are contained with one corporate entity than if they face one another across the chasm of a market boundary.

Granovetter (1985: 495) addresses the institutional economic view on opportunism[1] and argues that both in markets and hierarchically organised firms, social structural influences play a role. According to Granovetter, Williamson does acknowledge that (1) norms of trustworthy behaviour extend to markets and are enforced; (2) repeated personal contact across organisational boundaries support minimum level of courtesy and consideration between parties; (3) expectations of repeat business discourages efforts to seek a narrow advantage in any particular transaction; and (4) individual aggressiveness is curbed by the prospect of ostracism among peers, in both trade and social circumstances. The reputation of the firm for fairness is not to be dissipated (see Granovetter, 1985: 495).

Granovetter (1985: 502) claims that the inhibition of opportunism or malfeasance in economic life and the general existence of cooperation and order (social relationship or network) by the subsumption of complex economic activities in hierarchically integrated firms not can be used as distinguishing decision rule between firm and market. A high level of order can often also be found in the market. The social network also generates in markets and in contracts powerful pressures that limit opportunism (Hennart, 1993: 532). Trust plays a role both between and within organisations and the same is true for the reputation mechanism. Organisational theorists argue that Williamson took a too narrow view of human behaviour with opportunism as a basic assumption. Consequently, he could only see one alternative governance structure for the market: hierarchy (cf. Douma and Schreuder, 2002: 167). This means that the place and rule of opportunism as a distinguishing decision rule for choosing between the firm and the market in Figure 5.2 is disputable.

Finally, the bipolar approach of Williamson – markets versus hierarchies and price versus non-price coordination – does not acknowledge the large variety in mode of organisations of governance structures. To understand this variety we have to take into account the mix of the applied coordination and motivation mechanisms. This has been explained in Chapter 3 and will be more extensively discussed in Chapter 8.

---

[1] In the resource-based view of the firm, they also assume that opportunistic behaviour will not occur (Conner and Prahalad, 1996: 477).

To avoid this type of problems, organisational theorists often only use a qualitative way of reasoning to analyse transaction costs, the most suitable governance structure, why firms exist and the way in which organisational modes affect the knowledge that is applied in business activities[42]. However, a weak point is the withholding of an empirical testing. Therefore we will apply in Section 5.5 other approaches – as used in this section – for investigating transaction costs. These are based on the transaction as a *quid pro quo*; which activities have to be carried out and which types of costs are involved. The theoretical basis is still transaction cost economics.

5.4 Framework for determining attributes of transactions which are decisive for the choice of governance structures

According to transaction cost theory, the human characteristics of *opportunistic behaviour* and *bounded rationality* together with the transaction characteristics *asset specificity (transaction-specific investment), uncertainty and frequency* determine which governance structure is efficient. In the previous sections, we largely followed the approach of Williamson. In this section, we will extend and deepen this approach with other basic attributes and characteristics of goods. A central question in this section is: can we develop a coherent framework of transaction attributes that leads to efficient governance structures? Which attributes are decisive for the choice of such governance structures? For developing this framework we make use of some attributes mentioned before, and we will add some new ones which can be seen as a complement for building a coherent framework of transaction attributes. All together these attributes consist of:
1. level of asset specificity;
2. degree of uncertainty;
3. level of frequency and duration;
4. difficulty of measuring performance of the transaction;
5. level of connectedness of assets and co-specialised assets;
6. non-excludability and non-rivalry of the goods.

In general, a high level of these attributes will lead to higher transaction costs if a transaction occurs. Transaction costs, the level of the quasi-rent and the distribution of the quasi-rent determine which governance structure is preferable.

5.4.1 Asset specificity and connected hold-up problems and lock-in effects

As explained, the most important attribute of a transaction for determining the most suitable governance structure is the asset specificity attribute in connection with hold-up and lock-in effects. Assets are specific to certain uses if the goods and service they provide are highly valuable only in that use. The degree of specificity of an asset can be defined as the fraction of its value that would be lost if it were excluded from its major use. Suppose in a certain relationship, one of the parties would like to make an investment. An important question is what is the nature of the investment? If this investment is committed to a specific or narrow task it is a specific investment.

---

[42] See, for example Conner and Prahalad (1996).

We have already discussed some examples, but we will introduce some other ones, not only referring to private goods and private firms, but also to public goods and public enterprises. The first example is an oil well. The owner of the oil well concludes a contract with a firm called Jensen for the transportation of the oil. Jensen builds a special pipeline for the transportation of the oil. A second example concerns an isolated factory. In this case, the owner concludes an agreement with a firm called Smit. This firm builds a railway-line for transporting the products of the factory. A third example is a tenant who leases land from a landowner. The tenant builds a special stable for his milk cows. The pipeline, railway-line and the cowshed are specific investments with little or no alternative uses, and are, therefore, sunk investments.

When an asset is specific to a particular transaction, the party who has done the investment can be held-up:

a. The owner of the oil well might insist on lower transportation tariffs after the pipeline has been built;
b. The owner of the factory might insist on lower rail lines rates;
c. The landowner might insist on having a higher land rent because the tenant is able to milk more cows.

The owners of the oil well and the factory can threaten to transport their products by trucks, if the owners of the pipeline and railway-line do not accept this request. The landowner can threaten the farmer/tenant that after the contract period he will not renew the contract, but he would conclude a land lease contract with another tenant. These threats are powerful because, the pipeline, railway-line and cowshed are highly specific and would lose almost all their value, if the threats were carried out.

Hold-up and lock-in

The possibility of hold-up arises in every (contractual) relationship which is incomplete. The reasons may be diverse. As soon as a person has selected a specific technology or relationship, the discontinuation or termination of the relationship can be extremely expensive. Further, as a result of unforeseen circumstances, the position of one of the parties in the contractual relationship can result in a deterioration or change in the negotiation position of the parties over time. Termination of the relationship can indeed be costly. Given a relation between two parties, the arising of hold-up situation itself has often no effect on total value directly. It creates (opportunity) costs and will lead to a redistribution of income between the two parties. However, the fear of being *held-up* can prevent people from investing in highly specific assets. It will affect the total welfare in a society. These are the real social costs of a hold-up problem. Hold-up problems are very common and recur frequently, not only nowadays but in the past also. They refer to the same effect as in the transaction cost theory: efficient transactions will be not carried out.

In Section 2.5 we distinguished different types of lock-in. Lock-in means that your alternatives are strongly reduced. This can because of functional, technical, or institutional reasons (see Section 2.5). Lock-in effects can be the result of being *held-up*. It is an *ex-post* phenomenon, while hold-up is more of an *ex-ante* problem. Suppose the owners of the oil well and the factory, from our examples, have no other alternative for transporting oil and end products of the factory than the railway-line. If the owner of the railway-line increases the transportation tariffs, the owner of the factory is locked-in and he has to pay these higher tariffs. Similarly, if the landowner insists on a higher land rent, the tenant-farmer will have no other alternative. The only thing that he can do is pay this higher rent. He can hardly move to another landowner because of the investment of building a new stable. He is locked-in by the landowner and his own investment. Lock-in effects are also very common and recur frequently.

However, in these three examples – a, b and c – it is possible that both parties need each other strongly. The owner of the oil well needs the pipeline, and the owner of the factory needs the railway. Maximising the benefits requires using both assets together in that use. Suitable governance structures are therefore vertical integration into one firm or company, long-term contracts and a joint venture. The latter means that two companies set up a new business unit in a newly formed company.

If each side can use a powerful threat against the other, we can speak about co-specialised assets. It is a condition of two assets in which each is more productive when used with the other. Co-specialised assets are in some respect unique and are also complements. Both parties are often locked-in. In that case, any breakdowns in the transaction will lead to large costs on both sides (Milgrom and Roberts, 1992: 307). In the case of the oil well and the isolated factory, the conditions for co-specialised assets exist.

It is possible that these conditions do not exist in the landowner and farmer/tenant relationship. For example, the landowner can easily find another tenant. For efficient land use, the most suitable governance structure is a long-term contract with the possibility of renewing the contract at the end of the contract period, complemented with a lease regulation for (1) continuation rights for the tenant and (2) a compensation for asset specific investments in land, buildings (barns and sheds) and land-bounded investments, such as drainage and soil improvements at the end of the contract for reducing hold-up and lock-in effects (Slangen *et al.*, 2003: 27-28). Another mode of organisation is that the tenant becomes the owner of the land.

Box 5.4. Lock-in effects.

Since IT components often work together as systems, switching any one component often involves switching other components as well. This means that the switching costs associated with one component in IT industries may be quite substantial. For example, switching from Macintosh to a Window-based PC involves not only the hardware costs of the computer itself, but even more importantly, learning how to use a brand new system.

When switching costs are very high, users may find themselves experiencing lock-in, a situation where the costs of changing to a different system are so high that switching is virtually inconceivable. This is bad for the consumers, but is, of course quite attractive for the sellers of the components that make up the system in question. Since the locked-in user has a very inelastic demand, the seller(s) can jump up the prices of their components to extract consumer surplus form the user (Varian, 2003: 628-629).

Natural monopoly

The asset specificity, as a transaction attribute, also plays an important role in so-called natural monopolies. Natural monopolies are characterised, for a large part, by fixed costs and relatively small variable costs. The total average costs will decrease if the production capacity increases. Paul Joskow, a well-known economist, has produced a number of studies (1985a and b, 1987, 1988) in which he confronted the transaction costs approach with real-world evidence. He examined the specifics of the relationship between coal-burning electricity generating plants and the mines that provide the coal. In the mid-1980s, coal generated more than 50 per cent of the electricity consumed in the United States. Coal mines (suppliers) must sink investments in mining capacity. The electricity utilities (buyers) must commit specific investments in the amount of generating equipment and also in the adaption of boilers to a particular coal (FitzRoy, 1998: 257). The case of Joskow is an example of a natural monopoly[43].

Natural monopolies are a common phenomenon for the provision of electricity, gas, water and other 'network' service, such as railways. Different modes of organisation are possible. As we have seen in the last 15 years, the trend in utility regulation has been to encourage a vertically dis-integrated structure, encouraging competition where possible and subjecting the pure 'natural monopoly' assets to some form of public control. Interconnection charges for users of the network then become a primary problem. How should train companies pay for use of the railway infrastructure? Is it technically feasible and not too costly for competing gas producers and suppliers to contract with a gas-pipeline operator? Would it be possible to separate the operation of water pipelines from the businesses concerned with retailing, collection storage and the treatment of wastewater (Ricketts, 2002: 525)?

Even within a vertically dis-integrated structure there are different governance structures possible. We will provide four examples (cf. Ricketts, 2002: 525):
a. The national government is the legal owner[44] and the public utility company takes care of all the involved activities.
   This is the in-house production solution, with all the possible disadvantages, particularly with respect to public choice considerations (see e.g. Section 6.4) and low-powered incentives. Public ownership and in-house production of the government is not self-evidently worse than alternative governance structures. However, the lack of competition, little opportunity for innovation, cost savings by reducing the non-contractible quality and the absence of pressure from a loss of reputation (Sheifer, 1998b: 140) are all ownership and in-house production traits of a benevolent government. It is a matter of judgment whether the public choice problems associated with special interests might still render ownership and in-house production of the government less desirable that the alternative mode of organisation (Ricketts, 2002: 525).
b. The national government is the legal owner of the network and the network is leased to private operators.

---

[43] If coal is the only alternative for the plant than we have to deal with two co-specialised assets.

[44] Generally, the rights of full asset ownership consists of five elements: (a) the right to use the asset; (b) the right to appropriate the returns from the asset; (c) the right to change the form, substance, and location of the asset; (d) the right to exclude others; and (e) the right of transfer to others through markets or to their inheritances. This will be discussed more extensively in Chapter 9 and 10.

This is a variety of a franchise contract solution. The length of the contract often varies between 10 and 20 years and the private operator pays the government a fixed amount of money at the start of the relationship (which can function as a bond) and a percentage of the sales for the right to exploit the network. With large quantities of specific sunk investments, it avoids the capital valuation problems that would arise at contract renewal and reduces the fear of *ex-post* contractual opportunism or hold-up by the government. However, (government) ownership of the network (= durable investment) requires an intertemporal continuity for investment programmes to be undertaken. A problem can arise when the human capital of the network operators is highly specific and complementary with physical assets owned by the other party, i.e. the government. In these circumstances, the most suitable governance structure suggests that the human capital of the network operators and physical assets should be brought in under one business unit. This can also limit the moral hazard problems associated with the upkeep and maintenance of the network which an operator might let deteriorate over the period of its franchise term (Ricketts, 2002: 526).

c. The local government is the legal owner of the network

In some countries (e.g. in the Netherlands) the local government is the legal owner of the network facilities of water, gas and electricity and gas. The situations as described in a. and b. can be applied.

d. Parts of the bundle of property rights of ownership of the network assets are allocated to and operated by a franchisee.

An option is that the natural monopoly should be franchised – with the control rights over a certain part of the bundle of property rights and for a defined period over the network – by the franchise winner. Here the balance of advantages is the reverse of case b. Capital valuation problems of the investments, hold-up and intertemporal sustainability might be serious concerns ownership of the assets would encourage innovation. However, the bidding process becomes more complicated if the franchisee is to invest in a large amount of durable capital as the investment programme must be agreed as part of the franchise deal rather than announced by the government before bidding begins. Where the length of the franchise and the durability of capital can be equated, problems of asset valuation at the termination of the franchise are over come. Each bidder starts from scratch at the time of contract renewal. In situations where capital is not very long lived, where the environment is technically very dynamic, where human capital is highly complementary with the assets and where issues of non-contractible of the quality[45] are not very serious, this straightforward franchising system would be favoured. The more stable the environment and the less specific the investment, the longer can be the duration of this type of franchise solution (Ricketts, 2002: 527).

5.4.2 Uncertainty

Uncertainty has been discussed in the Sections 4.5 and 4.6, and also in Section 5.3 as a part of the transaction cost theory of Williamson. According to this theory, the degree of uncertainty is a result of the incompleteness of contracts and the possibilities of *ex-post* renegotiation.

---

[45] This will be explained in 5.4.4.

A standard way for two parties to organise a transaction is to make an agreement or a contract specifying what is expected from each. Sometimes such contracts are very simple. For example, today I ordered two loaves of bread in the bakery in my village and I will pick them up tomorrow. The uncertainty and complexity is small and it is easy to predict what type of performance I want from the bakery.

In practice, due to a number of reasons, uncertainty and complexity exist. Contracts can be very complicated, e.g. a contract for the construction of a railway-line from Rotterdam to Germany, or a new airbus with less or no irritating noise, and with less CO_2 emissions. In general, such a contract will give rise to uncertainty and complexity. In a complex and unpredictable world, it is difficult to forecast and take into account all possible events. Specific unforeseen events may not be taken into account. With perfect foresight, we could develop a better contract. However, mostly we have to deal with uncertainty and to make estimations of possible outcomes of the transactions.

The expected utility theory and prospect theory can be helpful for this type of analysis. Suppose, you are working on two transactions: A and B. As we know from the expected utility, it is important to know (1) the distribution of probability and (2) the risk-attitude. From the prospect theory, we know that most people have a loss aversion. Assume you are risk-neutral for gains, but for losses you have a loss aversion. You have an extreme loss aversion; you **weigh losses 5 times more than gains**. For both transactions we know the distribution of probability and the gains and losses. Table 5.5 summarises the figures.

For the simplicity, if we have only gains we apply the expected utility approach and if we have a loss we will make used of the prospect theory. The results for both transactions are:

A: EU = 0.2 × 10 + 0.8 × 6 = 6.8 million euro
B: V = 0.6 × 15 + 5 (0.4 × -5) = 9 – 10 = -1 million euro.

Based on the gains and losses, distribution of probabilities, risk-attitudes and loss aversion we can calculate that transaction A is preferable. Because we assumed risk-neutrality for gains, the

Table 5.5. Overview of the probabilities, gains and losses.

	Probability	Results (million euro)
Transaction A		
Gain 10 million euro	0.2	2
Gain 6 million euro	0.8	4.8
Expected utility (EU)		6.8
Transaction B		
Gain 15 million euro	0.6	9
Loss 5 million euro	0.4	-10
Total value (V)		-1

expected utility is equal to the expected value. Based on loss aversion, we can investigate that uncertainty, in terms of a chance on a loss, is an important aspect in the transaction cost theory.

Second, even if all events could be predicted, it is difficult for the parties to negotiate over so many possibilities. There would be far too many events to take into account in the contract, and further a common language would be needed to be able to describe all the diverse states of the world (Hart, 1995: 23). Both, the first and the second, arguments are a result of bounded rationality.

Third, even if the parties could take all possibilities in the future into account and negotiate over them, it would still be extremely difficult to write it all down in an agreement which in case of conflict of opinion, could be examined by an outsider, e.g. a court of law, with regard to the content and meaning of the agreement and enforced. As a result of these factors, the concerned parties generally formulate a contract which is incomplete (cf. Hart, 1995: 23). Not only the feasibility, but also the high transaction costs mean that a such contract is simply too difficult to achieve. This means that the contract will have gaps and that some provisions will be missing.

Generally, when uncertainty and complexity make it hard to predict what performance will be desirable, contracting becomes more complex. Specifying rights, obligations and procedures becomes more important than actual performance standards. The longer the time horizon between performance and counter performance (*quid pro quo*) the more uncertainty will arise, and the more trust is needed. If all relevant contingencies can be forecasted and planned a contract specifying what is required can be a good alternative. However, still the argument of high transaction costs remains. The question arises: which governance structure can reduce these transactions costs?

As explained in Section 5.3, when the asset specificity is low, transaction cost economics predicts the market as governance structure, even when there is a lot of uncertainty. The idea is that uncertainty as result of bad behaviour will be punished. In the future, other parties will not be inclined to do business with parties with a bad reputation. However, the market as governance structure in cases of high level of uncertainty is not undisputed. Other governance structures which are making use of, for example, common values and norms, reputation mechanisms and the build-up of trust are also possible, such as different types of contracts. Especially, the reputation is often seen as important mechanism for realising credible commitment for contract compliance. Under these conditions long-term contracts are suitable governance structures, even in the case of uncertainty. Another solution could be cooperation with other parties, such as a Public Private Partnership (PPP); in which it is possible to allocate the risk to the least risk-averse party. Finally it is possible to make of delegation for reducing the risk connected with uncertainty. The principle could be the same as in case of PPP; shifting the risk to a less least risk-averse party.

5.4.3 Frequency and duration

As explained in the previous section, some transactions are one-time affairs, as for example when you buy a house. Others are repeated frequently, involving some of the same parties under more or less the same conditions over a long period of time. In the first case, one expects the parties to use whatever general mechanisms are available in the community to control their actions. In particular, they likely will resort to a standard form contract, with any disputes between them to be resolved in court. One of these mechanisms for transactions which occur infrequently is making use of external intermediator. For example, suppose you would like to buy a house, and it is not your daily work. Most people only buy a house once or twice their lifetime. Intermediators, like a real estate agent, may reduce transaction costs, such as search costs, surveys, inspection costs and dispute resolving. An important incentive for them to do their job well is the reputation mechanism.

In case of parties who interact frequently, one expects quite a different sort of mechanism that is specially designed for the particular aspects of their relationship. A special purpose institution is often worthwhile because it can be tailored to the particular circumstances of the relationship or organisation. The period of time is also important. The longer the period over which (two) parties might interact, the more difficult it will be to foresee and to contract for all relevant contingencies. In such situations more trust is needed. However, a long time horizon also means that reputation can be a more effective control mechanism.

Parties involved in a long-term, close relationship with frequent interaction have many opportunities to grant or withhold favours to one another. The ability to reward faithful partners and to punish unfaithful ones in a long-term relationship greatly reduces the need for any kind of formal mechanism to enforce agreements between them. The parties can also develop understanding and routines that reduce the need for explicit planning to coordinate their actions. These practices can eliminate the need for formal, detailed agreements, both because parties understand what is expected of them and because they have no need to document those understandings for outsiders to enforce. Trust and reputation are necessary to support the practises. The costs savings that result can be considerable (cf. Milgrom and Roberts, 1992: 31).

5.4.4 Difficulty of measuring performance in a transaction

It is often difficult or too costly to measure the actual performance of transactions. However, for some governance structures such as incentive contracts, in which a variable payment depends on the effort or performance, it is important to measure the performance. Similarly, if you want to tie worker's pay to their performance it should be possible to measure actual performance (see also Section 4.2. and Chapter 6).

Measuring performance is an important factor for the choice between in-house provision and contracting out, because the option of contracts, as a governance structure, requires (1) that you know what you want; and (2) that the quality of the goods or services that you want are contractable. In the case that you do not know what you want, the contract will be very incomplete and the costs associated with renegotiations will be considerable, so that the transaction costs become very high. If you are not able to measure the performance, it is possible that the contract taker has a strong tendency to reduce the costs, and this is accompanied by a reduction in (non-contractible) quality. The adverse effect of cost reduction on quality could be significant. In this situation in-house production is likely to be a better solution. This will be discussed more extensively in Chapter 7.

For example, farmers in the EU have concluded management agreements with the government for preserving wildlife and landscape[46]. The results of these management agreements are often difficult to measure, due to the unobservable effort of the farmers, the uncertain weather conditions, predators, the rules of the agreements, etc. This example suggests it is hard to provide effective incentives if one can not measure the performance accurately. If measuring performance is difficult, people commonly arrange their affairs to make measurement easier or to reduce the importance of accurate measurements.

But suppose we are able the measure the performance, then the question arises what are effective incentives? Possible incentives are on the one hand rewards (the carrot), performance-based pay, career concerns, reputation building and on the other hand punishments (the stick). It should be noticed that performance-based pay could also result in a kind of punishment. The attributes of the transaction determine which of the possible solutions is best, or even whether any of them are workable.

In general, when it is relatively cheap to measure performance accurately, a performance-based pay is the best solution. If performance is difficult to measure we have to look to alternative solutions. The same holds for activities in which **care** is very important but difficult or costly to measure. However, as we know from the knights and knaves (Section 4.4), when the problem of motivating the person to honour his or her responsibilities is great, the best system may be to avoid offering any formal financial performance incentives (e.g. surgeons). As explained, motivation of people can be driven by external motives, such as financial incentives, and by internal motives, like the feelings to do your work well, trustworthiness and having or building up a good reputation. According to Le Grand (2003: 53 -55) there can be a trade-off between the two kinds of motivation, such that too heavy emphasis on extrinsic motivation can drive out internal motivation.

5.4.5 Connectedness and co-specialised assets

Transactions differ in how they are connected to other transactions, especially those involving investments which are highly asset specific. It is even possible that the assets or the services they yield are strongly complementary. A high level of one significantly increases the value of the other. Some transactions are largely dependent on others. As explained before, this gives rise to hold-up problems and lock-in effects. An example of connectedness is the relation between water and an irrigation system – including canals and pipes. A strong relationship exists between both assets. Without water, the irrigation system is useless or even worthless, and also the other way around. There is also a strong connection between water and land. Without an irrigation system and water, land in some dry regions is useless. This raises questions about the property rights, ownership arrangements and the best governance structure. For answering these questions we have also to take into account the type of the goods: private goods, pure public goods, common goods quasi-public goods and club goods. This will be discussed more extensively in Chapter 9.

---

[46] Unified ownership or do-it-yourself (by government or nature conservation organisations) could be an alternative to private provision by contracts with private landowners and farmers. For a discussion see Polman and Slangen (2007: 13-15).

Assets – or services they yield – are strongly complementary if a higher level of one significantly increases the value of the others. It is possible that there are may be multiple patterns of investments that are mutually dependent and consistent with each other and are forming coherent patterns. However, only one of these distinct patterns actually maximises the total value. When the involved parties have divergent interests the coordination problems become more difficult. This gives rise to higher transactions costs.

The connectedness of transactions can also be a result of the people involved. Human capital is one of the most important kinds of assets. Skills and knowledge of a person are often tied to the person in question. The transferability of human capital is problematic if those skills are specific to an organisation or asset. Co-specialised skills and knowledge are often characteristic for working in a team. Teams are very common in hospitals, research institutions, government bureaus and in firms. Mostly they are charged with specific tasks asking specific knowledge and expertise. The team is an organisational mode.

If each of the members of the team can use a powerful threat against the other members of the team, we have to deal with co-specialised assets. All the involved assets, when working together, are more productive than if used separately. The goods and service they provide are highly valuable. The involved co-specialised assets are in some respect unique and are also complements. Involved parties are often locked-in. In that case, any breakdowns in the transactions will lead to large costs (Milgrom and Roberts, 1992: 307). An indication of these costs is the value that would be lost if the members of the team are no longer working together.

5.4.6 Non-excludability and non-rivalry of the goods

Non-excludability refers to a lack of property rights. In the case of complete non-excludability, it is impossible to exclude people from the consumption of the good. If nobody can be excluded from the use of a good, no individual will be prepared to produce such a good, because the benefits of that good are available to all and one person cannot be excluded from consumption. From the producer's perspective, an important condition for producing a good is that people can be excluded, i.e. there are property rights which are transferable. Otherwise, nobody is prepared to pay for it. The degree of excludability is critical since in order for a well-functioning market to exist, individual property rights of goods must be specified and should be transferable (Varian, 2003: 606). The governance structure of the market is only suitable if a direct exchange of individual property rights can take place.

The lack of property rights or the degree of non-excludability is the crucial factor in determining which goods should be publicly provided. This means a governance structure in which the government in a certain way and level is involved. The choice of the market as a governance structure involves high transaction costs, because of the difficulties of the allocation of transferable property rights. In the case of a high degree of non-excludability, the level of transaction costs are often prohibitive.

For a transaction to occur, property rights have to be clearly exclusive; property rights over a good have to be specified in a way such that individuals who have not paid for consumption can be excluded (Boadway and Bruce, 1989: 110). Exclusion may not be feasible for technological reasons (e.g. national defence) or for an institutional reason (e.g. property rights can not be assigned). When exclusion is impossible, the free-rider problem and the associated prisoner's dilemma arise (Boadway and Bruce, 1989: 129-30). The failure of defining property rights is an important aspect of many externality situations, such as the free-rider problems and the tragedy of the commons.

Non-excludability on the consumer side means that it is impossible to exclude those who are not willing to pay for the use of a good. The benefits of the good (or the 'bad') are available to all. For example, a dike offers everyone protection against water nuisance or flooding. Nobody can be excluded. It also means that individuals can not reject the good or 'bad'. Suppose, you live in the neighborhood of an atomic power station, and an accident happens, you can not avoid the damages of the nuclear fall out. Similarly, if you are living in polder and suddenly the dike breaks, everyone in the polder will experience water nuisance or flooding. However, excludability on the consumer side means that it is possible to exclude people who are not willing to pay for the use of a good. It also means that individuals can reject the good. Figure 5.4 gives an overview of the classification of four types of goods based on non-excludability and non-rivalry.

Non-rivalry in production is caused by the imperfect divisibility (or lumpiness) in the production sphere, involving that for providing a good a certain scale is needed. A certain minimum size is necessary otherwise offering the good is not efficient. Making a railway and other network provisions such as for gas, water and electricity, for example, of five meters; a railway wagon for 1 person; a recreation area of one square meter are not useful. For many provisions such as networks and infrastructure, we have to deal with indivisibility. Just as with natural monopolies, they are often characterised by a large part fixed costs and relative small part variable costs, and often but not always they are natural monopolies. These fixed costs and indivisibility lead to non-rivalry in consumption; the marginal costs of use are zero.

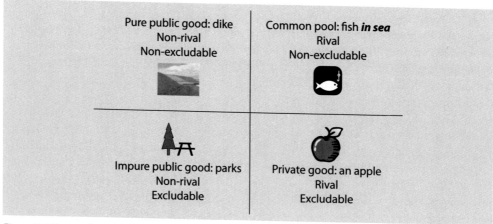

Figure 5.4. Types of goods, by characteristics: non-excludability and non-rivalry.

Non-rivalry in consumption is caused by the imperfect divisibility (or lumpiness) in consumption sphere. A good is non-rival or indivisible in consumption when a unit of the good can be consumed by one individual without detracting, in the slightest form, the consumption opportunities still available to others from the same unit (Cornes and Sandler, 1996: 8). At the same time several people can simultaneously make use of the goods; i.e. multiple consumption by several persons simultaneously is possible. An example is a dike as water protection, such as the IJsselmeer Dam. Table 5.6 summarises the most important characteristics.

Based on the properties of non-rivalry and non-excludability we can investigate which governance structure is suitable. For making use of the market governance structure, the following conditions are required:
- exclusion and rejection of the goods is possible;
- the goods have private and transferable property rights;
- the use of the goods is rivalry;
- the goods are divisible in marketable units.

If all these conditions are fulfiled, the market is the most suitable governance structure.

For pure public goods, direct government provision, i.e. the governance structure *in-house* production is preferable. Sometimes a contractual solution for pure collective goods is possible. However, this depends on the goals of the government and the contractibility of the quality of the good. For the quasi-public goods and common goods, the following governance structures can be used of:
a. private firms offer these goods and the government contributes in the financing on the basis of a contract, or a contractual agreement within a public-private partnership project;

Table 5.6. Types of goods and characteristics.

Type of the goods	Characteristics
Pure public goods	Non-excludable
	No property rights
	Non-rivalry
	Plural consumption is possible
Quasi-public goods	Exclusion is possible
	Use is not rivalry
Common goods	Exclusion is difficult
	Rule of the government make exclusion possible
	Use is rivalry
Private goods	Exclusion is possible
	Use is rivalry

b. goods are offered by a 'club'[47]. For example, in the Netherlands nature and landscape are provided by private nature conservation organisations and farmers environment cooperatives.

If the quasi-collective goods are nevertheless offered by the government via in-house production, then it must be questioned whether from an efficiency-consideration governance structure (a) or (b) is preferable.

It should be stressed that non-excludability and non-rivalry are very important attributes of transactions in our daily (e.g. environmental goods, climate issues). Both are interrelated; pure public goods are non-excludable and non-rivalry and pure private goods are excludable and rivalry. Non-excludability – and certainly if it is combined with non-rivalry – often results in high transaction costs; transaction cost can be so high that the transaction does not take place. The costs of establishment, delineation and enforcing of property rights often exclude transfer via the market. This is one of the problems with public goods. This will extensively be discussed in Chapter 9 and 10.

Finally, the 6 attributes of transactions described above are decisive for the choice of a governance structure. The asset specificity, including sunk investments, fixed assets, non-excludability and non-rivalry have the clearest implications for the mode of organisation or governance structure. These 6 attributes of transition can be considered as the building stones of a framework for determining the attributes of transactions which are decisive factors for the choice of governance structure. They are partly, but not completely, based on the transaction cost theory of Williamson.

5.5 Determining private and public transaction costs in practice

In this section we will present two approaches for determining transaction costs. In both approaches the government is the contract giver. The contract takers are private landowners or farmers. Quantitative estimation of transaction costs in government decision making for allocation of natural resources and environmental goods are rare (Challen, 2000: 189). It is common in the literature to make a distinction between private transaction costs, in this case borne by private landowners and farmers, and public transaction costs which are the transactions costs for the government (Mettepenningen *et al.*, 2008: 7-8).

Although some empirical work in transaction cost economics has been done, measuring transaction costs is not easy. The reasons for that are as follows: (a) there is no standard terminology on transactions costs; (b) it is difficult to separate them from production costs; (c) if transaction costs are high, the transaction probably will not take place and thus part of the transaction costs are not observable; and (d) different actors may face very different transaction costs so many estimates may be needed (Mettepenningen *et al.*, 2008: 10)[48].

---

[47] Clubs are an important phenomenon in different areas. Just think of sporting associations. The goods and services that they provide are closely connected to quasi-collective goods. The exclusion mechanism is the contribution. Those who do not pay are not members and are not allowed to participate.

[48] This article has to be published. It means the page number can change.

There are different ways of measuring transaction costs. One way is to estimate transaction costs by making use of the demand and supply curves of goods and services. This will be applied in the first example presented in this section. The difficulties here are the availability of the data and the estimations of the curve. A second method is using surveys or interviews. However, these methods involve high costs and they are time-consuming. Respondents in a survey and interview are asked to estimate future costs or remember costs of the past, which could lead to less reliable results (Mettepenningen *et al.*, 2008: 9). An advantage is that interviews and surveys enable us to investigate the perception stakeholders have on transaction costs. Managers very often don't know what transaction costs are, but they do take them into account, although not always in a numerical way. It shows that the perception of transaction costs is important, because it is this what determines *ex-ante* what the outcome of a decision will be (Mettepenningen *et al.*, 2008: 9). A perception of the height of transaction costs is important in deciding to enroll or to participate in a transaction, such as a nature management contract with the government. This method will be applied in the second example presented in this section. Finally, a possibility is to carry out simulation, in which researchers themselves go through all the steps of a transaction (Mettepenningen *et al.*, 2008: 9). We will leave this method further out of consideration.

Private and public transaction costs and nature management contract in the EMS

In 1990 the Dutch government started a nation-wide project for developing a network of nature protection areas. This network is called the Ecological Main Structure (EMS), which has the purpose of safeguarding the biodiversity and therewith the value of nature in the Netherlands. This network should be completed by 2018 and it concerns about 15% of the rural area in the Netherlands. Metaphorically speaking, the Ecological Main Structure (EMS) is the flagship of the most important nature conservation programme of the Netherlands.

Given that the Netherlands is determined to develop a complete system of protected nature areas for the conservation of biodiversity, a number of questions arise. First, how can we organise such a network? Which organisational modes can be used by the government? Possible governance structures are: (1) in-house production by the government (purchasing and converting agricultural land in nature and management by government agencies); (2) purchasing and converting agricultural land in nature and management by nature conservation organisations; (3) nature management by private persons; and (4) nature management by farmers.

Second, what are the transaction costs for activities to be carried out in each governance structure? Here we will only look to the transaction costs of nature and landscape management contracts between private landowners and farmers as contract takers and the government as the contract giver. According to the government planning process, this contractual arrangement should apply to approximately 130,000 ha, i.e. 20% of the total EMS (cf. Jongeneel *et al.*, 2005: 75). The transaction costs for the private landowners and farmers are called private transaction costs, and the transaction costs for the government are called public transaction costs.

With respect to transaction costs, a distinction can be made to the **supply side** of nature conservation practices on land and the **demand side**. The transaction costs can be included in a demand and supply framework (Bovenberg, 2002: 535). With respect to the supply side we suppose that farmers and other private landowners offer nature and landscape preservation on a contract-basis and the government demands for such contracts. The contract is the transaction mechanism. If by concluding a contract the farmers impose a **private transaction cost** of x on themselves, it is efficient to conclude such a contract only if the gains from participating $(d - s)$ exceed these transaction costs (see Figure 5.5, supply side). In the absence of transaction costs the market equilibrium is given by E, and the associated transactions are given by q_E. The impact of non-zero transaction costs is that they lead to a provision shortage of the good. With transaction costs the equilibrium quantity is q_T rather than q_E. All points in between q_T and q_E yield a positive gross surplus, which is however not sufficient to cover the transaction costs. At the margin q_T the gross surplus $p^d - p^s$ exactly offsets the transaction costs. The transaction costs can thus be measured analogous to a tax distortion, with the total transaction costs amounting rectangle ABCD in Figure 5.5. Besides this rectangle, the economic or efficiency costs also include the so-called Harberger triangle BCE, which represents the loss of surplus due to transactions that are crowded out by the implicit tax wedge x. It is also possible to redraw the supply curve (see dotted line in Figure 5.5, panel a) including the transaction costs. This supply curve then expresses supply as a function of the price, corrected for the transaction costs.

With respect to the demand side, a similar reasoning can be made (see Figure 5.5, demand side). Here the **public transaction costs** can be thought of as the organisational costs (overhead, contract design, bargaining cost) and costs of bureaucracy involved in generating the demand for nature conservation. Often it can be represented by a mark-up on the (labour) inputs used in the governance structure for realising nature conservation. These public transaction costs y can be simply modelled as a wedge between $p^{d'} - p^{s'}$, in a way analogous as was done at the supply side. Likewise on the supply side, also here the demand curve can be redrawn to include the transaction costs. Similarly, as with the supply side, the same applies to the demand side,

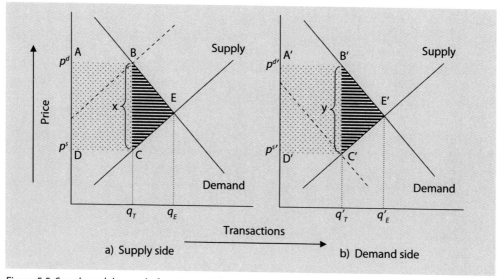

Figure 5.5. Supply and demand of contracts and transaction costs (Bovenberg, 2002: 535).

the presence of non-zero transaction costs implies the demand is underestimated. The public transaction costs amount A'B'C'D' and the efficiency costs are equal to A'B'C'.

This example shows the effects of private and public transaction costs. They result in a shift of the demand and supply curve. The emphasis is here on getting insight in the cost of running of the system, i.e. contracts between the government and the farmers for preserving nature and landscape. The next step is the calculation of the these costs. Based on that, we can investigate what governance structures are best suited for preserving nature, landscape and biodiversity. Cost-Benefit Analysis (CBA) provides a consistent analytical framework to compare the economic and financial impacts of different institutional arrangements for various nature conservation policies. A complete CBA taking into account the choice of governance structures within the EMS should include an analysis of transaction costs. However, the standard CBA does often not include transaction costs.

Private transaction costs in the EU nature and landscape management contracts

In this example to gain insight into transaction costs in practice, we will make use of the positive approach by investigating what people understand by these costs. As explained, they are not the production costs, but the costs connected with the transaction of goods and services from one agent to the other. A transaction is a two-sided mechanism: the transfer of goods or services from one individual to another or the trade-off between performance and counter performance, it is a *quid pro quo*.

Nature and landscape management contracts are often conducted between the government and private landowners and farmers. The governance structure is the management contract, or more precisely the contractual relationship between a contract taker (private landowner or farmer) and a contract giver (government). The 'step by step' transaction costs are given in Box 5.5. The costs of the activities from 1 to 7 are public transaction costs, and the costs from 8 to 12 are private transaction costs. It should be noticed that the compensation for the contract does not belong to the transaction costs. Compliance of the rules of the management agreement – including the resulting loss of income (foregone income) – by the contract taker belong to the costs of the delivered product, in short preserving nature and landscape. Opposite to this performance we have the counter performance of the government; it is the management compensation. The contract is the intermediary; i.e. the governance structure of the transaction.

Some costs arise for both parties; for example, the costs of monitoring. The farmers have often to keep records about their activities, for example the amount of fertiliser and manure used, and the number of meadow bird nests. They also spend time on accompanying control agencies to the field, etc. In addition, the government also incurs performance monitoring costs.

In most EU-countries, the government plays an important role in preserving nature and landscape by having ownership, planning, management, financing and production of forest and nature in its own hands. The governance structure used in this case is in-house production of the government. An alternative to public production or in-house production by the government is private provision by contracts with landowners or farmers. These contracts are meant for

---

Box 5.5. Transaction costs of nature landscape management contracts.

Step by step the transaction costs consist of:
1. developing the contract or menu of contracts by the contract giver;
2. offering the contracts by the contract giver;
3. negotiating the contracts by the contract giver;
4. concluding the contracts by the contract giver;
5. monitoring the contracts after being signed by the contract giver;
6. paying out compensation by the contract giver to the contract taker;
7. taking care of sanctions and conflict resolving mechanisms;
8. studying the contract by the contract taker;
9. filling in the contract by the contract taker;
10. negotiating about the contracts by the contract taker with the contract giver;
11. concluding the contracts by the contract taker;
12. monitoring the results of the management activities.
Note: this list does not indicate the order.

---

preserving environmental goods and rural amenities. The performances of farmers consist of a whole range of activities or restrictions oriented on preserving these goods and the counter performance consists of the compensation payment. In the EU, these voluntary measurements for preserving environmental goods and rural amenities are called Agri-Environmental Schemes (AESs). AESs can be considered as contracts between the government and farmers. Most of them have a duration of 6 years.

In the period 2004-2007 an EU-research project was carried out in 9 countries of the EU among farmers who participate in AESs[49]. One part of the project was oriented on determining the private transaction costs connected to these AESs. Given the numbers of respondents, more than 1300 farmers, it was one of the largest research projects for determining the transaction costs in practice. In addition to this large survey, a small follow-up research project involving more than 160 farmers from over 9 countries was carried out. These farmers were asked to keep during one year (2005-2006) detailed records on AESs implementation. They had to register costs and labour hours spent on several pre-defined tasks. All together they can be categorised in the classical typology of search, negotiation and monitoring costs. On average, these costs were about 40 euro per ha per year. Of the whole survey sample, about 40% of the farmers have made specific investments for AESs. The costs of these investments expressed in a yearly investment annuity was on average 39 euro per ha per year.

The average premium for the farmers for the AESs in the 9 countries was 151 euro per ha per year.[50] This amount can be used as reference point for the private transaction costs. The private

---

[49] The Design of Agri-environmental Schemes in EU: Lessons for the future. Project under EU 6th Framework Programme, STREP Contract no SSPE-CT-2003-5020, Integrated Tools to design and implement, Commission of the European Union, 2003.

[50] In the Netherlands, the average premium is much higher; about 480 euro per ha per year (Jongeneel et al, 2005: 75).

Box 5.6. Asset specificity and nature conservation.

Asset specificity refers to the degree to which an asset is committed to a specific task, and thus cannot be redeployed to alternative uses without sacrificing the majority of its value. For example, for nature conservation the following three types of asset specificity are relevant:

1. Site specificity, which refers to an asset that becomes committed to a particular use owing to its location. The land used for preserving wildlife and landscape, because of its 'use' but also because of its 'site', is asset specific. Valuable areas for wildlife and landscape are immobile and location tied (that is tied to a particular area).
2. Physical asset specificity, such as investments in machinery, equipment or land, and one that has a narrowly defined purpose. Investments in land or in machines used for wildlife and landscape preservation have a narrowly defined purpose, and are sunk investments.
3. Human asset specificity that arises through learning-by-doing. Preserving wildlife and landscape is a process of learning-by-doing; it requires an investment in human capital and time.

transaction costs consisting of classical typology of search, negotiation and monitoring costs amount to 27% of the yearly payment and yearly investment annuity for the specific investments amount to 26%. This means that the level of private transaction costs should not be underestimated. They represent a significant share of the compensation premium (Mettepenningen *et al*, 2008: 28-31; Polman and Slangen, 2007: 47-57). However, farmers are not compensated for these private transaction costs. The relative high percentage – compared to the premium – for the yearly investment annuity emphasises the meaning of the asset specific investments. The costs of these asset specific investments should be covered by the compensation premium. Both elements – no compensation for the pure private transaction costs and the compensation for the specific investments is part of compensation premium – mean that the average premium is 'quasi-rent'. It is questionable whether the distribution of the quasi-rent is in the advantage of the farmers.

Box 5.7. Key terms of Chapter 5.

Nexus of contracts

Transactions attributes

Human characteristics

Asset specificity

Uncertainty

Frequency

Duration

Measuring performance

Connectedness of assets

Co-specialised assets

Non-excludability

Non-rivalry

Opportunistic behaviour

Bounded rationality

Exogenous variables

Endogenous variables

Recoverable costs

Sunk costs

Sunk investments

Quasi-rent

Producer surplus

Consumer surplus

Reservation price

Hold-up

Lock-in

Fundamental transformation

Bargaining power

Ex-post renegotiation

Ex-post haggling

Switching costs

Vertical integration

In-house production

Joint venture

Natural monopoly

Franchise winner

Franchisee

Franchiser

Non-contractual quality

Distribution of probabilities

Risk-attitude

Loss aversion

Private Public Partnership

Teams and co-specialised assets

Private transaction costs

Public transaction costs

Transition costs

Appendix 5.1. Differences between transaction costs and transition costs.

A transaction is the transfer of goods services or rights from one individual to the other. The way a transaction is organised depends on its characteristics. For example, if one kind of transaction occurs frequently in a similar way, people develop routines to manage it effectively. Transaction cost economics subscribes the view that the transaction is the basic unit of the analysis (Williamson, 1991: 281). It should be noticed that transaction cost economics assumes that the institutional environment is unchanging, at least for the moment of analysis. It is a comparative static analysis. Changes in the institutional environment elicit shifts in comparative costs of governance (Williamson, 1991: 287).

There is some confusion about transaction costs and transition costs. They are not the same and they should not be mixed. Transaction cost (= cost of running a system) does not include the cost of creating, building up or changing a system or institutional structure (or an institutional provision that will change the institutional environment). Of course, if they have been created they can reduce transaction costs. For example, the costs of developing a land cadastre for determining and laying down of property rights of land (this is an institutional provision that belongs to the institutional environment) are not transaction costs but an investment or the production cost of provision. These investment cost are associated with the institutional change. However, neither in terms of Coase (1988) and Milgrom and Roberts (1992) nor in terms of Williamson are they considered to be transaction costs.

As said, transaction cost economics is a comparative static analysis. Based on this theory, we can investigate transaction costs associated with making and implementing decisions for resource allocation under a given institutional structure. It is a comparative-static analysis of different institutional arrangements to ascertain which institutional arrangements would minimise the transaction costs in resource allocation. An intriguing question is: how can we include an intertemporal dimension and assess the importance of *dynamic 'transaction costs'* in decisions for changes in the institutional environment? *Dynamic 'transaction costs'* can be defined as the cost arising in the transition from one institutional structure to another. These costs are generally refered to as **transition costs** (cf. Challen, 2000: 109).

The type and magnitude of **transition** costs will be determined by the nature of the proposed institutional change as well as the institutional status quo. Also, the magnitude of transition costs will be influenced by the process by which an institutional change is implemented. Transition costs are probably the most generally acknowledged and studied costs associated with institutional change. In some instances, procedures have been established for the estimation of particular **transition** costs as a component in the process of institutional change (Challen, 2000: 190). Of course, it is possible to use another definition of transaction costs or to stretch out the term transaction costs. However, in that case it is not consistent with the transaction cost economics (as a comparative static analysis), and it is missing a sound theoretical basis.

6. Principal-agent theory

6.1 Introduction

The principal-agent framework can be used in situations in which a person, the principal, has a certain relationship with another person, the agent. Agents can be a group of people or individuals. An agent performs a certain task, which leads to costs on behalf of the principal. However, the principal is not able to observe the actions of the agent directly. He can often only observe the output, which is (partly) the result of the actions of the agent, but it is sometimes even difficult to measure the output. The central problem in principal-agent relationship is how the contract should be designed to motivate the agent to act in a way that serves the interests of the principal best.

Hart and Holmström (1987: 73-74) consider the principal-agent theory a representative paradigm for organisational-theoretical aspects of contracts because of the lack of information. The principal-agent theory offers a comprehensive framework for a joint analysis of matters regarding how contracts are to be set up, and which incentives are to be offered given the existence of asymmetric information. It makes it possible to analyse situations from a more coherent perspective. For example, if one person, the principal, wants to stimulate another person, the agent, to carry out specific activities which are associated with costs for the agent, the principal-agent approach makes it possible to take into account, in a coherent way, issues such as hidden information, hidden actions, risk-attitude of the agent and providing incentives by the principal.

According to Douma and Schreuder (2002: 109), the principal-agent theory is a part of *agency theory*. Agency theory, in its simplest form, discusses the relationship between two people: a principal, and an agent who makes decisions on behalf of the principal. They distinguish within the agency theory two streams: the **positive theory of agency** and **the theory of principal and agent**. In the **positive theory of agency** the firm is viewed as a nexus of contracts. The main research questions of the positive theory of agency are: how do contracts affect the behaviour of participants, and why do we observe certain organisational forms in the real world? In general, it is assumed in the positive theory of agency that existing organisational forms are efficient. If they were not, they would not continue to exist. The positive theory of agency thus sets out to explain why organisational forms are as they are. The theory is not (yet) expressed in the form of mathematical models. Agency-relations can be found within an organisation (manager versus subordinates) or between organisations.

The **principal-agent theory** does not assume that existing organisational forms are efficient. This theory focuses on the analysis of situations whenever one of the following occurs: (1) conflict of interest between a principal and agent, for example, between an employer and an employee, a landowner and a farmer/tenant, a minister and his civil servants; (2) asymmetric information and uncertainty; (3) agreements are made or contracts are concluded; and (4) questions concerning how contracts influence the behaviour of the agents. If there is a relationship between the principal and agent, the central question is what should be the incentive system that the principal has to develop for the agent. How should the principal design the agent's reward structure?

In this chapter, the focus will be on the principal-agent theory. We will not closely follow the distinction made by Douma and Schreuder. Our approach is that the principal-agent setting can also be used to understand and explain organisational issues. This part of our principal-agent approach will be discussed in Section 6.2. Here we will present some simple formal mathematical models for dealing with expected utility and risk-attitudes. In Section 6.3 we extend our principal-agent approach with hidden information and adverse selection; in Section 6.4 with hidden actions and moral hazard; and in Section 6.5 with the optimal contract. In each of those sections, we will give some examples. The chapter will be concluded with an application of principal-agent theory (Section 6.6) to explain the ineffectiveness and inefficiency of the government.

Key questions:
- What types of problems can be analysed with the principal-agent theory?
- What are the differences between a first and second-best solution?
- What is the central problem of the principal-agent theory?
- What is the effect of a risk-averse agent on the compensation that he would like to receive?
- How can the hidden information problem of the agent be solved?
- How can the hidden actions problem of the agent be solved?
- How can an optimal contract be realised?
- What is time-inconsistency and what are its effects?
- Who are the principals and who are the agents if we apply principal-agent theory to the government and what can we learn from this analysis?

6.2 Principal-agent theory

The *principal-agent* theory makes it possible to analyse situations in which the driving force for specific participants is lack of information (regarding what others are doing, or what others know, or what their next-best alternative is) from a comprehensive perspective (Kreps, 1990: 578). It explains why an individual carries out, for a compensation, activities in the interests of one or more persons. Another possibility is that a person, the principal, wants to stimulate another person (the agent) to undertake specific actions which involve costs.

Within the principal-agent framework, we can analyse situations where a person, the *principal*, has a certain relation with an *agent*. The term agent can also refer to a group of individuals. An agent carries out a specific task, which involves costs, for the principal. The principal is not in a position to directly observe the activities of the agent, but instead observes the output which is fully or partly generated by the agent. The crux of the principal-agent problem is the development of a payment-incentive scheme by the principal such that the *agent* carries out the best activities from the point of view of the *principal*.

The principal-agent theory offers a framework for a comprehensive analysis of situations involving: (1) conflict of interest between principal and agent (for example, between an employer and an employee, a landowner and a farmer/tenant, politician and civil servants); (2) asymmetric information and uncertainty; (3) making an agreement or setting-up a contract; and (4) issues such as how contract design influences the behaviour of the participants.

The principal-agent situation

According to Rees (1985: 3-4), the theory of the principal and agent lends itself to any situation in which one or more individuals, called agents, must choose a particular activity (action (a)) from a specific set of actions. The particular outcome (x) resulting from this choice, depends not only on the activity (i.e. effort level) of the agent, but also on the elements of the surrounding factors (θ), prevailing at that time. Uncertainty is inherent in this situation. The outcome (x) generates utility or return for the principal. A contract is to be defined so that the principal makes a payment (y), to the agent. The utility level of the agent depends on the payment (y) and on the amount of effort (or costs) associated with the activity (a). It should be noted that the term 'contract' should be interpreted very broadly. It may refer to a formal contract, such as an insurance policy, an agreement for sharecropping, or a contract that characterises an employment relationship, or to some penalty-reward system that may not be a formal contract at all (Rees, 1985: 3-4).

The theory of the principal-agent assumes that the principal has a Von Neumann-Morgenstern (N-M) utility function $u(x-y)$ where risk-attitude and expected outcome affect the agreement. The agent has a N-M utility function $v(y,a)$, where it is assumed that the agent can only be risk-neutral or risk-averse. An important characteristic of the N-M-utility function is the *expected utility function*. We assume that the *expected utility property* holds for the N-M-utility function. This means that the *sub-utility indices*, in this case the utility of the expected incomes from each action, which are weighed and added to measure the total of the expected utility, are measured on a cardinal scale (see also Section 4.5).

Moreover, in principal-agent theory it is assumed that activity (a) generates disutility for the agent. In most applications (a) is interpreted as efforts or activities carried out by the agent as prescribed by the principal. The principal is not really interested in the agent's choice of (a) but rather in the outcome (x) and the amount (y) that he must pay to the agent, which could be an area of potential conflict of interest between the principal and agent. The principal wants the agent to do the task properly but this increases the costs for the agent. This conflict of interest, together with the immeasurable nature of the agents' efforts, is at the centre of the principal-agent

Box 6.1. Expected utility function.

The fact that we have to deal with decisions under uncertainty adds a special structure to the choice problem. In general, how a person values income in one state as compared to another will depend on the probability that the state in question will actually occur. Utility can be written as the weighted sum of income in each state, whereby the weights are given by the probabilities of each state. The weighted average is called the expected value. Expected utility functions are unique up to an affine transformation. An expected utility function is also called a Von Neumann-Morgenstern (N-M) function. One of the important properties of the von Neumann-Morgenstern expected utility function is that the 'sub-utility indices', which are weighted and added to measure the total of the expected utility, are measured on a cardinal scale. The principal-agent theory assumes that the principal has an expected utility function or (N-M) utility function u(x-y). A N-M utility function also applies to the agent v(y,a), where it is assumed that the agent can only be risk-neutral or risk-averse (see also Section 4.5).

problem. The agent will, supposedly, act in his own best interest. This will be expressed in the contract, since the disutility which the agent experiences due to activity (*a*) means that, without direction, he will not act in his principal's best interests (Rees, 1985: 5-6).

The principal-agent problem can be stated as follows (Rees, 1985: 5-6). The principal must formulate a payment schedule, where, in its most general form, he specifies the compensation of (*y*) to the agent, which depends on: x, a, and another variable, e.g. z. So we have:

$$y = f (x, \theta, a, z)$$

(6.1)

where: y = compensation for the agent
    x = outcome or result for the principal
    θ = surrounding factors, e.g. the weather or government policy
    a = activities carried out by the agent
    z = other variables

The variable z can in this case be (incomplete) information over *a* or over θ, which is freely (= costlessly) available. A central assumption in principal-agent theory is that the payment schedule depends upon variables which both parties can observe. It is assumed that the agent is acquainted with activity *a* and that he can observe x and θ. For this reason, only a limited number of possibilities regarding availability of information to the principal are possible. We limit ourselves to the following:

1. The principal can observe *a* (the activity of the agent) and the surrounding factors (θ). If we further suppose that the principal also knows the relationship $x(a,\theta)$, he can in turn also observe θ and a. In this case, the principal does not need z. Further (imperfect) information is superfluous. This means that the payment scheme only needs to be dependent on θ. The principal chooses the payment schedule and a value of activity (*a*) carried out by the agent in such a way that the principal's own expected utility is maximised, subject to the constraint that the agent receives at least the minimal expected utility in accordance with his *reservation price*, i.e. his next-best alternative. This restriction is called the *participation condition*. In this case a *first-best* optimum risk-sharing contract is possible, which resolves the *moral hazard* – or incentive problem by what is known as a *forcing contract* (Rees, 1985: 6). Under a 'forcing contract' the level of effort of an agent (= value of (*a*)) is equal to the optimal effort level of the agent from the point of view of the principal; assumed to be a_0. The principal then promises to pay an amount, say y_0, if the effort-level of the agent is at least a_0. He pays nothing if the effort level is smaller than a_0. Under such a contract, the agent is forced to bring up his effort-level to a_0 (Douma and Schreuder, 2002: 126).

2. The principal can observe neither (*a*) nor (θ) completely or not at all. Because of this, there is no complete information, no 'first-best' but only 'second-best' solutions are possible. In other words, a *moral hazard*-problem arises (Rees (1985: 6). A *moral hazard*-problem exists if the principal can observe neither the activity nor the surrounding factors. The principal must then recognise that, given the payment schedule, the agent will choose the nature and the level of effort of the activity (*a*) such that his own expected utility is maximised. In general, this will imply a value of the activity (*a*) that differs from the value that would make the payment schedule optimal. The inability to observe the activity (*a*) – and the surrounding factors (θ)

– means that the principal cannot directly correct for this, and so a constraint or an incentive, in the form of an **incentive-condition**, must be added to the **participation-condition** in the principal's optimalisation-problem. According to Rees (1985: 6), this additional incentive constraint then creates a *second-best* problem relative to case (1).

The addition of the **incentive-condition** implies that the principal must take into account that the payment schedule he chooses will determine the value of the activity (*a*) to the agent, via the maximisation-procedure of the agent, and thus affect the final equilibrium. In general, this will lead to a departure from the optimal risk-sharing solution: there is a trade-off between the gains from sharing the risks and the need to control how the agent carries out the activities.

In reality, situation (2) is more widespread. The central problem of the principal-agent theory is finding a payment schedule which will provide an optimal trade-off between the benefits of sharing risks and the costs of providing an incentive to the agent. This trade-off applies for many situations: for example, a principal would like to carry out an activity by contractors, a minister asks his civil servants to develop a policy measure, the government (as principal) wants farmers to contribute to nature and landscape preservation. Sharing the risk means that the risk-attitude is very important. The more risk-averse the agent is, the higher the compensation he will ask for bearing the risk. This means that the costs of providing an incentive to a risk-averse agent can become very high. It is usually most efficient to allocate the risk to the least risk-averse party. In that case, the compensation for bearing risk will be lower and with that the social costs will also be lower.

A risk-averse individual is an individual who, given a choice between an alternative with a fixed income, say y_2, and an alternative with an uncertain income with expected value equal to y_2, prefers the alternative with the fixed income (= y_2)[51]. For a risk-averse individual, the expected utility function is concave from the origin (see Section 4.5). A risk-loving individual is prepared to accept a lower expected return for more distribution in revenues. For a risk-loving individual, the utility function is convex from the origin. Risk-loving behaviour probably does not occur often. This risk-attitude, as we have said, is mostly excluded from the principal-agent approach.

In most principal-agent approaches, it is assumed that the principal is risk-neutral and that the agent is either risk-neutral or risk-averse (Douma and Schreuder, 2002: 128). Risk-neutral means that the person does not care about risk and does not require compensation for bearing risk. A risk-neutral individual ranks alternatives according to the expected income. In this case, we have a linear expected utility function. In contrast, risk-averse means that the person is not willing to take risks and wants to be compensated for bearing risk.

As explained, in a risk-neutral situation the N-M utility function is linear. This means that for a risk-neutral agent, the expected utility function can be defined as follows (Kreps, 1990: 582):

$$U(y,a) = y - a \tag{6.2}$$

---

[51] A risk-averse person prefer a fixed amount of money of € 10 above situation with 50% chance on €20 and 50% change on € 0.

where: U = expected utility

 y = expected income

 a = effort (e.g. the costs of performing the activity) which the agent must deliver

In a risk-averse situation, the utility function is concave. This property implies that a fixed amount of money is valued higher than an uncertain amount with weighted average yields of exactly the same value. An example of an expected utility function for a risk-averse agent is given in Equation 6.3. Other functional forms are possible as long as they have the mentioned property (see Kreps, 1990: 583):

$$U(y,a) = \sqrt{y} - a \tag{6.3}$$

The similarities of Equations 6.2 and 6.3 are linked to the 'expected utility property' of the N-M utility function. The expected utility functions (Equations 6.2 and 6.3) assume a cardinal utility notion. This means that not only the size of the outcomes indicates a ranking but also the differences in utility index values have a ranking connotation.[52]

Note that *a* is often expressed as a monetary value of the effort or costs of the agent. A risk-averse person has a decreasing marginal utility for income. The variable (y) defines the expected income, and variable (a) the costs. Weighing both has to make clear if the transaction delivers a positive contribution to the welfare of the agent. For two reasons, the costs or efforts are often not transformed into the expected utility function of the agent. Firstly, the expected utility function is based on marginal utility of income and not on effort or costs. However, it is possible to take for variable (y) the net income for the agent. In that case, it is assumed that a unit of the costs has the same value as the unit of the income. As explained in Section 4.6, this is not always the case. A second reason is that because of the simplicity, we leave the effort of the agent outside his expected utility function.

To show that it is extremely costly for the principal to expose the agent to risk if the agent is risk-averse, we assume that the agent has a concave expected utility function as in Equation 6.3. That is, we assume that the agent is risk-averse. Through this specification, large differences arise between the expected utility for the agent and the payment for the principal. Similar mathematical specifications lead to payments by the principal which are not very realistic (see also Table 6.1).

A risk-averse attitude implies a concave utility function. However, the degree of concavity is also very important. Mathematically, any function whose first-order condition is greater than zero and with a second-order condition of zero or less than zero, fulfils these conditions. That is, regarding the utility function U = U(y,a) the following conditions must be met:

$$\frac{\partial U}{\partial y} > 0 \text{ and } \frac{\partial^2 U}{\partial y^2} \leq 0 \tag{6.4}$$

---

[52] Both equations are used as an example. However, these equations can take many different forms. The square root can be expressed as an exponent (= $y^{0.5}$), but we can also use another number as an exponent, for example 0.8. Similarly, other types of the functions are possible. See also Box 6.3.

Box 6.2. The central problem of P/A theory.

According to Rees (1985: 7), the central problem of P/A theory is to find a payment schedule that provides an optimal trade-off between the benefits of risk-sharing and the costs of providing a good incentive to the agent. Under the assumption that costless observation is possible, he shows an application of optimal risk-sharing in which the marginal rates of substitution for income of the principal and the agent in each situation is the same. A risk-sharing optimum is a payment from the principal to the agent which is Pareto-efficient, i.e. which maximises the expected utility of the principal for some given minimum level of agent's utility (Rees, 1985: 7). Using the Edworth-Bowley-box approach, Rees proves that optimal risk-sharing with a risk-neutral principal and a risk-averse agent implies that the principal gives a fixed (= certain) income to the agent, i.e. an income independent of surrounding factors (in Equation 6.1 indicated by θ). In that case the principal bears all risks (Rees, 1985: 9).

Table 6.1. The expected utility and payments for different values of the exponent of y.

Value for the exponent of y (=x, where y^x) for the agent	Expected utility for the agent (euro)	Payments for the principal (euro)
0.50	1,500	2,336,014.30
0.60	1,500	201,017.87
0.70	1,500	3,390.37
0.80	1,500	9,400.51
0.90	1,500	3,390.35
0.95	1,500	2,207.20
1.00	1,500	1,500.00

Based on the above considerations and the assumed risk-averse behaviour (of the agent), one can establish intuitively that for the proper mathematical specification of the utility function the value for the exponent of y (= x), must lie between 0 and 1 (see Equation 6.5).

$$U(y,a) = y^x - a \qquad 0 < x < 1 \tag{6.5}$$

The example calculated in Table 6.1shows, that in the case of a risk-averse agent it is extremely expensive for the principal to expose the agent to a risk. Suppose the exponent is 0.95. Although the value of 0.95 is fairly arbitrary the following can be noticed. Any value close to 1 leads to a linear utility function and thus, a risk-neutral behaviour. Furthermore 0.95 fulfils the constraints specified in Equation 6.4.

If we assume y = 1500 euro, Table 6.1 gives in the case of a risk-averse agent, the payments for the principal for values of the exponent of y between 0.5 and 1, based on Equation 6.6:

$$y^{0.5} - a < y^x - a < y^{0.95} - a \tag{6.6}$$

The results of Table 6.1 make clear that in the case of a risk-averse agent, it is extremely expensive for the principal to expose the agent to risks. The payments are for the principal extremely high for all values of the exponent between 0.5 and 0.95. Empirical research on risk-attitudes is needed to indicate the value of the exponent. The given examples have only been chosen because of their straightforwardness.

As said, besides changing the value of the exponent, other mathematical specifications of the expected utility functions are possible (cf. Saha, 1993: 905). In the expected utility approach, an agent's risk-preference structure implies a set of restrictions on optimal responses to changes in prices, income or risk. The risk-preference structure which one assumes to apply has significant consequences. One of the reasons is that maximisation of expected utility is the underlying premise of much of the research on optimal choices under risk.

Both the principal and the agent have to deal with a lack of information, asymmetric information and uncertainty. The principal cannot (completely) observe the objective function of the agents. There are different types of agents with different types of utility and cost functions. This means, we have to deal with the type of incentive problem known as *hidden information*. Because the activities of the agents are not (or not completely) observable, the problem of *hidden actions* can arise. Therefore, transactions have to be carried out under conditions of *moral hazard*. Consequently, the principal has to deal with hidden information and hidden actions of the agent. However, the agent has also to deal with uncertainty: the type of contract; what do they have to do; how much will they lose in terms of property rights; who will get the residual income; and how is the compensation drawn up. Hidden actions can arise from the side of the principal; for example, time-inconsistency of the principal. In Section 6.3, we will discuss hidden information, in Section 6.4 hidden actions and also time-inconsistency of the principal.

Box 6.3. Other mathematical specifications of the expected utility function.

In the empirical risk literature, a wide variety of functional forms for a decision-maker's utility has been used. For example, Saha (1993: 906) proposed a flexible form of a utility function that exhibits decreasing, constant or increasing absolute risk aversion and decreasing or increasing relative risk aversion, depending on parameter values. This utility function will allow the data to 'reveal' not only the degree of risk aversion but also the structure of risk-preference (cf. Saha, 1993: 906).

Equation 6.7 gives the flexible form of a utility function for establishing the absolute and relative risk aversion.

$$u(y) = \theta - e^{-\beta y^{\alpha}} \tag{6.7}$$

The parameter restrictions of the utility function are:

$$\theta > 1, \alpha \neq 0, \beta \neq 0, \alpha\beta > 0 \tag{6.8}$$

where: u = the utility
  y = the income
  α, β = parameters

This utility function is called the '*expo-power*' (EP) utility function. Because the EP is unique to an affine transformation (i.e. a transformation can be applied which has no consequences for the nature of the utility functional form), the parameter θ does not play a role in characterisation of risk-attitudes or in determining of optimal choices. The Arrow-Pratt coefficients of absolute and relative risk aversion can also be derived from the EP utility function. Decreasing absolute risk aversion is said to occur when $\alpha <$ 1 and constant risk aversion when $\alpha = 1$. The EP utility function exhibits decreasing relative risk if $\beta < 1$ and, increasing relative risk aversion when $\beta > 0$. The EP utility function is quasi-concave for all values of $y > 0$ (Saha, 1993: 906-907).

The EP utility function offers possibilities for estimating the parameters for absolute or relative risk aversion in the utility function. Risk parameters are usually estimated assuming the risk-preference structure implied by the chosen utility function. In contrast, the EP utility function imposes no *a priori* restriction on how risk aversion changes with income. Estimates of the parameters α and β will allow the data to 'reveal' not only the degree of risk aversion but also the risk aversion structure. However, one should take into account the specification on the left hand side of Equation 6.7; information is needed about the valuation of the income. Estimating the parameters is difficult due to the non-linear functional form, so non-linear (parametric) optimisation techniques will have to be employed.

6.3 Hidden information and adverse selection

Firstly, we extend the principal-agent approach to situations with hidden information. In this case, one party is better informed than the other party. It is an information problem which exists before the agreement is signed; it is an *ex-ante* information problem. For example, the principal is unable to perfectly observe the objectives of the agent. There may be different types of agents with different utility and cost functions. The principal is supposed to develop an incentive scheme which, in general, is suitable for all types of agents. This type of incentive problem is identified as a hidden information problem.

The possibility of hidden information can lead to adverse selection (= incorrect selection). Adverse selection is an important characteristic within the principal-agent approach. It occurs when the agent, at the moment of choosing an action possesses any prior information, which if known to the principal, would influence the choice of action the principal would want the agent to undertake. This requires that the agent in some way lets the principal know that he possesses private information. Consequently, the selected effort of the agent, the achieved outcome from the agent and the compensation to the agent, may all depend on the signals or incentives the principal gives to the agent.

Suppose that a principal has to do with two types of agents (e.g. contractors) for carrying out a certain activity:
1. Highly productive agents (e.g. agent with a high output/input ratio or efficient agents);
2. Unproductive agents (e.g. agents with a low output;/input ratio or inefficient agents).

Agents from group (1) are able to produce the same amount of output at a lower cost than agents from group (2). Therefore agents belonging to group (1) are considered to be efficient, while those belonging to group (2) are considered to be inefficient. For the efficient agents, the marginal cost curves are lower than for less efficient agents. In Figure 6.1 the marginal costs are on the vertical axis and the output on the horizontal axis. The area under the marginal cost curve defines the costs. The reward for the (quasi) fixed production factors is defined by the area between the price line FG and the marginal cost curve. This area is the producers' surplus.

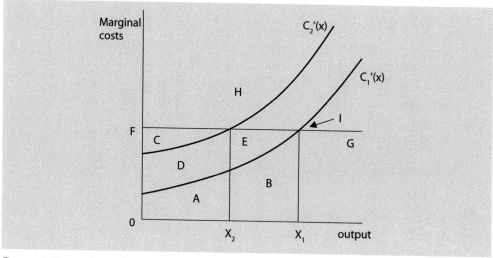

Figure 6.1. Marginal costs for two types of agents.

Institutional economics and economic organisation theory

The output is seen here as the value of the production. Suppose the value of the production is between 0 and 2000 and the average value is 1000. The marginal cost curve is also the supply curve. Efficient agents will be able to realise the production at lower costs than inefficient agents. The marginal cost curve for the efficient agent is $C_1'(x)$ and for the inefficient agent $C_2'(x)$. We have assumed that the demand curve for the product is entirely price elastic. The horizontal line FG is then also the price line. At the points where the line intersects the marginal cost curves, the marginal returns (= price) are equal to the marginal costs (MR=MC). The principal is prepared to offer the agents a compensation which fulfils the participation conditions. The amount which fulfils these conditions is the 'reservation price'. The reservation price for a producer or contractor is the minimum amount required to supply the product or carry out a certain activity. The supply curve indicates the reservation price for each unit of product. This means that inefficient agents have a higher reservation price than efficient ones.

The reservation price, for the principal, is the maximum amount he/she can afford to spend per unit of product. If the (market) price is higher than the reservation price then a transaction will not take place. This reservation price is indicated by the price line FG. We can assume that the principal is striving to minimise costs.

In terms of Figure 6.1, agent 1 receives a compensation of A+B which is exactly equal to the total production costs. Agent 2 receives A+D which is equal to his total costs. The problem with this scheme is that it does not satisfy the incentive compatibility. The reward for the inefficient agent just meets the participation conditions (C is small but positive), while the efficient agent opts for a compensation of $OFIX_1$ rather than one of $OFHX_2$. In terms of the diagram, the low-cost agent (= the efficient agent) could pretend to be the high-cost agent (= the inefficient agent) and only produce an output equal to X_2. This would yield him a surplus equal to the area of D.

The principal can fix the compensation based on the average agent. On the basis of the same norms each agent receives the same fixed compensation. However, let us assume that the principal wishes to make an agreement with efficient agents. One solution is to change the payments. The principal could decide to pay a compensation equal to A in Figure 6.1 if the output is X_2 and A+B+D if the output is X_1. This gives the efficient agent a net surplus of D. It then makes no difference to him whether to produce X_1 or X_2. However, this plan is not optimal for the principal.

Using Figure 6.2, the arrangement that leads to an optimal solution can be shown. Let us slightly scale down the output of the inefficient agent. We assume that the inefficient agent is operating in the area where price equals marginal costs. The reduction in the output produced by him is just balanced by the reduction in the amount that the principal is obliged to pay the inefficient agent. As shown in Figure 6.2, both output OX_2 and the area D have been reduced. The surplus that an efficient agent would receive if he chose to produce OX_2 is now smaller. By making the high-cost agent produce less, and paying him less, we make the target output less attractive to the low-cost agent.

Figure 6.2 shows that reducing the target output for the high-cost agent reduces profits received from the high-cost agent by the area ΔC, but simultaneously decreases profits from the low-cost agent by area ΔD. Hence, the principal will find it attractive to reduce the target output of the

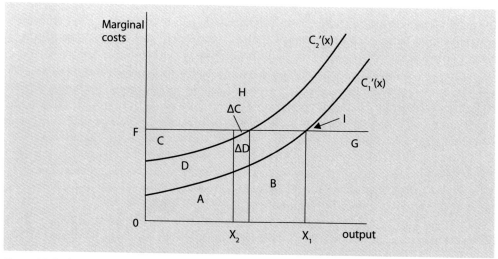

Figure 6.2. Reduction of the output for high-cost agent.

high-cost agent (to some amount) below the efficient level. By paying the high-cost agent less, the principal also reduces the amount he has to pay to the low-cost agent, if the low-cost agent were to opt for the output level of the high-cost agent.

The incentive problem can also be approached algebraically (Varian, 1992: 460). The basic incentive problem is that the low-cost agent may try to 'pretend' that he is a high-cost agent. If X_1 is the output that agent 1 is supposed to choose, then the principal must structure the payment plan so that by choosing X_1, the utility of agent 1 exceeds his utility if he chooses X_2, and similarly for agent 2. These conditions are a particular form of the incentive compatibility conditions, which are called the 'self-selection conditions'. The latter are composed of both the participation conditions and those incentive conditions that lead to contracts, so that the agents choose the contracts which are meant for them (see also Section 4.2.4). The revelation principle is important in this context. It says that whatever can be done with an indirect mechanism can also be done with a direct mechanism. We have a direct revelation mechanism if the participation and incentive conditions are formulated in such a way that truth-telling is the optimal strategy for the interacting parties (cf. Kreps, 1990: 684-696).

6.4 Hidden actions and moral hazard

The principal wants the agents to perform their job well. To achieve this, he wishes to make agreements with the agents. The degree to which agents perform their job well determines the value of the activities carried out for the principal. If an agent does little or nothing, then the agreement is of little or no value to the principal. If however an agent works hard and carefully on the activity that he/she has to do for the principal, then it will be useful for the principal to make agreements. The question is how the principal can stimulate the agents to provide a positive or even a great effort.

The principal could set up a contract which yields an amount, say 2000 euro, for carrying out the activity (be generous) to the agents and trust that the agent will work hard and do their job well. Trust is good and can have a stimulating effect, but it could also happen that agents with a 'who cares?' mentality continue their reckless ways of handling work, for example, by destroying nature and landscape or by delivering a low quality of the goods and services, to which the term moral hazard can be applied. This means that we need to suppose that there is a chance that things will not function as expected, for example, the agent does not take care for the environmental effects, the quality of the work or the product. If the principal offers the agent a fixed amount, say 2000 euro, which fulfils the participation conditions the agent will accept the agreement. The question now is: what will the effort level of the agent be? It is possible that the agent delivers a low level of effort with respect to the quality. In this case the principal pays the agent 2000 euro for a task that is worth much less, say 500 euro.

To control this problem we must add a second constraint in the form of a performance incentive or an incentive compatibility constraint. We can offer the agents a contract where their reward depends directly on the amount of effort they exert. The contract could be as follows. The principal is prepared to pay the agents 2000 euro for a task if they make a great effort (e.g. hard working and high quality), and (say) 500 euro, if they do very little. If the contract is enforceable then the agents will deliver an optimal contribution (in size and quality). Here they gain a utility level which is slightly higher than the next-best alternative while if they accept the contract and do not work hard they receive 500 – 0 = 500 euro. In the latter case they are worse off than in the next-best alternative.

This requires performance to be measured and be monitored, but how feasible is this, and how enforceable are the contracts? These considerations lead to an inclination to assume a certain probability distribution regarding the size of the production. For simplicity we disregard the quality, although it could be an important factor.

The underlying assumption is that a greater effort on the part of the agent increases the chances of value of production. We specify a certain agent who is willing to carry out an activity. The following assumptions should be considered to apply:
a. the principal is risk-neutral;
b. the size of the production is observable;
c. the reward to the agent can be made to depend on the size of production.

We suppose three possible outcomes:
1. there is no production;
2. the value of production is worth 500 euro;
3. the value of production is worth 2000 euro.

The differences in the outcomes reflect the effort required of the agent to realise these outcomes.

If the agent works hard this will result in a probability of:
• 0.6 that the production is worth 2000 euro;

- 0.3 that the production is worth 500 euro;
- 0.1 that the production is worth zero or there is no production.

If the agent does not exert himself very much this will result in a probability of:
- 0.1 that the production is worth 2000 euro;
- 0.3 that the production is worth 500 euro;
- 0.6 that the production is worth zero or there is no production.

We assume two situations; situation (1) refers to a risk-neutral agent and situation (2) to a risk-averse agent.

Situation (1): the risk-neutral agent

In addition to the principal, the agent is also risk-neutral. The expected utility function of the agent in this case is $u(y,a) = y-a$ (see Equation 6.2). We also assume that the agent has a next-best alternative; the best alternative outside the contract. The value of this alternative is 600 euro. To show the effect we will also use a next-best alternative of 1000 euro.

A high and a low level of effort of the agent corresponds to $a = 500$ and $a = 0$ respectively. The principal is prepared to conclude a contract and pay more than the 1000 euro, say 1100 euro if the agent works extra hard to realise the production. This would yield a net benefit to principal of $2000 - 1100 = 900$ euro. However, the principal is not willing to pay 600 euro (or 1000 euro), which is the minimum amount required to win the agent over to production, if the agent responds with a low effort level. The principal will surely not be pleased if the agent makes little or no effort for production after an agreement has been reached costing 1100 euro.

A simple solution exists. An agent who is considering signing a contract can choose from the following actions:
1. Refuse the contract, and take the next-best alternative of 600 euro.
2. Agree to the contract and work on the production at a low level. This gives a net expected utility of $(y-a)$, which is: $(0.1)(2000) + (0.3)(500) + (0.6)(0)-0 = 350$.
3. Agree to the contract and work hard towards production. This gives a net expected utility of $(0.6)(2000) + (0.3)(500) + (0.1)(0)-500 = 850$.

These outcomes have the characteristics of utility indices, and constitute a ranking. The agent, given the three choices, chooses option 3. With option 1 the agent receives an income of 600 euro, i.e. his next-best alternative. The principal will also consider option 3 as a good outcome. Given the outcomes of the three possible scenarios, it is in the agent's best interests to devote his energies towards the production for the principal. If the next-best alternative is no longer 600 euro but, for example, 1000 euro, then the agent will refuse the contract (since $850 < 1000$).

Situation (2): a risk-averse agent

The principal is risk-neutral and the agent risk-averse. In this case a concave expected utility function applies to the agent. We assume that this function can be described by a utility function of the form $u(y,a) = \sqrt{y}-a$ (see Equation 6.3). With the exception of the risk-attitude, we suppose that the underlying assumptions, including the probability distribution, are the same as in **situation (1)**. We assume that the principal can make the compensation to the agent dependent on the size of production by the agent. On the basis of these considerations the following comments can be made about **situation (2)**:

a. The most efficient agreement in a case where the principal is risk-neutral and the agent risk-averse is, the one where the compensation to the agent is fixed. In general this means that if one party is risk-neutral and the other risk-averse then it is efficient for the risk-neutral party to bear all the risks.
    Intuitively this can be illustrated by the following. If the principal gives a reward to the agent, the agent will value this amount as if it were his expected utility. As the agent is risk-averse, the risky reward will be valued at less than its expected value. If the principal is risk-neutral the costs of the reward will be seen as equal to the expected value of the reward. If we assume the expected value of the agent's reward has a value ē, then the principal would see this as an expense which is equal to ē, whereas the agent, because there is some amount of risk, would value the payment at less than ē.

b. On the other hand, if we give a risk-free compensation to the agent then there is no incentive for the agent to exert himself for production and if the agent does not work at nature production, for example, then the principal will not want to make the deal.

Case a) can be illustrated by the following. An agent who is considering signing a contract can choose from the following options:

1. Refuse the contract, and take the next-best alternative of 600 euro.
2. Agree to the contract and work on production at a low level. This gives a net expected utility of $(\sqrt{y}-a)$, which is: $(0.1)(\sqrt{2000}) + (0.3)(\sqrt{500}) + (0.6)(\sqrt{0}) - 0 = 4.47 + 6.71 = 11.18$.
3. Agree to the contract and work hard towards nature production. This gives a net expected utility of $(0.6)(\sqrt{2000}) + (0.3)(\sqrt{500}) + (0.1)(\sqrt{0})-500 = (26.83 + 6.71) - 500 = -466.46$.

These three outcomes constitute a cardinal utility ranking. Given the choice between these three alternatives the agent will prefer option 1. The expected utility resulting from options 2 and 3 are clearly lower than from option 1. This is due to the agent's utility function including his risk-attitude.

In **situation (1)**, it was possible to reach an agreement where the interests of the principal and the agent were parallel. The agent received the highest expected income and devoted himself to the production. This coincided with the interests of the principal. In **situation (2)**, this is not achieved. To convince a risk-averse agent to sign a contract, the given probability distribution needs to give a much higher compensation. This raises the question of how can an agreement be reached in this situation.

To stimulate the agent to exert some effort towards the size of the production we will have to sacrifice some efficiency. This can be achieved by letting the principal bear all risks. The question is: how can this be done as efficiently as possible? This can be done by minimising the expected compensation for the agent under two conditions (since we are looking at this from the perspective of the principal). The first condition is that the agent signs the contract and the second is that he

Box 6.4. Measuring, monitoring and enforcing.

The question to what extent monitoring is possible and the contract enforceable, is important. Some aspects of production, such as quantity, are easier to control than, for example, the quality. A simple solution exists. The principal can offer the following possibility: 'If you deliver bad quality then you have to pay me a fine, for example, 400 euro. If you deliver an acceptable quality you will get a bonus of 100 euro. If you deliver a good quality you will get a bonus of 2000 euro'. A prerequisite is that there are clear indicators for quality and rules for applying a fine and a bonus.

For example, in the case of nature and landscape management agreements, it is possible that there are farmers who sign the contract, exert no effort towards nature and landscape preservation, but claim that they have done so. For applying fines and a bonus, the government will need some tangible evidence about what the farmer is doing for nature and landscape preservation. Tangible evidence may not even exist or the government may not even have access to knowledge of how hard the farmers in question work for nature and landscape preservation.

chooses to make a greater effort. This means that the participation conditions must be fulfiled. In this case the production must deliver the agent a higher expected income than his next-best alternative. The second condition means that there is an incentive for realising a high level of effort. As explained, these conditions are called the participation constraint and the incentive constraint.

Both restrictions enclose the optimum which is relatively intuitive: the principal does not want to pay the agent more than absolutely necessary to get him to engage in the production. The principal also does not want to burden the agent with more risk than necessary to get his full effort because it is an expensive proposition for the principal to let the agent bear the risks. In the case of a risk-averse agent the principal will have to come up with a fixed compensation which will lure the agent into working hard on the production.

To show that, in the case of a risk-averse agent, it is an expensive proposition to saddle the agent with risks, we can follow, besides this intuitive approach, a more general one. We set up a contract whereby an agent is paid an amount of y_1^2 if he does not realise any production, an amount of y_2^2 if he realises small production, and an amount of y_3^2 with high production. Since we are dealing here with a risk-averse agent and given the utility function it is preferable to square the values[53]. We want to establish the best possible contract subject to the constraints that the agent will take the contract and put in a high level of efforts to production. That is, the participation constraint and the incentive constraint must be fulfiled. We minimise the payment of the principal:

$$0.1y_1^2 + 0.3y_2^2 + 0.6\,y_3^2 \tag{6.9}$$

subject to the participation (Equation 6.10) and incentive constraint (Equation 6.11):

---

[53] This is in accordance the approach of Equation 6.3.

$$0.1y_1 + 0.3y_2 + 0.6y_3 - 500 \geq 600 \; (\vee 1000) \tag{6.10}$$

$$0.1y_1 + 0.3y_2 + 0.6y_3 - 500 \geq 0.6y_1 + 0.3y_2 + 0.1y_3 \tag{6.11}$$

Given the aims of minimising the payments for the production (Equation 6.9) and fulfiling the two limiting conditions (Equations 6.10 and 6.11) we can calculate the values of y_1, y_2 and y_3. We assume two values for next-best alternatives; 600 and 100 euro. For the calculation, we use the Kuhn-Tucker conditions (cf. Chiang, 1984: 722-728). The results are shown in Table 6.2.

Under the defined conditions the expected payment, with the next-best alternative of 1000 euro, is: $0.1 \times 643^2 + 0.3 \times 1500^2 + 0.6 \times 1643^2 = 2{,}336{,}014.30$ euro. The expected utility from this amount for the risk-averse agent is equal to $0.1 \times 643 + 0.3 \times 1500 + 0.6 \times 1643 = 1500$ euro. We assume that the latter figure fits into the range of amounts paid out for such activities. This does not hold true for the expected payout figure of over 2 million euro. This figure is extremely high. The same is true if we assume the next-best alternative to be worth 600. From this we can conclude that, if the agent is risk-averse, it is better to pay him a fixed amount. The risks then come to rest with the principal. This excludes the option of an incentive to make the agent work hard, because the payment of the 'correct' incentives by the principal is in the case of a risk-averse agent, extremely expensive for the principal.

Table 6.2. The (non-squared) compensation for the production of the agent.

	Next-best alternatives (in euro)	
	1,000	600
y_1	643	243
y_2	1,500	1,100
y_3	1,643	1,243

Time-inconsistency

A special form of hidden actions or opportunistic behaviour is time-inconsistency. As explained in Section 4.3, time-inconsistency means that the rules of the game are changed by the party deciding the policy or rules. It is a phenomenon which affects all decision-makers who attempt to influence the behaviour of others. An important aspect of time-inconsistency is *credibility* of a pronouncement, intended policy, etc. The problem is that, if people realise it, they would anticipate a change in policy and would behave in such a way that politicians would not be able to achieve their objective.

A way to enhance the credibility of government policy commitment is to make use of delegation. Delegation occurs when a principal conditionally grants authority to an agent to act on his or her behalf which can take place between different types of principals and agents. The relations between a principal and agent are mostly governed by a contract defining the relationship between both parties.

As said in Section 4.3, the Dutch government has delegated tasks and authority to international organisations such as the European Commission, the European Central Bank, NATO, United Nations, etc. One of the reasons why governments delegate tasks and authority to international organisations is to enhance the credibility of its policy commitment. To increase credibility through delegation, two conditions must be met. **First,** the preferences of the agent must be stronger than those of the (national) government itself, so that left to its discretion the agent will adopt a policy that moves the outcome in the direction the national government knows it 'should' go but cannot implement itself. **Second**, there must be some costs to withdraw authority from the agent. It means in some cases delegation can be seen as solution for opportunistic behaviour or **time-inconsistency** of the (national) government. However, delegations can also create a principal-agent relationship with connected problems.

Time-inconsistency also occurs in principal-agent relationships. This means that a way for reducing time-inconsistency is making use of delegation and delegation subsequently creates a principal-agent relationship. The outcome of this process also depends on the level to which the above mentioned conditions are fulfiled. In practice there are a lot of examples of time-inconsistency in principal-agent relationships. Mostly, they refer to the government as principal; different types of agents conclude contracts with the government. The agents may expect that the government, once an agreement is concluded, will change the rules or lower the compensations. Agents can be anticipated to be extremely reluctant when it comes to concluding an agreement.[54]

This obviously has consequences regarding the willingness of agents to make agreements with the government. Agents can anticipate the uncertainties brought about by time inconsistencies of the government by adopting a more risk-averse attitude. Asking for a high compensation is a consequence of government's behaviour in the past and is an expression of risk-averse behaviour of the agent. The government may consider the plan too expensive then. However, the government should realise that a part of this strategic behaviour of the agent is due to its own past behaviour.

---

[54] Time-inconsistency of the government is also an important reason why firms and organisations are reluctant to conclude Public Private Partnership agreements. See also Chapter 4.2.5.

Box 6.5. Time-inconsistency and management agreements; an example.

Time-inconsistency also occurs in agreements between farmers and the government for nature and landscape preservation. It refers to changes in plan development, the program, the compensation level, the duration of the contract, and the supply of management packages. The duration of management agreements was before 1995 six years, from 1995 to 2000 five years, and from 2000 until now again six years. Farmers may expect that once the agreements have been signed, the government may lower the compensation payments. They can anticipate this change in policy by being very cautious and reluctant to sign management agreements with the government. The compensation of the management agreements were, up until 1989, based on the incomes of farmers in a comparable area.

In 1988 the government changed its manner of compensation from one based on 'comparison areas' to one based on three fundamental factors:
• production losses, i.e. decline in returns;
• extra labour-hours;
• difference in operating costs.

This adaptation led to a significant lowering of the compensations for management packages in areas with difficult production circumstances. Farmers whose agreements were based on income of farmers in comparable areas, were confronted with heavy cuts in their compensations after 1988. An important part of the pioneering and trend setting farmers, for nature and landscape preservation, terminated their agreements. These farmers felt cheated by the sudden drop in income especially considering the efforts invested in other areas to improve the external production factors, and thereby the income, of other farmers. The government was therefore not seen as a trustworthy partner. This obviously has consequences regarding the willingness of farmers to continue making management agreements with the government. Farmers anticipate the uncertainties brought about by time-inconsistencies of the government by adopting a more risk-averse attitude. Their strategic behaviour is partly due to the past behaviour of the government.

Another example concerns the protection of nests of meadow birds. In the Netherlands, many farmers had a contract for protecting nests of meadow birds. Recently, however, according to the European Commission (October 2006) it is not allowed anymore to give farmers a compensation, because protecting nests of meadows birds belongs to good farming practice, and is included in cross-compliance regulation. The policy of stretching out the concept of good farming practice to the protection of meadow birds, preserving nature and landscape, without any compensation, is a typical example of time-inconsistency of the government. Farmers perceived this as negative and the government will lose both its credibility and reputation. Of course the discretionary power of government makes such an intervention possible.

6.5 The optimal contract

Suppose that the government wants contractors to develop a recreation area of 100 ha. For the sake of simplicity we assume there are two contractors: an **efficient** contractor who is able to realise the recreation area at a cost of 1000 euro per ha (contractor A) and a **less efficient** contractor who can realise this area for 1500 euro per ha[55] (contractor B). These amounts are the participation conditions for each contractor. If the government knows the contractor's costs then the problem is simple to solve. The government can reach an agreement with the contractor who is able to develop the recreation area at the lowest costs. However, if the government does not know what the production costs are, it could ask the contractors to make their costs known. If the costs are the same then the government could divide the area between both contractors and pay the named costs. The contractor who reveals the lowest costs is granted the task to develop the recreation area and the government pays the costs.

Because of this, if the contractors are restricted to quoting either 1000 or 1500 euro per ha as their costs, they quote 1500 euro, regardless of what their actual costs are. If the costs are actually 1500 euro then there is no reason to quote 1000 euro, since this leads to a loss of:
- 25,000 euro if both contractors say that their costs are 1000 euro. In this case, the government divides the recreation area between the two contractors. Contractor B with a production costs of 1500 euro per ha will lose 1500 euro ha × 50 ha = 25,000 euro.
- 50,000 euro if contractor B says 1500 euro. In this case the government grants the recreation area entirely to contractor A. The loss of contractor A is therefore 500 euro per ha *100 ha = 50,000 euro if he quotes 1000 euro.

If the costs are 1000 euro then there is no reason to name 1000 euro. If the one contractor says 1500 and the other does too (the chance of this is ½) then the efficient contractor A makes a profit of 500 euro per ha * 50 ha = 25,000 euro. Both contractors will choose to name 1500 euro. The costs to the government are then 1500 euro per ha * 100 ha = 150,000 euro, i.e. it is Nash equilibrium to say 1500 euro.

Clearly, the government needs to come up with some kind of incentive to get the contractors to reveal their actual costs (cf. Krebs, 1990: 681-682). This condition is also known as the **self-selection condition** or the **strategy of truth-telling**. Consider the following scheme: If both contractors say 1500 euro then the assignment is divided and the government pays 1500 euro per ha. If both contractors say 1000 euro then the assignment is also divided between both contractors and the government pays x > 1000 euro per ha. That is, the government pays both contractors x euro per ha. If one contractor says 1000 euro and the other 1500 euro then the mandate goes to the contractor who said 1000 euro and the government pays y > 1000 euro per ha. That is, that one contractor receives y euro per ha. The question now is how large x and y should be in order to get both contractors to name or **reveal their real costs**, i.e. truth-telling.

For this we assume that contractor A believes that contractor B will name the real costs, but contractor A does not know whether contractor B is able to do it for 1000 or 1500 euro. (Suppose x,y ≤ 1500). Then contractor A, if its costs are 1000 euro per ha, can name 1500 euro and make a profit of 500 × 50 = 25,000 euro with a 50% chance. Or contractor A can name 1000 euro and make a profit of 50 (x-1000) with a probability of ½ (if the costs of the other contractor are 1000 euro per ha), and a profit of 100 (y-1000) with a probability of ½ (if the costs of the other

---

[55] In reality these amounts are much higher, sometime even 20 times. This does not matter for the calculation. By multiplying the calculated outcomes with this factor the results are close to the to actual situation.

Institutional economics and economic organisation theory

contractor are 1500 euro per ha). Assuming that both contractors try to achieve their maximum profits, contractor A will declare his actual costs (= truth-telling) if:

$$\tfrac{1}{2}\,50\,(x - 1000) + \tfrac{1}{2}\,100\,(y - 1000) \geq 25{,}000 \qquad (6.12)$$

The left side of Equation 6.12 (left of the $\geq$ sign) indicates the profit for contractor A, by being honest and the right side the profit when they lie about their costs. In this situation (Equation 6.12) a so called Nash equilibrium exists (Kreps, 1990: 682). This means that both contractors have no incentive to deviate from the chosen strategy. A unilateral deviation from the chosen strategy does not pay.

Assuming that the contractors declare their actual costs, the costs to the government will be as follows:

$$100\,(\tfrac{1}{4}\,x + \tfrac{1}{2}\,y + \tfrac{1}{4}\,1500) \qquad (6.13)$$

That is, with a probability of ¼, the government will pay x euro per ha, with a probability of ½ it pays y euro per ha, and with a probability of ¼, it pays 1500 euro per ha. The aim of the government is to minimise:

$$25x + 50y + 37{,}500 \qquad (6.14)$$

The truth-telling-inducing constraint can be written as follows:

$$25x + 50y \geq 100{,}000 \qquad (6.15)$$

Equations 6.14 and 6.15 indicate that we are dealing with a linear programming problem. It is obvious that each value of x and y which fulfils the constraint $25x + 50y = 100{,}000$ and the objective function of $25x + 50y + 37{,}500$ minimises the expected costs for the government. In the present situation these expected costs for the government for the recreation area of 100 ha are in total **137,500 euro**. That is an average of 1375 euro per ha.

The linear programming problem, in the form of Equations 6.14 and 6.15, is illustrated in Figure 6.3. Line segment AB indicates the constraint function. All the values for x and y which result in a value greater than 100,000 for Equation 6.14 are found in the shaded area above this segment (AB). The objective function for the government touches the segment AB or lies above it. Line segment OC indicates where x and y are equal to each other. Where segment OC intersects segment AB all the conditions are fulfilled.

On the basis of this point, the expected compensation per ha for contractors A can be calculated as follows. If we assume that y = x, which fulfils the conditions for a Nash equilibrium, then the expected compensation for contractor A in euro per ha is:

$$\tfrac{1}{4}\,x + \tfrac{1}{2}\,y + \tfrac{1}{4}\,1500) \qquad (6.16)$$

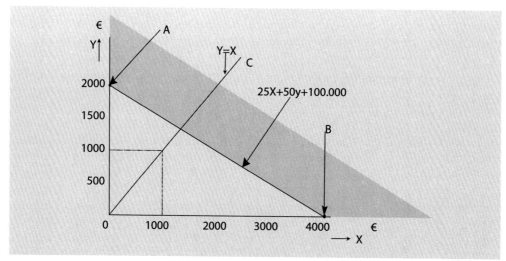

Figure 6.3. The expected value for contractor A and the expected costs for the government.

With this procedure the government minimises its expenses and ensures that efficient contractors will implement the development of the recreation area.

¾ 1333.33 +¼ 1500 = 1375)   (6.17)

The question is whether one can refer to a dominant strategy in the preceding example. A dominant strategy is said to exist if the payoff from this strategy, independent of the strategies chosen by all other players, is not less than any other possible strategy (for this player) (cf. Furth, 1994: 1163). There is no dominant strategy for each of the participating parties. If, however, a number of conditions are met, an optimal bidding strategy can be developed. For this the participating parties must be aware of their reservation price and the probability distributions of the reservation prices of the other participants. In general the participants involved in such a sign up will invariably ask more than their reservation price (Furth, 1994: 1163).

To achieve an optimal strategy we need to build in a mechanism which ensures that the participation conditions are met and that the incentive is such that truth-telling about the reservation prices is the optimal strategy for the participants. This mechanism is known as the revelation principle. It is also called a direct revelation mechanism; the word 'direct' indicates that everybody voluntarily chooses to be honest.

Referring to the above example we need to ensure first of all that both contractors wish to participate. To achieve this, a participation bonus could be given. If they decide to participate then an incentive must be given such that both parties simultaneously and independently declare their actual costs. To achieve this the incentive must be such that 'truth-telling' is the most profitable option for all participants. We now carry out the following modification.

A simple solution is that both contractors who participate will receive a participation bonus of 1000 euro[56]. If both contractors claim that their costs are 1500 euro per ha and it is the amount for which they are willing to implement the policy, then the task is divided evenly. Each contractor receives 1500 euro per ha. If both contractors claim 1000 euro per ha then the task is also divided and additionally they receive the participation bonus of 10 euro per ha. If one contractor states that his costs are 1000 euro per ha and the other 1500, then the one who said 1000 euro will be awarded the contract. This contractor then receives an extra bonus of 250 euro per ha. In total this contractor receives (1000 + 10 + 250 =) 1260 euro per ha.

We suppose now that contractor A has a cost price of 1500 euro. For this contractor it is better, regardless of what contractor B says, to state 1500 euro instead of 1000 euro. The participation bonus of 10 euro per ha euro makes it better to bid a price of 1500 euro than to refuse tendering a bid. If contractor A has a cost price of 1000 euro and assumes that contractor B will also state a cost price of 1000 euro it is better for contractor A to bid 1000 euro than 1500 euro and end up getting nothing. Should contractor A bid 1000 euro he makes a profit of 10 × 50 = 500 euro. If contractor A bids 1500 he receives nothing, with the exception of the 10 euro participation bonus.

Next, we suppose that contractor A has a cost price of 1000 euro. If contractor B says that he has a cost price of 1500 euro, it is better for contractor A to state a cost price of 1000 euro instead of 1500 euro. Stating 1500 euro, for contractor A, will result in a profit of 500 euro per ha × 50 ha = 25,000 euro while stating 1000 euro as the cost price will result in a profit of 260 euro per ha ×100 ha = 26,000 euro. According to this scheme truth-telling is the dominant strategy for both contractors. The expected benefit for contractor A is now (per ha):

¼ 1010 +½ 1260 + ¼ 1500 = 1275.50 euro (6.18)

The costs for the government for the total area of 100 ha then work out to be:

100 [¼ 1010 +½ 1260 + ¼ 1500] + 2000 = 127,750 (6.19)

This modification means that truth-telling becomes the dominant strategy for both contractors. The expected costs (= 127,750 euro) are much lower for the government than without these modifications (= 137,500 euro). This is a result of the participation bonus and the amount of money as incentive for truth-telling. This means that giving a participation bonus and a extra bonus of 250 euro per ha[57] as an incentive for truth-telling is very efficient for the principal.

---

[56] This amount of money can also be used for preparing the bidding or the tender.

[57] Both amounts of money are somewhat arbitrary. Slightly lowering both types of bonuses decrease the costs for the government.

> **Box 6.6. Principal-agent theory and transaction cost theory.**
>
> In the standard principal-agent approach the agents negotiate on a once-and-for-always basis where they take into consideration all possible future possibilities. Under specific assumptions the principal proposes a compensation (incentives)-schema where the reward of the agent depends on the results obtained. In this manner, a situation is created where the agent maximises not only his own utility but also that of the principal. Such contracts are considered complete because once they are set up, they can be directly implemented. There is no room for re-negotiation, and no new contract will be made (cf. Furubotn and Richter, 1997: 248).
>
> According to Hart (1995: 21), the standard *principal-agent theory* assumes that if variables are observable for both parties they can be set up in a contract without costs. However, this does not mean that the setting up of a good contract is without costs. The principal-agent theory assumes that comprehensive contracts can be set up. Comprehensive contracts do not need to be a first-best solution. For a *first-best* solution, there should be complete information or at least no asymmetric information. A comprehensive contract means that the duties for each party are carefully specified in all anticipated situations as completely as possible. As a result the parties have no need to revise or renegotiate as the future unfolds. The reason is that if parties should ever want to change the contract or add a contract clause, such changes or additions would already have been anticipated and built into the original contract (cf. Hart, 1995: 22).
>
> In reality, contracts are not comprehensive and complete; they are revised and renegotiated. Complete contracts in practise cannot be made because the contracting parties are not in a position to take all future events into account when setting up a contract, and even if they could foresee the future, it would be too expensive to write it all down at once in a contract (cf. Furubotn and Richter, 1997: 142).
>
> An important element which is missed in the standard *principal-agent approach* is, according to Hart (1995: 21), is the cost associated with writing or setting up of a contract. This cost, central in the transaction cost theory, is neglected in the standard *principal-agent approach*.

6.6 Principal-agent approach and functioning of the government

The *principal-agent* theory offers an explanation for why governments do not always function well. Another explanation is given in Box 6.7. Within the *principal-agent* theory, situations in government bureaus can be analysed when there is matter of a person, the principal, (or a group) who in a certain situation is faced with an agent. The term agent refers to individuals (or groups) who have a certain task to carry out for a principal, but with that task there are associated costs. Within the principal-agent framework, we can analyse different situations within government where a person, the *principal*, stands in a certain relationship to an *agent*. An agent carries out a specific task, which involves costs, for the principal (Schram *et al.*, 2000: 50-55; Wolfson, 2001: 96).

The principal within the government derives a certain task from his objective and asks the agent to carry this out. This takes place in a situation with uncertainty, imperfect and asymmetric information. Therefore, the principal can not (perfectly) observe the objective function of the

---

Box 6.7. Institutional lock-in.

In addition to the principal-agent approach we can explain the behaviour of civil servants by making use of institutional lock-in. More recently it has become clear that many formal rules of the institutional environment slow down rather than accelerate economic growth (North, 1990, in Shleifer and Vishny, 1998: 8). For example, in the Netherlands the laws and rules concerning spatial policy, and town and country planning extend over a long period and are rather inflexible. An explanation for the attachment to rules of laws is the path dependency and the institutional lock-in of civil servants. The public servant is familiar with the existent policy. Therefore continuing with the same type of policy in a new policy area brings about few additional costs, and the chance for unexpected effects and risks are small for the public servants. Furthermore, most public servants are risk-averse (Nentjes, 2004: 622-623). However, path dependency and the institutional lock-in of policy often lead to ineffectiveness and inefficiency.

---

agent. Furthermore there are different types of agents with different utility functions. These types of information problems are indicated as hidden information.

A second information problem that is characteristic for many principal-agent situations is moral hazard. It arises when the agent carries out an action that the principal can neither observe nor easily check. Instead of moral hazard the term hidden action is also used. Situations where we have to deal with moral hazard elicit unintentional or improper use of resources after an agreement has been made. In this way moral hazard is an *ex-post* information problem.

If the principal knows the objective function of the agent and can easily observe him or her, then there is a first-best solution possible, where the moral hazard problem can be solved by a forcing contract. Through a forcing contract the effort of the agent for carrying out of a certain activity (say a) is equal to the optimal effort level of the agent, seen from the perspective of the principal (say a_0). However, it is more often the case that the principal knows neither the objective function of the agent nor is he or she able to observe it. If information is incomplete, second-best solutions are only possible.

While much of the literature on the principal-agent approach refers explicitly to the organisation of the firm, Niskanen (1971) is one of the first authors who applied it to government bureaucracy. According to Niskanen (1971), ministers and other politicians are the principals and civil servants are the agents in a government bureaucracy. However, once in four years, during democratic elections, civil servants become principals by way of voting. In short, Niskanen's application of the principal-agent theory may be summarised as follows:
a. The civil servants of a government organisation, the agents, can have their own preferences and objectives other than those of the politicians, the principals, who determine the formal policy.
b. Therefore the principals, in practice, do not have complete information concerning the work and the objectives of the civil servants (asymmetric information) and have limited instruments to obtain this information.

Here the *principal-agent* problem is defined. The agent's objectives (meant by a and b) can be summarised by stating that the civil servants, in most cases, will pursue their individual interests through budget maximisation and/or broadening the extent of their service. Yet these objectives are normally not in accordance with the objectives of the politicians. Therefore these hidden actions often break the effectiveness and efficiency of government policy. The civil services (or their bureaus) often function in a monopolistic situation and can not go bankrupt. In this way, an environment is created that leads agents to the increase their departmental budgets and extend their jurisdiction (Niskanen, 1971: 31-36).

Niskanen further argues that civil servants have a strong time preference. Hence, the implicit discount rate used by government agents is always assumed to be smaller than the marginal return of capital in society. This assumption implies that government agents will always choose more capital intensive activities than what is efficient (Niskanen, 1971: 117). In support of Niskanen's propositions, Sandler and Tschirhart (1980: 14-97) and Cornes and Sandler (1986: 188) show that government services focus more on short-term objectives than other governance structures such as *clubs,* which consist of more generation-overlapping members.

While conflict of interest cases, such as those outlined above, are symptomatic of principal-agent problems, their causes are related to the sources of uncertainty that characterise principal-agent relationships. One of these uncertainties is related to the circumstances within which the activity must be carried out. In practice, the concrete execution of the order given by the principal depends on the frequently changing environment. Given that the principal is less informed about the changing circumstances than the agent, the principal must trust the agent's judgement in carrying out the task.

A second source of uncertainty concerns the objective that the agent actually pursues in practice. Government agents often enjoy fairly wide degrees of choice on whether or not to focus on the objective of the organisation. Given such flexibility, the principal knows little about how and to what degree the agent is going to carry out the order. This uncertainty creates the situation of asymmetric information in which it is especially difficult for the principal to check whether the work has been completed as is intended. In this way, the agent creates (or takes) the space to pursue his own objectives within certain boundaries.

A third source of uncertainty is related to the input or effort level of the agent (moral hazard). Their efforts in the organisation are a function of (1) personal characteristics (zeal, tendency to serve) and (2) the motivating elements in their environment (the style of the leader, the nature of the work and organisation, career possibilities). The level of uncertainty depends on how little is known about what the agent is doing. With little knowledge of the agents' interests and behaviour, forcing contracts and incentives are often not possible.

Further explanations for government inefficiency focus not only on the effects of uncertainty on principal-agent relationships, but also on the lack of accountability. The rational behaviour in a bureaucracy is according to Schram *et al.* (2000: 238) not only bounded by lack of information and inertia, but is also selective, because the individual effort in a certain sense is left to 'the politeness of mister'. This creates x-inefficiency. The x-inefficiency gives the degree of effort to work effectively and efficiently within a production or consumption household. In the case of government x-inefficiency, the real costs are higher than the minimal necessary costs. Yet government organisations feel less urgency to avoid this technical inefficiency (Schram *et al.*, 2000: 239).

According to Schram *et al.* (2000: 239) government organisations do not produce efficiently due to their lack of factual functioning. If their money providers (= principals) cannot observe the factual functions of their agent's outputs, then it is likely that agents receive a higher than necessary budget for production and therefore can deliver the facilities with much less effort. Budget enlargement will in that case lead to a more than necessary expansion of the use of production factors, by which the working pressure of the present staff is reduced.

Furthermore, according to Schram *et al.* (2000: 238-239) it is quite plausible that subordinates in a principal-agent relationship are not easily willing to provide information about their functioning to their principals. The asymmetrical information gives an advantage to the one carrying out the order or job (agent). In the public sector, the phenomenon of information asymmetry between the principal and agent will manifest itself stronger than in the market sector. The exact relationship between input and output will mostly not be known, further the output is often not (well) measurable, and therefore neither the relationship between the agent and output will be known.

If the output can not be measured (well), for example, for public services, nature and landscape preservation, etc., then the principal does not know to what degree the agents are productive. Consequently the principal will make-do with indicators that are more focussed on the input than on the actual output of the agents, because the latter is not easily measured. This may stimulate the agent to focus more on the input criteria and less on the output. Also, there is no 'discipline of the market' in the public sector. Government organisations do not have the concern of bankruptcy if they price themselves out of the market. Subsequently, there is less necessity to avoid technical inefficiency within the organisation.

Applied to public services, politicians are the principals. According to Schram *et al.* (2000: 51) it is often assumed, from the **normative** point of view, that principals promote the general public interest, according to the social welfare function. On the other hand, from the **positive** point of view, it is often assumed that their objective is to be re-elected. This assumption is often, according to the American Downs (1957), still particularised to the hypothesis of vote-maximisation. This hypothesis states that politicians strive for as many votes as possible. This would mean that politicians would try to realise the interests of their voters, rather than the interests of society as a whole.

Applied to the management of public services, civil servants are the agents. As such, they can pursue a range of objectives, including status, appearance and power. For the most part, these objectives are seen as being related to the size of the department (service) where they work. The size is again dependent on the budget that is granted from above. That is why Niskanen (1971: 42) concludes that civil servants pursue budget maximisation. With a larger budget, the extent of their departmental services increases. Similarly, the costs increase as the extent of the services increases. Thus it is argued that civil servants will pursue a budget so large that the services can just be financed. However, the politicians who function as principals, also must derive a certain amount of benefits from each level of a service.

Politicians, according to Niskanen (cf. Schram *et al.*, 2000: 52), will pursue net profit maximisation, meaning the total benefits minus the total costs. Figure 6.4 shows that the civil servants will pursue a larger extent of the budget than the politicians. The total costs, necessary for providing a certain level of service, are given by TC. It is assumed that these minimal costs increase constantly with the level of service provision. The total benefits for the politicians, which are equal to the maximum budget that they are willing to allocate to a certain level, are shown by the curve TB. It is assumed that the marginal benefits decrease with the level of the services as the level of the service is higher.

With complete information about the costs, politicians would like to increase the level of the service as long as the extra benefit of increasing a unit of service does not compensate the extra costs anymore (compare MB = MC). This is the case with Q_{pol}, where the slope of the TB-curve is equal to that of the TC-line. At that level, the marginal benefits are equal to the marginal costs. However, according to Niskanen (cf. Schram *et al.*, 2000: 52) civil servants will aim for a budget as large as possible. The TB-curve gives the budget that politicians are maximally prepared to allocate. Assuming that the costs of the services must be covered, the civil servants will attempt to maximise the level of their services under the requirement that TB ≥ TC. Their optimum is therefore reached with the level Q_{bur}. So we see that civil servants aim for a larger budget than the politicians ($Q_{bur}>Q_{pol}$).

The degree to which they can realise this depends on the degree of information asymmetry between the civil servants (agents) and politicians (principals) regarding the minimal costs, belonging to a certain level. In practice, (cf. Schram *et al.*, 2000: 53) because politicians have little information on the true budget costs, while civil servants are fully informed, it is likely that the latter will realise their optimum Q_{bur}.

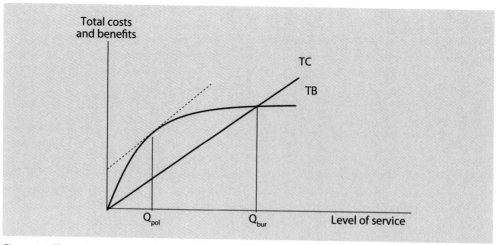

Figure 6.4. The optimal provision level for (quasi-)public goods for politicians and civil servants.

Box 6.8. Key terms of Chapter 6.

Principal	Optimal contract
Agent	Participation bonus
Expected utility function	Dominant strategy
Neumann-Morgenstern utility function	Nash equilibrium
Reservation price	Self-selection conditions
Participation condition	Revelation mechanism
Incentive condition or incentive compatibility	Truth-telling
Forcing contract	x-inefficiency
Hidden information and adverse selection	Institutional lock-in
Hidden actions and moral hazard	

6.7 Question for review: principal-agent approach and risk-attitude

a. What is an important issue in the Principal-agent-approach concerning risk?
    Suppose a principal would like to conclude a contract with two agents for carrying out activities. The estimated time for carrying out these activities is about one year. One agent is risk-neutral (named A) and the other is risk-averse (named B). The expected utility function for the risk-neutral agent (A) is given in Equation 6.2:
$$U(y,a) = y - a \qquad (6.2)$$
    and, the expected utility function for the risk-averse agent (B) is given in Equation 6.3.
$$U(y,a) = \sqrt{y} - a \qquad (6.3)$$
    where: U = expected utility
    y = expected income for the agent
    a = own costs for the agent.
    The principal states that agents can earn € 250,000 if they conclude the contract. It means y = € 250,000. For both agents the efforts (or costs) that they have to make are € 50,000 (thus a = € 50,000).

b. Calculate what both agents are going to do, participate or not, and explain your answer.

c. What should be **at least** the value of y to make sure that the risk-averse agent B would participate?

d. Explain the trade-off between risk-bearing and the cost of providing an incentive in the case of the risk-averse agent.

e. Why is it efficient to allocate the risk to the least risk-averse party?

f. Would in the case of a risk-averse agent, a fixed salary of 60,000 euro per year be a good alternative for both the principal and the agent? Who bears all the risk in this case?

g. Suppose the exponent of the risk-averse agent is not $y^{0.5}$ in Equation 6.3 but $y^{0.8}$. Would this agent participate or not? What would be the difference in risk compensation?

7. Contract theory

7.1 Introduction

In this chapter we focus on the institutional arrangement of 'contracts'. A contract is a governance structure and thus also a transaction mechanism for conducting an exchange. Any transaction which is of the type 'You scratch my back, I'll scratch yours' – also known as *quid pro quo* – can be considered as a contract. In the case of spot-markets, where the two sides of the transaction take place almost simultaneously, the contractual element is usually downplayed, presumably because it is regarded as trivial. However, whenever there is a long-term relation or a long duration between purchase and delivery (*quid* and *quo*), a contract is an essential element of the transaction relation (Hart and Holmström, 1987: 71). In the case of a lease contract, for example, for an office, the transaction involves a transfer of (a part of) the bundle of property rights from the landlord – such as the user and income rights – to the tenant. The performance (*quid*) is the transfer of a part of the bundle of property rights and the counter-performance of the tenant is mostly the rent (*quo*).

Contracts are becoming more and more important. For example, fiercer global competition, rapid technological developments and pickier customers are forcing firms to seek more efficient production and distribution structures. In recent years, industries have shown increasing collaboration on issues of product development, quality guarantee systems (certification) and improved logistics. Spot markets are being replaced by contract-production and systems of vertical coordination. More coordination and collaboration may lead to improved efficiency in production and distribution channels and to more product and market innovations. These vertical relationships can take many organisational forms, like strategic-alliances, long-term contracts, licensing, subcontracting, joint ventures, franchising, cooperatives and networks.

In this view, contracts not only play an important role in principal-agent approach (see Chapter 6) but also in the organisational modes as described above. The main part of contract theory is based on the assumption that parties agree to a (for them) Pareto-optimal contract for a specific period of time. Yet, for a number of reasons most of contracts are incomplete. In Section 7.2 we will explore these reasons and discuss the consequences of the incompleteness of contracts. Furthermore, we will address in this section the relationship between the incomplete contract theory and new property rights theory.

In Section 7.3 – based on five key elements – we will characterise three types of contracts: classical, neoclassical and relational. These five key elements used to characterise contracts are a matter of grading, and should be interpreted on a sliding scale. In Section 7.4 we will discuss a number of properties of contacts. These properties are analysed for the three types of contracts. In Section 7.5 we pay attention to the role of commitment for observing contracts. Section 7.6 describes ten rules of thumb for contracting.

In Section 7.7 we will present a comprehensive framework for analysing design principles for reducing contractual failures. This framework is based on the elements discussed in the previous chapters. We conclude this chapter with Section 7.8 consisting of an application of the contract theory; public provision versus contracting out or outsourcing.

Key questions:
- Why are contracts mostly incomplete?
- How do transaction costs, incomplete contract theory and principal-agent theory deal with the origin of quasi-rents and its distribution?
- What do the principal-agent and the contract theory assume about the completeness of contracts?
- Which key elements provide a basis for the classification of contracts and what types of contracts can be distinguished?
- What are characteristic properties of contracts? Which coordination mechanism is mostly used?
- What is the commitment problem, what are its constituent parts and can it be resolved?
- What is reputational capital?
- Which factors determine the value of reputation?
- Which rules of thumb are important as guidelines for contract design? Are they equally important for each type of contract?
- Which types of design principles are important for reducing contractual failures?
- In which two types of situations is direct government production likely to be superior to contracting out?

7.2 Complete and incomplete contracts

Complete contracts

The basic model of a perfect competitive market relies on a number of assumptions. These assumptions are maintained regardless of whether the market under consideration is a product or a factor market. If these assumptions are met, a market is perfectly competitive (cf. Katz and Rosen, 1994: 344). Perfect competition, with all the associated assumptions, results in a perfect market. However, a perfectly working market is an ideal-type situation.

Just as with the market, we can also start an analysis of contracts from an ideal-typical situation. In that case, we can speak about a perfectly complete contract in which all the coordination and motivation problems are resolved. In an ideal situation there are no problems concerning property rights. A complete contract specifies what each party is to do in every possible situation and arranges the distribution of realised costs and benefits in each contingency so that each party individually finds it optimal to abide by the contract's terms (Milgrom and Roberts, 1992: 127).

Consequently, with the ideal complete contract, every contingency is anticipated, all relevant information is available and all risks involved in the contract are divided in an optimal manner among the contracting parties, at the lowest costs (cf. Cooter and Ulen, 1997: 186). If the original plan is efficient then the complete contract implements it and brings about an efficient result. Such a contract is considered to be complete because, when signed, it can be immediately implemented.

All the ordinances in the contract are verifiable, so that one of the parties can call upon a third party, for example a court, to enforce the contract.

Incomplete contracts

In reality, most contracts are incomplete for several reasons. **First,** in a complex and unpredictable world, it is difficult to forecast and take into account all possible events. Specific and unforeseen events may not be factored into the contract agreement. With perfect foresight, we could develop a better contract (Hart, 1995: 22). **Second,** even if all events could be predicted, it is difficult for the parties to negotiate over so many possibilities. There would be far too many events to take into account in the contract, and further a common language (for which prior experience does not exist) would be needed in order to describe all the diverse states of the world (Hart, 1995: 23).

Third, even if the parties could take all future contingencies into account and negotiate over them, it would still be extremely difficult to write it all down in an agreement in such a way that the content and the meaning could be examined and enforced by an outsider, e.g. a court of law, should a conflict arise. As a result of these factors, the concerned parties generally formulate a contract which is incomplete (cf. Hart, 1995: 23). Not only is the feasibility of a complete contract in question, but also the high transaction costs mean that it is simply too difficult to achieve a complete contract. As a result, we come to the terrain of the incomplete contract, to which most contractual arrangements belong. This means that the contract will have gaps and that some provisions will be missing.

Summarising, incomplete contracts arise as a result of lack of information, bounded rationality and the high transaction costs of obtaining the required information, for monitoring and enforcing of the agreements. As a result, there are several factors which lead to incomplete contracts; some of which are more related to the transaction cost theory and others are more oriented to elements of incomplete contract theory. The transaction costs view emphasises that it is too costly to design a complete contract, while the incomplete contract theory focuses on all the contingencies that can arise that were not foreseen or not specified in the contract (cf. Lafontaine and Slade, 2007: 650). It is sometimes even impossible to take all the contingencies into account. For example, determining the probability that a certain contingency will occur, or the monitoring required to check if the other party complies fully with the agreement, are both difficult activities. Furthermore, the enforcement of contracts can be costly.

These arguments lead us to incomplete contract theory (cf. Hart, 1995: 23, 25). It is simply too expensive to take all events into account, specify what should happen in case of each specific circumstance and to control whether the other party or parties adhere to the agreement. The enforcement and observance of contracts can entail enormous costs (cf. FitzRoy *et al.*, 1998: 234). This incompleteness has important consequences. In a complete contract, income can be distributed in such a way that there is no return such as a residual income. If contracts are incomplete, at least two questions arise: (1) who has the residual control rights or residual power and (2) who has the residual income rights or to whom does the residual income accrue? According to Hart (1995: 6) this depends on who has the 'residual power'. The one with the 'residual power' has the 'residual rights of control' and the 'residual income rights' such that the residual-income accrues to him or her (Hart, 1995: 63-64).

Box 7.1. Transaction costs, incomplete contracts and principal-agent approach.

According to transaction cost theory, asset specificity generates a flow of quasi-rents that are associated with *ex-post* haggling and opportunism. This means that all forms of asset specificity associated with quasi-rents can lead to a dispute as each party to a contractual arrangement attempts to appropriate those rents (Lafontaine and Slade: 2007: 657). The bargaining power and opportunistic behaviour (including moral hazard) play an important role here. However, the predictions of transaction cost theory concerning the distribution of the quasi-rents are less robust than those of the incomplete contract theory.

Incomplete contract theory states that contracts are incomplete; there will be residual control rights and a residual income. This will lead to a dispute about who has the residual control right in a contract and who is able to capture the residual income. It depends on who has the *'residual power'*. The one with the *'residual powers'* also has the *'residual rights of control'* (Hart, 1995: 6). Hart presents theoretical arguments as to why in many cases one might expect the holder of the residual control rights to have significant residual income rights, i.e. residual control rights and residual income rights should often go together. An important reason is that if residual control rights and residual income are separated, a hold-up problem often arises (Hart, 1995: 64).

The incomplete contract theory is also labelled as the new property rights theory. The new property rights approach has been developed over the last fifteen years to explain the optimal allocation of asset property used in firms, organisations or contractual relations (Foss and Foss, 2001: 21). In the new property rights theory or incomplete contract theory having the residual control rights and the residual income is taken as a definition of ownership (Hart, 1995: 30). Residual control rights are like any other good; there will be an optimal allocation of them (Hart, 2002: 185). The new property rights theory is especially concerned with residual control rights and the residual income. This means that ownership is an important source of *power* if contracts are incomplete. We will come back to this topic in Chapter 9 and 10.

The standard principal-agent approach is usually based on the assumption of a complete contract. However, the assumption that a complete contract can be designed for all situations limits the applicability of the principal-agent approach (cf. Hart, 1995: 21). Consequently, the standard principal-agent approach assumes no quasi-rents, no residual control rights and no residual income. The crux of the principal-agent approach is that the actors have diverse objectives and interests, and the principal has insufficient information over the actions of the agent. Because of asymmetric information, an incentive problem arises.

These theories can complement each other quite well, certainly if in the principal-agent approach the assumption of complete contracts is relaxed.

Residual claimant

In an incomplete contract, benefits can arise from the residual income characteristic as a consequence of: (1) missing information; (2) the limited ability of people to absorb all available information; (3) the high transaction costs of acquiring the required information, controls on compliance for the agreements and the enforcement of contracts. A central question: is who is able to capture this residual income? As explained, it is the person who has the residual income rights and who is said to be the residual claimant.

Instead of *residual income* the term *residual return* is used. It is that part of the return that remains after all debts and costs and all other contractual obligations have been paid. Just as 'residual rights of control', the concepts of *residual return* or *residual income* is closely linked to incomplete contracting. As we have said, under complete contracting it is assumed that the division of the returns and costs in each eventuality is specified contractually and there are no returns and costs that could be usefully thought of as residual. In this view no residual income would remain.

Sometimes the concepts of *residual control rights* and *residual income* are a little vague. Suppose two parties (A and B) would like to set up a profit-sharing contract. The total profit is TP and it is agreed *ex-ante* that party A receives:

$$0.6(TP) \tag{7.1}$$

and party B receives

$$TP - 0.6(TP) \tag{7.2}$$

The question is: who is the residual income claimant? The answer is that both are. The setting up of a profit-sharing contract does not have to be expensive if the yield is completely verifiable. The *residual income* can thus be shared. However, it remains unclear how residual income is allocated if the profits are not very verifiable or if it is very expensive to monitor. Another problem can arise regarding *residual control rights*. These rights are not divisible in the same way as *residual income rights*. Hart (1995: 64) illustrates this with an example: suppose there are two parties and one *asset*, then it is reasonable that one party or the other has *residual control rights*. But it would be difficult or impossible to allocate 80% of the rights to one party and 20% to the other.

Given the incompleteness of contracts, contingencies can always occur which can be advantageous to the concerned parties, but are not considered in the contract. However, in some situations it may not possible to measure (or verify) all aspects of an asset's return. For example, suppose there is a contract between a landowner and a tenant. The advantage – in the form of an increase in value of the asset – will generally go to the owner of the asset. Arguably, most of the latter will accrue to whomever has the control rights, because this person can decide when or even whether to sell the asset.

According to the **new property rights approach**, the owner has the *residual control right* over the asset: the right to decide about the use of an asset to the extent that it does not conflict with the terms of the contract, customs and laws. The possession of *residual rights of control* is in fact perceived as the definition of ownership. This seems to be in contrast to the more standard definition of ownership, whereby an owner possesses the residual income from an asset rather than its *residual control rights*.

Although there is not always a one-to-one relationship between *residual income* and *residual control rights* there are – according to Hart (1995: 64) – theoretic arguments why *residual income* and *residual control rights* should both be conferred on just one person or organisation. **First**, if *residual income* and *residual control rights* are separated, then a *hold-up problem* arises. Briefly, if *control rights* and *income rights* are to a great degree complementary, then it is efficient to allocate both to one and the same person (cf. Hart, 1995: 64-65, evidence on p. 46). **Second**, in some situations it is not possible to measure or determine all aspects of the stream of returns from an asset. This return can consist of two components: a short-term income generated by current activities and a long-term component resulting from the value-appreciation of the asset. The long-term income accrues to the person who has *control rights*, because he can decide whether or not to sell the asset. The short-term income accrues to the person who *uses the asset*. This person will attempt to maximise this income, without regarding the long-term value of the asset. (This person actually has no control rights.) This may lead to a very inefficient outcome. It is better to bundle the short-*term income rights* with the *control rights*. **Third**, there are goods where it is not feasible to separate *residual income* from *residual control rights* (cf. Hart, 1995: 65).

Summarising, ownership is defined as having both the residual control rights and the residual income rights, i.e. the possibility to have the residual income. Incomplete contract theory emphasises the residual control rights. The allocation of these rights which confer the rights to make decisions about assets when contingencies arise, are the bridge between incomplete contract theory and new property rights theory. Both are closely related to each other and can be considered as having almost the same approach. In Chapter 9 and 10 we will re-visit the new property rights theory in more detail.

7.3 Types of contracts

In order to decide to which type of institutional arrangement a contract belongs, we must first know what sort of contract it is. Lyons and Metha (1997: 48), on the basis of the work of Macniel (1979), distinguish three types of contracts: classical, neoclassical and relational. The emphasis here is on the nature of the coordination mechanism, the nature of the contracting parties and their mutual relation keeping in mind the process of exchange in the future. According to Deakin and Mitchie (1997: 11), this classification provides a basis for a theory explaining **contract form, duration**, and the **distribution of power** in the relationship, **contractual duties** and **enforcement**. Lyons and Metha (1997: 49) make use of five key elements which characterise the three types of contracts. The three types of contracts can be characterised by the following five key elements:

- **Classical contract**
  - The identities and personal characteristics of the parties are irrelevant.
  - A discrete exchange or transaction is specified.
  - Contingencies and/or unexpected events and penalties for non-performance are specified.

- Written documents overrule any verbal agreement.
- Court of law arbitrates in the case of difference of opinion or in the event of disagreement.

- **Neoclassical contract**
  - The identities of parties is of importance/ matters.
  - Usually the duration is fixed. Normally it specifies a fixed duration (and /or task to be completed).
  - It is accepted that not all unexpected events can be specified (or accepted that not all contingencies can be specified).
  - Written documentation provides the status quo basis for further negotiation.
  - Arbitration procedures exist in case of differences in opinion or dispute.

- **Relational contract (Lyons and Metha (1997: 49)**
  - The identities and personal characteristics of the parties are crucial.
  - It is often of unspecified duration (or normally indeterminate duration).
  - Norms of behaviour, or shared codes of conduct specify the reaction to new developments, or inform responses to new developments as they unfold.
  - Written documentation is used as an official document of agreement, or is treated as a record of what has been agreed.
  - Values and norms of behaviour, or shared codes conduct are of greater importance than written documents in case of differences in opinion. They overrule written documents in settling disputes.

Identity

The **first** element is related to the identity and the personal characteristics of the contracting parties. For the classical contract, this is not important, but for the relational contract it is crucial. The classical contract usually involves discrete or one-term transactions with a low degree of *asset specificity, uncertainty, frequency* and *connectedness,* the *performances* are easily to measure, and the goods or services involved are rival and excludable (see Section 5.3). This is justified by 'identity does not matter'. The low frequency shows that little or no repetition of the transaction is to be expected. The short-term orientation of the classical contract means that all future rights and duties of the concerned parties are completely returned, or do not exist. Further, the absence of relation specific investments means that opportunistic behaviour can be effectively countered by the threat of exclusion (exit) from the market or appeal to a court of law (cf. Deakin and Mitchie, 1997: 11).

According to Menard (1996: 157), classical contracts are suitable in relations such as '*market-relations*'. The price is the determinant factor, there is no specific investment by the concerned parties (the *specificity of the asset* is negligible), and the need for contractual certainty is, due to the nature of the good, minuscule. A neoclassical contract is typically a longer term arrangement with the intent to pursue a continuous relationship, where the identity of the parties matters.

Duration

The **second** element concerns the duration. The duration of the relationship in a classical contract is specified, but it remains unspecified in a relational contract, or it is even infinitive. The duration of a classical contract can be extremely short, such as with the spot-market. Transactions, which take place in a similar manner as in the spot market, can be considered as classical contracts. The duration of neoclassical contracts is in-between the classical and relational contract.

How to deal with unexpected events

The **third** element focuses on how people are expected to deal with unexpected events or contingencies. This is especially important in situations with relation-specific investments. If investments are relation-specific, then the usefulness of the classical contract is limited, or even ineffective and inefficient. The reason is that the classical contract is not able to specify all possible future events. Moreover, no single party can use the market mechanism as an institutional arrangement to avoid or limit the threat of opportunism from the other party, because (1) this would put the relation-specific investment at risk; or (2) what has already been invested would be lost (cf. Deakin and Mitchie, 1997: 11).

In other words, when contracting parties make relation-specific investments which can not be redeployed at low cost, the usefulness of the classical contract is limited since the express terms of the contract can no longer specify all future contingencies. Nor can one party use the market mechanism of exit to limit the threat of opportunism by the other since this would mean foregoing the chance to realise relation-specific investments. These conditions give rise to 'neoclassical' contracts, in which parties accept at the out set that the agreement is incomplete, in the sense of being unable to specify their rights and obligations in all future states of the world (cf. Deakin and Mitchie, 1997: 11-12). Under these conditions, the role of norms of behaviour, shared codes of conduct, trustworthiness and reputation becomes more important.

The role of written information

The **fourth** element focuses on the role of the written documentation. The status of this documentation differs among the three types of contracts. In classical contracts written documents overrule any verbal agreement. In the neoclassical contract, it provides a basis for further negotiations, while in the relational contract it is used as an official document of agreement. However, an important difference is that in the relational contract, the relationship is often more important than the content of the contract (for example a marriage contract).

Differences in opinions

The **fifth** element relates to the procedure to be followed in case of conflict of opinion. Neoclassical contracts specify an arbitration procedure in anticipation of problems in dealing with changing circumstances (cf. Lyons and Metha, 1997: 49). Relational contracting is characterised by the substitution of the legal system. Its associated formal documents remain more in the background due to the use of informal agreements such as verbal promises, *letters of intent,* or *gentleman's* *agreements*. The identities and the characteristics of the contracting parties are of considerable importance. In the case of differences in opinion, values and norms of behaviour, shared codes conduct, reputation, trustworthiness and the relationship itself are of greater importance than written documents. Moreover, they overrule written documents in settling disputes. The success of the transaction depends on the extent to which both parties can trust each other, refrain from opportunistic behaviour and can rely on cooperative behaviour in the event of unexpected events (cf. Lyons and Metha, 1997: 51).

Spectrum of contracts

Just as with *governance structures*, we can distinguish a broad spectrum of different types of contracts. At one end of the spectrum, we have **classical** contracts, and at the other end, **relational** contracts. On the left side we have the classical contract for which the price is the most important coordination mechanism. The identity of the partner is not relevant. Duration is short, and asset specificity is small. Safeguards are not important. Shifting from left to right the role of the price as a coordination mechanism becomes less important while other elements become more important. Figure 7.1 gives an overview of the spectrum of contracts.

One of the characteristics of **neoclassical** contracts is the restricted role of prices as a factor of adjustment. This is caused by the presence of specific assets, while complete self-enforcing safeguards are difficult to implement. Combined, these factors have consequences for the usefulness of the role of the price mechanism for setting the price of these contracts and with

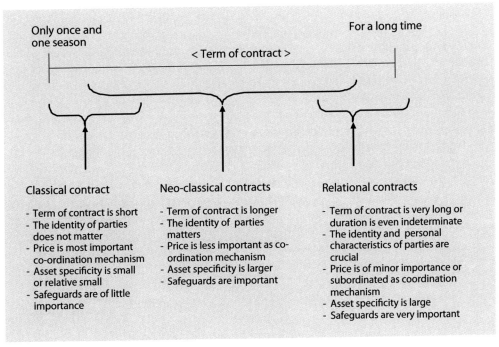

Figure 7.1. The spectrum of contracts.

that of the role of the price as coordination and motivation mechanism. We will return to this in Section 7.4.

In the case of a relational contract the relationship itself can be even more important than the content of the contract (compare it with a marriage). Contracts at the *relational* side of the spectrum include strong personal involvement, have a long duration and anticipate the possibility of events as a normal part of the continuing association between the parties. Marriages and long-term labour relations are examples of relational contracts (cf. Furubotn and Richter, 1997: 143). New Institutional Economics has led to a shift in attention from classical contracts toward the concepts of neoclassical and relational contracts.

The difference – on the spectrum of contracts – between the classical contract and the relational contract can be described as follows. The classical contract is almost 'everything included' or *complete*. The performance and counter performance are determined *ex-ante* and all the provisions for all events are specified for the duration of the contract. There are no specific investments made and there is no particular virtue in continuing the (business) relationship. Any concerns which remain open for the parties are covered by contract laws. It does matter if problems are ultimately resolved by court action (cf. Lyons and Metha, 1997: 51). The beginning and the end of the contract are clearly defined. This concept of the classical contract is also used in standard neoclassical economic theory. The ideal type of the *complete contract* can be seen as a result of the model of the perfect working market in which personal relations play no role (cf. Furubotn and Richter, 1997: 142).

In a *relational contract*, it is recognised that there are gaps in the agreement. However, the relationship between the involved parties, their identity, commitment, trustworthiness and reputation can overcome these problems. In general, reputation refers the general beliefs that others have concerning one's character. However, in the context of a contract, the concern is with a person's propensity to keep promises or with their reputation for being trustworthy (MacLeod, 2007: 609). In a relational contract, parties meet repeatedly over time and may modify contracts as a function of events as they unfold.

In our real world we see contracts used in many diverse fields and the type of the contract used depends upon the characteristics of the goods or service exchanged. Based on the key characteristics of classical, neoclassical and relational contracts, we can develop a framework for classifying and analysing contracts. As shown in Figure 7.1, the key characteristics are: duration of the contract, identity of the parties concerned, role of price as coordination mechanism, special characteristics of the object (degree of *asset specificity* or transaction-specific investment) and the importance of specific guarantees. These characteristics are inter-related. For example, the importance of specific safeguards increases with a rise in the asset specificity. This framework can be applied in many situations with just minor adjustments.

Box 7.2. An example: land lease contracts.

A well-known example of contracting is found in the leasing of land. For analysing the types and properties of lease contracts and the way in which specific terms are arranged (the organisational form), we make use of the framework in Figure 7.1. This framework can be applied in many other fields – e.g. the franchise and franchisor relationship, soccer players and soccer clubs – with just minor adjustments.

A **classical contract** is of short duration, and the identity of the parties and personal characteristics are of no importance. A classic example of such a contract is a transaction in a spot-market. In the case of lease, an example could be a bulb-grower who would like to lease land for one season (from October to July or from March to November) from a dairy farmer in the form of a cultivation-contract with an agreed-upon lease-price up-front. Neither one of the parties is strongly dependent on the other: there is no asset specificity. It is a contract with short-term orientation

In this case, there is little possibility for any residual income. It is clear who has the power of control in the contractual relationship and also over what. The bulb-grower uses the land one time and thereafter no more. In the classical contract, the price is the most important coordination mechanism (cf. Menard, 1996: 157). In general, the prices will be relatively high. The only thing that matters for the landowner is the return. Safeguards and written procedures are of limited meaning here. The economic advantage for both parties is the driving power of the transaction.

The **neoclassical contract** is more useful for renting and leasing of houses, offices and land. This can be a yearly repeated contract, or a contract for a longer period. The identity and personal characteristics of the parties matter and are important. These contracts are suitable for leasing building or plots of land. If the landowner is the owner of the buildings, then the contract should pay attention to management and maintenance of the buildings. If the tenant would like to make an investment in the land or buildings, then some arrangements must be made for the tenant's investment at the time when the contract ends. Otherwise, the investments in land and buildings will not take place and a *hold-up problem* arises[1]. As a result, there will be not an efficient use of production factors or a socially optimal land-use.

As investments in land and buildings increase, there will be a greater need for safeguards in the form of written documentation and legal rules (for example, to be included in a lease regulation) as protection against lock-in effects. Safeguards in the form of written documentation are also needed in the case of land which requires careful treatment or for preservation of nature and landscape. Furthermore, there is a need for an arbitration procedure or a conflict-solving mechanism in case of disputes. Price as a coordination mechanism is less important here as compared to the classical contract. As special characteristics increase (level of asset specificity or the relation-specific investment), the importance of 'safeguards clauses' increases, while the use of the price as coordination mechanism declines.

---

[1] The possibility of hold-up arises in every contractual relationship which is incomplete. The reasons may be diverse. As soon as a person has selected a specific technology or relationship, the discontinuation or termination of the relationship can be extremely expensive. Further, as a result of unforeseen circumstances, the position of one of the parties in the contractual relationship can result in a deterioration or change in the negotiation position of the parties over time. Termination of the relationship can indeed be costly.

> **Box 7.2. Continued.**
>
> A question that often arises in the case of neoclassical contracts is: who has the residual power in the contractual relationship? Lease contracts do not specify all matters and unforeseeable events. For example, the introduction of production rights for milk, sugar beets and manure, and income rights (known as single farm payments) were not foreseen, whereas they represent considerable value now. The person with residual power over these rights is able to capture the connected residual income. Another residual income is the increased value of the land and the difference between the free market value and the value of leased land under the current Lease regulation. If the landowner is able to sell leased land as unleased land he can appropriate this residual income[2]. If the landowner is patient (or if an institutional investor has at one's disposal a diversified portfolio with leased land) the investor can over time collect the residual income by selling the leased land as unleased.
>
> On the other side of the spectrum is the **relational contract**. These contracts could be intended for farmsteads and also for plots of land (for example, when the lease contract is continuously renewed). A partnership for a farm between father/mother and son/daughter is also a striking example of a relational contract. The price as coordination mechanism plays a subordinate role in the partnership. Relational contracts also include the long-term relationship where the landowner and the exploiter (farmer) undertake an agricultural (or horticultural) business under a joint account. The compensation for the owner of the land can vary from a fixed amount per hectare to an amount dependent on the returns, or costs, or both (= sharecropping). Sharing of the costs (and sometimes also of the returns) makes it possible to overcome the hold-up problem. The duration of a relational contract is left unspecified, but the identity and the personal characteristics are obviously of importance here.
>
> ———————
> [2] The Lease regulation 2007 for regular lease contracts specifies that a tenant, who has obtained an object by making use of his priority rights and sell it within 10 years, must pay a compensation to the landowner consisting of the difference in value between the unleased value of the land and the amount that he as tenant has paid for the land. The compensation steadily declines with the number of years since the sale.

7.4 Properties of contracts

A contract is a commitment to a mutual agreement which is enforceable and recognised by non-interested third parties. In general, a contract specifies the actions each party will take (for example the delivery of a good or service by one party and the payment to be made by the other party) and may assign decision-making powers (cf. FitzRoy *et al.*, 1998: 232). Contracts can be verbal or written and most of them possess the following properties:

Voluntary exchange

First, the closing of a contract is a *voluntary exchange.* Because it is voluntary, it is only accepted if the expected result of the agreement is individually and mutually advantageous for both parties (Milgrom and Roberts, 1992: 127) The *voluntary exchange* holds for classical, neoclassical and relational contracts. This exchange is an important difference with rules of law from the government or direct supervision in hierarchy.

Coordination mechanism

Second, contracts contain a coordination mechanism, and coordination is a central issue in Economic Organisation Theory (Milgrom and Roberts, 1992: 126-127). In Section 3.6, we gave an overview of four groups of coordination mechanisms. Coordination can take place by one of the four groups or a certain mix of them. As discussed, the four groups are: the '*handbook*', '*invisible hand*', '*handshake*' and '*visible hand*'. In general, the '*handbook*' group is the most important for the governance structure 'contract'. In this case, the coordination consists of rules, directives and safeguards. For detailed contracts, the emphasis is on the handbook. However, too much emphasis on the handbook allows distrust to develop among the contracting parties and contracts become solidified distrust.

However, contracts often also contain a price as a coordination mechanism. In this case, the coordination mechanism of contracts consists of a combination of '*handbook*' and '*invisible hand*'. In general, the type of contract determines which coordination mechanism will prevail and what the role of the price will be in the *quid pro quo* relationship. Price can be a compensation (only counter performance) or an incentive mechanism.

The '*handshake*' can also be used as a coordination mechanism for contracts. Important elements of this mechanism are common vales and norms and mutual adjustment. Common values and norms (based on repeated interaction promoting solidarity, consensus and trust) and codes of conduct can also serve as coordination mechanism to groups of people. *Mutual adjustment* refers to the coordination achieved by informal horizontal communication. For a detailed description of the '*handshake*' as a coordination mechanism and its application in practice, see Section 3.6 and Section 8.3.

The '*visible hand*' group is mainly used in firms and organisations based on hierarchy. By hierarchy we mean that the positions in the firm are ranked; higher order level commands lower level. In this case, the coordination will be carried out by authority or direct supervision. This group of coordination mechanisms is not relevant for contracts in general. After all, contract parties are not vertically integrated with the other party. Contract parties mostly retain their separate external identity.

However, the coordination mechanisms are not the same for classical, neoclassical and relational contracts. For classical contracts the price is probably the most important coordination mechanism, but also the '*handbook*' may play a role. Consequently, the coordination mechanism for a classical contract is a combination of the '*invisible hand*' and '*handbook*', but the emphasis is on the price as a coordination mechanism. For a neoclassical contract, the price as coordination mechanism is less important, compared to classical contracts. In that case, the coordination mechanism of neoclassical contracts consists of combination of '*handbook*' and '*invisible hand*', but there is a shift in the mix more in the direction of the '*handbook*' as a coordination mechanism, compared to classical contracts. Depending on the identity of the parties the mix can also include elements of the '*handshake*'.

The price as coordination mechanism often plays a subordinate role in relational contracts. In such contracts the relationship itself can be even more important than the content of the contract (compare with a marriage). Such contracts indicate a certain continuity in the relationship between the parties. It means the identity of the parties matters. For this reason, the 'handshake' is often used as a coordination mechanism for such types of contracts. However, the actual coordination is a mix of the 'handshake', 'invisible hand', and to a less degree the 'handbook'. The coordination mechanisms will comprehensively be discussed in Chapter 8.

Motivation mechanism

The next property of contracts concerns **motivation.** Motivation questions arise because individuals have their own private interests, which seldom correspond perfectly to the interests of other parties, the group to which the individuals belong or the society as a whole. Such problems arise because specific plans cannot be described in a complete enforceable contract (Milgrom and Roberts, 1992: 126-127).

Hence, the **third** property of contracts is that they contain a *motivation-element.* Many contracts often contain a steering mechanism which defines performance criteria and the means to measure the performance. Motivation can also be included in the specification of a reward-structure which marks the level of payment if a minimum level of performance is attained. The motivation elements are generally not the same for classical, neoclassical and relational contracts. For example, performance-based pay fits well with classical and – to a lesser extent – with neoclassical contracts, but not so well with relational contracts. In contrast, the characteristics of trustworthiness, having concerns about you career and a good reputation are more important for neoclassical contracts and especially for relational contracts.

The kinds of motivations in a contract can be internal to the individual concerned or external. The pressure or feelings to do your work well in a contractual relationship does not arise so much from financial incentives but from internal motivation also. Because of the trade-off between the two kinds of motivation, too much emphasis on extrinsic motivation can drive out intrinsic motivation. As explained in Section 4.3, motivations activated by external factors, such as monetary incentives, rules and direct order (as in hierarchical governance structure), can crowd out motivations that are internal to the individual, such as more **altruistic concerns.**

It is important to be aware of what can happen, if the motivation for contract compliance is based more on the stick than on the carrot. The threat of sanctions – as a type of motivation – which is mostly driven by external motives, can, given the trade-off between the external and internal motivation, have a negative effect on internal motivational elements, such as feelings to do your work well, trustworthiness and having or building up a good reputation.

A contract can be explicit or implicit

The **fourth** property of contracts is that the set of agreements in a contract can be **explicit** or **implicit**. An explicit contract is one in which there is a written document about the agreement. An implicit contract is one which has no formal record of the terms and conditions agreed upon by the parties. Such contracts are enforceable by the *reputation-mechanism* (Milgrom and Roberts, 1992: 139, 259). This raises the question whether and when a party is able and in a situation to develop and maintain a desired *reputation*. A party with a short-term horizon is less willing to invest in a reputation than a party with a longer-term horizon. Therefore reputation is less important for classical contracts. Similarly, investing in a reputation at the beginning of a game is more attractive than at the end. However, in order to build a reputation, the game has to be played several times.

Relational or detailed plans of actions

The **fifth** property is that the relationship in a contract is often more important than in a market transaction. Contracts are mostly incomplete and often relational in nature. Relational contracting means that the impossible task of setting up a complete contract is not attempted. Instead, an agreement is set up which frames the relationship. The parties do not agree on detailed plans of actions (Milgrom and Roberts, 1992: 131) but rather:

- on goals and objectives;
- on general provisions that are broadly applicable;
- on the criteria to be used in deciding what to do when unforeseen contingencies arise;
- on who has what power to act and the bounds limiting the range of actions than can be taken; and
- on dispute resolution mechanisms to be used if disagreements do occur.

Such contracts can in fact work quite effectively; at least when the potential conflicts are not too great and the parties are not inclined to be opportunistic in their dealings with on another (Milgrom and Roberts, 1992: 131). Of course, such contracts can be relational contracts only.

7.5 Commitment, contracts compliance and re-opening of the contract

As explained in Section 4.4, there are various forms of commitment; from traditional forms of commitment including trust, friendship, relationship, ethnicity, religion, to commitment in the language of game theory. Commitment rules out alternatives or forecloses an opportunity. Commitment alone is often not enough, it must also be credible, for example, by burning the bridges behind you in a warzone, you signal your credible commitment to battle. It is signal that you are willing to fight.

Part of the problems with contracts lie in the **credibility** of the compliance of all contractual agreements made. The commitment to which a contract is binding is often rather in doubt; which is related to the incompleteness of contracts. We can separated the commitment problem into two parts: one that is connected with reneging; and one that is called *ex-post* renegotiations (cf. Milgrom and Roberts, 1992: 133). The commitment problem as result of reneging can occur in all incomplete contracts. However, the commitment problem as result of *ex-post* renegotiations commitment is only a problem in neoclassical and relational contract. In classical contracts, this commitment problem does not arise, because of its short-term orientation.

7.5.1 Lack of commitment connected with reneging and the role of reputation

It is possible in a contract that the parties have in fact made an agreement but that one of parties no longer wants to comply with it. In such cases, the party reneges on the deal or agreement. A customer may simply not pay for services rendered, or a supplier may refuse to deliver the goods that are contracted for, perhaps because the costs of completing the contract are higher than anticipated.

This is a serious problem especially in **incomplete contracts** because what has to be done in diverse circumstances is not written down explicitly and so remains open to interpretation (cf. Tirole, 1993: 22-24). If reneging occurs by not carrying out the agreed-upon transactions, it clearly affects efficiency. However, often the problem with reneging is not that it impedes efficiency directly, but rather that it affects performance indirectly (cf. Milgrom and Roberts, 1992: 133). The threat of getting cheated may prevent an efficient transaction from ever occurring.

When parties fear that the contracting partner may renege on agreements made, they can perhaps rely on the reputation of those with whom they make the contract. Reputations are formed on the basis of behaviour displayed, and particularly on the perception of others regarding that behaviour. Reputation can be seen as an institutional device that may be considered as a part of human capital, or the capital stock of an organisation. Choosing contracting partners on the basis of their *reputation* is one defence against being exploited by a reneging contracting partner (FitzRoy *et al.*, 1998: 254). Reneging on the agreement, or capturing the quasi-rent or the residual income, is at the expense of the reputational capital.

Box 7.3. Reputational capital.

The economic theory of relational contracts focuses upon the enforcement benefits of repeated interaction between parties. Recent experimental work finds that the abilities of parties involved in relational contracts to act reciprocally is an important ingredient in sustaining cooperative behaviour. A second ingredient in a transaction is the acceptance or the belief that, for example, a fair price is demanded or a fair quality of the good or service is offered (also called fair trade), corresponding with the norms and beliefs of others (MacLeod, 2007: 609). Individuals with a good reputation are able to realise rent from keeping their reputation intact; reputational capital. The notion of reputational capital is similar to human capital – it is rent that a party receives for being trustworthy (MacLeod, 2007: 616)

7.5.2 Lack of commitment as result of ex-post renegotiation

The other commitment problem is more subtle. In specific circumstances, it is advantageous for both parties to *renegotiate* the contract *ex-post*. At least one of the parties would like the contract to continue, but with some changes in the provisions. New information may have become available, or some conditions may have changed. Re-opening or renegotiating the contract *ex-post* can appear attractive to both parties. At first, this does not seem to be a problem. If both parties really want to renegotiate, it is possible that the original contract includes the wrong incentives. In that case it is not possible to generate the desired behaviour with that contract (cf. Milgrom and Roberts, 1992: 133; FitzRoy *et al.*, 1998: 253). However, opening the possibility of renegotiating can also be – at same time – an incentive for opportunistic behaviour.

How to ensure credible commitment

As we have said, commitment alone is not enough, it also has to be credible. A self-organised group (such as local club taking responsibility for preserving the environment) could solve the commitment problem without external force. As we may expect with such a club, the members are supposed to be self-motivated in observing the agreement. However, does this also hold for partners in a classical or neoclassical contract? In reality, it will not always be the case. Monitoring, sanctions and conflict resolving mechanisms are mostly indispensable for supporting contracts. They are necessary for ensuring that the commitment is credible.

Trust

Trust can be important. It can increase credible commitment, but it also has another role. For example, trust lowers the cost of search and monitoring, because trusting people are less secretive and more ready to supply information. Trust reduces the costs of contracting and control because it lowers fears of opportunism and accepts more influence from the partner. In the case of trust, people will deliberate and renegotiate on the basis of give and take ('voice') rather than walk out ('exit') when conflicts arise. Trust based on friendship or kinship is often not enough to be the basis for cooperation. Conversely, material self-interest and coercion are seldom sufficient either. It is proposed here that you 'really' trust someone when you are willing to forego guarantees on the basis of coercion or self-interest (cf. Nooteboom, 1999: 30).

However, while trust is necessary and can work (although we try to think why it does), but we also have to take into account the possibility that trust may not always exist of its own accord (cf. Kreps, 1990: 580). In such cases, we can make use of direct control that one may exercise over conduct by contract, monitoring or threat (coercion). Trustworthiness may also include motives of self-interest that restrain the partner in his opportunistic behaviour; motives such as preservation of reputation and expectations of future reward from cooperative conduct in the present (Nooteboom, 1999: 29).

In a transaction, a decision-maker can honour trust in order to encourage future trading partners. In other words, an incentive exists to exhibit the characteristic of trustworthiness in order to maintain his or her reputation for honesty. In addition, if it is possible but costly to write detailed contracts, a good reputation can often allow the decision-maker to avoid not only that expense but also the use of costly and error-prone legal contract enforcement mechanisms (Milgrom and Roberts, 1992: 263). One of the ways people enhance the effectiveness of a system of reputations is by narrowing the range of people with whom they do business. Frequent transactions, if they are all of similar magnitude, allow trust to flourish (Milgrom and Roberts, 1992: 266-267).

Reputation

Reputation has also been discussed in Section 4.4. As said building up a good reputation is a way of showing commitment. For incomplete contracts, functioning in an environment of imperfect information in which people fear opportunistic or bad-behaviour, reputation is very important. A good reputation can overcome all the problems of opportunistic behaviour in an incomplete contract, while a bad reputation increases the chance of opportunistic behaviour and hold-up problems.

The value of a reputation for contracts and thus the costs incurred in building and maintaining a good one depends on how often it proves to be useful. This is related to:
- the frequency of similar transactions;
- the time horizon over which similar transactions are expected to occur; and
- the profitability of the transactions.

This implies that reputation is less important for contracts on an one time basis. The incentives to build and maintain a *reputation* are greater, the more frequent the transactions, the longer the time horizon, and the more profitable the transactions. Reputation is therefore more important in neoclassical and relational contract. These types of contracts also offer more possibilities for building reputation or reputational capital (see Box 7.3). It is clear that these arguments hold not only for contract takers but also for contract givers (e.g. the government).

Contracts (and thus transactions) between a contract taker and a contract giver are a two-sided mechanism. Looking at both sides from a reputation perspective, it is clear that the party which has the most to lose from a damaged reputation is likely to be the one with the longer time horizon, the more visibility, the greater size, and the greater frequency of transaction. However, it appears from case studies that even in repeated settings where reputation is important and where individuals share the norm of keeping agreements, reputation and shared values and norms are insufficient in themselves to produce stable cooperative behaviour in the long run (cf. Ostrom,1998: 93-94). For that reason, not only monitoring and sanctions are necessary, but also conflict resolving mechanisms.

Complexity

Special problems caused by insufficient commitment in a contractual relationship arise whenever individuals or organisations have to deal with:
- asset specificity and the connected hold-up and lock-in problems;
- uncertainty;
- frequency and duration;
- difficulty of measuring performance in the transaction;
- connectedness; and
- non-excludability and non-rivalry.

A high level of these attributes increases the complexity of writing and concluding contracts (cf. Lafontaine and Slade, 2007: 657). Often (as said in Section 5.4) asset specificity is cited as the most important one. It refers to specific investments in order to achieve a particular objective, known as relation-specific investments or investments which generate a yield over a long period for a specific application, but which are of little or no value if applied elsewhere. The relationship is in this case the contract. Specific investments within a contract can be related to a place, or in special machines or buildings, or special skills, etc. The specificity arises because there is no second-hand market or alternative application outside the contract to obtain a comparable yield.

Most of these attributes has largely been discussed previously in Section 5.4. A high level of complexity can lead to non-contractible assets (cf. Lafontaine and Slade, 2007: 650; 660). For example, for contracting it should be known:

a. what you want; in the case that you do not know what you want, the contract will be very incomplete, the costs associated with renegotiations are considerable, and thus the transaction costs become very high; and
b. whether the quality of the goods or services that you want is contractible. If the other contract party has a strong tendency to reduce the costs and this is accompanied by a reduction in the non-contractible quality, the results will be undesirable.

Specific investments in a contractual relationship can also connect parties strongly to each other; called **connectedness**. Parties which have undertaken such an investment can be forced to accept a worsening of the relationship. Since the other party can threaten to break the relation, they find themselves in an unfavourable negotiating position. This creates *hold-up problems* (*ex-ante*) and *lock-in effects* (*ex-post*). These problems arise due to incomplete contracts in combination with specific investments (cf. Milgrom and Roberts, 1992: 137). For complete non-excludable and non-rival assets it is impossible to conclude contracts. However, for quasi-public assets it depends on the factors described in (a) and (b).

How can we overcome the problems of contracting if we have to deal with *asset specificity, uncertainty, frequency, connectedness* and *performances* that are difficult to measure? A high level of commitment, reputation, and trustworthiness of the involved partners is important. From the story of the knaves and knights (Section 4.3.) we learned that knightly behaviour can deliver a valuable contribution. In reality, on the one hand we have knaves; self-interested individuals who are motivated to help others only if by so doing they will serve their private interests. Their motivations are activated by external factors, such as monetary incentives. On the other hand we have knights; individuals who are motivated to help others for no private rewards. They are mainly driven by intrinsic motivations. However, we have to take into account that not everyone is a knight. A way to overcome these problems is to consider a set of design principles for reducing contractual failures. In Section 7.7 we will demonstrate a comprehensive framework for analysing such principles. This framework is based on the elements discussed in the previous chapters.

7.6 Guidelines for contract design

Handling the complexity of real world contracting requires a systematic approach. Bogetoft and Oleson (2004: 18-41) have developed a checklist or a set of guidelines for contract design. They present them as ten rules of thumb; these are listed in Table 7.1.

Table 7.1 groups the ten rules into three categories corresponding to the objectives of coordination, motivation and minimising of the transaction costs. These three aspects are important for the following reasons:
- Coordination: to ensure that the right products are produced at the right time and place (rules 1-3 on the checklist).
- Motivation: to ensure that the parties have individual incentives to make coordinated decisions (rules 4-8).
- Transaction costs: to ensure that coordination and motivation are provided at the lowest cost (rules 9-10).

Table 7.1. Ten rules of thumb for contracting (Based on Bogetoft and Oleson, 2004: 23).

Coordination	1. Coordinate production and demand
	2. Balance pros and cons of the allocation of control rights
	3. Minimise the cost of risks
Motivation	4. Reduce the costs of pre-contractual opportunism
	5. Reduce the costs of post-contractual opportunism
	6. Do not kill cooperation
	7. Motivate long-term contract concerns
	8. Balance the pros and cons of renegotiations
Transaction costs	9. Reduce the cost of contracting
	10. Use transparent contracts

- **Coordinate production and demand**
  Perhaps the most important role of contracts is to coordinate the actions/activities of (independent) decision-makers. The contract should *coordinate* the activity (e.g. production or services) to make sure that the right producers are producing the right quantity and quality of the right products/services at the right time and place. An important aspect is the minimisation of production costs. Coordination can generally be achieved using instructions, rules or price signals, or a combination of these.

- **Allocation of control rights**
  The allocation of control rights is a key aspect of a contract. This refers to who has the authority to make most of the decisions and about what. A contract often involves a transfer of control rights over (a part of) the bundle of property rights of an asset; e.g. with leasing a house, an office or a plot of land. In general, control rights in a contract are the rights to make any decisions concerning use, returns or transfer of an asset that are not explicitly controlled by law (cf. Milgrom and Roberts, 1992: 289). As explained in Section 3.6, these control rights consist of (1) specific control rights and (2) residual control rights. The specific control rights are those rights specified by the contract. Consequently, residual control rights are the rights to make decisions concerning the asset's use, returns, transfer, etc., that are **not** explicitly assigned by the **contract**[58] (cf. Hendrikse, 2003: 248). An important question concerning a contract is: who has the residual control rights and who is able to capture the residual income. This type of analysis is part of the New Property rights Theory.

- **Minimise the cost of risks and risk sharing**
  Activities are subject to different types of risks. For example, agricultural production and marketing deal with biological, climate and weather, price and institutional risks. In addition, there is a behavioural risk, because one party does not know what actions the other parties are taking. Normally, an uncertain payment is considered to be less valuable than a certain payment with the same expected value, and a loss is valued differently than a gain. The parties can reduce the costs of risks and uncertainties in two ways. They can minimise the risk, or they can share the risk between them. One way of minimising risk and uncertainty is to choose a more robust contract that leads to reasonable outcomes even if the initial assumptions do not hold true. Information collection (or monitoring) is another way.
  Risk sharing is an important topic in contract design because it affects both the cost of risk-bearing and the motivation to behave in certain ways (incentives). An optimal arrangement (or contract) therefore involves a *trade-off* between the efficient (cost-minimising) *risk-sharing* and the *provision of incentives*. The more risk-averse an agent is (or a contract taker) the higher the compensation he will ask for bearing risk. Consequently, the cost for compensating risk will be higher for the principal (contract giver). The higher the cost of providing an incentive to the risk-averse party, the more advantageous it is that the principal (if he is risk-neutral or less risk-averse) bears all the risk, and gives the risk-averse agent a fixed amount of money. Minimising the cost of bearing risk also means reducing the possibility of providing incentives (e.g. performance incentives) to a party.

---

[58] For the simplicity, we leave here the rules of law outside consideration.

An efficient contract balances the costs of risk-bearing against the gain of providing incentives. From the efficient point of view of society, the least-averse party should bear the risk. Allocating of the risk to the least risk-averse party means that the compensation for bearing risk can be lower. It also means that the social cost will be lower, because the compensation for bearing risk is also a social cost.

- **Reduce the costs of pre-contractual opportunism**

 The problem of pre-contractual opportunism is also called adverse selection or hidden information. The literature on contract theory points to four ways for reducing the adverse selection problem. **First**, a party can collect information before the contract is signed. In this way the less informed party can reduce the informational advantage of the other party. **Second**, a party can use signalling to reveal his true type through his behaviour before the contract is signed. **Third**, a contract supplier can use rationing and offer a contract that is acceptable only to some 'good' types of contract takers. This reduces the ability of contract takers to extract rents by mimicking 'less' good types. In Section 4.2.4 we called this **screening**. Hence, rationing leads to fewer but better contracts. The fourth approach is **self-selection via screening**, where the contract supplier offers a menu of contracts. The contracts must be designed so that the contract takers reveal their true type through their selection of the contract. This is also called the *truth-telling condition*. This has also been discussed in Section 4.2.4 and 6.3.

- **Reduce the costs of post-contractual opportunism**

 An opportunistic party does not automatically take the action called for in the contract, i.e. **moral hazard** problems occur. The contracts should motivate the party to take the right action, even if they are unobservable. In order to provide incentives for unobservable actions, compensation to the agent (= contract taker) must be based on outcome. However, there is often a stochastic relationship between the actions and the resulting output. This implies that output-based incentives will expose the agent to risk, because the payment depends on factors outside the agent's control, e.g. the weather. When the agents are risk-averse, this risk carries a risk-premium. Hence, there is a trade-off between providing incentives and minimising the cost of risk.

 The optimal strength of the incentives depends primarily on three factors. **First**, the incentives should be strong if the additional effort has a high value. **Second**, the incentives should be strong if incentives have a strong effect on agents' behaviour. **Third**, the trade-off between providing incentives and reducing the cost of risk means that the incentives should be weak if the agent is very risk-averse or if the principal has only very imprecise information about the agent's behaviour.

- **Do not kill cooperation**

 As explained in the Section 7.3, the identities and the attributes of the contracting parties are of considerable importance. The success of the transaction often depends on the extent to which both parties can trust each other, refrain from opportunistic behaviour and can rely on cooperative behaviour in case of unexpected events (cf. Lyons and Metha, 1997: 51). Some rules, such as a system of certification, professional standards or rules, can be developed on the basis of a rational design. However, in the attempt to create conditions for 'process trust' to develop it should be emphasised that detailed contracts can be destructive and contracts can become solidified distrust.

If a contract to deliver performances contains directives that are too tight, it will have a negative influence on the cooperative behaviour and performance of the workers. Complete contracts are therefore not only unwanted from the point view of transaction costs, but also they hinder the workers' own initiative, often causing a passive attitude and lack of motivation. In such cases, incomplete contracts are perhaps preferable. The explanation lies in the idea of reciprocity. A principal who gives an agent freedom of action to carry out his task trusts that he will work properly. In exchange, the agent will do his best not to betray the trust of the principal.

It is also important not to break off trust, because trust reduces the costs of contracting and control as it lowers fears of opportunism and accepts more influence from the partner. People will deliberate and renegotiate on the basis of give and take ('voice') rather than walk out ('exit') when conflicts arise. Material self-interest and coercion are seldom sufficient either. You 'really' trust someone when you are willing to forego guarantees on the basis of coercion or self-interest.

- **Motivate long-term contracts**
  Contracts should induce parties to take the long-term effects of their actions into consideration. It is important that contracts encourage the right investments. A party who has invested in specific assets is vulnerable to the termination of contracts. This leaves the party with specific assets in a weak bargaining position in negotiations once the investment has been made. Long-term contracts can reduce hold-up problems because the terms are settled before one of the parties makes specific investments. Long-term contracts can also alleviate ratchet effects, i.e. the tendency to under-perform in early contracts to avoid tough contracts later on, and facilitate the development of know-how through planned experiments.

- **Balance the pros and cons of renegotiations**
  Renegotiations facilitate flexible contracts and enable the parties to adjust the contract to changes in the environment. Hence, the parties can remove *ex-post* inefficiencies through renegotiations. However, renegotiations also reduce commitment and may lead to strategic

---

Box 7.5. Hold-up problems and long-term contracts.

Hold-up problems can be reduced in different ways. First, long-term contracts can reduce the hold-up problem. Second, if both parties make specific investments, the balance of the bargaining position can remain unchanged. Third, the role of reputation may also prevent the parties from holding up the other party. A party with a good reputation may be reluctant to devaluate his reputation by holding up a contract partner, because this may ruin his chance of making contracts with other agents.

Long-term relationships require commitment. Commitment alone is not enough, it should also be credible. The crux for bringing about credible commitment in contracts is monitoring, graduated sanctions and conflict-resolution mechanisms. These activities should be carried out on a low cost level. Showing credible commitment creates reputational capital.

---

behaviour. If the parties know that the contract will be renegotiated, the parties do not act according to the incentives in the initial contract but according to the incentives they expect to receive in the renegotiated contract. Hence, renegotiations can lead to *ex-ante* inefficiencies. Often, powerful incentives rely on harsh penalties that are costly for both parties to implement, i.e. both parties are better off *ex-post* if the penalties are removed. If the parties foresee this as a result of renegotiations, the incentives will be weakened. The trade-off between risk-sharing and incentives demonstrates this. If the parties renegotiate after the effort has been provided, the parties can improve the *ex-post* efficiency by shifting risk from the risk-averse party to the risk-neutral party (Bogetoft and Oleson, 2004: 36-37).

- **Reduce the cost of contracting**
  The cost of contracting includes the time and money spent on collecting information, balancing the pros and cons, bargaining, concluding the contract, monitoring, sanctions and conflict resolution, i.e. the **transaction costs**. These costs should be kept down as much as possible because they do not directly generate a surplus. However, they are important activities as they provide information about the costs of the use of contracts as a governance structure.

- **Use transparent contracts**
  The contracts should take the *bounded rationality* of the parties into account. Contract parties act according to perceived incentives, which may differ from true incentives. Therefore, it is important to use a simple contract as possible, so that parties can easily relate their choice of action to the compensation scheme set out in the contract. However, simple contracts may also mean less complete contracts where more questions are unanswered in the contract. In order to affect the behaviour of the parties the incentives should be articulated *ex-ante* (Bogetoft and Oleson, 2004: 39).

Most efficient contracts

Reasoning along these lines, we can argue what is the most suitable and efficient contract. The most suitable and efficient contract does not always coincide. The most suitable contract strongly depends on the attributes of the transaction. For a simple transaction a simple contract is sufficient. Indicators for simplicity are: how are coordination, motivation and the enforcement of activities taken into account in the contract. An efficient contract contributes to optimising coordination and motivation in the cheapest way possible. In other words, it minimises the costs of planning, monitoring, and motivating, i.e. it minimises transaction costs.

However, in our real world we have not only to take into account efficiency arguments but also income distribution effects. For that reason the criteria for most suitable contracts should include income distribution arguments. Combining efficiency and income distribution arguments and making use of the discussed theories, the criteria for most suitable contracts are:
- suitable coordination and motivation mechanisms;
- low public and private transaction costs;
- reduced hold-up and lock-in effects;
- a fair distribution of residual income;
- minimised costs of risk;
- allocation of risk to the least risk-averse party.

7.7 Design principles for contractual failures

In this section we will develop a comprehensive framework for analysing design principles for reducing contractual failures. This framework is designed with the elements from Chapter 4 and this chapter. It summarises the elements and bring them together in a coherent way.

The chance of opportunistic behaviour, hidden information, hidden actions, lack of credible commitment and lack of trust, require that we develop design principles for effective and efficient contracts. Figure 7.2 gives an overview – based on the literature and theory – of ways or *design principles* for reducing the effects of hidden action (adverse selection), hidden information (moral hazard), shirking[59], lack of credible commitment and trust. In other words these are mechanisms for dealing with contractual failures as a result of incomplete contracts. As shown in Figure 7.2 there is some overlap in the various ways for reducing the effects shown in the columns. Some methods can be used for different phenomena. The list is not exhaustive, but reflects important principles.

An analysis can be made to determine in which way and on what level contracts or more in general, organisational modes (e.g. firms or clubs) take into account the *design principles* for reducing hidden information, hidden actions, lack of credible commitment and trust. A relevant question is to what extent do parties involved in designing contracts make use of design principles for reducing the effects indicated in Figure 7.2?

The effects indicated in Figure 7.2 (*hidden information, hidden actions, shirking, lack of credible commitment, and trust*) result from incomplete contracting. Incomplete contracts mostly involve hidden information and hidden actions. Hidden information is an *ex-ante* information problem and can lead to adverse selection. For example, in the case of membership of an environmental

---

[59] Shirking is a form of hidden actions, but the term shirking is more connected with team production.

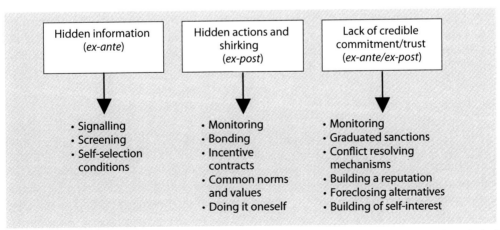

Figure 7.2. Design principles for reducing the effects of hidden information, hidden actions, shirking, lack of credible commitment, and trust.

club, the board of the club does not know if one of the (potential) members possesses private information which, if known, would influence the attitude and conduct of the board. Ways in which the problem of hidden information can be reduced are *signalling, screening* and *self-selection conditions.*

- **Hidden information**
  The first column in Figure 7.2 refers to the problem of hidden information. *Signalling* occurs when the better-informed party makes certain verifiable facts known, which when properly interpreted, may indicate the presence of other unobservable but desirable characteristics. In signalling, the privately informed party takes the lead in adopting behaviour that, when properly interpreted, reveals their information. For signalling to be effective, the receiver must believe that the signal is credible. That is, the observable characteristic must clearly point to the unobservable, desirable characteristic. A signal for the qualification of a potential member could be his education. For example, has he followed a course in wildlife and habitats management? In order to distinguish themselves as credible candidates for nature and landscape management contracts with the government, farmers may have to follow courses on wildlife management, or become on a voluntary basis a member of an environmental cooperative with membership dues.
  Screening refers to activities undertaken by the party without private information (mostly the principal) in order to separate different types (agents) of the informed party (= group of agents) along some dimensions. It is the uninformed party that undertakes activities to sort the informed parties into separate types. Screening means that one of the contracting partners demands certain elements in the set of observed characteristics that are correlated with unobserved but desirable elements. Screening is a strategy available to an uninformed party that, if successful, will encourage the better-informed party to reveal information. To allow the informed party to voluntarily reveal his private information, we need an information revealing mechanism.
  Simply making known to the relevant group what the organisation offers and what it expects, can induce some *self-selection* among potential candidate-members. Sometimes this can be a by-product of other policies. Self-selection is usually a type of behaviour in response to some screening activity that causes workers to choose from a menu of contracts and sign the one they like best. To assure that potential candidate-members choose the contracts intended, we need a particular form of the incentive compatibility condition, called *self-selection conditions.* The 'building-in' of self-selection conditions in contracts reduces the problem of hidden information.

- **Hidden actions**
  The second column in Figure 7.2 refers to hidden actions or shirking. These are *ex-post* phenomena. The problem of hidden actions or shirking can be reduced by monitoring, incentive contracts, bonding, common values and norms and in-house production. **Monitoring** can be carried out in different ways. For example, in the case of nature and landscape preservation contracts between farmers and the government, self-monitoring or mutual monitoring by farmers is one solution. Such a task can be carried out by or delegated to a group of farmers, e.g. an environmental cooperative. The advantages are reducing transaction costs for government and enhancing the social control among farmers. An alternative would be

making use of third parties[60], such as groups of volunteers of NGOs. In this case, it helps the credibility of the third parties if they consist of experts and are independent. This alternative can also reduce the transaction costs. Finally, the monitoring activities can be carried out by the government. However, this involves public transactions costs.

Incentive contracts are contracts based on a variable payment depending on the efforts or performances. The incomes become subject to random factors. Most people are risk-averse and dislike having their income depend on random factors. The risk created by incentive contracts is costly to these people. They are not as well off with a risky income as they would be receiving the same expected level of pay for certain, and they thus have to be paid more on average to convince them to accept these risks. From the contract giver's perspective, this extra income is a cost of using incentive pay (cf. Milgrom and Roberts, 1992: 187).

A **third** solution would be to require the posting of bonds to guarantee performance, to be paid back if the performance is satisfactory or if targets are reached. Using such solutions may still lead to incomplete contracts, but some self-enforcing elements will be incorporated. **Fourth**, in homogeneous groups, the incidence of hidden actions can be reduced by common norms and values. A **fifth** way to prevent some forms of moral hazard is to do all the work *by yourself*; the in-house production variant, or vertical integration.

- **Credible commitment**
  The third column in Figure 7.2 refers to credible commitment. If we look at the sources of commitment and trust, there is some overlap. Trust is closely related to social norms of behaviour, which is also an important element in commitment. In a contractual relationship we often have to deal with the problem of imperfect commitment. It refers to the inability of parties to bind themselves to follow through on threats and promises that they would like to make but which, they would like to renounce after they have made them. This problem affects both 'market relationships' and 'contractual relationships', although their nature and impact may differ between organisational forms. Long-term contractual relationships require a certain level of commitment.

Monitoring, sanctions and conflict resolving mechanisms

Commitment alone is not enough. It should also be credible. This can be done by making use of the triptych monitoring, sanctions and a conflict-resolving mechanism. It means that the crux for bringing about credible commitment in contracts is making use of monitoring, graduated sanctions and conflict-resolution mechanisms. However, these activities should be carried out on a low cost level. The role of monitoring and credible commitment should be emphasised; without monitoring there can be no credible commitment; without credible commitment there is no reason to propose new rules. Mutual monitoring or monitoring by volunteers reduces costs. Contract takers who violate the rules are likely to be subjected to graduated sanctions, depending on the seriousness and the context of the offence. If individuals are going to follow rules over a long period of time, there must be some mechanism for discussion and for resolving what constitutes a conflict or a difference of opinion.

---

[60] As explained in Chapter 4.2.6, the reported information is some times called fire alarm.

The presence of a conflict-resolution mechanism does not guarantee that parties will be able to maintain the agreements. However, it is difficult to imagine how any complex system of rules can be maintained over time without such a mechanism, even quite an informal one. One possibility would be that those who are selected as the leaders are also the basic mediators or resolvers of the conflict. Another possibility is the **use of third parties.** To be useful and reliable the third party has to be **independent,** and **an authority or expert.** To make promises trustworthy, credible commitments need to be established. This is not a problem if the courts can make agreements binding, but in many relational contracts, such courts-assured solutions are difficult to attain (Furubotn and Richter, 1997: 276).

External coercion is also a frequently cited theoretical solution to the problem of commitment. However, in the case of a self-organised group, for example, farmers who would like to take care of the environment – by making use of an environmental cooperative – this solution does not address what motivates the external enforcer to monitor behaviour and impose sanctions (cf. Ostrom; 1998: 44). A self-organised group must solve the commitment problem without an external enforcer. The members have to motivate themselves to monitor and be willing to impose graduated sanctions to keep conformance high. They have to be self-motivated to observe agreements without the use of an external enforcer.

Building a reputation

Building a **reputation** is one way of showing commitment in a contract. **Reputation** is the view formed of an individual or organisation by another based on past experience and is often used as a basis for forecasting future behaviour in contractual arrangements. This impression is made credible by actions in an early period or a long run relationship. As explained, the incentives to build and maintain a *reputation* are larger, the more frequent the transactions, the longer the time horizon, and the more profitable the transactions are. These arguments hold for both the contract taker and the contract giver.

Contracts (and thus transactions) between a contract taker and a contract giver are a two-sided mechanism. If we look from a reputation perspective at both sides, the party with the longer time horizon, the more visibility, the greater size, the greater frequency of transaction party has the most to lose from a damaged reputation. This outcome also indicates which party in contracting should have the discretion to direct activities in unforeseen events. It is the one with the most to lose from a damaged reputation. In the case of nature and landscape preservation contracts between the government and farmers, this is mostly the government. This discretion power can also create a special form of opportunistic behaviour of the government called **time-inconsistency.**

It appears from case studies that even in repeated settings, where reputation is important and where individuals share the norm of keeping agreements, reputation and shared values and norms are insufficient in themselves to produce stable cooperative behaviour in the long run. For that reason, not only monitoring and sanctions are necessary, but also conflict resolving mechanisms. The latter are also meant for reducing the problems of time-inconsistency created by the government.

Foreclosing alternatives

A well-known example of foreclosing alternatives is Julius Caesar decision to burn the bridges behind him as his army advanced on the enemy, thereby forcing his army to attack (see Box 4.9). This commitment is achieved by foreclosing the opportunity to run away. However, commitment alone is often not enough, it must also be credible.

Credible commitment can also be realised through more formal rules and through foreclosing alternatives. If the government makes the external production circumstances more difficult, for example, by increasing the water level in peat land areas or if the government threatens with re-zoning of the land use, it forecloses alternatives and makes certain nature and landscape preservation contracts more attractive. By doing so the government creates a kind of credible commitment.

Building-in of self-interest

The final way to reduce lack of credible commitment and trust is to build-in self-interest. This means that people are doing things that are of interest to themselves. These interests can vary from financial benefits to a *license to produce*. The latter is also connected to the concept of *responsible entrepreneurship*. The understanding of '*responsible entrepreneurship*' is related to a diverse and complex phenomenon. In general, it suggests that a firm should not only think of economical value of the firm (mostly represented by the profit of the firm), but also of the social and ecological values as result of the firm's activities on social and ecological quantities. This is pointed out through the 'triple-p bottom line'. The three p's stand for *profits, planet* and *people*, i.e. the extent to which firms are able to realise sustainable developments from economic (profits), ecology (planet), and society (people) points of view. From this viewpoint, firms function in a socially responsible manner (*responsible entrepreneurship*) if the economic, social and ecological values that it produces fulfil the expectations of the stakeholders. Satisfying the social and ecological criteria creates in fact a 'permit' to carry out activities (see Huylenbroeck and Slangen, 2003: 114).

7.8 Applications of the theory; public provision versus contracting out

Unified ownership or do-it-yourself (for example, by the government itself), can be an alternative to private provision by contracting out. The choice between in-house provision and contracting out[61] has proven to be controversial. Hart *et al.* (1997: 1127-1161) have developed a theory of government ownership and contracting that sheds light on the cost and the quality of the service under alternative provision schemes. In their model, the provider of the service – whether it is a government employee or a private contractor – can invest his time either to improve the quality of the service or to reduce its cost. Both types of improvements prior to implementation require the approval of the owner of the asset.

If the provider is a government employee, he or she needs the government's approval to implement any improvement or cost reduction, since the government retains residual control rights over the

---

[61] Instead of contracting out the term outsourcing is often used.

asset. As a result, the employee receives only a fraction of the return of either the cost reduction or the quality improvement. By contrast, if the provider is a private contractor, he or she has the residual control rights over the asset, and hence does not need to get government approval for a cost reduction. At the same time, if a private contractor wants to improve quality and to get a higher payment, he needs to renegotiate with the government since the government is the buyer. As a consequence, the private contractor generally has a stronger incentive to reduce costs as well as to improve quality compared to the government employee (Hart *et al.*, 1997: 1129).

There are **two situations** in which direct government production (= in-house production of the government) is likely to be superior (Shleifer, 1998: 13; Van Damme, 1998: 811). **First,** the government may not know what it wants. In that case, a contract will be very incomplete and the costs associated with renegotiations are considerable, so that contracting becomes very expensive. **Second**, the contract party may have a strong tendency to reduce costs, accompanied by a reduction in (non-contractible) quality. The adverse effect of cost reduction on quality is significant (see also Hart *et al.*, 1997: 1142). In both situations, government production is likely to be a better solution.

This analysis emphasises the self-interest of politicians and bureaucrats as an important factor in understanding government failure. However, a complete theory of non-market failure also requires an analysis of the internal organisation of the government. The allocation of (residual) control rights, the insight on who is able to capture the residual income, and the communication channels between the government agencies and the interest groups, all affect the behaviour of the government agencies. As explained in Section 6.4, the principal-agent theory offers a good explanation for this type of government failure.

Unified ownership or the do-it-yourself option (for nature preservation by government) can be an alternative to private provision by contracting out with private landowners and farmers. For example, if more nature is wanted, agricultural land on a large scale could be converted into nature areas. However, if the government does this, there will be not only important financial and economic consequences (cf. Oskam and Slangen, 1998: 129), but it also has negative effects on rural employment and income, and it will lead to a loss in typical rural landscapes. It could be an expensive alternative compared to contracting out with private landowners and farmers, but it also creates the problem of government failure, which is in the domain of public choice theory.

Most of the contracts for preserving nature and landscape are neoclassical contracts. A broad variety exists in the types of contracts. light management agreements such as contracts for preserving the 'less favoured areas', simple maintenance activities such as lopping wooded banks and carrying out a precisely prescribed task (e.g. no grazing animals in grassland, not mowing the grass before 10th of June). In most of the contracts prescribed above, the measures that have to be carried out are often easily to monitor. However this does not hold for the output in terms of quality of nature and landscape. In general, the results of these management agreements are often difficult to measure, due to the influence of the effort of the farmers, the weather conditions, predators, the rules in the agreements, lack of good indicators, high monitoring costs, etc.

As said, one of the characteristics of neoclassical contracts is the restricted role of prices as a factor of adjustment. This is caused by the presence of specific assets, while complete self-enforcing safeguards are difficult to implement. These factors have consequences for the role of the price mechanism for setting the price of these contracts, and with that of the role of the price as coordination and motivation mechanism.

In Section 5.4 we presented some results of agri-environmental schemes in the EU. Most of these schemes (including contracts for nature and landscape preserving) have a flat rate per ha as reward-structure. Based on the discussed theories this can explained by:
1. The quality of nature and landscape preservation is difficult to determine and the measure.
2. Risks and uncertainties. One source of risks and uncertainties can be attributed to weather conditions, biological factors (e.g. predators, diseases) and the rules in the agreements. Other ones are the asset specificity, trust in and reputation of the government, sometimes connected with time-inconsistency of the government.
3. Farmers are risk-averse. They would ask a high compensation if the payments become depending on the performance in terms of the quality of nature and landscape.

These findings suggest that it is hard to provide effective incentives if one cannot measure the performance accurately. If measuring performance is difficult, people commonly arrange their affairs to make measurement easier or to reduce the importance of accurate measurements by paying a fixed compensation.

Box 7.6. Key terms of Chapter 7.

Complete contracts	Safeguards
Incomplete contracts	Voluntary exchange
Residual power	Coordination mechanisms
residual control rights	Motivation mechanism
Residual income	Explicit or implicit contracts
Quasi-rents	Relational or detailed contract
Residual claimant	Reneging
Residual return	*Ex-post* renegotiation
New property right approach	Credible commitment
Hold-up problems	Trust
Classical contract	Reputation
Neoclassical contracts	Reputational capital
Relational contracts	Rules of thumb for contracting
Identity of parties	Design principle for reducing contractual failure
Asset specificity	Contracting out

---

8. Coordination mechanisms and organisational modes

8.1 Introduction

This chapter deals with coordination mechanisms and governance structures or modes of organisation. An important difference between coordination mechanisms and governance structures is that coordination – a central issue in economic organisation – is more oriented on the nature of the coordination mechanism such as the price, mutual adjustments, the contract rules or safeguards and direct supervision. On the other hand, the governance structure or organisational mode often consists of more than just the coordination mechanism. It also includes – in the case of a firm – the formal rules concerning legal ownership, corporate status and tax regimes. However, between coordination mechanisms and governance structures a mutual relationship also exists. The nature of the coordination mechanism determines, for a large part, the type of governance structure. For example, in a contractual relationship, the nature of the coordination mechanism largely determines the type of the contract that comprises the governance structure.

In Section 8.2 we will analyse why coordination, motivation, and the organisation of transactions are so important, and what links them together. Coordination and motivation can sometimes make use of the same steering mechanism. For example, a price for carrying out an activity can be used for coordination but also as a financial incentive for motivation. The way in which transactions are organised is revealed in the applied governance structure. In Section 8.2, we will make clear that for each type of governance structure there are certain coordination mechanisms, transaction costs, and formal rules concerning legal ownership, corporate status and tax regimes.

In Section 8.3 we focus on the relationship and differences between governance structures and coordination mechanisms. Understanding the distinction between governance structures and coordination mechanisms is key to understanding the different governance structures and the potential possibilities of combining coordination mechanisms into governance structures. In Section 3.6 and Section 7.4, we have already introduced the four groups of coordination mechanisms: the invisible and visible hand, the handbook and the handshake. In Section 8.3 will discuss them more extensively and we will formulate some propositions that lay the foundation for the relationship between coordination mechanisms and governance structure.

In Section 8.4 we will give an overview and a typology of a continuum of governance structures from spot market to vertical integration based on the following key elements: the coordination mechanisms used, the type of motivation, the identity of the partners, the duration of the transaction, the enforcement mechanism, financial participation and the level of vertical integration. Most of these elements have been discussed in previous chapters.

A number of modes of organisation are contractual relationships. As said in Chapter 7, contracts are becoming more and more important. Fiercer global competition, rapid technological developments and more discerning customers are forcing firms to seek more efficient production and distribution structures. In recent years, industries have shown increasing collaboration on issues of product development, quality guarantee systems (certification) and improved logistics.

Spot markets are being replaced by contract-production and systems of vertical cooperation. More coordination and collaboration may lead to improved efficiency in production and distribution channels and to more product and market innovations. These **vertical relationships** can take many forms, like strategic alliances, long-term contracts, licensing, subcontracting, joint ventures, franchising, cooperatives and networks. Not only the contractual aspects play an important role in these types of relationships, but most of them can also be seen as alternative modes of organisation.

The options from spot markets to complete vertical integration – also called *in-house production* – present a continuum of governance structures. The two ends of the continuum have been analysed in many ways historically by many authors. Important subjects of research were the classic **make versus buy** decision and the specifics of vertical integration. The background of the **make or buy** decision is the choice a firm must make about whether it should *make* an intermediate good in-house or secure it in some market or via contracts. The insight is growing that a variety of hybrid governance structures between spot markets and vertical integration or *in-house production* can been identified. The mentioned key elements can be used for classifying these hybrid modes of organisation. They also show that there are different 'ways to organise'.

In spite of our emphasis on the spectrum of governance structures from spot markets to vertical integration, the conceptual approach in Section 8.4 can also be applied to horizontal relationships. The above mentioned key elements can be used for typifying governance structures applied in horizontal relationships, such as networks and certain clubs. Finally, the choice of the governance structure is an important strategic decision for a firm or organisation.

The governance structure or organisational mode also includes the formal rules concerning legal ownership, corporate status and tax regimes, etc. To make this clear – and to show that governance structures are more than only coordination and motivation mechanisms – we will give in Section 8.5 an overview of the characteristics of six organisational modes based on ownership, corporate status, liability, fiscal aspects, transaction costs and costs of capital. The criteria for classification are derived from institutional economics, Economic Organisation Theory and property rights theory. An intriguing question here is; what determines the choice of a specific governance structure from the various possibilities? Table 8.2, in Section 8.5, gives an answer to this question for six possible organisational forms of firms ranging from single owner to private limited company. We conclude the chapter with an application of a special governance structure; the dominance of the family farm.

Key questions:
- Why is coordination a central issue in Economic Organisation Theory?
- What types of motivation mechanisms can be used in a governance structure?
- Why is it important to make a distinction between coordination mechanisms and governance structures?
- Why is it important to pay attention to the relationship between coordination mechanisms and governance structures? For example, why is there not a one-to-one correspondence between them?

- Which (groups of) coordination mechanisms can be distinguished and what are the possible corresponding governance structures?
- Which key elements can be used for classifying and characterising governance structures?
- Can these key elements be used for both vertical and horizontal relationships?
- What is the role of coordination mechanisms concerning the residual control rights and residual income?
- Why do intermediaries have a greater incentive to invest in reputation than individual transaction partners?

8.2 Coordination, motivation and the way of organising

An economic analysis of the most fundamental unit, i.e. the transaction, should be focussed on coordination, motivation, and the way in which these transactions are organised. These issues matter, not only for a single transaction, but also for each organisational mode, like a contract or a firm. It should be noticed that the firm can also be seen as metaphor for any organisational mode or governance structure in which transactions are carried out. An intriguing question is why these issues are so important and what the linkage between governance structure, coordination and motivation is.

8.2.1 Coordination

Coordination is a central issue in the Economic Organisation Theory. It includes what needs to be coordinated, how coordination is achieved in spot markets, in organisations and in hybrid forms (such as contracts), which alternatives there are for achieving coordination between organisational units and how each part of a system fits together. As explained in Section 7.4, the coordination mechanism is not the same for each governance structure, not even for classical, neoclassical and relational contracts. The price is the most important coordination mechanism in the classical contract. However, the price is less important as a coordination mechanism for the neoclassical contract and the price often plays a subordinate role as a coordination mechanism in relational contracts. The relationship itself could be even more important than the content of the contract.

Therefore, we would like to know what kind of coordination mechanisms we have, how we can classify them, what is the relationship with motivation, and whether there is a one-to-one correspondence between the governance structure and the coordination mechanism, or if a given governance structure may use a combination of coordination mechanisms?

8.2.2 Motivation

This includes what and who needs to be motivated, which incentives are needed, what alternative kinds of incentive mechanisms there are, and what needs to be done to make incentive mechanisms effective and efficient. Each governance structure contains a *motivation-element*. For example, many contracts have a steering mechanism which defines performance criteria and the means to measure the performance. Motivation is also often included in the specification of a reward-structure which marks the level of payment if a minimum level of performance is attained.

Each governance structure can make use of two kinds of motivations: intrinsic to the individual concerned and extrinsic. In a firm or organisation the pressure or desire to do your work well does often not arise so much from financial incentives and direct order, but rather, from internal motivation. In Section 4.3 it has been argued that there may be a trade-off between the two kinds of motivation, such that too heavy an emphasis on extrinsic motivation can drive out intrinsic motivation. Motivations activated by external factors, such as monetary incentives or direct order (as in hierarchical governance structure), can crowd out motivations that are internal to the individual, such as more **altruistic concerns.**

8.2.3 The way how to organise matters

The way in which transactions are organised and carried out is revealed in the applied organisational mode or governance structure. Governance structures are a response to various transactional considerations. That is also the focus of transaction cost theory. It must be pointed out that the coordination mechanism plays an important role in the governance structure, because the nature of the coordination mechanism determines, for a large part, the type of the governance structure. On the other hand the organisational mode often consists of more than just the coordination mechanism. It also includes the formal rules concerning legal ownership, corporate status and tax regimes for the firm. A central issue in Economic Organisation Theory is that the 'way to organise matters'. It also means that the boundary of the firm is a subject of analysis. Reasoning along this line, we can also see the firm as a metaphor for any institutional arrangement or governance structure.

Based on the above, we can conclude that coordination and motivation partly overlap each other. For example, the price can be used as a coordination mechanism, but it is also an element of motivation. However, coordination mechanisms and motivation-elements fulfil different functions within a governance structure. It can be observed based on a number of arguments – which are partly mutually dependent – that the way how transactions are organised and carried out matter. This is revealed in the applied governance structure. **First** of all, the nature of the coordination mechanism characterises, for a large part, the type of governance structure.

Second, governance structures have to take into account the characteristics of human decision-makers and the attributes of the transactions. According to transaction cost theory, governance structures are a response to various transactional considerations. Transaction cost economics (TCE) tries to explain which institutional arrangement is most efficient for carrying out transactions. The empirical object of TCE is formed by the transactions carried out in governance structures[62]. The variety of ways of organising transactions found in the world reflects the fact that transactions differ in basic attributes. Based on this framework of attributes, we can determine which governance structure or organisational mode is efficient or able to add value for parties involved.

Third, governance structures often consist of more than just the coordination mechanism. For example, if the governance structure is a contract, it should also specify the contract agreements,

---

[62] The governance structure is the dependent variable, see also Chapter 5.2.

such as duration, what has to be done, etc. If the governance structure is a firm, it also includes the legal entity, the formal rules concerning ownership, the corporate status and tax regimes for the firm. We will come back to these aspects in Section 8.5.

8.3 Four groups of coordination mechanisms

As previously said, this chapter deals with coordination mechanisms and governance structures, and governance structures are also modes of organisation. A broad spectrum governance structures can be distinguished, consisting of the spot market at one end of the spectrum and organisations based on 'command and control', also called hierarchies, at the other end. In between, we have the so-called hybrid governance structures, such as contracts, clubs, partnerships, cooperatives, joint ventures, etc. As discussed, the nature of the coordination mechanism determines, for a large part, the type of governance structure. It characterises the governance structure.

The nature of the coordination mechanism can refer to different elements such as the price, mutual adjustments, rules in a contractual relationship or direct order (as in a hierarchical governance structure)[63]. In Section 3.6 and Section 7.4 we already paid attention to coordination mechanisms. In this section, we explore in more detail what kind of coordination mechanisms we have, how we can classify them, what the relationship is to motivation, and whether there is there a one-to-one correspondence between coordination mechanisms and the governance structure.

The relationship between coordination mechanisms and governance structures deserves attention for different reasons. Firstly, there is no one-to-one correspondence between the two, because certain governance structures can combine different coordination mechanisms or make use of a mix of them (Hennart (1993: 531). Secondly, the distinction between governance structures and coordination mechanisms is key to understanding the different governance structures and the possibility of combining coordination mechanisms into governance structures (cf. Borgen and Hegrenes, 2005: 12-13). Thirdly, coordination is a central issue in a governance structure. It includes what needs to be coordinated and how coordination is achieved in governance structures such as spot markets, firms and contracts.

As shown by Figure 8.1 we can distinguish four groups of coordination mechanisms (cf. Borgen and Hegrenes, 2005: 12). On **the left side** we have the 'invisible hand' group. The coordination mechanism here is the price. In the pure or ideal-typical situation, the corresponding governance structure is the spot market. This extreme is the realm of most traditional theoretical economic analysis: there is perfect information, lots of competition and little, if any, room for opportunism (FitzRoy, 1998: 258). In this ideal-typical approach, the spot markets predominantly rely on prices. The standard neoclassical economics supposes, under perfect market conditions, no motivation problems. Everyone is striving for utility or profit maximisation.

At the **bottom** of Figure 8.1, we see the 'handbook' group. In this case, the coordination mechanism consists of rules, directives and safeguards. As explained in Section 7.4, the 'handbook' – as a coordination mechanism – is often used for the governance structure 'contracts'. However, contracts

---

[63] See Mintzberg (2006: 3-7).

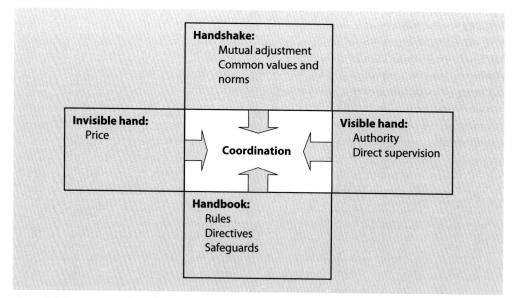

Figure 8.1. Four groups of coordination mechanisms (adapted from Borgen and Hegrenes, 2005: 12).

often contain a price as an additional coordination mechanism. In that case, the coordination mechanism of contracts consists of a combination of the 'handbook' and the 'invisible hand'. Generally speaking, the type of contract determines which coordination mechanism will prevail and what the role of the price will be in the relationship *quid pro quo*. The price could be a compensation (counter performance) or an incentive mechanism (= motivation element).

As explained in Section 7.4 the coordination mechanism is not the same for each type of contract. In a classical contract the price is the most important coordination mechanism. For a neoclassical contract, the price is less important as a coordination mechanism, compared with the classical contract; the coordination mechanism is more a combination of 'invisible hand', 'handshake' and 'handbook'. In relational contracts the price as a coordination mechanism often plays a subordinate role. The relationship itself could even be more important than the content of the contract. For relational contracts, reputational capital is also a supporting element in the coordination.

At the **right side** of Figure 8.1 we see the 'visible hand' group, used in firms and organisations based on hierarchy. It means hierarchy is the corresponding governance structure: the positions in the firm are ranked; higher order level commands lower level. In this case, the coordination will be carried out by an authority, direct supervision or direct order. According to Figure 8.1, the invisible and visible hands are the polar cases of the vertical spectrum of coordination mechanisms. In this ideal-typical approach, the spot markets predominantly rely on prices and firms on hierarchies (cf. Borgen and Hegrenes, 2005: 13).

Box 8.1. Standardisation of values and norms.

Standardisation of values and norms leads to common values and norms. Dasgupta (1991: 75, 79) interprets social norms as being implicit social contracts to cooperate, embedded in customs and rituals, and resulting from repeated interactions. If people are not extremely myopic, it is the self-interest of each member of the group to keep the norms; in other words, the norms are self-enforcing. Common values and norms diminish the incidence of opportunistic behaviour between the members of the group. Effective coordination based on common values and norms coincides with a strong internal motivation and high commitment of individual members of a group to achieve their common goals.

At the top of Figure 8.1, we see the 'handshake' as a coordination mechanism. Important elements are common values[64] and norms, and mutual adjustment. Common values and norms pertain to a congruent set of preferences within a group of people. They form guiding coordination principles that guide a group or community. Such a group can range from a family to a club (based on self-organisation or a more formal one), from a church to a volunteer group, or team of people working towards a common goal. Common values and norms – based on repeated interaction promoting solidarity, consensus and trust – and codes of conduct can serve as a coordination mechanism for groups of people. The standardisation of norms and values means that codes of conduct are usually shared for the entire organisation, so that everyone functions according to the same norms of behaviour. The motivation, trust and commitment underlying the operation of this organisation can be understood as evolving from the standardisation of values and norms or shared codes of conduct through selection (see Douma and Schreuder 2002: 171). To work effectively, such a horizontal organisation could be partly based on formal rules, but they must be complemented by informal rules (sanctions, conventions, norms or codes of behaviour) that supplement them and reduce transaction (e.g. enforcing) costs (cf. North 1993: 20).

Mutual adjustment refers to the coordination achieved by informal horizontal communication. Small organisations, such as partnerships, consultancy firms, architectural bureaus, can rely on mutual adjustment as the main coordination mechanism. By doing so, it can maintain a spirit of innovation (cf. Douma and Schreuder, 2002: 42). Mutual adjustment is also the important coordination mechanism in peer groups. A peer group is a group of people working together without hierarchy. There is no boss, so there can not be any direct supervision. The peer group sells out its output, the proceeds of which are shared among the members of the peer group according to some sharing rules. Examples of peer groups are small partnerships for lawyers, auditors, doctors, etc. (cf. Douma and Schreuder, 2002: 155)[65].

Coordination mechanisms consisting of elements such as mutual adjustment, common values and norms, are often found in organisations with highly motivated people. A strong sense of

---

[64] According to Ouchi (1980: 132), organisations can in some instances rely to a great extent on socialisation as principal mechanism of mediation and this 'clan' form can be very efficient in mediating transactions between individuals. Reciprocity and common values and beliefs are the coordination mechanisms (cf. Ouchi (1980: 137).

[65] Most rock and other bands are often organised as partnerships. However, some rock bands are organised as hierarchies with one band member acting as entrepreneur and the other members receiving wages as workers. An interesting question is what are the advantages and disadvantages of partnerships versus hierarchies (cf. Douma and Schreuder, 2002: 179)?

> **Box 8.2. Role and meaning of trust in carrying out transactions.**
>
> Nooteboom (1999: 24-25) emphasises the role and meaning of trust in carrying out transactions. Because trusting people are less secretive and more ready to supply information, this role has the effect of lowering the cost of search and monitoring. Trust reduces the costs of contracting and control because it decreases fear of opportunism and leads to the acceptance of more influence from the partner. People who trust each other will deliberate and renegotiate on the basis of give and take ('voice') rather than walk out ('exit') when conflicts arise.
>
> Common values and norms, and trust are not only important for the handshake coordination, but also in helping the market mechanism function well. The same also holds for other governance structures. If people do not trust each other or if cheating each other is normal, then the market mechanism can not work well. A recent example is Russia[1] where the market as a transaction mechanism has not managed to get off the ground properly. If people do not hold common values and norms, such that they can trust one another and their government, the economy will undermine its own institutional basis. The same also holds for other governance structures.
>
> ---
>
> [1] The high score of Russia on the 'Transparency International Corruption Perceptions Index' supports this view.

mission, *esprit de corps* or ideology, which individuals share, tells them how to act together and dispense with the need for other forms of coordination (cf. Douma and Schreuder, 2002: 44). The motivation underlying the operation of such organisations can be understood as evolving from the standardisation of values and norms or shared codes of conduct through selection (see Douma and Schreuder, 2002: 171).

Mutual adjustment is also often used for coordinating activities within extremely complex organisations, for example for activities with a complicated division of labour, in which many specialists carry out several specific tasks. Another application of mutual adjustment is the coordination within an organisation that has to carry out a very difficult job. At the beginning it is not exactly known what has to be done. The knowledge develops as the work progresses. Mintzberg (2006: 4) gives as an example the organisation which has to send the manned spacecraft to the moon. However, this is only one application. In practise, we often see such type of organisations.

While we can distinguish four groups of coordination mechanisms in Figure 8.1, in practice we often observe a certain combination of these four groups. Nevertheless, based on the above analysis and Figure 8.1, we can formulate some propositions that form the basis for the relationship between coordination mechanisms and modes of organisation or governance structures, and for the analysis of hybrid governance structures (cf. Hennart, 1993: 531; Borgen and Hegrenes, 2005: 13-15):

- As mentioned earlier, one must distinguish between coordination mechanisms (invisible hand, handbook, visible hand and handshake) and mode of organisations or governance structure (markets, hybrid governance structures, and firms as hierarchies). There is not always a one-to-one correspondence between the two. A given governance structure may, under specific circumstances, use a mix of elements of the four groups of coordination mechanisms.

- The two extreme governance structures (spot markets and hierarchies) use different coordination mechanisms to organise economic activities.
- Spot markets are governance structures that predominantly use the price coordination mechanism. Firms as hierarchies predominantly rely on the direct supervision/order coordination mechanism. However, because of diminishing returns to measuring output and constraining behaviour, both firms and markets will often use a mix of 'price driven incentives' and 'direct supervision constraining behaviour'. The firm's mix will contain a high proportion of 'direct supervision constraining behaviour' relative to price incentives, the mix in markets will be biased towards 'price driven incentives'. This means that the application in practice is often a question of gradation.
- The combination of prices, rules, direct supervision and mutual adjustment as coordination mechanisms defines a wide variety of governance structures along a continuum which goes from pure spot markets to traditional firms, respectively firms based on vertical integration (= in-house production).
- There is a wide variety of organisational modes under which legally autonomous entities do business among themselves in a particular way: they mutually adjust with the help of the different coordination mechanisms (e.g. mutual adjustment, prices, rules and direct supervision), and they share or exchange means of production, capital, products and services, but still without a unified ownership. A wide range of hybrids is found in the real world, such as clubs (based on self-organisation or a more formal one), peer groups, cooperatives, contracts, networks, franchising and collective trademarks.

In the next section, we will discuss a variety of governance structures – with corresponding coordination mechanisms – along a continuum which goes from spot markets to firms based on vertical integration (= in-house production) in the next section. This continuum, presented in Figure 8.2, consists of a number of hybrid governance structures also.

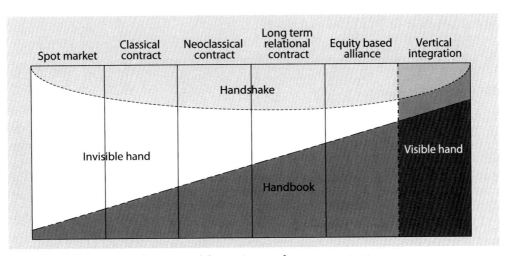

Figure 8.2. Coordination mechanisms and the continuum of governance structures.

8.4 A continuum of governance structures

Figure 8.1 shows that the invisible and visible hand are the polar cases along the spectrum of coordination mechanisms. In the ideal-typical approach, the spot markets predominantly rely on prices and firms on hierarchies. It means that on a continuum of governance structures the 'spot markets' and 'firms as hierarchies' have a one-to-one correspondence with the coordination mechanisms 'price' and 'direct supervision' respectively. Vertical integration is a way to have full direct supervision over all the stages of the production process in which you want to be involved. Based on these polar cases, we can provide a ranking of the governance structures from the left to right and map the relevant coordination mechanisms based on propositions discussed in Section 8.2 and 8.3.

Figure 8.2 gives an overview of the continuum of governance structures with at the one end the **spot market** and at the other end **vertical integration** or **in-house production,** and the so-called **hybrid forms** in-between them. The ranking of the six governance structures from the left to right is also determined by the intensity of coordination; the intensity will increase from the invisible hand to the visible one. The intensity of the coordination mechanism the 'handbook' can be considered as less intensive than those of the 'visible hand', because going from the left to the right, this type of coordination is increasing and in a hierarchy, the coordination is carried out by authority. At the same time, the role of the invisible hand is decreasing.

The role of the 'handshake' in the different governance structures is more open, because it can be combined with the other coordination mechanisms, or support, or even sometimes partially substitute them. However, for spot markets this is less likely, because of the anonymity and the identities of the partners do not matter. Going from left to right in Figure 8.2, we will indicate for each governance structure the decreasing role of the invisible hand and the increasing role of the handbook and the visible hand, and the continuous role of the 'handshake'.

Figure 8.2 is only based on coordination mechanisms. Table 8.1 gives a more comprehensive overview based on 8 key elements characterising the six governance structures. The key elements concern coordination, motivation, the identity of partners (personal relation or not and *ex-ante* restrictions on a choice of a partner), duration, enforcement (by court or reputation), financial participation (in the form of equity) and the degree of vertical integration.

Spot markets

The invisible hand of the market determines price and broadly acceptable performance standards. With spot markets, the coordination based on the handbook and the visible hand is low or even absent. As explained in Section 8.2, coordination is a central issue in a governance structure, including what needs to be coordinated and how coordination is achieved. Making use of the coordination mechanism means that we have to cope with control rights[66]. However, the control

---

[66] In general, control rights are the rights to make any decision concerning the use, returns, transfer of an asset that are not explicitly controlled by law (cf. Milgrom and Roberts, 1992: 289). **Specific control rights** are those rights specified by contracts. These rights (and the accompanying obligations) can be observed and verified, for instance by a court of law.

Table 8.1. Typology of governance structures.

	Spot market	Classical contract	Neoclassical contract	Relational contract	Equity based alliance	Vertical integration
Main coordination mechanism	invisible hand	invisible hand/ handbook	invisible hand/ handbook	handshake/ handbook	handbook/ visible hand/ handshake	visible hand
Motivation (intrinsic / extrinsic)	extrinsic	extrinsic	extrinsic/ intrinsic	intrinsic/ extrinsic	extrinsic/ intrinsic	extrinsic/ intrinsic
Impersonal relation	Yes	Yes	No	No	No	No
Ex-ante restrictions on choice of a partner	No	No	Yes	Yes	Yes	Yes
Duration	Short	Short	Moderate	Long	Long	Long
Enforcement	Court	Rules/court	Rules/court	Reputation/ court	Court	Authority
Equity participation	No	No	No	No	Yes	Yes
Vertical integration	No	No	No	No	Partly	Full

rights in a spot market are less intensive or small, or even almost absent. This is reflected in the coordination mechanism used.

Parties on each side of a transaction can engage with price discovery and make either a yes or no decision to enter into the transaction. In this sense, the opportunity to exercise control rights occurs almost entirely *ex-ante* to the transaction. The only *ex-post* control right decision is whether or not to repeat the transaction with the same party if such a repetition is needed in the future. In cases of less than pure competition, e.g. monopoly, one actor can have a major influence over the establishment of the coordination conditions. To actors with this market power, it would seem that they have some rights to specify some of the terms of exchanges. However, in spot markets, the weaker actor retains the right to walk away from the exchange, and the availability of substitute products puts another type of limit on the control rights that can be exercised (cf. Peterson *et al.*, 2001:152). For transactions governed by the spot market, there exists hardly a role for the handshake.

Table 8.1 gives the outcome of the governances structure 'the spot market' based on 8 key elements. As expressed in Figure 8.2 also, the coordination mechanism is the invisible hand. The use of intrinsic or extrinsic motivation depends on the involved persons. Mostly it will the extrinsic one, because the standard neoclassical economics supposes under perfect market conditions no motivation problems. Everyone is striving for utility or profit maximisation. The assumption of the anonymity means: the identity of the partners does not matter; it concerns impersonal relations and there are no *ex-ante* restrictions on the choice of the partner. The duration of the transaction is short. If one of the parties fails to perform, a third party will be sought; this can be the court. There is no financial participation and vertical integration is completely absent.

Contracts

The next step, moving to the right along the continuum, is suggested to be the hybrid governance structure '**contracts**', consisting of **classical contracts**, next **neoclassical contracts** and a step again further to the right, the **relational contracts**. We **first** discuss the global principles for the three types of contracts. Later we will specify characteristics for each type.

The specification of contracts involves the legally enforceable establishment of specific and detailed conditions of exchange. The specification also concerns the control rights; determined, for example, by the rules, directives and contract safeguards. With the specification of contracts, the intensity of coordination markedly increases from that of spot markets. In general, the most important coordination mechanism for contracts is the 'handbook'. However, the emphasis on this coordination mechanism is not the same for the three types of contracts.

Classical and neoclassical contracts

The classical contract as a governance structure is more closely located to the spot market than the neoclassical contract. Subsequently, the role of the price coordination mechanism is more important for classical contracts than it is for neoclassical contracts. For classical contracts, the price is still the most important coordination mechanism (see Figure 8.1 also) and the role of the handbook is moderate. However, for neoclassical contracts, the role of the price decreases and the role of the handbook increases. At the same time, overly detailed handbooks for contracts can easily be interpreted as solidified distrust.

If it is possible to make use of the 'handshake' as a coordination mechanism, it can replace the role of the 'handbook' by making use of common values and norms, credible commitment and reputation building. These elements can function as coordination mechanisms, overcome problems of imperfect information and reduce opportunistic behaviour. At the same time, they will also reduce the transaction costs. However, repeated transactions have to occur for building a reputation. The size of the reputational capital – i.e. the costs of building and maintaining a good one – depends on the frequency of the transactions, the time-horizon over which transactions are expected to occur and the profitability of transactions.

As said, making use of the coordination mechanism means that we have to cope with control rights. The control rights specified by contracts are called the specific control rights. Because of this specification, the control rights in a contract are more intensive than in a spot market. This is reflected in the coordination mechanism used. The parties to a contractual transaction can exercise control rights through the *ex-ante* negotiation of contract specifications (i.e. rules, directives and safeguards) and mutually agreed upon incentives for meeting the specifications.

Box 8.3. Motivation in the governance structure 'contracts'.

The kinds of motivations in a contract can be intrinsic or extrinsic to the individual concerned. Mostly the motivation elements are different for classical, neoclassical and relational contracts. Performance-based pays fit well with classical and neoclassical contracts, but not so well with relational contracts. In classical and neoclassical contracts, motivation can be included in the specification of a reward-structure. However, trustworthiness and reputation are more important for neoclassical contracts and especially for relational contracts.

The parties must invest time and due diligence beyond mere price discovery and a yes or no decision to transact.

Ex-post, the parties exercise control rights through (1) proper monitoring of contract execution and (2) related decisions to renew or renegotiate the contract, or (3) seek third party enforcement if one of the parties fails to perform. In this sense, *ex-post* control rights are more intense than under spot markets. However, the success of specification of contracts is largely dependent upon the *ex-ante* control process. The contract specifications and incentives, once established, become the immutable standards upon which all *ex-post* control activities depend. The most extreme *ex-post* control rights even lie beyond the transacting parties themselves, because often the ultimate enforcement of performance is delegated to a third, external party represented by the legal system (Peterson *et al.*, 2001: 153). Coping with these control rights requires more of the coordination mechanism. This is expressed in the handbook approach.

Table 8.1 summarises the characteristics of 'classical and neoclassical contracts' for the 8 key elements. The coordination mechanism consists of a mix of the invisible hand and the handbook, although in a neoclassical contract the role of the price can be smaller than in a classical contract. The use of intrinsic or extrinsic motivation depends on the people involved. Mostly, the extrinsic motivation will dominate. In the classical contract, the identity of the partners does not matter given the impersonal relation and no *ex-ante* restrictions on the choice of the partner[67]. However, this does not apply for neoclassical contracts. The duration of classical contract is short while it is moderate for a neoclassical contract. Both have the same enforcement mechanisms; rules and the court. Further, both are mostly characterised by no financial participation. Finally, vertical integration is absent.

Relational contracts

The fourth portion of the continuum concerns the **relational contracts**. In this governance structure, a relationship exists between the parties that can be typified as a relation-based alliance. It can be defined as an exchange relationship in which the parties (firms or individuals) involved, share risks and benefits emanating from mutually identified objectives. To be **relation-based,**

---

[67] Classical contracts are often considered to be closely related to spot markets transactions. The assumptions standard neoclassical economics are: perfect market conditions, no motivation problems, because everyone is striving for utility or profit maximisation and anonymity meaning that the identity of the partners does not matter.

the relationship must exhibit at least the following characteristics: (1) mutuality in objective identification; (2) mutuality in the coordination mechanism; as well as (3) mutuality in sharing risk and benefits. Following this definition, coordination in relational contracts or relation-based alliances arises from a mutually accepted 'handbook' or the 'handshake'. As shown in Figure 8.2 the price often plays a minor role. Sometimes (depending on the parties) the handbook can be substituted by the handshake as coordination mechanism. The analogy of a marriage is appropriate when discussing relational contracts or relation-based alliances. The partners agree to work together and thus must find some means to resolve internal differences and concerns. Yet, both parties retain their separate, external identity. In spite of the relational contracts, or relation-based alliances arising from mutual interests, coordination is not always handshake oriented.

The question is what will dominate: either the 'handbook' or the 'handshake' and what will be the trade-off? Detailed handbooks for long-term relational contracts are typical examples of contracts as solidified distrust. In principle, the coordination in mutual interest driven and relational contracts could be carried out by the handbook, but in practice it would hardly be a workable approach. The role of the price of as coordination mechanism in a relational contract is less important than for the neoclassical and classical contracts. More than in the case of classical and neoclassical contracts, the 'handshake' as coordination mechanism can substitute the role of the 'handbook', by making use of mutual adjustment, common values and norms, and building-up credible commitment and reputation.

The intensity of coordination needed to align and maintain mutual interests, involves processes that are more complex than those for spot markets, classical and neoclassical contracts. It is in this sense that the coordination must reach another level. Whether it is higher or lower, depends on the possibilities of applying the 'handshake' as a coordination mechanism. The focus becomes the relationship itself between the parties with the immediate transaction being only one element of the relationship. The relationship itself is often more important than the content of contract.

The control rights in a relational contract are often different from those of classical and neoclassical contracts. This is reflected in the coordination mechanism. *Ex-ante*, the control rights involve building the relationship to help assure that mutual interests are in fact present. Arriving at mutual objectives and setting informal parameters for judging the on-going nature of the relationship and its effectiveness in transacting also become key control activities. *Ex-post,* monitoring the relationship and transaction performance is essential, and when coordination results are less than expected, mutual resolution of concerns or a mutual decision to dissolve the relationship must occur. In the *ex-post* control activities, the informality of *ex-ante* activities implies that no third party judge can be of much assistance and only internal resources of the parties can be brought to bear on coordination error resolution. If successful coordination is to be achieved, parties in relational contracts or a relation-based alliance must invest significant time and commitment to both the *ex-ante* and *ex-post* control rights. However, a strong orientation on the handbook could have a negative trade-off effect on the 'handshake' coordination mechanism. In the final situation, it is the relationship that determines coordination and not any specific transaction *per se* (cf. Peterson *et al.*, 2001: 153).

Table 8.1 summarises the characteristics of 'relational contracts' for 8 key elements. The coordination mechanism consists of a mix of the handshake and the handbook. Consequently, the role of the price will be smaller than in a neoclassical contract. The use of intrinsic or extrinsic motivation depends on the involved persons, it is to be expected that the intrinsic ones will dominate, or at least play an important role. In a relational contract, the identity of the partners matters; as do personal relations and *ex-ante* restrictions on the choice of the partner. The duration of a relational contract is long. The enforcement mechanisms consist of the reputation mechanism (Macleod, 2007: 610) and the court. Relational contracts are mostly characterised by no financial participation. Finally, the relationship can be vertical, but full vertical integration is absent.

Strategic alliances and contracts

Concerning the relationship between strategic alliances and contracts we have to make the following remark. Many strategic alliances between firms include some form of contract as part of their relationship. This does not mean that a strategic alliance can be regarded as a relation-based relationship. Instead, it depends on the type relationship and the type of contract. If strategic alliances are merely limited to the nature of legal classical supplier contracts, neither firm would achieve the broader working relationship that each wants for long-term viability. A neoclassical contract could make a difference; however, this depends on the contract specifications and the duration. Therefore, the existence of a contract in an exchange relationship does not necessarily mean that the relationship is a relation-based alliance.

Equity-based alliances

The fifth position along the continuum is that of the **equity-based alliances**. They consist of a mixture of organisational forms that include joint ventures, business groups (see Douma and Schreuder, 2002: 167-176), partial ownership relationships, some forms of franchising, and other organisational forms that involve some level of shared equity capital between the actors in an exchange relationship. The distinguishing feature between this portion of the continuum and relation-based alliances is the presence of a formal organisation that has an identity distinct from the exchange actors and that is designed to be their joint agent in the conduct of the coordination activity. For the first time along this continuum, the centre of coordination is accomplished by a **formal organisation structure.** However, the parties still maintain a separate identity. For that reason, the most important coordination mechanism is the handbook. Policies, procedures, rules and safeguards (i.e. handbook as coordination mechanisms) are formally put in place for the conduct of exchange between parities. An equity commitment makes the defining of control rights and responsibilities more clear cut than in the case of a relation-based alliance. Agricultural cooperatives clearly lie at this point on the continuum as do joint ventures (cf. Peterson *et al.*, 2001: 154).

The key to understanding this type of coordination, including what needs to be coordinated and how coordination is achieved, is that, although coordination can now be accomplished organisationally, the coordination is often decentralised. Making use of the coordination mechanism means that we have to cope with control rights among the ownership parties and the ownership parties still maintain a separate identity that allows them to walk away from the exchange if they desire to do so. This is reflected in the used coordination mechanism.

The ability to walk away, however, has been dramatically reduced by the existence of substantial investments in the new independent identity. This is called the lock-in effect. The establishment and maintenance of this independent organisation (as a result of which not only the handbook but also the visible hand as coordination mechanism becomes more important) changes the coordination mechanism as compared with relational contracts or relation-based alliances. The visible hand is becoming more important.

The focus of the coordination within an equity-based alliance is on the property rights of stakeholders within the independent entity created by the parties. A key question here is: who has the residual control rights and who is able to capture the residual income? *Ex-ante*, the control rights consist of negotiating the formation of the formal decentralised organisation that will govern the *ex-post* resolution of any coordination concerns. The coordination of transactions – e.g. between a farmer and his cooperative – is delegated to the new, limited organisation with the ability of the ownership parties to monitor results and adjust policies and procedures *ex-post*. In this strategy, the real coordination is exercised through the *ex-post* processes and not the *ex-ante* ones. Take the marketing or environmental cooperative as an example. Producers come together to form the new cooperative entity without giving up their own separate business identities. The *ex-ante* activities focus on the legal formation of the cooperative (including its governance structure), a business plan, and initial financing which establishes the equity contribution of the individual members. The producers then exercise *ex-post* coordination rights through an executive committee and/or a board of directors that sets policies and procedures for the execution of all transactions (cf. Peterson *et al.*, 2001: 155).

For the 'equity-based alliance' governance structure, the coordination mechanism is a mix of the 'handbook' and the 'visible hand' The invisible hand plays a minor role. The question would be: what could be the role of the 'handshake'? It should also be emphasised here that the use of the 'handshake' coordination mechanism can support or even replace the role of the 'handbook' by making use of common values and norms, building-up credible commitment and the reputation mechanism. As said, these elements can function as coordination mechanisms, overcome problems of imperfect information and reduce opportunistic behaviour. At the same time, they will also reduce the transaction costs. The value of having a good reputation could be very important for, as an example, an agricultural cooperative, given the frequency of the transactions, the time-horizon over which transactions are expected to occur and the profitability of transactions. Building-up and preserving *reputational capital* is very important for such an organisation or club, especially if they function as an intermediary (cf. Spulder, 1996: 48; Brousseau, 2002: 361).

Table 8.1 summarises the characteristics of 'equity-based alliance' for 8 key elements. The coordination mechanism consists of a mix of the handbook, the visible hand and the handshake. The role of the price will be smaller than in a neoclassical contract. The use of intrinsic or extrinsic motivation depends on the involved persons, size and type of the organisation. Is it a small-scale club based on self-organisation or a more formal club with a strong business orientation? In the last case, it is to be expected that extrinsic motivation will dominate, or at least play an important

---

Box 8.4. Motivation in the governance structure the firm.

In the governance structure 'the firm', which uses the 'visible hand' coordination mechanism, we have also two kinds of motivations: one internal to the individual concerned and one external. The pressure or desire to do your work well in a firm can arise by way of a direct order with a financial incentive (= external motivation) and by internal motivation. However, the problem of the trade-off between the two kinds of motivations is also present.

---

role. In the 'equity-based alliance' governance structures, the identity of the partners matters; as do personal relations and *ex-ante* restrictions on the choice of the partner. The duration of a relationship is long. The enforcement mechanisms consist of the court and also the reputation mechanism in a small-scale club. Finally, this governance structure is mostly characterised by financial participation in the form of equity, and a partial vertical integration, because the parties still have a separate identity.

Vertical integration

The final portion of the continuum is vertical integration, i.e., the creation of one organisation that has the coordination (by direct supervision or authority) over all the transactions. It is also called *in-house production* and it is the *making by yourself solution* in the **make versus buy** decision. The *unified ownership* or the *do-it-yourself* option involves bringing two or more separate organisations under unified direction (Milgrom and Roberts (1992: 92).

Extending the reasoning from the prior portions of the continuum, vertical integration results in the two parties to a transaction becoming one party and thus true or complete hierarchy is achieved. This can result from the merger of two parties, the acquisition of one party by the other, or one party internally committing resources to replace the market function of the other party. Coordination is exercised within policies and procedures of a single organisation (= the visible hand coordination mechanism; direct supervision, direct order, and authority). For the first time in the discussion of the continuum of governance structures, coordination can be conceived of as being centralised.

Next, there are no separate parties to the transaction that retain independent control rights. As with an equity-based alliance, the focus of coordination is on the property rights of the key stakeholders with the key questions: who has the residual control rights and who is able to capture the residual income? However, now these rights are in one surviving entity rather than in a limited separate entity (as in an equity-based alliance). The intensity of *ex-ante* and *ex-post* coordination processes are thus increased even further in that the scope of coordinating decisions rights and the difficulties of re-separating the parties, make the coordination tasks even more complex. *Ex-ante,* the coordination involves negotiating the formal centralised *ex-post* governance structure. *Ex-post,* coordination results from effective execution of governance policies and procedures for the centralised organisation (cf. Peterson *et al.*, 2001: 155).

Note that the above description of vertical integration relies on a centralised organisation rather than the more traditional or classical notion of single ownership (as in the classical capitalistic firm). This is a subtle but critical change in description. Vertical integration in this version of the continuum is a strategy that relies upon centralised coordination. This is what economists have most often meant by true hierarchy – a command and control system within a **single organisation.**

Table 8.1 summarises the characteristics of 'unified ownership' for 8 key elements. The coordination mechanism consists of the visible hand. Also here the use of internal or external motivation depends on the involved persons, size and type of the organisation. Is it a small-scale organisation or a more public limited company with a strong business orientation? In the last case, it is to be expected that extrinsic motivation will dominate, or at least play an important role. In the 'unified ownership' governance structure, the identity of the partners matters; as do the personal relations and *ex-ante* restrictions on the choice of the partner. The duration of a relationship is long. The enforcement mechanisms consist of the authority. Finally, this governance structure is characterised by financial participation in the form of equity and vertical integration.

In sum, the above discussion illustrates – within the proposed continuum – the shifting coordination mechanisms used in governance structures across the continuum. The coordination mechanisms move from the invisible hand in spot markets to the visible hand in vertical integration. In-between them we find the 'handbook' for classical, neoclassical and relational contracts and equity-based alliances. The 'handbook' and 'visible hand' coordination mechanisms can be supported, partially substituted, or complemented, by the handshake. However, this is less likely for spot markets because the identity of the partners does not matter. The role of the 'handshake' is often under-estimated. It can be important for different reasons, for example, it can strongly reduce the coordination costs, or in terms of *quid pro quo* the transaction costs. However, the choice of the governance structure, including the (mix of) coordination mechanisms, belongs to the strategy of a firm or organisation.

In spite of our emphasis on the transition from spot market to vertical integration, the conceptual approach in this section – concerning coordination mechanisms and governance structures and the other key elements for classifying the mode or organisation – can also be applied to horizontal

---

Box 8. 5. Coordination, residual control rights and residual income.

The incomplete contract and new property rights theory predict the existence of residual control rights and residual income. An intriguing question is: are coordination mechanisms able to cope with these phenomena? If they, in practice, *ex-ante* can be predicted, it could be possible to take them into account by rules in the contract and by direct supervision in a firm. However, given the incompleteness of contracts and the definition of ownership based on having residual control rights and residual income, this will often be very difficult. Whether coordination mechanisms are able to cope with residual control rights and residual income depends on: to what extent they are residual, who is the residual claimant and what is the type of governance structure. The coordination mechanism should minimise possible negative effects of the distribution of residual control rights and residual income as far as possible.

relationships such as networks, clubs based on self-organisations and more formal clubs. For these modes of organisation the handshake is an important coordination mechanism. Instead of contracts we can also make use of intermediaries. Intermediaries have greater incentives than an individual contract taker to invest in reputation. They have more transactions and the probability of re-transacting with a buyer is greater than the probability of re-contracting between a contract giver and a contract taker (cf. Spulder, 1996: 48; Brousseau, 2002: 361; MacLeod, 2007: 616). Finally, we can analyse all these modes of organisation with the 8 key elements of Table 8.1.

8.5 Five organisational modes

One of the salient characteristics of the history of industry is the transition from family firms to large factory-style corporations. Large corporations dominate modern economies. For a long time, agriculture has largely resisted the transition to large corporate ownership. Household-firms still dominate in agriculture, but there has been a remarkable shift in organisational mode. For a comprehensive framework for analysing the organisational mode of (agricultural) firms and its development we have to include (1) the formal rules of the institutional environment (e.g. government rules concerning corporate status or legal entity, liability, fiscal regime, environmental issues, agricultural and rural policy); (2) the advantages and disadvantages of different organisational modes concerning property rights, principal-agent issues, transaction costs and the costs of capital; (3) characteristics of the human decision-maker; and (4) attributes of the transactions in the firm and hold-up and lock-in effects.

Farm organisation can vary from a single owner or simple partnership, where labour is paid by the residual claims or income, to a public corporation with many anonymous co-owners and specialised wage labour. Note that the same holds true for firms in trade, industry and any service sector. Based on criteria derived from the Economic Organisation Theory and institutional economics, including the theory of property rights, we can typify the organisational forms of farms. Table 8.2 gives an overview of these criteria. The organisational forms are based on legal definitions of organisational modes. We can distinguish seven organisational modes: single owner, partnership, partnership firm, limited partnership, private limited company, public limited company and cooperatives. In this section, we will leave the farm as a public limited company and as a cooperative out of consideration, because they are hardly found in Dutch agriculture and horticulture. Furthermore cooperatives have been discussed in the previous section. In this section, the five organisational modes are put into a theoretical perspective and relevant findings in the literature are discussed.

For the theoretical perspective we have made use of the new property rights theory, developed over the last fifteen years to explain the optimal allocation of asset property used in firms. This approach is labelled as the incomplete contract theory (Foss and Foss, 2001: 21). In the new property rights theory, the definition of ownership is taken as having the residual control rights and the residual income. In the case of a firm or organisation, where different stakeholders are often involved and different assets are brought in, it is not always simple to indicate who has the residual control rights and who can capture/appropriate the residual income. Properties (and property rights) are seen as the possibility to practice residual control rights and to capture or appropriate the residual income. However, having the residual control rights and residual income

Table 8.2. Summary of the five organisational modes.

	Single owner	Partnership	Partnership firm	Limited partnership	Private limited company
Ownership	One farm head	Co-ownership; more farm heads; organisation mode for succession	Co-ownership; more farm heads	Difference between silent and active partners	Separation of ownership and management; shares not traded publicly
Corporate status	Non-legal entity	Non-legal entity	Non-legal entity	Non-legal entity	Legal entity
Liability	Farm head personally liable	Farm heads personally liable for their share	All farm heads personally liable for their entire estate	Silent partners for their brought-in capital. Active partners for their entire estate	Shareholders only liable for their brought-in capital
Fiscal aspects	Profit taxed by income tax	Profit taxed by income tax	Profit taxed by income tax	Profit taxed by income tax or corporation tax	Profits taxed by corporation tax; dividends also taxed
Transaction costs	Relatively low	Increase with more members	Increase with more members	Sharing partnership's profits by active partners limits agency cost	Incentive problems if ownership and management separated
Cost of capital for the farm	Relatively high	Relatively high	Relatively high	Relatively high, but partly lower because of silent partners	Lower; risk-bearing costs are lower

characterises ownership. Against this theoretical background, the selected organisational forms are further reviewed below and results are summarised in Table 8.2.

Single owner

A 'pure' family farm is the simplest case, where a single farmer owns the output and controls all farm assets, including all labour assets. The most important characteristic of a single owner is the presence of only one farm head. Other persons present at the farm are always employed by the owner. The farm head is personally liable for all of the farm's debts (cf. Kerkmeester and Holzhauer, 2002: 63). The farm head has the full control rights, full income rights, full transfer rights and also the residual control rights and he appropriates the residual income.

The simplest family farm (= single owner family farm) avoids hidden information and hidden actions of labour, because the farmer is the only residual claimant. Quasi-rents are completely held by the farmer. The transaction costs of recruiting, screening and contracting personnel are relatively low for a single owner, because there is generally very few personnel (employees). If there are personnel, incentive costs and monitoring costs will exist, because employees do not share in the farm's residual income. Therefore they are not fully motivated for the farm's cause.

Partnership

A partnership (*maatschap*) is a non-legal entity; all the members of the partnership bring in something of their own, such as land, buildings, labour or capital. Each member is personally liable for an equal share of the farm's debts and losses. Each member is entitled to carry out duties concerning normal farming activities. Only together the members can decide over important management decisions concerning means of production (labour, capital and non-factor inputs), investments, and financial means of the partnership. Partnership is often chosen as an organisational mode when there are a number of farm heads, who often have a kinship relationship. A partnership is also a suitable organisational mode to use for family succession.

In the case of a partnership, ownership does not coincide with individual property. The bundles of property rights of all assets do not belong to one person. Rather, there are two or more co-owners. This has also consequences for who has the *residual rights of control* and who is able to capture the *residual income*. An important difference with the single owner family farm is the sharing of the residual rights of control and the residual income and the existence of the incentive problem. The profits are usually divided by the members according to their share in the partnership. The profits are taxed according to the (progressive) income tax rates. The best incentive for each member to work hard is to divide the profits according to their share in the partnership. However, it is often difficult to measure each individual's contribution (hidden actions). More complex rewarding systems are more difficult to implement and lead to a rise in decision-making costs. As the number of members of a partnership increases, incentive problems also increase.

Partnership firm (vennootschap onder firma)

A partnership firm is a partnership that is operating under a common name, and must be registered by the Chamber of Commerce. The ownership and management (including directorship) are shared by all members of the farm; they are co-owners. Contrary to a partnership, all of the members of the partnership firm are personally liable for their entire (personal) estate, and not for an equal share of the farm's debts and losses. A creditor can address each member of the partnership firm for his credit and not only the member he has done business with.

Concerning co-ownership, residual income, residual control rights and the existence of the incentive problem, the partnership firm is similar to the partnership described above. The same problems as for partnership hold for sharing profit, paying taxes, measurement problems of each individual contribution, rewarding systems, decision-making costs and incentive problems. It means the economic organisational motives to choose for a partnership firm are largely the same as those for a partnership. The monitoring costs will increase with the number of partners, because each member is allowed to act on behalf of the partnership firm and because each member is liable for his entire estate. This implies that all risks are shared equally by the members of the partnership firm (Kerkmeester and Holzhauer, 2000: 68-69).

Limited partnership

A limited partnership is a special form of a partnership firm with one (or more) active partners and one (or more) silent or limited partners. The silent partners are not allowed to be actively involved in the management of the partnership and are therefore only liable for their brought-in capital. The active partners are responsible for daily decision-making within the partnership and are liable for their entire (personal) estate. Within families, a limited partnership is sometimes used when younger generations want to take to over the farm and the older generation acts as a silent partner who brings in buildings and/or land.

The profits are shared and taxed in a similar way as in the case of a partnership firm, with the exception that the silent partners can also be taxed according to corporation tax. The economic organisational motives to choose a limited partnership are largely the same as those for a partnership (firm). For the silent partners, a favourable aspect of the limited partnership is their entitlement to a share of the profits instead of a fixed interest percentage. To limit agency costs the active partners are allowed to share in the partnership's profits (Kerkmeester and Holzhauer, 2000: 70).

Private limited company

A private limited company is a legal entity and can be viewed as an institutionalised form of cooperation which is recognised as a legal personality by law. A legal entity has its own capital, and accompanying rights and obligations. A private limited company is a legal entity with its share capital divided by the shareholders. The company is not permitted to offer its shares for sale to the public and shares are listed to a certain shareholder, so they cannot be traded publicly. A private limited company must have a shared capital of at least € 18,000. The company has to be founded in the presence of a Notary Public and the company and its statutes have to be registered legally. Because a private limited company is a legal entity, it has its own possessions and debts. In exchange for a share in the firm, shareholders make means of production, like capital and land, available to the firm. The shareholders are only liable for their share in the capital of the private limited company.

The advantage of limited liability is that it increases the possibilities for more large scale activities. A single owner with unlimited liability would be expected to undertake fewer or smaller scale activities than would be the case for a private limited company. Even if the available activities were identical in the two cases, the additional risks faced by the single owner will induce him or her to apply a higher discount rate, and fewer of the activities will yield expected returns which exceed the 'cost of capital'. Thus the cost of capital to the firm is likely to be lower in the private limited company; this is just another way of saying that risk-bearing costs are lower for the decision-makers (Ricketts, 2002:110).

The shareholders are the legal owners (= owners in a juridical sense) of the company and are responsible for appointing the board of directors. Often a private limited company involves separation of ownership and management. However, farms with a private limited company as organisational mode often have one shareholder (but more are also possible) who also acts as director. In case of non-separation of ownership and management, incentive problems are generally not an issue.

If there is more than one shareholder, ownership does not coincide with individual property. Together with the separation of ownership and management, this organisational mode has consequences for those who have the *residual rights of control* and those who are able to capture the *residual income,* and it also creates an incentive problem. Profits are divided among the shareholders according to their share in the company. The profits are taxed according to the corporation tax rate. The dividends received by the shareholders are also taxed.

Summary of organisational forms

Table 8.2 provides a summary of the five organisational forms according to six criteria in the left column. The typology of organisational forms can also be seen as spectrum ranging from single owner to a private limited company.

Based on the theory presented and Table 8.2, the following general conclusions can be drawn concerning the spectrum of organisational forms. These conclusions should be interpreted as moving from the left to the right across the spectrum:
- Separation of ownership and management will increase as the organisational form shifts from single owner towards a private limited company.
- Co-ownership offers the possibility of building up reputation.
- Separation of ownership and management will increase.
- Who has residual control rights and who is able to capture the residual income become less clear.

- Transaction costs increase because of (1) reducing the problems of adverse selection and moral hazard and (2) giving incentives, both caused by making use of workers and managers.
- More possibilities of sharing risk. An important difference between a private limited company and other organisational forms (to the left of the spectrum) is the reduced liability and therefore risk, which in turn implies a lower cost of capital and possibilities for more large scale activities.
- More possibilities for specialisation of work and management.
- More possibilities to spread fixed costs over more transactions.
- The governance structure becomes more complex and more robust.

8.6 An application; the dominance of the family farm

The possible explanations of the domination of the family farm as an organisational mode in agriculture and horticulture can be divided into three categories (Allen and Lueck, 1998: 347-349): (1) the nature of the agricultural production process; (2) economic-organisational factors; and (3) costs of production factors. These three factors are more or less overlapping.

The **nature of the production process** influences the possibilities for economies of scale. First, the advantages of scale are limited by the spatial extent of land-bounded agriculture. This rapidly leads to relatively high internal transport costs. A second explanation is the season-bounded character of the different phases of agricultural production processes (Allen and Lueck, 1998: 346-347).

These different phases bring us to **economic-organisational factors. First** of all, it is not always technically possible to separate the successive phases of the agricultural production process in marketable or contractable transactions, especially for land-bounded activities. If it is technically possible at all than it usually involves **high transaction costs.** In order to overcome the transaction costs the successive phases of the agricultural production process can take place in one firm. In that case, the successive phases of the agricultural production process are being coordinated within one firm and not via the market or contracts. This is a matter of vertical integration. Holdings that are able to specialise, will increase in size more easily than those that are not.

Secondly, the uncertainty and complexity of the production processes influence the level of transactions costs. Uncertainty by seasonal influences plays an important role in agricultural production. If the random and systematic effects of nature cannot be controlled, farming is dominated by family farm production. Generally speaking, family farm production provides many opportunities for avoiding moral hazard and few for exploiting economies of size (Allen & Lueck, 1998: 347). It means that some types of farming are more suitable for family farms than other types of production. Seasonal influences are especially relevant for arable farming, vegetable and fruit growing in open orchards.

In those cases where nature's seasons and uncertainty can be controlled, agricultural production tends to be organised as large-scale firms as in much of the modern economy (Allen & Lueck, 1998: 347). This is the case with glasshouse horticulture and factory farming, where technological advances and new means of production limit seasonal influences on production processes and reduce transaction costs.

However, when the complexity of production processes decreases, the transaction costs of labour will also decrease. In glasshouse holdings and factory farms activities tend to be accomplished routinely and simply, thus transaction costs at these farms will be relatively low compared to farms with complex activities. Family farming is less preferable when the number of (routine) activities per product increases (glasshouse horticulture and factory farming fulfil this condition).

The same holds true for the number of production cycles per year. When they increase, activities tend to be done more routinely and it is easier to hire employees to perform those activities. This leads to a high level of specialisation, which (in combination with routine activities) enables the realisation of economies of size. With an increase in farm size, an organisation mode of a limited partnership, a partnership firm or a (private or public) limited company tends to be more suitable. When the number of cycles is low, like at arable farming, the advantages of specialisation will be limited (Allen and Lueck, 1998: 363) and an organisational mode of a single owner or a partnership is more suitable.

Costs of production factors are the third category that can be used to explain the dominant mode of organisation in the agricultural sector. Farmers (temporarily) bring their own labour, capital and land to their company for a much lower price than the common market price. An explanation for this can be found in: (1) the preference to be a farmer or market grower; (2) mobility bounded values and norms of the group to which farmers belong; and (3) the production factors are for an important part asset specific – the costs of these production factors have become sunk costs, they have low opportunity cost, or a low salvage value. It is also a matter of lock-in effects.

According to the standard neoclassical approach; most of the studies oriented to the development of agricultural firms see the farm as a technical production function. However, little attention is paid to other possible factors underlying the change (such as structural characteristics relating to the farmer, the farm, and the attitudes, managerial ability and decision-making behaviour of the farmer) of the organisational mode. Based on the new institutional economic and Economic Organisation Theory we constructed a comprehensive framework for analysing different organisational modes.

In the agriculture sector we have to deal with specific circumstances that determine the choice of the organisational mode. We will discuss two examples. First, the organisational mode is often adapted for handing over of the farm from parents to their children (mostly they make use of partnerships). Furthermore, the changes of organisational mode (e.g. from single owner to private limited company) does not always mean a separation of ownership and management. For example, in a private limited company, it is still possible that we have one shareholder who is at the same time director and manager also.

Second, in the EU, but also in USA and Australia we had a strong decline in the price support of the government. However, on the supply side, there is a continuing strong increase in productivity in Western countries. This increase, together with a nearly constant demand for agricultural products, led to decreasing real prices. In order to survive, one option for farmers is farm enlargement. This necessitates a re-organisation, from a single owner 'family farm' to a partnership firm, or even to a private limited company. A change in farm organisation implies a change in the contractual relationship between labour, capital, and management of the farm. The liberalisation of the EU-price policy leads to more price uncertainty. More robust governance structures can help to adapt the farm structure and to reduce the risks of this price uncertainty.

Although the family farm remains the dominant organisational mode for farms there are changes in the legal mode of organisation. Important factors for explaining the different modes of organisation are (limited) liability, risk-bearing costs, transaction costs, and residual control and income rights. These findings were supported in an empirical study, based on a sample of 3100 farmers in the Netherlands. This study also included the impact of farmer's attitudes, the farm advisory network, and structural variables on organisation choice. Findings from this research also demonstrated the significant role financial advisors appear to play in the choice of organisation mode. Other factors were age, branch (horticulture, factory farming), and farm size (Jongeneel *et al.*, 2006).

Box 8.8. Key terms of Chapter 8.

Governance structure or mode of organisation
Coordination mechanisms
Motivation mechanisms
Ways how to organise matter
Invisible hand
Visible hand
Handbook
Handshake
Spot market
Classical contract
Neoclassical contract
Relational contract
Strategic alliances and contracts

Vertical integration
Personal relationship
Ex-ante restrictions on choice of partner
Duration
Enforcement
Rules/Court
Reputation capital
Financial participation in the form of equity
Residual control rights
Residual income
Clubs
Intermediaries
Equity based alliance

9. Ownership

9.1 Introduction

Ownership is a complex concept. On the one hand it can be considered as a bundle of property rights and on the other hand it is intimately associated with contractual incompleteness. In the more modern literature, the first point of view is strongly connected with the old property rights theory, and the second one with the new property theory. We make use of both property rights theories. In this chapter we will focus our attention on the concepts of ownership, the optimal allocation of ownership, what are the incentives of ownership, and the question of who is the owner and whose interests should count.

In Section 9.2 we will pay attention to the economic notion of ownership for simple assets like a bike or a horse, and more complex ones such as a firm. We will show that it is often useful to interpret 'owning an asset' as having residual control rights and residual income. Section 9.2 will be concluded with some reasons why a system of private ownership is not always efficient for the society. In Section 9.3 we will analyse the question of whether we can realise a kind of efficient filling-in of ownership, i.e. an optimal allocation of ownership. Can we structure ownership in such a way that it minimises distortions in investment decisions caused by attributes of transactions? Or, stated in a more positive way: can we develop an ownership-theory that maximises the value of the assets used within an organisational mode?

In Section 9.4 we will analyse the question: who 'owns' a project or a firm? Answering this question is not always easy. This is especially the case if the payoffs for an asset are multi-dimensional. The question even becomes problematic when we consider the complex agglomerations of assets of a modern corporation, such as a public limited company. The final section of this chapter deals with the question whose interests should count: all the people involved in a project or firm, or only the managers and shareholders? The rise of investment funds makes the question 'whose interests should count?' an important one.

Key questions:
- What are the two economic approaches to ownership?
- What is the relationship between the incomplete contract theory and the new property rights theory?
- Why is the concept of ownership complicated?
- Which two rights are often seen as marking ownership?
- What is the problem with monitoring if we see the firm as a form of team production and how can it be solved?
- Why is a system of private ownership not always efficient?
- Which two guidelines are important for the structure of ownership and what is the general principle?
- What has been the starting point for the discussion on the separation of legal ownership and management, and whose interest should count?
- Which two important types of view can be distinguished concerning whose interests should count?

- What is the role of the so-called activistic hedge funds and what type of countries are more sensible for such funds?
- Which four sets of circumstances determine whether government ownership is likely to be superior to private ownership?

9.2 The concepts of ownership

The concept of ownership is complicated, even for simple assets. A person who owns something has certain rights and obligations concerning its use. For example, if you own a horse, you are free to ride it, to stable it, to feed it, to lend it to others, to transfer your rights to another party, but you have the obligation to take care for it. For a simple physical asset, like a car – if you own the car – you are free to drive it (provided that you have a license and obey the traffic laws), to park it (in a legal parking space), to paint and decorate the car (provided that you keep the windows clear and do not offend the public morality), to choose where and how often to have it serviced (provided that you obey the emission control and safety laws), to lend it to others for driving (if the borrower is a licensed driver), to transfer your rights to another party (either permanently through gift or sale or temporarily through rental), and so on (Milgrom and Roberts, 1992: 289).

Similarly, if you own a firm, you have the right to hire and fire its employees (subject to legal limitations on discrimination and wrongful discharges and the terms of any employment contract), to determine the products, prices, and policy of the firm (subject to regulation), to transfer the profits or other resources of the firm to your personal account (subject to the tax laws and any restrictive clauses in the firm's loan agreements or other contracts), and so on. For economic analysis, it is often useful to interpret 'owning an asset' to mean having the residual control rights – that is the right to make any decisions concerning the use, returns, transfer of an asset that are not explicitly controlled by law or assigned to another by contract – (cf. Milgrom and Roberts, 1992: 289) – and having the residual income. The residual income is the amount that remains from the gross-return of a company, activity, good or service after all the remaining contractual commitments are fulfiled.

This property rights approach has been developed over the last fifteen years to explain the optimal allocation of asset property used in firms, organisation or contractual relations[68]. The meaning of having **residual control** or **decision rights** appear in the link between decision rights and asset ownership. According to this property-rights view, the owner of a non-human asset has residual rights of control over the asset, i.e. the right to make all decisions concerning that asset which have not been specified in a contract or are not in conflict, or inconsistent, with the laws, existing legal rules or the contract. (When there are multiple owners of an asset or firm, they will typically delegate some of the residual control rights to e.g. directors, managers, board of directors.)

Properties (and property rights) are seen as the possibility to practice *residual control rights* and to capture or appropriate the residual income. The opposite is perhaps more important: those who

---

[68] This approach is also labelled the new property right theory. This is based on the idea that it is often difficult to make and to write complete and enforceable contracts. The new property right theory is also called the incomplete property right theory (Foss and Foss, 2002: 21). In the incomplete contract theory having the residual control rights is taken as a definition of ownership (Hart, 1995: 30).

Box 9.1. Economic approaches to ownership.

There are two important economic approaches for ownership. One is based on the old property rights theory and the other on the new property rights theory. The old one deals with (1) ownership as a bundle of property rights and the new one with (2) ownership as having residual control over and having residual income of an asset. The latter is intimately associated with the contractual incompleteness.

According to the old property rights theory, ownership can be considered as a bundle of property rights. Based on the property theory – as will be explained in more detail in Section 10.2, the rights of full asset ownership consist of five elements: (a) the right to use the asset; (b) the right to appropriate the returns from the asset; (c) the right to change the form, substance, and location of the asset; (d) the right to exclude others; and (e) the right of transfer to others (through markets) or to their inheritances.

The new property rights approach focuses on having residual control right and residual income. This theory has been developed over the last fifteen years to explain the optimal allocation of asset ownership in firms, organisations or contractual relations. An important application of the new property rights approach is the property right theory of the firm (Grossman and Hart, 1986; Hart and Moore (1990; 1999). A firm is identified as a collection of non-human assets under a certain type of ownership.

Within this approach – also labelled as the incomplete contract theory (Foss and Foss, 2001: 21) – is having the residual control rights and the residual income taken as a definition of ownership (Hart, 1995: 30). In the new property rights theory, ownership is seen as the possibility to practice *residual control rights* and to appropriate the residual income. This can also be the other way around: those who can practice the *residual control rights* and capture the residual income can be considered as the owners.

Residual control or decision rights are like any other good; there will be an optimal allocation of them (Hart, 2002: 185). Tying together residual control and residual income is key to the incentive effects of ownership. These effects are very powerful because the decision-maker bears the full financial impact of his or her choices. When it is possible for a single individual to have both the residual control and the residual income, the residual decisions made will tend to be efficient ones. Generally speaking, for efficient and effective ownership, properly combining of residual control rights and the residual income is required.

can practice the *residual control rights* and capture the residual income are the owners or have the ownership (and the property rights). The problem is that, in practice, *residual control rights and residual income* can be quite fuzzy and vague concepts. The same holds for the allocation of residual control. In the case of a firm or organisation, where often different stakeholders are involved and different assets are brought in, it is not always simple to indicate who has the *residual control rights* and who can capture/appropriate the *residual income*. That means that the ownership of a firm, organisation, or contractual relationship is often a vague concept. However, having the residual control rights and residual income, characterises ownership.

Tying together residual control and residual income is the key to the incentive effects of ownership. These effects are very powerful because (at least in the simple cases) the decision-maker bears the full financial impact of his or her choices. When it is possible for a single individual to have both the residual control and the residual income, the residual decisions made will tend to be efficient ones. This means that for efficient and effective property a properly combining of the two aspects of ownership the **residual control rights** and the **residual income** is required: (cf. Milgrom and Roberts, 1992: 291 -292).

If ownership means having residual control rights and having residual income, then its importance must derive from the difficulty of writing contracts that specify all the control rights. Suppose that for some particular business relationship it is cheap and easy both to write and to enforce complete contracts – ones that specify what everyone is to do in every relevant eventuality at every future date and how the resulting income in each such event should be divided. In that hypothetical situation, there would be no unforeseen contingencies, no eventualities for which plans has not been made, no unexpected gains and losses, and no difficulties in ensuring that the agreed actions and divisions of income would be implemented. Residual control rights would mean nothing because no rights would be left unspecified. Nothing would be residual (Milgrom and Roberts, 1992: 289).

As explained before, the total control rights consist of (1) the specific control rights and (2) residual control rights. The specific control right are those rights specified by contract or law. These rights (and the accompanying obligations) can be observed and verified, for instance by a court of law. The residual control rights are the rights to make decisions concerning the use, returns, transfer of an asset that are not explicitly controlled by law or assigned by another contract. The question of who has the residual control rights in **complete contracts** is quite simple, because there are no residual control rights and residual income.

However, as argued in Chapter 7, complete contracts are generally impossible for transactions of any significant complexity that occur over a period of time longer than a few days. Complete contracting requires insight in all contingencies that may arise during the contract terms:
• Costlessly determining the appropriate actions and division of income to take in each contingency.
• Describing all these verbally with enough precision to make sure that the terms of the contracts are clear.
• Arriving at an agreement on these terms.
• Doing all this in such a way so that the parties to the contract are motivated to follow its terms.

Each of the presumed conditions is probably impossible on its own, and their conjunction is certainly so. Finally, the problems of information asymmetries plague contracting. All together, and in line with the basic arguments in Section 7.2, the unavoidable conclusion is that contracts are necessarily incomplete. Consequently, arrangements that leave all control rights that are not otherwise assigned to a single, distinguished individual – i.e. eliminating the need to negotiate and reach agreement for every unplanned event – enjoy significant cost advantages (cf. Milgrom and Roberts, 1992: 289). In that case, there is only one single person who has the residual control rights and the residual income. Nothing has to be negotiated and to be redistributed. This is a strong advantage or incentive of full ownership.

Box 9.2. Who is the owner?

Ownership is a source of power if there are residuals; applied to contracts if they are incomplete. The person who gets the residual income is defined as the residual claimant. If a person is the only owner of a firm, then he is the 'residual claimant' and has the 'residual rights of control'. He has the right to decide about the use of the means of production, hiring and firing of people.

However, there are three complications. **First**, who is the owner? In the classical capitalistic firm (cf. Alchain and Demsetz, 1972) it was clear. One person had: the (1) full *control rights* (i.e. final authority over all of the policies pursued by the firm); the (2) full *income rights* (i.e. the non-restricted right to the firm's residual); and the (3) full *transfer rights* (i.e. complete freedom to assign his rights, in whole or in part, to others). The owner of a classical capitalistic firm has therefore not only the (residual) control rights over the bundle property rights but also the right to the residual income. In a firm or organisation different stakeholders are often involved and different assets are brought in. The same holds for modern companies, such as public limited company where different groups of people are involved; workers, managers, shareholders, creditors, etc. The question is who has the residual control rights and who is able to capture the residual income? Is it equally distributed among all the people involved? **Second**, ownership is often a complicated concept. Ownership of e.g. a firm is often a vague and unclear concept. The reason is that the allocation of the residual control rights and the allocation of the residual income rights can be fuzzy. Which group of people in a firm have these rights? This is not always clear. However, having the residual control rights and residual income, characterises ownership. A **third** complication is that the bundle of rights which form the property rights differs from country to country and changes over time. Summarising ownership is often a fuzzy and a complex concept.

The notion of ownership as residual control rights and residual income is relatively clear and meaningful for a simple asset like a bike. However, it gets fuzzier when we apply the concept of ownership to something complicated, like a large firm. Large firms bundle together many assets, and who has what control rights is often unclear. In the case of a firm the control rights of different categories of decisions may be poorly specified or may lie with various parties. An additional complication is that the rights that come with ownership vary among countries and over time. A firm's owner may have the right to hire employees but not the right to lay them off or fire them at will (cf. Milgrom and Roberts, 1992: 290).

Box 9.1 gave an overview of the rights constituting ownership as a bundle of property rights (cf. Cooter and Ulen, 1997: 72). All these rights have not only legal but economic consequences also. It means we can look at rights from a legal point of view and from an economic one. Especially the **income and transfer rights**[69], are often emphasised as marking the **economic meaning of ownership**. These rights are discussed in more detail in Section 10.2.2. The effects of these rights is that one has the right to capture the return of the asset by using the asset or to rent it out to a third party and get a return, and the right to transfer the asset to others and get a (market) value of the asset. The main economic consequence is that it enables the owner to receive and keep the residual income from the asset. This may be:

---

[69] Only the owner is allowed to sell an asset. It also means that ownership is restricted to physical assets.

- Directly, by a current cash flow – as result of return of using the asset or renting it out to third party. It supposes that the owner can refuse the use of an asset to anyone who will not pay the price the owner demands.
- Indirectly, by changes in the future flows or changes in the current value of the asset.

These returns are the basis of the **economic notion of ownership**. According to this notion, the one who is entitled to receive any net income that the firm produces is the **residual claimant.** Net income is conceived as the residual income. It is the amount that is left over after everyone else has been paid. Like residual control, the notion of residual income is tied to contractual incompleteness. Under complete contracting, the division of the income or change in value in each eventually would be specified contractually, and there would be no residual income (cf. Milgrom and Roberts, 1992: 291).

Just as the allocation of residual control can be fuzzy, the notion of residual income is fuzzy as well. One problem is that recipients of the residual income may vary with the circumstances. For example, when a firm is unable to pay its debts, increases in its earning may have to be paid to the lenders. It means – in this case – the lenders are the residual claimants. Another example is the success of a firm. It may affect the market's perception of its managers' abilities and thereby their future opportunities and income. Thus, the managers become residual claimants on a proportion of the total return. For these reasons, the ownership of something as complicated as a firm is a vague and often unclear concept (cf. Milgrom and Roberts, 1992: 291). It also means that if people are speaking about ownership a logical question would be: 'What do you mean'?

Tying together residual income and residual control is not only key to understanding ownership but also key to the incentive effects of ownership. These effects could be powerful because – at least in simple cases – the decision-maker bears the full economic burden of his or her choices. When it is possible for a single individual both to have the residual control and to receive the residual income, the residual decisions made will tend to be efficient ones. In contrast, if only part of the costs or benefits of a decision accrue to the party making the decision, then that individual will find it in his or her personal interest to ignore some of these effects, frequently leading to inefficient decisions (cf. Milgrom and Roberts, 1992: 291).

The incentive effects of ownership can be illustrated by a car and the firm as a form of team production. Having residual control rights and residual income explains the incentive effects of an **owner** of a car versus those of a **renter.** One important attribute of a rental transaction is the extreme *difficulty of performance measurement*, i.e. the impossibility of establishing exactly how much the car's value has depreciated during a rental. For this reason, the rental company is unable to base its charges on its actual costs. Instead, it bases them on things it can observe, such as days and hours of the rental, miles driven and obvious collision damage. Such a charge does not give a good incentive to any single actual use, and its effect, to be as careful as possible is not fully rewarded and rough use is not fully charged. The one who decides on how the asset is actually used – the renter – has residual control (for a time) but is not the residual claimant. In contrast, the owner of a car has both the residual control and the residual returns (cf. Milgrom and Roberts, 1992: 292). Properly **combining** the two aspects of ownership – **residual control** and **residual**

returns -provides strong incentives for the owner to maintain and increase an asset's value. This does not only hold for simple assets but also for more complex ones like a firm.

We can consider a firm as a form of team production (compare Alchican and Demsetz, 1972). It means the output is the joint product of several workers' contributions, and the outputs of each team member is difficult to define and certainly hard to observe. As a result, team production creates the **incentive problem of shirking.** If individual output is observable, it could be easily overcome by giving each worker the title to what he or she produces. This is not always easy, and often involves high transaction costs. A solution in this case would be that one member of the team undertakes a specialised function:

1. to *monitor* the other workers; and
2. to have the authority to expel members of the team who perform unsatisfactorily and replace them with new members.

This creates another problem: who will monitor the monitor? However, according to Alchian and Demsetz (1972) the monitor is motivated by receiving the residual returns. So monitoring is not necessary. This results in what economists call the *classical firm*: an organisation in which a boss hires, fires, and directs workers who are paid a fixed wage. The boss receives the residual returns (cf. Milgrom and Roberts, 1992: 293). It is the full ownership solution.

As explained, ownership creates strong individual incentives. However, this does not mean that a system of private ownership is always efficient for society as a whole. At least the following reasons can be mentioned why a system of private ownership is not always efficient:

1. Pure public goods have the characteristics of non-excludability and non-rivalry. It is because of the non-excludability of these goods that it is impossible to define and specify private property rights. This will discussed more extensively in Section 10.4.
2. Providing some goods and services involves very high and often for a large part fixed costs. This is a result of non-rivalry or indivisibility of the goods. The consequence can be that the private sector will not provide such goods. Examples of such goods are railways, high ways, networks for the supply of gas, water and electricity, large irrigation systems, etc.
3. Having a single decision-maker bearing all the risk in an asset's value may be incompatible with efficient risk sharing and impractical if the amounts are large.
4. Increasing the value of a particular asset often involves undermining competitors, setting monopoly prices, polluting or destroying the environment, all activities that bring about inefficiencies.

It should be noted that the above arguments are partly overlapping, but all have in common that private ownership will bring about inefficiencies.

Yet, in spite of these four reasons for private ownership inefficiencies, a generally well-accepted rule is that 'getting the property rights right' can improve our welfare. The assumption is that a system of clear, enforceable and tradable private property rights will generate a socially efficient outcome. This is the basic idea of the Coase theorem as described in Box 9.3. This theorem states that if parties bargain to an efficient agreement, then outcomes they will agree upon do not

> **Box 9.3. Coase theorem.**
>
> In its 'strong' form, the Coase theorem asserts that the initial assignment of property rights make no difference to efficiency because identical Pareto-optimal allocations will emerge. In order for this interesting outcome to be realised, some far reaching assumptions have to be made. The key assumptions cited in the literature are: (1) costless negotiations, (2) fully defined property rights, and the absence of wealth effects. In this special environment, transaction costs are zero and the negotiating parties have quasi-linear preferences, so that the distribution of the income occasioned by trade doe not affect marginal valuation (Furubotn and Richter, 2005: 128). In the literature there are different versions of the Coase theorem. A simple presentation is that clear a definition of property rights is in principle sufficient to ensure efficiency by bargaining (Cooter and Ulen, 1997: 82). Yet, that is only the case if the transaction costs are zero (Furubotn and Richter, 2005: 129).

depend on the bargaining power of the parties or on what assets they owned when bargaining began. However, the reasons that may prevent efficient agreements are:
1. whether there are clear, enforceable property rights that can be transferred easily;
2. transaction costs can be high;
3. most people have loss aversion, this has been explained in Section 4.6;
4. weak institutions at different levels; and
5. a weak or bad government.

In Section 10.3 we will discuss the Coase theorem in more detail.

9.3 The structure of ownership

As explained, ownership is often not only a vague concept, but also a broad concept. It can refer to a bundle of property rights or having residual control rights and residual income. However, ownership of an asset or a firm can also refer to modes of organisation, varying from single ownership to co-ownership, such as in a partnership or in a public limited company. From an economic point of view, we have to look at efficient ways of structuring ownership in such a way that there will be an optimal allocation of residual control rights and residual income.

The question is, can we structure ownership in such a way that it minimises distortions in investment decisions caused by attributes of transactions? Or formulated in more positive way; can we develop an ownership-theory that maximises the value of used assets when applied in an organisational mode? Two important guidelines are:
1. If is it possible for a single individual to have both the residual control and to receive the residual income, then the residual decisions made will tend to be efficient ones.
2. Properly **combining** the two aspects of ownership – **residual control** rights and **residual income** – provides strong incentives for the owner to maintain and increase an asset's value.

These guidelines do not only hold for simple assets but also for more complex ones like a firm.

The attributes that determine efficient ownership are largely the same as those used for the framework for determining attributes of transactions which are decisive for the choice of the governance structure (see Section 5.3); asset specificity; uncertainty, frequency and duration; difficulty of performance measurement; connectedness and co-specialised assets; non-excludability and non-rivalry of goods; and human capital. However, the ownership-theory is focused on the basic concepts of the incomplete contract theory or the new property theory; **residual control** rights and **residual income.** As said in the chapters before, the predictions of these theories are more robust than those of the transactions costs theory.

9.3.1 Asset specificity and associated with hold-up and lock-in problems

The most important attribute of transactions for studying asset ownership is the asset specificity attribute. Assets are specific to a certain use if the services they provide are exceptionally valuable only in that use. In Section 5.4 we took as examples (1) a railway line that carries cargo to and from an isolated factory; (2) an oil well and a pipeline; and (3) a tenant who is investing in land and buildings. The *degree of specificity* of an asset is defined to be the fraction of its value that would be lost if it were excluded from its major use.

When an asset is specific to a particular use, as the railroad line is specific to serving the factory, the owner can be held up. The factory owner might insist on lower rail rates, threatening to ship the factory's output by truck, if the railroad owner does not accept this request. This threat is powerful because the rail line is highly specific and would lose almost all its value if the threat was carried out. As a result, the railway-line owner might indeed be forced to make concessions to the factory owner. If the factory's product is too large or heavy to ship by truck, however, the assets of railway-line and factory are co-specialised, in which case each side can use a powerful threat against the other. Any breakdowns in bargaining will lead to large costs on both sides.

This creates two types of problem: hold-up and lock-in problems. A hold-up problem itself has often no effect on total value directly. It causes income redistribution effects between the involved parties. The direct effect of the hold-up problem caused by the factory owner is that the railroad owner receives less of the total value and the factory owner more. The efficiency itself is unaffected, however there are income redistribution effects between the parties involved. Despite this, hold-ups can lead to value-destroying consequences. The fear of hold-ups can hinder people from investing in highly specific assets. It will reduce the value of the asset, the value of the firm, and the total net added value in the society. These are the real social costs of the hold-up problem. It prevents people from conducting efficient investments.

As explained in Section 5.4, lock-in means that the alternatives are strongly reduced. A lock-in effect is an *ex-post* phenomenon, while hold-up is more of an *ex-ante* problem. Suppose, the owners of the oil well and the factory from our examples have no alternative for transporting oil and end products of the factory, other than the railway-line. If the owner of the railway-line increases the transportation tariffs, then they are locked-in and will have to pay these higher tariffs.

What is the solution in this case? Firstly, when an asset is specific to a particular use, hold-up and lock-in problems for that asset can be avoided by having the assets in one organisation, i.e.

the user owns the asset also. Secondly, when two assets are both highly specific to the same use, the maximising value of assets requires using both together in that use. The two assets are then said to be *co-specialised*. Specificity and co-specialisation are important because they give rise to hold-up and lock-in problems. Central to ownership-theory is that there will be a tendency for specific assets to be owned by those who use them and for two co-specialised assets both to be **owned by the same person or organisation having both the residual control rights** and **residual income.** This is often called the ownership solution. The hold-up and lock-in analysis is central to analyzing efficient ownership. Its application requires a detailed evaluation of the context, which involves studying other attributes and related transactions.

9.3.2 Uncertainty

If all relevant contingencies can be forecasted and planned, a contract specifying what is required can be a **good alternative** to ownership. Contracting can be applied between the railway company and the owner of mine or factory. The same holds for the oil well and pipeline. Long-term contracts are often a good substitute for full ownership; meaning they combine **residual control** rights and **residual income** in one organisational mode. For example, landowners use long-term land tenure contracts for the lease of farmland by farmers. Similarly, the relationship between a franchisor and franchisee is covered by a contract. Long-term contracts can create incentives to treat each other fairly and subsequently overcome problems of hidden actions and hidden information by way of the repeated relationships between the same parties over a period of years (which means a long-term relationship), trust and building reputational capital. A good reputation can overcome all the problems of opportunistic behaviour, while a bad reputation increases the chance of opportunistic behaviour and hold-up problems. Trust is important for a long-term relationship, because the longer the time horizon between performance (quid) and counter performance (quo), the more **trust** is needed.

9.3.3 Frequency and duration

The **longer** the time period over which two parties might interact, the more difficult it will be to foresee and contract for all the relevant contingencies. Thus, the less likely it is that a (classical or neoclassical) contracting solution will be satisfactory. Consequently, some **other governance structures** including **co-ownership** may be preferred, especially when the fixed costs of creating a solution can be spread over more individual transactions. However, a long time horizon also means that **reputation** may be more effective as an enforcement mechanism. The incentives to build and maintain a *reputation* are larger, the more frequent the transactions, the longer the time horizon, and the more profitable the transactions; this is expressed in the concept of reputational capital.

9.3.4 Difficulty of performance measurement

Even when the assets are not highly specific, the assignment of ownership as a bundle of property rights can still matter. If a **nonspecific** asset is used by **a single person** to produce **marketable output,** then an easy way to provide proper incentives is to make this person the owner, and let him have both the residual control and being the residual claimant. The person will have a proper interest in maximising the residual value of the asset.

The ownership solution – in terms of having of **residual control** rights and **residual income** – has also some disadvantages. Firstly, transferring ownership also means transferring the risk of fluctuations in value of the asset to a single individual who may find the risk very costly to bear. Secondly, the person who takes care for the asset has also other responsibilities in which performance is sometimes difficult to measure. These other responsibilities will be neglected unless strong enough incentives are established for the asset owner to devote some effort to them. When performance in the other responsibilities is difficult to measure, these incentives are costly and represent an added cost of transferring asset ownership.

An alternative to the ownership incentive could be the use of explicit performance-based pay. This alternative requires attempting to measure the person's performance. Compared to transferring ownership, the disadvantage of this system is that it incurs an added measurement cost. **Generally**: (1) when it is relatively cheap to measure performance accurately and (2) when the risks associated with asset ownership are relatively large, it is better to base compensation on measured performances than to shift to ownership. These risks could involve a reduction in the non-contractible quality[70]. This rule means, for example, you should never make soccer players the owners of a soccer club, because the performances of the soccer players can quite easily be measured.

When care is especially difficult or costly to measure and the risks of asset ownership are not too great, then the ownership solution should be preferred, tying residual control rights and residual income together. Examples are medical specialists with their own clinics, or farmers who offer care possibilities for handicapped persons at their farm. When the motivation of the person to honor his or her other responsibilities is high, the best system may be **to avoid** offering any formal **financial performance incentives**. Many doctors, surgeons, teachers and scientific researchers are driven by intrinsic motivation. This refers to our discussion about knaves and knights in Section 4.3. The knaves are driven by intrinsic motivation and they derive no benefit from the fact that the activity is of use to others. On the other hand, knights are driven by external motivation such as financial incentives. That is they derive some rewards from the fact that others benefit from the activity (in contrast to the knaves).

Incentive contracts are one example of how financial performance incentives can be applied. It means a variable payment depending on the efforts or performances. The incomes become subject to random factors. However, most people are risk-averse and dislike having their income dependent on random factors. The risk created by incentive contracts is costly to them. They are not as well off with a risky income as they would be by receiving the same expected level of pay for certain. Thus, they have to be paid more, on average, to convince them to accept these risks. From an employer's perspective, this extra income is a cost of using incentive payment schemes.

---

[70] This refers, for example, to the choice between contracting out versus in-house provision, discussed in Chapter 7.8.

9.3.5 Connectedness

Transactions differ in how they are connected to other transactions, especially those involving investments which are highly asset specific. It is even possible that the assets or the services they yield are strongly complementary. This means that if one transaction has a high level of connectedness, then it will significantly increase the value of the other. Some transactions are largely dependent on others. As explained before, this gives rise to hold-up problems and lock-in effects. An example of connectedness is the relation between water and an irrigation system – including canals and pipes. There is a strong relationship between both assets. Without water, the irrigation system is useless or even worthless, and also the other way around. There is also a strong connection between water and land. Without an irrigation system and water, land is, in some regions, useless. In developed countries there is also a strong connectedness between the provision of electricity, gas and water and the network facilities of these goods. This raises questions about the best ownership structure.

If assets – or services they yield – are strongly complementary, a higher level of one significantly increases the value of the others. It is possible that there may be multiple patterns of investments that are mutually dependent and consistent with each other and are forming coherent patterns. However, only one of these distinct patterns actually maximises the total value. When the involved parties have divergent interests, the coordination problems become more difficult, for example, particularly for the distribution of quasi-rents. According to transaction cost theory, this gives rise to high transactions costs associated with *ex-post* haggling and opportunism.

The connectedness of transactions can also be a result of the people involved. Human capital is one of the most important kinds of assets. Skills and knowledge of a person are often tied to the person in question. The transferability of human capital is problematic when those skills are specific to an organisation or asset. Co-specialised skills and knowledge are often characteristic for working in a team.

A general principle is that ownership rights should be structured to minimise distortions in investment decisions caused by **hold-up** and **lock-in** problems. The connectedness of assets can lead to **hold-up** and **lock-in** problems. In the case that multiple patterns of investments that are mutually dependent and consistent with one another and forming coherent patterns, in practice, mostly one of these distinct patterns actually maximises the total value. In the case that we have to deal with decision-makers with divergent interests, the coordination problems become much more difficult. This means that, other things being equal, **strongly complementary assets should be brought under co-ownership** and thus tying residual control rights and residual income together in one mode of organisation. Sometimes we can make use of alternative sophisticated governance structures which can be excellent substitutes for ownership, and these alternatives may avoid some of the influence costs of ownership. We can think about relational or global contracts, peer groups, partnerships, networks, franchising, joint ventures and certain clubs. In these cases, the components of social capital such as trust, commitment and reputational capital are very important.

9.3.6 Non-excludability and non-rivalry

Non-excludability and non-rivalry are characteristics of pure public goods. For this type of goods, private ownership is impossible. In the case of full non-excludability and non-rivalry we have to deal with the problem of 'nobody's ownership' and at the same time with 'everyone's ownership'. For example, a dike protects people against flooding. It is impossible to allocate ownership to the good 'protection' to someone and to exclude others. The same holds for clean air; it is impossible to allocate ownership.

9.3.7 Human capital

Human capital is one of the most important kinds of assets. However, a person's set of skills and knowledge consists of assets that can only be owned by the person him- or herself. Non-transferability of human capital is problematic when those skills are specific to an organisation or asset. Examples are co-specialised skills and knowledge such as in a team of excellent researchers at a university. Ownership rights in a firm or its assets do not include the human capital of all the workers. Hence, the impossibility of transferring ownership of human capital leads to the question: *in whose interest should firms be run?* This question will be discussed in Section 9.5.

9.4 Who 'owns' a project or a firm?

If the payoffs from an asset are **not one-dimensional** e.g., if not all returns are in terms of money, there may be different **residual elements** associated with each dimension. For example, two professors form a partnership for writing a text book together. The result will be a variety of rewards (royalties, prestige, a successful course, status etc.). Both persons will get royalties. The question is how to distribute these royalties. It is also possible that one professor uses the book for a course, attended by many students. His prestige and status will increase by making use of the book and a successful course. So he will have more **residual elements.**

Such a simple venture gives rise to complications. Most business transactions will be equally or even more complex. A manager who carries out a particular project **gains expertise.** This can have a high value in the future, because he can exploit it. The returns from projects carried out by a firm are not alone revenues and costs of a firm, they also generate residuals that may be claimable by shareholders, but have an affect on the manager's future earnings opportunities. The first question is: are they observable to the firm or the different stakeholders within the firm, or even to the manager? The next question will be: for whom are the residuals? Who has the residual control rights and who is able to capture the residual income? Or in other words who 'owns' a project or a firm?

Who owns a public corporation?

The concept of ownership becomes problematic when we consider the complex agglomerations of assets of a modern corporation, such as a public limited company. Shareholders nominally, and by law, own a corporation. However, their rights are in fact quite limited. They can **vote** to change the corporation character and can **elect** the board of directors and remove them by majority vote.

They usually have the **rights** to vote on substantial 'organic' changes, such as mergers in which the company disappears or the sale of most of the corporation's assets.

However, shareholders cannot set the dividends that are paid out for them. They have no role in investments or acquisitions decisions. They do not **hire and fire** the managers or set their pay, and have no say in setting prices. They have no rights in deciding on issues that are crucial in running the business. By electing the directors, who are empowered to hire and fire management, they can indirectly affect decisions that are made. If the directors they elect do not follow their wishes, the stockholders can replace them as the opportunities arise. However, the formal definitions of residual rights are in terms of residual control rights and residual income that **are not explicitly** vested by contract or law. The shareholders are still the 'legal' owners, but the written contracts leave them **few** or no residual rights. Shareholders' **rights** are not **residual**; instead, they are often strictly delimited and enumerated.

If any group could be considered to have residual control in a corporation, it might be the board of directors. They have the power to set dividends, to hire and fire the managers, to set the compensation of the senior executives, to decide to enter new lines of business, and to reject merger offers or instead approve and submit them to stockholders. If the directors have residual control rights, however, they do not have claims to all the residual returns. Let us take the case of bankruptcy. If a corporation is liquidated what will happen with the receipts? Debts and taxes have to be paid.

Many firms are financed by a combination **debt** and **equity**. The debt holders – banks, the purchasers of the firm's bonds, input suppliers who offer credit – are lenders. They provide cash in return for a promise to be repaid a fixed amount (perhaps with interest) at a later date. The equity holders get to keep whatever profits are left after paying the debt obligations. In a corporation, the equity is lodged with the shareholders, who elect the board of directors to represent their interest in setting policy and in a hiring manager to run the firm. However, **bankruptcy** can be seen as an institutional arrangement to protect the value of assets. Forcing a firm into bankruptcy is an ultimate measure. Once a firm is forced into involuntary bankruptcy, the creditors gain many of the *decision rights and control rights* that normally belong to equity holders or the managers. It also means the directors are not free to appropriate the profits for their own use because in the case of bankruptcy, they will not be able to capture the residual returns.

Based on the discussion above, the question is who really has the residual control rights and can capture the residual income; the shareholders or the board of directors?. A right that cannot be exercised is of no or little significance. For most purposes, the directors must rely on the officers of the firm. The manager and the employees provide them with the information needed to make decisions. By controlling the **flow of information** to the board and **setting** the agenda, the senior executives have **effective control over many decisions.** Moreover, the board members are chosen by the senior executives, and totally beholden to them. In return, the officers are dependent on the corporation's employees to develop the information in question and to carry out the decisions that are made. Sometimes, the plans of senior managers are highly resisted by lower-level employees. Perhaps the managers or senior executives are really the residual decision-makers. Maybe they have the **residual control rights** and are able to capture the **residual income.**

Box 9.4. Ownership is complex.

The question 'Who owns a large corporation'? is often difficult to answer. First, we have to deal with the question what is ownership? Ownership can be defined as having the residual control rights and the residual income rights. This would also be the answer if we follow the new property rights or the incomplete contract theory. The shareholders often do not have these rights. Second, the question 'Who owns a large corporation'? is also difficult to answer, because different types of stakeholders are involved in a large corporation: shareholders, board of directors, managers, employees, banks, input suppliers, buyers, etc, and a large corporation has also many assets. Different stakeholders have different interests, different types and levels of information and different rights. The question will be who has the residual control rights and the residual income rights? It means ownership can often be very fuzzy.

Having the **residual control rights** and **residual income** in a large corporation is a topic concerning the Corporate Governance. **Ownership** is defined by **residual control rights** and **residual income rights.** The idea of the owners being those with residual claims is not always fully satisfactory. If the residual claimants are not in a position to control the decisions that effect the value of the asset, then the incentive properties that have been claimed for ownership are certainly weakened. It may be **impossible** to identify any individual or group that is the unique residual claimant or to identify the benefits and costs of a decision and so compute the residuals.

Summarising, the situation is often **fuzzy** for a profit corporation. How does the concept of ownership apply to a university, a church, or another **non-profit organisation**? In such organisations, no private parties have a right to appropriate the residuals after debts are paid. Residuals must remain in the organisation, and if the organisation is dissolved, any remaining funds go to the state. If there is a residual claimant, it would be the state. However, the state does not have the residual control in such an organisation any more than it does in a profit organisation.

9.5 Whose interests should count?

This is an old discussion. Marx considered the origination of the public limited company as a step in the direction to socialism, because in this construction ownership became a collective character. However, most firms chose for the public limited company construction, because it was easier for them to recruit capital. The changes in the governance structures of large firms were originally charted by Berle and Means (1932), with their famous book 'The Modern Corporation and Private Property'. They found a separation between legal ownership and those who managed the firm. The study of Berle and Means (1932) confirmed this separation empirically and is considered as a starting point of the discussion of separation of legal ownership and management, and the question whose interest should count.

Nowadays we see a new development. Investment funds or hedge funds try to takeover parts of the shares of firms (e.g. Stork in 2006 and ABN Amro in 2007). By doing so, they try to get control over the firm. The next step is that they try to strip or split up the firms assets and sell off the best parts of the firm – or make other decisions creating high short-term profits. With the takeover of the strategic part of the shares of a company, investments funds or hedge funds do not have the intention of controlling the firm for a long time. The acquisition of the strategic part of the shares in a firm is only meant for realising short-terms profits. The only interests that count are those of the shareholders of the investment funds.

The conflict of interests between activistic shareholders and the firm is at odds with the stakeholder model[71]. Within this model, the management has a central position: it determines the strategy, but is tied to the interests and the continuity of the company, and it weighs the interests of all of the involved people in the company. Consequently, the stakeholder interests that comprise the firm as a whole, not only the interests of the shareholders, are considered. The stakeholders consist of the workers, shareholders, managers, input suppliers, clients and creditors (Mouthaan, 2007: 578). In this view, profit maximisation of a firm does not correspond with maximisation of the shareholders interests, but with maximisation of value of all the stakeholders (Baarsma and Theeuwes, 2008: 69).

This phenomenon is different from a hostile takeover which means the acquisition of enough of the shares in a public limited company to give controlling interests (ownership) in the firm. Successful hostile takeover attempts often result in the replacement of the target firm's senior management and the appointment of a new board of directors. Hostile takeovers can often be interpreted as a corrective response to managerial moral hazard: the takeovers displace managers who were pursuing their own interests at the expense of the shareholders.

Both examples point out a conflict of interests. These conflicts refer not only to shareholders and managers but also to the employees. One could argue that companies, and especially publicly held corporations, should not be run simply in the interests of their shareholders. People who agree with that consist of at least two groups: (1) the managers and employees of the corporations, and maybe other stakeholders such as banks and input suppliers; and (2) a variety of academics and activists who believe that the pursuit of profits is either socially inappropriate or immoral. Both groups may characterise stockholders as uninvolved, absentee owners with no loyalty to the firm and no concerns but their narrow selfish interests in short-term financial gains (an example is given in Box 9.5). They are either unworthy of having their interests predominate or incapable of realising where their long-term interests actually should lie. Instead, the company should pursue **social aims** or **should care for the interests of the all people who are actually involved in the organisation.**

Against these positions is another opinion proposed by investors (both private and institutional) along with the investment funds and stock-brokerage industries, as well as a set of free-market economists. This alliance argues that maximising the value of the firms enhances economic efficiency. Having managers pursue anything other than maximisation of the value of the firms entrusted to them is to invite calamitous self-serving moral hazard. What results is that the

---

[71] A central question in the stakeholder model is who should be included as a "stakeholder" ? For example, it may be argued that the people who are living in the surroundings of a factory and experience negative externalities should be included as stakeholders.

Box 9.5. ABN Amro.

ABN Amro was one of the largest banks in the Netherlands. In the beginning of 2007 an activistic hedge fund (named TCI; The Children's Investment Fund) which had less than 2% of shares, sent a letter to the shareholders in which it complained about the low profits (low dividends and low share prices) for the shareholders. It proposed to split up the ABN Amro and to sell the best parts of the firm to create high short-term profits for the shareholders. At the same time, the managers – perhaps under the pressure of the discussion among the shareholders as a result of the letter – started a merger procedure with Barclays Bank. At the end of April 2007, both ABN Amro and Barclay achieved an agreement. Meanwhile the share prices strongly increased, because of the rumours about merging the two firms. In the last week of April, another candidate-buyer emerged; a consortium consisting of Fortis, the Royal Bank of Scotland and Santander. The consortium offered a bid of 72.2 billion euro which was about 13% more than the bid of Barclays. However, in that case, the ABN Amro would be split up. This alternative had the preference of most of the shareholders (because of the higher value for the shareholders) and they went to the court to block the merger of ABN Amro and Barclays Bank. According to Business Law, shareholders have the right to be consulted. However, the Business Chamber of the court declared the request of the shareholders not admissible. In October 2007 Barclays Bank announced to withdraw his bid on the ABN Amro. The bid of the consortium was much higher and the take-over of the ABN Amro by the consortium was a fait accompli. However, interests of the workers, (lower) managers and other stakeholders were passed-by. The central question here is who is the owner and whose interests should count; those of the shareholders, those of the managers, those of the workers and/or those of other stakeholders?

managers will simply pursue their own interests, perhaps adjusted to account for the interests of their allies (Milgrom and Roberts, 1992: 316).

Ownership, externalities and corporate social responsibility.

In a system of complete, competitive markets, the arguments for running the firm to maximise profits or the value of the firm are largely undisputed. Similarly, if bargaining costs are low and property rights well established, secure and tradable, so that the Coase theorem would apply, there would be no basis for complaints about a firm pursuing the interests of its shareholders. Unfortunately we do not live in such a world (Milgrom and Roberts, 1992: 316).

In reality, the decisions that are made in firms can affect many different people in ways that the market as a governance structure does not adequately coordinate; i.e. the problems of market failures or externalities. Externalities, such as polluting the environment are one example. A firm that chooses to pollute may increase its value at others' expense, and this course of action is unlikely to promote overall efficiency when we cannot count on the mechanisms of bargaining to ensure that the firm recognises the full costs and benefits of its actions. Similarly, if the firm is dealing with unsophisticated, badly informed customers, it might maximise its gains while decreasing efficiency by selling them shoddy or even dangerous goods. In such situations, a social responsible course of action may be more efficient.

> ## Box 9.6. The role of activistic hedge funds.
>
> In Europe, the number of active hedge funds in the period 2000-2006 increased from about 250 to almost 1500 (Ter Weel, 2007: 401). During the last few years, a special group of hedge funds have drawn attention: the activistic hedge funds. These funds take positions in firms quoted on the stock exchange. They try to change the strategies of these firms or to sell important parts of these firms. For the Netherlands, the problems of activistic hedge funds are especially large, because Dutch companies have a relatively open shareholders structure. Therefore, they are more sensible for activistic funds. These funds go along with undervalued share prices, lack of focus (therefore it is possible to split up certain parts of the firm), much liquid assets (liquid capital), a stable cash flow and still available borrow capacity (gearing) (cf. Mouthaan, 2007: 574). Activistic hedge funds create a lot of commotion in firms such as Stork, ABN Amro and VNU. These funds aim for high short-term profits for the shareholders. They make clear that they have other interests than the managers or the workers in a firm.

The question is whether asking for such behaviour, or even realistic, might not bring unintended consequences. Suppose that the firm's managers are directed to promote social efficiency. Do they have the information to do so? How can they learn about the costs and benefits to other parties of various courses of action when there are neither prices nor explicit bargaining with the affected parties to guide them? How is all this monitored effectively, and by whom? Who has the information and the incentive to tell whether the managers who are not pursuing profits are behaving appropriately or are instead serving their owner interest? (Milgrom and Roberts, 1992: 316).

What are possible alternatives?

In many countries, private firms are regulated by law. This can be complemented or even substituted by building-in self-interest. As a result, people are doing things that are of interest to themselves. As explained in Chapter 7, these interests can vary from financial benefits to a *license to produce*. The latter is also connected to the concept of *responsible entrepreneurship*. In general, one understands that among these, a firm should not only think of economical value of the firm (mostly represented by the profit of the firm), but also of the social and ecological values as result of the firm's activities on social and ecological quantities. From this viewpoint, firms function in a socially responsible manner (*responsible entrepreneurship)* if the economic, social and ecological values that it produces fulfil the expectations of the stakeholders.This fits with the above mentioned corporate social responsibility.

Another alternative, but that is located at the other end of the spectrum, is in-house production of the government. The coordination mechanism is the visible hand applied by the government or a supervisor. Profit maximisation is not an objective, but the quality and accessibility of the provision of the services with public good characteristics are important, which often means the involvement of different interest groups (Baarsma and Theeuwes, 2008: 69). Sheifer (1998a: 11) concludes in his article about state versus private ownership that in four sets of circumstances government ownership is likely to be superior to private ownership:

1. opportunities for cost reductions that lead to non-contractible deterioration of the quality of the provision are significant;
2. innovation is relatively unimportant;
3. competition is weak and consumer choice is ineffective;
4. reputational mechanisms are also weak.

As explained in previous chapters, contracting out could be an in-between solution.

Box 9.7. Key concepts of Chapter 9.

Ownership as a bundle of property rights
Ownership as having residual control rights
   and residual income
Incentive effects of ownership
Economic meaning of ownership
Residual claimant
Team production
Full ownership solution
Ownership theory
Asset specificity
Non-contractibility
Complementary assets
Non-excludability and non-rivalry

Ownership of a project
Ownership of a public corporation
Stakeholders interest
Shareholders interest
Managerial moral hazard
Activistic hedge funds
Whose interests should count in a firm?
Corporate responsibilities
Responsible entrepreneurship
Government versus private ownership
Quality and accessibility of the provision of services
   with public good characteristics

10. The economics of property rights

10.1 Introduction

Property rights form an important part of the work of the NIE. In this chapter, we will first focus on two important approaches to the property rights theory. In the literature these approaches are called the old and new approach. We will address both approaches in Section 10.2, and show that both can be seen as complements to one another. In the **first** approach, which considers **property as a bundle of rights,** the rights are especially seen as a juridical matter with important economic consequences. In the **second** approach, the **new property rights theory** focuses on what it means to own or to have the property rights over an asset in an economic sense; it is the ability to exercise residual control rights over the asset and to have the residual income.

According to the Coase theorem, not only the types of property rights are important, but also the specification, delineating, allocation, assignment and enforcement of these rights. In addition to efficiency, we must also pay attention to the income distributional effects, or equity effect of property rights. Further it is important to know that in modern constitutional states and parliamentary democracies where laws and rules limit the government's monopoly of power, the government protects and enforces property rights, but it can also assign new property rights.

In Section 10.3 we will give a numerical example of the Coase theorem starting from a free or open access situation, i.e. there are no property rights defined. According to this theorem, it does not matter who will be granted the user rights of an asset as far as it concerns the allocation efficiency. For reasons of equity or income distribution effects, we can also assign the rights to the poorest group in our society. If the rights have been assigned and these rights are tradable, the Coase theorem assumes that negotiations will lead to efficient allocation of these rights. Yet, as we have already explained, transaction costs are important for the transfer of property rights.

Property rights only have a value and a function in the economic process if they are specified, protected, and enforceable. However, as explained in previous chapters, some goods are characterised by non-excludability. It is impossible to allocate (full) property rights to a non-excludable good. Consequently, the concept of 'excludability' has a direct relationship with property rights. In Section 10.4 we will discuss the concepts of excludability and rivalry, through which it is possible to classify goods and resources. In Section 10.5 we give some applied examples of property rights in practice; the tragedy of the commons, single ownership, and group ownership. Finally we conclude with some lessons from the Coase theorem and with the question of whether everything we see is efficient?

Key questions:
- What types of property rights theories can be distinguished and what are the differences?
- Why is it useful to combine both types of property rights theories for analysing the role of property rights and their effects;
- Which conditions have to be fulfiled for common property regimes to function well?
- Which factors determine the quality of a bundle of property rights, and which of these factors are related to the Coase theorem?

- What determines the validity of the Coase theorem?
- What types of goods can be distinguished and which characteristic of a good determines whether it is possible to allocate property rights?
- Which factors may prevent efficient agreements concerning property rights?
- What lessons can we learn from the Coase theorem and what are the alternatives?
- Do property rights only refer to economic efficiency or are other issues also important?

10.2 Property rights theory

10.2.1 Old and new property rights theory

Work on the economics of property rights flourished in the 1960s. Looking back on the last 40 years, property rights were viewed both as the conceptual key that unlocks many of the puzzles of economic organisation and as the means to realise superior economic performance (Williamson, 1998: 28). Nowadays, there are two important approaches to the property rights theory. The first one is called the old property rights theory and second one the new property rights theory.

In the **first** theory, property is seen as a juridical matter with important economic consequences. The central question in the **first** approach is: what does it mean to possess a good? Identifying the differences between the types of rights and property regimes, and analysing their effects is an important part of this approach. In this approach, property rights are conceptualised as social relations pertaining to the use of scarce resources, and supported (enforced) by formal laws, morals and customs of a social system (Foss and Foss, 2001: 21). Foss and Foss (2001: 21) name this approach the '**old property rights approach**'. Box 10.1 describes the origin of the old property right theory.

The **first** – or old property rights theory – approach deals with:
1. *Property as a bundle of rights;* In the case of *property as a bundle of rights,* property is seen as a set of rights. These rights describe what people may and may not do with resources; the extent to which they have them at their disposal, can use, transform, transfer them or exclude others from their property.
2. *Property regimes; Property regimes* refer to property systems for resources or for firms in a nation or in a region. Property regimes consist of government, private, common, or non-property regimes. A bundle of certain property rights is used within a certain property regime. The rules of the game within a certain property regime also determine how the game with the bundle of property rights can be played.

There are two important differences between *property as bundle of rights* and *property regimes.* A **first** difference is that *property regimes* are found at a higher aggregation level than property as a bundle of rights. As said, a bundle of certain property rights is used within a certain property regime. Property as a bundle of rights refers to the rights of an individual, which include the type of rights and permitted actions (e.g. the way a good may be used and the right to exclude others). A **second** important difference is that property regimes are not transferable via the market (this is because they are at a higher aggregation level, where the market is not used as a governance

Box 10.1. Central thesis of old property rights view.

Property rights are an important part of the work of New Institutional Economics. The origin of the work on property rights goes back to Coase (1960), Alchian (1965), Alchian (1967), Demsetz (1967) and Alchian and Demsetz (1972). The central thesis of the property rights view is that the particular structure of the property rights in an organisation (in the form of a team, firm, government organisation, etc.) or an economy influences the allocation and utilisation of assets in specific and predictable ways (Furubotn and Pejovich, 1972: 1139). As a result, ceteris paribus, the value of traded goods depends on how the property rights over these goods are defined. Since individuals try to maximise utility not only as consumers but also as members of organisations (e.g. private firms, government bureau, university), any change in the system of property rights will have a specific and predictable influence on the allocation of resources, the composition of the goods produced and the distribution of income. Therefore, lack of property rights or the 'taking' of them by the government, without any compensation, influences efficiency and equity.

structure) whereas the rights which make up part of the bundle of property rights are often tradable via the market.

The **second** approach is oriented towards: what does it mean to own an asset? The economic importance of ownership depends on the owner's ability to exercise residual control rights over the property rights and having the residual income. In many cases, the holder of residual control rights will, to a large extent, also have the residual income rights. Both are often complementary, therefore residual control and residual income often (should) go together. According to Foss and Foss (2001: 21) the new property rights theory is also named the incomplete contract theory. As explained, this theory starts from the basic idea that it is often difficult to write enforceable comprehensive contracts.

Central in this approach is the question of who has the *residual control rights* and the *residual income rights*. Having the *residual control rights* is the right to make any decision concerning an asset that is not explicitly controlled by law or assigned to another person (or organisation) by contract. The *residual income rights* are related to residual income, which is the amount that remains from the gross-return of a company, activity, good or service after all the remaining contractual commitments are fulfiled.

Properties (and property rights) are seen as the possibility to practice *residual control rights* and to capture or appropriate the residual income. The opposite is perhaps more important: those who can practice the *residual control rights* and capture the residual income can be considered as the owners. The problem is that, in practice, *residual control rights and residual income* can be quite fuzzy and vague concepts. The same holds for the allocation of residual control and residual income rights.

Tying together residual control and residual income is the key incentive for an efficient use of a bundle of property rights. These effects are very powerful because (at least in simple cases) the decision-maker bears the full financial impact of his or her choices. Consequently, when it is possible for a single individual to have both the residual control and the residual income,

Box 10.2. The emergence of property rights.

In historical terms, property rights may be viewed as a response to scarcity. In primitive economics, characterised by small numbers of inhabitants, it was usually possible for individuals to use the resources available without having many conflicts in terms of rights of access. Grazing land, for example, was probably not fenced or 'defended'. Population growth, together with advances in technology, gave rise to a more intensive use of resources, and land in particular. This tended to give rise to both more frequent disputes about resource use and to 'over-utilisation' of certain scarce resources. Higher and also more sustainable levels of output means that ways must be found to avoid these disputes and over-utilisation. It can be argued that the most efficient way (at least in a strictly economic sense) is a system of private property rights (cf. Whynes and Bowles, 1981: 33).

The pioneers in the field of property rights focused primarily on the role of property rights within organisations such as firms and within team production. Important questions that they raised were who bears the costs within an institutional arrangement, who receives the profits and who has the right to, or power over, the net-profits? Demsetz (1967: 347-348) points to the close relationship between property rights and external effects, and the function of property rights: 'A *primary function of property rights is that of guiding incentives to achieve a greater internalisation of externalities'*. This relation and the function of property rights with respect to environmental issues and the use of natural resources, has received considerable attention in recent literature.

the residual decisions made will tend to be efficient ones. Generally speaking, for efficient and effective use of a bundle of property rights, properly combining the two aspects is required: the **residual control rights** and the **residual income**.

10.2.2 Property as a bundle of rights

The most common view on *property* considers only *the legal meaning of a bundle of rights*. These rights describe what people may or may not do with resources; the extent in which they have these resources at their disposal, may use them, transform or transfer them, or exclude others from their property. These rights are not fixed, they may change from one generation to the next (Cooter and Ulen, 1997: 72). This is expressed, among other things, in the way the government recognises and protects property rights. An important viewpoint in this approach is that property is a juridical matter, but this often disregards important economic consequences.

There are various categories of property rights. Generally, the bundle of rights of full asset ownership consists of five elements: (a) the right to use the asset (usus), (b) the right to appropriate the returns from the asset (usus fructus), (c) the right to change the form, substance, and location of the asset (abusus), (d) the right to exclude others; and (e) the right of transfer to others through markets or to their inheritances. Element (d) means that property rights define the manner by which the owner can prevent others from making use of his property, or in specific cases who may or may not be excluded from the property. The last element (e) implies that the owner has the freedom to transfer all his property rights (e.g. to sell a house), or some property rights (e.g.

to rent out a house) in assets to another individual at a mutually agreed upon price[72]. Table 10.1 gives a short overview of the rights and its naming based on the above-mentioned arguments (cf. Furuboth and Richter, 1991: 6; 1997: 16; 2005: 20).

Property rights mostly have a broader scope than ownership. Furubotn and Richter (1997: 5; 2005: 5) define property rights as follows: 'Property rights, in the economist's wide sense of the term, embrace the rights to use and to gain benefits from physical objects or intellectual works and the rights to demand certain behaviour from other individuals'. They (1997: 16; 2005: 20) outlined the basic elements of their property rights approach as given in Table 10.1. Furuboth and Richter (1997: 77; 2005: 85) make a distinction between absolute property rights, such as ownership of physical and intangible assets, and relative property rights, such as contracts. In fact, ownership rights can only be considered as absolute property rights to physical objects.

The concepts of property, ownership and possession often lead to confusion. They could be different. Property rights are a condition for economic exchange. They give incentive for economic initiatives and are therefore a condition for economic growth. Property does not always imply possession or ownership. Only in the case of private property of private goods we can speak of possession[73]. Possession only concerns assets and cannot be extended to human beings (leaving slavery out of consideration).

As appears from Table 10.1, property rights have certain characteristics, among which is the possibility of transfer via the market. Furthermore, they can be set up by the government as a policy instrument to realise certain goals. Important questions then are: who receives the rights, who will receive effective protection from the government, and how will that be implemented? Property rights indicate who must pay whom in order to control the benefits that flow from these

---

[72] Eggertsson (1990: 34) distinguishes three categories of property rights: first, the rights to use an asset, including the right to physically transform it; second, the right to earn income from an asset and to enter into agreements with other individuals involving the asset; and third, the right to permanently transfer ownership rights over an asset to another party – that is, to alienate or sell an asset.

[73] Individuals in a marital relationship refer to my wife, my husband or my children. But this does not mean that the man is the owner of his wife. Together they have children, but the children are not their property. In fact, ownership can only be considered as absolute property rights to physical object or animals. With pure public goods, there is no private ownership or possession.

Table 10.1. Rights of a bundle of property rights.

Description	Type of right	Latin name
The right to use the asset	User rights	*Uses*
The right to capture the returns of the asset	Income rights	*Usus fructus*
The right to change the form, substance and location of the asset	Alteration rights	*Abusus*
The right to exclude others from the use of the asset, or in certain cases who can and who cannot be excluded from the property	Exclusion rights	
The right to transfer the asset to others through market, or to heirs through inheritance	Transfer rights	

rights. As explained in Box 9.3, the Coase theory states that regardless to whom the rights are assigned, trade in the rights internalises the value of these rights and leads to an optimal Pareto situation (see Section 10.3).

Rights can only be effective if there is an authority in place prepared to protect or enforce the interests of rights holder in certain specific situations. In Western countries this is mostly the government. This means that a person in a specific situation has a right to turn to the government (in this case external enforcer) to make sure the claim on the right is protected. The effective protection, which he obtains from the authority, is merely the correlated duty for all others who are interested in his right. This means rights refer not so much to the relation between a person and an object, but much more to the relations between the concerned persons and others in relation to that object.

The meaning of having ownership should include the control rights over (a part of) the bundle of property rights, for example over a benefit or an income-stream. Whether the rights – mentioned in Table 10.1 – are valid in practice is a part of the analysis. The **first** reason why these rights do not always hold could be (the quality of) the type of bundle of property right and a **second** reason the way how property rights are specified, granted or allocated and protected. More in general, property rights can provide an answer to five fundamental questions (cf. Cooter and Ulen, 1997: 71-72):

1. What types of property rights can be distinguished and established?
2. What can be privately owned?
3. What may owners do with their property?
4. What are the effects of property rights?
5. What are the remedies for the violation of property?

10.2.3 Synthesis of old and new property rights approaches

The old property rights approach (a bundle of rights) assumes: (1) the rights of the property holder and obligations of the other people in relation to the object are at the forefront; (2) they are instrumental by nature; and (3) they are protected by the government.

With the new property rights approach, the **economic meaning of property** refers to 'having control over an asset and having the residual income at one's disposal'. The question: **what does it mean to be an owner?** is crucial here. The answer is determined by the residual control rights, but more by the ability to appropriate the residual income. Having the residual rights of control but no access to the residual income makes ownership an empty concept.

These two approaches are not so much a matter of a contrast, but rather, they can be seen as being complementary. The pioneers in this area (see Box 10.1) focused on the role of property rights within organisations like firms, and within team production. A number of important questions are: who bears the costs within an institutional arrangement, to whom do the returns accrue and who has right to these, or the power over the net-yield? This often refers to the marketable costs and benefits.

The approach based on the new property rights theory is focussed on residual control rights and residual income. Both are powerful concepts for analysing the incentive and distributional effects of property rights. This is expressed in having the residual control rights over a bundle of property rights and having rights to the residual income; without both sets of rights, ownership over a bundle of property rights is meaningless.

A number of examples will make clear that it is important to make use of both approaches and that they can be seen as being complementary. They are two sides of the same coin. The **first** example is the old classical capitalistic firm. In a such firm the owner has: (1) full *control rights* (i.e. final authority over all of the policies pursued by the firm); (2) full *income rights* (i.e. the non-restricted right to the firm's residual), and (3) full *transfer rights* (i.e. complete freedom to assign his rights, in whole or in part, to others) over all the assets (cf. Furuboth, 2002: 84). The owner of a capitalistic firm has therefore not only the bundle of property rights but also the right to the residual income. This means that in the case of private property (= property regime) the bundle of property rights (with all rights) is completely allocated to one person. This person also has the *residual rights of control* and the *residual income* at his disposal.

A **second** example concerns a firm with more owners such as a Public limited company (Plc). A Plc is as an enterprise private property (= property regime). However, in this case private property does not coincide with individual property. The bundles of property rights of all assets do not belong to one person. After all, different groups of people such as shareholders, managers, commissioners, employees, external capital providers, suppliers and buyers are involved in the exchange of assets (cf. Kerkmeester and Holzhauer, 2000: 13). It is an organisation in which various parties (also called stakeholders) are working together. There is not one person who has the user right, the right to capture the profits, the right of changing the form, substance and location of assets that are used in the firm, or the right to exclude others and the transfer rights.

Similarly, the shareholders[74] can not hire and fire people. In modern large firms, the shareholders (= owners in a juridical sense) are no longer the ones who have, or practise, the power of decision-making (Kerkmeester and Holzhauer, 2000: 78). This brings up the question of who is the owner of a firm such as a public corporation? To answer this question, it is better to make use of the concepts **having residual control rights** and **residual income** for determining the ownership of such firms or organisations. The ability to have the residual control rights and to capture the residual income determines *in fact* which people, or groups of people, are the owners. This example shows the strong relationship between ownership as explained in Chapter 9 and the bundle of property rights.

A **third** example is the leasing of land. In the old classical capitalistic firm approach, the owner of a large agricultural farm has the complete control rights over all production means, the complete control rights over the residual income and complete transfer rights. With the leasing of the land to a tenant-farmer, the landowner transfers a part of the bundle of property rights to the tenant. It concerns the control rights over a part of the bundle of property rights, including the income

---

[74] Reality teaches us that shareholders are mostly not the ones who have the residual control rights in a Plc nor are they able to appropriate the residual income.

rights (see Table 10.1). Leasing out (a part of) the bundle of property rights to another party is a two-sided transaction mechanism: the transfer of (a part of) the bundle of property rights versus the counter performance (quid pro quo). The counter performance is the lease price being paid. For land, as well as for many other assets, it is possible to lease the user rights out to another party for a certain period of time, without leasing out the full transfer rights, which include the right to 'sell' the asset.

Also very important in a tenant-landowner relationship are the *residual control rights* and the *residual income*, because those who have the residual control rights can often capture the residual income. There are different types of residual incomes for land and land related production and income rights:
1. The residual income in the short-term arising from current land use.
2. The long-term residual income arising through the increase in the value of the land.
3. The value (plus increase) of the production rights[75] and the income rights (such as the single farm payments (SFP)[76].

Ex-ante (before the transaction), it is often very difficult to foresee who will have the residual control rights and the residual income. As explained in Section 7.2, the *ex-post* results in terms of residual income, are often more evident than those for the residual control rights.

The person who can capture the residual income often differs. In the case of land, the short-term residual income goes to the farmer-tenant who generates marketable products, while the long-term residual income arising from the increased value of the land, the residual income in terms of the value of the production rights, and the income rights of the SFP, all accrue to the landowner. However, recently the tenants got a right to a fifty/fifty compensation of the value of production and income rights, see footnote 75 and 76.

Based on above we can state that the landowner has the residual control rights, because he can decide whether or not to sell the assets and he is able to capture the residual income described in (1) and (2). However, the decision to sell the land, and the production of income rights are

---

[75] In the agriculture, the introduction of production rights for milk (introduced in 1984), sugar and manure has led to the origin of new property rights. The production quota connected with these rights are transferable and represent a value. Concerning the milk quota, the tenant is obliged to return the milk quota in full to the landowner at the end of the lease-contract. The tenant has a right to a fifty/fifty compensation of the value of this production rights.

[76] The SFP was introduced January 2006. In the Netherlands, the discussion about the ownership of the SFP lasted more than one and a half year. On September 25th 2007 the Agricultural Land Tribunal decided that the rights on SFP – after the end of the lease agreement – belong to the landowner. However, the tenant has a right to a fifty/fifty compensation of the value of these SFP. In Spring 2008, it became clear that the European Commission did not agree with this judgment: 'A landowner who leases out his land would, in our opinion, not have any say in what happens to payment entitlements allocated to his tenant, not even on expiry of the lease agreement' (Min. LNV, 25th March 2008: 1-2). Tenants have a strong argument for a new procedure to the European Court of Justice about the ownership of these rights. This example illustrates the complexity of ownership and the importance of opening the 'black box' of property rights.

Box 10.3. Renting of asset by an owner and the value of an asset.

The option to rent out a part of the bundle property rights and the way in which it is done, is important for the value of an asset (e.g. a house or a plot of land). Concluding lease contracts between an owner and a tenant means that a part of the bundle of property rights is transferred for a given period of time. The type of contract also determines the value of a bundle of property rights that is left over for the landowner. It means that the contract specifies the allocation of the property rights over the land between the landowner and the tenant. For instance, an expected increase in the value of the *transfer right* consisting of 'selling an asset without a user', in the short run, makes a short-term contract more attractive compared to a long-term contract, because in a short-term contract the owner will earlier have the possibility to sell the land or house 'without a user'.

The value of lease contracts for the landowners depends on the content of the bundle of property rights. The more control rights for the landowner, the less protection for the tenant, the shorter the duration of the contract, the higher flexibility of the contract, and the higher the level of property rights transferability, the higher is the value of the bundle of property rights for the landowner (Slangen and Polman, 2008).

Box 10.4. Residual control rights and residual income conferred on one person or firm.

Hart (1995: 64-65) gives two arguments why *residual income* and *residual control rights* should both be conferred on just one person or organisation. First, if *residual income* and *residual control rights* are separated, then a *hold-up problem* arises. Briefly, if *control rights* and *income rights* are to a great degree complementary, then it is efficient to allocate both to one and the same person. Second, in some situations the return of an asset can consist of two components: a short-term income generated by current activities and a long-term component resulting from the value-appreciation of the asset. The long-term income accrues to the person who has *control rights*, because he can decide whether or not to sell the asset. The short-term income accrues to the person who *uses the asset*. This person will attempt to maximise this income, without regarding the long-term value of the asset. (This person actually has no control rights.) This can be an inefficient outcome. It is better to combine the *short-term income rights* with the *control rights* (see also Section 7.2).

restricted [77]. Given the price increase of land and the value of land-bound production and income rights, these types of (long-term) residual income for the landowner are substantial.

When both residual control rights and residual incomes are notably large, there is some strong pressure present by efficiency considerations to unite both incomes in one person. In practice, it appears that the value of the land-bound production rights and the appreciation of the land prices are important *incentives* for the tenant-farmer (= land user) to unite the use and ownership of land to one person, by becoming the land user/owner. This is especially true when the land

---

[77] This means that the law restricts the control rights of the landowner. For example, according to the Dutch lease regulation, in the case of a land sale, the tenant has a priority right to purchase the land. In case of a sale of the production and income rights, the landowner has to compensate the tenant, see footnote 75 and 76.

Box 10.5. Land use concepts as basis for new institutional arrangements.

Land lease is an age-old phenomenon. It has been the basis for important economic theories: for example, the theories of Ricardo and Von Thünen. Modes of organisation such as joint ventures, and franchising have their basis in concepts such as sharecropping and fixed lease price contracts. In many text books, the application of the principal-agent approach is explained by taking the following setting: the principal is an owner of a plot of land and the agent wants to use the land. For analyzing the effects of the reward structure on the behaviour of an agent, different settings can be chosen: sharecropping or fixed lease price contracts. Both have different effects. New theories such as incomplete contract theory or the new property rights theory increase the insights in this exchange phenomenon.

---

user/tenant can buy the land against the leased value (by making use of his priority right)[78] The purchase of leased land is a possibility for the tenant to appropriate this residual income. Because of a large price difference between the non-leased and leased value, the size of the residual income is noteworthy.

According to the two property rights approaches, it becomes clear that property rights, resources and technology exercise a direct effect on the alternatives open to decision choices of individuals in society. Moreover, the property rights approaches open a method of analysis that can be applied to a wide range of different organisational structures. Thus, the themes that appear in discussions on the *'classic capitalistic firms'* (Alchian and Demsetz 1972: 783) are repeated, with certain variations, in other areas. In each instance, we often have to deal with: (1) combined input; (2) various input-suppliers; (3) one party who knows all contracts for the combined input; (4) one party who has the right to renegotiate over each input-contract, independent of the contracts with other input-suppliers; (5) the question who has the *residual control right*, and who is able to appropriate the *residual income?* and (6) the question who has the right to sells the rights which define the property of the object?

10.2.4 Four property regimes

In Section 10.2, we defined the differences between a bundle of property rights and property regimes. Both belong to the old property rights theory. According to Bromley (1991: 23), four possible property regimes can be distinguished:
1. government property regimes;
2. private property regimes;
3. common property regimes;
4. non-property regimes.

With a *government property regime* the control over the bundle of property rights mentioned in Table 10.1 is in the hands of the government. For firms and natural resources, including land, the government can leave the management, financing, production and exploitation with government firms or government agencies. Individuals and groups may be able to make use of

---

[78] In the Netherlands, this right is part of the lease regulation for regular lease contracts.

natural resources, but only at the forbearance of the government. The government can rent out the natural resources to groups of individuals and offer them the *usus* and *usus fructus* for a certain period of time, for example. Government or state property regimes, remove most managerial discretion from the user, and generally convey no long-term expectations in terms of tenure security. With government property regimes, the user's freedom of management is often limited or barely present (Bromley, 1991: 23).

The *private property regime* is found at the other end of the spectrum and is the most well known regime. Private property[79] is the legal and social permitted right to exclude others, permitting the owner to force others to go elsewhere. Private property does not always coincide with individual ownership. With a partnership, a limited partnership company, public limited company (Plc.) or a limited liability company (Ltd.) there is private property; often several individuals are involved as owners. It is a cooperative relationship of various interested stakeholders, and is managed as a group.

For example, a public limited company is a private property enterprise, but is a cooperative venture of parties with diverse interests and is managed and administrated as a group. It appears to be obvious to consider private property as the complete and absolute 'control rights' over the complete bundle of property rights over assets granted to the owner. An owner is often confronted with all types of restrictions and obligations. The positive results of the private control over land and related natural resources is a result of the fact that the individual (or group) owner can take management decisions and make investments with the knowledge that good management will result in a private reward (cf. Bromley, 1991: 24-25).

The third regime is *common property*. Firstly, common property represents private property for the group of co-owners. All others are excluded from decision-making and use. Secondly, individuals have rights and duties in a common property regime, where the exclusion of non-owners is the common factor with private property. Common property can be seen as a collective group property or a corporate group-property. The property-owning groups vary in nature, size, and internal structure across a broad spectrum, but they are social units with definite membership and boundaries, with certain common interests, with at least some interaction between the members, with some common cultural values and norms, and often with their own endogenous authority system (Bromley, 1991: 26).

In order for a common property regime by group ownership to function well, it is necessary that the behaviours of all members of the group are subject to accepted rules and open for all to observe. Conformity with group norms at the local level is an effective mechanism against anti-social behaviour. A viable common property regime has a built-in structure of economic and non-economic incentives that encourage compliance to conventions and rules. Unfortunately, in many settings, those rules and incentives have become inoperative – or dysfunctional – largely

---

[79] Private property is not necessarily theft, as Proudhon put it, but a good deal of theft has ended up as private property rights. This is especially true in the western world where European colonisers appropriated vast terrain inhabited by tribal peoples (Bromley, 1991: 25).

because of pressures and forces beyond the control of the group, or because of internal processes that the groups were not able to master (Bromley, 1991: 27).

Essential for any property regime is an authority system that is able to ensure that the expectations of rights holders are met. Compliance, protection and enforcement by an authority system is a necessary condition for the viability of any property regime. Private property would be nothing without the requisite authority system to make certain that rights and duties are adhered to. The same requirements hold also for common property. If the authority system does not function well or if it breaks down – for whatever reason – then the management, or self-management of the resource use cannot be exercised any longer. Common property in that case degenerates into 'open access' (Bromley, 1991: 27).

Property rights in terms of a bundle of rights (in this case common or shared rights) are not the only important elements for compliance and 'wise use' of natural resources. The *common property regime* as a system is broader than the set of possession entitlements that is its core. It also includes user's rights, exchange rights, distribution of entitlements/rights, a management sub-system and authority instruments as means of management. When any part of this complex system is undermined or destroyed, the entire system malfunctions up to a degree at which it ceases to be what it was (Bromley, 1991: 27-28).

According to Bromley (1991: 28), there are two problems related to the *common property regime*. First, a breakdown in compliance by co-owners may be difficult to prevent. When due to developments elsewhere in the economy, the co-owners have hardly any alternatives, maintaining the rules of property regime will lead to loss of opportunities. For example, the process of privatising the common resource, meaning individual use rights rather than collective use rights, may not coincide with the characteristics of the resource. If such a process prevents seasonal adaptation to fluctuating resource conditions then overuse of a local resource by members of the group might result. Secondly, if the government holds common property in low esteem – that is – if the government disregards the interests of those segments of the population largely dependent upon common property resources – then external threats to common property will not receive the same governmental response as would a threat to private property. The willingness of the government to protect and enforce the *common property regime* is smaller than with private property regimes

According to Bromley (1991: 29), *private property regimes* are more stable and can adapt better. They have the social and legal mechanisms required to exclude others (e.g. because of excess population) and can effectively resist unwanted intrusions due to the power of the government behind them. This power has often been eroded for common property regimes. Common property is in essence 'private' property for the group. It is a group-decision regarding whom shall be excluded. The difference between private and common property regimes is not to be found in the nature of the rights and duties as much as in the number of people to which inclusion or exclusion applies.

In the *open access-regime* there is no ownership. Because there are no property rights, it is often said: *'everybody's property is nobody's property'*. The willingness to invest in or to improve resources depends on their institutional dimension. If property and management are not determined, investment in the form of a capital-good will not take place. Because of the institutional vacuum of *open access*, a user's level resulting in the exhaustion of the natural resources exists. *Open access* results from the absence, or the breakdown, of a management or authority system whose very purposes was to introduce and enforce a set of norms of behaviour among the participants with respect to that particular natural resource. When valuable natural resources are available to the first party to effect capture, these resources become *open access* because: (1) these natural resources have never been incorporated in the regulated social system or; (2) due to the institutional failure that have undermined former collective or individual management regimes (cf. Bromley, 1991: 30).

The four types of property regimes are described in Table 10.2. A major distinction among the first three is the decision-making process. In the private property regime, usually the private owner decides what shall be done. The common property regime requires consensus among all the co-owners before a specific action can be taken. The **transaction costs** associated with this and the solution of the **problem of group-size** and **free riding** are seen as disadvantages of the common property regime (cf. Bromley, 1991: 31).

In a situation with *open access*, each potential user has the complete autonomy to use the resource since no-one has the legal ability to exclude potential users and to keep them out. The natural resource is subject to the rules of capture and belongs to no-one until it is in someone's possession. In the case of air-pollution, in the absence of regulation, the polluter has the privilege to pollute the air, and others have no rights. When pollution is made illegal, polluters have a duty, while others now have a right. In open-access fishing, the fish belongs to the party that catches it. There are no property rights in this regime, only possession (cf. Bromley, 1991: 32).

Table 10.2. Four types of property regimes (Bromley, 1991: 31).

Government property	Individuals have a *duty* to observe use/access rules determined by controlling/managing government agency. Government agencies have the *right* to determine the use and access rules
Private property	Individuals have the *right* to undertake socially acceptable uses, and have the *duty* to refrain from socially unacceptable uses. Others (called 'non-owners') have the *duty* to refrain from preventing socially acceptable uses, and have the *right* to expect that only socially acceptable uses will occur
Common property	The management group (the 'owners') has the *right* to exclude non-members, and non-members have the *duty* to abide by exclusion. Individual members of the management group (the 'co-owners') have both *rights* and *duties* with respect to use rates and maintenance of the thing owned
Non property	There is no defined group of users or 'owners' and no benefit stream is available to anyone. Individuals have both *privilege* and *no right* with respect to use rates and maintenance of the asset. The asset is an 'open access resource'

With common property forests, pasture land, fisheries, etc. some natural resource degradation arises from population growth within the social unit having rights to the resource. The entailed increase in the use of the given natural resources cannot be stopped (or only with difficulty) because of the nominal right of every villager to take what he/she needs to survive. The ability of the renewable natural resources to grow annually to add to the assets – or to sustain its annual yield – is then doubtful, or there may even be a depletion of the resource. If the group or village believes that everyone from the larger population has the right to take what he or she requires, in a situation where the supply of the resource remains stable (or declines), then it is obvious that very soon the right to expropriate this natural resource for the inhabitants cannot be satisfied any longer. He/she can only take this right if he/she can capture it by being first. Situations where the right of every inhabitant cannot be honoured place a burden on existing institutions. Failure to deal appropriately with the change in **group-size** affects equilibrium and integrity of the system. Because of that the effectiveness of the rules and conventions in regulating the total use is undermined. A common property regime for the group then becomes an *open access* regime for those within this group (Bromley, 1991: 32).

A condition to bring about improvement in a situation of *open access* is the introduction of another property regime. Converting an open access situation into another property system is a complex process. Which regime is preferred depends on: (1) the nature of the resource itself; (2) the demand and supply conditions of the resource; (3) the characteristics of the users of the resources; and (4) the characteristics of the legal, political and institutional environment in which the users reside. With respect to the nature of the resource, if *open access* is to be converted to an effective common property regime, the important conditions are: the existence of clear resource boundaries, small (manageable) resource size and scope, and accessible information about the conditions of the resource. For the demand and supply conditions, the relative scarcity in the light of demand is important. Regarding the characteristics of the users, the conversion of an *open access* into an open common property regime is easier if: (a) the size of the group is relatively small; (b) the users are homogenous; and (c) the users live in the neighbourhood of the resource (Bromley, 1991: 33-34).

10.2.5 The quality of bundle of property rights

The quality of the rights can refer to the content or the value of the bundle of the rights or a part of it, such as the user rights. An important difference between renting and full ownership is the control rights over the bundle of property rights connected to an asset. This holds for a house, an office or a plot of land. In the classical *capitalistic firm approach,* the owner of the farm has the full control rights over all means of production, the full control rights over the residual income and the full transfer rights (cf. Furuboth, 2002: 84).

A landowner who would not like to use his land as a farmer for different reasons can lease out his land. However, leasing out land to a tenant-farmer means that the landowner transfers these rights, in part or almost entirely, to the tenant, mostly on a contractual basis. It means he will lose a part of the bundle of property rights. Intriguing questions are: (1) who has the control rights in incomplete contracts such as lease contracts; (2) what does leasing out under different types of lease contracts mean for the right of transfer; (3) how do landowners value the different bundles of property rights connected with a lease contract for a plot of land or a house; (4) what is the value of a rented house or office and to what extent does the value for sale depend on the type of the lease contract?

Important for the quality of the bundle of property rights is also the institutional environment, consisting of the informal and formal rules in the society, for example the lease regulation. The informal and formal rules also determine the level of theft. The quality of the property rights is influenced by the level of theft. Theft is a not only transfer of an asset, but it has also a direct efficiency consequence, because, a high level of theft means weak or insecure property rights. It also brings a society in a hold-up situation. The reluctance to invest when property rights are insecure results in inadequate maintenance and development of assets.

Furthermore, for the quality of the bundle of property rights, the way people think about status and the allocation of the property rights is also important. The institutional environment – in which the property rights are embedded – is not a constant factor, nor is the status and the allocation of the property rights. Property rights are a bundle of rights. These rights describe what people may and may not do with certain resources: the extent in which they may have these resources at their disposal, use, transform or transfer them, or exclude others from their property. Because of the changes in the institutional environment, these rights are not fixed; they may change from one generation to another. This is revealed in the way that the government recognises and protects property rights.

The status and allocation of the property rights can also change as a result of shifting of people's preferences. For example, citizens are feeling that the environmental quality (e.g. greenhouse problems) is going to decline, and they want to prevent this. This is revealed in a shift of people's preferences. Shifting preferences lead to a change in the *optimal level* of environmental quality. This means that by shifting preferences the *reference level* also changes. The status quo of property rights arrangements which have served agriculture so well exist for historical reasons and may not necessarily be appropriate for the future. Shifting values and changing perceptions of the role of agriculture will surely bring about a shift in property rights and policy entitlement.

When the government or another organisation takes away a part of the bundle of property rights of a resource from a specific person or a group without compensation, it has an adverse effect on property rights. In Chapter 11 we will extensively discuss *titular takings* and *regulatory takings* including the question of what extent must the original owner or user be compensated?

The quality of the bundle of property rights influences the level of transaction costs also. For example, a low degree of excludability of goods and services is a characteristic that arises from a lack of property rights (Boadway and Bruce, 1989: 110). Allocating property rights to these types of goods and services would involve huge transaction costs. A low protection and enforceability of property rights will also involve higher transaction costs. This means there is a relationship between the quality of the property rights and transaction costs. The quality of the bundle of property rights can be described in terms of:

- **Degree of control rights**

  In general, control rights are rights to make any decisions concerning use, returns or transfer of an asset, and the right to exclude others. These control rights consist of (1) specific control rights and (2) residual control rights. The specific control rights are those rights specified by law or by contract. Rights specified by law can be very important[80], because they limit the residual control rights.

  For example, concerning property rights over land, control rights indicate to which level a person has the right to make any decisions on the bundle of property rights of land and land related property rights. A lease contract involves a transfer of control rights over (a part of) the bundle of property rights of land and land related rights. The introduction of production rights (for milk, sugar and manure) and income rights (the SFP) has led to the question who has the control rights over these new property rights. The residual control rights are important, because those who have the residual control rights can often capture the residual income.

- **Division of rights**

  Property rights can be considered as a bundle of rights. From this bundle, certain rights can be separated out. For many resources, the user's rights can be separated out from the bundle of property rights. Land, houses, buildings and offices can be leased or rented. For example, for land or a house the user's rights can be separated from the bundle of property rights attached to land or a house. The property rights that a tenant leases mainly consist of user rights. His right to transfer and the right to exclude others are much more restricted than those of an owner/user. This affects the (residual) control rights and the residual incomes of land or houses for tenant/user and owner/user and thus the ways in which the existing property rights are valued.

  The level to which certain rights can be separated out also depends on the degree of excludability. This refers to the extent to which the rights are exclusive, i.e. to what extent can others be excluded from use. The lack of excludability leads to incompleteness of property rights. Firstly, there can be shared or common property rights; two or more individuals together have the property rights of an asset. Secondly, the incomplete divisibility of the property rights means that some attributes cannot be specified in excludable rights for individual property right holders. The result of these effects is that some attributes are lying in what Barzel (1997: 5) calls the 'public domain'. This causes the free-rider problem.

- **Protection of the rights**

  Property rights can be created by the government, and in such a form that they can function as a policy instrument for achieving certain goals. Important questions are: who gets these rights and who will get the effective protection from the government? Property rights also indicate who must pay to whom in order to have access to the interests that are issued from the rights. Important aspects are: to what extent are the rights respected, can they be enforced, are individuals compensated for a loss of a right and to what extent can the rights serve as a basis for a loan in the economic process? All these questions determine the quality of the rights.

---

[80] For example, see footnote 6.

Box 10.6. Reference level and protection of property rights.

The increased concern for the environment is linked to the relationship between the status and allocation of private property rights between firms (including farmers), the government and the *reference-level*. The *reference-level* can be defined as the level of quality of the environment that the society feels should be present. The *reference-level* can also be the *status quo situation*, or a standard or expectation of the provision-level of an environmental good. In other words, it all depends on what people find 'normal' or think it should be.

Through shifting of citizens' preferences, also the *reference-level* changes and hereby also the opinion and attitude of the allocation of property rights between firms and the government changes. If the *reference-level* of a society for the quality of the environment rises (the measuring rod is at a higher level), the property rights of these goods will be situated more in the public domain. The result is that people feel that environmental goods belong more to the society, even though they are located e.g. on the land of the farmers. Through such a shift in preferences the allocation of property rights is not fixed. Through changes in allocation of the property rights, the relative control rights of farmers on the use of their land diminish. Farmers will say: this *is my land; I have the full property rights*. Through the characteristics – non-rivalry and (to a certain extent) non-excludability – wildlife and landscape are not pure private goods however. Citizens will for this reason, and also because of the shifting of ownership rights, say: it *is my wildlife and landscape*. This has definite consequences for the value of property rights of certain assets.

- **Duration**
  Is the disposal of a bundle of property rights of asset (or part of it) restricted to a specific period, and if so to what period? The periods for which (part of) the property rights of an asset are leased out or rented can diverge strongly. The duration of land-use contracts for a farmstead is 12 years and for plots of land it can, at least in the Netherlands, vary from 6 years to one year. For other assets like houses or offices, the duration can diverge strongly. The duration has consequences for quality of the rights. Mostly, the duration has an inverse effect on the value of the bundle of property rights over the land of the landowner.

- **Flexibility**
  Flexibility refers to the formal rules of the institutional environment. Are there changes in these rules? For land, houses and offices, the flexibility is determined, for example, by the lease regulation. What consequences does a change or an adaptation of the formals rules have for the regulation and by that for the flexibility? Which changes appear in all rights or in the rights concerning land leases for example, and what does that mean for inheritance and ownership? Furthermore, a change in the norms and values in a society can affect the formal rules and by that the flexibility.

- **Enforceability**
  The enforcement of property rights makes it possible to exclude others from use. Exclusive ownership requires expensive measures for the delineation of resources and enforcement of property rights. The value of exclusive property rights depends, ceteris paribus, on the costs of enforcement of the rights, in this case, the cost of excluding others. This ultimately depends on

the deployment of force. Individuals as well as the government usually undertake enforcement of exclusive property rights. Enforcement by the government increases the value of privately owned assets and constitutes one of the corner stones of the market-economy. In areas where the government does not help to enforce contracts, or even property rights, this outright prohibits possession and exchange, due to high transaction costs. The costs of enforcement of exclusive rights are lower if the population follows the social norms, which coincide with the basic structure of rights that the government attempts to maintain. The disintegration of social norms can have important economic consequences (cf. Eggertsson, 1990: 35).

- **Degree of transferability**

  To what extent and how are the property rights transferable – partly or fully – from one party to another party, e.g. by lease, sale and purchase, inheritance, etc.? Some of the property rights of an asset can be transferred via a market. If laws reduce the transferability of property rights, for example, it will have consequences for the content of the bundle of property rights and its value. The Coase theorem (1960) states that irrespective of who has these rights, the rights can be traded. In that way, the value of these rights can be internalised; this can result in a Pareto-optimal situation.

  The Coase theorem is based on a number of assumptions. First, it is assumed that transaction costs are zero. The absence of transaction costs is an important assumption of the standard neoclassical approach. However, this assumption is often unrealistic. Transaction costs include e.g.: (1) information costs; (2) negotiation costs; and (3) observance or enforcement costs. The second assumption is that the assignment of rights has no effect on (efficient) allocation and has no wealth effects. The Coase theorem only refers to efficiency, and does not evaluate the fairness in the assignment of the rights. By awarding property rights for land, water, fishing and so on, a society can achieve a more equal income distribution. Keeping fairness considerations in mind, property rights can be allocated in such a way as to achieve a more equitable income distribution without adversely affecting allocation efficiency. As will be explained, this fits within the second welfare theorem.

  The third assumption is that a gain in property rights will be valued the same as a loss in property rights. It means people have no loss aversion. The Coase theorem is often used in the analysis and design of policy reforms, including those that are related to environmental goods: the final entitlements result from costless exchanges being independent of initial allocations and gains and losses of property rights are valued the same.

10.3 Property rights and the Coase theorem

As explained in Section 10.2, within the property rights theory there are two important approaches. The **first approach** is oriented towards: (1) the type of property right and the permitted actions, e.g. the way a good may be used and the right to exclude others and (2) property regimes (government, private, common, or no ownership).

The **second approach** is oriented towards the economic importance of ownership: it depends on the ability to exercise residual rights of control over the assets and having the residual income This approach to property rights is particularly important with regard to incomplete contracts, when

Box 10.7. The basic idea of the Coase theorem.

The important 'discovery' of Coase was to point out that the right, for example, to clean air and quiet, and the right to undertake activities that generate harmful effects, are property rights and are thus completely parallel with other rights that go with property ownership (such as the right to till land or to cut timber). Such rights can be given away or sold to another party just as any other good can. Transfers can be anticipated. According to Furubotn and Richter (2005: 102), there is no reason to assume that the initial endowments of rights should be Pareto efficient. In general, gains can be achieved through exchange, thus people will often find it advantageous to trade their rights to such things as clean air and quiet for money (Furubotn and Richter, 2005: 102).

not all the costs and benefits of certain events will be specified. Often this leads to the question: who will bear the costs of the non-specified events and who will appropriate the benefits?

For the application of the Coase theorem, we will mainly address the first approach[81]. We assume that: (1) the rights of the property holder and obligations of the other people in relation to the object are at the forefront; (2) they are instrumental by nature; and (3) they are protected by the government. The application will show that the specification, delineation, assignment and enforcement of the rights are important. For the allocation efficiency, it does not matter to whom the rights to use the asset be granted (under the condition of transferability). If the transfer of property rights is governed by a contract, then we also need the second approach.

The case: property rights over water

In a certain area, bulb growing is a very important activity. Both the soil and climate are very suitable for growing bulbs. The bulb growers have a sufficient supply of good quality water at their disposal, which can be used for sprinkling bulbs during dry periods in spring and summer, and also for washing the bulbs. In that same area, a wood-processing factory is established. It uses a lot of water, resulting in a reduction of the groundwater level, thus causing a considerable decline in profits for the bulb growers.

Before the wood-processing factory was established in that area, the annual net return of the bulb growers was 3 million euro (we assume that net return is expressed in Net Value Added, NVA). As a result of the water use by the factory, this return drops to 1.5 million euro annually or in other words, the bulb growers suffer an annual loss of 1.5 million euro. The factory also has a net return (NVA) of 3 million euro. The factory can also obtain water elsewhere by making use of a pipeline, which would incur costs of 1 million euro per annum.

We will analyse three situations: (1) there are no property rights over the water (i.e. free access); (2) the bulb growers have the water property rights, meaning the property rights are allocated to

---

[81] It is possible that for the application of the Coase theorem (incomplete) contracts are used, but for reason of simplicity we ignore this here.

the bulb growers by the authorities; (3) the factory has the water property rights, meaning that the property rights are allocated to the owners of the factory by the authorities.

In situation (1) the law of the jungle will exist. There is free access. We assume that the factory is the winner and continues to take the same amount of water. The bulb growers suffer a drop in yield of 50%. This is reflected in column (1) of Table 10.3.

As far as the total income of the area is concerned it is not the best solution. The factory has caused annual losses of 1.5 million euro. However, these losses could have been avoided by an annual amount of 1 million euro, meaning that the allocation is not efficient. Note that this situation can be seen as an example of an external effect. The bulb growers bear the negative effects without any compensation. The winner takes all.

The question is: how can we eliminate the negative effects? In the Netherlands, the most obvious measure would be legislation whereby either the bulb growers would cease their activities or the factory is required to alter its water supply. Another solution would be to end free access to the water and to assign the property rights concerning water to one of the two parties. There are two possibilities:
1. The property rights (the right to have access to the water and to use it) are assigned to the injured party (i.e. the bulb growers). The bulb growers have the right to exclude the factory from using water in that area. This is reflected in column 2 of Table 10.3.
2. The property rights (the right to have access to the water and to use it) are assigned to the factory. The bulb growers must suffer the losses. This is reflected in column 3 of Table 10.3.

What are the consequences of the different solutions? As a basis we can take the situation before the specification and assignment of the property rights. It is the free access situation or no property rights situation. The contribution of the Coase theorem is that as far as allocation efficiency and the wealth of the society (in this case the income of the area) is concerned it does not matter who has the property rights. It is possible to give the rights to the injured party (the bulb growers) or to the factory. The result in terms of income of the area is the same. Column (2) and (3) in Table 10.3 reflect this.

Table 10.3. Income of the area under different water property rights of the water (in million euro).

Income	Free access (1)	Property rights for the bulb growers (2)	Property rights for the factory (3)
For bulb growers	1.5	3	$3 - 1 = 2$
For factory	3	$(3 - 1) = 2$	$(3 - 1 + 1) = 3$
Total	4.5	5	5

Property rights for the bulb growers (injured party)

If the bulb growers gain the rights to the use of water they can exclude the factory from doing so. This delineation of property rights may be the result of a court ruling instituted by the bulb growers against the factory, or the result of a new law or legal principles, i.e. government intervention. The property right to use the water allows the use to be transferred to others. It also means that the bulb growers can offer the factory access to the water at a charge.

The factory has the following options:
- Cease business; the (opportunity) costs are in this case 3 million euro.
- Compensate the bulb growers for their loss; the costs would then be 1.5 million euro at the most. The remaining income for the factory in this case would be 1.5 million euro (3 – 1.5 = 1.5 million euro).
- Obtaining water from elsewhere by making use of a pipeline, which would cost 1 million euro per annum.

Obtaining water from elsewhere would be the best alternative. The total return for both parties is given in column (2) of Table 10.3. By delineation, specification and assignment of property rights the water will be used in ways other than those in the situation of free access. The allocation will change; by altering the allocation, the value of the production increases from 4.5 to 5 million euro. The regional product (in NVA)) is increased with 0.5 million euro.

What is the reason for this? In the situation of free access and unclear property rights, water was a free good. The factory did not take the losses incurred for the bulb growers into account in its calculation, which was crucial for the continuation of their business. In the new situation (with clear property rights for the bulb growers) the factory must take the social cost resulting from the losses caused to the bulb growers into account. Measures to reduce these costs are economically attractive for the factory. Because of the assignment of the property rights it is economically efficient for the factory to consider the interests of others.

Property rights for the party that causes the losses

What will happen if the property rights are assigned to party that cause the losses (in this case the factory)? The factory gains the right to use the water; the bulb growers must bear the losses.

The bulb growers have the following alternatives:
- Close their business; in that case their returns are zero.
- Bear the losses; their returns decrease from 3 to 1.5 million euro.
- Purchase the water rights; in other words the right to water is purchased by compensating the factory for the costs of obtaining water from elsewhere by making use of a pipeline. The cost of this is 1 million euro. The return for the bulb growers, compared with bearing the losses, is 0.5 million euro (-1 + 1.5 = 0.5).

The last alternative is a little better or, given the situation, the best alternative for bulb growers. It does not harm the factory because its position does not get any worse. The bulb growers continue to grow bulbs and they compensate the factory for the cost of water provision. Table 10.3, column (3) shows that the total value of the net production in region is 5 million euro. The allocation of the production factors is the same; the factory is working (with water from elsewhere) and the bulb growers are growing bulbs.

Efficiency and equity

What is the conclusion based on the Coase theorem? In case of the use of a rival good, lack of (well-defined) property rights can result in a waste (i.e. inefficient use of resources). This can be avoided by allocating the property rights to one of the parties involved. Specifying, assigning and protecting the property rights can realise a more efficient allocation and greater social welfare than in a situation of free access. For efficient allocation (i.e. level of income in the region) it does not matter which party will gain the property rights. The initial distribution of the property rights does not influence efficient allocation.

Social welfare is defined here as the net production of the region or the Net Value Added. An increase in the NVA means an increase in social welfare. If by establishing property rights the net benefits of the group or citizens increase, it is always possible that those who benefit from the delineation of property rights can compensate for the losses of the ones who suffer from this process. If this compensation is awarded we speak of a Pareto-improvement: the welfare of A increases without the welfare of B decreasing. A measure taken is Potential Pareto-efficient if the advantages for A are large enough to compensate B and there is still something left over of the advantage for A. It is not necessary that compensation takes place in reality.

If, as in column (1) of Table 10.3, we assume the situation with free access as starting point, then the specification and assignment of the property rights to the factory is not only a Pareto improvement, but it is also Pareto-efficient. It is Pareto-efficient, because the bulb growers are better off than with free access and the factory remains at the same level. When specification and assignment of the property rights to bulb growers is compared with free access a Potential Pareto-efficient situation exists as well. The bulb growers are better off than with free access and, based on their increase in income, they could fully compensate the factory. However, the compensation is not carried out. This is why it is called Potential Pareto-efficient.

The results of our application only tell us something about the efficiency (the effect on the amount of NVA). However, it does not say anything about the equity of the solution. The three variants in Table 10.3 differ in the consequences for the incomes of the two parties. This means that the allocation of the property rights has large effects on the income distribution. It is possible to take into account income distribution effects (or equity considerations), and to make a choice between the two situations that are both efficient. It means that it is not necessary to have a conflict between efficiency and equity criteria.

The Pareto efficient situation realised by specification and assignment of the property rights is related with the First Welfare Theorem. The First Welfare Theorem states that if there is a market for every commodity, and all producers and consumers act as price takers, then the allocation of resources will be Pareto efficient (Katz and Rozen, 1994: 410). This means that the government does not always need to intervene using legislation. An efficient situation can also arise by bargaining between parties. This is an important element in the Coase theorem. However, the First Welfare Theorem itself says nothing about fairness (Katz and Rozen, 1994: 414).

The Second Welfare Theorem states that, under certain conditions, every Pareto-efficient allocation of resources can be attained by some set of competitive prices. This Second Welfare Theorem is important because of its implication that, at least in theory, the issues of efficiency and distributional fairness can be separated. If society deems the current distribution of resources to be unfair, it needs not to interfere with market prices and impair efficiency. Rather, society should transfer resources (including property rights) among people in a way deemed to be fair (Katz and Rozen, 1994: 416).

Summarising, the applied example of Coase theorem only refers to efficiency, and does not evaluate the fairness in the assignment of the rights. However, by awarding property rights for land, water and fishing areas in a free assess situation, a society can achieve a more equal income distribution. Property rights can be allocated in such a way that it is possible to achieve a more equitable income distribution without adversely affecting allocation efficiency. This can be used by the government as an important instrument.

Coase theorem on a continuous scale

In the numerical example we stated an *all or nothing* situation: 100% water of good quality or nothing. In reality there are *in between* solutions. We will show how the Coase theorem works on a continuous scale. In Figure 10.1 AQ_1 gives the marginal return for the factory and OB gives the marginal losses for the bulb growers as a consequence of the water use by the factory.

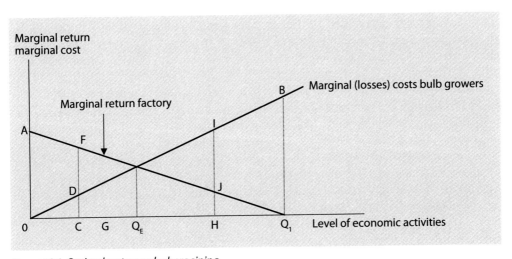

Figure 10.1. Optimal water use by bargaining.

Water property rights assigned to bulb growers

Assume that the bulb growers are allocated the water property rights. The starting point in Figure 10.1 is the origin (point 0). The bulb growers will prefer no activity at all, because any activity by the factory will result in losses for them. The bulb growers have gained the water property rights; their view will hold the greatest influence. But now consider whether the two parties (bulb growers and factory) could bargain about the level of activity of the factory (water use by the factory). Assume that the issue is whether to move to point C or not. If they move to C, the factory would gain 0CFA in total profit, but the bulb growers would lose 0CD. But since 0CFA is greater than 0CD, there is potential for bargaining. Very simply, the factory could offer to compensate the bulb growers by an amount greater than 0CD, and less than 0CFA and the factory would still have a net profit. Moreover, the bulb growers would be better off: although they would lose 0CD, they would gain more with compensation. If such a bargain could be struck, the move to C would be seen as an improvement for both parties (such a move is known as a Pareto-improvement, since at least one party is better off and no party is worse off).

But if the move from 0 to C is a social improvement so is the move to G (simply repeat the argument). Indeed, so is a further move to Q_E. But any move to the right of Q_E is not feasible because the factory's net gain then becomes less than the bulb grower's losses – hence the factory cannot compensate the bulb growers to move beyond Q_E. Thus, if we start at 0 and the property rights of the water belong to bulb growers, there is a 'natural' tendency to move to Q_E, the social optimum.

Water property rights assigned to the factory

Now imagine that the water property rights are vested to the owners of the factory. The starting point is Q_1 because that is the point to which the factory will go given that he has every right to use the water for his products. The factory will expand its activities to the point where the marginal return of each extra unit is equal to 0, MR = 0. That is point Q_1. At that point losses for bulb growers are $0Q_1B$ (i.e. 1.5 million euro).

But it is now possible for the two parties to meet again and consider the move from Q_1 *back* to H. But this time the bulb growers can compensate the factory by giving up a certain amount of activity. Since the bulb growers would have to bear a loss of $HIBQ_1$ if the move to H does not go ahead, they would be willing to offer any amount less than this to make the move. The factory would be willing to accept any amount greater than HJQ_1, the profits that it would have to surrender. The potential for bargaining exists once more and the move to H will take place. But if the move to H is a social improvement, so is the move from H to Q_E. Hence Q_E is once again the level of activity to which the system will gravitate.

As long as we can establish a bargaining position between both parties, the market will bring us, based on the above argument, to Q_E which is the social optimum. The potential importance of the argument can now be seen, for *regardless of who hold the property rights, there is an automatic tendency to the social optimum*. This finding is known as the *Coase theorem*, after Coase (1960; cited in 1988: 157-163). If it is correct, we have no need for government regulation of externalities, for the market will take care of itself. It is also important that the initial vesting has no influence on the allocation efficiency that arises as a result of the negotiations between the parties.

Transaction costs

One of the assumptions of the Coase theorem is that transaction costs are zero. However, each transaction of goods or service involves costs. Transaction costs can be split up according to *ex-ante* and *ex-post* types. *Ex-ante* types are the costs of drafting, negotiating, and safeguarding an agreement. These costs arise before the transaction takes place. In that phase, the parties concerned have to deal with search costs. These include costs for acquiring information about product, price, quality, time and place. Such costs arise in the first phase of the transaction (exchange) process; also called the contact phase.

The second phase of the transaction process is the contract phase, which means concluding the agreement. In this phase, costs can arise as a result of efforts to recognise *ex-ante* problems, uncertainties, and risks and to take measurement to avoid or control them. *Ex-post* costs arise after concluding an agreement. These costs belong to the third phase of the transaction process. They include the cost of monitoring, re-negotiations, costs of arbitrage, costs of a court, etc. These costs have been discussed in Chapter 5.

Transaction costs of transferring property rights consist of private and public transaction costs, including the following elements:
1. The cost of specifying, delineating and establishing of the property rights.
2. The cost of obtaining information and finding a contract partner. In case of the bulb growers, they need to investigate what the losses are, who causes these losses, what is a reasonable offer for the owners of the factory, etc.
3. The cost of negotiations, formulating and writing a contract.
4. Monitoring cost and, if necessary, the enforcement costs.

High transaction costs will results in transactions not taking place. Assume that in our case the transaction costs are 0.6 million euro and that this amount must be paid by the party taking the initiative to the transaction. Table 10.4 gives an overview of the alternatives available to the factory and the results if the factory takes the initiative.

Based on these results, the factory will opt for obtaining water from elsewhere. In the case of assigning water property rights to the factory, it is not attractive for the bulb growers to buy

Table 10.4. Factory takes initiative.

Alternatives	Return mln €	Net return mln €
Stop production	0	0
Compensating bulb growers plus transaction costs	3 – (1.5 + 0.6)	0.9
Obtaining water from elsewhere	3 – 1	2

out the water use of the factory. The alternatives of the bulb growers and the results are given in Table 10.5.

The cost of buying out the water of factory by the bulb growers is 1 + 0.6 + 1.6 million euro. This is higher than the losses incurred by the factory when extracting the water. This means that the factory will continue to extract water.

We can conclude that the transaction costs are an obstacle to bargaining over water property rights. If the transaction costs are so high that any one party's share of them outweighs the expected benefits of the bargaining, that party will withdraw from the bargaining, or not even start. Moreover, it seems likely that the transaction costs will fall on the party that does not have the property rights. But transaction costs are real costs – we have no reason for treating them any differently to other costs in the economy. Thus, if transaction costs are very high, all we appear to be saying is that the costs of bargaining outweigh any benefits. In that case no bargaining is optimal.

Table 10.5. Bulb growers take initiative.

Alternatives	Return mln €	Net return mln €
Stop production	0	0
Bearing the losses	3 – 1.5	1.5
Buying out water use for the factory plus transaction costs	3 – (1 + 0.60)	1.4

Validity of Coase theorem and equity

The Coase theorem has some critical points. First, depending on the version, it starts from a free access situation or there are already private rights (cf. Cooter and Ulen, 1997: 79). Second, one of the key assumptions is that transaction costs are zero. However, each transaction of goods or service involves costs. This certainly holds for transfer of property rights over land, water, fishing areas and so on. It means that in practice this assumption is often not right. Third, it is assumed is that a gain in property rights will be valued the same as a loss in property rights. However, most people have loss aversion. Fourth, the equity effects of the assignment, trade and finale entitlements are ignored.

Box.10.8. Coase and the zero transaction costs assumption.

Different scientists formulate the Coase theorem differently. Coase did not believe the zero transaction costs (ZTC) assumption to be a representation of the real world. He called it an unrealistic assumption (Coase, 1960:15; 1988: 114) and used it only as a convenient device to point out what would happen in a neoclassical ZTC world. He writes that once the costs of carrying out market transactions are taken into account, it is clear that such a rearrangement of rights will only be undertaken when the increase in the value of production consequent upon the rearrangement is greater than the costs which would be involved in bringing it about (Coase, 1960:15; 1988: 115). This approach raises the general question of alternatives to market solutions such as the firm or direct government regulation. Relative to government intervention, he argues that such action is not the only, or necessarily the best, way to solve the problem of externalities: 'All solutions have costs and there is no reason to suppose that government regulation is called for simply because the problem is not well handled by the market or her firm' (Coase, 1960:15; 1988: 118). The debate on the logic of the Coase theorem is still going on (cf. Furubotn and Richter (2005: 108).

10.4 The characteristics of goods: excludability, rivalry and property rights

Excludability and rivalry are important concepts in the classification of goods and in specifying which type of property rights apply and which type of property rights are preferred. Goods and services, and also natural resources, can be classified on the basis of technical characteristics – excludability and rivalry. Excludability means that it is possible to exclude individuals from goods, service and natural resources also, e.g. persons who do not want to pay for the use of the good. Non-excludability is the property of a good by which benefits of that good can not be easily excluded and, therefore, are made available to all. Once the good is provided the benefits are available to all.[82] Non-excludability is, due to the lack of property rights, the exclusive factor for deciding which goods must be publicly provided. Excludability could be impossible for technical or for institutional reasons. In both cases it is not possible to assign property rights. When exclusion is not possible, problems such as free-riding and prisoner's dilemma can occur (Boadway and Bruce, 1989: 129-130). Free-riding means that individuals (free-riders) can use or consume the good without paying for it.

Rivalry refers to the subtraction of benefits associated with his its use. Non-rivalry suggests the possibility for multiple users without subtraction of benefits; i.e. the possibility that a good, a factor of production or natural resource, can be used not only by individual A, but also, at the same time, by several other persons. For example, sunsets are non-rival or indivisible when views are unobstructed. With divisible goods, that is: goods which can be technically divided into marketable units, rivalry is clearly present. In the ideal typical situation of a market with perfect competition in all markets, all goods, factors of production and natural resources are completely rivalrous. One person's right to the good is always at the cost of the other person. This is not the case with non-rivalry; several individuals can then use a good at the same time. Multiple use, i.e. use by several persons simultaneously, is then possible. An important measure of rivalry is

---

[82] This does not refer to positive goods only, but also to bad things.

the marginal cost. For non-rival goods, the marginal costs of the use are nil. Non-rivalry and indivisibility are largely interchangeable expressions.

Once the characteristics *rivalry* and *excludability* of goods are defined, the so-called spectrum of goods can be distinguished. Pure public goods have the properties of *non-rivalry* and *non-excludability*. Pure private goods are fully rival and excludable. Different types of goods (or bads) occupy the in-between points along this spectrum. Goods whose benefits are non-rival and (partially) excludable are called impure public goods. There are also goods whose benefits are (partially) rival and non-excludable. These are called common goods. Figure 10.2 gives an overview of the different types of goods.

An important subclass of goods whose benefits are excludable but partially non-rival are the *club goods* (Cornes and Sandler, 1996: 9). The essential difference between club goods and pure public goods depends on the existence of an exclusion mechanism. The characteristics of clubs have been discussed in Section 3.7. As explained, a club is a voluntary group of people deriving mutual benefits from sharing costs of the activities, the members' characteristics (e.g., members like playing soccer, golf, preserving the environment, etc.) or a good characterised by excludable benefits. These excludable benefits are mostly internal, i.e. for the members. Besides, the benefits of a club can also be external such as preserving environmental goods.

Non-excludability is a characteristic that arises from a lack of property rights (Boadway and Bruce, 1989: 110). From the institutional point of view, it is interesting to look at circumstances that may constitute obstacles to the establishment of private property rights. It is clear that in order to set a price for a commodity, it must be possible to exclude those who do not pay a price. For some goods, exclusion is possible but costly. The metering of water use, tolls for routes and brides, introduction of milk quota and CO_2 emission quota, etc. are examples of costly, and

Rivalry / Excludability	Non-rivalry (indivisible) goods 0% ←	Rivalry (divisible) goods → 100%
Impossibility of: - exclusion - rejection 0%	(1) Pure public goods	(2) Common goods, common resources and open access resources
Possibility of: - exclusion - rejection 100%	(3) Impure public goods	(4) Pure private goods

Figure 10.2. Characteristics of goods.

not always universally adopted, exclusion devices. Exclusion might be possible at a cost in a situation involving environmental pollution or congestion. There are, however, other goods for which exclusion is intrinsically impossible. If citizens are excluded from a public park, then it is, by definition, no longer a pure public park. National defence is another commonly quoted example of a good from which exclusion is not possible. In any event, if exclusion is impossible or too costly to be privately profitable, an essential precondition for the establishment of effective property rights is lacking (Cornes and Sandler, 1996: 43).

The failure of property rights to be well defined is then an important ingredient of many externality situations. In Section 10.5 we discuss some examples. However, such a failure is not a sufficient reason to conclude that there is an inefficiency and hence a scope for government intervention. The government can also fail and this might be even worse than market failure. However, government intervention does not necessarily mean that the government deals with all the aspects that can be distinguished in the production of goods and services. The most encompassing way of government intervention takes place when ownership, management, financing and production are in government hands. Only for purely public goods it is reasonable to expect that ownership, management, financing and production and services are in the hands of government.

Concerning correcting market failure the government has a broad range of instruments at its disposal. The instruments can be grouped in: (1) research, extension, education and persuasion; (2) direct regulations (rules of laws, licenses and quota systems); (3) fiscal facilities; (4) subsidies and levies (taxes); and (5) government provisions. Instruments such as transferable emission rights, water and fishing quota, production rights and income rights can be seen as combination of (2) and (4), further the market is used as a governance structure and the price as a coordination mechanism.

In Figure 10.2 we provide a classification of goods and natural resources based on the concepts of rivalry and excludability. We indicate what type of good it is, whether the market can be used as governance structure, government intervention has preference, including which type of intervention, or if other governance structures – like clubs – are possible and suitable.

As Figure 10.2 shows, it can be concluded that based on the 0 or 100% situations four types of goods can be distinguished: pure public goods, impure public goods, groups or common goods and pure private goods. The question is whether excludability or rivalry should be treated as the decisive characteristics for the classification of goods. The degree of excludability is actually quite critical for obtaining insight into problems regarding the property rights characteristics of goods. Non-rivalry becomes interesting only in combination with the possibility of exclusion.

The question is which transaction mechanism or governance structure is best for different types of goods. For the market to function well as a governance structure, it must be a matter of pure private goods. This means that:
- exclusion and rejection should be possible;
- there are private property rights and these can be transferred;
- the use of the good is rival;
- the good is divisible.

A market is in fact a transaction mechanism that provides for direct exchange of individual rights (property or user rights). For exchange to occur, property rights have to be clearly exclusive. This assumes the possibility of specifying private property rights and rights on a good so that individuals who have not paid for it can actually be excluded (Boadway and Bruce, 1989: 110). Deciding on, paying for and consuming of the goods then go together. This is the reason to treat excludability as the distinguishing factor in Figure 10.2, with the following type of goods:

- **Pure public goods**
  Exclusion is not possible and/or not efficient and the use is non-rival. No one can claim individual property rights and private property rights are not possible. Examples of pure public goods are:
  - national defence;
  - specific landscapes and e.g. the sunset;
  - open space;
  - dikes as water protection, such as the Afsluitdijk/Barrier Dam as a dam for water protection;
  - daylight.

  Examples of public bads are:
  - radioactive fall-out from nuclear stations in case of a disaster;
  - emission of a greenhouse gas.

  The property rights for pure public goods are difficult or impossible to define; it means there are no property rights. Concerning the public bads, it can be said there exists no property rights on clean air. The lack of property rights can lead to external effects (Boadway and Bruce, 1989: 112). The goods that fall under category (1) are also non-rival. That is, the use is not limited or restricted (to an individual). Non-excludability and non-rivalry are, however, a matter of degree. If we maintain non-excludability and permit rivalry to go to 100%, we come into cell (2).

- **Common goods and resources**
  Exclusion is not possible and/or not efficient and the use is rival. This means the use of good is not restricted, but the use by one individual is at the cost of others. An example is the sea-fishery in the North Sea where fishermen were rivals without any government regulation. Nowadays the fishing areas have been divided and there is an active (EU) volume-policy based on output quotas for each fishery. Another example relates to the surface and groundwater in many countries. The drying-up of river beds is considered an environmental problem as a result of intensive use of the water. The use of water from surface and pools of groundwater is rival.

  For this type of goods, individual property rights do not exist (too expensive or unverifiable). Often for such types of goods, common property regimes are applied. The inability of exclusion often results in government intervention, which leads to the creation of property rights such as user or production rights. Some examples are:
  - user rights for fishing areas, sometimes combined with fish quota;
  - milk quotas;
  - hunting rights;

- concessions licences for chalk, oil, minerals, sand and gravel winning and for wood-harvesting;
- permits for sprinkling and irrigation with surface or groundwater, i.e. user rights of water;
- pollution rights, e.g. CO_2 emission rights.

Such types of government intervention lead to private property rights, which sometimes are tradable such as in the case of milk quotas and CO_2 emissions rights. However, the bundle of rights is often restricted to user rights and the right to exclude others.

The use of common goods can be so intensive that not only rivalry arises, but also congestion, meaning that the use of a good by individuals has a negative effect on the use by others. Congestion is also a public bad. Examples of congestion are hiking or biking with a large group of individuals in a recreation or nature park area, or whale watching with large numbers of individuals and over-loaded trains or roads. For trains and roads in principle exclusion possibilities exist. This brings us to good in cell (3).

- **Quasi or impure public goods**
  Exclusion from the good is in principle possible and the use is non-rival. It means that property rights can be specified and delineated. If the use of the good by one person is not at the cost of the other (non-rival), then the marginal-costs for an extra additional user will be nil (Boadway and Bruce, 1998: 118). In that case, multiple consumption of the good is possible. It is a result of the indivisibility of the concerned good. When claims on provisions are not, or only to a limited extent rival, the social efficiency is not served by exclusion-sanctions even if these were possible.
  Examples of goods or provisions for which exclusion is possible and the use is non-rival are:
  - education;
  - highways during the night;
  - afsluitdijk/Barrier Dam as a road;
  - outdoor recreation projects and parks;
  - nature and landscape.
  There are also goods or resources where exclusion is possible and the use is non-rival to a great extent. However, intensive use of these goods can lead to congestion. These goods are known as club goods. Examples are: sport associations, environmental associations/cooperatives and agricultural cooperations. Members can easily be excluded (for non-payment or due to misconduct). Membership fee is an exclusion mechanism, see also Section 3.7. If the number of members reaches a certain limit however, additional members are likely to reduce the advantages to the existing members (i.e. congestion).

- **Pure individual or private goods**
  Exclusion is possible, appropriate and efficient, and the use of the good is rival. The latter also means that the good is divisible in consumption and transferable in marktable units. For individual goods, where individual property rights exist, the use by one individual excludes the possibility of use by another. As explained, the market is the best governance structure.
  In the standard neoclassical approach, it is assumed that all resources fall under private property regimes, and individuals have property rights to use them for diverse purposes, and can also sell the right to others. For a complete overview of the rights see Table 10.1. It means

the property rights are perfectly defined, completely in private possession and enforceable (De Allesie, 1983: 65; Eggertsson, 1990: 84; Gravelle and Rees, 1992: 10). However, often (private) property rights are missing or are not specified, protected or enforceable. Often the value of the good depends on how the property rights are defined.

For a market to function well, firms and consumers must be in a position to transfer property rights for using production factors or consuming of goods. This requires a good system of property rights (Boadway and Bruce, 1989: 110). Single property rights of assets must be specifiable, enforceable and transferable. Property rights are human artefacts. The institution 'ownership' accompanied by guaranteed property rights is the most common and effective institution which provides an incentive to individuals to make goods, to maintain them and to improve them. The specification of this rights indicates how the costs and benefits are to be divided amongst the parties within the institutional arrangement.

10.5 Application in practice

The Coase theorem states that if the parties bargain to an efficient agreement (for themselves) the results of bargaining will not depend on (1) the bargaining power of the parties, or on (2) what assets each owned when the bargaining began. This has been proved in Section 10.3. Efficiency alone determines the choice of activities. However, the distributional fairness is also important[83]. This also includes decisions about how costs and benefits are to be shared. A number of reasons can prevent efficient and fair agreements. First, the premises that people can bargain, implement, and enforce their agreements are not always valid. There can be significant transaction costs that arise from bounded rationality, hidden information, hidden actions and opportunistic behaviour (Milgrom and Roberts, 1992: 293).

The second reason that may prevent efficient agreements has to do with a lack of clear and enforceable property rights that can be transferred easily. Figure 10.2 indicates that for some goods it is impossible or very difficult to allocate property rights; they are pure public goods. If we do not have clear and enforceable property rights that can be transferred easily, then efficiency may not be realised. If no one clearly owns a valuable asset no one has an incentive to guard its value properly. If property rights are not tradable there is little hope that assets will end up with those people who can make the best use of them and so value them most. If property rights are not secure, owners will not invest great amounts in assets that they may lose with no compensation, or they may sink valuable resources into protecting their claims (Milgrom and Roberts, 1992: 293). The reason is they have in that case only costs and no benefits. As explained in Box 4.3, insecure property rights create hold-up problems.

These responses to insecure property rights explain the efficiency costs of theft. Theft is a not only transfer of an asset, but it has also a direct efficiency consequence, because, a high level of theft means weak or insecure property rights. It also brings a society in a hold-up situation. The reluctance to invest when property rights are insecure results in inadequate maintenance and development of assets. For example, car owners in cities who refrain from installing navigation

---

[83] For example, to whom will the government allocate the property rights?

systems in their vehicles for fear that they will be stolen are foregoing a transaction that would be valuable if their rights were secure. Another example is the threat of takings by government without adequate compensation. They hinder investments and development of assets. The threat of takings is a real problem in China and in many other countries.

This brings us to the third reason preventing efficient agreements. This reason has to do with weak or inadequate social embeddedness (informal rules) and institutional environment (formal rules). The last reason that hinders bargaining to efficient agreement is a weak and bad government. These reasons are more or less mutually dependent. A weak government, and an inadequate social embeddedness and institutional environment will lead to high transaction costs. The same holds for unclear and very difficult to transfer property rights. The transaction costs can prohibit the transactions.

One of the saddest incentive problems resulting from untradable, insecure, or unassigned property rights is known as the *common-resource problem*, the *public-goods problem*, the *free-rider problem*, and the *tragedy of the commons*. On the one hand when many people have the right to use a common pool resource, there is an incentive for overusing the resource. On the other hand when many people share the obligation to provide some resources, it will be under-supplied. A consequence is that a concentration of ownership rights can lead to increased efficiency. A well-known example is the economics of ocean fisheries. We will analyse the application of three property regimes. These regimes have been discussed in more detail in Section 10.2.6.

The group or common ownership approach

One way to solve problem of overfishing would be to vest a fishery association made up for the members of a local fishing fleet with the exclusive right to control the fishery. This would include rights to determine who may fish in the area, the total catch size and various rules affecting the method of fishing, such as the hours or seasons when fishing is permitted, and so on. Individuals could then have rights to partake in the total allowed catch. The advantages of this kind of arrangement are easy to see. As a group, the association has a collective incentive to safeguard the fish population. The best fishing arrangements may be those that maximise the joint profits of the fisherman, taking into account the full effect that this season's harvest has on future harvests (Milgrom and Roberts, 1992: 295).

The disadvantages are firstly that it may be costly to keep out interlopers – who would want to fish although they have no right to do so. Secondly, moral hazard problems could arise among the individual members of the association, depending on how the catch is shared. If a quota is used there will be an incentive for overfishing by cheating on the quota. The possibility of refusing fishing rights to anyone caught cheating provides incentives for obeying the rules. It means resources must be used to enforce the rules. An alternative is: give each association member a fixed share of the total catch. In that case, the incentives are to cut back on effort, crew sized, and so on, because all the savings accrue to the individual and the costs in terms of a smaller catch are spread over the whole fleet (compare milk quota system). However, it excludes the possibility of realising scale advantages.

A third difficulty with vesting fishing rights with the fleet as a group is disagreements among the members about the rules to govern the exploitation of their fishery. Fishing boats differ in their costs of fishing, and their owners may vary in their expectations about future fish prices and their outside job opportunities. They may also have differing ideas as to what rate of fishing the population can sustain. These differences mean they will disagree about possible policies. There will be no consensus among the members about the appropriate rules to govern the exploitation of their fishery.

As explained in Section 10.2.6 common property can be seen as a collective group property or a corporate group-property. The property-owning groups vary in nature, size, and internal structure across a broad spectrum, but they are social units with definite membership and boundaries, with certain common interests, with at least some interaction between the members, with some common cultural values and norms, and often with its own endogenous authority system. In order for a common property regime by group ownership to function well, it is necessary that all members of the group are in compliance with the accepted rules and their behaviour is observable. Conformity with group norms at the local level is an effective mechanism against anti-social behaviour.

Essential for any property regime is an authority system able to ensure that the expectations of rights holders are met. Compliance, protection and enforcement by an authority system is a necessary condition for the viability of any property regime. Private property would be nothing without the requisite authority system to make certain that rights and duties are adhered. The same requirements hold also for common property. If the authority system does not function well or if it breaks down – for whatever reason – then the management, or self-management, of the resource use cannot be carried out any longer. Common property in that case degenerates into 'open access'.

Single or private ownership

An alternative that avoids this problem of inefficiencies is to assign the rights to a single individual, e.g., one of the members of the fishing fleet. The 'single-owner' solution works well for ordinary items like automobiles, houses, and furniture. Applied to fishing rights, it has the same general advantages as the system that allows the community to determine the size of the total catch and fishing rules. The single owner would avoid overfishing that destroys future harvest. The major problem is who is the lucky one who gets the rights?

The solution of allocating the rights by rotating them among the possible candidates from year to year is a very inefficient solution. This would encourage overfishing because the current holder of the rights would not gain at all from preserving the population for next year. Another possibility would be to auction the rights to the highest bidder and compensate the losers by distributing the returns of the auction among them. This would ensure the most efficient use of the rights, because the winner will be the one for whom the rights are most valuable. Another solution would be to give each fisherman fishing rights based on a reference level. If the government thinks that this level will lead to overfishing, it can reduce the rights with a certain percentage. The next step

Box 10.9. Water use in France.

Since the 1992 Water law, France has been slowly setting up tools to implement a so-called balanced management of water between users. Access rules are locally negotiated by water councils of users who design water management schemes. In the south Parisian Basin, for example, contingents of water are administratively allocated to individual irrigators on a yearly basis. The total agricultural contingent is decided according to the common aquifer level that is monitored by an independent Government Agency. However, this tool is not finely tuned enough to provide an efficient management of drought events. In such cases, government authorities take emergency measures by limiting or forbidding irrigation with very significant negative consequences on irrigated farm profits, like for example in 2005[1]. The allocation of water use is not directly based on the economic value of water. Rather, the allocation between users depends on political compromises while emergency measures depend on the appreciation of the government in its role of protecting the water as a common resource.

---

[1] INRA (2006). Sécheresse et Agriculture, Expertise collective de l'INRA pour le Ministère de l'Agriculture et de la pêche, October, 2006)

could be make the fishing rights tradable. This method is also applied for milk quota and CO_2 emission quota.

While it might seem that analyzing fishing rights is a very particular case which does not apply exactly to other situations, this is not true. There are many comparable situations. For example, a correlated situation concerns groundwater. Pools of underground water are a major source of water for drinking and irrigation. In the western part of United States, a number of aquifers are being drawn down much more quickly than they are refilled by natural seepage from surface. The problem is just as with fisheries: no ones owns the aquifer, so no one guards it properly. For example, it is especially acute in California. This state does not have a program for groundwater management. However, we see, for example, in large parts of France comparable problems, especially in hot and dry summers like the summers of 2003, 2005 and 2006.

In both California and France the farmers have rights to use the water. However, in most cases the farmers' rights to the water are limited. For example, they do not have the right to transfer the rights to another person, firm or organisation. Farmers are not generally allowed to sell their water to the highest bidder. What would happen if farmers had the rights to sell the water? The marginal value of a cubic meter groundwater is likely to be higher for residential and industrial users than for farmers. In that case, some farmers would find it profitable to cut back their production, change the crops they raise to less water-intensive ones, or switch to more efficient methods of irrigation. They could then sell rights to water they would save to others users who value it highly. According to the Coase theorem, efficient use of water is what should be expected if water rights are secure and tradable (Milgrom and Roberts, 1992: 297).

Untradable and insecure rights

According to the Coase theorem, assets will tend to be acquired by those who can use them best. If a person owns a good or right that is more valuable to his or her neighbour, then there is a price at which the two would both find it profitable to trade, and the goods would move to where they are most valuable. However, firstly the bundle of rights constituting ownership is not always transferable. Secondly, property rights are often insecure, so that they might be restricted or lost at some future point without fair compensation being paid. *Insecure rights* weaken the owner's incentive to invest in developing and maintaining the asset. This is also known as the hold-up problem. There is always the danger that both the asset and the returns it generates will be lost.

Lessons from the Coase theorem and alternatives

An important assumption of the Coase theorem is that the costs of arriving at and enforcing an efficient agreement are **low**. From this follows the conclusion that resources will be allocated efficiently, even in the absence of competitive markets and regardless of the initial allocation of property rights or distribution of bargaining power. However, in practice we often have to deal with transaction costs. Analysing the major sources of transaction costs serves **three** functions. First, it helps us to identify where to expect inefficiencies to be found. Second, it helps us to explain (a) a whole range of practices and formal rules including those that arise to minimise transaction costs and (b) certain **government regulations** (designed to achieve as much as possible in an institutional environment) where bargaining among individuals would be too difficult, complex, or costly to be a realistic possibility. Finally, it lays a foundation for an important part of the institutional economics: *property rights theory*, including *getting the property rights right*. If the allocation of bundle of property rights does affect value, then one possible objective is to assign them in a way that creates value.

Transaction costs are often an obstacle and are often limits for the Coase theorem. Determining, writing, and enforcing an agreement in a world of bounded rationality, imperfect information and opportunistic behaviour involves transaction costs. The relevant parties have to be identified. They must reach agreement on the basic relationship that tie actions to desired outcomes and determine a set of plans in light of a complex and unpredictable world. Then the actions that each party is to take and the distribution of the resulting returns must be determined, accepted, and specified with sufficient clarity for all to understand them and know what to do and what to expect. Finally, some mechanisms must be put in place to enforce the agreement and to resolve disputes (cf. Milgrom and Roberts, 1992: 301).

In some situations these costs are small compared to the benefits that result: transactions are carried out. In others, however, the transaction costs may be large or even overwhelming. For example, it would be quite costly for passengers in an airplane (or on an airport) to negotiate whether the flight (or airport) should permit smoking. If smoking is not forbidden, should non-smokers be compensated for being hindered? How should the compensation be determined? Who should pay the compensation – the airline (or airport) or the smokers? If it is the smokers, how much should each of them pay? How is this to be determined?

To reduce these transaction costs people seek **other** institutional arrangements. The airlines and airports make rules about smoking in an airplane and on an airport. A similar analysis justifies the creation of formal rules (laws) by the government that specify how e.g. in the USA property owners must maintain the public sidewalks crossing their properties and the damages that must be paid if the laws are violated and an injury results. In the UK, private landowners have to accept and to maintain public footpaths that cross through their property. The laws governing product safety, among others food safety, can be analysed similarly. These laws mostly specify rights that are not tradable; a person can often not accept a lower safety standard for a product in exchange for a lower price. An alternative would be private contracting. However, private contracting between an individual consumer and an individual food producer (e.g. farmer) would sometimes involve high [, especially excessive costs in controlling and enforcement.

Is everything we see efficient?

Answering this question can not be detached from the question are the property rights right? But given the state of the art of the property rights allocation, if we take into account transaction costs, the current situation is often efficient because the reason why a 'better' outcome was not achieved is that the transaction costs of achieving it are too high. In cases – like smoking, food safety, and other cases where the problem arises frequently, people may devise rule-making or law-making principles that are intended to resolve situations at low costs. For example, the rule *smoking is forbidden* is a cheap solution from the viewpoint of transaction costs. Furthermore, as explained in Chapter 9, an organisational mode is a governance structure. The type of the governance structure is a variable choice. According to transaction cost theory, the choice is determined through the transaction costs. For that reason, it is improper to ignore the costs of an institutional arrangement such as running the organisation.

Transaction costs and efficient assignment of ownership claims

When transaction costs are low, the Coase theorem holds that the initial assignment of property rights is irrelevant to efficiency, as long as the rights are clearly assigned, secure, and transferable. When there are impediments to efficient bargaining, however, it may be crucially important that these rights be assigned properly initially. In well-functioning societies, the initial assignment of property rights is typically a task of the government. Governments not only protect property rights, they also create new property rights, for example, through patents, trademarks and copy-rights laws. The holders of patents or copy-rights can use courts to prevent others from using their invention without compensation. On the one hand, these property rights in fact result in short-term inefficiency. Once the idea is created, **it is efficient to have it employed as widely as possible** because there is no opportunity cost to its further exploitation. On the other hand, this solution would mean that inventors and developers would receive only a tiny fraction of the returns to investments. This would remove much of the incentive for creative and innovative activity, and the long-term impacts would be bad.

Other examples of **new property rights**, created by governments are production quota, such as for milk, fish, sugar beets, manure quota (including allowed use of manure per ha land), the single farm payments and property rights for pollution, such as CO_2 emission rights, see Box 10.10.

> **Box 10.10. European trade system on greenhouse gases.**
>
> In January 2005, the European Commission started the European transfer system (ETS) for greenhouse gases, meant for reducing emissions as efficient as possible. In the ETS, participants are allowed to emit if they have the required emission rights. The rights are transferable. There are a number of important key questions for implementing such a system of property rights. Firstly, how is the total allowed space for emissions determined, for example, the CO_2 ceiling? Instead of 27 national ceiling in the period 2008 -2012 there will be one ETS ceiling for the whole EU. Secondly, how are the emission rights assigned? The initial assignment to firms is based on a historical reference year.
>
> Firms using more energy than 20 MW_{th} are obliged to participate in the ETS. This holds for all sectors, including the aviation sector. This means, for example, that a greenhouse grower with more than 10 ha glasshouses also have to participate. Thirdly, is the assignment for free? The granting for emission rights is for free. However, it is possible that a firm has grown after the historical reference year. Consequently, the firm has to buy emission rights. Granting for free based on historical reference year is called grandfathering. Fourth, are the rights are transferable? In the in the ETS the emission rights are transferable.
>
> In the applied ETS, the rights are assigned according to a historical reference year and they are transferable. However, the granting of emission rights for free creates windfall profits, if these rights are transferable and have a market value, and if this market value can be calculated in product price. This creates an incentive for enlargement, certainly if the European Commission propose to provide more rights for free at a ratio of future performance. This takes away the incentives for reducing volumes of emissions and strongly decreases the efficiency of the system. Granting free emission rights subsidises the activities, for example the transport of passengers (Davidson *et al*, 2007:553).

Assigning these rights to private persons or firms is often an efficient system compared with other solutions. On the other hand, governments also often alter or remove existing property rights (= takings). This is the subject of Chapter 11.

Finally, property rights have – besides economic efficiency and fairness – ethical significance as well. On the one hand, supporters of free market systems see private property as a fundamental right, not just a mechanism for generating incentives. On the other hand, many people worldwide believe that private property is fundamentally immoral. According to Proudhon 'property is theft!' (Bromley, 1991:25). Even when the institution itself is not fundamentally questioned, ethical issues arise.

Property rights are also a major **point of conflict** between the industrialised world and the less developed nations. What rights have rich corporations and rich countries to exploit oceans, the tropical rain forests, and other important natural resources? However, often only developed countries have technologies and resources to exploit these opportunities. Lack of or incomplete property rights result in *common-resource problems, public-goods problems, free-rider problems,* and the *tragedy of the commons.* Solutions could be introducing property rights regimes, such as state property, common property or private property. Important questions are: what are the pros and cons of each regime, what are the institutional conditions fulfiled, and what type of bundle of property rights can we specify within the regimes? However, for some goods it will be impossible or very difficult to determine clear and enforceable property rights.

Box 10.11. Key terms of Chapter 10.

Property as a bundle of rights
Property as having residual control rights
  and having residual income
Property regimes
Government property regimes
Private property regimes
Common property regimes
Non-property rights regimes
Open access
Transferability of property rights
Coase theorem
Pareto efficiency
Equity
Social optimum
Transaction costs

Property rights and non-excludability
Los aversion
Non-rivalry
Pure public goods
Impure public goods
Common goods
Private goods
Tragedy of the common
Common ownership solution
New property rights
Production quota
Income rights
Emission quota
Emission rights
Efficient rules

---

11. The economic theory of takings

11.1 Introduction

As explained in Chapter 10, property rights only have a value and a function in the economic process if they are specified, protected, and enforceable. This is where the government plays an important role. In this chapter we examine a completely different role of the government; it has the power to take-over property *(titular takings)* and to enforce limitations in the use of property rights *(regulatory takings)*.Takings are the opposite of assigning of property right by the government. The lack of property rights or the act of *taking them away* by the government, without any compensation, influences both efficiency and equity in a society. In this chapter we will explain the economic effects of government takings, according to new institutional economics and Economic Organisation Theory.

In Section 11.2 we will distinguish two types of takings: titular and regulatory takings. The titular takings are most far-reaching. In the Western world, the general rule is that the act of taking private property is only allowed on two conditions: (1) the private property is taken for a public purpose; and (2) the owner is compensated. This indicates that the power of the government cannot be interpreted as an unlimited natural power to operate in the public interest without taking the interests of individuals into account. For analysing the effects of takings, we will – based on the new institutional economics and Economic Organisation Theory – construct an economic theory of takings. It will include the economic arguments that form the foundation of these two conditions, worked out in Section 11.3 and the incentive effects of takings, as described in Section 11.4.

In Section 11.5 we will compare the Coase theorem, takings and land reform. They have some common elements, but also characteristic differences. For example, the working of the Coase theorem can be better explained by the theory of the firm and that of land reform with the theory of the state. In Table 11.1 we give a brief and stylised comparison of Coase theorem, takings and land reform. Finally, Section 11.6 gives some applications of the theory of takings.

Key questions:
- Why does the government need resources?
- What types of takings can be distinguished?
- What are the economic arguments behind the rules that private property should only be taken (1) for a public purpose; and if (2) the owner is compensated?
- Why are taxes less disruptive than takings if the government need resources?
- What are crucial differences between applying the Coase theorem, takings and land reform?

11.2 Two forms of takings: titular and regulatory takings

In Chapter 10, we emphasised the importance of the role of the government in specifying, protecting and enforcing property rights. These activities are associated with scale advantages. When a specific organisation, in this case the government, specialises in providing these services, the total income in a society will be higher than if every individual protects his/her own property.

The task of the government in a modern democracy goes further. Briefly, the most important reasons for government intervention are market failure and the achievement of the government's own objectives. This is mostly revealed in the delivery of public goods.

There are various types of explanations for the forming and functioning of governments, ranging from the neoclassical to the public-choice approach. To explain and understand government intervention, we must study the objectives, motives, and behaviour of the people who form the government as an *organisation*. Market failure is at the centre of the neoclassical economic explanation of the government, whereas New Institutional Economics has made several important contributions to the explanation of government failures, see e.g. principal-agent theory in Section 6.4 and the institutional lock-in as described in Box 6.7. The *public choice*-theory assumes that the activities of the government are developed and implemented by people – politicians, judges, bureaucrats, civil servants, and others. In this approach, individuals or groups of individuals maximise their utility at the costs of the other inhabitants. Insight in the role and importance of interest groups is then essential (cf. Furubotn and Richter, 2005: 475-476).

The forming and functioning of the government requires a transfer of resources from private to public hands. Private property must be transformed for public use. This can take place via takings or via taxes. The government needs the means of production for preparing and carrying out her tasks and has to regulate the activities of people. In this view, there are two ways for having the disposal over the required means of production: (1) imposing taxes and using the tax returns for buying the means of production and hiring people for fulfiling the tasks of the government; and (2) making use of takings. In the last case, the government has the direct disposal over the means of production and labour.

If the government is not able to obtain sufficient resources through voluntary donations or market transactions, then government authority is required to acquire the resources (Epstein, 1985: 4). This means that the government not only has the power to specify, protect, and enforce the property rights, but also the power to take away property itself or regulate its use. The power of the government to take away property or to regulate its use, affects the clarity and certainty over property rights. However, the social losses associated with the losses of these rights reflect the economic costs of the power of the government to take property and regulate its use. So we have on the one hand these economic costs, and on the other hand the advantages of the delivered public goods. On the basis of these two (losses and profits) elements, it is possible to formulate an economic analysis of *takings*.

Two forms of *takings* can be distinguished (Cooter and Ulen, 1997: 149):
- *Titular takings*. In this case, all the property rights are removed. The government takes land from many owners in order to provide public goods, such as military bases, airports, highways, dams, schools and nature areas. Such expropriation regularly occurs in the layout and purchase of land by the government for setting up rail roads, highways, industrial terrains, nature areas, etc.
- *Regulatory takings*: it means the removal of a part of the property rights. In such cases, there is a restriction on the use of the property without taking the title from the owners. This means a loss of a part of the property rights.

As we have said, property rights only have an effect if there is an authority that is prepared to protect and enforce these rights. Usually, this authority is the government. The same government also has the power to take property or to regulate its use. In many countries, the Constitution circumscribes the government power to take private property. Mostly the thrust is that the Constitution prohibits the government from taking private property for public use, without just compensation. The rule is that the act of taking private property is only allowed under two conditions: (1) the private property is taken for a public purpose; and (2) the owner is compensated. This indicates that the power of the government cannot be interpreted as an unlimited natural power to operate in the public interest without taking the interests of individuals into consideration (cf. Epstein, 1985: 109). We provide five economic arguments that form the foundation for these two conditions (cf. Cooter and Ulen, 1997: 149-155). The first four are more related to *titular takings* and the fifth to *regulatory takings*.

11.3 Five economic arguments for restricting takings and compensation

11.3.1 Compensation

To understand the compensation requirement we must contrast takings and taxes. Taxes are assessed on a broad basis, such as income, sales, profit, property, wealth or bequests. Every subject is confronted with the same schedule of tax rates. In contrast, a *taking* involves a particular piece of property in possession or owned by a particular person. Tyrannies or dictators sometimes finance governments and enrich officials by taking property from individuals. To finance the government by *takings,* the private owner whose property is appropriated must not receive compensation. If the owner of the private property receives compensation equal to the market value of the property, then the government could not profit from taking the property. The requirement of compensation can be seen as a directive to use taxes for the financial needs of the government and not by *takings* (cf. Cooter and Ulen, 1997: 150).

There are good economic reasons for the financing of the government by taxes rather than *takings*. Any kind of expropriation distorts the incentives of the people and causes economic inefficiency. Imposing taxes distorts far less than uncompensated *takings*, especially if these taxes are based on a broad base. To see why, consider the basic principle in public finance that focused taxes distort more than broad taxes. Applying this principle, a given amount of revenue can be raised with less distortion by a tax on food rather than vegetables, or a tax on vegetables rather than carrots. This principle follows from the fact that avoiding broad taxes is more difficult than avoiding narrow taxes. For example, avoiding a tax on food requires eating less, whereas avoiding a tax on carrots requires eating another vegetable such as cucumbers (Cooter and Ulen, 1997: 150).

It means that broad taxes distort behaviour less because many people cannot change their behaviour to avoid these types of taxes. Thus, efficiency requires the government to collect revenues from broad taxes such as income or consumption. However, if we broaden the tax-base there will be some distortion. The distortion from taxes is termed as *excess burden*. In Figure 11.1 the effects of imposing taxes and the arising of excess burden is worked out.

Box 11.1. Excess burden of taxes.

Suppose that SS in Figure 11.1, under perfect competition, represents the social opportunity costs of the production of a good, and DD the demand curve of the same good under conditions which do not limit the consumer sovereignty. For simplicity we assume that the good is a some kind of food. The result is a Pareto-efficient equilibrium in which Q_1 is sold against a market price P_1. Next a price increasing tax is imposed (e.g. a tax added value; TAV), the size of the tax is t per unit. With the new P_2 a quantity of Q_2 can only be sold, with a tax return of P_3P_2AB. With the price increase induced by the imposed tax the situation for consumers deteriorates with P_1P_2AC. It is a loss in their consumer surplus. Opposite to the loss in utility we have the tax return of P_1P_2AE paid by the consumers. A useful spending of the tax revenue by the government can lead to a positive income effect of this tax revenue for the consumers. The rest – AEC – is the *excess burden* or *dead weight loss* of the taxes.

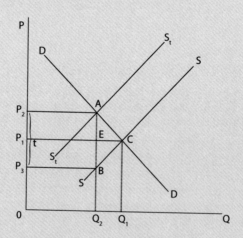

Figure 11.1. The excess burden of taxes.

In same way we can deduce that the producer surplus is reduced with P_1P_3BC in Figure 11.1. The share in the total tax return produced by the producers is P_1P_3BE and the excess burden of the tax BEC.

The total income effect of the tax in Figure 11.1 is equal to the total tax revenue P_3P_2AB. However, beside that we have an excess burden for the consumers and producers with the size of ABC. This excess burden represents the results of the substitution-effect: the plans of individual agents which as result of the tax pressure can not be carried out (e.g. consumers have less possibilities for consuming and saving; they miss utility and interest return, and producers have less possibilities for investments; they will miss profits). The excess burden introduces an extra cost, without a tax revenue for the government on the other hand.

In contrast, *takings* have a very narrow base. Individual owners will often do everything they can to prevent the government from taking their property without compensation. Because of the possibility of uncompensated *takings*, people will put in less effort and resources will be withdrawn from production, so that they cannot be used anymore as an instrument of the politics of redistribution

(Cooter and Ulen, 1997: 150). Welfare theory considerations also call for compensation. If the extra benefits in a project resulting from a *taking* are insufficient to compensate the losers, then the project is not worth implementing. In addition to the welfare-theory considerations, there are also justice considerations for compensation (cf. Epstein, 1985: 4-5).

Summarising, the government needs resources. If we balance takings against taxation, taxation gives fewer distortions, is less inequitable, has less negative incentives and less uncertainties resulting in less hold-up problems. In the case of takings, the person whose property has been taken has bad luck. Taxation provides a better spreading of the risk than the act of taking properties. The risks are shared by all the tax payers. If the government needs resources for carrying its tasks, taxation is by far preferable to takings.

11.3.2 Public use

The compensation-requirement does not preclude other political misuse. The government can take a person's possession and sell it to someone else. To appreciate the problem, consider the difference between a taking and a sale. Sales are motivated by mutual gain, which is created by moving property from lower-valued to higher valued uses. To illustrate, suppose Blair has a nice painting and Clinton would like to buy it. Clinton's purchase of the painting creates a surplus because Clinton values it more than Blair. The fact that both parties must consent to the sale guarantees mutual gains. In contrast, a taking does not require the consent of the property owner, so unilateral gain can motivate a taking. A property owner may value his or her property more than whoever takes it.

Let us take another example. We assume that Blair has a family estate and he values this estate at € 100,000. By taking Blair's estate and giving it to Clinton, the government transfers property from one private person to another, so that Clinton has to pay Blair's subjective price for the estate. The requirement of compensation at market prices does not prevent this abuse, which occurs because the owner's subjective value can exceed the market price paid as compensation. To eliminate the abuse, the government could compensate the owner's subjective price rather than the market price. However, no one but the owner knows the subjective price. In a voluntary sale, the owner receives at least the subjective price or does not sell. If the state wanted to compensate at least the owner's subjective price, the government would have to buy the property, not take it (cf. Cooter and Ulen, 1997: 151).

The 'public-use' requirement avoids the abuse in this example. Clinton's use of Blair's estate is private, not public. Consequently, the taking in this example violates the public-use requirement. The public-use requirement forbids the use of takings to bypass markets and transfer private property from one private person to another. Instead, property must be taken for a public use. For example, Blair's estate could be taken for a park, school or highway (Cooter and Ulen, 1997: 151).

The public-use requirement does not solve the problem of inefficiency of involuntary transfers. To illustrate, suppose that motorists would be willing to pay € 50,000 to use a highway through Blair's estate, the market value of which is € 40,000. By taking the land, paying Blair € 40,000, and building a highway, the government anticipates a surplus of €10,000. In reality, Blair values his estate at € 100,000, so the net social loss will equal to € 50,000, and Blair will lose € 60,000 (cf. Cooter and Ulen, 1997: 151).

In most countries, the government buys most of the resources that it uses to supply public goods. For example, the government buys cement, stones, furniture, pencils, computers, labour, land, etc. However, there are still countries in the world where takings occur.

Summarising, the public-use requirement means that use (i.e. takings) of private property is restricted to public purpose. This is necessary for preventing mis-use. However, this requirement does not solve the problem of inefficient involuntary transfer. For that, full compensation is necessary. It prevents the government from taking too much and creating hold-up problems.

11.3.3 Hold out

The government must often purchase large parcels of land from many owners in order to provide public goods, such as airports, harbours, highways, industrial terrain and wilderness areas. The projects often require 'contiguity', which means that the parcels of land must touch each other. In these cases, the last owner can *hold out* the entire process if the government needs contiguous parcels for a project. Even when owners do not hold out, the possibility of doing so can dramatically increase the transaction costs of purchasing contiguous parcels. Accordingly, the taking-power of the government can eliminate this problem (Cooter and Ulen, 1997: 151).

However, as we have learned from (1) and (2), takings lead to inefficiency. So the government should resort to compulsory purchase only when there are many sellers, each of whom has resources that are necessary to the project. In general, the government should only take private property with compensation to provide public goods when transaction costs preclude purchasing the necessary property (Cooter and Ulen, 1997: 151-152).

11.3.4 Insurance

People typically purchase insurance for assets whose value constitutes a significant proportion of their wealth, such as a house. Most homeowners purchase fire insurance. Similarly, people want insurance against takings. Private companies provide fire insurance, whereas the government provides insurance against takings by compensating property owners. Why does the private sector provide insurance against fires, and the government provide insurance against takings? This question challenges us to relate takings to the economics of insurance (Cooter and Ulen, 1997: 152).

Insurance reduces the risks of the policyholders. It spreads the risk among them. In general, spreading risks more broadly reduces the amount of risk that anyone must bear individually. Similarly, the government can spread the risk of *takings* among all the taxpayers. This would result in greater risk spreading than with all the policy holders in an insurance company. Thus, the degree of risk spreading is a sound argument for public insurance. However, administrative efficiency argues for private insurance. The discipline required for economic competition results in a higher level of administrative efficiency with private insurance as compared to insurance provided by the government (Cooter and Ulen, 1997: 152).

Risk spreading and administrative costs are not decisive. Rather, the decisive case for public insurance against takings rests upon incentive effects for the government. Decisions about takings are made primarily by the government. If the government did not have to pay compensation, it might take property to finance itself, or use the property itself, or take property for redistribution to friends of politicians, or it might end up with too many public goods at its disposal (Cooter and Ulen, 1997: 152).

11.3.5 Regulations

Regulations restrict the use of the property without taking title (= all the property rights) of the owner. It is a less profound intervention than the titular takings. Regulations limit the control rights of someone over a bundle of property rights. These control rights consist of (1) specific control rights and (2) residual control rights. Regulations belong to the specific control rights; rights specified by law or rules of law based on the regulation.

Regulations typically cause a decline in the value of some target properties, which may prompt a law suit for compensation. To illustrate, an entrepreneur who acquires land to build a factory may be blocked when the local government rezones the land as a nature area, and forbids industrial use. The entrepreneur may sue for damages, alleging that the government took the value of the property but not the title. When courts find cause for the plaintiff in such cases, they say there was a 'taking'. When courts find cause for the defendant in such cases, they say there was a 'regulation'. The difference is that a taking requires compensation and a regulation requires no compensation (Cooter and Ulen: 1997: 153).

As explained in Section 10.4, market failure could be a reason for government intervention. For correcting market failure, the government has a broad range of instruments at its disposal: among them, direct regulations and contracts between the government and private parties. The direct regulation of provisions, or activities, that could also be realised by contracting out, frequently seems to occur as a direct response to high transactions costs and observed impediments to smooth transactions. This can be observed in cases where long-term contracting involves extensive investments in specific or relational assets and where the outcome of the contract is hard to predict due to unanticipated contingencies (cf. Görtan and Hägg, 1997: 351).

Based on the Coase theorem, the contracting solution could involve high transaction costs or a low level of adaptation. In such cases, direct **government regulation** (designed to achieve as much as possible within a certain institutional environment), where bargaining among individuals would be too difficult, complex, or costly to be a realistic possibility, could be the most efficient approach. For example, in cases such as smoking, food safety, animal health and other cases where the problem arises frequently, governments may devise rule-making or law-making principles that are intended to resolve situations at low costs. As explained, the *no smoking* rule is a cheap solution from the viewpoint of transaction costs. However, an important difference between regulation and contracting out is the voluntariness and the compensation for the loss in property rights.

11.4 Incentive effects of takings

Compensated restrictions (takings) and uncompensated restrictions (regulations) result in different incentive effects. If the government does not need to compensate for restrictions, then it will likely impose too many of them. If there are too many restrictions, resources will not be put to their highest-valued use or resources will not be used optimally. Thus, uncompensated restrictions result in inefficient use of resources. Firstly, no compensation means no costs for the government which then creates an incentive to take too much. Secondly, it will lead to fewer investments by people, in the short-term, possibly creating the hold-problem. Moreover, no compensation also creates the risk problem of 'who has bad luck'?

Conversely, if the government must compensate the property owners it will prevent mis-use by the government. If the government must compensate fully for restrictions, then property owners or users will be indifferent (if they are risk-neutral) about whether or not the government restricts them. If property owners are indifferent about whether or not the government restricts them, they will improve their property as if there were no risk that restrictions will prevent the use of the improvements. If restrictions subsequently prevent the use of improvements, the investment will be wasted. Thus, compensated restrictions can result in wasteful improvements (Cooter and Ulen, 1997: 153).

Both uncompensated and compensated takings of private property should be restricted to public purpose. It prevents mis-use by the government. Besides violating the public-use requirement[84], uncompensated restrictions result in inefficient use, and in the case of risk-neutral owners/users, the compensation of restrictions can lead to useless improvements.

The effect of two legal instruments from the institutional environment – regulation and takings – is quite different for private persons and the government. For private persons, the uncertainty about the behaviour of the government plays an important role. In practice, there is often uncertainty regarding whether the government will introduce a change in regulations (for example, by re-zoning and limitations on user rights or other rights see Table 10.1). Risks will be internalised in the investment level. Complete compensation means that the risks are zero. The investment level will then be the highest. However, the rule of no compensation will result in smaller investments as a result of the internalisation of the risks at the investment level (Cooter and Ulen, 1997: 154-155). This creates a hold-up problem.

No compensation for the loss of value in investments, caused by the uncertainty of governmental action, provides incentives for the entrepreneur to ensure that the private investment is efficient. This can result in a lower investment level. On the other hand, full compensation for the loss of value in investments, caused by uncertain governmental actions, provides incentives to increase

---

[84] See previous Section 11.3, point 2

private investments (Cooter and Ulen, 1997: 155). However, the effect of the incentive also depends on the risk-attitude and the loss aversion of the private person.

This argument concerns incentives for private persons, not for the government. If the court decides that the alteration in allowable uses of land (in the relevant area) is a mere regulation, so that compensation need not be paid, then the alteration costs the government nothing. On the other hand, if the court decides that this particular action is a taking, so that compensation must be paid, then this type of action is very costly to the government. Obviously, the non-compensability of a regulations gives government officials an incentive to overregulate, whereas the compensability of takings makes government officials internalise the full cost of expropriating private property. When government action is likely to be judged as a taking, the government internalises the costs of its actions and thus restrains its taking of private property. On the other hand, when government action is likely to be judged as a mere regulation, the government lacks incentives to conserve its use of valuable private property rights (Cooten and Ulen, 1997: 155).

If the government compensates property owners for governmental takings, property owners have an incentive toward improvements, whereas if the government does not compensate, the government has an incentive to overregulate private property. This is the paradox of compensation (Cooter and Ulen, 1997: 155). A general rule, based on the assumption that the government chooses to maximise the social welfare, is that the compensation in the event of a taking should be set at the full market value of the asset (Lueck and Miceli, 2004: 49-50). However, it is questionable whether this rule takes the loss aversion of individuals into account.

11.5 Land reforms, Coase theorem and takings

The concept of land reform means to shift or alter property rights over land. According to Perkins *et al.* (2006: 619), the main motive for initiating land reform usually is political, not economic Therefore, the type of political regime is important for the content and the purpose of reform measures and the kind of land tenure system being reformed. History has shown us that two types of politics lead to reform. In one type, a society with a large tenant and landless labourer population that is controlled by other classes, may find itself faced with increasing rural unrest. In this type of land reform, to keep this unrest from escalating into a revolution, property rights over land are allocated to the peasant class to reduce conflict and give them a stake in continuous stability. In the second type, land reform takes place after a revolution supported by the rural poor has occurred. The main purpose of reform, in this case, is to consolidate support for the revolution among the rural poor and eliminate the economic base of one of the classes, the landlords, most opposed to the revolution.

For example, the motive behind the Mexican land reforms of the twentieth century was largely of the first type. It was largely meant to minimise the political uprising among different classes. Prior to the Mexican Revolution of 1911, land in Mexico had become increasingly concentrated in large haciendas ranging in size from 1,000 to over 400,000 acres. Although the revolution of 1911 was supported by those who had lost their land and other rural poor, those who took power after the revolution largely were from upper-income groups or the small middle class. To meet the continuing unrest, the new Mexican government periodically redistributed some arable land. Mexican land-tenure relations, however, continued to be characterised by large estates existing alongside small peasant holdings. Reform eliminated some of the more extreme forms of pressure for more radical change, but Mexican agriculture still includes a large, poor, and not very productive rural peasant class (Perkins *et al.*, 2006: 620)

The Chinese land reform of the 1940s and early 1950s under the leadership of the communistic party, was characteristic for the second type of political motives. The communist revolution had been built primarily on the poor, and the landlord class was one of the pillars of support of the existing Kuomintang government. Prior to the reform some 40 percent of arable land had been farmed by tenants, who typically paid half of their main crop to the landlord as land rent (= sharecropping). The landlord, either a resident in the village or an absentee, contributed little or nothing else than the land. After the reform, and prior to the collectivisation of agriculture in 1955-56, land was owned by the tiller and the landlord received no compensation whatsoever. In fact, many landlords on trial publicly in the village were either executed or sent off to perform hard labour under harsh conditions (Perkins *et al.*, 2006: 620).

A more recent example of land reform with compensation occurred in Zimbabwe. At the turn of the twenty-first century, president Mugabe encouraged landless individuals to simply seize the land of the large farms owned by white farmers. With the government unwilling to enforce their private property rights, the white farmers had little choice other than to flee their farms or risk their lives by defending them. Whether those who received land will have secure property rights and farm the land efficiently remains to be seen, but the initial results contributed to famine in Zimbabwe (Perkins *et al.*, 2006: 620).

The Japanese land reform that followed World War II differed in important respects from the Chinese experience. Land reform in Japan was carried out by the U.S. occupation forces. The occupation government believed that landlord classes were an important supporter of the forces in Japanese society that brought about World War II. Small peasant proprietors, in contrast, were seen a solid basis on which a future democratic and stable Japan could be built. Since the Americans had won the war, Japanese landlords were not in a position to offer resistance to reform, and a large scale land reform was carried out. While compensation for landlords was provided for in legislation, inflation soon had the effect of sharply reducing the real value of the amounts offered. As a result, Japanese land reform also amounted to confiscation of landlord land with little compensation (Perkins *et al.*, 2006: 621).

The impact of land reform on agricultural production depends on what kind of system is being reformed as well as the content of the reform measures. Land reform has the greatest positive impact on production where the previous system was one of small peasants, with high rates of insecure tenancy (for example, one-year contracts) and absentee landlords. Under such conditions reform has little impact on cultivation practices since farms are small both before and after reform. The elimination of landlords also has less affect on efficiency because they have little to do with farming. On the other hand, turning tenants into landowners provides them with well-defined and secure property rights and hence with a greater incentive to invest in improvements (Perkins *et al.*, 2006: 622). In that case, they have both residual control rights and residual income and consequently no hold-up problems.

At the other extreme, there are reforms that break up large, highly efficient modern estates, or farms, and substitute them with small and inefficient producers. In many parts of the developing world highly mechanised estates using the most advanced techniques arise over time. The incentive problems inherent to the use of hired farm labour, at least partially, are overcome by the use of skilled professional estate managers. Often these estates are major suppliers of agricultural produce for export and hence a crucial source of the developing country's foreign exchange. If land reform breaks up these estates and turns them over to small peasant proprietors who know little about modern techniques and lack the capital to pay for them, the impact on the efficiency and the agricultural production can be catastrophic (Perkins *et al.*, 2006: 622). But there are also examples, as in the Kenyan highlands, where the breaking down of large estates into small peasant holdings actually increased the production, mainly because the small holdings were farmed much more intensively than the large estates. In between these two extremes are a myriad of variations with different impact on efficiency, both positive and negative (Perkins *et al.*, 2006: 622).

Land reform has a major impact on the distribution of income in rural areas, particularly if land is taken from landlords without compensation, or at least without anything close to full compensation. If former tenants are required to pay landlords the full market value of the land received, the society's distribution of wealth is the same as before. The tenants receive land together with a debt equal to the value of land, hence no change in net wealth of the former tenants. The former landlords surrender land but acquire an asset of equal value in the form of a loan to the tenants (Perkins *et al.*, 2006: 622).

Two critical remarks have to be made. **First**, the society's distribution of wealth is only the same as before if both tenants and landlords value gains and losses equally. **Second**, the process of land reform assumes frictionless transactions. In reality, there can be high transaction costs to create and enforce the new situation, including new property rights. The power of the political actions and the threat of violence creates such high enforcement costs for the existing landowners that they have no other choice than to leave their land and allow property rights to shift accordingly. An important side-effect can be that people become hesitant in carrying out productive activities, as they are afraid the ruler could seize any returns. Society gets a kind of hold-up problem. In other words, lack of property rights or the erosion of these rights creates a negative incentive for people to undertake productive activities or investments (see also Box 1.2).

Reform with full compensation may be desirable on efficiency grounds because of the advantages of strengthening property rights through landowner rather than tenant cultivation, but initially at least, the new owner is just as poor and the new landlord just rich as before. On the other hand, if the land lord is compensated with bonds paid out of general tax revenues, the former tenants's income share may rise, provided that the taxes to pay for this do not fall primarily on the tenants. The best-known successful land reforms commonly have involved little or no compensation for confiscated assets of landlords. Such was the case in Russia after 1917 and China after 1949, as well as in the Japanese and South Korean reforms after World War II. The discussion of land-tenants relations and land reforms often focuses on the use of better techniques and more inputs. However, the land use system must provide farmers with well-defined, secure and enforceable property rights, and hence, the incentive to introduce those techniques and inputs, and use them efficiently (Perkins *et al.*, 2006: 623).

In Table 11.1 we give a brief and stylised comparison of the Coase theorem, takings and land reform. The criteria are given in the left column of this table. We assume in the start situation for the Coase theorem 'free access', i.e. assets (resources) are used freely, without property rights, like we did in the water case in Chapter 10. However, this is not the case in the *ex-ante* situation for takings and land reform. In both cases, there are property rights for the assets; private or common property rights. Yet, it is possible that these rights have not been registered. Sometimes these rights only consist of the user rights while property regimes are government property. Government agencies have the right to determine the use and access rules.

The purpose of the Coase theorem is to realise a more efficient situation as explained in the previous chapter. For takings, the purpose is to produce public goods and for land reform the purpose is often to maintain political power. According to the Coase theorem, the rights will be traded; in the bargaining process the price will be the coordination mechanism[85]. In case of takings and land reform, the coordination mechanism will be the visible hand of the ruler, see Box 11.2. The transaction mechanism for property rights within the Coase theorem is the market and for takings and land reform the government.

---

[85] For the relationship between the transaction mechanisms or governance structures and the price as coordination mechanism see Chapter 8.

Table 11.1. Comparison of Coase theorem, takings and land reform.

	Coase theorem	Takings	Land reform
Start situation	Free access	Private/common property rights	Private/common/state property rights
Purpose	Efficiency	Public goods	Maintain politic power
Transfer in property rights	Trade among parties; carried out by bargaining	Enforced transfer	Enforced transfer
Transaction mechanism	Market	Government	Government
Economic basis	Yes	Yes	No
Compensation	Reservation price	Compensation rules in constitution	It depends
Valuation of gains and losses	Is to be assumed equal	Unclear	Not important /does not matter
Income distribution	Is considered	Depends on compensation	Has an impact only without compensation
Theory of the firm or the state	Theory of the firm	Mix of theory of the firm and state	Theory of the state

Box 11.2. The theory of state and government as ruler.

Normally the coordination mechanism the 'visible hand' is used in firms and organisations based on hierarchy. However, we can also apply this mechanism within the theory of the state. This theory has been explained in Box 1.3. The government is the designer and the ruler. We posit here a ruler who recognises that substantial benefits can be obtained by organising some activities. If a ruler gains a monopoly on the use of force, the ruler can use coercion as the fundamental mechanism to organise a diversity of human activities that will produce collective benefits. In our case, the activities consist of takings and land reform.

The compensation for the transfer of property rights from one party to the other one, within the Coase theorem, will be the reservation price. For the takings approach, most countries apply the compensation rule; a compensation equal to the market value of the property. Without this rule the government has the incentive to take too much, because compensation is not necessary and the government could profit from taking the property. No compensation will also create a hold-up problem for the party who will loss his assets. For land reform, compensation is often not applied.

The valuation of the gains and losses are assumed to be equal in the Coase theorem. However, this is a doubtfully assumption, given the loss aversion of people. For takings, the valuation of the gains and losses is not clear. The compensation rule 'equal to the market value of the property' assumes that gains and losses are considered to be equal. For land reform, the valuation of gains and loss does not matter for the political ruler. However, one can imagine, that landlords' loss of land and their estates has an enormously impact on their welfare.

As said, Table 11.1 gives a brief and stylised comparison of the Coase theorem, takings and land reform. We assumed for the Coase theorem free access. Releasing this assumption can be considered as the next step in applying the Coase theorem; bargaining (cf. Cooter and Ulen, 1997: 79-83). It is also possible that a land reform process is carried out by a democratic government and that landowners whose land has been taken are compensated. Even if a compensation is granted to the landowner, the transaction cost of securing the property rights can be high for the government. However, if no compensation is granted, the landowner will likely have high transaction costs in the attempt to secure and enforce his or her property rights from the government take-over, often through legal action. In general, the land reform process occurs at the cost of the existing landowners' loss. Such losses are not likely to be frictionless transactions. Rather, landowners are likely to attempt protecting their rights, resulting in high transaction (enforcement) costs. By doing so, the cost of capturing these property rights also increases. In countries such as Zimbabwe, in which the government regime supported land reform, extreme levels of social violence created such high enforcement costs that landowners had no alternative but to vacate the land.

11.6 Application of the theory

In the Netherlands, Article 14 (1) of the Constitution allows expropriation only with insured compensation. This article provides citizens with equal bargaining power. Further, it supports the view that the government should be seen as a methodological individual, as a player and not as an institution above the citizens, representing abstract general interests (Kerkmeester, 1993: 98). In the Netherlands, both titular and regulatory takings occur. Titular takings occur with expropriation for general objectives; they are radical and all embracing. Compensation often takes place at the market price or higher. Regulations are not so invasive, only a part of the property rights are affected. Further, it is not always clear whether or not the loss of property rights must be compensated. However, in practice these losses and the resulting economic effects can be considerable.

This can be illustrated with some different examples. First, an individual who purchases a plot of agricultural land can incur a substantial loss of his property rights if the government changes the zoning of this land (for example, to forest or nature area). Every year, a number of farmers in the EU make use of the subsidy-regulation for temporary forestation. Yet, what is the consequence if the government declares by re-zoning this to be a permanent forest, i.e. forbids cutting and reduces the grants for replanting only? What is the loss in value of the bundle of property rights? To give an idea of the loss, in the Netherlands, the price of agricultural land is about 40,000 euro per ha while the price of permanent forest land is about 10,000 euro per ha. Consequently, a change in the bundle of property rights of an asset can have important economic consequences.

The second example refers to the instruments of spatial and environmental policy. Regulations are important instruments for both areas. With direct regulations, the government either prohibits specific behaviour or permits behaviour under certain rules. Among these rules are the well-known set of interdictions, obligations and licences. These prescriptions are direct in character. They have a direct and compulsory influence on the behaviour of producers and consumers. A characteristic of legal regulations is that they impose considerable limitations on property rights. These are regulatory takings. In most EU-countries, we see their applications reflected in the instruments that the government has applied for the preservation of the quality of soil, water, air, nature and landscape, animal welfare and health, and human health (food safety and consumer trust).

Prohibitions and obligations dominate the environmental policy advocated. Licences have so far been applied very little as instruments of environmental policy in the Netherlands and the EU. However, this is changing. For more and more activities, it is becoming necessary to have a license or a right to produce emissions. Licences can be seen as property rights. The application of licences or permits is not meaningful in the case of any material or activity that can be lethal to man and environment in very small concentrations. Licences or permits can consist of the right to carry out certain activities like cutting trees and emission rights for CO_2 and the restricted use of the minerals N, P and K (because of the manure regulation) on land. In principle, emission and pollution rights can be tradable. Pollution rights, being tradable, bring flexibility in the allocation of the limited quantity of emissions tolerated. This has been discussed in Chapter 10.

Legal measures comprise regulations amounting to physical limitations, for example quotas. A distinction can be made between regulations under public and private law. The governments' role in public law, combined with the behavioural mechanism of 'compulsion', results in direct regulation. In private law regulations, the role of government is limited to legislation; it adopts the role of facilitator for a private implementation process. In this approach, tradable production or pollution rights are a combination of the public and private law role of the government. There is a limitation on total pollution, for example, a CO_2 ceiling enforced by public law (the quantity of licenses determined unilaterally by government) and private law for the trade in licenses. As the target group is confronted both with compulsion (not to exceed the volume permitted) and with the opportunity to realise transactions (trade in licences), aspects of both behavioural and transaction play a role.

A special application of direct regulation in the EU is cross-compliance coupled with good farming practice. It is a tool to improve compliance with existing standards for preserving the quality of soil, water, air, nature and landscape, animal welfare and health, and human health (food safety and consumer trust). Fulfiling these standards is called **good farming practice**. Good farming practise can be described as maintaining agricultural land, especially land which is no longer used for production purposes, in good agricultural and environmental condition. The criteria used to define and instruments used to address these issues differ between countries. The chosen criteria reflect the differences in national priorities and geo-climatic and eco-system conditions. The most common measures are the establishment of a certain level of green cover during winter, the control of unwanted shrub and tree encroachment, and restrictions on machinery use and on stubble burning. In some cases, the selection of measures was probably also guided by how easy they were to control and enforce. Some countries used the implementation of good farming practice to introduce new requirements for farmers while others used existing standards.

The cross-compliance mechanism refers to the linking of environmental conditions, animal welfare and health, and human health (food safety and consumer trust) to agricultural support payments; the so-called single farm payment. Compliance with a series of restrictions related to the environment, food safety or animal welfare is required to be eligible for the single farm payments programmes[86]. It means *ex-ante*, each farmer has to compare additional costs involved by the compliance mechanism to the additional benefit from the support scheme. This instrument influences private behaviour and indirectly results in the provision of positive externalities. Nevertheless, the voluntary nature of the cross-compliance mechanism may be questioned. Indeed, where support payments are high, it is very close to a mandatory tool. For that reason, it fits within the instrument 'direct regulation' and it is a form of takings.

Fourth, consider the regulations about Nature 2000 sites in the EU. This Directive requires member states to maintain or restore sufficient biodiversity and to take special management measures to establish special protected zones. This focuses on the protection of important areas for wildlife, nature and landscape. The choice of the areas is based on the rarity of the animal and plant species or the importance of certain habitats. For Nature 2000 sites, the Dutch government wants to designate a number of protected areas in which a number of activities will be forbidden. These regulations mean a loss in the bundle of property rights. For farmers, forest-owners and landed estate owners it can mean a loss in return on one hand (some activities are not allowed anymore) and on the other hand an increase in the risks of damage from wildlife or diseases.

---

[86] This can also be considered as an attempt of the government to create incentives for self monitoring and as a way for reducing transaction costs; this is comparable to the 'no smoking rule'.

Landowners, including farmers, forest and landed estate owners, believe that this regulation should be accompanied by compensation.

Box 11.3. describes a completely different form of takings. It refers to takings of labour in Ethiopia. In the past these types of takings were common in more countries. See also Box 1.2.

Box 11.3. The labour quota system in Ethiopia.

Widespread environmental degradation is among the major factors for the poverty prevalence in many developing countries. There are different ways to struggle with these problems. In Ethiopia, for example, a labour quota system exists. It is a system of labour pooling peasant households for resource management. Every active adult household member is expected to contribute 20-27 adult person-day per year. At minimum of 30% of the active adult labour in a village is expected to be mobilised. The mobilised labour is utilised mainly for constructing soil and water conservation structures on cultivable and non-cultivable land, afforestation activities, dam construction, rural road construction and maintenance and other infrastructural works. Communities have labour quota by-laws which are approved by the village assembly and controlled by local courts. Nevertheless, the non-compliance level is high. About 50% of the households contribute less then the half of the agreed quota of person-days (Tesfay, 2006: 113).

In the above case, two situations can be considered. First, the local government can force households in the rural areas to provide free labour service (apparently without any compensation) for example in building community terraces for soil and water conservation. This is purely labour taking. The (local) government is not compensating for the labour provided by the rural households. This labour quota system is a kind of taking. People are being forced to provide labour in some activities without compensation. No compensation in these activities means no costs for the government, but also an incentive to take too much (because there are no costs for the government). People who have to work have bad luck.

Second, households are compensated for their labour service in such activities as road or dams construction in rural areas. This compensation method is famously called in Ethiopia 'Food for work'. At times, the (local) government requires such type of labour takings (free provision of labour service in soil and water conservation) as a prerequisite for compensated labour services in road or dams construction. So, it means people who did not participate in the free provision of labour service will not be allowed to participate in the compensated activity. You could really observe such kind of compensated and uncompensated labour taking activities in Ethiopia.

However, comparisons with the situations in Western countries would be not correct in some cases. While it is not difficult to compensate for any takings here in the West, it could be the case that (local) governments in countries like Ethiopia simply do not have the resources to compensate labour takings for constructing soil, water conservation elements and roads.

A fifth example is the discussion in the U.S. regarding the status of various species in private lands, and the associated potential conflicts over private property rights, regulations, takings and compensation. The Endangered Species Act of 1988 does not provide compensation for owners of private land, which incur income and wealth losses as a result of the measures for habitat protection on their land. Innes *et al.*, (1998: 36) estimate that these measures of the government have resulted in a loss of value of private property to the extent of 20-33%. This has consequences for the legitimacy of regulatory takings without compensation. The compensation-debate focuses on three questions: (1) Should takings be compensated? (2) If so, then how should compensation be made? (3) Is there a need for (juridical or constitutional) conditions to ensure that the government has an incentive to choose for efficient takings and a compensation policy (Innes *et al.*, 1998: 37)? This discussion is still going on.

Finally, the use of government takings and regulations are still very common. However, their original purpose has changed. In the past, labour takings were commonly used in the Western world. For example, most countries had – and some have still have – compulsory military service. This is a kind of takings certainly if the compensation is very low or almost zero. Similarly, in areas such as traffic rules we see a lot of regulations. Some of them of involve considerable limitations of your property rights. For example, on some roads you are not allowed to drive faster than 80 or 100 km per hour with your car. The no-smoking regulation is a comparable example. However, because of transaction costs (negotiating, monitoring and enforcement) such rules are preferable to a bargaining process through which these property rights are negotiated (e.g. rights over road use and smoking rights).

Box 11.4. Key terms of Chapter 11.

Titular takings	Re-zoning
Regulatory takings	Paradox of compensation
Excess burden	Types of land reforms
Compensation requirement	Transfer of property rights
Public-use requirement	Transaction mechanism of property rights
Hold out	Theory of the state
Compensated restrictions	Income distribution
Uncompensated restrictions	Valuation of gains and losses

References

Alchian, A.A., 1965. The basis of Some Recent Advances in the Theory of Management of the Firm. Journal of Industrial Economics, 14: 30-44.

Alchian, A.A., 1969. Corporate Management and Property Rights. In: Economics Policy and Regulation of Corporate Security. American Enterprise Institute, Washington, D.C., pp. 337-360.

Alchian, A.A. and H. Demsetz, 1972. Production, Information Costs, and Economic Organisation. American Economic Review, 62: 777-795.

Alessi, L. de, 1983. Property Rights and Transaction Costs. The American Economic Review, 73: 64-81.

Allen, W.D. and D.L. Lueck, 1998. The nature of the farm. Journal of Law and Economics, XLI: 343-386.

Allen, D.W. and D. L. Lueck, 2002. The Nature of the Farm; Contracts, Risks, and Organisation. The MIT Press. Cambridge, 258 p.

Arrow, K.J., 2000. Observations on Social Capital. In: P. Dasgupta and I. Serageldin (eds.), Social Capital. A Multifaceted Perspective. The World Bank, Washington, pp. 3-5.

Assem, M.J. van den and G.T. Post, 2005. Miljoenenjacht: voer voor economen. Economisch Statistische Berichten, 90: 538-539.

Baarsma, B. and J. Theeuwes, 2008. De verwarde onderneming. Economisch Statistische Berichten, 93: 68-71.

Bargeman, B., 1996. Associates in de vrije tijd. Vrijetijd Studies, 14 (Hardloopverslaving, verenigingsleven, stedetoerisme): 34-49.

Barzel, Y., 1997. Economic Analysis of Property Rights. Second Edition, Cambridge University Press, Cambridge, 161 p.

Bates, R.H., 2003. Social dilemmas and rational individuals. In: J. Harriss, J. Hunter and C.M. Lewis (eds.), The new institutional economics and third world development. Routlegde, London, pp. 27-48.

Baumol, W.J., J. Panzar and B. Willig, 1982. Constestable markets and the Theory of Industry Structure. Hartcourt Brace Jonanovich, New York, 575 p.

Beers, C.P. van, J.J.M. Theeuwes, 1998. Natuurlijke werkloosheid in Nederland. Economisch Statistische Berichten, 83: 352-355.

Berle, A. A. and G.C. Means, 1932. The modern corporation and private property. MacMillan, New York, 391 p.

Beugelsdijk, S., 2003. Culture and Economic Development in Europe. Proefschrift, Faculty of Economics and Business Administration, Universiteit van Tilburg, 200 p.

Black, J., 2002. A Dictionary of Economics. Second edition. Oxford University Press, Oxford, 511 p.

Brickley, J.A., C.W. Smith and J.L. Zimmerman, 2001. Managerial Economics and Organizational Architecture. Second Edition. McGraw-Hill, New York, 616 p.

Binmore, K., 1992. Fun and Games; A Text on Game Theory. D.C. Heath and Company, Lexington, Massachusetts, 602 p.

Bijman, J., 2002. Essays on Agricultural Co-operatives; Governance Structures in Fruit and Vegetable Chain. Proefschrift, Erasmus Universiteit Rotterdam, 185 p.

Blanchard, O. and J. Wolfers, 1999. The role of shocks and institutions in the rise of European unemployment: The aggregate evidence. Working Paper 7282, National Bureau of Economic Research, Cambridge, Massachusetts, 34 p.

Boadway, R.W. and N. Bruce, 1989. Welfare Economics. Second Edition, Blackwell, Oxford, 344 p.

Bogetoft, P. and H.B. Olesen, 2004. Design of Production Contracts; Lessons form Theory and Agriculture. Copenhagen Business School Press, Copenhagen, 207 p.

Bourdieu, P. 1986. Forms of Capital: In: J.C. Richardson (ed.), Handbook of Theory and Research for the Sociology of Education. New York: Greenwood Press, pp. 241-258.

Borgen, S.O. and A. Hegrenes, 2005. How can transaction costs economics add to the understanding of new contractual formats in the Norwegian Agri-food System. Working Paper 2005-7, Centre for Food Policy, Norwegian Economics Agricultural Economic Research Institute, 49 p.

Boschma, R.A., 1997. Evolutionaire Theorie. Economisch Statistische Berichten, 82: 313-315.

Boschma, R.A., K. Frenken and J.G. Lambooy, 2002. Evolutionaire economie. Coutinho, Bussum, 252 p.

Bovenberg, A.L. and C.N. Teulings, 1999. Concurrentie als alternatief voor rechtsprincipes. Economisch Statistische Berichten, 84: 364-367.

Bovenberg, A.L., 2002. Norms, values and technological change. De Economist, 150: 521-553.

Bromley, D.W. and I. Hodge, 1990. Private property rights and presumptive policy entitlement; reconsidering the premises of rural policy. European Review Agricultural Economics, 12: 197-214.

Bromley, D.W., 1991. Environment and Economy; Property Rights and Public Policy. Basil Blackwell, Cambridge, Massachusetts, 247 p.

Brousseau, E. 2002. The governance of transactions by commercial intermediaries; An analysis of the re-engineering of intermediation by electronic commerce. International Journal of the Economics of Business, 9: 353-374.

Brousseau, E. and J-M. Glachant (eds.), 2002. The Economics of Contracts; Theories and Applications. Cambridge University Press, Cambridge, 584 p.

Brouwer, M., 1990. Theorie van de industriële organisatie. In: L. van de Geest (ed.), Economische theorie: stand van zaken. Academic Service, Schoonhoven, pp. 233-275.

Bruinsma, D.J., 2000. Grenzen verleggen voor vernieuwing. Economisch Statistische Berichten, 85: 4-8.

Buchanan, J.M. 1965. An Economic Theory of Clubs. Economica, 32: 1-14.

Caballero, R.J., 1996. The Macroeconomics of Specifity. Working Paper 5757, National Bureau of Economic Research, Cambridge, Massachusetts, 46 p.

Caves, R.E. and M. Porter, 1976. Barrries to exit. In: R.T. Masson and P.D. Qualls (eds.), Essays on Industrial Organization in honor of J.S.Bain. Ballinger Publisher Co. Cambridge, Massachusetts, pp. 39-69.

Cayseele P. van and H. Schreuder, 1990. Strategisch Management. In: L. van de Geest (ed.), Economische theorie: stand van zaken. Academic Service, Schoonhoven, pp. 307-327.

Challen, R., 2000. Institutions, Transaction Costs and Environmental Policy; Institutional Reform for Water Resources. Edward Elgar, Cheltenham, 233 p.

Chapman, T.L. and D. Reiter, 2004. The United Nations Security Council and the Rally' Round the Flag Effect. Journal of Conflict Resolution, 48: 886-909.

Clarkson, K.W. and R. LeRoy Miller, 1982. Industrial Organization; Theory and Evidence and Public Policy. McGraw-Hill, Singapore, 518 p.

Coase, H.R., 1937. The Nature of the Firm. Economica, 4: 386-405.

Coase, H.R., 1960. The Problem of the Social Cost. The Journal of Law and Economics, 3: 1-44.

Coase, H.R., 1988. The Firm, the Market and the Law. The University of Chicago Press, Chicago, 217 p.

Coase, H.R., 1992. The Institutional Stucture of Production. The American Economic Review, 82: 713-719.

Coase, H.R., 1996. The Nature of the Firm. Economica. In: L. Putterman and R.S. Kroszner (eds.), The Economic Nature of the Firm. Cambridge University Press, Cambridge UK, pp. 89-104.

Coleman, J.S., 1988. Social Capital in the Creation of Human Capital. American Journal of Sociology, 94 (Supplement): S95-S120.

Conner, K.R and C.K. Prhalad, 1996. A recource-based theory of the firm: Knowledge versus Opportunism. Organizational Science, 7: 477-501.

Cooter, R. and Th. Ulen, 1997. Law and Economics. Second Edition, Addison-Wesley, Reading Massachusetts, 481 p.

Cornes, R. and T. Sandler, 1996. The theory of externalities, public goods and club goods. Second Edition. Cambridge University Press, Cambridge, 590 p.

CPB, 1997. Challenging Neighbours: Rethinking German and Dutch Economic Institutions. Springer, Berlin, 592 p.

Damme, E.E.C. van, 1990. Speltheorie. In: L. van de Geest (ed.), Economische theorie: stand van zaken. Academic Service, Schoonhoven, pp. 363-381.

Damme, E.E.C. van, 1998. Kruisvaarders met koud water vrees. Economisch Statistische Berichten, 83: 811.

Damme, E.E.C. van and A. Heertje, 1994. Speltheorie in beweging. Economisch Statistische Berichten, 79: 936-941.

Dasgupta, P., 1991. The Environment as a Commodity. In: D. Vines and A.A. Stevenson (eds.), Information, Strategy and Public Policy, Basil Blackwell, pp. 71-103.

Dasgupta, P.S., 1997. Economic Development and the Idea of Social Capital. Working Paper. Faculty of Economics, University of Cambridge.

Dasgupta, P., 2000. Economic Progress and the Idea of Social Capital. In: P. Dasgupta and I. Serageldin (eds.), Social Capital. A Multifaceted Perspective. The World Bank, Washington, pp. 325-424.

Dasgupta, P. and I. Serageldin (eds.), 2000. Social Capital. A Multifaceted Perspective. The World Bank, Washington, 440 p.

Davidson, M., B. Boon and J. Faber, 2007. Toedeling van emissierechten aan de luchtvaart. Economisch Statistische Berichten, 92: 552-554.

Davis, L.E. and D.C. North, 1971. Institutional change and American economic growth. Cambridge University Press, London, 283 p.

Deakin, S. and J. Michie, 1997. The Theory and Practise of Contracting. In: S. Deakin and J. Michie (eds.), Contracts, Co-operation, and Competition; Studies in Economics, Management and Law. Oxford University Press, Oxford, pp. 1-39.

Demsetz, H., 1967. Toward a Theory of Property Rights. The American Economic Review, 57: 347-359.

Devlin, R.A. and R.Q. Grafton, 1998. Economic Rights and Environmental Wrongs; Property Rights for the Common Good. Edward Elgar, Cheltenham, UK, 189 p.

Dixit, A., 2002. Incentives and Organisations in the Public Sector: An Interpretative Review. The Journal of Human Resources, 37: 696-727.

Douma, S.W. and H. Schreuder, 1992. Economic Approaches to Organizations. Prentice Hall International, London, 185 p.

Douma, S.W. and H. Schreuder, 1998. Economic Approaches to Organizations. Second Edition, Prentice Hall International, London, 238 p.

Douma, S.W. and H. Schreuder, 2002. Economic Approaches to Organizations. Third Edition, Prentice Hall International, London, 282 p.

Eggertsson, T., 1990. Economic behaviour and institutions. Cambridge University Press, Cambridge, 385 p.

Eggertsson, T., 1997. Sources of Risk, Institutions of Survival, and A Game Against Nature in Nature in Premodern Iceland, Paper presented NIE Meeting, Saint-Louis, 19-21 September.

Epstein, R.A., 1985. Takings; Private Property and the Power of Eminent Domain. Harvard University Press, Cambridge, Massachusetts, 362 p.

Falk, A. and U. Fischbacher, 1999. A Theory of Reciprocity. Working paper. University of Zurich, Institute for Empirical Economic Research, 42 p.

FitzRoy, F.R., Z.J. Acs and D.A. Gerlowski, 1998. Management and Economics of Organization. Prentice Hall Europe, London, 598 p.

Foss, K and N. Foss, 2001. Assets, Attributes and Ownership. International Journal of the Economics of Business, 8: 19-37.

Frey, B., 1997. From the Price to the Crowding Out Effect. Swiss Journal of Economics and Statistics, 133: 325-350.

Fudenberg, D. and J. Tirole, 1996. Game Theory. MIT Press, Cambridge Massachusetts, 579 p.

Furubotn, E.G., 2002. Entrepreneurship, transaction-cost economics, and the design of contracts. In: E. Brousseau and J-M. Glachant (eds.), The Economics of Contracts; Theories and Applications. Cambridge University Press, Cambridge, pp. 72-95.

Furubotn, E.G. and S. Pejovich, 1972. Property Rights and Economic Theory: A Survey of Recent Literature. Journal of Economic Literature, 10: 1137-1162.

Furubotn, E.G. and R. Richter, 1991. The New Institutional Economics: An Assessment. In: E.G. Furubotn and R. Richter (eds.), The New Institutional Economics: A collection of articles from the Journal of Institutional and Theoretical Economics. More (Siebeck), Tubbingen, pp. 1-32.

Furubotn, E.G. and R. Richter, 1997. Institutional and Economic Theory: The Contribution of the New Institutional Economics. The University of Michigan Press, 542 p.

Furubotn, E.G. and R. Richter, 2005. Institutional and Economic Theory: The Contribution of the New Institutional Economics. Second Edition, The University of Michigan Press, 653 p.

Furth, D., 1994. De winner's curse. Economisch Statistische Berichten, 79: 1162-1164.

Germis, J. and E. Vermeylen, 2002. Rollenpatronen succesfactor voor PPS in Vlaanderen. Economische Statistische Berichten, 87: 860-863.

Graafland, J.J., 2001. Vier strategieën voor maatschappelijk ondernemen. Economische Statistische Berichten, 86: 28-31.

Granovetter, M., 1973. The Strength of Weak Ties. The American Journal of Sociology, 78: 1360-1380.

Granovetter, M., 1985. Economic Action and Social Structure: The Problem of Embeddedness. The American Journal of Sociology, 91: 481-510.

Gravelle, H. and R. Rees, 1992. Microeconomics. Second Edition, Longman, London, 752 p.

Groenewegen, J. (ed.), 1996. Transaction Cost Economics and Beyond. Kluwer Academic Publishers, Dordrecht, 389 p.

Görant, P. and T. Hägg, 1997. Theories in the Economics of Regulation; A Survey of the Literature from European Perspective. European Journal of Law and Economics, 4: 337-370.

Grossman, S. and O. Hart, 1986. The Cost and Benefits of Ownership: Theory of Vertical and Lateral Integration. Journal of Political Economy, 9: 691-719.

Hanley, N., H. Kirkpartrick, I. Simpson and D. Oglethorpe, 1998. Principles for the Provision of Public Goods from Agriculture: Modeling Moorland Conservation in Scotland. Land Economics, 74: 102-113.

Hanneman, W.M., 1999. The Economic Theory of WTP and WTA. In: I.J. Bateman and K.G. Willis (eds.), Valuing Environmental Preferences. Oxford University Press, Oxford, pp. 42-96.

Hart, O., 1995. Firms, Contracts, and Financial Structure. Oxford University Press, Oxford, 228 p.

Hart, O.A., 2002. Norms and the Theory of the firm. In: E. Brousseau and J-M. Glachant (eds.), The Economics of Contracts; Theories and Applications. Cambridge University Press, Cambridge, pp. 180-192.

Hart, O. and B. Holmström, 1987. Theory of contracts. In: T.F. Bewley (ed.), Advances in Economic Theory; Fifth World Congress. Econometric Society Monographs No. 12, Cambridge, pp. 71-155.

Hart, O. and J. Moore, 1990. Property Rights and the Nature of the Firm. Journal of Political Economy, 98: 1119-1158.

Hart, O. and J. Moore, 1999. Foundations of incomplete contracts. Review of Economic Studies, 66: 115-138.

Hart, O., A. Shleifer and R.W. Vishny, 1997. The proper scope of government: Theory and an application to prison. The Quarterly Journal of Economics, 11: 1127-1161.

Hawkings, D., D.A. Lake, D. Nielson and M.J. Tierney, 2003. Delegation Under Anarchy: States, International Organisations, and Principal-Agent Theory. www.internationalorganizations.org.

Hay, A.D. and D.L. Morris, 1991. Industrial Economics and Organization; Theory and Evidence. Oxford University Press, Oxford, 686 p.

Hayek, F., 1945. The use of knowledge in society. American Economic Review, 35: pp. 519-530.

Hazeu, C.A., 2000. Institutionele Economie; Een optiek op organisatie- en besturingvraagstukken. Uitgeverij Countinho, Bussum, 143 p.

Hazeu, C.A., 2007. Institutionele Economie; Een optiek op organisatie- en besturingvraagstukken. Tweede druk, Uitgeverij Countinho, Bussum, 153 p.

Hendrikse, G.W.J., 1992. Concurrentiestrategieën. Academic Service, Schoonhoven, 180 p.

Hendrikse, G.W.J., 1993. Coördineren and Motiveren; een overzicht van de economische organisatietheorie. Academic Service, Schoonhoven, 319 p.

Hendrikse, G.W.J., 2003. Economics and Management of Organizations; Co-ordination, Motivation and Strategy. The McGraw-Hill Companies, London, 507 p.

Hendrikse, G.W.J. and H. Schreuder, 1990. Economische Organisatietheorie. In: L. van de Geest (ed.), Economische theorie: stand van zaken. Academic Service, Schoonhoven, pp. 277-290.

Hennart, J. 1993. Explaining the Swollen Middle: Why Most Transactions are a Mix of 'Market' and Hierarchy'? Organizational Science, 4: 529-547.

Hirshleifer, J. and J.G. Riley, 1995. The Analytics of Uncertainty and Information. Cambridge University Press, Cambridge, 465 p.

Hodgson, G.M., 1998. The Approach of Institutional Economics. Journal of Economic Literature, 36: 66-192.

Holmström, B., 1982. Moral Hazard in Teams. Bell Journal of Economics, 13: 324-340.

Innes, R., S. Polasky and J. Tschirhart, 1998. Takings, Compensation and Endangered Species Protection on Private Land. Journal of Perspectives, 12: 35-52.

INRA, 2006. Sécheresse et Agriculture, Expertise collective de l'INRA pour le Ministère de l'Agriculture et de la Pêche, October, 2006.

Jensen, M. and W. Meckling, 1976. Theory of the Firm: Managerial Behaviour, Agency Cost and Capital Structure. Journal of Financial Economics, 3: 305-360.

Johnson, G.L., 1958. Supply Function – Some Facts and Notions. In: E.O. Heady, H.G. Diesslin, H.R. Jensen and G.L. Johnson (eds.), Agricultural Adjustment Problems in a Growing Economy. The Iowa State College Press – Ames, Iowa, USA, pp. 74-93.

Johnson, M.A. and E.C. Pasteur, Jr., 1981. An opportunity cost view of fixed asset theory and the overproduction trap. American Journal of Agricultural Economics, 63: 1-7.

Jongeneel, R.A., L.H.G. Slangen, E. Bos, M. Koning, T. Ponsioen and J. Vader, 2005. De Effecten van Natuurprojecten op de Economie: Financiële and Economische analyse van kosten and baten, Leerstoelgroep Agrarische Economie and Plattelandsbeleid and LEI, Wageningen Universiteit, ISBN-10: 9090196595, Wageningen, 157 p.

Jongeneel, R.A., N.P.B. Polman and L.H.G. Slangen, 2006. Explaining the changing institutional organisation of Dutch farms: the role of farmer's attitude, advisory network and structural factors. Agricultural Economics and Rural Policy, Wageningen University, 18 p.

Jongeneel, R.A., N.P.B. Polman and L.H.G. Slangen, 2008. Why are Dutch farmers going multifunctional? Land Use Policy, 25: 81-94.

Joskow, P.L, 1985a. Vertical integration and long term contracts: The case of coal-burning electric generating plants. Journal of Law, Economics and Organizations, 1: 33-80.

Joskow, P.L, 1985b. Long term vertical integration and the study of industrial organization and government regulation. Journal of Institutional and Theoretical Economics, 141: 586-593.

Joskow, P.L, 1987. Contract duration and relationship-specific investments: Empirical evidence from coal markets. American Economic Review, 77: 168-185.

Joskow, P.L, 1988. Asset specificity and the structure of vertical relationships: Empirical evidence. Journal of Law, Economics and Organizations, 4: 95-117.

Joskow, L., 1995. The New Institutional Economics: Alternative Approach. Journal of Institutional and Theoretical Economics, 151: 248-259.

Kahneman, D. and A. Tversky, 1979. Prospect theory: an analysis of decisions under risk. Econometrica, 47: 263-292.

Kasper, W. and M.E. Streit, 1998. Institutional Economics; Social Order and Public Policy. Edward Elgar, Cheltenham, UK, 517 p.

Katz, M.L. and H.S. Rosen, 1994. Microeconomics. Second edition, Irwin, Burr Ridge, 705 p.

Kerkmeester, H.O., 1993. De Grondwet als een sociaal contract. Rechtseconomische Verkenningen 3, Gouda Quint, Arnhem, 130 p.

Kerkmeester, H.O. and R.W. Holzhauer, 2000. De economische structuur van het ondernemingsrecht, Een inleiding in de economische theorie van de onderneming. Rechtseconomische Verkenningen 9, Gouda Quint, Deventer, 113 p.

Khalil, E., 1995. Organizations versus Institutions. Journal of Institutional and Theoretical Economics, 153: 445-466.

Knack, S. and P. Keefer, 1997. Does Social Capital Have an Economic Payoff: A Cross Country Investigation, Quarterly Journal of Economics 112: 1251-1288.

Knetsch, J., 1999. Behavioural Economics: Implications for analysis and weighing of environmental values. Mansholt Lecture, The Mansholt Graduate School, Wageningen, 36 p.

Kreps, D.M., 1990. A Course in Microeconomic Theory. Harvester Wheatsheaf, New York, 850 p.

Kydland, F.W. and E.C. Prescott, 1977. Rules rather than discretion: The inconsistency of optimal plans. Journal of Political Economy, 85: 473-491.

Lafontaine, F. and M. Slade, 2007. Vertical integration and firm boundaries: The evidence. Journal of Economic Literature, XLV: 629-685.

Landes, D.S., 1998. Arm and Rijk; Waarom sommige landen erg rijk zijn and andere erg arm. Het Spectrum, Utrecht, 700 p.

La Porta, R., F. Lopez-de-Silanes, A. Shleifer and R.W.Vishny, 1997. Trust in Large Organisations, American Economic Review Paper and Proceedings, 87: 333-338.

La Porta, R., F. Lopez-de-Silanes, A. Shleifer and R.W.Vishny, 1999. The Quality of the Government, Journal of Law, Economics & Organization, 15: 222–279.

Langlois, R.N., 1986. The New Institutional Economics: An Introduction Essay. In: R.N. Langlois (ed.), Economics as Process: Essays in the New Institutional Economics. Cambridge University Press, New York, pp. 1-25.

Le Grand, J., 2003. Motivation, Agency and Public Policy; Of Knights and Knaves, Pawns and Queens. Oxford University Press, Oxford, 191 p.

Loucks, L.A., 2005. The Evolution of the Area 19 Snow Crab Co-management Agreement: Understanding the Inter-relationship Between Transaction Costs, Credible Commitment and Collective Action, PhD Dissertation, Simon Fraser University, http://ir.lib.sfu.ca/handle/1892/713.

Loucks, L., 2007. Patterns of Fisheries Institutional Failure and Success: Experience from the Southern Gulf of St. Lawrence Snow Crab Fishery, in Nova Scotia, Canada, Marine Policy, 31: 320-326.

Lueck, D. and Th.J. Miceli, 2004. Property Rights and Property Law. Cardon Reseach Papers in Agricultural and Resource Economics, Reseach Paper 2004-01 September 2004. Department of Agricultural and Resource Economics, University of Arizona, 71 p.

Lyons, B. and J. Mehta, 1997. Private Sector Business Contracts: The Text Between the Lines. In: S. Deakin and J. Michie (eds.), Contracts, Co-operation, and Competition; Studies in Economics, Management and Law. Oxford University Press, Oxford, pp. 43-66.

Macleod, W.B, 2007. Reputations, relationship, and contract enforcement. Journal of Economic Literature, XLV: 595-628.

Mas-Colell, A., M.D. Whinston and J.R. Green, 1995. Microeconomic Theory. Oxford University Press, New York, 981 p.

McAfee, R.P. and J. McMillan, 1991. Optimal Contracts for Teams. International Economic Review, 32: 561-577.

Milgram, S., 1967. The Small World. Psychology Today, 2: 60-67.

Ménard, C., 1994. Organizations as coordinating devices. Metroeconomica, 45: 224-247.

Ménard, C., 1995. Markets as institutions versus organizations as markets? Disentangling some fundamental concepts. Journal of Economic Behaviour and Organization, 28: 161-182.

Ménard, C., 1996. On Clusters, Hybrids, and Other Strange Forms: The Case of the France Poultry Industry. Journal of Institutional and Theoretical Economic, 152: 154-183.

Ménard, C., 1997. The Enforcement of Contractual Arrangements. Paper presented NIE Meeting, Saint-Louis, 19-21 September 1997, Centre ATOM University Paris.

Mettepenningen, E., A. Verspecht and G. van Huylenbroeck, 2008. Measuring private transaction costs of Agri-Environmental Schemes. Journal of Environmental Planning and Management (in press).

Milgrom, P. and J. Roberts, 1992. Economics, Organization and Management. Prentice Hall International, Englewood Cliffs, New New Jersey, 621 p.

Ministerie van Landbouw, Natuur and Voedselkwaliteit, 2008. Pacht and Bedrijfstoeslagrechten. Brief aan de Voorzitter van de Tweede kamer van de Staten – Generaal, 25 maart 2008, Kenmerk TRCIZ/2008/845, Den Haag, 2 p.

Mintzberg, H., 2006. Organisatiestructuren. Pearson Education Benelux, 325 p.

Moe, T., 1984. The New Economics of Organization. American Journal of Political Science, 28: 739-777.

Moerland, W., 1992. Economische theorievorming omtrent de onderneming, Deel 1 and Deel 2. Maandblad voor Accountancy and Bedrijfseconomie, 66: 57-65 and 116-125.

Mouthaan, E, 2007. Corporate Governance: de grenzen van aandeelhoudersactivisme. Maanblad voor Accountancy and Bedrijfseconomie, 81: 574-581.

Nabli, K.M. and J.B. Nugent, 1989. The New Institutional Economics and Economic Development: An Introduction. In: M.K. Nabli and J.B. Nugent (eds.), The New Institutional Economics and Development. Elsevier Science, no.183, New York, pp. 3-33.

Nelson, R., 1995. Recent Evolutionary Theorizing about Economics Change. Journal of Economic Literature, 23: 48-90.

Nelson, R. and S.G. Winter, 1982. An Evolutionary Theory of Economic Change. Harvard Press, Cambridge, Massachusetts, 437 p.

Nentjes, A., 2004. Milieubeleid start zich blind op regels. Economisch Statistische Berichten, 87: 620-623.

Niskanen, W.A., 1971. Bureaucracy and Representative Government, Aldine, Chicago, 241 p.

Noordhaven, N.G., 1997. Economische and Neo-institutionele organisatietheorie. Maandblad voor Accountancy and Bedrijfseconomie, 71: 236-245.

Noort, van den, P.C., 1969. Inleiding tot de landhuishoudkunde. De Erven F. Bohn N.V., Haarlem, 172 p.

Noort, van den, P.C., 1984. Inleiding tot de algemene agrarische economie. Tweede druk. H.E. Stenfert Kroese BV, Leiden, 209 p.

Nooteboom, B., 1999. Inter-firm Alliances:Analysis and Design. Routledge, London, 239 p.

North, D.C., 1990. Institutions, Institutional change and Economic Performance. Reprinted in 1995, Cambridge University Press, Cambridge, 152 p.

North, D.C., 1991. Institutions. Journal of Economic Perspective, 5: 97-112.

North, D.C., 1993. Institutions and Credible Commitment. Journal of Institutional Economics, 149: 11-23.

North, D.C., 1994. Economic Performance Through Time. The American Economic Review, 84: 359-368.

North, D.C., 2003. The new institutional economics and third world development. In: J. Harriss, J. Hunter and C.M. Lewis (eds.), The new institutional economics and third world development. Routlegde, London, pp. 17-16.

North, D.C. and R.P. Thomas, 1973. The Rise of the Western World: A new economic history. Cambridge University Press, Cambridge, 171 p.

Olson, M, 1965. The Logic of Collective Action: Public Goods and the Theory of Groups. Harvard University Press, Cambridge, MA, 212 p.

Olson, M., 1982. The Rise and Decline of Nations: Economic Growth, Stagflation and Social Rigidities. Yale University Press, New Haven, 273 p.

Olson, M., 1996. Distinguished Lecture on Economics in government: Big bills left on the sidewalk: Why some nations are rich, and others poor. Journal of Economic Perspectives. 10: 3-24.

Oskam, A.J. and L.H.G. Slangen, 1998. The financial and economic consequences of a wildlife and development and conservation plan: a case study for the ecological main structure in the Netherlands. In: S. Dabbert, A. Dubgaard, L.H.G. Slangen and M.C. Whitby (eds.), The economics of landscape and wildlife conservation. CAB International, Oxan, pp. 113-133.

Ostrom, E., 1998. Governing the Commons; The Evolution of Institutions for Collective Action. Cambridge University Press, Cambridge, 280 p.

Ostrom, E., 1998. A Behavioural Approach to the Rational-Choice Theory of Collective Action. Presidental Adress, American Political Science Association, 1997. American Political Science Review, 92: 1-22.

Ostrom, E., 2000. Social Capital: A Fad or a Fundamental Concept? In: P. Dasgupta and I. Serageldin (eds.), Social Capital. A Multifaceted Perspective. The World Bank, Washington, pp. 172-214.

Pearce, D.W. and R.K. Turner, 1990. Economics of Natural Resources and the Environment. Harvester Wheatsheaf, London, 378 p.

Perkins, D.H., S. Radelet and D.L. Lindaurer, 2006. Economics of Development. Sixth Edition, W.W. Norton & Company, New York, 864 p.

Peterson, H.C., A. Wysocki and S.B. Harsh, 2001. Strategic choice along the vertical coordination continuum. International Food and Agribusiness Management Review 4: 149-166.

Polman, N.B.P. and L.H.G. Slangen, 2002. Self-organising and Self-governing of Environmental Co-operatives: Design Principles. In: K. Hagedorn (ed.), Environmental Co-operatives and Institutional Change. Edward Elgar, Cheltenham, pp. 91-111.

Polman, N.B.P and L.H.G. Slangen, 2007, The Design of Agri-environmental Schemes in EU: Lessons for the future. Project under EU 6TH Framework Programme, STREP Contract no SSPE-CT-2003-5020, Integrated Tools to design and implement, Commission of the European Union, Wageningen, May 2007, 72 p.

Polman, N.B.P and L.H.G. Slangen, 2008. Agri-Environmental Schemes in the EU; A contractual approach. Journal of Environmental Planning and Management (in press).

Pope, R.D., 1982. Empirical Estimation and Use of Risk Preference: An Appraisal of Estimation Methods that Use Actual Decisions. American Journal of Agricultural Economics, 64: 376-383.

Portes, A. and J. Sensenbrenner, 1993. Embeddedness and Immigration: Notes on the Social Determinants of Economic Action. The American Journal of Sociology, 98: 1320-1350.

Pratt, J., 1964. Risk Aversion in the Small and the Large. Econometrica, 32: 122-136.

Pretty, P., 1999. Reducing the Cost of Modern Agriculture: Towards Sustainable Food and Farming Systems. In: A.K. Dragun and C. Tisdell (eds.), Sustainable Agriculture and Environment: Globalisation and the Impact of Trade Liberalisation. Edward Elgar, Cheltenham, pp. 79-100.

Putman, R.D., 2000. Bowling Alone: The Collapse and Revival of American Community. New York: Simon and Schuster, 540 p.

Putman, R.D., R. Leonardi and R. Nanetti, 1993. Making Democracy Work; Civil Traditions in Modern Italy, Princeton, NJ, Princeton, University Press, 258 p.

Putterman, L. and R.S. Kroszner (eds.), 1996. The Economic Nature of the Firm. Cambridge University Press, Cambridge UK, 390 p.

Rabin, M., 1997. Psychology and Economics (Berkely Department of Economics Working Paper No. 97-251) Berkeley: University of California. Shorter version published in Journal of Economic Literature, 36: 11-46.

Rajan, R.G. and L. Zingales, 1998. Power in a theory of the firm, The quarterly Journal of economics, 113: 387-432.

Rees, R., 1985. The theory of principal and agent, part I. Bulletin of Economic Research 37: 3-26.

Ricketts, M., 2002. The Economics of Business Enterprise; An introduction to Economic Organisation and the Theory of the Firm. Third Edition. Edward Elgar, Cheltenham UK, 590 p.

Rodrik, D., 1998. Why do more open Economies have bigger Governments? Journal of Political Economy, 16: 997-1032.

Rutherford, M., 1994. Institutions in Economics; The old and new institutionalism. Cambridge University Press, Cambridge, 225 p.

Sadoulet, E. and A. de Janvry, 1995. Quantitative Development Policy Analysis. The John Hopkins University Press, Baltimore, 397 p.

Saha, A, 1993. Expo-Power Utility: A 'Flexible' Form for Absolute and Relative Risk Aversion. American Journal of Agricultural Economics, 75: 905-913.

Saleth, M.R. and A. Dinar, 2004. The Institutional Economics of Water; A cross-country analysis of institutions and performance. A co-production of World Bank and Edward Elgar, Cheltenham, 398 p.

Sandler, T. and J.T. Tschirhart, 1980. The Economic Theory of Clubs: An evaluated survey. Journal of Economic Literature. XVIII: 1481-1521.

Shleifer, A., 1998 a. State versus Private Ownership. Department of Economics, Working Paper 1841, Harvard University, Cambridge Massachusetts, 32 p.

Shleifer, A., 1998 b. State versus Private Ownership. Journal of Economics Perspectives, 12: 133-150.

Shleifer and R.W. Vishny, 1998. The Grabbing Hand: Government pathologies and their cures. Harvard University Press Cambridge, Massachusetts, 278 p.

Schotter, A., 1981. The Economic Theory of Social Institutions. Cambridge University Press, Cambridge, 177 p.

Schram, A.J.H.C., H.A.A.Verbon and F.A.A.M. van der Winden, 1991. Economie van de Overheid. Academic Service Economie and Bedrijfskunde, Schoonhoven, 224 p.

Schram, A.J.H.C., H.A.A.Verbon and F.A.A.M. van der Winden, 2000. Economie van de Overheid. Tweede Editie. Academic Service Economie and Bedrijfskunde, Schoonhoven, 322 p.

Slangen, A.H.L., 2005. Studies on the Determinants of Foreign Entry Mode Choice and Performance. Proefschrift, Faculty of Economics and Business Administration, Universiteit van Tilburg, 111 p.

Slangen, L.H.G., 1994. The Economics Aspects of Environmental Co-operative for Farmers. International Journal of Social Economics, 21: 42-59.

Slangen, L.H.G., 1997. How to organise nature production by farmers. European Review Agricultural Economics, 24: 508-529.

Slangen, L.H.G. 2001. Sustainable agriculture – Getting the institutions right. CEESA Discussion Paper No.1, 1/2001, ISSN 1616-9166, Humboldt University Berlin, 35 p.

Slangen, L.H.G. and N.B.P. Polman, 2002. Environmental Co-operatives: a New Institutional Arrangement of Farmers. In: K. Hagedorn (ed.), Environmental Co-operatives and Institutional Change. Edward Elgar, Cheltenham, pp. 69-90.

Slangen, L.H.G. and N.B.P. Polman, 2008. Land lease contracts; properties and the value of bundles of property rights. NJAS Wageningen Journal of Life Science. 55: 397-412.

Slangen, L.H.G., G.C. van Kooten, P. Suchanek and R van Oosten, 2001. Institutions of sustainability in Central and Eastern European Countries (CEESA). Project under EU 5TH Framework Programme Contract no: QLK5-1999-01611, Commission of the European Union, Wageningen October 2001, 60 p.

Slangen, L.H.G., N.B.P. Polman and A.J. Oskam, 2003, Grondgebruik, pachtcontracten and pachtprijszettings-mechanismen. Rapport in opdracht van het Ministerie van Landbouw, Natuurbeheer and Voedselveiligheid, Leerstoelgroep Agrarische Economie and Plattelandsbeleid, Wageningen Universiteit, 113 p.

Slangen, L.H.G., G.C van Kooten and P. Suchanek, 2004. Institutions, social capital and agricultural change in Central and Eastern Europe. Journal of Rural Studies, 20: 245-256.

Simon, A.H., 1961. Administrative Behaviour. Second Edition, Macmillan Company, New York, 259 p.

Shubik, M., 1975. The Equilibrium Model is Incomplete and Not Adequate for Reconciliation of Micro and Macroeconomic Theory. Kyklos 28: 545-573.

Soest, D. van, 2007. De aanpak van het subsidy-freerider problem. Economisch Statistische Berichten, 92: 407-409.

Spulber, D.F., 1996. Market Microstructure and Intermediation. The Journal of Economic Perspectives, 10: 135-152.

Spulber, D.F., 2002. Introduction: Economic Fables and Public Policy. In: D.F. Spulber (ed.), Famous Fables of Economics; Myths of Market Failures. Blackwell, Oxford, pp. 1-31.

Stiglitz, J.E., 1974. Incentives and Risk-sharing in Sharecropping. Review of Economic Studies, 41: 219-256.

Stiglitz, J.E., 2000. Formal and Informal Institutions. In: P. Dasgupta and I. Serageldin (eds.), Social Capital. A Multifaceted Perspective. The World Bank, Washington, pp. 59-68.

Sutinen, J.G. and K. Kuperan, 1999. A socio-economic theory of regulatory compliance. International Journal of Social Economics, 26: 174-193.

Szpiro, G., 1986. Measuring Risk Aversion: An Alternative Approach. Review Economics and Statistics, 68: 156-159.

Tesfay, G., 2006. Agriculture, Resource Management and Institutions; A socioeconomic analysis of households in Tigray, Ethiopia. PhD Thesis, Wageningen University, 155 p.

Teulings, C., L. Bovenberg and H. van Dalen, 2005. De cirkel van de goede intenties; De economie van het publiek belang. Amsterdam University Press, Amsterdam, 155 p.

Tiebout, C.M., 1956. A Pure Theory of Locale Expenditures. Journal of Political Economy, 64 (5), 416-424.

Tirole, J., 1993. The Theory of Industrial Organization. The MIT Press, Cambridge, Massachusetts, 479 p.

Titmuss, R., 1973. The Gift Relationship: from human blood to social policy. Harmondsworth, England. 366 p.

Transparancy International, 2008. The 2006 Transparency International Corruption Perception Index. www.infoplease.com/ipa/A0781359.html.

Uzzi, B., 1997. Social Structure and Competition in Interfirm Networks: the Paradox of Embeddedness. Administrative Science Quarterly, 42: 35-67.

Uzzi, B. and J. Gillespie, 2002. Knowledge Spillover in Corporate Financing Networks: Embeddedness and the Firm's Debt Performance. Strategic Management Journal, 23: 595-618.

Uzzi, B. and R. Lancaster, 2004. Embeddedness and Price Formation in the Corporate Law Market. Amercian Sociological Review, 69: 319-344.

Uzzi, B., L.A. Amaral and F. Reed-Tsochas, 2007. Small-world Networks and Management Science Research: A Review. European Management Review, 4: 77-91.

Van Huylenbroeck, G. and L.H.G. Slangen, 2003. Nieuwe Institutionele Arrangementen in het landelijke gebied. Tijdschrift voor Sociaal Wetenschappelijk Onderzoek van de Landbouw (TSL), 18: 107-121.

Varian, H.R., 1992. Microeconomic Analysis. Norton & Company, New York, 506 p.

Varian, H.R., 2003. Intermediate Microeconomics; A Modern Approach. Sixth Edition, Norton & Company, New York, 688 p.

Weel, B. ter, 2007. Activistische Hedgefondsen in Europa. Economisch Statistische Berichten, 92: 401.

Whynes, D.K. and R.A. Bowles, 1981. The Economic Theory of the State. Martin Robertson, Oxford, 236 p.

Williamson, O.E., 1987. The Economic Institution of Capitalism. The Free Press, New York, 450 p.

Williamson, O.E., 1991. Comparative Economic Organization: The Analysis of Discrete Structural Alternatives. Administrative Science Quarterly, 36: 269-296.

Williamson, O.E., 1996. The Mechanisms of Governance. Oxford University Press, New York, 429 p.

Williamson, O.E., 1998. Transaction Cost Economics: How it Works; Where it Headed. De Economist, 146: 23-58.

Williamson, O.E., 2000. The New Institutional Economics: Taking Stock, Looking Ahead. Journal of Economic Literature, XXXVIII: 595-613.

Wiseman, J., 1957. The Theory of Public Utility Price – An Empty Box. Oxford Economic Papers, 9: 56-74.

Witteloostuijn, A. van, 1994. De economische theorie van marktwerking en het gedrag van organisaties. Economisch Statistische Berichten, 79: 770-774.

Wolfson, D.J., 2001. Theorie and toepassingen van de economische politiek. Uitgeverij Coutinho, Bussum, 255 p.

Woolcock, M., 1998. Social Capital and Economic Development: Toward A Theoretical Synthesis and Policy Framework. Theory and Society, 27: 151-208.

Woolcock, M., 2001. The Place of Social Capital in Understanding Social and Economic Outcomes. Canadian Journal of Policy Research. 2: 11-17.

Zerbe, R.O. and D.D. Dively, 1994. Benefits-costs Analysis; In Theory and Practice. Harper Collins College Publishers, New York, 557 p.

Zingales, L., 1998. Corporate Governance. In: J. Eatwell, (ed.), The New Palgrave of Law and Economics. Macmillan, London, pp. 497-503.

Glossary

Acquistion cost:
The value of an asset at the moment of decision making. If the asset must be on the market, the acquisition cost is equal to the market price.

Activistic shareholders:
When shareholders take an active role in the firm's operation and attempt to secure drastic changes in the organisation, they are said to participate in shareholder activism. A well-known example is the case of investment or hedge funds that try to takeover the shares of firms. After securing control over the assets, they try to strip or split up the firm's assets and sell them off. Activistic shareholders do not have the intention of controlling the firm for a long period of time.

Adverse selection:
This term originates from the insurance industry and refers to the tendency of those who seek to buy insurance to be a nonrandom selection from the population. More specifically, it refers to be those who expect to have the highest expected claims. Adverse selection also refers to the kind of *pre-contractual opportunism* that arises when one party to a bargain has private information about something that affects the other's net benefit from the contract. In such cases, adverse selection refers to those whose private information implies that the contract will be especially disadvantageous for the other party agreeing to a contract.

Agency costs:
A general name given to the costs involved in monitoring the behaviour of some party acting on your behalf.

Agency relationship:
As used in economics, an agency relationship is one in which one person (the agent) acts on behalf of another (the principle). For example an employee is an agent of his or her employer and a doctor is the agent of a patient.

Agency theory:
It deals with problems of asymmetric information between two parties having a certain relationship, for example a contractual one.

Agent:
A person who acts on behalf of another.

Altruism:
It is the opposite of self-interested behaviour. Altruistic people are prepared to help others and they derive some personal benefit from activities that help others.

Alienable property rights:
These are private property rights that can be transferred (sold or given) to other individuals.

Allocation:
In the neoclassical model of a private ownership economy, an allocation consists of the lists of the amount of each commodity to be bought and sold by each consumer and each firm. More generally, an allocation is a complete specification of how resources are to be used.

Arbitrage:
Originally, this term referred to buying and selling the the same item in different markets simultaneously in order to profit from a difference in prices between the markets. A pure arbitrage transaction involves no risk and no net investment. The term is now applied more broadly to trading that takes advantage of discrepancies in pricing among groups of assets that are close substitutes.

Asset:
This is a possession of value, both real and financial. Real assets include the ownership of land, buildings or machinery. Financial assets include cash and securities and credit extended to customers. It also refers to a potential future

flow of benefits and services, including the article giving rise to the stream. For example, shares of stock or machines are assets. The term asset is also used in a metaphorical and usually favourable sense to describe things that cannot actually be owned, for example the skills and loyalty of the employees of a firm.

Asset specificity: It refers to the degree to which a resource is committed to a specific task and thus cannot be redeployed to alternative uses without a substantial reduction in its value. Asset specificity is the most critical dimension for describing transactions. It occurs in so many ways that five types of specific investments are distinguished: site specificity, physical asset specificity, human asset specificity, dedicated asset specificity and brand name capital specificity.

Asymmetric information: The relative holdings of data by individuals, when at least one party to an agreement has superior knowledge of some dimensions of the agreement. It refers to a situation in which not all the parties involved have the same information.

Authority relation: An arrangement in which one party (the superior) has the right, within reasonable bounds, to direct the behaviour of, punish and reward the other (the subordinate).

Backward integration: To bring the supply of an input under the ownership and management of the input purchaser (in this situation the organisation produces its own inputs). It is a form of *vertical integration*.

Bankruptcy: A situation in which a firm is unable to pay its bills and must go out of business. Consequently, shareholders lose their investments, creditors have a long fight to recover debt, and managers may lose credibility.

Bargaining area: It is the sum of areas of consumer surplus and the producer surplus.

Bargaining costs: The transaction costs involved in negotiations between or among different parties. These include the time spent on bargaining, resources expended during bargaining or in trying to improve a bargaining position, and any losses incurred as a result of failure or delay in reaching otherwise efficient agreements.

Bargaining failures: It occurs due to asymmetric information; parties fail to reach an agreement, even when in principle a contract could be constructed that would be mutually advantageous – *See*: precontractual information problems.

Barriers to entry: Factors that limit the entry of new firms to a market, even though the existing firms are making economic profit.

Behavioural theory of the firm: In standard microeconomics it is assumed that firms are holistic entities that seek to maximise profits. By contrast, the behavioural theory of the firm postulates the firm as a coalition of (groups of) participants, each with their own objectives. Theories of firm behaviour are based on considering the objectives of individuals and groups within firms. They consider the motives of managers and other groups within the firm. In small firms, a preference to remain one's own master may limit ambition. In a large firm, the pursuit of managerial perquisites, or empire-building based on love of power or prestige, may lead to maximisation of turnover rather than profits. It also argues that lack of information leads firms into choice based on satisfying rather than on maximising behaviour.

Being trapped:	It is a resource allocation where resource values in use have fallen bellow the acquisition costs, but not below salvage values.
Bilateral governance structure:	This a governance structure in which two parties are involved.
Benchmarking:	The identification of the best practices of firms operating within similar environments, so that the benchmarking firm can learn from the experience of others.
Board of directors:	The governing body of a company which appoints the company's officers. Most board of directors are elected by shareholders. They act in the interest of the company by being a part of the internal control mechanism.
Book value:	One way to place a value on a firm; the historical accounting valuation of the firm's assets including accumulated depreciation charges and owners' equity.
Bonds:	A way to link parties to each other and to limit hidden action problems is the posting of bonds (bonding) to guarantee performance. This can be achieved by a guarantee deposit or by the posting of bonds. The bond is a sum of money that is forfeited in the event that inappropriate behaviour is detected, i.e. the deposited amount can be confiscated if undesired behaviour (*shirking* or *cheating*) is discovered. Posting bonds can be a very effective way to provide incentives.
Bonus:	A payment to a firm's employees in addition to their normal pay. Bonuses may be linked to performance and provide an incentive to employees both to exert themselves and to stay with the firm rather than looking for another job elsewhere.
Bounded rationality:	The limitations on human mental abilities that prevent people from foreseeing all possible contingencies and calculating their optimal behaviour. Bounded rationality may also include those limitations on human language that prevent perfect communication on those things that are known.
Brand:	A name used to identify the maker or distributor of a good.
Business environment:	The technology, markets (product and input) and regulations facing the firm.
Business (unit) strategy:	The way the firm competes in a given line of business.
Building-in of self-interest:	This means that people are doing things that are of interest to themselves. These interests can vary from financial benefits to a *license to produce*. The latter is also connected to the concept of *responsible entrepreneurship*.
Capital goods:	Goods intended for use in production, rather than by consumers.
Capital structure:	The mix of debt and equity financing chosen by a firm; the higher the ratio of debt to equity, the more leveraged the firm.
Cartel:	A group of firms in the same industry that cooperate in order to maintain (high) prices or market shares.
Cash flow:	Accounting net income plus any allowances for depreciation. Essentially, the amount of money generated by the operation that is currently available for investing, servicing any new debt taken on, or disbursing to owners.
Ceteris paribus:	Latin for 'other things being equal'. This means that other things which could change are for the moment being assumed not to.
CEO:	Chief Executive Officer, the highest in officer of a corporation. The CEO is typically either the company president, or the chair of board, or both.
Centralised decision system:	A decision system that assigns the most important decisions to senior executives within the organisation.

Certainty equivalent:	Given a choice between an uncertain or random income and a certain, non-random one, the amount of certain income that would make the chooser just indifferent between the two alternatives. Also called the *certain equivalent*. It is the certain out come which would confer the same utility as an actual distribution of expected outcome. In the case of a person with a linear utility function, the certainty equivalent of a distribution of uncertain outcomes equals the mean expected value of the uncertain outcomes. Such a person is risk-neutral. Is the utility function characterised by a decreasing marginal utility, the certain equivalent is less than the mean expected outcome of a distribution of uncertain outcomes and the person is risk-averse.
Classical contract:	This is a short-term contract in which the identities, the personal characteristics are not important and the price is the most important coordination mechanism. It is close to a spot market transaction.
Classical firm:	A conception of the firm in which the actions of the firm are those that would be taken if a single individual had decision making authority and paid fixed wages to workers and prices to suppliers and received as profit any excess of the firm's receipts over its expenditures.
Club:	A club is a voluntary group of individuals who derive mutual benefits from sharing one or more of the following: (1) production costs of activities and services; (2) the members' characteristics (e.g. they like playing soccer or golf); (3) a good characterised by benefits. These benefits can be internal and excludable, which means only for the members. The benefits can also be external and non-excludable. The latter means that also non-members can enjoy of the benefits (e.g. a club that preserves environmental goods).
Club goods:	The benefits are excludable but partially non-rival. The essential difference between club goods and pure public goods depends on the existence of an exclusion mechanism.
Coase theorem:	A proposition that if there are no wealth effects and no significant transaction costs, then (apart from distributional considerations) the outcome of bargaining or contracting is independent of the initial assignment of ownership, wealth, and property rights, and is determined solely by efficiency.
Collateral:	The property of a borrower that is contractually forfeited to the lender if the loan payment terms are not met. It is also called the security of the loan.
Collusion:	An agreement or cooperation amongst individuals or firms to further their own goals at the cost of others.
Commitment:	It is a determination or promise to follow a particular course of action.
Common property regime:	It represents private property for a group of co-owners. All others are excluded from decision-making and use. Individuals have rights and duties in a common property regime, where the exclusion of non-owners is the common factor with private property. Common property can be seen as a collective group property or a corporate group-property. The property-owning groups vary in nature, size, and internal structure across a broad spectrum, but they are social units with definite membership and boundaries, with certain common interests, with at least some interaction between the members, with some common cultural values and norms, and often with its own endogenous authority system.

Common resource problem: A situation in which several different parties can use a resource for their individual benefit and property rights are not sufficiently well defined and enforced to ensure that individuals bear the full costs of the actions and receive the full benefits they create. Also called a free rider problem (especially in situations where excluding parties who fail to pay for the resource is difficult) or a public good problem. The resulting inefficiencies have led to the term of tragedy of the commons. This refers to the danger of over-exploitation of resources due to a lack of property rights over them.

Commons: Resources which are neither privately owed nor owned by the government but are left open for free use.

Company: A form of organising business, with a legal personality distinct from the individuals taking part in it.

Comparative performance evaluation: The practice of evaluating an individual's performance by comparing it to the performance of others doing similar work.

Comparative advantage: A theory used to explain international trading patterns; choose what to produce by determining those goods in whose production they have an advantage (in terms of the opportunity cost of other, lost outputs) over other countries.

Comparative costs: A comparative advantage expressed in terms of costs.

Competitive equilibrium: A list of prices, consumption plans, and production plans such that (1) every individual consumes the goods he or she prefers subject only to the limits of his or her budget, (2) every firm makes goods and uses inputs in the way that maximises its profits, and (3) the total quantity supplied of each good is equal to the total quantity demanded.

Competition: The situation when anybody who wants to buy or sell has a choice of possible suppliers or customers. With perfect competition there are so many suppliers and customers that all the traders are able to buy or sell any quantity at price which they can not influence. They act as price-takers. Such intensive competition is rather unusual in real life.

Competitive market: A market structure in which no buyer or seller has market power (all trades are made at the going market price); it is characterised by a large number of potential buyers and sellers, low costs of entry and exit, product homogeneity, and rapid dissemination of accurate information at low cost.

Complementarities: The relationship between two groups of activities in an organisation in that one activity experiences feedback from changes in the other activity.

Complements: Products that tend to be consumed together; a price reduction of one good tends to increase the quantity demanded of the other good.

Complete contract: A hypothetical contract that describes what action is to be taken and payments made in every possible contingency.

Concentration: Economic term referring to the importance of large producers in a market; said to increase when fewer, larger producers dominate a market.

Congestion or crowding: It implies that one user's utilisation of the club good, decreases the benefits or quality of services still available to the remaining users.

Connectedness: Two assets can be strongly connected: railways and trains, network facilities and goods such as water, gas and electricity. The expected loss incurred from failing to coordinate a particular group of decisions concerning the use of assets.

Constant returns to scale:	A situation in production where increasing inputs by x per cent will result in increasing output by x per cent. If inputs are doubled, for example, outputs will double.
Consumer surplus:	Consumer surplus can be measured by the area below the demand curve but above the price. The demand curve shows the valuation put by consumers on successive units of goods. The area below the demand curve and above the price line is the excess of the benefits consumers gain from purchases of goods over the amount paid for them.
Contestable market:	For having a contestable market some conditions should be fulfiled. First, outsiders notice the change of making a profit. This means that information is costlessly available to potential entrants, there are no sunk costs, and incumbent firms are not able instantly to match a new entrant's price. Second, 'hit and run' entry is possible. This means a newcomer can enter the market, supply the good or service for a short period of time and escape without loss when the incumbent firm retaliates. There are no effective barriers to entry or exit in term of highly specific investments and sunk costs. Third, there is some period of time over which an entrant can make a profit.
Contracts:	Formally, contracts are legally enforceable promises. They may be oral or written, and they typically must involve obligations on each party – for example, to provide a good or service on the one hand, and to pay for it on the other. See complete, incomplete and implicit contract.
Contracting costs:	The out-of-pocket and opportunity costs of negotiating, drafting, and enforcing contracts; they include search and information costs, bargaining and decision costs, and policing and enforcement costs, and the efficiency losses that result because incentive conflicts are not completely resolved.
Contracting problems:	These occur within contracts because individuals have incentives to take actions that increase their well-being at their contracting partner's expense; they occur within both explicit and implicit contracts.
Control rights:	The rights to make any decision concerning use, returns and transfer of an asset, and the right to exclude others. Control rights over a bundle of property rights indicate to which level a person has the rights to take any decision over the bundle of property rights of an asset.
Cooperatives:	A form of commercial organisation in which only customers (or sometimes suppliers) are eligible to be among the owners and any earnings are distributed in proportion to sales or membership or through price reductions, rather than in proportion to the owners' investments.
Coordination mechanism:	Economic activities have to be coordinated. Each mode of organisation makes use of a coordination mechanism or of a mix of them. Coordination mechanisms are needed to match supply and demand as well as to align the activities of the different partners to a transaction. Coordination can take place by the following coordination mechanisms: the 'handbook', 'invisible hand', 'handshake' or the 'visible hand', or a certain mix of them. Coordination mechanisms are a crucial part of a governance structure. For example, in the governance structure the market, the coordination is accomplished by prices, expressed as the invisible hand.

Corporate control:	This refers to the authority over the decisions of a firm, typically attained by purchasing (either alone or with allies) a large fraction of the firm's shares.
Corporate culture:	A set of shared beliefs and values, precedents, expectations, stories, routines, and procedures in a firm that help define that firm's way of doing things and serve as a guide to behaviour for those within the firm.
Corporate strategy:	The plan of action for a firm; the primary consideration is the degree of corporate diversification chosen by the firm (the determination of which business activities the firm will undertake).
Corporation:	An organisation that allows the enterprise to act as a legal entity separate from its owners, who enjoy limited liability for the corporations' debts. A public corporation is government-owned body; a private corporation is a synonym for a company.
Corruption:	The use of bribery to influence politicians, civil servants and other officials.
Cospecialisation:	A condition of two assets, each of which is more productive when used with the other. Cospecialised assets must be unique in some respect and must be also complements.
Cost of capital:	The cost to an organisation of obtaining financial recourses. Usually stated as an interest rate.
Credible commitment:	This type of commitment is achieved by foreclosing alternatives. It means that your are motivated to keep conformance of the rules and contracts compliance high.
Debt:	A form of financing a firm; it represents an agreement requiring regular payments.
Decision control:	This encompasses the ratification and monitoring of decisions. It is part of the control rights.
Decision management:	This encompasses the initiation and implementation of decisions.
Decision rights:	The authority to decide how resources will be used in organisations. It is part of the control rights.
Delegation:	It occurs when a principal conditionally grants authority to agent to act on his or her behalf. Delegation is a way to enhance the commitment or credibility of the government policy. The relations between a principal and agent are mostly governed by a contract defining the relationship between both parties.
Doing it oneself:	The principal is doing the work by him self. It is also called in-house production and it is the make decision. Unified ownership or the do-it-self option involves bringing two separate organisations under unified direction.
Dominant strategy:	This occurs when it is optimal for a firm to choose a particular strategy no matter the choices of its rivals – especially used in game theory.
Downstream:	An activity that follows the reference activity in the sequence of steps producing raw materials to delivering a finished product to the customer.
Economic Darwinism:	The economic counterpart of the biological theory of natural selection; an organisation selects features that increase its ability to survive within its environment; the basic idea is that a competitive marketplace creates pressures that favour organisations that are relatively more efficient.
Economies of scale:	The reduction in average cost that is achievable when a single product is made in large quantities.

Economies of scope:	The reduction in total cost that is achievable when a group of products are all made by a single firm, rather than being made in the same amounts by a set of independent firms.
Economic meaning of ownership:	Having the income rights and the transfer rights are often emphasised as marking the economic meaning of ownership.
Edgeworth box:	A graphical depiction of the total amount of two factors of production going to the production of two outputs. If an individual or a firm has two type of resources, and uses them for two different purposes, the box shows the amount s of resources available on its axes. Each point in the box represents a possible allocation of resources.
Efficiency principle:	The working hypothesis that organisations and institutional arrangements that persist tend to be efficient ones. The logic is that if an arrangement is inefficient, then there are gains to be realised from changing.
Efficiency wages:	Wage premiums paid to reduce shirking because employees are afraid that if they are caught, they will be fired and lose this premium; efficiency wages also discourage employee turnover.
Efficient:	An allocation, contract, or organisation is efficient if there is no feasible alternative that everyone finds to be at least as good and that at least one person strictly prefers.
Efficient resource allocation:	A situation in which it is not possible to reallocate available resources so as to achieve one or more objectives without accepting less of another. Efficiency is also referred as Pareto optimal.
Efficient market hypothesis:	The hypothesis that prices in asset markets, and particularly share markets, fully and accurately reflect all information relevant for forecasting future returns.
Employee owned firm:	A firm in which the providers of labour services hold at least a controlling interest.
Endangered species:	A species which is in danger of extinction.
Endogenous:	Arising from within the system. This is contrasted with exogenous, which means imposed on a system from outside.
Endowment:	In the competitive equilibrium model, the amounts of various goods that a consumer owns initially, before trade opens.
Equal compensation principle:	The principle in incentive contracting that if an agent is to allocate effort among different activities, then each must ring the same marginal return to effort. Otherwise, the agent will focus exclusively on the one that yields the greater impact on his or her income.
Equity:	(1) The value of real property in excess of any legal claims against it for debts owed; (2) Resources contributed to a firm in exchange for an ownership claim. It is a form of financing for a firm; it represents a stake in a corporation made by an investor who obtains some rights to dictate the policies and operation of the firm; (3) Securities issued by a firm that represent ownership rights (such as stocks) or that are convertible into such securities.
Equity (fairness):	The concept of distributive justice used in welfare theory. It refers to how income distribution affects the welfare of individuals.

Equilibrium:	A stable situation in which no party has a reason to change its strategy. For example, in a competitive market, this occurs when the quantity supplied of a product equals the quantity demanded.
European Court of Justice:	This is the highest **court** in the **European** Union (EU).
Evolutionary theory of the firm:	It is the newest and least developed of the accepted theories of the firm; it is the view that the survival of firms is an evolutionary process. The unit of analysis is the firm and its productive processes. This theory focuses on three related aspects of organisations: the structure, their strategy, and their *core competency*. Firms are able to survive only if they change appropriately in response to changes in demand and technology; in short they must adapt and find new productive scope for their core competencies – the things they do well, in order to succeed.
Ex-ante:	The *ex-ante* value of a variable is what the person or organisation expects it to be. *Ex-ante*, meaning as viewed before the event is contrasted with *ex-post*, meaning as viewed after the event.
Ex-post:	The value of a variable as it appears after the event, that is, what actually occurred.
Excess burden of taxes:	The excess burden represents the real costs of imposing taxes. Consumers have less possibilities for consuming and saving (loss in utility and interest) and producers have less possibilities for investments (loss in profits). The excess burden (EB) is equal to the sum of the consumers surplus (CS) and producers surplus (PS) minus the tax return (TR); EB = (CS + PC) – TR. It is the distortion as a result of imposing taxes.
Exit barriers theory:	This theory is similar to the fixed asset theory. Emphasis is placed on the limited salvage value of durable assets. Resources become durable, because once purchased, their value in use exceeds their salvage value. This creates an exit barrier.
Exclusion mechanism:	A mechanism whereby non-members and non-payers can be barred.
Expected value:	The weighted average of possible realisations of a random variable, where the weights are the probabilities.
Expected utility:	This measure weights the expected euro benefits not only by their probability but also by the marginal utility of income. It represents the mean level of utility expected from future activities, when only the distribution of possible values of these activities are known. The expected utility is often seen as a solution for choice problems in the face of uncertainty. A Von Neumann-Morgenstern (N-M) utility function is a particular form of an **expected utility function.** An important property of the N-M expected utility function is that sub-utility indices, which are weighted and added to measure expected utility, are cardinally measurable. It means that not only the amount of the outcome of expected utility function represents a ranking, but the differences in utility indices have also a meaning of ordering.
Explicit contracts:	Formal written agreements with a party related to the firm (for example, employees, customers, suppliers, and capital providers).

Externalities:	Costs or benefits from the actions of one party that affect the utility or production possibilities of another party and are not mediated through markets. Externalities might be positive or negative.
Extrinsic motivation:	Motivation activated by external factors such as monetary incentives, rules or direct order.
Fire alarm:	Reported information of a third party which is independent, an authority, and an expert also. It is also called a third party alarm.
Firm:	A basic organisational unit of production; it is often a focal point for a set of contracts. Many firms are run by single owners and partnerships; larger firms are usually organised as companies.
Firm-specific assets:	Assets that are significantly more valuable in their current use within the firm than in their next-best alternative use outside the firm.
Firm-specific capital:	Human or physical capital that is less productive when it is used outside a particular firm.
First-best situation:	A situation of the economy in which all the necessary and sufficient conditions for efficiency are satisfied simultaneously. If all but one such a condition was satisfied, it would always be beneficial to satisfy the remaining one.
First welfare theorem:	It states that if there is a market for every commodity, and all producers and consumers act as price takers, then the allocation of resources will be Pareto efficient. The First Welfare Theorem itself says nothing about fairness.
Fixed cost:	A cost incurred by a firm that does not vary with output.
Fixed input:	An input that does not vary with output, such as size of land area of a factory.
Fixed asset:	An asset is said to be fixed if the asset is 'trapped' or sunk in a certain use or relationship.
Fixed asset theory:	This theory can be used to explain why fixed resources are 'trapped' or sunk in a certain use or relationship. Important concepts in this theory are acquisition costs and salvage value. The fixed theory focuses on resource allocation where resource values in use have fallen below the acquisition costs, but not below salvage values.
Fixed costs:	Those costs which do not vary with output over the time horizon of analysis.
Forcing contract:	In a forcing contract the level of effort of the agent is equal to the optimal effort level of the agent from the view point of the principal. The agent is forced to this effort level by the payment schedule of the principal.
Formal authority:	The power that comes from explicitly assigned decision rights within the organisation.
Forward integration:	This occurs when the firm begins to conduct additional finishing work or to market its own goods (under the ownership and management of the firm) – also called downstream integration.
Franchise agreements:	Contracts between the franchisor (parent) and the franchisee that grant to the franchisee the right to use the parent's name, reputation, and business format at a particular location or within a stipulated market area.
Free cash flow:	Cash flow, plus after tax interest expenses, less investments.

Free cash flow problem:	Incentive conflicts between owners and managers over retaining cash within the firm beyond that is necessary to fund value-increasing investment projects; managers prefer to take projects which expand firm size beyond that which maximises the firm's value, rather than to distribute the cash to owners.
Free-rider problems:	This occurs in team efforts; each member of the team has an incentive to shirk because each receives full benefit from shirking, but bears only a part of the costs (see common-resource problem).
Full-cost transfer prices:	Full cost is the sum of fixed and variable costs. The full cost is used to value goods exchanged between business units.
Fundamental theorem of welfare economics:	The proposition that the allocation associated with a competitive equilibrium is efficient.
Fundamental Transformation:	Williamson (1987) uses this term to describe the effect of asset specificity on supplier negotiations. For example, a fundamental transformation occurs in the labour market if a previously unskilled employee acquires a set of skills and knowledge specific to the firm. Such human asset specificity strengthens the bargaining power of the employee, which creates the fundamental transformation in the supply of the employees' services.
Game theory:	A general analytical approach to modelling social situations in which the information, possible actions, and motivations of the actors or players and how those actions lead to outcomes are all specified in detail. In contrast, the competitive equilibrium model does not specify what would happen if the demands of consumers exceeded the available supply.
General human capital:	In contrast with human asset specificity, it consists of skills, training, education and qualifications that are useful across a wide variety of occupations and different firms.
General knowledge:	In contrast with specific knowledge, it is relative inexpensive to transfer.
General purpose capital:	It is in contrast with asset specificity, it is a non-specific asset.
Goal congruence:	A situation in which the objectives of different individuals or organisations are sufficiently aligned so that they are led to pursue common goals.
Governance structures:	They are institutional arrangements, or transaction mechanisms for carrying out transactions, such as a market or a firm, and they often contain a certain structure for administrating the transactions. Standard forms of governance structure are markets, firms and contracts. Governance structures are also called modes of organisation.
Government property regime:	The government has the control over the bundle of property rights in her own hands. For firms and natural resources, including land, the government can leave the management, financing, production and exploitation with government firms or government agencies. Individuals and groups may be able to make use of natural resources, but only at the forbearance of the government. The government can rent out the natural resources to groups of individuals and offer them the use and income rights for a certain period of time.
Gross domestic product:	It one of the main measures of economic activity in a country or region. Gross indicates that it is calculated without subtracting any allowance for depreciation of capital goods; domestic indicates that it measures activities located in a

country regardless of their ownership. The Gross national product measures the income of the residents of a country including incomes earned abroad but excluding payments made to those abroad.

Group incentive pay: It bases employee compensation on group performance.

Hidden information: This is a form of information asymmetry. One party has more information than the other. This party has no incentive to disclose information if it is to his or her disadvantage.

Hierarchy: (1) An idealised arrangement of authority in which each person has only one boss and the organisation has a single top officer. (2) A system of ranking employees.

Holding company: A company which owns several other companies but exercises little or no management control over them.

Holding problems: Conflicts that occur when parties invest in specific assets; for example, after the investment is made, the buyer might be able to force a price concession, since it will be in the interests of the seller to continue to operate as long as variable costs are covered.

Hold out: Governments often need large parcels of land for airports, highways, industrial terrains, etc. These projects often require 'contiguity', parcels must touch each other. The last owner can hold out the project.

Hold-up problem: The problem that arises when the party who makes a relationship-specific investment is vulnerable to threats by other parties to terminate that relationship. Given a relation between the two parties, the hold-up situation itself has often no effect on total value directly. It creates (opportunity) costs and will lead to a redistribution of income between the two parties. However, the fear of being *held-up* can prevent people from investing in highly specific assets. Therefore hold-up is an *ex-ante* problem. It will affect the total welfare in a society. These are the real social costs of a hold-up problem.

Hostile takeover: A change in corporate ownership that is opposed by the current management and board. This is usually accomplished by buying a sufficiently large fraction of the shares from the current stockholders to be able to control the election of board members. It can be interpreted as a corrective response to managerial moral hazard.

Horizontal integration: (1) In antitrust economics, an expansion of a firm by acquisition of or merger with competitors. (2) In business usage, an expansion into related activity that does not involve vertical integration.

Human asset specificity: *See:* specific human capital and asset specificity.

Human capital: The amount of knowledge, skills, education, training and experience held by an individual enabling that person to become more productive, earn higher future income, lead a more meaningful life, and have improved decision-making ability. It is a term that characterises individuals as having a set of skills and knowledge that make an individual more productive and can benefit employers.

Imperfect commitment: Parties' limited abilities to bind themselves to future courses of action, especially to bind themselves to avoid opportunistic behaviour.

Implementation problem: The mathematical problem of minimising the cost born by a principal while still inducing a self-interested agent to perform in a particular way. Also called a minimum cost implementation problem.

Implicit contract: A type of agreement with no formal statement of terms and conditions agreed to by the parties. It consists of promises and shared understandings that are not expressed by formal legal documents but that are considered by parties to be binding on one another's conduct.

Incentive or incentive compatibility conditions: Limitation on the set of contracts that can be implemented that arise from the necessity of giving individuals appropriate incentives to induce them to adopt the desired course of action. These constraints are particularly important where there are information asymmetries or incompleteness, so that individuals might misrepresent their private information or take unobservable actions that are different from those desired by the other parties. It is also called the performance incentive.

Incentive contracts: These are contracts with a variable payment depending on the efforts or performance.

Incentive intensity principle: The principle in incentive contracting is that the intensity of incentives should increase with the marginal productivity of effort and with the agent's ability to respond to incentives and should decrease with the agent's risk aversion and the variance with which performance is measured.

Incomplete contracts: They do not specify actions under all possible contingencies. They arise as a result of lack of information, bounded rationality and the high transaction costs of obtaining the required information, for monitoring and enforcing of the agreements. There are several factors leading to incomplete contracts; some of which are more related the transaction cost theory and others are more oriented to incomplete contract theory. The transaction costs view emphasises that it is too costly to design a complete contract, while the incomplete contract theory focuses on all the contingencies that can arise that were not foreseen or not specified in the contract. It is sometimes even impossible to take all the contingencies into account. Furthermore, the enforcement of contracts can be costly.

Influence costs: The costs incurred in attempts to influence others' decisions in a self-interested fashion, in attempts to counter such influence activities by others, and by the degradation of the quality of decisions because of influence.

Informational asymmetries: Differences among individuals in their information, especially when this information is relevant to determining an efficient plan or to evaluating individual performance.

Informational incompleteness: Lack of complete information, especially when this information is relevant to determining an efficient plan or to evaluating individual performance.

Informational rent: A return in excess of opportunity costs that accrues by virtue of an individual having access to precontractual private information. The private information means that the individual must be given incentives not to take advantage of the informational asymmetry, and providing these incentives results in rents.

Information failures:	This refers to the case when information asymmetries and adverse selection lead to a breakdown of markets and the failure to consummate potentially beneficial exchanges.
Innovations:	According to evolutionary theory, innovation are sources of new variations in the economy. They can be compared with mutation in evolutionary biology.
Institutions:	This a broad concept. It includes the informal and the formal rules of the institutional environment (rules of the game), and the institutional arrangements (play of the game) also.
Institutional environment:	The formal rules of the game that structure human behaviour. It is also said they are the rules of game.
Institutional arrangements:	Arrangements between people or groups of people that govern the ways in which people cooperate and carrying out transactions. These are the plays of the game.
Institutional lock-in:	Public servants are familiar with existent policy. Therefore continuing with the same type of policy in a new policy area brings about few additional costs, less risks less unexpected effects. It is also a form of path dependency.
Intensity of incentives:	The rate at which expected income changes with improved performance under an incentive contract.
Intrinsic motivation:	This type of motivation is more internal to the individual, such as the altruistic concerns. It includes the desire to do your work well, trustworthiness and having or building a good reputation.
Investment:	An expenditure of resources that creates an asset.
Jobs:	The basic roles and responsibilities of employees; jobs have at least two important dimensions: the variety of tasks that the employee is asked to complete and the decision authority that is granted to the individual to complete the tasks.
Joint ventures:	A business where the provision of risk capital and the decision making activities is shared between two or more firms. The firms joining in such a venture may provide different forms of expertise.
License to produce:	This is connected to the concept of *responsible entrepreneurship*. Firms function in a socially responsible manner if the economic, social and ecological values that it produces fulfil the expectations of the stakeholders. Satisfying the social and ecological criteria creates in fact a 'permit' to carry out activities.
Limited liability:	The condition of a person whose liability for the debts of a partnership or other organisation is limited to the amount of capital that the person has invested.
Limited partner:	A partner in a limited partnership who supplies financing and enjoys a share of the partnership profits but who exercises no control of partnership decisions and who has limited liability for partnership assets.
Limited partnerships:	A partnership consisting of both general partner and limited partners.
Lock-in:	Lock-in means that your alternatives are strongly reduced. This can because of functional, technical, or institutional reasons. Lock-in effects can be the result of being *held-up*. It is compared to hold-up as an *ex-post* problem.
Long run:	A term used to describe the time frame over which all inputs to the production process are not in fixed supply to the firm.
Loss aversion:	People feel the pain of loss stronger than the joy over a profit; they have a loss aversion. Loss aversion is a central concept in the prospect theory.

Make or buy decision:	The choice a firm must make about whether it should make an intermediate good in-house or secure it in some market.
Managerial misbehaviour:	Managers serve their own interests and not the interest of the shareholders or the workers of the firm.
Marginal cost:	The increase in the total costs of production resulting from raising output by one unit.
Marginal product:	The change in total product, or output, resulting from the use of one more unit of a variable factor, other things being equal.
Market:	All firms and individuals who are willing and able to buy or sell a particular product, including the interaction of one or more buyers with one or more sellers.
Market based transfer prices:	These are the external market prices used to value goods exchanged between business units.
Market failures:	Markets fail because of externalities, public goods, monopolies, and information failures; they keep markets from providing an efficient allocation of resources.
Market for corporate control:	Refers to the possibility of changing corporate control through buying the stock of the firm in the securities markets.
Market structure:	The basic characteristics of the market environment, including (1) the number and size of buyers, sellers and potential entrants, (2) the degree of product differentiation, (3) the amount and cost of information about product price and quality and (4) the conditions for entry and exit. It is also used when referring to size distribution and mode of competition.
Measurement costs:	Cost involved in determining the quality of a good or service that a party incurs to improve its bargaining price.
Menu of contracts:	A system for compensation in which individual employees may choose which of several different formulas will be used to compute their pay.
Missing markets:	A situation when no market exists in which to transact in a particular good or service.
Monitoring:	An activity for the purpose of determining whether the contractual obligations of another party have been met.
Monitoring intensity principle:	The principle of incentive contracting that indicates that more resources should be used to reduce the errors in measuring performance when stronger performance incentives are being given.
Monitoring rights:	The opportunity to oversee whether the obligations of another party have been met.
Monopolistic competition:	A market structure that is a hybrid between competitive markets and monopoly; firms have downward sloping demand curves for their differentiated products, but economic profits are limited by entry and competition.
Monopoly:	A type of market structure in which there is a single seller facing the market demand; there is only one firm in the industry.
Moral hazard:	Originally, an insurance term referring to the tendency of people with insurance to reduce the care they take to avoid or reduce insured losses. Now, the term refers also to the form of *postcontractual opportunism* that arises when actions required or desired under the contract are not freely observable.

Motivation:	It is argued that there are two kinds of motivations for action: intrinsic and extrinsic. Between both there can be a trade-off, such that too heavy emphasis on extrinsic motivation can drive out intrinsic motivation. Motivations activated by external factors, such as monetary incentives or direct order (as in hierarchical governance structure), can crowd out motivations that are internal to the individual, such as more **altruistic concerns**. Motivation questions arise because individuals have their own private interests, which seldom correspond perfectly to the interests of other parties, the group to which the individuals belong or to society as a whole.
MW_{th}:	MW means megawatt and th is thermal energy. It is a measure for the used energy.
Nash equilibrium:	A strategic situation in which each decision-maker's planned strategy is best from his or her point of view in light of the strategies that he or she expects others to employ, and these expectations are correct.
Natural monopoly:	Natural monopolies are characterised by a large proportion of fixed costs and relatively small proportion of variable costs. Many provisions, such as networks and infrastructure, have to deal with indivisibility or lumpiness.
Negotiated transfer prices:	These are prices set by negotiation between the two business units to value goods exchanged between them.
Neoclassical contract:	This is a contract with a fixed duration, the identities of the parties matter, the price is less important as a coordination mechanism and the asset specificity is larger compared to the classical contract.
Neoclassical market model:	A model of market exchange in which utility-maximising consumers and profit-maximising producers transact at prices over which each party perceives itself to exercise little control.
Neoclassical theory of the firm:	The standard neoclassical theory of the firm is perhaps the oldest and most established view. In its simplest form, the firm is regarded as a blackbox, a production function, without an internal structure but able to produce a large variety of outputs using different combinations of inputs. The theory assumes that every economic agent has perfect information; that is, all agents know all technical feasible production and consumption plans and all prices in every market. Information is distributed symmetrically and every party has access to the same data. The role of the managers, given their (and everyone else's) full information in the neoclassical theory, is simply to maximise the profits or market value of the firm by choosing the optimal production plan.
Net Added Value (NAV):	The total sales of a firm minus (1) purchases of inputs from other firms and (2) the capital consumption (= depreciation). National income is the sum of NAV in all enterprises and of the government in the economy.
Network facility:	A durable system for the provision of water, gas and electricity and other 'network' service such as railways. It also is a natural monopoly.
Network organisations:	Organisations which are organised into work groups based on function, geography, or some other dimension; the relationships among these work groups are determined by the demands of specific projects and work activities, rather than by formal lines of authority; these relationships are fluid and frequently change with changes in the business environment.

Net present value:	The worth today of a clash flow stream, computed as a weighted sum of the cash flows in each future period, using weights that depend on interest rates.
Nexus of contracts:	A nexus is a connected group. Armen Alchian and Harold Demsetz have identified the firm as a connected group (explicit or implicit) of contractual relations among suppliers, customers and workers; the firm as a nexus of contracts.
Nomina:	Amounts measured in some currency, rather than in units of actual purchasing power.
Non-excludability:	Non-excludability refers to a lack of property rights meaning it is impossible to exclude people from the consumption of a good. Non-excludability can have a technical or an institutional reason. In both cases it is either not possible or it is very expensive to assign property rights. When exclusion is not possible, problems such as free-riding and prisoner's dilemma can occur. Free-riding means that individuals (free-riders) can use or consume the good without paying for it.
Non-recoverable costs:	These costs are the so-called sunk costs. The non-recoverable costs are equal to the fixed costs if these cannot be redeployed to alternative uses.
Non-rivalry in production:	Non-rivalry in production is caused by the imperfect divisibility (or lumpiness) in the production sphere, involving that for providing a good a certain scale is needed. A certain minimum size is necessary otherwise offering the good is not efficient. Just as with natural monopolies, they are often characterised by a large part fixed costs and relative small part variable costs, and often but not always they are natural monopolies. This fixed costs and indivisibility lead to non-rivalry in consumption; the marginal costs of use are zero.
Non-rivalry in consumption:	This is caused by the imperfect divisibility (or lumpiness) in the consumption sphere. A good is non-rival or indivisible in consumption when a unit of the good can be consumed by one individual without detracting, in the slightest, from the consumption opportunities still available to others from the same unit. At same time several people can simultaneously make use of the goods; i.e. multiple consumption by several persons simultaneously is possible. The good can be used by different users at the same time.
Non-specific assets:	Assets that are equally useful when employed in combination with any of various other assets or in any of several different relationships. See specific asset, firm-specific capital, and cospecialisation.
No wealth effects:	The condition on preferences that means that choices among non-monetary alternatives are unaffected by the individual's wealth or income.
Objective performance measure:	A measure that is easily observable and quantifiable.
Oligopolistic market:	A market structure that has only a few firms which account for most of the production in the market; products may or may not be differentiated; firms can earn economic rent.
Open asset:	It is open for everyone. There is no ownership and there are no property rights. There is no defined group of users.

Opportunistic behaviour:	Self-interested behaviour unconstrained by morality. Opportunistic behaviour includes providing selective and distorted information, making promises which are not intended to be kept, and posing differently from what the person actually is.
Opportunity costs:	The value of the resource in its next-best alternative use. Under the quasi-rent concept, a distinction between sunk costs and opportunity costs must be kept in mind. A cost is to be sunk if, once paid, it can never be recovered. An opportunity cost of an activity is the value of the next-best alternative. When an individual assesses the quasi-rents of some particular activities, she ignores any sunk costs and focuses instead on the payments in excess of what she could earn elsewhere (= opportunity costs).
Option:	A financial contract giving a right which need not be exercised unless the holder chooses to do so.
Organisational architecture:	Comprises the three critical aspects of corporate organisation: (1) the assignment of control right within the company, (2) the methods of rewarding individuals, and (3) the structure of systems to evaluate the performance of both individuals and business units.
Outsourcing:	Moving an activity outside the firm that formerly was done within the firm: it can also refer to an outgoing arrangement for using external firms either to supply inputs or distribute products. It is also called contracting out.
Ownership:	There are two approaches for considering the ownership of an asset: (1) as having a bundle of property right of the asset; (2) as having the residual control rights over and the residual income of an asset.
Pareto dominated:	A situation from which it is possible to increase strictly the welfare of some party without diminishing that of any other party.
Pareto efficiency:	A situation in which there is no feasible alternative that keeps all individuals at as least as well off but makes at least one person better off.
Pareto optimal:	A situation from which it is impossible to increase the welfare of any party without decreasing that of some other party.
Participation conditions or constraints:	Limitations on contracts or other organisational arrangements arising from the fact that participation is voluntary and so individuals must expect to do at least as well as under their next-best alternatives or they will refuse to participate.
Partnership:	A form of organisation in which some or all of the multiple owners, the partners, accepted unlimited liability for the organisation's debt and exercise management control. All members of the partnership bring assets in such as land, buildings, labour or capital. Each member is personally liable for the firm's debts and losses. Only together the members can decide over important management decisions concerning means of production (labour, capital goods and other inputs), investments, and financial means of the partnership.
Path dependency:	Economic behaviour relies on knowledge and experience built up in the past. Path dependency means that history matters.
Perfect capital markets:	A theoretical idea in which all individuals can borrow and save on the same terms, with these terms being unaffected by the amounts involved.

Perfect competition: An ideal market situation in which buyers and sellers are so numerous and well informed that each can act as price taker, able to buy or to sell any desired quantity without affecting the market price. Buyers and sellers have perfect information, products are homogenous, and entry and exit are free without costs.

Perfect information: When every participant in a market becomes aware of every price, product specification and buyer and seller location at cost.

Postcontractual information problems: Agency problems that occur because of asymmetric information after the contract is negotiated; individuals have incentives to deviate from the contract because the other party has insufficient information to know whether the contract was honoured – also called moral hazard problems.

Postcontractual opportunism: Opportunistic behaviour by a party that takes place after a contract is signed. Moral hazard and the hold up problem are two particular problems of postcontractual oppportunism.

Posting of bonds: Setting aside a sum of money (a bond) to guarantee performance under a contract.

Potential entrants: All firms that pose a sufficiently credible threat of market entry to affect the pricing and output decisions of incumbent firms.

Precontractual information problems: Contracting problems that occur because of asymmetric information at the time the contract is being negotiated; these problems include adverse selection and bargaining failures.

Precontractual opportunism: Opportunistic behaviour by a party that takes place before a contract is signed. Adverse selection is a problem of precontractual opportunism.

Present value: *See*: net present value.

Price discrimination: This occurs whenever a firm's prices in different markets are not related to differentials in production and distribution costs; it involves charging different consumers different prices based on their elasticities of demand.

Principal: The party whose interests are meant to be served in an agency relationship.

Principal-agent theory: This theory offers a framework for a comprehensive analysis of situations involving: (1) conflict of interest between principal and agent (for example, between an employer and an employee, a landowner and a farmer/tenant, politician and civil servants); (2) asymmetric information and uncertainty; (3) making an agreement or setting-up a contract; and (4) issues such as how contract design influences the behaviour of the participants.

Principle of risk sharing: The principle that when many people share in a number of independent risks, with each taking a small part of each risk, the total cost of bearing the risk is reduced.

Private good: Exclusion of this type of good is possible, appropriate and efficient, and the use of the good is rival. The latter means that the good is divisible in consumption and transferable in marketable units. For individual goods, where individual property rights exist, the use by one individual excludes the possibility of use by another. The market is the best governance structure.

Private property regime: Refers to a private property system for resources or firms in a nation or in a region. Private property is the legal and social permitted right to exclude others, permitting the owner to force others to go elsewhere. It is the most well known

	property regime. Private property does not always coincide with individual ownership. For example, with a partnership, a limited partnership company, public limited company or a limited liability company there is private property. However, often several individuals are involved as owners. It is a cooperative relationship of various interested stakeholders, and is managed as a group.
Private information:	Private information belongs to hidden information. It refers to information which is relevant for the potential transaction and to which one party is privy to, is not observable, and introduces risks for the other party. It is information that is relevant to determining efficient allocations that is known only to some subset of parties involved.
Prisoners' dilemma:	A strategic situation modelled as a normal form of game in which each party or player has a dominant strategy – one that is best no matter what behaviour is expected from the others – but playing out these dominant strategies results in an outcome that is Pareto dominated by an outcome that would be achieved under some other (dominated) strategies.
Private transaction costs:	These are the transaction costs born by private parties.
Producer surplus:	The area above the supply curve and below the market price line. It represents the difference between the minimum amount the seller will accept for any given unit sold and its actual price.
Profit sharing:	An element of a compensation plan in which employees receive bonuses that are in aggregate tied to firm profits.
Property rights theory:	Two important approaches can be distinguished: (1) the old property right theory, which considers property as a bundle of rights; and (2) the new property rights which asks the central question who has the residual control rights and who is able to capture the residual income?
Property regimes:	Refers to property systems for resources or firms in a nation or in a region. Property regimes consist of government, private, common and non-property regimes.
Property rights:	These are parts of the bundle of property rights over an asset consisting of (a) the right to use; (b) the right to appropriate the income; (c) the right to change the form, and substance; (d) the right to exclude others; and (e) the right to transfer the asset to others through markets or to their inheritances.
Prospect theory:	According to prospect theory, the (subjective) classification whether the outcome is a profit or a loss plays a role in the risk-attitude. People feel the pain of loss stronger than the joy over a profit; they have a loss aversion.
Public corporation:	A corporation whose shares are bought and sold through an organised exchange and so may be held by any investor.
Public goods:	They consist – based on the characteristic of non-excludability and non-rivalry – of pure and impure public goods. Both share the characteristic of non-rivalry; meaning the consumption of the good by one person does not diminish the amount available for others.
Public goods problem:	The core problem is the lack of excludability resulting in free-riding.
Public Private Partnership:	It is a hybrid institutional arrangement in which the government works together with private parties on a project. The mode of organisation, the legal entities and the interests of involved parties are different. In most cases, the

government has to fulfil different roles: a large interest in the realisation of the project; controlling the quality of the project, keeping the legal procedures and contractual agreements, and maintaining the public support. and plays different roles often: (1) it has a large interest in the realisation of a project; (2) it has to control the quality of the project, the legal procedures and contractual agreements; (3) it has to take care for maintaining the public support.

Public transaction costs:	These are the transaction costs for the government.
Quasi-rent:	The return of an activity in excess of the minimum needed to keep a resource in its current use. It behaves like a rent because in the short run the factor of production or resource will not disappear if the payments were decreased. These payments are not true rent since in the long run they have to be sufficient to induce new investments. The quasi-rent is always at least as large as the rent. For firms operating in the short run, quasi-rents are simply the excess of the total receipts over the total variable costs.
Quasi-public good:	Exclusion from the good is in principle possible and the use is non-rivalry. In principle, property rights can be specified and delineated, depending on transaction costs. If the use of the good by one person is not at the cost of the other (non-rival), then the marginal-costs for an extra additional user will be nil. This is due to the indivisibility of the concerned good or provision and multiple consumption of the good.
Ratchet effect:	This refers to basing next year's performance standard on this year's actual performance; such standard setting can induce employees to restrict production in the current period in order to limit the increase in their future performance benchmarks. That is agents or employees see that good performance to day will punished by stronger norms in the future.
Real:	Real, as opposed to nominal amounts, represent actual purchasing power by allowing for price changes.
Recoverable costs:	These costs are the total costs minus the sunk costs. In a short-term view the recoverable costs are equal to the variable costs.
Reciprocity:	Usually the word *reciprocity* is used to describe *I'll scratch your back if you'll scratch mine*. People provide a service to others, expecting to get something in return. If the service a person provides is not reciprocated to his or her satisfaction, then the service will be withdrawn. It is said that this type of reciprocity (a good deed is always rewarded) is the glue that holds human societies together.
Reference level:	This can be the status quo, a standard situation or historical reference year. It can also be based on what people find *normal* or what it should be. Behavioural economics shows that utility is derived from a change compared to the status quo, see prospect theory.
Relational contract:	In this contract the duration is long or even indeterminate, the identity and personal characteristics of parties are very important, price as a coordination mechanism less significant and asset specificity is often large. It is a contract that specifies only the general terms and objectives of a relationship and specifies mechanisms for decision making and dispute resolution.
Relative price:	The price of a good as compared to another.

Renege:	To deliberately choose not to carry out a promise or contract to the detriment of the other party. It is a form of *ex-post* opportunistic behaviour.
Renegotiate:	To bargain to determine new terms which will replace those of an existing contract. If no agreement is reached, the previous one remains in force.
Rent:	A return received in an activity that is in excess of the minimum needed to attract the resources to that activity.
Rent-seeking behaviour:	An attempt by some interested party to alter the allocation of rents in a contractual agreement; in general, it does not create value in a organisation.
Reorganisation:	To redesign the relationships, authority, responsibilities, and lines of communication in an existing organisation. In a reorganisation in bankruptcy, the bankrupt firm renegotiates the amount of its debts and the timing of its payment obligations and may reorganise its activities for forecasting future behaviour.
Reputation:	The view formed of an individual or organisation by another based on past experience, especially as a basis for forecasting future behaviour. It is a way of showing commitment.
Reputational capital:	Individuals with a good reputation are able to realise rent from keeping their reputation intact; reputational capital. The notion of reputational capital is similar to human capital – it is rent that a party receives for being trustworthy.
Reservation price:	The maximum price that a buyer is willing to pay for an item, given preferences, income and price of other goods, or the minimum that a seller is willing to accept, given.
Residual claimant:	One who has the legal rights to the profits of the enterprise once the fixed claimants of the firm (for example, bondholders and employees) are paid.
Residual income:	It is the amount of income that is left over after everyone has been paid.
Residual loss:	The dollar equivalent of the remaining loss in value that results because incentive problems have not been completely resolved by out-of-pocket expenditures on monitoring and bonding.
Residual return:	Income from an asset or business that remains after all fixed obligations are met. It is that part of the return that remains after all debts and costs and all other contractual obligations have been paid.
Residual rights of control:	The rights to make any decision concerning an asset's use that is not explicitly assigned by law or contract to another partner.
Resource allocation problem:	The problem of using limited resources efficiently or in a way that maximises some fixed objective.
Resource based view (RBV) of the firm:	According to the RBV of the firm, a competitive advantage is always based on the possession of certain resources, such as a large-scale plant or experience. It is a way of describing a company's strengths. The extent to which a competitive advantage is sustainable depends on how difficult or costly it is for other firms to obtain the same resources. In RBV of the firm, resources are defined quite broadly. These include financial resources, tangible resources (such as plant, equipment, buildings) and intangible resources (such as patents, know-how, brand names, experiences and organisational routines).
Responsible entrepreneurship:	In general, this suggests that a firm should not only think of the economic value of the firm (mostly represented by the profit of the firm), but also of the social and ecological values that result from the firm's activities on social and

ecological quantities. This is pointed out in the concept of triple-p objectives: *profits, planet* and *people*. Firms function in a socially responsible manner if the economic, social and ecological values that it produces fulfil the expectations of the stakeholders.

Returns to a factor:
This defines the relation between output and the variation in only one input, holding other inputs fixed.

Returns to scale:
The relationship between output and a proportional variation of all inputs taken together.

Revelation principle:
The principle that any outcome can be achieved by some mechanism under the self-interested strategic behaviour that is induced by the mechanism can also be achieved by a mechanism employing an honest mediator to whom the parties willingly report truthfully and who then implements the outcome that would have resulted from the original mechanism. The incentive that we have to give parties to find out who they really are or what their costs really are is also termed the *truth-telling condition* or the *strategy of being honest*. A direct revelation mechanism means that everybody voluntarily choose to be honest.

Risk:
The results of any action are not certain, but they may take more than one value. Risk is usually used to describe the form of uncertainty when, while the actual outcome of an action is not known, it is expected that it will be determined as the result of a random drawing from a set of possible outcomes whose distribution is known. Where this information is supposed to come from is usually not discussed.

Risk-averse:
The preference of a certain income to a risky outcome with somewhat higher expected value. It is a person who is willing to offer some explicit or implicit amount to have the risks reduced or removed. Risk-aversion means that marginal utility is decreasing in outcomes, so that of any two actions with equal mean outcomes, that with the lower dispersion will be preferred. An absolute risk-aversion means that risk-aversion might vary with the level of wealth: (1) with a constant absolute risk-aversion the willingness to carry out actions with uncertain outcome at higher levels of wealth does not change; (2) an increasing absolute risk-aversion express a lower willingness to carry out the same actions with increasing level of wealth; (3) and a decreasing absolute risk-aversion express a higher willingness to carry out the same actions with increasing level of wealth.

Risk-neutral:
The characteristics of a person who is indifferent between receiving a fixed sum of money or a risky prospect with an expected value equal to the fixed sum.

Risk-preference:
This person prefers an action or project with dispersed possible outcomes to a certain action or project with the same mean return.

Risk-sharing optimum:
This is a payment from the principal to the agent which is Pareto-efficient, i.e. which maximises the expected utility of the principal for a given minimum level of agent's utility. Optimal risk-sharing with a risk-neutral principal and a risk-averse agent implies that the principal gives a fixed income to the agent.

Risk premium:
The difference between the expected value of a risky income stream and its certainty equivalent.

Risk tolerance:	A measure of willingness to bear risk. Measured as the inverse of the coefficient of absolute risk aversion.
Routines:	Standardised rules for decisions and actions that, although they may vary to a limited degree with the particular circumstances, are applied across a period of time without further fine-tuning.
Regulatory takings:	The removal of a part of the property rights leading to a restriction on the use of the property without taking the title from the owners. This means a part of the property rights are lost.
Salvage value:	The salvage value of an asset is based on the current opportunity costs. In general, the salvage value for an asset is lower than the acquisition costs.
Satisfying behaviour:	People do not strive for utility of profit maximisation but are searching for choices that meet various aspiration levels and are therefore acceptable. For example a preference for an easy life, a desire to remain one's own master or preferring safer returns, comprise a set of additional preferences that need to be satisfied even if they mean smaller financial returns on average (see also risk-averse).
Screening:	The less-informed party attempts to induce the other party to voluntarily disclose information. To ensure that the other party voluntarily discloses information, we need an information-revealing mechanism. These conditions are called self-selection conditions, for example, offering a menu of contracts or options with the intention of encouraging self-selection.
Second-best:	The second-best is in contrast with the first-best. A second-best optimum is one where the best decisions are made about whether or not to satisfy some optimum conditions when others cannot be satisfied.
Second welfare theorem:	It states that, under certain conditions, every Pareto-efficient allocation of resources can be attained by some set of competitive prices. This Second Welfare Theorem is important because of its implication that, at least in theory, the issues of efficiency and distributional fairness can be separated. If society deems the current distribution of resources to be unfair, it need not interfere with market prices and impair efficiency. Rather, society should transfer resources (including property rights) among people in a way that is deemed to be fair.
Selection:	In evolutionary theory, it is seen as an enormous evolutionary mechanism that investigates the pattern of organisations at every point of time as it where, and test their ability to fulfil their role.
Selection environment:	The forces influencing competition processes are called the selection environment in evolutionary theory. They consist of markets, institutions and the spatial environment. The selection environment specifies which routines and innovations will survive and which will not.
Self-selection:	The pattern of choices that individuals with different personal characteristics make when facing a menu of contracts or options. Self-selection occurs when people with differential private information identify themselves to outsiders by choosing contracts that best fit with their private information. For example, workers who face a choice between a job with a fixed hourly wage and one with piece rate incentives will tend to prefer the former if they expect to be relatively unproductive and to prefer the latter in the opposite case.

Semistrong form of efficient markets hypothesis: The hypothesis that stock prices (or those of other assets) fully reflect all publicly available information. This hypothesis implies that unless an investor has inside information, he or she cannot expect to earn better rates of return (on a risk adjusted basis) from any active investment policy than from one of simply buying and holding a fully diversified, market portfolio.

Separation of ownership and management: A situation in which the residual returns and residual rights of control belong to different parties. More particularly, the common condition of modern corporations in which shareholders are the residual claimants but effective control of decision making lies with the top managers of the firm.

Shareholder rate of return: The rate of return on holding a stock over a period, calculated as the change in share prices plus any dividends received, all divided by the initial price of the shares.

Shareholder activism: When shareholders become so dissatisfied with the action of the corporation's management, they actively attempt to influence, or even to eliminate, management. It occurs because of separation of ownership and management.

Short run: The operating period during which at least one input (frequently a capital good) is fixed in supply.

Shirking: It is a form of *ex-post* opportunistic behaviour arising because of imperfect monitoring; one party puts in less effort than it otherwise might if its actions were perfectly observable.

Shut-down point: The minimum price that a firm will produce output for the short run, equal to the average variable costs at the chosen level of output; a further decrease in price causes losses larger than the fixed cost and below this minimum price the variable costs can no longer be recovered.

Signaling: It occurs when the better-informed party makes certain verifiable facts known, which when properly interpreted, may indicate the presence of other unobservable but desirable characteristics. For example, a worker who accepts a job that begins with several weeks of unpaid, specific training signals an intention to work for the firm for a long period of time.

Site specificity: A form of asset specificity; the condition of being limited to a particular location.

Social capital: Social capital is the shared knowledge, norms and values, and expectations about patterns of interaction that groups or individuals bring to repeated activities. The most important component of social capital is trust between people and, to a lesser degree, trust of people in the government, and trust in processes. A small amount of social capital within a group, organisation or society leads to higher transaction costs. If people trust each other they are prepared to exchange information, cooperate with each other and to carry out transactions with lower transaction costs.

Social costs: The total cost of an activity. This includes not only private costs which directly fall on the person or firm conducting the activity, but also the external costs, which fall on other people, who are not able to exact any compensation for them,

Social embeddedness:	This is the first level of institutional analysis. It is the level in which cultural norms, customs, morals, traditions and more informal code of conduct emerge. The term refers to the social relationships within which economic transactions are embedded. At this level we also find social capital.
Sole proprietorship:	A firm is owned by a single individual.
Specialisation:	(1) The division of tasks on the basis of comparative advantage. (2) The process of narrowing (and presumably, deepening) the range of tasks that a particular individual or machine can perform.
Specific assets:	Those assets that are worth more in their current use than in alternative uses.
Specific human capital:	This is created by learning things that are expected to be useful only within a specific contractual relationship – see asset specificity.
Specific investment:	An investment that creates a specific asset.
Specificity:	The extent to which assets are specific. When the principle of value maximisation holds, specificity is measured by the loss in value entailed in shifting the asset to another use.
Specific knowledge:	The knowledge which is relatively expensive to transfer.
Spot market contract:	A contract for the immediate exchange of goods or services at current prices.
Stakeholders:	Any individual or group who has a direct interest in a firm's continuing profitable operations (including shareholders, board of directors, managers, lenders, employees, customers, input suppliers, banks communities where the firm employs workers, and so on). Different types of stakeholders are involved in a large corporation and they have different interests, different types and levels of information and different rights.
Statistically independent:	A condition holding between random variables under which knowledge of the realised value of one variable gives no information about the probability of different realisations of the other.
Strategic alliances:	Any of a variety of agreements between independent firms to cooperate in the development and/or marketing products.
Strategy:	The general policies that managers adopt to generate profits; rather than focus on operation detail, a firm's strategy addresses broad, long-term issues facing the firm.
Strategy of truth-telling:	It is a condition that gives agents an incentive to reveal their costs, their real ability, or capacity.
Strong form efficient market hypothesis:	The hypothesis that stock prices (or those of other assets) fully reflect all information, including both publicly available information and information held by insiders.
Strongly complementary:	A group of activities is strongly complementary when increasing the levels of some activities in the group greatly increases the marginal returns to the remaining activities.
Structure-conduct-performance approach:	This approach argues that structure, conduct and performance of firms are mutually dependent. There is a path from structure to conduct, from conduct to performance, from performance to structure, but also from conduct to structure. Structure refers to characteristics of a sector, such as the number and size distribution of firms in that sector and the barriers that impede other firms entering that sector. Conduct refers to the behaviour of firms in a

	sector. Aspects of firms conduct are collusion (that is, the extent to which firms cooperate), costs and price strategy of the firms in a sector and product variety. Performance refers to results of firms in a sector in terms of profitability, growth in output and employment.
Substitutes:	Goods that compete with each other; if the price of one good is increased, the consumer will tend to shift purchases to the other good.
Sunk costs:	Non-recoverable costs that have already been incurred and the resources have no alternative use. Under the quasi-rent concept, a distinction between sunk costs and opportunity costs must be kept in mind. A cost is to be sunk if, once paid, it can never be recovered. An opportunity cost of an activity is the value of the next-best alternative.
Sunk investments:	These are investments which generate profits in the case of a particular application but have little or no value in another application. Sunk investments are related to concepts of fixed asset and asset specificity.
Survival of the fittest:	A principle implied by the concept of economic Darwinism; companies have the greatest chance of survival if they are organised efficiently given their particular environment.
Takeover premium:	The amount by which the price paid for a firm's shares in a takeover exceeds the total market value of the firm's shares in the absence of a takeover.
Takings:	Takings are the opposite of assigning of property right by the government. The government takes them away.
Team production:	A production process in which the individual outputs cannot be separately identified. For such a process, any individual incentives must be based on some measure of the effort or diligence of the workers.
Tender:	This is a bid for the right to carry out certain projects. One must estimate the costs and the benefits based on (often limited) available information to arrive at his bid. The one with the lowest is usually awarded the contract for the project but possible for a price which is less than the actual costs.
Tenure:	(1) It is a legal right to use a particular piece of land or to live in a particilar building during a fixed period of time. (2) The condition of being protected from termination of employment in a job, regardless of general performance, subject only to meeting certain minimal standards of acceptable behaviour.
Theory of the firm:	A group of theories belonging to institutional economics and Economic Organisation Theory. It includes the transaction cost theory, the principal-agent theory, the incomplete contract theory, the old and new property rights theory and economic theory of takings.
Theory of the state:	This theory focuses on a ruler who recognises that benefits can be obtained by organising activities. The ruler can use force as a fundamental mechanism to organise activities that will produce (collective) benefits. He obtains taxes, labour, or other resources from subjects by threatening them with sanctions if they do not provide the resources. The ruler keeps the residuals.
Three legs of the stool:	An analogy used to characterise the organisational mode; like a balanced stool, a well designed organisation should have a mode in which the three components (the assignment of control rights, the reward system, and the performance-evaluation system) are coordinated.

Time-inconsistency:	It is special form of hidden actions or opportunistic behaviour. An important aspect of time-inconsistency is the credibility of a pronouncement or intended policy. It occurs when a policy originally seemed optimal but after a time, is no longer considered optimal by the policy makers. As a result, the rules of the game are changed by the party deciding to continue or terminate the policy.
Tit-for-tat strategy:	This can be described as I'll-scratch-your-back-if-you-'ll-scratch-mine or as reciprocity.
Titular takings:	In this case, all the property rights are removed. The government takes land from many owners in order to provide public goods, such as military bases, airports, highways, dams, schools and nature areas. Such expropriation regularly occurs in the layout and purchase of land by the government for setting up rail roads, highways, industrial terrains, nature areas, etc..
Total value maximisation:	A goal of economic behaviour to increase to a maximum the total value of a transaction.
Tournament:	A contest in which the prizes received depend only on ordinary ranking (first, second, third, etc.) and not on absolute performance. A policy of promoting the person who is judged best qualified creates a tournament, as do sales contests in which a prize is given for achieving the largest sales volume.
Tragedy of the Commons:	*See:* common resource problem.
Transaction:	(1) is synonymous with the economic concept of exchange involving goods, services, or money. It is a two-sided mechanism: the transfer of goods and services (performance) for one individual to another and mostly money as counter performance; *quid pro quo* and (2) The largest unit of economic activity that cannot be subdivided and performed by several different people.
Transaction costs:	The costs of carrying out a transaction or the opportunity costs incurred when an efficiency-enhancing transaction is not realised. Transaction costs arise because of: information is needed, negotiations have to be made, contracts or agreements have to be concluded, inspections have to carried out and agreements have to be made to sort out differences in opinion.
Transaction cost theory of the firm:	There are costs linked to the use of the market mechanism. Firms as a mode of organisation can exist only if they can carry out transactions at lower costs than other governance structures.
Transfer price:	The amount that one business unit pays another for goods and services that are exchanged between them.
Transition costs:	These are the costs of creating, building up a system, an institutional structure or building up provision that will change the institutional environment.
Trilateral governance structure:	This a governance structure in which three parties are involved, for example a buyer and a seller and both are making use of an intermediator.
Trust:	Is the expectation of someone about the action of another that affects the first person's choice, when an action must be taken before the actions of other are known. Trust lowers the cost of search, monitoring, contracting and control; i.e. it reduces transaction costs.
Truth-telling condition:	The incentives that we have to give parties to find out who they really are or what their costs really are. Is also called the strategy of being honest.

Unlimited liability:	The condition of a person whose liability for the debts of a partnership or other organisation is not limited to the amounts he or she has invested.
Upstream:	An activity that precedes the reference activity in the sequence of steps from producing raw materials from natural sources to delivering a finished product.
Upstream integration:	*See*: backward integration.
Utility:	An index of personal well-being.
Utility function:	A numerical representation of an individual's preferences over different possible choices of situations. It is the relationship between an individual's well-being (utility) and the level of goods consumed.
Variable costs:	All costs incurred in production by firms that vary directly with the output.
Variable inputs:	Inputs that varies with quantity of output.
Variance:	A mathematical measure of the amount that a random variable is likely to vary around its mean value. The variance is equal to the expected value of the square of the difference between the variable and its mean.
Vertical chain of production:	The series of steps in the production process.
Vertical integration:	The process in which either one of the input sources or one of the output buyers of the firm is moved inside the firm. Vertical integration may involve forward integration, for example, an oil company running filling stations; or backward integration, for example, a fish processing firm running its own fishing boats.
Vertically integrated firms:	These are firms who participate in more than one successive stage in the vertical chain of production.
Von Neumann-Morgenstern (N-M) utility function:	This is a particular form of an expected utility function. An important property of the N-M expected utility function is that sub-utility indices, which are weighted and added to measure expected utility, are cardinally measurable. It means that a ranking represents not only the amount of the outcome of expected utility function, but the differences in utility indices have also an ordering of meaning.
Vote-maximisation:	This hypothesis states that politicians strive for as many votes as possible.
Weak form efficient market hypothesis:	The hypothesis that current asset prices reflect fully all the information that is embodied in past prices. An implication is that observing past prices cannot help in forecasting future prices. In particular, price changes should not display any predictable patterns. This implies that technical analysis cannot be the basis of a profitable investment strategy.
Wealth effects:	The variation in the amount a consumer is willing to pay for some object or in the quantity that the consumer may wish to buy at a particular price as a result of a change in the consumer's wealth.
Willingness To Accept (WTA):	WTA refers to the monetary compensation an individual would require to accept a welfare deterioration, or equivalently, to forego a welfare improvement.
Willingness To Pay (WTP):	WTP refers to the amount of income an individual would be willing to pay for having a good or to secure a welfare improvement, for example, by getting a better quality of environmental goods.
Willingness to sell:	It refers to the minimum amount of money a seller requires for selling a good.

Windfall profits:	These are gains arising from an activity which exceeds the minimum required to attract resources to that activity. They are also called rents. Payments for people with exceptional and scarce talents, such as artists and soccer players whose fees often exceed what they could earn in other occupations, plus a normal rate of return on the cost, can also be considered as rents or windfall profits.
Winner's curse:	The tendency of the winning bidder in a contracting competition to be the one who has underestimated the cost of doing the job, because bidders who overestimate the cost usually bid too high. Similarly, the tendency of the winning bidder in an auction to be one who has overestimated the utility of the object being sold.
X-efficiency:	This is defined as efficiency which consists of getting the maximum output technically possible from any given inputs, or producing a given output with the fewest possible inputs.
X-inefficiency:	The operation of the firm is less efficient than what is possible. See x-efficiency.
Zoning:	A system of specifying that certain activities can be only carried on in particular areas. Some activities create negative effects on the environment. Zoning tries to minimise the harm or negative externalities of these activities.

Keyword index

Printed in the United States
by Baker & Taylor Publisher Services